AF361325

IDEOLOGY AND THE RATIONALITY OF DOMINATION

IDEOLOGY AND THE RATIONALITY OF DOMINATION

Nazi Germanization Policies in Poland

Gerhard Wolf

Translated by Wayne Yung

Indiana University Press

The translation of this work was funded by Geisteswissenschaften International—
Translation Funding for Work in the Humanities and Social Sciences from
Germany, a joint initiative of the Fritz Thyssen Foundation, the German Federal
Foreign Office, the collecting society VG WORT and the Börsenverein des
Deutschen Buchhandels (German Publishers & Booksellers Association).

This book is a publication of

Indiana University Press
Office of Scholarly Publishing
Herman B Wells Library 350
1320 East 10th Street
Bloomington, Indiana 47405 USA

iupress.indiana.edu

Manufactured in the United States of America

Library of Congress Cataloging-in-Publication Data

Names: Wolf, Gerhard, 1954- author. | Yung, Wayne, 1971- translator.
Title: Ideology and the rationality of domination : Nazi germanization
  policies in Poland / Gerhard Wolf, Wayne Yung.
Description: Bloomington : Indiana University Press, 2020. | Title of
  original work: Ideologie und Herrschaftsrationalität :
  Nationalsozialistische Germanisierungspolitik in Polen, 2012, Hamburger
  edition. | Includes bibliographical references and index.
Identifiers: LCCN 2019054996 (print) | LCCN 2019054997 (ebook) | ISBN
  9780253048073 (hardback) | ISBN 9780253048080 (ebook)
Subjects: LCSH: Poland—History—Occupation, 1939–1945. |
  Germany—Relations—Poland. | Poland—Relations—Germany. | Holocaust,
  Jewish (1939–1945)—Germany. | Holocaust, Jewish (1939–1945)—Poland. |
  World War, 1939–1945—Poland. | Germany—Politics and
  government—1933–1945.
Classification: LCC D765 .W61713 2020 (print) | LCC D765 (ebook) | DDC
  940.53/438—dc23
LC record available at https://lccn.loc.gov/2019054996
LC ebook record available at https://lccn.loc.gov/2019054997

ISBN 978-0-253-04807-3 (hdbk.)
ISBN 978-0-253-04808-0 (web PDF)

1 2 3 4 5   25 24 23 22 21 20

Original title: Ideologie und Herrschaftsrationalität:
Nationalsozialistische Germanisierungspolitik in Polen

für C&L

Administrative division of the annexed West Polish territories and the General Government on March 1, 1940. Map by Peter Palm.

Contents

Preface to the English Edition

My book had hardly come out in German when Paula Bradish from my German publisher Hamburger Edition looked for ways of funding an English translation. I am very much indebted to her for taking the initiative and to the amazing program *Geisteswissenschaften International* for awarding a translation prize making my research accessible to an English-reading audience. I would also like to thank Professor Mark Roseman for his consistent support, this time for putting me in touch with Indiana University Press, where I was assisted by the efficient Ashante Thomas, who guided the book to publication. And it is published right on time—shortly after the edited volume *Beyond the Racial State* by Mark Roseman, Richard F. Wetzel, and Devon O. Pendas has demonstrated how fruitful a critique is that questions the paradigm of National Socialism as a *racial state*—which is also the argument of my book.

My final thanks are to Wayne Yung. When writing in English or reading English books on this topic, I am always struck by just how translation ends up becoming interpretation—often by intent, too often by accident. Finding the right words not just for the atrocities the Germans committed during the Second World War but also for the language they spoke and the terminology they used is exceedingly difficult if one tries to retain—and not narrow down—the many allusions terms like *völkisch* or *Volksgemeinschaft* invoke in German. With this translation, Wayne has done exactly this.

Gerhard Wolf, Brighton, 2019

Acknowledgments to the German Edition

I have always been conscious of how fortunate I have been in being able to devote my time—in fact, a long time—to a research topic that had already preoccupied me during my undergraduate studies, and to do so not on my own but with the help of like-minded people, along with a great deal of support from family, friends, and colleagues, as well as a still strong network of institutions that enabled the financing of this work and/or provided the space in which to write it. The circle of those who made these years a stimulating reward for me, and not only intellectually, has constantly grown over the years. It is truly a great pleasure to now have this opportunity to thank them publicly as well.

My first thanks go to my academic supervisor, Michael Wildt. He took up my project when the first steps had already been taken—but it was in conversations with him that it really took shape. His studies of the SS complex and the "Volksgemeinschaft" were crucial for my own research, and our frequent meetings in Berlin and Hamburg offered both an intellectual challenge and a sheltered haven. His inquisitiveness about my work and discussions and constructive criticisms of my hypotheses had a lasting impact on my thinking and repeatedly gave me the necessary self-confidence to embark on the next stage of work.

I would also like to thank Jörg Baberowski, who agreed at very short notice to become the second examiner for this project. His feedback was important for the revisions undertaken before publication. Further thanks go to Gabriele Metzler as the third examiner and to Wolfgang Wippermann, who helped me get this project underway. But for the idea behind it, my gratitude goes to Götz Aly and his trailblazing studies on Nazi population policy. These had already made a deep impact on me during my undergraduate studies, and his extensive archive, which he generously made available to me, allowed me a flying start.

An unfortunate reality for my line of work is that academic research is often a lonely occupation—from searching through the archives to composing the final text. This made it all the more helpful when there were opportunities that allowed me to present my interim results and to also learn from the ongoing efforts of others. In Germany, I would like to specifically acknowledge: the doctoral colloquium of Birthe Kundrus and Michael Wildt at the Hamburg Institute for Social Research, particularly my exchanges with Alexa Stiller, Andreas Strippel, and Regina Mühlhäuser; the invitations to present my project from Hans Henning Hahn, Johannes Tuchel, and Peter Steinbach; and my discussions with Andrej Angrick and Peter Klein.

Very heartfelt thanks go to my new colleagues at the History Department of the University of Sussex, who supported me in every conceivable way during the completion of my dissertation and its later revision. This plunge into the Anglo-American academic world was an immense intellectual enrichment for me. I would also like to mention the opportunity to discuss my work at the University of Oxford's Modern German Research Seminar, at the Modern German History Seminar of the Institute for Historical Research in London, and particularly at the conference "Beyond the Racial State: Rethinking Nazi Germany," which was organized by Devon Pendas, Mark Roseman, and Richard Wetzell at Indiana University. For their comments on specific sections of my work, I am particularly indebted to Hester Barron, Donald Bloxham, Paul Betts, Geoff Eley, Dirk A. Moses, and Darrow Schechter.

However, the ones who accompanied this undertaking the longest were my friends: Barbara Fried, who honed my theoretical thinking; Henrike Gremse, who helped me with translations; Christian Ehrlich, who coded a database to help me with my archival research; as well as Juliana and Greg Caplan, Anna Frank, Merle Keck, Steffen Küssner, Daphne Moench, Ilka Saal, Ralf Schweimeier, and Uwe Schulte, who read parts of my work and/or offered me a refuge.

Without the financial assistance of many institutions, I would not have been able to write this work. I would like to thank Manfred Heinemann and the Go East program at the DAAD, the German Historical Institutes in Warsaw and Moscow, and above all, Jan Philipp Reemtsma, Matthias Kamm, and the Hamburg Foundation for the Promotion of Science and Culture, who supported me so generously and unbureaucratically for the longest period of time. This is also why it is a particular pleasure for me that my book has been accepted for publication by the editors of "Studies on the History of Violence in the Twentieth Century" and that it is being published by Hamburger Edition. Here, sincere thanks also go out to my proofreader, Sigrid Weber.

I would also like to thank the staff at the various archives, particularly the German Federal Archives in Berlin, the State Archives in Poznań, and the Special Archive in Moscow. A special thanks also to Martin Dammann and Christopher Nesbit from the Archive of Modern Conflict. And what would I have done without the Berlin State Library?

I have saved my greatest thanks for the end, namely to my parents, Traute and Artur Wolf. They have encouraged my interests since my earliest memories, often sparking them in the first place. This book is dedicated to them.

Abbreviations

AOK	*Armeeoberkommando* (Army Command)
AR category (RuSHA classification)	*Altreich* (Old Reich: RuSHA category for those deemed racially suitable for labor deployment in the Reich and future assimilation into the German *Volksgemeinschaft*)
BdS	*Befehlshaber der Sicherheitspolizei und des SD* (Commander of the Security Police and the SD)
CdZ	*Chef der Zivilverwaltung* (Chief of Civil Administration of an occupied territory)
DUT	*Deutsche Umsiedlungs-Treuhand Gesellschaft* (German Resettlement Trust Company)
DVL	*Deutsche Volksliste* (German People's List)
EWZ	*Einwandererzentralstelle* (Central Immigration Office of the SS)
HSSPF	*Höherer SS- und Polizeiführer* (Higher SS and Police Leader)
IdS	*Inspekteur der Sicherheitspolizei* (Inspector of the Security Police)
IKG	*Israelitische Kultusgemeinde* (Jewish community [Vienna])
JdP	*Jungdeutsche Partei für Polen* (Young German Party for Poland)
NSDAP	*Nationalsozialistische Deutsche Arbeiterpartei* (National Socialist German Workers' Party, or Nazi party)
OHL	*Oberste Heeresleitung* (Army High Command)
RuS-Beratung	*Rasse- und Siedlungberatung* (Race and Settlement Advisory Unit of RuSHA)

RuSHA	*Rasse- und Siedlungshauptamt* (Race and Settlement Main Office of the SS)
RKFDV	*Reichskommissar für die Festigung deutschen Volkstums* (Reich Commissioner for the Strengthening of Germandom of the SS)
SD	*Sicherheitsdienst* (Security Service of the SS)
SdF	*Stellvertreter des Führers* (Deputy Führer)
SS	*Schutzstaffel* (Protection Squadron)
SSPF	*SS- und Polizeiführer* (SS and Police Leader)
UWZ	*Umwandererzentralstelle* (Resettlement Central Office of the SS)
VDA	*Volksbund für das Deutschtum im Ausland* (Volk Alliance for Germandom Abroad)
VoMi	*Volksdeutsche Mittelstelle* (Ethnic German Liaison Office of the SS)
VR	*Volksdeutscher Rat* (Ethnic German Council)

City Names

German Name	Contemporary Name
Bendzin	Będzin
Bielitz	Bielsko
Breslau	Wrocław
Briesen	Wąbrzeźno
Bromberg	Bydgoszcz
Danzig	Gdańsk
Dirschau	Tchew
Gdingen	Gdynia
Gladau	Głodowo
Glowno	Główna
Gosslershausen	Jabłonowo Pomorskie
Gotenhafen	Gdynia
Grätz	Grodzisk Wielkopolski
Hohensalza	Inowrocław
Jarotschin	Jarocin
Kalisch	Kalisz
Kempen	Kępno
Kolmar	Chodzież
Königsberg	Kaliningrad
Krakau	Kraków
Krotoschin	Krotoszyn
Kulmhof	Chełmno
Lissa	Leszno
Litzmannstadt	Łódź
Lodsch	Łódź
Marienwerder	Kwidzyn
Mewe	Gniew
Neumark	Nowe Miasto Lubawskie

Neustadt	Wejherowo
Nürnberg	Nuremberg
Oppeln	Opole
Petrikau	Piotrków
Posen	Poznań
Potulitz	Potulice
Saybusch	Żywiec
Schrimm	Śrem
Schroda	Środa
Stettin	Szczecin
Teschen	Cieszyn
Thorn	Toruń
Wollstein	Wolsztyn
Wongrowitz	Wągrowiec
Zoppot	Sopot

SS Ranks

SS Rank	Translation	US Equivalent
Reichsführer-SS	National Leader of the SS	
Obergruppenführer	Senior Group Leader	General
Gruppenführer	Group Leader	Lieutenant General
Brigadeführer	Brigade Leader	Major General
Oberführer	Senior Leader	(none)
Standartenführer	Regiment Leader	Colonel
Obersturmbannführer	Senior Assault Unit Leader	Lieutenant Colonel
Sturmbannführer	Assault Unit Leader	Major
Hauptsturmführer	Chief Assault Leader	Captain
Obersturmführer	Senior Assault Leader	First Lieutenant
Untersturmführer	Junior Assault Leader	Second Lieutenant
Hauptscharführer	Chief Squad Leader	Master Sergeant
Oberscharführer	Senior Squad Leader	Sergeant First Class
Scharführer	Squad Leader	Staff Sergeant
Unterscharführer	Junior Squad Leader	Sergeant
Rottenführer	Section Leader	Private First Class
Sturmmann	Storm Trooper	Private

IDEOLOGY AND THE RATIONALITY OF DOMINATION

Introduction

Among those persons earmarked for induction into Section 3 of the Deutsche Volksliste [German People's List], there are some who are racially unsuitable for incorporation into the German Volksgemeinschaft [ethnonational community]. But an influx of undesirable blood into the German Volkskörper [ethnonational body] must be prevented without fail.[1]

These thoughts were written by Heinrich Himmler on September 30, 1941, as he tried to take control of the selection process applied to the local populace in occupied western Poland.

By this point, the "incorporated eastern territories" had long since become an arena of fierce wrangling between the various relevant German authorities. Occupied during the invasion of Poland and already incorporated into the Reich in October 1939, this territory was transformed into a "training ground" ("Exerzierplatz") for Nazi population policy: here, the populace was subjected to a systematic selection process; here lay the focus of Nazi deportation policy; and here was also where the first steps were taken toward the mass murder of political opponents, sanitarium patients, and later the Jewish populace.[2] The conceptual threads behind this explosion of violence intersected at two central concepts of Nazism: "Volksgemeinschaft" and "Lebensraum," meaning "ethnonational community" and "living space." Although Poland was not the first eastern neighbor to fall victim to the Reich's aggressive policies, nor even its primary target, this country—or more precisely, its western part—was nonetheless the first one earmarked for Germanization, the first one upon which the Nazis projected their horrifying dystopian vision of a "German Lebensraum in the east."

The Nazi project of Germanizing the annexed territories certainly covered a very wide range of activities, from the theft of Polish assets to attempts at replacing the local education system with a German one, and from stamping a "German character" onto towns to reshaping the rural landscape.[3] But at the heart of all German efforts stood the Germanization of the populace. This essentially meant applying a selection process to the local populace, sorting them into those considered "Fremdvölkische" (the "ethnonationally foreign"), who were to be expelled or exterminated, and those considered "Germans," who—together with the ethnic

Germans brought here from Eastern Europe and the settlers from the Reich itself—were to form the core of the "Volksgemeinschaft" to be established here.

In view of the importance assigned to this particular complex in the ideology of Nazism and in the justification given for the war, it would not have been surprising if, immediately after annexation, this territory had been subjected to a coherent and systematic Germanization policy prepared long in advance.[4] In fact, Hitler had already provided the relevant framework in 1922, fixing it in writing a few years later.[5] According to him, if the "foreign policy of the ethnonationally oriented state [völkischen Staates]" is to establish "a healthy, viable, natural relationship between the number and growth of the population on the one hand, and the size and quality of the soil and territory on the other," then a return to the borders of 1914 would not suffice.[6] In fact, such a suggestion was "political nonsense," as any potential success would still be so "miserable that it would not be worth it . . . to invest the blood of our people for this again."[7] Instead, a Nazi foreign policy would turn its "gaze toward the land to the east. We are finally ending the colonial and trade policy of the prewar period and moving to the territorial policy of the future."[8] In *Mein Kampf*, Hitler was still vague about what should happen to the populace already living there, although he did argue in brief passages for a strictly racial approach: "Germanization" must not be misinterpreted as chiefly the "superficial acquisition of the German language"—a criticism primarily alluding to attempts by Prussia and the Habsburg empire to assimilate their non-German-speaking populations, by force if necessary. He went on to write that "Germanization can be undertaken only with the soil, and never the people." From a racial point of view, the failure of this earlier Germanization policy was neither surprising nor regrettable. After all, it was a "hardly credible error in reasoning to believe that . . . out of a negro or a Chinese a German emerges because he has learned German." Furthermore, the necessarily associated "blood mixing" ("Blutsvermischung") would have meant "the lowering of the level of the higher race" as well as the annihilation of the "cultural strengths" of the "German people," and if that had happened, "it would hardly have been possible to call it a cultural factor anymore."[9] Hitler was even more explicit in his "second book" (although it remained unpublished in his lifetime): "The ethnonationally oriented state can under no circumstances annex the Poles with the intention of turning them into Germans one day. Instead, it must make a decision to either sequester these racially alien elements so that the blood of one's own people is not undermined again and again, or else to immediately remove them entirely and thereby assign to one's own ethnonational comrades [Volksgenossen] the land and territory freed as a result."[10]

Even if these statements by Hitler were more about criticizing the previous Germanization attempts by Prussia and the Habsburg monarchy than about defining a political agenda, one thing was still clear: the areas in Eastern Europe to be occupied by a Nazi Germany had to be depopulated if they were to fulfill their function as an expanded "German Lebensraum" for a "people without space" (*Volk ohne Raum*, the well-known title of a 1926 right-wing novel), and they had to be settled by "Germans" in order to secure them in the long run.

Of course, the realities of Hitler's Germany were something else. For example, the Nazi regime's own structural idiosyncrasies were already hindering all attempts at defining long-term plans for the postwar future. After Poland's capitulation, a multitude of actors immediately claimed precedence in taking charge of the territory's Germanization: the most important of these included the Reich Interior Ministry (Reichsinnenministerium), the provincial administrations, and Heinrich Himmler in his new role as the Reich Commissioner for the Strengthening of Germandom (Reichskommissar für die Festigung deutschen Volkstums, or RKFDV). This point also shows how misleading and simplistic it is to assume that the Nazi Party's policies after its coming to power were simply a pure implementation of Nazi ideology, or even a direct translation of slogans contained in the party platform or in *Mein Kampf*, ideas written at a time when Hitler and his followers were little more than an insignificant faction in the Weimar Republic's lunatic fringe, with no need or opportunity to actually realize their slogans on the national political stage.

This was particularly evident in the way that Nazi Germanization policy was formulated and implemented in annexed western Poland. With the diverging centrifugal forces of competing political interests built into this polycratically structured regime, there was no way they could be reconciled through common recourse to the central elements of Nazi ideology. On the contrary, it was precisely the incoherence of Nazi ideology that allowed rival actors to use it for legitimizing even contradictory policy proposals. The typical consequence was years of wrangling in which even the most basic questions could find no agreement, questions that were finally resolved not by a decision from the highest authority in Berlin, but by one from Moscow—with the invasion of the Red Army.

Himmler's directive, cited at the beginning, points to one instance of this wrangling. At issue was the selection criteria used by the German People's List (Deutsche Volksliste, or DVL), an institution meant as a tool for cataloguing the local "Germans." His directive brings up a number of questions. For one, how could it be that in September 1941—after two years of German occupation—the relevant German agencies had still not agreed on a set of selection criteria? But more important, how did it come to pass that the implemented selection process did not actually conform to Hitler's guidelines and limit itself to the "Germanization of the soil," but had instead apparently aimed at the assimilation of non-Germans, so that Himmler then found it necessary to issue this course correction and demand the exclusion of "undesirable blood"? What role was played by "race" as a selection criterion? And was Himmler's intervention actually successful?

In fact, not so much. As I will show, there were other priorities, for example, among the "ethnocrats" (to borrow an apt term from historian Michael Burleigh) who were working in the Wartheland. Already with the first instructions issued to the local bureaus of the DVL in January 1940, it was stated that "racial markers cannot be used as a reliable basis for assessing German ethnonational membership."[11] In the other two annexed provinces, Himmler's directive would fail even more dramatically: in Upper Silesia, it was declared that the "induction of persons of German ethnonationality into the DVL can fundamentally not be made dependent on the result of a racial evaluation," while in Danzig–West Prussia, the DVL offices were instructed that the results of racial appraisals, "for the decision making of the DVL, are not to be seen as binding."[12]

The DVL was certainly not some minor undertaking but instead was at the heart of all Nazi efforts to Germanize the populace of annexed western Poland and establish a "German Volksgemeinschaft." Founded in late October 1939 immediately after the civil administration was installed, it initially existed only under the Reichsstatthalter (Reich governor) of the Wartheland, before expanding a year and a half later to cover all of annexed western Poland, registering almost three million "Germans" by the war's end—out of a total population of over seven million. This made it by far the largest Germanization project of the Nazi regime.[13]

Of course, Nazi Germanization policy in the annexed territories of western Poland was aimed not only at the inclusion of "Germans," but also at the settlement of "Volksdeutsche" (ethnic Germans) who had been attracted from Eastern Europe by the "Homeward into the Reich" ("Heim ins Reich") campaign and, above all, at the exclusion of the "Fremdvölkische" living there. At least in theory, this established a (coerced) circular flow of resettlement, an "organizational unity of so-called positive and negative population policy," as Götz Aly described it.[14] In this regard, I will confine my investigation to the treatment of the local non-Jewish populace; in terms of implementing bodies, I will focus on not only the DVL, but also the activities of the Resettlement Central Offices (each known as an Umwandererzentralstelle, or UWZ), which were tasked with the identification and deportation of the "Fremdvölkische."[15]

After the murder sprees of the first two months had taken tens of thousands of victims, and before the anti-Jewish policy was ultimately radicalized with the establishment of the Kulmhof extermination camp (near Chełmno nad Nerem, Poland) in late 1941, the German occupiers had intended to get rid of unwanted population groups by deporting them to the territory of the General Government.[16] To this end, UWZs were established in the targeted provinces, but unlike the DVL, these were subordinated not to the civil administrations, but to the local SS offices.[17] Of course, they were confronted with the same question facing the DVL: According to what criteria should it be decided whether a person was to be exempted from deportation as a "German," or should fall victim to it as a "Pole"? For persons not (or not yet) registered by the DVL, this decision was delegated to the ethnocrats of the SS apparatus. In view of Himmler's attempt to reorient the selection practices of the DVL in favor of using racial criteria, one might expect that the criterion of "race" would dominate at least the selection practices of the UWZs.

But this too would be an overhasty conclusion. Although it is true that a few months later, Himmler's direct orders would mean that those classified as "Deutschstämmige" (the "German-descended") were to be exempted from deportation, it was otherwise generally not racial criteria, but instead pragmatic ones, that ultimately decided who would be deported and when. One consequence of this was that, despite instructions to the contrary from SS headquarters in Berlin, relatively few Jews were expelled from the annexed territories in the beginning.

* * *

This short outline may seem surprising, as it contradicts a historiographic trend that has asserted itself since the 1980s, one that stands against a research approach shaped by social history while instead attributing a new (and simultaneously old) explanatory power to the role of Nazi ideology, particularly—as claimed by this trend—its racial core.[18] Although this "return of ideology" need not necessarily boil down to a narrow view that attributes violent policies solely to ideology, racism is nonetheless assigned the central role here, not only in terms of the demand to winnow "life unworthy of life" ("lebensunwertes Leben") from persons deserving of life, but also in terms of legitimizing the state policies that implemented such demands.[19] The appeal of this metanarrative is obvious: it enables an integrated representation of Nazi rule, so that large-scale atrocities like the Shoah, as well as the mass murders of Soviet POWs, "antisocial elements," and all those declared a threat to the "German Volksgemeinschaft," can be analyzed as various aspects of a *single* policy of violence, one aimed at establishing a racist utopia through "the final solution of the social question."[20] The widespread influence of this new paradigm is reflected in a multitude of studies in which Nazi Germany is now presented as primarily a "racial state," to borrow the title of a 1991 book by Michael Burleigh and Wolfgang Wippermann.[21]

There are two dangers with this approach. First, it is often used as the basis for an understanding of ideology where the unquestionably irrational premises of *völkisch* ("folkish," meaning ethnonationalist) or racial ideology are seen to also contaminate the policies they fuel and justify, thereby overlooking the fact that—as Werner Röhr wrote in regard to racism—its "delusional aspects . . . precludes neither their functionality in regard to its articulated goals nor the possibility of rational calculation within its framework."[22] The connection between ideology and power, so essential to the critique of ideology, threatens to be lost completely, so that ideology becomes an irrational force, one that instead of dressing up conduct serving the functional needs of power, works to threaten such conduct instead.[23] The relationship between ideology and the rationale of power is no longer understood as a shifting field of contention, but is instead reduced to a straightforward dichotomy, resulting in a historiographically simplified confrontation between "ideologues" and "pragmatists."

Second, a privileging of racism also threatens to obscure what Lutz Raphael described as the "weakly regulated pluralism within a whole array of Nazi worldviews," although it was precisely this plurality that made the Nazi Party so attractive to contemporaries.[24] This relates above all to the fact that a focus on race leads to a marginalization of antisemitism and anti-Jewish violence, and begs the question why the regime chose genocide in the case of the Jews but was able to make compromises in the handling of other enemy groups. But even more relevant to the present investigation is the marginalization of the more "traditional" nationalist aspects of Nazi ideology, as embodied by terms like *Volk* (folk, but variously meaning people, nation, or ethnonation) and "Volksgemeinschaft." Although the discursive framework within which the determinants of German identity could be articulated had certainly been narrowed after the 1933 Nazi takeover, one cannot say there had been a real paradigm shift. In neither the general public's understanding nor in the multitude of official Nazi publications was membership in the German Volk defined in exclusively or even primarily racial terms: instead, it was built much more upon social practices and above all cultural ones as well, stretching as far back as to the German philosophers Johann Gottfried Herder and Johann Gottlieb Fichte.

During World War II, this ideological patchwork would also turn Germanization policy into an ideological battleground, one in which the highlighting of "Volk" or "race" represented two contrasting rulership techniques for subjugating the local populace. This conflict was not a new one. As Cornelia Essner writes, völkisch ideologues like longtime Nazi Party and SA member Friedrich Merkenschlager had mobilized against the rise of racial anthropology and its popularization, even in its early days. In his 1926 polemic *Götter, Helden und Günther: Eine Abwehr des Güntherschen Rassegedankens* (Gods, heroes, and Günther: a refutation of Günther's racial ideas), Merkenschlager attacked the work of Hans F. K. Günther, whose 1922 book *Rassenkunde des deutschen Volkes* (Racial science of the German people) had become by far the most popular racial anthropology work in Germany during the interwar period, and it also made a lasting impact on political debate.[25] In it, in response to contemporary research, Günther outlined a topological racial anthropology of the German people, which in this view no longer formed a single organic entity (as claimed by Merkenschlager and other völkisch ideologues), but instead represented a "racial mix" comprising the various racial components of unequal value, ranging from a "Nordic" race to an "East Baltic" one.[26] Günther amplified this idea with his 1925 publication, *Der nordische Gedanke unter den Deutschen* (The Nordic idea among the Germans), which opened him to criticisms that his call for "Nordification" ("Aufnordung") was driving a wedge in the German "Volk."[27] This clash of ideas was in full swing by the time the Nazis came to power and now also engulfed the party's different wings and their respective organs. The party's leaders soon realized that calls for a "Nordification" of the German "Volk" threatened the building of broad-based support for their new government—particularly as fears began to spread that new laws like the one permitting forced sterilization could be tied to the dystopian vision of a "Nordic Germany."[28]

Essner claims that—with the help of influential allies like Heinrich Himmler and the new Reich Interior Minister Wilhelm Frick, and despite all pacifying efforts such as those by the Racial Policy Office (Rassenpolitisches Amt)—the "Nordics" soon achieved the upper hand, so that "race" and not "Volk" became the theoretical polestar for Nazi ideology.[29] I find this highly questionable because there can be no doubt that völkisch criteria, in the imagination of the German "Volk," had lost none of its plausibility. In fact, the present investigation of Nazi Germanization policy will instead demonstrate the opposite. This is despite such instances as when the racists at the SS Race and Settlement Main Office (Rasse- und Siedlungshauptamt der SS, or RuSHA) quickly took the initiative as early as October 1939 by equipping its Poland-assigned suitability inspectors (*Eignungsprüfer*) with a racial criteria catalog that was meant to help them separate "Germans" from "Poles" in the annexed territories. For example, blue was not the only acceptable eye color: but if they were brown, it was important to carefully distinguish what shade. Here, "black-brown, which mostly looks sinister and tends more toward black," was to be rejected. According to Berlin, this appeared "mostly in cases of a foreign blood element (non-European) and among colored races." Meanwhile, "among us is . . . a rich, velvety brown (cow eyes) generally the darkest color."[30] This guidance was hardly practicable, as was the policy formulated on its basis. Neither this nor similar selection procedures would find wide application. In deciding who would now be considered "German," the occupiers were not guided by racial anthropology criteria, but instead focused on the willingness to collaborate and perform, on submissiveness, and on the eagerness to acquire German language skills—a selection procedure that clearly harked back to Prussia's Germanization policies.

* * *

The conflict over DVL selection criteria, as alluded to at the beginning of this introduction, not only illustrates the differences between the relevant actors in such a key area as Germanization policy, it also reveals the fruitlessness of trying to interpret the practices of German occupation organs by looking primarily at the Nazi regime's central ideological writings. The structure and dynamics of the Germanization policy in annexed western Poland cannot be understood if they are read simply as the physical implementation of ideological dictates. Although Nazi Germanization policy clearly revolved primarily around the two ideologically loaded ideas of "Volk" and "race," it is equally clear that the various actors did not use these terms in the same way and could not agree on how they related to one another.

It is against this background that I will analyze Nazi Germanization policy by situating it in the conflicted zone between ideological premises and the rational needs of power. Therefore, I will not treat the selection practices of the DVL and the UWZs as a linear implementation of doctrinaire demands by Nazi ideologues, nor will I analyze ideological justifications as purely window dressing for courses of action motivated by entirely unrelated rationales; instead, I will highlight the dialectic interplay between selection practices and their ideological justifications. In this context, I want to evaluate the effectiveness of völkisch and racial ideologies in shaping selection practices, while also showing, through examples of the relevant hegemonic practices, which ideologies were able to assert themselves as being particularly functional in terms of serving the needs of power. Specifically, the following questions will be at the heart of the investigation:

> 1) What was the process for formulating the selection criteria that separated "Germans" from "Poles," and how were these criteria handled in practice? Why were the relevant actors unable to agree upon a common set of selection criteria valid for all provinces and for the entire duration of the war? Why were they constantly changing, often varying greatly according to time and region?
>
> 2) How important was the ideological justification for these selection criteria (whether only stipulated or actually implemented), and how "flexible" did Nazi ideology turn out to be, in giving an ideologically consistent face to the real-world necessities that faced the German occupiers?
>
> 3) How did these criteria, which could be fixed only temporarily in time and space, relate to the power politics between different institutions, as well as between the actors who tried to assert their interests? Can the actions of these institutions be understood as part of the German occupation strategy for establishing permanent possession of these territories and exploiting them economically? In this regard, did the relevant population policy measures prove to be functional for serving the needs of power?

Existing Scholarship

It is only gradually that such questions are being raised in research on Nazi Germanization policy in Poland. In the first writings on this topic, such as in the wartime underground press (as investigated by Andrzej Gąsiorowski) and the publications of the Polish government-in-exile in London, a prominent role was assigned to the DVL, which was often denounced as a tool for the occupiers to encourage collaboration in the Polish populace.[31] The rapid expansion of the DVL seems to have precipitated a Polish reevaluation of Nazi occupation policy in annexed western Poland, as later publications by the government-in-exile perceptively observed that the German occupiers were increasingly orienting themselves toward a more "traditional German approach, the Germanization of the Poles themselves."[32] There was the mistaken assumption in London, however, that this shift was simply Berlin's reaction to the failures of its deportation program, thus overlooking the bitter wrangling between various German agencies over competing strategies for achieving "German Lebensraum."

After the war, this was another area that saw important advances initially in the courtroom.[33] Especially significant here were the proceedings against the heads of the RKFDV Staff Main Office (Stabshauptamt des RKFDV), the Ethnic German Liaison Office (Volksdeutsche Mittelstelle, or VoMi), and RuSHA during the "subsequent" Nuremberg trials of 1946–49, when the spotlight already began turning to the "close connection between resettlements and evacuations," as well as highlighting the rationale of the DVL and the "re-Germanization campaign" ("Wiedereindeutschungsaktion") for serving the needs of power.[34] After all, this allowed the Reich "to bring labor to Germany, at the same time depriving Poland of masses of its citizens and attempting to effect a forced Germanization of these foreign citizens."[35] But by assuming that this brutal population policy had been prepared long in advance in Berlin, the US prosecutors failed to understand the logic of its dynamics, which is why to them the gap between ideological dictates and policy practices necessarily appeared "somewhat inconsistent," thereby remaining unexplained.[36]

For subsequent scholarly research, these trials were decisive trendsetters—in both positive and negative respects. Little attention was again paid to the ideological dimension and to its role as a battlefield for the Nazi power blocs competing for hegemony in this area. Instead, both Robert L. Koehl, in his 1957 study of Himmler's RKFDV apparatus and its actions, and Martin Broszat, in his study of the Nazi regime's Poland policy shortly thereafter, tended to emphasize the strategic importance of population policy for German occupation policy and the Reich's war capacities, although the latter scholar did also address the DVL in more detail for the first time.[37] Without access to the archives of Eastern Europe, both Koehl and Broszat were left to rely on the records of the regime's central authorities in Berlin, which is why they only had a rough sense of the major role played by each local Gauleiter (Gau leader, the head of a Nazi Party regional subdivision known as a Gau).[38]

Despite its shortcomings, Broszat's study was nonetheless remarkable in the German context, representing an early attempt to confront German crimes in Eastern Europe at a time when Germans were more interested in discussing their own sufferings: after all, it was more advantageous during the Cold War to highlight the mass expulsion of Germans from Eastern Europe, thereby scoring political points against the Soviet Union.[39] This phenomenon is reflected in the multitude of studies on population groups that had been brought into the occupied territories for settlement during the war and who in this view were equally counted among the "Vertriebene" ("expellees"), an appellation that is both misleading and symptomatic.[40] But because of a failure to adequately situate these resettlement efforts within the broader totality of Nazi population policy, the self-contradictions of these actions could be interpreted only through the racial worldview of the occupiers themselves, making them seem like—as described for example by Jachomowski—"one of the strangest escapades of Nazi ethnopolicy."[41] In a framework like this, questions about how such population transfers served the rational demands of power within German occupation strategy cannot even be asked in the first place.

What has proved more important in this regard are the scholarly contributions from those countries most affected by Nazi plans for more "Lebensraum," scholarship so often overlooked in Western historiography. After the war, Poland saw determined efforts to rebuild and expand its institutions of historical research, which soon came out with several important volumes of reprinted source materials, alongside a number of publication series.[42] In the early postwar period, these institutions were in demand as centers for scholarly policy advice.[43] For example, while the Polish authorities may have found it easy to deport people registered in Sections 1 and 2 of the DVL, meaning those who seemed particularly loyal to the Germans, it did not seem the right way to handle the more than two million people registered in Sections 3 and 4, who were considered "Germans on probation." They had been enrolled by the Germans because the region's economy would have collapsed without them, and now Zygmunt Izdebski, as a rapporteur for Poland's Ministry for the Recovered Territories (and also the head of the Polish Western Association in Silesia and a member of the Silesian Institute), used similar reasoning to argue vehemently against their expulsion, pointing to his study of the massive terror that had left many with no alternative but to apply for DVL membership.[44] After it was generally decided to integrate members of Sections 3 and 4 into Poland's postwar society, discussion of the DVL faded away, as did scholarly research into it.[45]

Research efforts, particularly in Poland, into German occupation policy then shifted in the subsequent period to its even more violently imposed aspects and took three fundamental hypotheses as their basis. The first one claimed that "the German imperialists . . . had detailed plans for expansion and conquest and tried to implement them consistently," with examples ranging from the preinvasion compilation of extensive wanted-person lists to detailed geopolitical plans in the form of the "General Plan for the East" ("Generalplan Ost").[46] The second hypothesis, because of the "General Plan for the East" and the great number of persons murdered, assumed that German policy aimed at the genocide of the Polish people and of Slavic populations in general who stood in the way of the dystopian vision of a "German Lebensraum" in the east. Borrowing from the Nuremberg war-crimes trials and particularly from Raphael Lemkin's definition of genocide, but generally without mentioning him, many scholarly studies spoke of a "direct annihilation" and an "indirect annihilation" of the Polish people, citing the targeted liquidation of its elites, the mass deportations, and the measures for the repression of Polish culture.[47] In that line of reasoning, it was not uncommon to additionally claim that those measures were even more urgent for the German occupiers than, for example, their anti-Jewish goals.[48] In the studies following the third hypothesis, insights into the functional aspects of Nazi population policy were frequently and unquestioningly placed alongside the claim that they had been predetermined by the racist ideology of the occupiers and had been guided by "National Socialist race theory."[49] In these studies, theoretical ideology and practical interest stand alongside one another, but their interrelationship is not explained and remains unexplored.

The results of my investigation diverge from these hypotheses, sometimes considerably. As I will show, it is hard to identify any uniform Germanization policy, as the SS apparatus was unable—and the Reich Interior Ministry even less so—to maintain control over the wayward powers on the periphery and the competing power blocs in Berlin or to steer them onto prescribed paths. In this regard, my study is more inspired by Czesław Madajczyk's work *Die Okkupationspolitik Nazideutschlands in Polen 1939–1945* (Nazi Germany's occupation policy in Poland, 1939–1945), still considered a standard reference today.[50] To a much greater degree than most Polish researchers before him, he investigates not only the relevant Berlin head offices, but also their interactions with regional and local offices. As Madajczyk later stated in a personal rereading of his research, it was this approach that first allowed him to unravel the "discrepancy between the program formulated in advance . . . and the modifications forced on it by the actual conditions of war."[51] Nonetheless, Madajczyk's research also has gaps, with only fragmentary analysis of the roles played by the UWZ and the DVL.

It was after the implosion of Eastern Europe's states that the wider research field experienced a quantum leap. The reasons are easy to identify, ranging from the so-called "deideologization" of historiography in a post–Cold War world to the greater accessibility of Eastern Europe's archives.[52] It is often the more narrowly focused in-depth studies that have proved the most innovative, with investigations of specific policy areas leading to more generalized conclusions about Nazi rule.

Of particular importance for me have been—first—investigations of the role played by Germany's intelligentsia and scholarship in formulating plans. In this regard, particular praise goes to Götz Aly and Susanne Heim, whose book *Architects of Annihilation* (originally published as *Vordenker der Vernichtung* in 1991) not only highlighted a "new" class of perpetrators, but also contextualized the regime's decision to annihilate the Jews within the wider framework of Nazi population policy, which itself was no longer treated as merely an addendum to occupation policy, but instead put at the focus of investigation.[53] But the question of how important scholarly advice was in shaping policy, as explored in that and later studies, remains largely unresolved.[54] On this point, I will argue more cautiously, because scholarship was often requested only when the purpose was to legitimize decisions already made.

Tied closely to those investigations are—second—studies that, while focusing on the Shoah, depart from earlier approaches that tried to explain it solely as a dynamic of antisemitic violence and embed it instead within the dystopian project of expanding "German Lebensraum." Worth noting here is another work by Götz Aly, which spotlights the relationship between wider population planning and the annihilation of the Jews, with the faltering program of deportation and resettlement then made responsible for the decision to commit mass murder.[55] Although Aly may have overstated the causative connection, he nonetheless achieved an important advance in uncovering the radicalizing influence of deportation and resettlement policies.[56]

The detailed demonstration of the importance of Nazi population policy has had a decisive impact, with—third—most published studies in the last two decades on the German occupation of Eastern Europe likewise devoting more attention to that aspect. The effect can be seen first and foremost in scholarly investigations of the various SS main offices (*SS-Hauptämter*, the top-level departments of the SS) that were directly involved in Germanization policy as a result of Himmler's parallel roles as the RKFDV and as overall head of the SS. Noteworthy examples here include the study by Valdis O. Lumans on VoMi, and especially Michael Wildt's study of the Reich Security Main Office (Reichssicherheitshauptamt), which had a major role in the planning of population policy.[57] Building on Wildt, who has already highlighted the importance of the Reich Security Main Office in the expulsion of local "Fremdvölkische" and the selection of the "Volksdeutsche," I will demonstrate for the first time that it also played an important role in the wrangling over the DVL. Another gap in research was addressed by Isabel Heinemann with her investigation of RuSHA; although I think she overestimated its importance, for it did not in fact become the "coordination headquarters for the settlement and race policy of the SS" or the "key institution" of Nazi population policy.[58] Instead, the marginalization of all racially oriented selection processes would also push RuSHA to the sidelines.

Also proving helpful are—fourth—regionally focused studies that show, to a greater or lesser degree, the close connection between Nazi Germany's racist plans for the east, its resettlement policy, and its mass murder of Jews. While Czesław Łuczak, for example, fails to examine more closely the difference between the regime's racial theories and its actual policies on the ground, taking instead the former as an explanation for the latter and thus mistakenly claiming that the selection practices of the DVL were oriented toward the "racial criteria applicable to Germans in the Reich," Sybille Steinbacher takes this complicated relationship as a defining topic.[59] For her, it is clear that the German occupation's selection and deportation policies certainly did not represent some strange "wartime experiment by irrational fantasists," but instead must be analyzed as an undertaking "founded upon the concrete interests of power politics."[60] In all these studies, the central roles played by the UWZ and the DVL are made quite clear. None of them, however, conducts a deeper study of these institutions.[61]

Recent years have finally seen a number of studies that, in analyzing specific fields of activity or policy by the German occupiers, such as the invasion of Poland, economic policy, labor policy, and policies on education and culture, also investigate how these connect to Germanization policy or else make it their main topic.[62] When these studies do focus on population policy issues, they tend to concentrate more on deportation, resettlement, and colonization aspects, leaving the DVL in a kind of blind spot. The only exception here is an article by Werner Röhr on Nazi population policy in the Wartheland, which also contradicts for the first time the widespread scholarly assumption that the DVL conducted its selection process according to racial criteria. Even Röhr, however, gives few details about what this selection process looked like in practice.[63]

Source Materials

Since a basic premise of my study is that any analysis of Nazi Germanization policy must start with the practices actually conducted on the ground, I have striven from the very start to consider not only the planning and decision-making processes undertaken by the top-level authorities in Berlin and at the various provincial administrative capitals, but also and especially the happenings in the governmental regions and rural counties (*Regierungsbezirken* and *Landkreisen*, Germany's mid- and low-level administrative divisions). Overall, the source materials of three institutional complexes have proven to be decisive: those of the top-level Reich authorities, particularly the Reich Interior Ministry; those of the SS apparatus, ranging from the various SS main offices in Berlin to the individual SS posts and police stations on the periphery; and, above all, those of the civil administrations in the annexed regions, here too ranging from the administrative capitals down to the cities and rural counties.

The greatest part of these materials is housed in Polish archives, often in astonishing amounts. This is most conspicuous in the surviving materials on the DVL. For reasons of economy, my study focuses on the records left by the top-level heads of the three provinces in the annexed western Polish territories, one or two midlevel heads in each province, and selected low-level heads of urban and rural counties, each of whom supervised a DVL central office, a regional office, or a branch office. The surviving records of the civil administration in Posen (today Poznań, during the war the capital of the Wartheland) are exceptionally extensive and include an enormous number of DVL membership files, but those of the civil administrations in Danzig–West Prussia and Upper Silesia are somewhat scantier. The main developmental stages of selection policy in Danzig–West Prussia can be reconstructed through the parallel records of multiple sources, particularly those of the local Gauleiter's offices, as well as those of the *Regierungspräsident* (governmental region president) and various city and county administrations in Bromberg Governmental Region, in addition to the postwar trial documents of Albert Forster, former Reichsstatthalter and Gauleiter of Danzig–West Prussia. This was more easily done for Upper Silesia, where documentary gaps—particularly in the records of its *Oberpräsident* (senior president, the head of a province)—could be filled by the "Special Archive" holdings at the Russian State Military Archive in Moscow.

The particular weight given to events in the Wartheland are explained not only by its particularly extensive surviving records, but even more by the great importance the province had for Germanization policy. The province is where the DVL and UWZ were first established, it is where by far the greatest number of locals suffered expulsion, and it was also the location of the RuSHA field office whose analysis would prove invaluable for understanding not only the selections that RuSHA did for the UWZ but also those done at the DVL.

Whereas Michael Alberti, in his investigations of the annihilation of the Jews in the Wartheland, was often frustrated to discover that the destruction of files at the end of the war primarily involved those records that documented the most heinous of German crimes, my experience was a very different one.[64] To understand just how selective the Germans must have been in destroying incriminating evidence, one can examine the surviving records of the ethnonationality unit (*Volkstumreferat*) at the Wartheland Reichsstatthalter's offices, which includes not only the documents of the local DVL central office, but also a number of memoranda about the future of the Wartheland's German and Polish populations, dystopian fantasies that eclipsed all DVL measures conducted to that date while also sketching out the ways in which the entire remaining populace would be subjected to a complicated selection process. Therefore, although the surviving source materials may have occasional gaps on specific institutions and regions, it nonetheless appears complete enough on most key issues to attempt a comprehensive analysis of Nazi Germanization policy in the annexed territories of western Poland.

Notes

1. Directive 50/I by Himmler as RKFDV, September 30, 1941, APP 406/1114, 5–6, reprinted in Pospieszalski, *Hitlerowskie "prawo" okupacyjne*, 144–45.

2. The term "Exerzierplatz" ("training ground") was already used during the war to describe (for example) the Wartheland, in order to highlight the trailblazing role of the province (Alberti, "Exerzierplatz des Nationalsozialismus"; Röhr, "Reichsgau Wartheland 1939–1945"; Hansen, "Damit wurde das Warthegau").

3. Recent studies of the confiscations include Dingell, *Zur Tätigkeit der Treuhandstelle Ost*; Rosenkötter, *Treuhandpolitik*. On the education system, see Kleßmann and Długoborski, "Nationalsozialistische Bildungspolitik"; Harten, *De-Kulturation und Germanisierung*; Hansen, "Schulpolitik im besetzten Polen." The stamping of "German character" is specified in the confidential guidelines of Chief of Civil Administration Arthur Greiser, September 29, 1939, AGK NTN/11, 1–2. On the rural landscape, see Hartenstein, *Neue Dorflandschaften*.

4. In the following investigation I will speak of *the* ideology of Nazism, although it was of course a theory complex drawing on very diverse streams of thought while trying to combine often contradictory approaches whose relative importance was generally not decided through intellectual debate, but instead through confrontations between various factions of the regime. For a broader look at Nazi ideology, see, for example, Weber, *Faschismus und Ideologie*; Raphael, "Nationalsozialistische Weltanschauung"; Kroll, *Utopie als Ideologie*; Jäckel, *Hitlers Herrschaft*.

5. Kershaw, *Hitler: Hubris*, 246–50. See similarly Jäckel, *Hitlers Weltanschauung*, 37–57.

6. Hitler, *Mein Kampf*, 728.

7. Ibid., 738.

8. Ibid., 742.

9. Ibid., 429–30.

10. Hitler, *Zweites Buch*, 81.

11. Guidelines for registering German ethnonationals in the DVL, headquarters copy, official use only, undated (probably late January 1940), APP 406/1106.

12. Memo from Bracht, undated (probably January 25, 1943), APK 117/140, 16; Forster to DVL regional and branch offices, February 9, 1943, APB 9/380, 243.

13. Besides the annexed regions of western Poland, a DVL has also been shown to exist in Ukraine and northern France, while a comparable model was similarly launched in the General Government and in southeastern European territories under German occupation civil administrations.

14. Aly, *Endlösung*, 381. Although such terminology is frequently used by researchers, it is also misleading, because it helps veil the frequently violent character of even "inclusivist" measures.

15. For an investigation of the selection process applied by the UWZ to the "Volksdeutsche" destined for settlement in the occupied territories, see Strippel, *Einwandererzentralstelle*.

16. On the early murder sprees, see particularly Jansen and Weckbecker, "Der Volksdeutsche Selbstschutz"; Mallmann, Böhler, and Matthäus, *Einsatzgruppen in Polen*;

Böhler, *Auftakt zum Vernichtungskrieg*; Rossino, *Hitler Strikes Poland*; on the origins and function of Kulmhof, see Kershaw, "Improvised Genocide?"

17. UWZs were later established for the same purpose in the annexed territories of Lower Styria and Upper Carniola with logistical and staffing support from the Polish bureaus, whose personnel were also involved with the deportations out of Moravia, Hungary, and other occupied territories (Marczewski, *Hitlerowska koncepcja*, 267).

18. See here particularly Caplan and Childers, *Reevaluating the Third Reich*, which brings together many newer research articles. Also see, for example, Friedlander, *The Origins of Nazi Genocide*; Proctor, *Racial Hygiene*; Schmuhl, *Rassenhygiene, Nationalsozialismus, Euthanasie*; Bock, *Zwangssterilisation*; Bridenthal, Grossmann, and Kaplan, *When Biology Became Destiny*.

19. Stone, "Beyond the Auschwitz syndrome," 454.

20. Peukert, "Genesis der Endlösung," 25.

21. Burleigh and Wippermann, *The Racial State*. This book restricts its investigations to the inside of the Reich itself, without making any assertions about Nazi population policy in occupied Eastern Europe.

22. Röhr, *Faschismus und Rassismus*, 64. In the present investigation, I will use the word "racial" to denote those exclusionary practices that, from the perspective of the relevant actors, were the direct products of a—however internally coherent—"race theory." This applies particularly to the proponents of racial anthropology, which presumed that primarily somatic and biometric markers can be used to divide humanity into distinct groups, while also defining them, attributing immutable characteristics to them, and establishing a hierarchy for them. Thereby, I also intend to establish a certain distance from the otherwise commonly used term "racist," because this has acquired a considerably wider meaning not only in common parlance, but also increasingly among scholars as well: in this view, "racist" is basically every argumentation or behavior that discriminates against targeted groups by attributing such "immutable" personal traits—even when these are argued at least formally in cultural terms. For this expanded usage, see those studies that particularly emerged in response to the rapid rise in antimigrant attacks seen in many Western countries during the "crisis decades" (Hobsbawm) that followed the 1973 oil crisis. For example, see Taguieff, "From Race to Culture," highlighting the central role played by New Right thinkers (especially Alain de Benoist) in France. Similarly, for the UK, see Martin Barker, *The New Racism*. In both cases, the conceptual thrust was clearly the same: through the biologization of divergent social practices, one could justify not only expulsions, but also assaults and lethal attacks. This inclusion of cultural differences, be they alleged or real, makes such an expanded definition of "racism" largely unusable for my investigation, because it excessively blurs the distinctiveness of another social differentiation practice that took as its reference point not "race" but "Volk" (folk here meaning ethnonation).

In a similar vein, the term "völkisch" (folkish, meaning ethnonationalist) describes in-group selection practices that, from the perspective of the relevant actors, derive from a theory, however coherent, that revolves around "Volk" as its central reference point, framing it as a historical subject and as a community of both descent and destiny, one united by shared traits and a shared language, as well as an awareness of being carriers of a historical "mission." Although such an invocation of a community of descent clearly has essentialist elements and therefore overlaps with racial ideologies, nonetheless, as Manfred Hettling recently asserted: "Descent is not to be equated with race." Instead, from the viewpoint of a völkisch population policy (and key to the present investigation), the Germanization of Poland was not only possible, it was virtually demanded—and not only during the German Empire period, but also the Nazi one.

23. Actions serving the rational (or functional) needs of power are here understood as actions in the political sphere that are calculated to not only secure the continued existence of the relevant institution or political regime, but also, if possible, increase its power.

24. Raphael, "Nationalsozialistische Weltanschauung," 31.

25. Essner, "Im Irrgarten der Rassenlogik," 90–91. Furthermore, Merkenschlager was not alone in his critique, with similarly oriented ones also expressed by other scholars, especially those from southern Germany and Austria (certainly not by chance, as southerners were often deemed racially inferior to northerners), see ibid., 88–89; also Weisenburger, "Rassepapst," 170–71 and 179.

26. Günther, *Rassenkunde des deutschen Volkes*, 39–73, 171–78, and 230–45. Günther relied particularly on the research of Eugen Fischer, Erwin Baur, and Fritz Lenz, with their 1921 work *Grundriss der menschlichen Erblichkeitslehre und Rassenhygiene* (see Essner, "Im Irrgarten der Rassenlogik," 82–83). But Günther certainly took a few liberties in interpreting this research, as seen in his hierarchical ranking of the races allegedly existing in the German populace. This seemed not to disturb the original authors, with at least Eugen Fischer (who would later support Günther) commenting benevolently: "The poet always resonates within him" (cited in Weisenburger, "Rassepapst," 173). For a more detailed overview of Günther's "research results," see Hutton, *Race*, 35–55; on Fischer's relationship with Günther, see Massin, "Rasse und Vererbung," 190–94.

27. Essner, "Im Irrgarten der Rassenlogik," 88–97; Essner, *Nürnberger Gesetze*, 62–63; Weisenburger, "Rassepapst," 175–79; Hutton, *Race*, 113–29. Writing later on the corrosive effect of racism, see also Arendt, *Elemente und Ursprünge*, 271, who drew a critical response in Moses, "Hannah Arendt, Imperialism, and the Holocaust."

28. Essner, "Im Irrgarten der Rassenlogik," 92–97; Essner, *Nürnberger Gesetze*, 63–64. For a more detailed look at the confrontation between völkisch and racial ideologues, see Breuer, *Volkischen in Deutschland*, 113–25; Breuer, *Radikale Rechte*, 234–44.

29. Essner, "Im Irrgarten der Rassenlogik," 92–97.

30. Directive from Hofmann giving instructions for suitability assessment of returnees (*Rückwanderer*), confidential, October 14, 1939, SMR 1372-6/26, 16–19.

31. Gąsiorowski, "Niemiecka lista narodowa."

32. Polish Ministry of Information, *The Quest for German Blood*, 8. See also other ministry publications: *German Invasion*; *Black Book*; *German New Order*.

33. This refers not only to the Nuremberg trials, but also the Eichmann trial and especially those conducted in Poland.

34. *Trials of War Criminals*, 5:129.

35. Ibid., 5:132.

36. Ibid., 4:624.

37. Koehl, *RKFDV*, 3. On the re-Germanization program, see ibid., 123. His accounts of the DVL and the UWZs were quite cursory, see ibid., 104–7, 119–21, and 139–41. The book drew on several of his earlier articles, for example, Koehl, "Colonialism inside Germany," "Politics of Resettlement," and "Deutsche Volksliste in Poland." Here also Broszat, *Nationalsozialistische Polenpolitik*, 86–90 and 95–96. Two years later, Broszat embedded this

study in a broader outline of modern German-Polish relations, *Zweihundert Jahre deutsche Polenpolitik.*

38. A good example of this is Broszat's accounts of the DVL, which always become fuzzy in its concrete activities on the ground (such as his account of the DVL's founding in the Wartheland, which he wrongly attributed to the local Sicherheitsdienst) and Broszat also gives no details of its selection practices (Broszat, *Nationalsozialistische Polenpolitik*, 115).

39. See the multivolume *Dokumentation der Vertreibung der Deutschen aus Ost-Mitteleuropa* (Documentation of the expulsion of Germans from east central Europe), published by West Germany's Federal Ministry for Displaced Persons (under Minister Theodor Oberländer), and compiled by a commission that included Werner Conze, Theodor Schieder, and Hans Rothfels. This documentation project brought together people who knew each other when they used their scholarly arguments first to justify German supremacy in Eastern Europe and then during wartime to offer direct support to Nazi population policy (with the exception of Rothfels, who was forced into exile), even—as in the case of Oberländer—helping to impose it with gun in hand. On the various individuals, see Haar and Fahlbusch, *Handbuch der völkischen Wissenschaften.*

40. See, for example, Frensing, *Umsiedlung der Gottscheer Deutschen*; Loeber, *Diktierte Option*; von Hehn, *Umsiedlung der baltischen Deutschen*; Jachomowski, *Umsiedlung der Bessarabien-, Bukowina- und Dobrudschadeutschen*; Stossun, *Umsiedlung der Deutschen aus Litauen*; Döring, *Umsiedlung der Wolhyniendeutschen.*

41. Jachomowski, *Umsiedlung der Bessarabien-, Bukowina- und Dobrudschadeutschen*, 137.

42. For example, the Głównej Komisji Badania Zbrodni Niemieckich w Polsce (Central Commission for the Investigation of German Crimes in Poland, founded by Poland's Ministry of Justice), the Instytut Zachodni (Western Institute) in Poznań, and the Instytut Śląski (Silesian Institute) in Opole (formerly in Katowice). These organizations released several volumes of reprinted source materials, which were often the only way for Western researchers to access the holdings of Polish archives. Of particular importance here are the multivolume *Documenta Occupationis Teutonicae* from the Western Institute and the *Biuletyn* of the Central Commission. Similarly important are the journals of the Western Institute, such as its flagship *Przegląd Zachodni*, whose offshoot was soon published in English, French, and German. See also the journals *Studia Historica Slavo-Germanica* and *Studia Historiae Oeconomicae* from Adam Mickiewicz University in Poznań, which published articles in various languages and became important conduits for knowledge transfer between Polish and international scholars. For a general overview, see Czubiński, "Polnische historiographie des Zweiten Weltkrieges"; Haubold-Stolle, "Imaginative Nationalisierung."

43. For example, see Hadler, "Drachen und Drachentöter."

44. Izdebski, *Niemiecka lista narodowa.* For example, the Bishop of Katowice, Stanisław Adamski, encouraged his German-speaking clergy and parishioners to enroll in the DVL as a way to protect them against the feared negative consequences and saw this as not a "betrayal" but a "defense" of Polish identity in difficult times, see Adamski, *Pogląd na rozwój sprawy narodowościowej*, 17. See also the article by Adamski's personal secretary, Romuald Rak, "Deutsche Volksliste."

45. Scholarly interest shifted in subsequent years more toward the postwar reintegration of DVL Section 3 and 4 members into Polish society. See, for example, Boda-Krężel, *Sprawa volkslisty*; Romaniuk, *Podzwonne okupacji*; Stryjkowski, *Położenie osób wpisanych.*

One exception is Dzieciński, *Łódź w cieniu swastyki*, whose study of Łódź under German occupation also contains a relatively detailed section on the wartime DVL, including a short description of its selection criteria.

46. Czubiński, "Poland's Place in Nazi Plans," 21. This debate was triggered by Pospieszalski, "Hitlerowska polemika," and Madajczyk, *Generalplan Ost*. For an attempt to relate the deportations conducted in the Wartheland and especially in the General Government to the evolving General Plan, see Marczewski, *Hitlerowska koncepcja*, 263–78. Around the same time in West Germany, scholars like Helmut Heiber downplayed the General Plan as the "daydreams" of German bureaucrats drunk on power (Heiber, "Dokumentation: Der Generalplan Ost"). But in East Germany, this discussion resulted in an eight-volume series (begun a year before the Berlin Wall fell and completed in unified Germany) on Nazi occupation policy, in which the authors likewise assigned great significance to the General Plan (Schumann and Nestler, *Europa unterm Hakenkreuz*). In 1994, Czesław Madajczyk finally put out a compilation of original source materials on the General Plan for the East, uniting all the versions found until that point, along with submitted commentaries by various other bodies (Madajczyk, *Vom Generalplan Ost zum Generalsiedlungsplan*).

47. On genocide and its implementation in Poland, see Lemkin, *Axis Rule*, 79–81.

48. For precisely such sentiments, see, for example, Datner, Gumkowski, and Leszczyński, *Genocide 1939–1945*, 41; Łuczak, *Polityka ludnościowa i ekonomiczna*, 29; Marczewski, "Nazi Nationality Policy," 33; Marczewski, "Hitlerowska polityka narodowościowa," 59; Chrzanowski, "Wypędzenia z Pomorza." This discussion was continued more recently by two US historians: Lukas, *Forgotten Holocaust*; Piotrowski, *Poland's Holocaust*. Here, see also Dobroszycki, "Polish Historiography."

49. Marczewski, *Hitlerowska koncepcja*, 248. Marczewski is atypical in his assertion that the Germans did not invade Poland with a preformulated occupation plan. He does, however, believe that one was completed within the first few months of the occupation (see ibid., 11), an interpretation that does not really allow enough space for the evolutionary changes seen in German occupation policy. Marczewski is also more explicit than others in emphasizing the differences in Nazi population policy that separated the Wartheland from the other two provinces of annexed western Poland; see ibid., 11 and 253.

50. Madajczyk, *Okkupationspolitik Nazideutschlands*. This is an adapted German translation of his two-volume study *Polityka III Rzeszy w okupowanej Polsce*.

51. Madajczyk, "Zur Besatzungspolitik der Achsenmächte," 304.

52. Instead of a "deideologization" of historiography, it would probably be more accurate to describe it as an ideological shift. Especially among East German and Polish historians, one can see that the prehistory of the war, the Soviet Union's relationship with the Reich, and the even the implementation of antisemitic policies, had now acquired a very different meaning. At the same time, the collapse of "actually existing socialism" put into question all Marxist-inspired historiographies, leading to, for example, a regional revival of totalitarianism theory, which had been rejected for good reason: see Wippermann, *Totalitarismustheorien*; Roth, *Geschichtsrevisionismus*.

53. Aly and Heim, *Vordenker der Vernichtung*. It says much about the atmosphere in West Germany during the 1960s (including the academic one) that the first studies in this area were published abroad: for example, Goguel, *Über die Mitwirkung deutscher Wissenschaftler*; Goguel, "Bedeutung der Reichsuniversität Posen"; Goguel, "Nord-und ostdeutsche

Forschungsgemeinschaft" ; Burleigh, *Germany Turns Eastwards*. See also Fahlbusch, *Wissenschaft im Dienst*; Haar, *Historiker im Nationalsozialismus*; Roth, "Heydrichs Professor"; Mackensen, Reulecke, and Ehmer, *Ursprünge, Arten und Folgen*.

54. A good example of this are the investigations into the General Plan for the East, particularly into the relationship between its two planning centers, with one run by Dr. Hans Ehlich at the Reich Security Main Office and the other run by Prof. Konrad Meyer at the RKFDV Staff Main Office, as well as their relationship with the criminal practices of the SS units, especially their murder sprees in the Soviet Union. Putting it simply, the unresolved question is: Who led the way in these massacres, the planning groups in Berlin or the murderers on the ground? Did German units follow a plan, be it finished or not, or was it the dynamics of violence on the ground that forced the agenda for Berlin's geopolitical planners, who in many ways were always one step behind the realities and constantly having to adjust their plans accordingly? On this, see Roth, "Generalplan Ost—Gesamtplan Ost." On skepticism about the influence of scholarly policy advisers, see also Leniger, *Nationalsozialistische Volkstumsarbeit*, 13.

55. Aly, *Final Solution*. Here, Aly was able to build on earlier scholarship, because this link was already described in Broszat's *Nationalsozialistische Polenpolitik* and even more exhaustively in Christopher Browning's research. Nonetheless, Aly's analysis is a new one, in that Broszat primarily highlights the link between deportation and resettlement policies without discussing the effects it had on the course of anti-Jewish policy; meanwhile, although Browning does underline the radicalizing effects that the former's failure had on the decision to commit mass murder, he does not explicitly point out that the problems of resettling ethnic Germans may have accelerated or otherwise influenced this process; see Browning, "Nazi Resettlement Policy."

56. See also the critical counterpoint in Wildt, *Generation des Unbedingten*, 462.

57. Lumans, *Himmler's Auxiliaries*; Wildt, *Generation des Unbedingten*.

58. Heinemann, *Rasse, Siedlung, deutsches Blut*, 42 and 10. Also worth mentioning here is Longerich's biography *Heinrich Himmler*, which devotes much space to population policy.

59. Łuczak, *Pod niemieckim jarzmem*, 60.

60. Steinbacher, *Musterstadt Auschwitz*, 94; see also 118–19.

61. See, for example, Esch, *Gesunde Verhältnisse*; Kaczmarek, "Zwischen Altreich und Besatzungsgebiet." See also the biographies written about the Gauleiters (who were simultaneously the Reichsstatthalters) of Danzig–West Prussia and the Wartheland: Schenk, *Hitlers Mann*; Epstein, *Model Nazi*.

62. On the invasion of Poland and the population policy aspects of the Reich's warfare, see, for example, Rossino, *Hitler Strikes Poland*; Böhler, *Auftakt zum Vernichtungskrieg*. On economic and labor policy, see Röhr, "Zur Rolle der Schwerindustrie"; Röhr, "Zur Wirtschaftspolitik der deutschen Okkupanten"; Kaczmarek, "Die deutsche wirtschaftliche Penetration"; Stefanski, "Nationalsozialistische Volkstums- und Arbeitseinsatzpolitik." On educational and cultural policy, see Harten, *De-Kulturation und Germanisierung*.

63. Röhr, "Reichsgau Wartheland." See also Kaczmarek, "Niemiecka polityka narodowościowa"; Leniger, *Nationalsozialistische Volkstumsarbeit*; Lempart, "Deutsche Volksliste"; Strippel, *NS-Volkstumspolitik*.

64. Alberti, *Verfolgung und Vernichtung*, 17.

1   The German Quest for Polish Land

Anti-Polish Germanization Policy: The Path toward the German Nation-State

Modern German-Polish relations are rooted in the partitions of the Polish-Lithuanian Commonwealth that took place from 1772 to 1795. These territorial seizures were cemented in 1815 by the Congress of Vienna, making the czar of Russia thenceforth king of the newly created "Congress Poland" in personal union while furthermore reaffirming Austria's annexation of Galicia as well as Prussia's annexation of West Prussia and the Grand Duchy of Posen.

It was Prussia that profited most from Poland's dismemberment. Although West Prussia was immediately assimilated into the kingdom's administrative structure as a new province, King Frederick William III showed a certain amount of forbearance to the populace in the Grand Duchy of Posen on May 19, 1815, when he declared that they would not need to "deny [their] nationality," that their "religion is to be preserved," and also that their "language is to be used, alongside German, in all public proceedings."[1] Attacks against these "supreme sanctities of a nation" aimed at "denationalizing a people" would achieve precisely the opposite of what Prussia's education minister Karl vom Stein zum Altenstein described as Berlin's sole desire: "perfectly good subjects."[2]

Neither Prussia's initially conciliatory policy nor Russia's harsher one could hinder the emergence of a Polish national movement, which soon succeeded in making the Polish question a perennial concern on the European agenda. The partitioning powers came to feel this by 1830 at the latest, when the July Revolution in France also inflamed Poland, ultimately leading to an uprising against the Russian occupation troops. European reactions were divided, the German lands not excepted: while the government in Berlin feared that the disturbances could spread to the Prussian part of Poland, the bourgeois nationalist opposition felt great sympathy for the Polish insurrectionists and saw Poland as a key battleground through which Europe's entire restorationist order might be overturned.[3] In this camp, a potential reestablishment of the Polish state was not considered a threat at all: instead, it was to be welcomed as a positive step forward in their own struggle for German unification.[4] Regardless of whether this really reflected "cosmopolitanism" (as Michael G. Müller claims) or was instead more about "pan-nationalism" (as described by Reinhart Koselleck), the Prussian government found both equally suspect.[5] Appointed Oberpräsident of Posen Province in December 1830, Eduard von Flottwell was sent there with the mission of nipping feared irredentist aspirations in the bud by intensifying the assimilation of the local populace and marginalizing the Polish aristocracy and the Catholic Church. Flottwell's measures marked a radical turnaround in Prussia's Poland policy, putting the Prussian state on an ill-fated collision course with a large part of its own populace in the eastern provinces.[6]

The sympathy shown by the German bourgeoisie would prove less durable than the uncompromising stance of the Prussian state. Although the former would flare up briefly once more with the arrest and conviction of Polish conspirators in 1846–47, the situation changed fundamentally when the Poles, during the turmoil of the March Revolution (1848), took action by setting up parallel administrations and establishing armed units in parts of the Grand Duchy. Prussia's liberal "March government" offered the granting of autonomy rights, not to the entire Grand Duchy, but to its eastern part around the city of Gniezno; but Polish nationalists indignantly rejected the concession as inadequate and decided to pursue open struggle.[7] The violent suppression of the uprising in Prussian Poland happened simultaneously with the antidemocratic backlash reversing the German revolution. The realization that the fulfillment of Polish ambitions would collide with the political goal of German unification ultimately extinguished even the one last brief flare-up of friendly feelings toward Poland, so that the former image of freedom-loving Poles gave way to an image of brutal rebels against a legitimate order.[8]

The change in feeling was also apparent in the debates of the Frankfurt Parliament (1848–49). Polish calls to be left out of a German Empire that was to be founded on the principle of a common nationality were dismissed. The idea of a restored Poland that incorporated some Prussian territory was denigrated as "feeble-minded sentimentality" by left-wing nationalist parliamentarian Wilhelm Jordan, who declared the Poles to be "mortal enemies" of a united Germany.[9] The German revolutions of 1848–49 were thus derailed by not only social conflicts, but also national ones.[10] Forced to choose between liberty and unity, the majority chose unity and ultimately lost both to the counterrevolution.[11]

The 1871 establishment of the German Empire as a nation-state naturally rekindled the debate over national minorities. Just as they had done in Frankfurt in 1848, Polish parliamentarians protested the incorporation of Polish-majority regions into an entity that was explicitly based on a nation-state concept and that was unwilling to grant minority rights to national groups.[12] On April 1, 1871, the Polish parliamentarian Alfred von Zoltowski declared that he and his colleagues would certainly be "the last ones" to fail to rejoice in what the Franco-Prussian war had achieved, namely, "the most powerful reaffirmation of a principle for whose upholding we have always stood up. . . . I mean the nationality principle"— but, in his view, the principle also had to apply to the Polish nation within the

German Empire.[13] In the newly established Reichstag, such demands met with peremptory rejection, thereby demonstrating how the former bourgeois opposition had now come to identify with the new state. It was with general approval that Zoltowski's protest was rebutted by Otto von Bismarck himself, who made clear to the Polish faction that in the eyes of the government they belonged "to no other people than the Prussians, among whom I also count myself." Echoing the ostensible "civilizing mission" of the medieval German eastward expansion that was rediscovered in the late nineteenth century, Bismarck threatened that the Prussian government would "continue in its efforts to spread the blessings of legal security and of civilized behavior, among both the grateful and the ungrateful."[14]

Bismarck's invocation of the old Prussian supranational conception of citizenship pointed to a model that had already become historically obsolete in 1871, no longer authoritative even for the new imperial government that he led. On the contrary: with the achievement of unity on the external stage, it was now time to push for it internally as well. In this context, external war played an important part in the developing of a German national consciousness and the founding of the German Empire, and it was a warlike logic that shaped the imperial government's integration policy: the internal opponent was "declared an 'enemy of the Empire' and put under police supervision" in a policy aimed not only at Catholics, Social Democrats, and Jews, but also at the ethnic minorities, of which the Poles were by far the largest.[15]

The Catholics were the first group to be labeled enemies of the new nation-state. Although it might be an exaggeration to say that Bismarck targeted Catholics because doing so would hit the Polish Prussians in particular, it nonetheless remains undisputed that the relevant measures had a "clearly anti-Polish edge" and that no part of the German Empire suffered the consequences more dramatically than Prussian Poland did.[16]

One focus of this conflict was the imperial government's secularization of schooling. During consultations on school legislation, Bismarck maintained the opinion that the slow progress in assimilating the Polish-speaking populace was due to the obstructionism of the Catholic Church. According to him, "the influence of the local clergy hinders . . . the usage of the German language, because the Slavs and the Romanics, in league with Ultramontanism, are trying to maintain coarseness and ignorance, and are fighting everywhere in Europe against Germanicism, which is trying to spread enlightenment."[17] In March 1872, the churches lost their authoritative role in the running of schools, which in the eastern parts of Prussia became instruments of Germanization policy. That same year, the province of Silesia declared German to be the language of instruction, and the provinces of Posen and Prussia did so in 1873. At that point, Polish was permitted only during religion classes, but soon afterward, they too had to be conducted in German.[18] Finally, on August 28, 1876, German was declared the sole official language, thereby abolishing the bilingualism that had existed at least in principle in the province of Posen.[19] The path was cleared for a policy of repression that was dressed up as a civilizing mission.[20]

But even after the state took control of school supervision, its attacks on the Catholic Church did not ease up. With what became known as the "May Laws," in 1873, the Prussian government started massively intervening in the church's internal administration for the first time, not only by regulating the training of the clergy, but also by subjecting them to the disciplinary authority of the state. Disobedient clerics were either arrested or exiled, thereby decimating the Catholic clergy over the following decades—in the Archdiocese of Gnesen (Gniezno) alone, the policy removed about one-third of the clergy.[21]

Even Heinrich Class, however, the head of the radical Pan-German League (Alldeutscher Verband), later believed that "Bismarck, in the heat of the battle, had chosen the wrong instrument."[22] And it was true that from the state's point of view, the outcome was disappointing, for the domestic political costs of this confrontation with the Catholic Church forced Bismarck into a compromise by the late 1880s. In domestic politics, these attacks had led to an increase in support for political Catholicism and to the founding of the Center Party (Zentrumspartei), and, in Prussian Poland, they had failed to advance the Germanization campaign or to isolate the Catholic Church from the Polish-speaking populace—instead, they consolidated the relationship.

But the failures of the state's coercive measures against the Polish-speaking populace led not to a revision of the policy course, but instead to its radicalization. No longer trusting solely the assimilative power of German culture, the Prussian government decided to "incorporate eradication measures into governmental policy" and direct them against those who either seemed incapable of assimilating or whose assimilation was not wanted.[23] The earlier skepticism that had already been directed toward the idea of assimilating the clergy and aristocracy was now expanded to include other classes as well.

This reorientation of Germanization policy reached its first climax with Bismarck's decree of February 22, 1885, in which he ordered the deportation of Poles residing in Prussia's eastern provinces who had still not acquired Prussian citizenship.[24] The failures of Prussia's assimilation policy were blamed on migrants from the Russian and Austrian partitions, evoking fears of an "inundation by Slavicdom."[25] Bismarck openly stated that it was necessary to expel those who "are Polonizing the border provinces, the Germanization of which is our governmental task."[26] The first expulsions began in February and March 1885 and sometimes included families who had lived there for generations. Around forty-eight thousand people in total were expelled from Posen, West Prussia, and Upper Silesia, including some nine thousand Jews—a relatively large number, in light of their much lower percentage of the population, thereby underlining the antisemitic undercurrent of the actions.[27] Although these expulsions met with heated protests, not only from the Social Democrats and Center Party members in the Reichstag, but also from the Prussian Junkers who were losing farmworkers in a region already short of labor, the expulsions nonetheless continued until 1887, with a few scattered instances thereafter.[28]

Besides these deportations, the decades leading into World War I would see Germanization policy combining with another concept, one that is commonly associated with Nazi ideology: the "Germanization of the soil."[29] The attacks on the Catholic Church had resulted in particularly harsh measures in Prussian Poland, because the state authorities believed that the lack of progress in assimilating the Polish populace could be explained only by the resistance of the Polish elites. In pursuit of the same goal, attention now turned once again to the Polish aristocracy. After its political power had been broken in the 1830s under Oberpräsident Flottwell, the time had now come to eliminate its economic influence as well and "rid the land of the trichinosis of Polish aristocracy," as proclaimed by Bismarck in a further biologization of the political discourse.[30]

Bismarck's original idea was to push through a legislative package against the Polish aristocracy, which was similar to the 1878 Socialist Laws aimed against the Social Democrats, but the plan was ultimately superseded by a proposal put forward in 1885 by two ministers in the Prussian state government, Robert Lucius and Gustav von Gossler. The proposal provided for the targeted purchasing of Polish estates, which would then be subdivided and allocated to German colonists.[31] The relevant legislation was passed by the Reichstag on April 26, 1886. The Prussian government initially put up 100 million Reichsmarks for the land purchases and established the Prussian Settlement Commission (Preußische Ansiedlungskommission), based in the city of Posen (today Poznań), which was to select the properties, subdivide them, prepare them for settlement, and finally sell them cheaply to German farmers.

From the Prussian perspective, satisfactory results were achieved only during the early period. Over time, the Settlement Commission began to face a formidable challenge from the constantly growing number of Polish self-help organizations, which had been pursuing what was called "praca organiczna" ("organic work") since the mid-1860s as a way to strengthen national self-assertion through intensive educational efforts in culture and scholarship, as well as the development of a modernized "Polish" economy.[32] With the foundation of various farmers' associations, credit cooperatives, and banks during this period, "the tide was basically turned against the Germanization campaign," so that after 1896, more "German" lands were falling into Polish hands than vice versa.[33] The Settlement Commission was starting to lose the "economic turf war over land ownership."[34]

The effect of these new setbacks on large swaths of the German Empire's political elite, particularly on the right wing, can hardly be overestimated. In the political upheavals after Bismarck's downfall—characterized by the collapse of the ruling right-wing coalition, the politicization of large parts of the populace, the formation of mass-membership parties, the rise of social democracy, and the formation of interest groups and trade unions—these failures accelerated a structural reorientation, within the right wing as well, that expected from the government a decidedly nationalist policy orientation both at home and abroad and strove to achieve it through the establishment of nationalist pressure groups.[35] For these radical nationalists, the Polish question quickly became "by far the most important 'national battleground,'" and it also dominated the first congress of what was probably the most influential of these groups, the Pan-German League, founded in 1891. Its members demanded a radicalization of existing policy, claiming that this would remain unsuccessful as long as it targeted only the Church and aristocracy but not the strengthening Polish middle class, for it was the latter that was enabling Polish tenacity.[36] The Pan-Germans then argued above all that the economic ruination of every affluent Pole was essential for a successful Germanization policy, and that long-term success could be achieved only with measures showing the Polish-speaking populace that "voluntary" assimilation into the German majority was in their own interests.[37]

Pressure groups like the Pan-German League, then, stood at the forefront of a movement that called on the state to wage economic war against the Polish minority. One of its founders, Alfred Hugenberg, already a key player on the Settlement Commission, demanded through an unsigned article in 1899 that the state be given the right to expropriate large Polish landholdings—an idea that was initially taken up only by Ferdinand Hansemann, one of the cofounders of the German Eastern Marches Society (Deutscher Ostmarkenverein), another radical nationalist group.[38] The discussion then shifted to a proposal from the Settlement Commission to restrict the construction activities of Polish land purchasers.[39] When this discriminatory measure also failed to achieve the desired result, and the Settlement Commission was instead forced to admit in its twentieth annual report that Polish organizations had outpaced it in terms of total land purchases, and that even with its own land acquisitions in the past year, up to 90 percent was bought from Germans, Hugenberg's demand was taken up once again.[40] The Eastern Marches Society brought back his campaign and stated in its mouthpiece publication *Die Ostmark*: "The weapon for slashing and for attacking, the weapon for regaining at least a part of the soil that has been alienated from us, is offered solely by the right of expropriation."[41] Finally, in late 1907, a bill was introduced in the Prussian legislature that would expand the definition of the "public interest"—a necessary justification for expropriations—to now include the "ideal of national homogeneity."[42] When the law was passed in March 1908, it represented a further erosion of the equality guaranteed by the Prussian constitution—even though this particular law was applied "only" four times and the expropriations were still tied to compensation payments.

Together with the deportations of the late 1880s, these events represented the climax of anti-Polish repressive measures during the nineteenth century, as well as a significant turning point in the Germanization policy of Prussia and Germany. To be sure, the preunification Kingdom of Prussia had already seen a gradual nationalistic shift in its anti-Polish policies, which were increasingly oriented toward the linguistic and cultural assimilation of the Polish populace. There had never been any doubt, however, that the members of this demographic group—although Polish-speaking—were in fact Prussians, individuals whose complete integration into the German-speaking majority was not only desirable, but virtually a necessity.

The radicalization effectively declared the bankruptcy of the existing policy, which had assumed that gradual assimilation was the natural course of history. Certainly, a flurry of increasingly fevered writings had appeared, recalling the German people's past as a settler folk, highlighting the ostensible superiority of German culture and defending the goal of assimilating the Polish-speaking populace. Pointing to the nine million Germans who had already been lost to emigration, Ernst Hasse (chairman of the Pan-German League from 1893 to 1908) wrote that it was only right and proper to counterbalance "about half of this loss through the Germanization of aliens, as an equivalent." In this context (and particularly interesting for the present volume's investigations), Hasse also defended this course of action against a criticism that had newly flared up on the right, that the assimilation of non-German groups might represent a racial threat:

> There are fears that the Germanization of the Poles will lead to a deterioration of the German race. We maintain that this does not apply to the Poles who live on the German Empire's territory. In many cases, these are only linguistically Slavs, and in ethnographic regard, are of no worse a blood mixture than the greater part of western Germandom. The German part of their blood stems from the time of Germanic settlement in the Vistula region before the Migration Period, from the countless German colonists in this region since the year 800. In cultural terms too, the Poles are standing entirely on German shoulders.[43]

The Polish-speaking Prussians, however, seemed less convinced by such sentiments. The enforcement of the German language laws, as well as cultural and educational policies in general, had to be increasingly delegated to the police, and when student strikes affected half the schools in the province of Posen during the 1906–7 school year, the truant children were beaten and their parents were delivered to the local gendarmerie.[44] Results from economic discrimination were no better. Although the Settlement Commission had devoured a billion Reichsmarks by 1913, twice as much as the empire's entire colonial revenue from overseas, it was just as much a failure.[45] Significantly, the Prussian government not only let itself be outmaneuvered by Polish landowners, banks, and cooperatives, it also encountered increasing difficulties in finding any "Germans" at all for its already rather modest number of land parcels.[46] The constantly trumpeted "German settler impulse [Siedlungswille]" was ultimately realized on the backs of ethnic Germans from Russia, who had few alternatives as newcomers.[47] Meanwhile, the constitutional integrity of both Prussia and the empire had fallen by the wayside. The Polish parliamentarian Anton Sulkowski addressed the fatal dynamic as early as 1908 in the Prussian upper chamber: "Millions upon millions are being sacrificed, but the millions don't suffice—these power plays are devouring point after point of constitutional law."[48]

* * *

As Peter Walkenhorst rightly emphasizes, disillusioning experiences like these were an important factor in causing radical nationalists like Heinrich Class (Hasse's successor) to hope for war, which would enable measures that were unachievable in peacetime. What Class had in mind was not so much a return to Bismarck's deportation policy but rather its complete radicalization. An indication can be found in the original version of a pamphlet Class wrote during the 1911 Agadir Crisis, in which he advocated that areas to be annexed after the upcoming war with France be handed over "free of people."[49] The phrase disappeared under governmental pressure but then reappeared a little later in his anonymously published book *Wenn ich der Kaiser wär'* (If I were the kaiser), this time also directed against Russia and referring to Eastern European territories that should be ceded to the German Empire.[50]

With the outbreak of World War I, such ideas flowed seamlessly into discussions of German war goals, lending the debates a distinctly anti-Polish edge. As elucidated in the plans of Chancellor Theobald von Bethmann-Hollweg, dated September 9, 1914, the German Empire's goal in Eastern Europe was to push back "Russia from the German border," producing a power vacuum that would allow the emergence of a string of states permeated by German capital and politically tied to the German Empire, thereby ensuring long-term German hegemony over Europe.[51] Although Berlin and Vienna may have diverged on the concrete details of this vision, the German Empire nonetheless insisted on a "rounding off" of its eastern border through the future annexation of what was euphemistically called a "border strip" ("Grenzstreifen"). Among the German Empire's political leadership, the concept was found for the first time in meeting notes written by Bavarian state premier Georg von Hertling, who met with Bethmann-Hollweg on December 3, 1914, and recorded that the latter was thinking of a "border adjustment" in the east. In the same sentence, Hertling added that "the narrow territory falling to Prussia should be evacuated by the Russians."[52] Although the phrasing is not entirely unambiguous, in that (as pointed out by Imanuel Geiss) it cannot be said without a doubt whether Bethmann-Hollweg meant the expulsion of only the ethnic Russians or also of Poles holding Russian citizenship, the further course of their discussion pointed to the latter. Two central issues defined subsequent plans prepared by the German Empire's governing bodies: the preferred width of the Polish zone and how to deal with the Jewish and Polish people living there. Hertling and Bethmann-Hollweg were of one mind, however, in their desire to push the German border as far east as possible and, after the disappointing results of Prussia's Germanization policy, to also deport as much of the local non-German populace as possible.

In all probability, Hertling's meeting notes represent the end of a political deliberation process that began within the Imperial Chancellery, during which the annexation of Polish territories was decided. The second step was now to discuss matters of practical implementation: for this purpose, various offices were asked to prepare expert opinions on potential cessions of land on the empire's eastern border. Here it is worth taking a closer look at two of the resulting responses, in an excursus that is important in shedding light on the background of the population shifts that were actually implemented during World War II. In my view, particular importance needs to be attached to these expert opinions in any discussion about the continuities and discontinuities of German imperialist policy in Eastern Europe.

Among the first responses received was that of Adolf von Batocki (Oberpräsident of East Prussia), dated December 20, 1914. In the "interests of world peace," he called for the annexation of a border strip covering some thirty-six thousand square kilometers, in order to create in Eastern Europe the "maximum possible conformity between state borders and linguistic ones." He wrote that not only was this border strip of military strategic value, but annexing it would also satisfy the alleged settler impulse of the empire's German populace and could furthermore serve as a catchment area for the ethnic Germans coming from Eastern Europe, who were to be resettled here in order to rescue the "white" race from the "so massively predominating colored races."[53] The non-German inhabitants of this border strip, whom Batocki calculated to be more than 85 percent of the population and thus almost two million people, were to be removed from the strip through a "generously dimensioned resettlement." This large-scale plan for the ethnic cleansing of Eastern Europe met with approval (according to Batocki) from the German chancellor.[54] Just a few months later, on March 25, 1915, Friedrich von Schwerin, head of the Frankfurt Governmental Region (Regierungsbezirk Frankfurt, a subdivision of Brandenburg Province, with its capital at Frankfurt an der Oder), presented his own no less radical proposal. In the view of Schwerin, who had begun his civil service career at the Settlement Commission and remained a vehement supporter of "internal colonization" his entire life, it was in the east, with the pushing back of Russia and the expansion of territory, that the foundation would be laid for the German Empire to become a world power. The annexed border strip would be resettled through a population exchange, replacing the non-German populace with ethnic Germans from as far away as the Volga colonies.[55] The resulting German settlement belt would isolate the Prussian Poles, forcing them to choose complete assimilation or—once again—emigration to Polish territories beyond the border.

The apparent readiness of the German Empire's leadership to radicalize the Germanization policy of the prewar era, and to make it a goal even in the midst of World War I, was not only shaped and reinforced by the support of Prussian administration heads but also influenced by a particular and at least semipublic debate of the period, one whose participants were often members of the relevant pressure groups and thus had good connections to governmental bodies. One example here was a very early initiative by Ludwig Bernhard, a Berlin professor and member of the Eastern Marches Society, who was one of many who refused to be silenced by an early wartime edict banning public discussion of German war goals; he circulated a memorandum revealingly called *Land ohne Menschen* (Land without people), which called for the annexation of Polish territory and a replacement of the local population with ethnic Germans from Russia. The memorandum made an impression on the German chancellor.[56] Bernhard's proposals were taken up also in other memoranda, such as the notorious *Intellektuellendenkschrift über die Kriegsziele* (Intellectuals' memorandum on war aims), dated July 8, 1915. Friedrich Meinecke's article of May 6, 1915, also deserves particular attention, for it went further by calling for the Prussian Poles to be expelled even from the provinces of Posen and West Prussia. Meinecke concluded his remarks by writing that "earlier, one would have considered this fantastical, and yet it is not unfeasible after all."[57] With this, Meinecke had casually surpassed the initial positions of even the Pan-German League and the Eastern Marches Society, which had likewise supported a policy of annexation and expulsion but had made an exception for the Prussian Poles.[58]

When the participants of an interministerial conference gathered at the imperial chancellery on July 13, 1915, in order to evaluate the submitted memoranda and decide on the next course of action, the consensus-building process was already well advanced. The conference endorsed the annexation of a border strip and the envisaged resettlement measures, that is, replacing the local non-German populace primarily with ethnic Germans from Russia. The German civil administration in occupied Congress Poland was instructed to quietly hinder the ethnic German inhabitants of the border strip from moving away and, where possible, to already start expelling the Polish and Jewish populace, in order to create a fait accompli for use in future peace talks.[59] Although it seems these instructions were not executed (or not to any great extent), the German Empire had nonetheless shown—at least at the planning level—that it was ready to pursue a policy of large-scale ethnic cleansing.

The enduring importance of the Polish border strip in Germany's agenda during subsequent stages of the war is shown by the tenacity with which the relevant parts of the German leadership continued holding fast to this ambition, even after it had long since proved to be a clearly dysfunctional policy, since it torpedoed every attempt to win over the Poles beyond the empire's borders as allies. By 1917, the increasingly hostile mood of the populace in the occupied Polish territories had finally forced a rethinking within the empire's leadership circles. Although population policy motivations meant they could not bring themselves to entirely abandon the idea of annexing a border strip, there was a call to at least reduce its extent. Thus, while the empire's leadership had not yet abandoned its plans for a large-scale resettlement project, one that envisaged the resettlement of ethnic Germans from Russia and even from the non-German regions of Austria-Hungary, Bethmann-Hollweg at the same time pushed the Army High Command (Oberste Heeresleitung, or OHL) in April 1917 for a significant reduction of the border strip. This emerging shift in priorities within the German Empire's civilian leadership quickly led it into an increasingly serious conflict with the OHL. Of course, the government's shift in priorities was nothing other than a direct reaction to the military's worsening situation on the eastern front. When this suddenly improved in 1918 with Russia's military collapse, the new chancellor, Georg von Hertling, immediately let himself be swept up in the OHL's confident predictions of victory. Besides large-scale expropriations, General Erich Ludendorff also called for a comprehensive resettlement program. And even after the Allies succeeded with their first major breakthroughs and the western front began to falter, the empire's leadership still stood firm—against the Poles. At a time when the imminent German defeat "was really obvious to every thinking person" (as Geiss wrote), Foreign Minister Paul von Hintze made a fool of himself during a meeting with the Polish representative in Berlin, Count Adam Ronikier, by officially introducing German demands—even as late as September 19, 1918—for the ceding of Polish territories. The subsequent reaction in Polish circles was that "even on their deathbed, the Germans are still thieving."[60]

* * *

Knowing what happened during World War II, when Poland played an even bigger role in Germany's war agenda, it makes sense to search for such lines of continuity. Hans-Ulrich Wehler, for example, sees in the ideas of the Eastern Marches Society an early manifestation of the Nazi "Lebensraum" ("living space") ideology, and Philip T. Rutherford, in presenting one of the most recent studies of Nazi population policy in Poland, notes that the commonalities are "so striking that a connection seems almost undeniable."[61]

But it can be pointed out with at least equal justification that even the Eastern Marches Society, right up to the end, had pushed for an assimilation of the Polish-speaking populace. According to Harry K. Rosenthal, "since the notion of 'blood' remained foreign to this group, this view prevented any easy identification of [them] with the later Nazis."[62] And the resettlement plans of the German Empire's civilian and military leadership, which bore the closest resemblance to the subsequent policy of the Nazis, remained exactly that: plans. Just as state conduct was still subject to legal constraints before the war, so was the German leadership likewise unprepared to actually annex Polish territory during the war or to put into action the already existing deportation plans.

It is certainly true that "Bismarck and Hitler were not interchangeable," but the radicalization of Prussian and German Germanization policy since the 1890s, with its plans for an ethnic cleansing of Europe, would nonetheless prove to be decisive in influencing later developments: its experiences formed the background against which the Nazis would later formulate their own Germanization policy.[63]

Poland's German Minorities as Accomplices and Instruments of German Aggression

Ethnonationalist foreign policy is a modern phenomenon. As late as the German Empire period, ethnic Germans abroad still did not play an appreciable role in foreign-policy considerations.[64] This would change with Germany's defeat in World War I. Greatly weakened and subjected to the restrictions of the Versailles Treaty, it was initially the Weimar Republic and then Nazi Germany that, in the effort to mobilize all available resources, identified the German minorities in the newly created states of eastern central Europe as an extension of their own aggressive interests and found active collaborators within these groups.

Revisionism in the Weimar Republic

The Treaty of Versailles meant that Germany had to bury all hopes of German domination in Eastern Europe. Instead of a greater German economic sphere, Berlin was now confronted by a string of independent states, which France had furthermore drawn into alliances meant to block any subsequent German pushes to the east. This new constellation of Eastern European states drew its legitimation from Woodrow Wilson's Fourteen Points. In proclaiming the right to national self-determination, the US president believed that a solution had also been found to the many nationalist confrontations that he considered had contributed to the outbreak of war.[65] But this was certainly not the case. As recently noted by Eric D. Weitz, the Treaty of Versailles marked a "move from the Vienna system to the Paris system," in which state sovereignty was no longer defined primarily—let alone solely—in territorial terms but also had to prove itself in terms of the resident populace, or in terms of the resident ethnically or religiously defined demographic groups.[66] New states answering the call for national self-determination arose from the liquidation of old empires in Central and Eastern Europe, but at the same time, nationalism was to be held in check by the various minority rights agreements imposed on these states.[67] But this policy was unsuccessful in the face of "the genie that would not go back into the bottle."[68] Particularly in a state that derived its legitimacy from its people, or more precisely from its *Volk* (folk, but variously meaning people, nation, or ethnonation), defined in ethnic terms, it was easy to see the existence of local ethnic minorities as a threat. This is how the ideal of ethnically homogeneous nation-states came to lie "at the heart of inter-war European politics."[69]

Revising the Treaty of Versailles became the main foreign-policy goal for each successive government of the Weimar Republic. It was not only about the annulment of treaty limitations on German sovereignty, but also the recovery of lost territories. The latter aspect soon solidified into an anti-Polish policy aimed at retaking formerly Prussian territories.

In view of the impending referenda in the eastern border regions, as well as the futile attempts by a multitude of paramilitary *Selbstschutz* (self-defense) and *Freikorps* (free corps) groups—backed by the German military—to reverse territorial changes by force, the German delight at the Soviet invasion of eastern Poland, while surprising at first glance, also becomes understandable. Unhappy with the eastern border drawn by the victorious Allied powers, the Polish army had invaded the Soviet Union, but only barely escaped a complete military catastrophe after a series of Soviet victories—which were celebrated in Berlin "as if these were German military successes."[70] The unexpected reversal just outside Warsaw in August 1920, however, along with the subsequent peace treaty favoring Poland, did not cause German foreign policymakers to give up on their cherished belief in the Polish state's imminent collapse. Instead, Berlin turned to reviving the old German-Russian policy of encircling Poland.[71] This received a decisive boost with the Treaty of Rapallo, signed in April 1922. Hans von Seeckt, the German army's commander in chief, who immediately after the war had transferred regular troops into Border Defense East (Grenzschutz Ost) and commanded them in the fight against Polish armed units, expressed German hopes as follows: "Poland's existence is intolerable, and incompatible with Germany's living requirements. It must disappear, and will disappear through its own weaknesses and through Russia, with German assistance."[72] Here, von Seeckt was not only reflecting the revanchist mood of the German military, but also describing the core of governmental policy, as was confirmed by Joseph Wirth, a liberal parliamentarian from the Center Party who was chancellor of Germany when he signed the Treaty of Rapallo and declared thereafter that "Poland must be dealt with. It is toward this goal that my policymaking is geared. . . . On this point, I am entirely in agreement with the military, especially with General von Seeckt."[73]

It was only with the accession of Gustav Stresemann, who was initially both chancellor and foreign minister before continuing as the Weimar Republic's longest-serving foreign minister, that a major shift occurred in 1924 in the German attitude toward Poland. As Stresemann made clear during a confidential meeting of all German national-level and Prussian state-level ministries shortly after entering office, he also felt that a revision of the Versailles Treaty was necessary: "The creation of a state whose political borders encompass all parts of the German people, meaning those who live within a contained settlement area in central Europe and desire union with Germany, is the distant goal of German hopes."[74] He was willing, however, to accept the politically feasible as the basic premise of a new German foreign policy. Instead of an undifferentiated course of overall confrontation, he pursued a policy that combined cautious rapprochement with a step-by-step revision of Versailles, a strategy that essentially aimed to create a split in Europe. It was hoped that concessions in Western Europe, particularly in satisfying France's security needs, would engender sympathy for Germany's desire to change the status quo—without military force—in Eastern Europe.[75] This tactical shift showed great promise, as shown by the signing of the Locarno Treaties in December 1925, through which the Weimar Republic formally recognized its new western border in exchange for (among other things) its acceptance into the League of Nations and the withdrawal of French troops from the Rhineland. In contrast, plans for an "eastern Locarno agreement," meaning comparable border guarantees for Poland and Czechoslovakia, fell through in the face of German resistance. Speaking to the Reichstag's Foreign Affairs Committee, Stresemann himself rejected any explicit renunciation of force in amending Germany's eastern border, for this would have implied a recognition of the existing land possessions.[76] Therefore, it would not be an exaggeration to identify Locarno as the starting point for the "decline of the European security framework."[77] After all, the Weimar Republic had thereby taken the "first step on the path toward the desired revision of the Versailles Treaty," and Poland was forced to accept the subordination of its own security interests to those of its Western allies, thereby downgrading Poland's western frontier to a "second-class border."[78]

The Weimar Republic thoroughly exploited the newfound latitude resulting from the détente on its western border. Having learned from experience that Poland was certainly not just a "one-season state" ("Saisonstaat"), as it had been scornfully called after the war, Berlin now tried to take advantage of Warsaw's economic difficulties by suspending German-Polish trade.[79] According to Stresemann, economic relations were to be suspended until "Poland's economic and financial emergency has reached the maximum degree and brought the entire

Polish state edifice to a condition of powerlessness," making the country "ready for a settlement of the border question according to our wishes."[80] Although it did not bring the Weimar Republic any closer to its goals, this economic war was nonetheless able to count on widespread support from all political parties, for the "demand for a comprehensive revision of the eastern border" had long since become "one of the few truly national integrating factors."[81]

The Weimar Republic tried to establish moral legitimacy for its anti-Polish destabilization policy by pointing to the German minorities. It was argued that these people had not only been forced into the Polish state in direct violation of Wilson's Fourteen Points, but had also been subjected to an assimilation process that the ratified minorities treaties should have prevented. This invocation of Wilson, however, did not hold water, for his peace program had explicitly provided for the establishment of a sovereign Polish state with access to the sea; furthermore, the minority treaties did not endow collectives of any description with group rights but instead—and in accord with the Western understanding of liberalism—focused on the legal person of the individual, securing the individual's right to choose his or her own ethnic identity.[82] The intention of the treaties was "to prevent the oppression of minorities, not the assimilation of ethnic groups"; in fact, the latter was seen as an unavoidable process by supporters of the League of Nations, one that was even to be welcomed—if it proceeded peacefully—as a solution for the nationalist tensions of the period.[83] The interpretation was different at Germany's Foreign Office. According to a memorandum from July 1928, the German minorities were to be maintained "through all means," for doing so represented "the prerequisite for a favorable solution to the Corridor Question and Upper Silesia Question."[84] Because of their function as "the living symbol and bridgeheads of revisionist claims," the German minorities received Berlin's undivided attention and massive support.[85] As Martin Broszat put it, "behind this minorities policy stood the border question, and it was only through the latter that the former also became politically explosive."[86]

It is therefore unsurprising that the mass exodus of Poland's German populace immediately after Germany's defeat in World War I aroused great concern in Berlin. According to Christian Jansen and Arno Weckbecker, the reasons behind this exodus were once attributed mainly to Polish governmental policy, especially in German historiography immediately after World War II, but more recent research has attributed its causes "primarily to the Germans themselves and their mentality."[87] Even the German military's transition commissioner back in 1919 who witnessed the German populace fleeing in a near panic could not help but feel that these people had become accustomed to massive state subsidies and were "trained to be dependent" on them.[88] On the other hand, Przemysław Hauser places more emphasis on an unwillingness to adapt to a future in which Germans were forced to live "without the status of a master race."[89]

The Weimar Republic was not prepared to resign itself to this development. As early as September 1920, the German embassy in Poland sent a status report explaining that the country's German minorities still had to learn—as Albert Kotowski summarized this missive—that "holding out in Poland is their primary national duty."[90] In order to support such policy goals, Berlin tightened its immigration, passport, and visa requirements in April 1921 and also tied abandoned-property compensation payments to declarations from the local German organizations in Poland, which had to certify that the emigrant had no choice but to leave.[91] Berlin soon realized, however, that only with a drastic improvement of the situation in Poland could a final exodus of the remaining Germans be prevented. Achieving such an improvement meant building across Germany and Poland an interconnected network of organizations with multiple components and strong financial backing.

Richard Blanke's proposition that the developments of Poland's German minorities should be investigated "apart from the usual foreign policy context" is particularly mistaken in the ways such groups were organized.[92] On the contrary, their "opposing fronts," as Hans-Adolf Jacobsen aptly describes the relations between the frequently feuding organizations of the Germans in Poland, cannot be understood without their foreign-policy dimension and are comprehensible only within the context of German-Polish relations and the close ties and dependencies between the German minorities and Berlin.[93]

This latter point became particularly apparent even in the early days after the war. In 1919, before the final border was even known, parliamentarians from Prussia's constitutional convention as well as Germany's Weimar National Assembly joined forces to create in Berlin a cross-party Parliamentary Action Committee for the East (Parlamentarischer Aktionsausschuss Ost).[94] But Allied control of Germany's budget prevented direct political and financial support of the Germans in the ceded territories; therefore, a front organization called the Konkordia Literarische Gesellschaft (Concordia Literary Society) was founded in January 1920 under Max Winkler.[95] At his disposal were considerable financial resources, earmarked for the acquisition of German newspapers abroad in order to secure their continued existence, which enabled Konkordia to become an immense newspaper group within a very short time, one that controlled almost the entire German press abroad.

Even more decisive was the Deutsche Stiftung (German Foundation), founded in November 1920 under Erich Krahmer-Möllenberg, formerly a senior official in the provincial government of Posen at Bromberg and then in the Prussian Interior Ministry and, like Winkler, another gray eminence of ethnopolicy (*Volkstumspolitik*). In contrast to Konkordia, however, the Deutsche Stiftung had closer ties to governmental authorities and acted—according to a memorandum from 1925—as a "camouflaged agency" of the Foreign Office.[96] It was the task of the Deutsche Stiftung to help "the Germans now of Polish citizenship . . . to strengthen them in being German and to maintain the German ethnic group as an independent cultural factor."[97]

Discussion of a single German minority in Poland was in itself already misleading, in that it suggests a group whose members felt a mutual bond for historical, religious, or other reasons. Germans in Poland felt such bonds only to a very small extent. According to Valdis O. Lumans, they actually represented "the most diverse of all German minorities."[98] They were scattered across the country in six regions, with the Upper Silesians in particular belonging to the Catholic faith, Protestants in the west following the Evangelical Consistory of Posen, and those in the east the Evangelical Church of the Augsburg Confession in Poland.[99] Beyond their religious and cultural differences, there were also strongly contrasting political preferences: Upper Silesia, strongly marked by heavy industry, remained until 1918 a stronghold of the Center Party, which was then locally succeeded by the German Catholic People's Party (Deutsche Katholische Volkspartei), while in agrarian Wielkopolska and Pomerelia the German National People's Party (Deutschnationale Volkspartei) dominated, and in Łódź there was even the founding of a German Workers' Party (Deutsche Arbeiterpartei), which played a particularly strong role among the workforce of the textile factories.[100]

Therefore, except for a short period in the early 1920s, these German minorities were unable to agree on a single nationwide association. In Wielkopolska and Pomerelia, for example, the immediate postwar period saw German parties, ranging from Social Democrats to the radical right, coming together with the free labor unions to form a Central Working Group of German Parties (Zentralarbeitsgemeinschaft deutscher Parteien, or ZAG), a loose alliance with a certain distance to Berlin that was supposed to coordinate a common approach. When the nationalist factions pushed for closer ties to Germany and failed to achieve this inside the ZAG, they withdrew from the alliance and pulled to their side the support of Germany's Foreign Office, which had since become the leading ministry handling all matters pertaining to the German minorities. The ministerial officials in Berlin torpedoed the mediation efforts of the socialists, who were pleading for a compromise within the ZAG framework, and demanded instead that its member organizations transfer into a new organization before then dissolving the ZAG. All factions except for the left-wing parties complied with these demands, thereby forming in May 1921 the Germandom Federation for the Protection of Minority Rights in Poland (Deutschtumsbund zur Wahrung der Minderheitenrechte in Polen), which became the "sole contact" for all financial transactions with the Foreign Office.[101] According to Norbert Krekeler, nothing more clearly demonstrates the idea that the development of the German organizations in Poland was "less an autonomous process among the ethnic

Germans and more a development steered largely from Berlin, one whose direction resulted primarily from the needs of Germany's foreign policy."[102]

Although the generous monetary transfers were crucial in stopping the wave of emigration, they also awoke new desires for further assistance among Poland's German minorities. Poland's economic situation was in fact quite strained, for the country faced enormous tasks upon its reestablishment. The different administrative, legal, financial, transport, and education systems of the three former partitions now had to be brought together, and the economy's structural inadequacies and imbalances needed to be overcome.[103] The latter aspect was further exacerbated by the fact that, with their incorporation into the new Poland, the country's major economic centers had lost their old markets in Germany and the former Russian Empire. The loss affected not only the textile factories in Łódź and the mining industry in Upper Silesia, but also the highly productive agricultural sector of the northwest. Therefore, the downward spiral experienced by local German agricultural enterprises was less a product of discriminatory measures by Warsaw and more a symptom of the general crisis affecting Poland's entire agricultural sector, one that also threatened socially explosive consequences, for most people lived from agriculture. The problem was further compounded by inequality in land ownership. The richest 1 percent of the agricultural populace owned 50 percent of the arable land, and the poorest two-thirds were crowded onto just 15 percent of it. The poorest two-thirds, then, often owned just enough for their subsistence, with no hope of surplus production or capital accumulation.[104] German landownership was part of this problem: in 1921, of all farms over 50 hectares (ca. 120 acres) in Wielkopolska, 36 percent belonged to German owners, and in Pomerelia, it was 43.7 percent.[105] A land-reform bill was passed on December 28, 1925, but it had been so softened by the dominant conservative forces that it failed to fundamentally change the situation. Nonetheless, its central provision allowing for the subdivision of large estates over 150 hectares (ca. 370 acres) was a very sensitive one in regard to large German landholdings, especially because the reform was basically an invitation to tie the expropriation issue to the minorities one. The reform had little effect, however, on the strong position of the German landholders: although the German share of the population had fallen to 10 percent in both Wielkopolska and Pomerelia by 1931, Germans still controlled 29 percent of the arable land in Wielkopolska, with estate sizes generally exceeding 100 hectares (nearly 250 acres); meanwhile, 22 percent of the arable land in Pomerelia, including 60 percent of the land in large-scale estates exceeding 180 hectares (nearly 445 acres), remained in German hands.[106] If the economic situation of the German great estates in Poland nonetheless worsened, the real cause was Poland's general economic situation, not to mention the economic war unleashed by Germany in 1925, which had led to even more troubles for export-oriented enterprises in particular.

In any case, the new demands of the situation accelerated a shift in Berlin in its treatment of the German minorities. By the time the Locarno Treaties were signed at the latest, all hopes for a quick collapse of the Polish state had to be set aside, and the financial support of the ethnic Germans now had to be adapted to the new realities. If Germans were to be stopped from leaving Poland so that enough still remained to legitimize demands for a treaty revision, then financial support for cultural matters would no longer suffice; emigration would need to be backstopped through massive subsidization of economic livelihoods, which soon became clear to the planners at Germany's Foreign Office.

The Polish authorities, aware of Berlin's increasing influence over German minority organizations, had dissolved the German Federation for the Protection of Minority Rights in 1923. Trying to take its place in 1924, but with little success, was the German Union in the Sejm and Senat (Deutsche Vereinigung in Sejm und Senat), a loose umbrella organization of German parliamentarians.[107] Germany's Foreign Office found itself confronted with an array of smaller organizations, which is why it made any further funding contingent on the formation of a central committee. The contingency ultimately led to the founding of the Quintet Committee (Fünfer-Ausschuss), which, as the highest authority of all German economic associations in Wielkopolska and Pomerelia, became the German minority's most important committee; it followed the guidelines of the Foreign Office in awarding loans exclusively to politically loyal "conscious Germans" ("bewusste Deutsche").[108]

To provide even more generous financial support to the ethnic Germans, the Ossa company was founded in 1926, likewise acting as an "auxiliary structure of the Foreign Office" under the management of Krahmer-Möllenberg and Winkler.[109] In the beginning, it was mostly big landowners who had profited from Berlin's generosity, while Upper Silesia's industrial companies, for example, were still being explicitly excluded from the loan program as late as 1926 by Foreign Minister Stresemann himself, from fears in Berlin of the capital requirements. Even this last reservation fell away, though, with the founding of Ossa: by April 1933, ethnic German industrialists in East Upper Silesia had received some sixty to seventy million Reichsmarks.[110] By 1928 at the latest, when Krahmer-Möllenberg admitted that these payments had "lost the character of genuine loans" and had become pure subsidies, the wholly political purpose of the payments became openly apparent.[111]

If even more proof of this were necessary, one could look toward events of the Great Depression, which brought additional hardships to Poland's German minorities. As Chancellor Heinrich Brüning's government radicalized Stresemann's foreign-policy agenda and completed its transition to a "Grossraumpolitik" (a "wider spatial policy" asserting a hegemonial influence beyond one's own borders), and heated discussions of the Danzig Corridor broke out in public debate, representatives of the Germans in Pomerelia saw an opportunity to present Brüning with new demands in late 1930: either grant additional cheap loans and an import quota for reduced-tariff wheat shipments, or it would become necessary for their "followers to be told the truth, and given back their complete freedom to act as they wish."[112] After that, the Ossa company was instructed to increase its disbursements in Wielkopolska and Pomerelia.[113]

Reversed Relations: Reconciliation with Poland as a Prerequisite for Nazi "Lebensraum" Policy

It may seem paradoxical that the Nazi seizure of power, of all things, would be what brought an easing of relations with Poland, if only temporarily. Unlike earlier German chancellors, Hitler felt he could not afford to further aggravate mutual relations and thereby endanger his expansionist foreign-policy goals. The Nazis ended the economic war with Poland and signed a nonaggression pact in January 1934, in which Germany for the first time ruled out a border change by force; it represented a conspicuous break with the foreign policy of the Weimar Republic and was certainly the "most important, the only important turnaround in Germany's handling of its eastern partner."[114]

Although appearing incomprehensible to many contemporaries, the pact fit logically into the Nazi foreign-policy agenda.[115] In his long-unpublished "second book," Hitler outlined the general thrust of Nazi foreign policy: instead of a rigid fixation on restoring the borders of 1914, which he criticized as "insane" because it would preserve the entire victorious coalition as an ongoing enemy, he called for a shift "to a clear, far-seeing spatial policy [Raumpolitik]" and set his sights beyond Pomerelia and Upper Silesia to target the Soviet Union.[116] Poland, whose political elite held strongly anticommunist sentiments and had still not given up all hope of expanding at Soviet expense, must have appeared to represent the ideal junior partner in this endeavor.

Of course, the interests of the German minorities became secondary to this strategic reorientation. In order to prevent any inconvenient protests from ethnic German spokespersons, Rudolf Hess strove to subjugate any remaining ethnic German associations not already under direct state control, as Hitler had not only named him Deputy Führer on April 27, 1933, but had also entrusted him with supervising matters of ethnopolicy. The first result was the founding in October 1933 of the Ethnic German Council (Volksdeutscher Rat, or VR), at the suggestion of Karl Haushofer, a theoretician of the "Lebensraum" concept, and Hans Steinacher, head of the Volk Alliance for Germandom Abroad (Volksbund für das Deutschtum im Ausland, or VDA), which was by far the largest private-sector organization in the Reich promoting "Germandom" ("Deutschtum").[117] The great expectations of both Nazi Party figures and ethnopolicy advocates were soon thwarted, however, by the ministerial bureaucracy, which would not let itself be pushed out of this policy field. During an interministerial conference, the representatives of the VR were told to align their actions with the Foreign Office's policy positions. Their hopes of having a say in the disbursement of state funding were likewise dashed. Steinacher was advised that he had probably interpreted his powers "a bit too optimistically" and that his prospective participation in the allocating of funds would "under no circumstances come into consideration."[118] It was mainly this decision that doomed the newly created VR to powerlessness.

* * *

In Eastern Europe, the ethnic Germans greeted Hitler's coming to power with "panegyric exclamations and loyalty declarations."[119] That they did so is hardly surprising, for Nazi ideology emphasized the importance of the *völkisch* (the "folkish," meaning the ethnonationalistic), a concept that legitimized these minorities' efforts to maintain their ethnic homogeneity and simultaneously affirm their ostensible role as bringers of culture to the east. Coupled with strong resentments against a modernity represented by industry and big cities, along with a hatred of communists and Jews, Nazism could thus be assured of success among rural residents in particular, who happened to make up the bulk of ethnic German minorities, and not only in Poland.[120] The success of this ideological expansion among the German minorities can also be read in the new political semantics that was now disseminating a völkisch and racist vocabulary among the ethnic Germans in Poland as well, words that had either gained mass appeal through Nazism or been reshaped by it: the term "Auslandsdeutscher" (a "German abroad") was replaced by "Volksdeutscher" (a "member of the German ethnonation"), the concept of the "minority" by that of the "Volksgruppe" ("ethnonational group"), which furthermore was involved in a "Volkstumskampf" ("ethnonational struggle") abroad.[121] The message behind this terminological change was clear. It highlighted one's membership in a "larger whole existing beyond the border," namely the German "Volksgemeinschaft" ("ethnonational community"), as it was now called.[122]

This voluntary Nazification process certainly did not lead the German minorities in Poland to an overcoming of their traditional fragmentation. A development like that seen in Czechoslovakia with Konrad Henlein's Sudeten German Party (Sudetendeutsche Partei) failed to materialize in Poland. Instead, the 1921 founding of the German National Socialist Association for Poland (Deutscher Nationalsozialistischer Verein für Polen) in Bielsko (formerly Bielitz) would prove to be a catalyst for increasingly stormy disputes. Conflicts with the Polish authorities may have forced the organization's renaming in 1928 to the Young German Party for Poland (Jungdeutsche Partei für Polen, or JdP), but the agenda of the party now led by Rudolf Wiesner had not changed, including its support for the development of a "Volksgemeinschaft," the pursuit of radical antisemitism, and the struggle against Marxism.[123] The party's expansion beyond its home region led to conflicts with the established—and often fragmented—interest groups of each local German minority. Emboldened by Hitler's coming to power, Wiesner's followers acted as if they were "young guns" rebelling against the sclerotic power structures of the "old-timers"—a pretense that was increasingly contrived as the relevant German associations in Wielkopolska and Pomerelia all became less and less different from the JdP in their political agendas, as a result of their self-chosen Nazification. This certainly did nothing to blunt the mutual antipathy, which sometimes even led to bloody skirmishes. For example, a Polish newspaper smugly noted that the local police had to be summoned to break up a brawl at a hall in Sępólno Krajeńskie (formerly Zempelburg), which took place under a banner reading "Wir wollen sein ein einig Volk und Brüder" (We want to be a united people and brothers).[124]

The VR would prove incapable of ending the general escalation, which from Berlin's viewpoint was highly undesirable in its threat to paralyze the German minorities and spin them out of Berlin's control.[125] Its inability to assert itself, particularly in the face of Nazi Party agencies like its Foreign Organization (Auslandsorganisation der NSDAP), prompted Hess in October 1935 to transfer the coordination of ethnopolicy from the dissolved VR to party member Otto von Kursell, whose agency, the Kursell Bureau (Dienststelle Kursell), was put at least nominally under Joachim von Ribbentrop, the appointee in charge of foreign-policy matters on Hess's staff. Thus, what had been an "autonomous, nonpartisan, honorary institution" had now become a "special party agency" to which "only party comrades belonged and which was led by an 'Alter Kämpfer' [an 'old fighter' from the Nazi Party's early period]."[126] Kursell was now able to threaten recalcitrant representatives of the German minorities with the severance of all contact and the withdrawal of financial grants unless the infighting stopped immediately. Although the change did not open a new era of cooperation (as hoped by Berlin) between groups like the JdP and others, the intensity of their disputes did subsequently lessen to a noticeable degree.[127]

Kursell was a member of not only the Nazi Party but also the SS, which was a situation that Heinrich Himmler, as head of the SS, wanted to exploit in order to expand his influence into the field of ethnopolicy. From his perspective, the attempt to extend his power over the more than ten million members of German minorities was a logical one as it would not only enhance his position within the Reich but also provide the intelligence arm of the SS with access to a network of informants in countries across Europe. And Himmler must have ultimately recognized an opportunity to give political force to an idea that was also widely anchored in the SS with the founding of RuSHA (Rasse- und Siedlungshauptamt, the Race and Settlement Main Office), namely the tying of settlement planning to racial selections, thereby concretizing the Nazi conception of "Lebensraum."[128] During a conflict with the SS about its interference in the ethnopolicy of Czechoslovakia, however, Kursell made it clear that he did not want to take up the role intended for him by Himmler, who then pointedly withdrew his confidence in him.

Hess had already learned during the fight over the VR that ethnopolicy could not be implemented in the face of opposition from the relevant components of the Nazi Party, but only with their support, and so he did not want to make the same mistake twice. Instead of engaging in a confrontation with Himmler, he relieved Kursell of his office and accepted Himmler's candidate for a successor. In 1937, when SS Senior Group Leader Werner Lorenz took over the former Kursell Bureau, which had since been renamed the Ethnic German Liaison Office (Volksdeutsche Mittelstelle, or VoMi), the handling of ethnopolicy fell completely within Himmler's sphere of influence. Although the tasks had remained the same, the founding of VoMi signaled a qualitative leap in the ethnopolicy of Nazi Germany. The reason was, first, it dovetailed with a new stance of the German government: on February 20, 1938, Hitler broke his five-year silence on the fate of the "Volksdeutsche" in Eastern Europe, and during a speech to the Reichstag, he made himself a champion for the rights of the "Germans" in Austria and Czechoslovakia. Second, Lorenz—unlike his predecessor—could soon justify the pursuit of his mission by pointing to a direct order from Hitler, dated July 2, 1938: VoMi was tasked with the "unified organizing of all state and party agencies, as well as with the unified deployment of all resources available to these agencies for the handling of ethnopolitical and borderland issues"—meaning that a party organization had been granted authority over state offices.[129] For the first time, Lorenz's agency also had control over extensive financial resources, which had always been the most effective instrument of ethnopolicy.[130] In 1938 alone, this meant control over 50 60 million Reichsmarks, a sum that approximated the budget of the Foreign Office.[131] A half year later, a decree from Hess completed this "Gleichschaltung" ("enforced conformity") of ethnopolitically oriented organizations: in accordance with the main focus of their activities, all existing bodies were to be incorporated into either the VDA or the Alliance of the German East (Bund deutscher Osten), both of which were placed under VoMi.[132]

With the support of the state, the party, and the SS, this "bastard organization" was assured a new level of power that gave Lorenz more freedom of action than either Steinacher or Kursell had before him.[133] In place of a "loose collaboration based on the principle of reciprocity," according to Hans-Adolf Jacobsen, "there appeared the unilateral directive, and the command backed by threat of reprisals."[134] The effects were felt not only by Germandom organizations like the VDA, but also by the German minorities in Poland. As early as April 1937, Lorenz had invited the nine most important groups to Berlin in order to persuade them of the need for a common nationwide committee. After some initial failures, his tone became sharper. In a missive dated May 18, 1938, to the representatives of each organization, Lorenz threatened that this was his "first, but also his last, suggestion," and that anyone who abstained from this accord was putting himself outside the "Volksgemeinschaft" and must bear the consequences.[135] With this, although Lorenz had not yet risen to level of "complete master of the ethnic German organizations in Poland," the path toward the founding of a loose umbrella organization in August 1938 was now open.[136]

Kotowski's observation that Warsaw's policy stance toward the German minorities was a variable dependent on German-Polish international relations is as true for the second half of the 1930s as it is for the entire preceding period.[137] It is therefore unsurprising that as Berlin's increasingly aggressive foreign policy and the advancing spread of Nazi ideology were matched by an increasingly irredentist stance among Poland's German inhabitants and that both taken together would ultimately affect Warsaw's minorities policy. Between March and June 1936 alone, the Polish government banned the National Socialist German Workers' Federation (Nationalsozialistischer deutscher Arbeiterbund) and dissolved thirty-three local branches of the German Union for Posen and Pomerelia (Deutsche Vereinigung für Posen und Pommerellen), the biggest political organization of the German minorities in Wielkopolska, which Warsaw accused of inciting the Kashubian populace against it.[138] Other measures aimed at reducing German influence, especially in the economy, and also at controlling the German-language school system. Beyond efforts to prevent Polish-speaking children from attending German schools, however, the relevant guidelines actually contained little that could cause umbrage: German schools were instructed to observe Polish public holidays, use approved textbooks only, and keep out all Nazi influences. In comparison with Prussia's Germanization policy, the approved measures proved to be—contrary to Kotowski's assessment—relatively harmless, and they were ultimately impotent when faced with German minorities that largely supported Nazism and whose leading organizations were already under Berlin's control.[139]

The Decision for War

Soon after the German occupation of western Czechoslovakia eliminated one more political buttress for Warsaw, Poland itself fell into Berlin's sights.[140] Ribbentrop's stance toward his Polish opposites was initially more restrained than the demands that had been presented to Prague: in return for the surrender of Danzig, permission to build an extraterritorial road and rail connection to East Prussia, and Poland's entry into the Anti-Comintern Pact, Germany would offer—and this was a rather bold move from the German side—definitive recognition of Poland's western border. Martin Broszat has rightly warned that the border recognition should not be mistaken as "from the outset a false offer from

Hitler, one that anticipated rejection to be followed by violence."[141] After all, the anti-Soviet proposition also fit the central goal of Nazi foreign policy, namely the acquisition of new "Lebensraum," and in previous years had become almost a leitmotif in the discussions that Hitler, Konstantin von Neurath, and Hermann Göring held with Polish representatives.[142] Despite repeated overtures, Warsaw had consistently rejected this offer, which would have made Poland completely dependent on Berlin. When Ribbentrop returned "empty-handed" from yet another visit to Warsaw in January 1939, the path to war was laid.[143] In late March, Hitler informed the German army's commander in chief, Walther von Brauchitsch, that if circumstances dictated, he wanted to resolve the "Polish question" through war; in early April, he instructed the Wehrmacht's High Command to undertake the planning of "Fall Weiss" ("Case White," the strategic plan for invading Poland), before he subsequently revoked the German-Polish Nonaggression Pact as well as the Anglo-German Naval Agreement.[144]

If Berlin had still expected in late 1938 that it could build an eastern empire on the rubble of the Soviet Union with Poland's help, Warsaw's categorical refusal had now forced a change of German plans. From the role of a potential ally, Poland's position shifted to that of the next victim of German aggression. But because of the guarantee that the United Kingdom made to Poland on March 31, 1939, German planning first required a nonbelligerence agreement with precisely the power that was the actual target of Nazi expansion efforts: the Soviet Union. As a result, the German-Soviet Nonaggression Pact—or "aggression pact," as Rainer Schmidt calls it—was signed on August 23, 1939.[145] This "U-turn of all time" sealed Poland's fate in two ways at once: whereas the dystopian vision of a "'living space' further east dropped for the foreseeable future out of the equation," an attack on the neighboring Poland had now become a calculable gamble.[146] These dreams of carnage were now projected on Poland, as seen in Hitler's address to the Wehrmacht leadership on the eve of the pact's ratification: "Accordingly, I have placed my Death's Head Units [Totenkopfverbände] in readiness . . . with an order to send every man, woman, and child of Polish descent and language to their deaths, mercilessly and without compassion. This is the only way for us to gain the Lebensraum we need."[147]

These developments led to immediate consequences for the German minorities in Poland, now that the Polish state was reacting to all provocations with a much shorter temper, and right up until the final weeks before the outbreak of war, it was forcefully dissolving the bulk of German minority organizations.[148] The Polish government was wrong in believing that dissolving the minority organizations would ensure its security, for it failed to see that doing so had not interrupted the various intelligence efforts and conspiratorial operations conducted across Poland by a number of German agencies. The German efforts proved useful in projects like the compilation of proscription lists, filled by German units with the names of persons who were later to be arrested and often executed. In August 1939, Rudolf Wiesner even suggested to VoMi that he could take up a role corresponding to the one played by Henlein in Czechoslovakia.[149]

Meanwhile, Germany's security agencies had begun arming members of German minorities and bringing them together into paramilitary units known as K-organizations (engaged in *Kampf* or "combat") and S-organizations (engaged in sabotage). Although the Polish Interior Ministry still believed it could put away any fears about Germans in Poland forming military groups, the K- and S-organizations in Upper Silesia already had 4,474 members, and the K-organizations in Poznań Voivodeship had 2,324 men under arms in seventy-two localities.[150] When the Wehrmacht attacked Poland on September 1, 1939, this fifth column sprang into action by blowing up bridges, blockading streets, occupying industrial zones, and even taking over an entire city before the Wehrmacht's arrival, as was the case in Katowice, the biggest city in Upper Silesia and known in German as Kattowitz.[151]

Notes

1. Quoted in Broszat, *Zweihundert Jahre*, 85.
2. Ibid., 90.
3. Kolb, "Polenbild und Polenfreundschaft," 113.
4. For example, see the many Pole-friendly references at the 1832 Hambach Festival in Majewski, "Sage nie," and Asmus, *Hambacher Fest*. For an overview of the many supportive organizations in Baden, which was particularly liberal at the time, see Brudzyńska-Němec, *Polenvereine*.
5. M. Müller, "Deutsche und polnische Nation," 74; see also ibid., 71–72, as well as Kolb, "Polenbild und Polenfreundschaft," 111–13. On "pan-nationalism," see Koselleck et al., "Volk, Nation," 7: 404.
6. Broszat, *Zweihundert Jahre*, 101–2.
7. Lukowski and Zawadski, *Concise History*, 142–44; Schmidt-Rösler, *Polen*, 82–83.
8. Trzeciakowski, "Polnische Frage," 63–64.
9. Quoted in Wippermann, *Ordensstaat*, 144–45. Müller and Schönemann, *Polen-Debatte*, explores the events more comprehensively.
10. Sauer, "Problem," 422–23.
11. On this, see also Ther, "Beyond the Nation," 53–54.
12. Hoensch, *Geschichte Polens*, 231.
13. Zoltowski to the Reichstag on April 1, quoted in *Verhandlungen des Reichstages*, 1: 97.
14. Ibid., 1: 98. On the rediscovery of the medieval German eastward colonization, see Wippermann, *Der deutsche Drang*, esp. 82–116; Kopp, "Arguing the Case," 151.
15. Sauer, "Problem," 431.
16. Wehler, "Deutsch-polnische Beziehungen," 204.
17. Trzeciakowski, *Kulturkampf*, 119.

18. Hoensch, *Geschichte Polens*, 232. For the effects on Silesia, see Matuschek, "Polnisch der Oberschlesier," part 1, 110–11, and part 2, 194. For the importance of language in emergent nationalism, see particularly Anderson, *Erfindung*, 72–87, and Hobsbawm, *Nationen*, 60–83; for Germany, see, for example, Puschner, *Völkische Bewegung*, 27–48. For a concise overview of research on the role of language in the assertion of nationalist worldviews, see Day and Thompson, *Theorizing Nationalism*, 90–92.

19. On this, see Leuschner, "Sprache."

20. Trzeciakowski, *Kulturkampf*, 52–53; Broszat, *Zweihundert Jahre*, 134; Lindemann, "Preußisch-deutsche Reichsgründung," 30.

21. Trzeciakowski, *Kulturkampf*, 57–59.

22. Einhart, *Deutsche Geschichte*, 286.

23. Trzeciakowski, *Kulturkampf*, 6.

24. Here, Kopp points to an interesting simultaneity, for this escalation of inner colonization policy coincided with the overseas expansion of the German Empire. The existence of a causal relationship, however, is debatable ("Arguing the Case," 149).

25. Broszat, *Zweihundert Jahre*, 143.

26. Neubach, *Ausweisungen*, 32.

27. Lindemann, "Preußisch-deutsche Reichsgründung," 35.

28. Ibid.; see also Wehler, "Von den 'Reichsfeinden,'" 187.

29. See, for example, the contemporary argument in Hasse, *Das deutsche Reich*, 56–58.

30. Wehler, *Das deutsche Kaiserreich*, 116.

31. Broszat, *Zweihundert Jahre*, 148.

32. Hagen, "National Solidarity," 42–43.

33. Berghahn, *Kaiserreich*, 186; see also Davies, *God's Playground*, 130; Broszat, *Zweihundert Jahre*, 141–42 and 152–53.

34. Broszat, *Zweihundert Jahre*, 153.

35. Eley, *Reshaping*, 41–48; Walkenhorst, *Nation—Volk—Rasse*, 68–69.

36. Alldeutscher Verband, *Zwanzig Jahre*, 13–22.

37. Ibid., 114–25.

38. Walkenhorst, *Nation—Volk—Rasse*, 264. Hansemann's support appears in the January 1900 issue of *Die Ostmark*, cited in Oldenburg, *Der deutsche Ostmarkenverein*, 136.

39. The relevant legislation was passed by Prussia's House of Lords on June 28, 1904, specifying that the construction of residential buildings in the provinces of East Prussia, West Prussia, and Posen, as well as parts of Silesia, Brandenburg, and Pomerania, required permission from the local Regierungspräsident—which, of course, was not granted to Polish applicants. More comprehensively in Hofmann, "Ansiedlungsgesetz."

40. Tims, *Germanizing Prussian Poland*, 152–55; Wehler, "Von den 'Reichsfeinden,'" 188.

41. From page 62 of the August 1907 issue, quoted in Oldenburg, *Der deutsche Ostmarkenverein*, 137.

42. Wehler, "Von den 'Reichsfeinden,'" 191. See also Walkenhorst, *Nation—Volk—Rasse*, 273–74.

43. Hasse, *Das Deutsche Reich*, 57.

44. Davies, *God's Playground*, 135. The events are examined more comprehensively in Kulczycki, *School Strikes*. The Alldeutscher Verband even called for Polish children to be released from compulsory education, arguing that strike participants should be "permanently excluded from school attendance" (Alldeutscher Verband, *Zwanzig Jahre*, 299).

45. Laak, *Über alles*, 86.

46. Boysen, "Geist des Grenzlands," 109.

47. Broszat, *Zweihundert Jahre*, 166.

48. Oldenburg, *Der deutsche Ostmarkenverein*, 140.

49. Quoted in Walkenhorst, *Nation—Volk—Rasse*, 222.

50. Frymann, *Wenn ich der Kaiser.*

51. Quoted in Fischer, *Griff nach der Weltmacht*, 93. According to Robin Prior and Trevor Wilson, Bettmann-Hollweg's September program was a "terrifying document uncannily foreshadowing the policy of conquest on which Adolf Hitler embarked twenty years later" (Prior and Wilson, "Review Article," 325). On the topicality of Fischer and the "Hamburg school" of historiography, see Berghahn, "Ostimperium und Weltpolitik." For an overview of the various scholarly interpretations of the September program, see Mombauer, *Origins*, 132–33, a book that also provides a concise survey of the general state of research into the causes of World War I.

52. Geiss, *Der polnische Grenzstreifen*, 72.

53. Ibid., 75.

54. Ibid., 77.

55. Ibid., 83.

56. Hagen, *Germans, Poles, and Jews*, 286.

57. Wehler, "Von den 'Reichsfeinden,'" 197.

58. See, for example, Geiss, *Der polnische Grenzstreifen*, 49; Fischer, *Griff nach der Weltmacht*, 141; Oldenburg, *Der deutsche Ostmarkenverein*, 225–27.

59. Geiss, *Der polnische Grenzstreifen*, 91–96.

60. Quoted in ibid., 147.

61. Wehler, "Von den 'Reichsfeinden,'" 191; Rutherford, "Race, Space, and the Polish Question," 51.

62. Rosenthal, *German and Pole*, 41.

63. Forgus, "German Nationality Policies," 107.

64. Seckendorf, "Kulturelle Deutschtumspflege," 116.

65. Sharp, "Genie That Would Not Go Back," 10–11. Similarly Zimmer, *Nationalism in Europe*, 60; Hobsbawm, *Nationen*, 132–33.

66. Weitz, "From the Vienna to the Paris System," 1314.

67. On the minorities agreements, see, for example, Riga and Kennedy, "Tolerant Majorities"; on Poland, see Fink, "Minorities Question." For a contemporaneous view, see Woolsey, "Rights of Minorities."

68. Sharp, "Genie That Would Not Go Back," 9.

69. Mazower, *Dark Continent*, 41.

70. Kotowski, *Polens Politik*, 197.

71. Peukert, *Weimarer Republik*, 201.

72. Broszat, *Zweihundert Jahre*, 218.

73. Quoted in Bundeszentrale für politische Bildung, *Deutsche und Polen*, 28.

74. Quoted in Haar, "Leipziger Stiftung," 379.

75. Wright, *Gustav Stresemann*, 269–71, 314–15, and 409–12. On Stresemann's past in the Pan-German League, see ibid., 52–54.

76. Wagner, "Weimarer Republik," 41.

77. Schramm, "Kurswechsel," 31.

78. Hoensch, "Deutschland, Polen und die Großmächte," 20 and 10.

79. See Puchert, *Wirtschaftskrieg.*

80. Quoted in Zorn, *Nach Ostland,* 48.

81. Hoensch, "Deutschland, Polen und die Großmächte," 23.

82. This rather narrowly defined limitation of the minority treaties did not prevent post-1945 Polish historians from also sharing the interwar Polish government's view that these treaties offered the great powers an opportunity "to interfere in the internal affairs of new states . . . under the pretext of acting in the interest of minorities residing in those states" (Czapliński, "Protection of Minorities," 126).

83. Komjathy and Stockwell, *German Minorities,* x. See also Mazower, *Dark Continent,* 53–54, and 57; Sharp, "Genie That Would Not Go Back," 25.

84. Quoted in Broszat, *Zweihundert Jahre,* 228.

85. Zimmer, *Nationalism in Europe,* 62.

86. Broszat, *Zweihundert Jahre,* 228.

87. Jansen and Weckbecker, *Volksdeutsche Selbstschutz,* 22.

88. Quoted in Broszat, *Zweihundert Jahre,* 212.

89. Hauser, "Deutsche Minderheit," 68.

90. Kotowski, *Polens Politik,* 197.

91. Krekeler, *Revisionsanspruch,* 50–53. See also Trevisiol, *Einbürgerungspraxis,* 187–88.

92. Blanke, "German Minority," 88.

93. Jacobsen, *Nationalsozialistische Außenpolitik,* 580. See also Hauser, "Deutsche Minderheit," 67.

94. Fiedor, "Attitude of German Right-Wing Organizations," 248; Hauser, "Deutsche Minderheit," 69; Krekeler, *Revisionsanspruch,* 13.

95. Winkler soon became one of the central figures in ethnopolicy circles and would implement the economic plundering of Poland during the Nazi occupation as head of the Main Trust Office for the East (Haupttreuhandstelle Ost, see Rosenkötter, *Treuhandpolitik;* Dingell, *Zur Tätigkeit*).

96. Krekeler, *Revisionsanspruch,* 16.

97. Ibid., 21.

98. Lumans, *Himmler's Auxiliaries,* 93.

99. These six regions were Posen and Pomerelia (ca. 342,000 Germans in 1926), Upper Silesia (ca. 300,000), Bielsko-Biała (ca. 30,000), Central Poland (ca. 350,000), Volhynia (47,000–60,000), and Galicia (ca. 60,000)—Jacobsen, *Nationalsozialistische Außenpolitik,* 582. Such figures were highly contested. For example, in Poland's official census of 1931, persons counting toward the German minority were numbered at only 254,522 for Central Poland and 91,207 for Upper Silesia combined with Cieszyn Silesia (Hauser, "Deutsche Minderheit in Polen," 87).

100. For an overview of German minority associations in Upper Silesia, see Greiner and Kaczmarek, "Vereinsaktivitäten"; on the ethnic conflicts in Łódź, see, for example, Kossert, "Protestantismus in Lodz," 89; on the German Workers' Party, see Kotowski, *Polens Politik,* 16–17; Hauser, "Deutsche Minderheit," 73.

101. Krekeler, *Revisionsanspruch,* 27.

102. Ibid.

103. Hoensch, "Deutschland, Polen und die Großmächte," 20.

104. Jansen and Weckbecker, *Der Volksdeutsche Selbstschutz,* 14.

105. Wynot, "Polish Germans," 30.

106. Ibid. The ownership situation was similar in the part of Upper Silesia that fell to Poland, with more than 55 percent of heavy industry still in German hands by 1939 (Kaczmarek, "Deutsche wirtschaftliche Penetration," 260).

107. Wynot, "Polish Germans," 51.

108. Krekeler, *Revisionsanspruch*, 67.

109. Ibid., 96.

110. Ibid., 96 and 104.

111. Ibid., 120.

112. Krekeler, *Revisionsanspruch*, 132. See also Peukert, *Die Weimarer Republik*, 202.

113. Funding for this region totaling 37.5 million Reichsmarks from 1925 to 1931, it increased to 13 million for 1932, and to 16 million for 1933 (Krekeler, *Revisionsanspruch*, 145).

114. Schramm, "Kurswechsel," 23.

115. Wollstein, "Politik des nationalsozialistischen Deutschlands," 795.

116. Quotations are from Hitler, *Zweites Buch*, 163. For the impact of "Lebensraum" ideology on Hitler's worldview, see Jäckel, *Hitlers Herrschaft*, 29–54; Kershaw, *Hitler: Hubris*, 149–51 and 240–50; Smith, *Ideological Origins*, 83–111; Walkenhorst, *Nation—Volk—Rasse*, 166–72; Puschner, *Völkische Bewegung*, 151–55, which also looks at the importance of this thinking for ethnonational rights during the German Empire period.

117. On Haushofer and his influence on Hitler's conception of "Lebensraum," see H. Herwig, "Geopolitik." For a comprehensive survey of the VDA's history from its beginning to the 1990s, see Goldendach and Minow, *Deutschtum erwache!*

118. Jacobsen, *Nationalsozialistische Außenpolitik*, 182.

119. Ibid., 167.

120. Lumans, *Himmler's Auxiliaries*, 28–29.

121. Seckendorf, "Kulturelle Deutschtumspflege," 115; also Kotowski, *Polens Politik*, 17.

122. Jansen and Weckbecker, *Der Volksdeutsche Selbstschutz*, 25. For a brief description of the Nazification of Upper Silesia's German associations, see, for example, Greiner und Kaczmarek, "Vereinsaktivitäten," 235.

123. Jacobsen, *Nationalsozialistische Außenpolitik*, 585.

124. Niendorf, *Minderheiten*, 211.

125. Jacobsen, *Nationalsozialistische Außenpolitik*, 586.

126. Ibid., 230.

127. Ibid., 593–94.

128. Lumans, *Himmler's Auxiliaries*, 38–39.

129. Jacobsen, *Nationalsozialistische Außenpolitik*, 243. See also Brown, "Third Reich's Mobilization," 133. Lorenz actually had even greater ambitions, originally pushing for the establishment of a dedicated Reich Commissariat and later wanting to become a state secretary for ethnopolitical issues (Staatssekretär für Volkstumsfragen). Therefore, Hitler's decree (see NG-972) was actually only a partial success for him; see also Stuhlpfarrer, *Umsiedlung Südtirol*, 238–40.

130. Lumans, *Himmler's Auxiliaries*, 67–68.

131. Jacobsen, *Nationalsozialistische Außenpolitik*, 243–44.

132. BArch NS 19/2307, 7–9, directive from Hess, February 3, 1939.

133. Koehl, *RKFDV*, 97.

134. Jacobsen, *Nationalsozialistische Außenpolitik*, 237.

135. Ibid., 241.

136. Koehl, "Deutsche Volksliste," 354. See also Lumans, *Himmler's Auxiliaries*, 97.

137. Kotowski, *Polens Politik*, 348.

138. Ibid., 242–44.

139. Ibid., 247–54.

140. Leitz, *Nazi Foreign Policy*, 73–74.

141. Broszat, *Zweihundert Jahre*, 255.

142. Ibid., 247; see also Wollstein, "Politik des nationalsozialistischen Deutschlands," 806.

143. Kershaw, *Hitler: Nemesis*, 166. In those same weeks, Hitler gave three speeches to Wehrmacht officers during which he clearly expressed his desire for war (ibid., 166–67). See also Czubiński, "Poland's Place in Nazi Plans," 31 and 37–38.

144. Hillgruber, "Deutschland und Polen," 54.

145. Schmidt, *Außenpolitik*, 341.

146. Kershaw, *Hitler: Nemesis*, 206 and 238.

147. Hitler's second speech to Wehrmacht heads, August 22, 1930, L-3, reprinted in *Akten zur deutschen auswärtigen Politik*, ser. D, 7: 171–72.

148. Kotowski, *Polens Politik*, 313 and 336.

149. Ibid., 338–39; also Seckendorf, "Kulturelle Deutschtumspflege," 132.

150. Kotowski, *Polens Politik*, 341. See also Szefer, "Dywersyjno-sabotażowa działalność," 297–308 and 310–24.

151. Szefer, "Dywersyjno-sabotażowa działalność," 335. See also Pospieszalski, "Nazi Attacks," 111–12.

2 War

*Projecting the "Lebensraum"
Dystopia onto Poland*

In CONTRAST TO the invasions of Austria, the Sudetenland, the Memel territory, and finally the Czech rump state, the attack on Poland was seen by the Nazi leadership as the first step in the final battle to acquire a life-or-death necessity for the German "Volk": new "Lebensraum" in the east. In the short time from the invasion's start on September 1, 1939, to the taking of Warsaw on September 28, to the capitulation of the last Polish units on October 6, German goals underwent a dramatic radicalization. Despite countless discussions throughout World War I, the German Empire had not been able to bring itself to do what Nazi Germany had launched in just a few short weeks, namely the expulsion or murder of persons considered "undesirable" on political or racial grounds, the systematic registration of resident "Volksdeutsche," and finally the resettlement of ethnic Germans from Eastern Europe. In what would become the annexed western Polish territories, an entire population was subjected to a comprehensive selection process for the first time, wherein the first step was to register those who in any case must be rendered "harmless" or given the right to preferential treatment as potential members of the "Volksgemeinschaft" that was to be installed here.

The Genesis of the "Lebensraum" Policy during the War

Just a few weeks after Hitler had instructed the German army's commander in chief to draw up an operational plan for waging war against Poland, the SS Security Service (Sicherheitsdienst, or SD) also began its preparations, as it had done in earlier military campaigns. As in the invasions of Austria, the Sudetenland, and the Czech rump state, the Wehrmacht was to be followed by SS units in Poland as well, in order to help police the rearward territory and take action against political opponents.

Under the code name "Operation Tannenberg," preparations at SD headquarters included the compilation of a proscription list known as the *Sonderfahndungsbuch Polen* (Special prosecution book for Poland).[1] The overall coordination of this effort was taken over in early June by Werner Best, the head of the Gestapo's Department I (administration and personnel) and Department III (counterintelligence), who was second only to Reinhard Heydrich as the most important figure in the Security Police (Sicherheitspolizei). In the end, there were seven *Einsatzgruppen* encompassing sixteen *Einsatzkommandos* (deployment groups and deployment commandos, respectively), altogether comprising some 4,250 persons, of which 2,250 came from the Ordnungspolizei ("order" police, or uniformed law enforcement officers) and the rest primarily from the Gestapo and the Kriminalpolizei (criminal police, or plainclothes investigators), while the SD mainly supplied the leaders of the Einsatzgruppen and Einsatzkommandos.[2]

Of particular interest are the instructions these men brought with them into the war zone, for they allow conclusions to be drawn about the kind of warfare that Germany was intending to wage, and thus about its envisaged war goals. The foreign-deployment guidelines for the Security Police and the SD were issued at the end of August, after consultations between Heydrich and Colonel Eduard Wagner, the responsible officer in the Army High Command (Oberkommando des Heeres, or OKH); here, the Einsatzgruppen were tasked in very general terms with the "combating of all anti-Reich and anti-German elements rearwards of the fighting troops."[3] Expressions like "völkische Flurbereinigung" ("ethnic cleansing of the soil"), which became so common just a few weeks later, are entirely missing here, as are any mentions of the Jewish populace. Instead, it was explicitly written that "mistreatment or killings of apprehended persons are strictly forbidden."[4] These guidelines contain no hint of the mass murders that these same units would commit just a few weeks later. It cannot be ruled out, however, that these written instructions may have served as cover for the SS, with a supplementary "killing order" issued orally by Himmler and Heydrich.[5]

In the latest research, this interpretation is most forcefully argued by Alexander B. Rossino. One piece of evidence is the testimony on a meeting with Einsatzgruppen leaders on August 18, 1939, who were apparently informed by Heydrich about further alleged atrocities committed against the ethnic Germans, leading him to expect heavy resistance from paramilitary Polish groups; in order to suppress them, "everything was permissible, meaning executions as well as arrests," according to Lothar Beutel, leader of Einsatzgruppe IV.[6] Another attendee of that meeting, however, the liaison chief of Einsatzgruppe IV, Dr. Ernst Gehrke, denied having received a "general liquidation order," but added that "back then it was not the usual way, expressing such things so openly."[7] No further clarity on Rossino's contentions is provided by a message from Heydrich to the chief of the Ordnungspolizei Kurt Daluege on July 2, 1940, in which he makes retrospective mention of the murders in Poland. Certainly, Heydrich does write that the "instructions for police deployment were extraordinarily radical (e.g., liquidation order for many Polish leadership groups, going into the thousands)"—this is not in doubt.[8] But the real question is when these instructions were actually issued, whether before the war or after it was already in progress—on this point, the message offers no clue. Although Rossino's interpretation cannot be entirely discounted on the basis of the surviving documents, I think it nonetheless fails to adequately consider the processual character that shaped the development of violence during these weeks. In this view, killing campaigns are primarily seen as the end product of a well-defined process of decision and command, one that is ascribed to the headquarters, with little attention paid to events on the periphery or to the personal initiative of agents on the ground; as a result, a more complex model of interaction between the hub and the periphery is no longer considered.

In my view, it seems much more likely that Heydrich initially refrained from issuing wholesale killing orders to those gathered on August 18, especially since he could not yet be sure at that point whether such a thing was actually enforceable against the will of the Wehrmacht. Instead, one can assume that it was more about readying these men for a deployment that was clearly unlike those that had come before. And it certainly cannot be ruled out that the prohibition against killing, as specified in the guidelines, was explicitly qualified with potential exceptions. Speaking in favor of this was an order issued on August 18 by Best to the SS units stationed on occupied Czech territory, in which he expanded the circle of those considered enemies. Every person who politically opposed the German occupation was now to be treated as an "enemy of the state," including all communists and left-wing social democrats, as well as all Jews.[9] Although one can hardly assume that any greater deference was ordered in regard to the Polish populace, this still does not mean that a general killing order necessarily existed for the deployment in Poland.[10]

But it was not only the SS units that were caught up in this radicalization process. The Wehrmacht too had long since begun unshackling itself from the "constraints" of international war conventions. After an order had already been issued as early as February 16, 1939, specifying the separation of war prisoners according to "racial" criteria (which was actually implemented after September 1 with the systematic selection of Jewish prisoners), the Army High Command (Oberkommando des Heeres, or OKH) as well as individual commanders began preparing their soldiers for the war against Poland on an ideological level.[11] Thus, in a handbook from the Wehrmacht High Command (Oberkommando der Wehrmacht, or OKW) dated July 1, 1939, the Polish populace was vilified as "fanatically hate-filled" and was also accused of "destroying and poisoning food stockpiles." It was because of this that any "accommodating treatment" would in fact be "construed as weakness."[12] For the Army High Command, it was just a short leap to then declare on August 9, 1939, that the rules of the Hague Conventions were to be obeyed at most "in spirit."[13] To ensure that the individual commanders in chief also understood what the upcoming war was about and how it was to be waged, Hitler invited them to a meeting on August 22. His speech to them must have cleared up any last doubts among the Wehrmacht leadership about the character of the impending war: "Poland's destruction at the fore. Goal is the elimination of all living forces, not the reaching of a certain line . . . shut the heart against pity. Brutal actions . . . Any newly reemerging living Polish force is to be immediately exterminated again."[14]

The German leadership thus wanted a war that was aimed not only at the extinguishing of Poland's armed forces, but also at already laying the groundwork for a German-dominated Eastern Europe, whose borders—at least for now—had been defined by the pact with the Soviet Union. But beyond that, vagueness dominated in Berlin. There was certainly no hint of any "detailed plans of expansion and conquest" that Antoni Czubinski claims to have found, nor anything else that resembled a plan, however coherent, about the future war aims.[15] There was consensus on only two aspects: the annexation of large parts of western Poland beyond the borders of 1918 and the homogenization of the populace there.

*   *   *

Thus, although the SS Einsatzgruppen probably did not have a wholesale killing order when they crossed Poland's borders on the early morning of September 1, they were nonetheless committed to waging a war that violated all rules of international law. And the Wehrmacht had set out on a similar course. As already demonstrated decades ago by Polish historians, and also proved more recently by two impressive studies, the Wehrmacht was certainly not just a bystander in the mass murders committed by the SS and police units during the war against Poland.[16]

One of the first major war crimes occurred in the city of Bydgoszcz, known in German as Bromberg. The shooting of retreating Polish soldiers by ethnic Germans, in which forty to fifty soldiers were killed, had led to Polish retaliatory attacks on September 3, in which anywhere from one hundred to three hundred people were killed.[17] During the Wehrmacht's conquest of the city soon thereafter, a war crime was already committed by a unit from Einsatzgruppe IV, which executed more than fifty defenders of city hall, mostly youths.[18] Further attacks on German personnel were answered with ever more radical terror measures, until the local Wehrmacht commander apparently gave free rein to the head of Einsatzkommando 1, which ultimately led to a mass execution on September 12 in a forest outside Bromberg, involving an estimated nine hundred Polish civilians previously arrested during roundups.[19] Of course, German propaganda focused instead on the alleged Polish atrocities, fabricating what it called the "Bromberger Blutsonntag" ("Bromberg Bloody Sunday"), during which allegedly fifty-eight thousand "Volksdeutsche" had been brutally murdered.[20]

Bromberg's explosion of violence under German orders was embedded in a general escalation of German warfare, which was primarily justified by the alleged threat of "franc-tireurs," a word known to Germans from two earlier wars. In an astounding parallel to the radicalization of German warfare seen during World War I, a more brutal approach by the Einsatzgruppen was ordered by Himmler on September 3, the day of the massacres in Bromberg.[21] He stated that "Polish insurgents caught in the act or with a weapon" were henceforth "to be shot on the spot," and that an insurgent was anyone who "attacked the lives of German occupation personnel or of Volksdeutsche, or threatened vital facilities or goods in the occupied territories."[22] A day later, the Wehrmacht followed suit by issuing its first "criminal order," which stated that "Polish civilians" suspected of having shot at German soldiers were no longer to be handed over as before to the Security Police for "clarifying the question of perpetration," but were instead to be shot by one's own troops; this also applied to civilians who were only "located at the houses and farmsteads from which our troops had been fired on."[23]

This first radicalization of German warfare had fatal consequences for the civilian populace. Although Polish soldiers—as long as they were not Jewish—retained at least the most basic rights upon capture, more and more of the civilian populace was now finding itself subject to German aggression. Not entirely settled, however, is the exact relationship between the Polish quashing of the ethnic German uprising in Bromberg and the explosion of violence from the German side, which began on the same day.[24] Nonetheless, it can be assumed that the outrage over the alleged crimes committed against the "Volksdeutsche" in Bromberg and, more generally, the anger at the allegedly unlawful warfare conducted by Polish "irregulars" behind the German front line were a pair of factors that mutually reinforced one another while also contributing to the unfettering of violence on the German side—even though both were the result of the regime's own ideological production and had little to do with reality.[25]

Unlike later events in the Soviet Union, this radicalization in Poland was marked by sometimes intense conflicts between the Wehrmacht and the SS. In the eyes of the SS, the Wehrmacht was endangering the political goals pursued by the Reich in Poland. As Heydrich informed his departmental heads on September 7, the "leading social class . . . must be rendered harmless as much as possible" and could "certainly not remain in Poland, but instead must be brought to German concentration camps."[26] Here, the ostensibly conscientious Wehrmacht was seen only as an obstacle, as reflected in the writings of military counterintelligence officer Helmuth Groscurth, who complained a day later that Heydrich "continues inciting against the army in the most outrageous way."[27]

The Wehrmacht complained not only about the conduct of the SS Einsatzgruppen, but also the actions of the so-called Volksdeutscher Selbstschutz, or Ethnic German "Self-Defense" Force. The potential of these militia formations had been immediately recognized by the SS leadership, which had also initiated some of them and supplied them with weapons. They were all put under SS command on September 9 and ultimately subordinated to the Ordnungspolizei (a Main Office of the SS) on September 26, 1939, under the chief of the Ordnung-spolizei Kurt Daluege and his local commanders on location.[28] Despite what their name might suggest, the Volksdeutscher Selbstschutz units were not primarily meant to provide "defense" for the local Germans but instead to act as a "complement to the Einsatzgruppen." Unlike the Einsatzgruppen, the Volksdeutscher Selbstschutz soon grew to include more than a hundred thousand members, thereby extending the reach of the SS into every locale.[29] Such units supported the SS through their local knowledge, particularly in assisting with the selection process applied to the resident populace, as well as the arrest of allegedly "anti-German elements"; they would soon help with the deportations as well and ultimately took part in the executions.[30]

Various voices in the Wehrmacht protested this continual expansion of the SS sphere of action, but to no avail.[31] During a discussion aboard the "Führer train" on September 12, 1939, Admiral Wilhelm Canaris, chief of military intelligence, reported to Colonel General Wilhelm Keitel, chief of the Wehrmacht High Command, that "extensive executions by firing squad were planned in Poland, and that especially the nobility and clergy were to be eradicated." Keitel was not surprised, for Hitler had apparently already informed him of the radicalization of warfare against the civilian population, as well as the associated population policy goals. Canaris learned that "this matter was already decided by the Führer . . . that if the Wehrmacht wanted nothing to do with this, it must also accept that the SS and Gestapo would make an appearance here."[32] A marginal note on the minutes of this conversation includes an expression that would appear more and more often, one that described the German policy goal in Poland: "political cleansing of the soil" ("politische Flurbereinigung").[33]

Conflicts also arose over the brutal treatment of the Jewish populace, especially after the mass murders committed in Bendzin (today Będzin) by the Einsatzgruppe z.b.V. (*Einsatzgruppe zur besonderen Verwendung*; Einsatzgruppe on special assignment) under SS Senior Group Leader Udo von Woyrsch. It would soon turn out, however, that the Army High Command was criticizing more Woyrsch's methods than the general direction of SS policy and itself issued an order dated September 12, 1939, for Jews "to be deported over the San river," the demarcation line between German and Soviet occupied Poland.[34] It thereby pivoted toward the policy defined by the Reich Security Main Office (Reichssicherheitshauptamt) on September 11, when Heydrich met with SS Brigade Leader Bruno Streckenbach, Kraków's Commander of the Security Police and SD (Befehlshaber der Sicherheitspolizei und des SD, or BdS), to discuss the expulsion of the Jews across the San.[35] In the end, the Wehrmacht even ordered its soldiers to shoot anyone coming back, "also outside of the bridges."[36] Hans Umbreit's assessment that the Wehrmacht's treatment of the Jews "bordered on criminality" is therefore too mild.[37] Indeed, it had taken less than two weeks for the Wehrmacht leadership to also agree with the ethnic cleansing policy pushed by the Nazi regime's top leadership. Aimed not only at alleged irregulars and the Polish elite, but also the Jewish populace, this was not simply a "political cleansing of the soil," as it was still described on the same day in the meeting notes of another military intelligence officer, Lieutenant Colonel Erwin von Lahousen.

The matters still needing discussion, as communicated by the Wehrmacht to Himmler and Hitler in the following weeks, were thus limited to delineating this division of labor and arranging an orderly exit of the German military. When Wagner received confirmation from Heydrich on September 19 of something that he already knew, namely that the Einsatzgruppen had in fact received orders to take action against the civilian population, he asked only that implementation be delayed until a German civil administration was established, so that the Wehrmacht no longer had to carry any responsibility for it.[38] The resolution was recorded as follows in the notes of Franz Halder, the army's chief of staff:

> b) Cleansing of the soil: Jews, intelligentsia, clergy, nobility.
>
> c) Army's demands: cleansing after the army's withdrawal, and after handover to a stable civil administration. Early December.[39]

It was probably for similar reasons that Walther von Brauchitsch, the army's commander in chief, sought a meeting the next day with Hitler, who immediately updated him on the war plans. There had been an important development: a telegram had arrived from Friedrich-Werner von der Schulenburg, the German ambassador in Moscow, who reported that the Soviet foreign minister Vyacheslav Molotov had "intimated" he was no longer interested in the "original inclination toward allowing a rump Poland to exist" and had asked for negotiations on its partitioning.[40]

This initiative from the Soviet Union had an immediate impact on German war planning. During the meeting aboard the "Führer train" on September 12, Foreign Minister Joachim von Ribbentrop had explained to Keitel that three choices existed at the time: partition Poland once again; allow for an "independent rump Poland"; or pursue the establishment of a Ukrainian state and the realignment of Lithuania's borders.[41] After Moscow's change of heart, Brauchitsch was faced with a new permutation, one that strove toward "resettlement on a large scale."[42] All those who had moved to the formerly German territories after 1918 were to be deported, with the Jewish Poles destined for induction into ghettos, although this was "not yet clarified in the particulars."[43] To replace all these people, Germans were to be brought in for resettlement.[44] Hitler had thereby outlined for the first time the upcoming program of forced population transfers, a concept that had already appeared in similar form among the radical nationalists and during the discussions of a Polish "border strip" during World War I but would now be undertaken by the Nazis. Like Wagner on the previous day, Brauchitsch seemed to have cared only about delaying the policy's full implementation until after the military administration wound up. And this was precisely the assurance he received. According to Hitler, the Wehrmacht would not be burdened with this "cleansing" ("Bereinigung").[45] That same night, Wagner drafted an order in which the Wehrmacht disempowered itself by authorizing the police and SS units to carry out "certain ethnopolitical assignments on behalf of the Führer and according to his instructions" and also to establish drumhead courts-martial.[46]

* * *

The SS knew how to exploit its newly expanded opportunities. On September 21, it was once again up to Himmler and Heydrich to extrapolate a population policy program from Germany's broader war objectives in Poland. As Heydrich announced to his departmental chiefs and gathered Einsatzgruppen leaders, the Polish territories in the German sphere of interest were to be divided: while "the former German provinces" were to be absorbed into the Reich, central Poland would see the establishment of "a Gau with a foreign-language populace" (a *Gau* was a geographic administrative subdivision)—not as a Polish rump state, but "as practically a no man's land" under German control. In one big push, he then sketched a comprehensive program of ethnic cleansing, one that for the first time included the Reich's own territory while also taking the "solution to the Polish problem" and tying it to a racial deportation policy.[47] Thirty thousand German Sinti and all German Jews were to be deported "with freight trains" from the (expanded) Reich to central Poland, with the latter group to be ghettoized in larger municipalities alongside Jewish Poles. For at least a portion of the Jewish Poles, however, a further deportation across the demarcation line had apparently been "authorized by the Führer."[48] The "end goal," as Heydrich put it in a letter to the Einsatzgruppen on the same day, was to be kept strictly confidential.[49] It consisted of deporting all Jews to a "Jewish state under German administration," as he wrote a day later to Brauchitsch.[50] As for the remaining Polish populace, the surviving "Polish leadership class" was to be eliminated first; "in addition, lists of the middle class: teachers, clergy, nobility, legionnaires, returning officers, etc." were to be compiled, so that they could be "arrested and deported to the leftover area."[51] On the other hand, the "primitive Poles" were to be "incorporated into the labor process as migrant workers and will be gradually relocated from the German Gaus into the foreign-language Gau."[52] Thus, while Phillip T. Rutherford is entirely correct in writing that Heydrich had thereby presented "the first detailed description of Nazi plans for a racial 'New Order' in newly conquered territory," Heydrich's designs were certainly not limited to that.[53] In this meeting focused on pragmatic concerns, which was primarily meant to give immediate operational instructions to the Einsatzgruppen in Poland, Heydrich also addressed the organizational structure of the forced expulsion measures. Here, he was able to announce a further victory in reporting that Himmler had been installed as the Settlement Commissioner for the East (Siedlungskommissar für den Osten), which would make the SS complex a decisive actor in Nazi population policy.[54]

Germany's war goals were further radicalized by developments in late September. As Hitler told Birger Dahlerus (a Swedish informal mediator between Germany and the United Kingdom) after the arrival of Schulenburg's telegram, England would have to resign itself to the fact that "Poland could no longer be resurrected." The only possible goal left was to ensure "order in the east" through a "reasonable regional arrangement of the nationalities." For this, however, an "ethnonational cleansing of the soil" ("volksmäßige Flurbereinigung") would be necessary—and this seems to be the first time the term was used—which would also involve the settling of Germans in the ostensibly thinly populated regions of western Poland.[55]

Although it is unclear from the transcript exactly what Germans Hitler was thinking about here, it was probably the ethnic Germans living in the Polish territories earmarked for the Soviet Union.[56] That same night, however, this particular aspect would also become more concrete. According to the testimony of Dr. Erhard Kroeger, leader of the German minority organization in Latvia and later an SS senior leader, he was summoned by Himmler, who revealed to him at the Hotel Casino in Zoppot (today Sopot), which served for a few days as Hitler's headquarters, that the Baltic states were now to be entirely left to the Soviet Union. To Kroeger's surprise, the initial intention was not to evacuate all ethnic Germans from the region, but only those who belonged to the Nazi movement or had dangerously "exposed themselves in ethnopolitics."[57] Appalled, Kroeger urged Himmler not to let the remaining people "fall into the hands of the Bolshevists" and asked that he appeal to Hitler for the resettlement of all the ethnic Germans.[58] The next day, Himmler communicated Hitler's approval to him.[59] A resettlement program had thus taken shape that just a few weeks later would discharge the first load of Baltic "Germans" at the port of Gdingen (today Gdynia).

It was probably only with the determination of Eastern Europe's final partitioning between Germany and the Soviet Union, as laid out in the German-Soviet Frontier Treaty of September 28, that the decision to implement a large deportation program and the destruction of Poland had been finalized in Berlin. On the very next day, Hitler spoke to Alfred Rosenberg about wanting to divide Poland into "three strips," with the western one annexed to the Reich as a "broad belt for Germanization and colonization," thereby making room for "good Germans from around the world." In contrast, the Jewish populace, along with all "somehow unreliable elements," were to be deported to the eastern strip, while a space remained between for an unspecified "Polish statehood."[60] Heydrich chose blunter words in a briefing of his departmental heads, calling the eastern strip a "nature preserve or 'Reich ghetto'" that was now to be established in the region around Lublin, after the modification of the demarcation line.[61]

It is against this backdrop that one must interpret Hitler's well-known speech to the Reichstag on October 6, 1939, which was promulgated as a "speech for peace."[62] In a continuation of the argumentation that he had already tested on Dahlerus, Hitler claimed that his only concern was the "pacification of the entire region" through "a new ordering of the ethnographic circumstances."[63] Michael Wildt has pointed out that Hitler was seeking justification in terms of the rightful self-determination of peoples, a concept that had been used to justify the dismantling of Eastern Europe's multiethnic empires after World War I.[64] Hitler's speech could be paraphrased as arguing that if an equitable and peaceful international order could be achieved only when each territory's populace was ethnically homogeneous and thus had a right to its own state, an impossibility in an ethnically variegated Europe, then political leaders had to create the desired situation retroactively. For Hitler, this "new ordering of the ethnographic circumstances" meant nothing other than a "resettling of nationalities." Such an effort could not be "restricted to this region," and also had to include the retrieval of "unsustainable fragments of Germandom" from all of Eastern Europe, because it was "unrealistic to believe that one could readily assimilate these members of a high-grade Volk."[65] This passage is of central importance because it implied a deportation program that went far beyond Poland, while also offering legitimation for Germany's expansion. It also makes clear that the envisioned "ordering of the entire Lebensraum according to nationalities" was aimed not only at an ethnic homogenization, but also at an ethnic hierarchization.[66]

Perpetuating the Reign of Terror: The Establishment of the German Occupation Regime

If Hitler had hoped that his speech of October 6 could convince the United Kingdom and France to accept a separate peace, then he was mistaken. In any case, the conclusion of war hostilities brought no relief to Poland. On the contrary: after the Wehrmacht had already decided on a mode of warfare that adhered at most "in spirit" to the international laws of war, the subsequent occupation regime further perpetuated the reign of terror.

The main agent of the oppressive measures was to be the upcoming civil administration, which developed from the civil administration teams that were brought along by the Army Higher Commands (Armeeoberkommandos) during the attack on Poland. The war's early days, however, saw some decisive shifts in power. For example, the Wehrmacht found itself confronted in the north by Albert Forster, Danzig's Gauleiter (Gau leader, the head of a Nazi Party regional subdivision), who had begun expanding his sphere of influence on his own initiative with the launch of the German invasion, so that by September 2 he had already taken over the municipal administration of nearby Dirschau (today Tczew). He was unconcerned by the fact that this was actually the job of the civil administration staff attached to the Fourth Army, which was assigned to the region. Just two days later, he contacted Col. Wagner and demanded that he be installed as the area's Chief of Civil Administration (Chef der Zivilverwaltung, or CdZ), in place of the current chief, SS Senior Leader Fritz Herrmann—a demand that was ultimately pushed through by Hitler, prevailing over the Army High Command. Meanwhile, although a less prominent role was played by Arthur Greiser (who would later become the Wartheland's Gauleiter and Reichsstatthalter, or Reich governor), he too was not the Wehrmacht's intended choice for CdZ in his region but was instead brought into play by the Reich Interior Ministry.[67] These circumstances can certainly be taken as further evidence of the vague and improvised nature of the political leadership's planning efforts.[68] But more important, the appointments of these "Alte Kämpfer" ("old fighters" from the party's early period) demonstrated the readiness of Hitler and the party leadership to install a control apparatus in the occupied territories that was entirely oriented to Nazi principles.

Thus, the military administration established on September 25 was for Hitler only an interim solution, one to which he attached "not much significance."[69] Just a short time later, he signed his "decree on the subdivision and administration of the eastern territories," which would dissolve military administration on November 1, 1939, while providing for the transition to a civil administration. Only two days after claiming at the Reichstag that he was striving primarily for the "creation of an unconditionally guaranteed peace and a feeling of security" in Europe, he had sealed the annexation of large parts of Poland's territory and handed them over to his close confidants, along with the task of "Germanizing" these areas.[70]

It is characteristic of the dynamics within the top political leadership that for them, even these three weeks soon became too long; Hitler therefore issued a new decree moving the start of civil administration to October 26, bringing it forward by one week. In their view, the war was still far from over, despite the capitulation of the Polish army. The upcoming annexation of western Poland and its transformation into a "German Lebensraum" demanded a stronger focus on those who were seen as a threat to the German project of total domination, or who otherwise had no place in this German dystopia for ideological reasons. And although the Wehrmacht had proved open to the ethnic cleansing policy during military hostilities, it was nonetheless seen as "too soft and lenient" for the further continuation of this campaign.[71]

The same was also true of the Reich Interior Ministry's planners, who likewise lagged behind the Nazi leadership in their radicalness. Certainly, the ministry's memorandum of October 2, on the "responsibilities of the civil administration in the occupied territories," showed no qualms about pursuing the "reconstruction and strengthening of Germandom" by calling for a "complete and final Germanization."[72] This thinking was still, however, very much rooted in Prussian Germanization policy, as shown by the addendum that only the "areas separated from the Empire in 1918" were meant.[73] Thus, while the ministry was still pondering how a "special status for Germandom" could be achieved in the policy sphere, and how the dispossession of major Polish landowners could be expedited through the use of Polish legal frameworks, Hitler's inner circle had already forged a few steps ahead. The Polish elite was now either murdered or expelled, and with the founding of Göring's Main Trustee Office for the East (Haupttreuhandstelle Ost) along with the installation of Himmler's Land Office (Bodenamt), the Polish populace was simply robbed of its property.[74]

New Borders

The Reich Interior Ministry also proved conservative in defining the new borders, an issue that had been forced onto the agenda by Forster's push for the civilian administration's early installation.[75] Hitler seemed little impressed by an ethnographic map showing western Poland's ethnic composition, which Wilhelm Stuckart, a state secretary at the Reich Interior Ministry, presented during a meeting; after all, the Nazi regime's "Lebensraum" policy was primarily aimed at expansion onto non-German-occupied territories, which were to be transformed into "German settlement land."[76] How very much the "Lebensraum" idea was tied to the expansive demands of the regime's imperialist eastern policy was then shown by a blue line drawn far to the east, with which Hitler in one imperial gesture took the agriculturally most productive regions of Poland as well as four-fifths of its industry, including its entire coal production, and added them to the Reich.[77]

Further development of this plan was assigned to a commission under Ministerial Director Ernst Vollert, head of Department VI at the Reich Interior Ministry, which covered ethnonationality and border demarcation (Abteilung VI: Volkstum und Grenzziehung).[78] Vollert had just recently returned to Berlin, having fallen out with Forster after just fourteen days as his deputy; Vollert had been a replacement for Fritz Hermann, who had been demoted to deputy when Forster took his role as CdZ.[79] This brief personal experience might very well have strengthened Vollert's skepticism about such large-scale annexation plans. In any case, his position paper, "Vorschlag zur territorialen Begrenzung von Westpreussen" (Proposal on the territorial demarcation of West Prussia), dated October 6, 1939, undershot even the demands once put forward by imperial and Prussian hardliners and argued instead for a correction of Hitler's preliminary decision.[80]

Certainly, Vollert likewise considered the "chief task" to consist of making "this old German land as quickly as possible back into a German land again," and he also did not shrink from suggesting the "resettling of a considerable portion of this Polish populace"—meaning up to 4,861,000 people, according to his own figures. But Vollert had underestimated the expansive power of the "Lebensraum" vision when he thereby called for Germany's limitation to the borders of 1914 and labeled it "inexpedient" to extend the future province by incorporating the counties of Lipno, Nieszawa, Rypin, and Włocławek, and thus "to add purely Polish, meaning formerly Russian areas," to it.[81]

Just as futile as Vollert's position paper was another one prepared by the Reich Interior Ministry's own think tank, the Dahlem Publication Office (Publikationsstelle Dahlem), on the same question. In order to strengthen the persuasiveness of its own stance, it had dispatched the young Dr. Theodor Schieder, head of the East Prussia Provincial Office for Postwar History (Landesstelle Ostpreussen für Nachkriegsgeschichte), to the city of Breslau (today Wrocław), where his meeting partners on September 28, 1939, included the local university professors Walter Kuhn and Hermann Aubin.[82] "Academia cannot simply wait until it is asked, it must also speak up," was what Aubin had written on September 18, 1939, to Albert Brackmann, director-general of the Prussian State Archives, under whom the Publication Office was also placed.[83] The meeting in Breslau was to develop a common position on the German handling of Poland, which intermediaries would then bring into the political decision-making process.[84] And in fact, there did seem to be a strong desire for advice within policymaking circles, as Aubin learned when he was told on October 4 that a short position paper was immediately desired by "several senior Reich offices"—probably referring to Vollert's department at the Reich Interior Ministry.[85] Schieder's resulting position paper demonstrated only a minor break with Berlin's past intentions, reflecting demands that had already been articulated by the Pan-Germans and also during the border strip discussion of World War I.[86] His position on the proposed border demarcation was similar. Schieder saw as a "first requirement . . . the *clear delimitation between Polishdom and Germandom*," and although he did mention the old border of 1914, he nonetheless argued for the border not to be extended further eastwards still, but on the contrary, to cede some former German territory by drawing it further west along what was called the "Plate Line" ("Plate'sche Linie"), which was a dividing line between German-speaking and Polish-speaking Prussians as established by the census of 1910.[87] Of course, voicing such opinions was no way to win influence in the shaping of "Lebensraum" policy in the Nazi state. In any case, Hitler left both Vollert's and Schieder's position papers far behind in his Reichstag speech of October 6. As even Johannes Papritz, director of the Dahlem Publication Office, was forced to realize, the Nazi leadership did not need scholarly policy advice in order to arrive at radical decisions. A cover letter he had already prepared for Schieder's position paper was now notated with the comment: "Not sent, because obsolete!"[88]

A day later, the territories were officially annexed: Hitler's "decree on the subdivision and administration of the eastern territories," dated October 8, 1939, reestablished the provinces of West Prussia and Posen (later renamed Danzig–West Prussia and the Wartheland), and appended the governmental regions of Kattowitz and Zichenau to Silesia and East Prussia respectively.[89] And as demonstrated by the remaining squabbles over the exact course of the border, the Nazi leadership chose to ignore not only Vollert's warnings in regard to Danzig–West Prussia, but also the similarly reasoned arguments against an expansionary solution in the border demarcation of Silesia and the Wartheland. Economically important areas from the former Russian partition were added to the province of Silesia against the will of its Oberpräsident Josef Wagner, while the industrial city of Lodsch (today Łódź) was added to the Wartheland in early November for the same reasons, even though both areas contained exclusively, or at least primarily, Polish-speaking populations.[90]

Reich Commissioner for the Strengthening of Germandom

Despite what Hitler had claimed at the Reichstag on October 6, when he misled the world about Germany's willingness to make peace, he not only subsequently ordered the annexation of western Poland and the establishment of a civilian administration, but he was also already raising the second pillar of the German occupation regime by entrusting Himmler with the "ordering of the entire Lebensraum according to nationalities" (as it had been described in his speech). His "decree on the strengthening of Germandom," dated October 7, 1939, expanded on this passage and tasked Himmler with "the settling of ethnonational groups [Volksgruppen] in such a way that better boundaries between them can be achieved"—meaning that the concept of the "Germanization of the soil" was now to be put into political practice.[91] That Germanization was to happen primarily at the expense of the ostensibly non-German populace was now a matter of course, as was the attendant recklessness that had been inconceivable to Vollert just a day earlier.

The idea of installing Himmler as a "settlement commissioner" was certainly not a new one but instead first arose in previously debated plans for resettling the ethnic Germans of South Tyrol. Italy's significance as Germany's most important ally had prompted Hitler, in advance of the Munich Agreement, to finally iron out a major stumbling block in their bilateral relationship, and so he promised Mussolini that these ethnic Germans would be transferred from Italy to the Reich. Ideological demands were once again subordinated to strategic considerations; in Hitler's view, politics was ultimately not about "sentiments, but only hard-heartedness," and here the "claptrap about South Tyrol" was harming Germany.[92] Just as Berlin had duped the ethnic Germans in Poland by signing the German-Polish Non-aggression Pact, the ethnic Germans in South Tyrol now learned that when push came to shove, relying on the "protection" of Germany would cost them their existence.[93]

What made such pragmatism even easier for the Nazis was that not only political factors but also economic ones seemed to necessitate it. The boom generated by Germany's rearmament had already led to the first labor shortages in the agricultural sector by 1933.[94] In the following years, it gave rise to increasingly acute crises in the rest of the economy as well, ultimately provoking ever more direct control of the labor market.[95] The intensified recruitment of foreign labor, particularly from Poland, was straining Germany's foreign exchange balance and posed—at least in the opinion of the SS and police—great risks, which allegedly could be best resolved through the targeted engagement of ethnic Germans from abroad.

It was in early 1937, at this intersection of "security-related" and economic concerns, that Himmler established a Four-Year-Plan Office (Dienststelle Vierjahresplan) under SS Senior Leader Ulrich Greifelt, in order to stimulate, "primarily in the area of agricultural labor deployment, . . . measures for the increased acquisition of agricultural workers"; the office was placed under Himmler's Personal Staff of the Reichsführer of the SS (Persönlicher Stab Reichsführer-SS).[96] Then, when Hitler entrusted Himmler with the resettlement of the "Volksdeutsche" from South Tyrol (at first informally), it was certainly not by accident that Himmler—after initially considering the Ethnic German Liaison Office (Volksdeutsche Mittelstelle, or VoMi)—passed the assignment down to Greifelt on July 23, 1939, especially since the war was imminent at that point, which meant that further shortfalls were to be expected in the labor market.[97] In the ensuing tussle with the Reich Chancellery and the affected ministries, Himmler tried to translate Hitler's assignment into the widest possible mandate; he ultimately achieved his designation as Reich commissioner in the final draft text of August 17, with the agreement of Hans Heinrich Lammers (head of the Reich Chancellery), as well as a great deal of latitude with the ministerial bureaucracy.[98]

The war delayed promulgation of this decree at first, only to catapult the resettlement of the South Tyroleans into an entirely new context. After the Nazi leadership had come to the decision that large parts of western Poland were to be annexed and "Germanized," and—at around the same time, but initially without any causal relationship—Hitler had also decided to resettle the ethnic Germans from the Baltics, it was only a short leap to the realization that these undertakings complemented one another and thus needed to be coordinated. Much as the resettlement of the "Volksdeutsche" from Russia had already appeared in the memoranda of the Prussian Interior Ministry even before World War I, when the discussion had focused on increasing the number of "German" farmworkers while also boosting the "German" populace in Prussia's eastern borderlands and then focused also on the "Germanization" of a "border strip" that was to be annexed in the future, this time too, the decision to annex the western Polish territories flowed seamlessly into deliberations about how they could be settled with "Germans," which ultimately pointed to the ethnic Germans beyond the Reich's borders. The South Tyroleans were now no longer to be settled in the Reich itself or perhaps somewhere like Moravia, but instead in a newly established "Beskidengau" (named after the Beskids, in the Carpathians) south of Kattowitz.[99] Meanwhile, the Baltic Germans were destined for Danzig–West Prussia and the Wartheland.[100]

Thus, when Hitler signed the "decree on the strengthening of Germandom" on October 7, it was only logical that Himmler be commissioned with the task. Himmler had already set up an agency of his own that was handling the resettlement of the South Tyroleans under Greifelt, and he also possessed the necessary tools (including coercive ones) for the planned program of resettlement, expulsion, and mass murder. Although still unspecific at the start of the war, these measures were now concretely outlined in the decree: first, the "bringing back" of the "Germans" abroad who qualified for "homecoming" into the Reich; second, their settling in Poland and with this the "arranging of new German settlement areas"; and third, the "eliminating of the harmful influences of . . . population segments alien to the Volk." Himmler was thereby authorized to issue any "general directives" needed to achieve these measures.[101]

The assignments that resulted from the authorization were delegated by Himmler to the SS apparatus. Greifelt's Coordination Office for Immigration and Return Migration (Leitstelle für Ein- und Rückwanderung), established for the resettlement of the South Tyroleans and subordinated to Himmler's Personal Staff, was designated as the coordinating authority, which was then transformed on October 17 into the Agency of the Reich Commissioner for the Strengthening of Germandom (Dienststelle des Reichskommissars für die Festigung deutschen Volkstums, hereafter the Agency of the RKFDV]), which functioned as the RKFDV headquarters.[102] Although this Reich Commissioner title was not mentioned in Hitler's decree, it did appear in the draft decree on the resettlement of the South Tyroleans, which was apparently justification enough for Himmler to now bestow it on himself and probably also the reason behind the lack of protest from other Reich bodies. Based in Berlin, the Agency of the RKFDV originally saw the establishment of three departments, namely, Planning (Planung), Land Office (Bodenamt), and Immigrant Allocation (Einwandererverteilung), but the last was soon renamed Human Deployment (Menscheneinsatz), which again underlines the importance that Himmler ascribed to the exploitation of labor. Himmler delegated the practical implementation of population policy to

VoMi, which at this point was not yet exclusively in the SS orbit, but instead stood at least formally under Rudolf Hess, and delegated as well to the Race and Settlement Main Office (Rasse- und Siedlungshauptamt, or RuSHA) and the Reich Security Main Office, both of the SS. Heydrich had already established on October 11, 1939, the EWZ for the Northeast (Einwandererzentralstelle Nordost, or Central Immigration Office for the Northeast), which, at the behest of Himmler as the RKFDV, was to conduct the systematic selection of "Volksdeutsche" to be resettled from the Baltics.[103] In order to ensure optimal cooperation with the other SS bodies, and also to establish a regional contact person for this area of responsibility, Himmler additionally named the Higher SS and Police Leaders (Höherer SS- und Polizeiführer, or HSSPF) to be his RKFDV appointees, each of whom soon established multiple branch offices that were structured similarly to the RKFDV headquarters in Berlin.[104]

The decree of October 7 would decisively bolster Himmler's power and become a key gateway for the expansion of SS influence. Himmler soon ignored one of the decree's most important restrictions, namely the prohibition against establishing his own agencies, but he also used it to justify his issuing of general directives to offices that were not part of the SS complex, but whose activities—at least in his opinion—touched on the "strengthening of Germandom." In annexed Poland, there was hardly any area that could have been excluded from the strengthening of Germandom.

Establishing the Civilian Administration

By the time the military administration was replaced by a civilian one on October 26, 1939, several important factors had already been established that would later allow for the intensifying of repressive measures in order to "Germanize" the occupied territories as quickly as possible. But the structure and responsibilities of the civil administration organs were still unclear. Due to the haste of this changeover, the Reich Interior Ministry was only able to furnish the civil administration with the necessary provisions after it had already been established.

The Reich Interior Ministry was primarily interested in significantly strengthening its own administration heads (i.e., Reichsstatthalters and Oberpräsidents) and in fact argued for keeping the CdZ structure, but without the military commander on top. As early as February 14, 1935, in the first regulations issued to a CdZ by the Reichswehr (later renamed the Wehrmacht), the entire civil administration was subordinated to the head of the administration, including—unlike the administration heads in the Reich, for example—the offices of specialized ministerial authorities such as finance and justice. Instructions from Berlin's central ministries had to be issued through him, and he could also issue his own direct orders to the various local offices in his territory.[105]

In this, the Reich Interior Ministry was colliding with other ministries that were affected: they demanded the emulation of ordinary Reich conditions after the departure of the military—as had happened in the Sudetenland—meaning direct control of their own regional offices. For the Reich Interior Ministry, however, this collision was simply one more reason to hold fast to its own vision. In fact, according to its plans, the proposed centralization of administration was also to serve as a test case, preparing the way for later changes in the Reich itself. With the support of the Nazi Party, the Reich Interior Ministry was ultimately able to win this confrontation.[106]

More than a week went by before Reich Interior Minister Wilhelm Frick was able to sign the implementing provision "for the subdivision and administration of the eastern territories" on November 2, 1939, thereby filling in the details of Hitler's decree of October 8. Here, the Reich Interior Ministry's strategic goal was very clear, namely, to strengthen the Reichsstatthalters specifically and the heads of general administration more broadly. Besides placing the Reichsstatthalters directly under Hitler (an innovation introduced with the annexation of the Sudetenland), the offices of specialized ministerial authorities on the provincial and county levels were placed directly under the administrative heads and not under the relevant ministries as was otherwise customary in the Reich. Furthermore, each Reichsstatthalter and his subordinated Regierungspräsidents (governmental region presidents) was given more control over the respective administrative levels assigned to them.[107]

But the support of the Nazi Party came at a price. As Hess let Stuckart know, "political leadership and political administration are to be conducted in personal union [by the same person]."[108] The party was of the same mind, wanting to implement in the annexed eastern territories the structural changes that did not yet seem achievable in the Reich itself, so that they might ultimately be applied there as well. The achievement of this goal did in fact promise great potential: if every state office were linked to a corresponding party office, then the party would secure the direct right to propose and veto candidates for every administration post, thus completing its seizure of power at every level. Working in tandem with each Gauleiter, who was simultaneously the local head of administration, namely the Reichsstatthalter or Oberpräsident, the party launched a running battle over the appointment of each Landrat (rural councilor, the head of a rural county), during which the Reich Interior Ministry soon realized how very much the strengthening of the Reichsstatthalters—which it had itself pursued—was ultimately diminishing its own control over such affairs. In order to strengthen their grip on the state administration, the Gauleiters, in their role as administration heads, systematically torpedoed the Reich Interior Ministry's nominations and installed trusted allies instead. In the Wartheland, around half the Landrat posts were filled with candidates from the party apparatus, while in

Danzig–West Prussia the figure reached 88 percent, and in many counties the same person held both offices, that of Landrat and that of Kreisleiter (county leader, the head of a Nazi Party county-level branch).[109]

This considerable strengthening of the "frontier Gauleiters" ("Grenzgauleiter")—to borrow a contemporary term—happened largely at the expense of the Reich-level ministries in Berlin, along with their subordinated offices and other self-administering bodies (i.e., communal-level administrations) in the provinces.[110] On the other hand, it was highly symptomatic of the envisaged policy that the thereby strengthened Reichsstatthalters and Oberpräsidents nonetheless had to accept diminishment in one particular area, in comparison with the situation in the Reich itself, namely in their relationship to the policing apparatus and the entire SS complex. With the rampages of the Einsatzgruppen, Himmler had created a power base that reached into every village through the Volksdeutscher Selbstschutz, which soon included, for example, 80 percent of the male "Volksdeutsche" populace in Danzig–West Prussia.[111] Himmler's position was further strengthened with his installation as RKFDV, for it allowed him to extend his activities beyond the security sphere and to even make use of other agencies.

The massive presence of the various SS formations had led, even before the establishment of the military administration, to the expansion of the SS administrative structure, especially with the appointment of HSSPFs: these were "Himmler's regional representatives," to whom were subordinated Inspectors of the Security Police (Inspekteur der Sicherheitspolizei, or IdS) and Inspectors of the Order Police (Inspekteur der Ordnungspolizei, the regional representatives of the SS Reich Security Main Office and SS Order Police Main Office), analogous to the inspectors inside the Reich itself.[112] Although they were also "personally and directly subordinated" to the administration heads as in the Reich, they were able to establish much greater freedom of action in Poland, as a result of the still unsettled power structures.[113] After the territorialization of the Einsatzgruppen on November 20, 1939, the annexed territories were likewise overlaid with a security police network, one that stood in a hybrid relationship similar to that of the general administration. Thus, each chief of a Gestapo Command Office (Stapo-Leitstelle) also became a policy adviser to the local Reichsstatthalter, and each chief of a Gestapo Office (Stapo-Stelle) became a policy adviser to the local Regierungspräsident. Their embedding in the SS apparatus, however, meaning their subordination to the IdS and the HSSPF, took priority: orders from Department IV (Amt IV) of the Reich Security Main Office took precedence over those from the general administration.[114]

The general understanding that the envisaged "Germanization" of the annexed provinces was to be achieved primarily through force had led to a massive expansion of powers for the general administration heads in annexed provinces compared to the powers of their counterparts in the Reich. The fact that specifically the SS and police were not weakened as a result, but instead were given considerable additional powers as well, hints at the methods through which the Nazi leadership wanted to achieve "Germanization."

Notes

1. Wildt, *Generation des Unbedingten*, 421; Wildt, "Radikalisierung und Selbstradikalisierung," 16; Rossino, *Hitler Strikes Poland*, 10–11.

2. Rossino, *Hitler Strikes Poland*, 11–13; also Krausnick, *Hitlers Einsatzgruppen*, 27–28. On the selection criteria for these duties, see Rossino, *Hitler Strikes Poland*, 53–57.

3. Unsigned guidelines for foreign deployment of Security Police and the SD, undated (probably early August 1939), German Federal Archives, Berlin [hereafter, BArch], R 58/241, 169–75.

4. Ibid.

5. Rossino, *Hitler Strikes Poland*, 15.

6. Quoted in Herbert, *Best*, 592–93.

7. Ibid.

8. Heydrich to Daluege, July 2, 1940, quoted in Krausnick, *Hitlers Einsatzgruppen*, 207.

9. Decree from Best, August 8, 1939, quoted in Herbert, *Best*, 239.

10. Rossino, *Hitler Strikes Poland*, 265.

11. Order quoted in Böhler, *Auftakt zum Vernichtungskrieg*, 39; implementation described by Alberti, *Verfolgung und Vernichtung*, 248.

12. German Army High Command, leaflet on the particularities of Polish warfare, quoted in Böhler, *Auftakt zum Vernichtungskrieg*, 40.

13. Ibid., 39.

14. Domarus, *Hitler*, 1238.

15. Czubinski, "Poland's Place in Nazi Plans," 21.

16. Rossino, *Hitler Strikes Poland*; Böhler, *Auftakt zum Vernichtungskrieg*.

17. Ibid., 136, using figures from Poland's Institute of National Remembrance.

18. Krausnick, *Hitlers Einsatzgruppen*, 48.

19. Wildt, *Generation des Unbedingten*, 442–47.

20. According to a statement by the former head of the German Union in Posen, Dr. Kurt Lück, published on January 9, 1940, in the *Ostdeutscher Beobachter* (the Nazi Party mouthpiece in the Wartheland), the initial figures totaled some 1,030 "Volksdeutsche" killed and 858 missing, see Pilichowski, "Nazi Genocide," 189. Berlin considered this to be much too low, as Lück would soon discover to his astonishment when the Foreign Office first spoke of 5,437 "Volksdeutsche" victims in its documents, which Goebbels' propaganda machine then arbitrarily inflated tenfold to 58,000. This "Bromberg Bloody Sunday" then evolved into an important motif in Nazi propaganda, used as justification for the ever-increasing radicalization of actions against the civilian populace. On Nazi propaganda to disguise war culpability, see Czubiński, "Poland's Place in Nazi Plans," 43–44.

21. Horne and Kramer, *Deutsche Kriegsgreuel 1914*. Horne and Kramer also go more specifically into the origins of the franc-tireur mythos during the Franco-Prussian War, and are then able to demonstrate (more convincingly than Böhler, for example) how anxious presuppositions, also by younger officers in particular, were seemingly confirmed in the

early days of World War I, not only by a series of misunderstandings, but also by the unique military situation, for example when the Schlieffen Plan's required rapid troop movements led to disorientation, or when modern long-range rifles put the snipers out of view and provoked German troops into acts of vengeance in the immediate vicinity, see ibid., 139–259. On the significance of this mythos in the destruction of Leuven, see Kramer, *Dynamic of Destruction*, 6–30.

22. Krausnick, *Hitlers Einsatzgruppen*, 36–37.

23. Böhler, *Auftakt zum Vernichtungskrieg*, 149.

24. See also Herbert, *Best*, 240; Longerich, *Politik der Vernichtung*, 244.

25. Böhler, *Auftakt zum Vernichtungskrieg*, 54. See also Wildt, *Generation des Unbedingten*, 447–49.

26. Quoted in Wildt, *Generation des Unbedingten*, 449.

27. Groscurth, *Tagebücher*, 201.

28. Jansen and Weckbecker, *Der Volksdeutsche Selbstschutz*, 49 and 51; for overviews of local structures, see also 165 and 167.

29. Ibid., 168.

30. Ibid., 102–4.

31. Rossino, *Hitler Strikes Poland*, 90–91.

32. Lahousen's file note on meetings aboard "Führer train" on September 12, 1939, quoted in Groscurth, *Tagebücher*, 358.

33. Broszat, *Nationalsozialistische Polenpolitik*, 20.

34. Quoted in Böhler, *Auftakt zum Vernichtungskrieg*, 215.

35. Rossino, *Hitler Strikes Poland*, 92.

36. Directive from 10th Army Command, September 26, 1939, quoted in Böhler, *Auftakt zum Vernichtungskrieg*, 217.

37. Umbreit, *Deutsche Militärverwaltungen*, 208.

38. Rossino, *Hitler Strikes Poland*, 117.

39. Halder, *Kriegstagebuch*, 1: 79.

40. Schulenberg to Foreign Office, September 20, 1939, reprinted in *Akten zur deutschen auswärtigen Politik*, ser. D, vol. 8, doc. 104, 82. See also Rutherford, "Race, Space, and the 'Polish Question,'" 70–71.

41. Lahousen's file note, September 12, 1939, quoted in Groscurth, *Tagebücher*, 357.

42. Halder, *Kriegstagebuch*, 1: 81. See also Wildt, *Generation des Unbedingten*, 457.

43. Halder, *Kriegstagebuch*, 1: 82.

44. Krausnick, *Hitlers Einsatzgruppen*, 53.

45. Quoted in Wildt, *Generation des Unbedingten*, 458.

46. Commander in chief of the army to commanders in chief and military commanders, September 21, 1939, quoted in Mallmann, Böhler, and Matthäus, *Einsatzgruppen*, 146. See also Krausnick, *Hitlers Einsatzgruppen*, 54.

47. Minutes of departmental head meeting with Einsatzgruppe leaders under Heydrich on September 21, 1939, BArch R 58/825, 26–30; see also Krausnick, *Hitlers Einsatzgruppen*, 59; Wildt, *Generation des Unbedingten*, 457–58.

48. Minutes of departmental head meeting with Einsatzgruppe leaders under Heydrich on September 21, 1939, BArch R 58/825, 26–30.

49. Quoted in Wildt, *Generation des Unbedingten*, 459.

50. Quoted in Krausnick, *Hitlers Einsatzgruppen*, 61.

51. Minutes of departmental head meeting with Einsatzgruppe leaders under Heydrich on September 21, 1939, BArch R 58/825, 26–30.

52. Wildt, *Generation des Unbedingten*, 458. See also minutes of departmental head meeting with Einsatzgruppe leaders under Heydrich on September 21, 1939, BArch R 58/825, 26–30.

53. Rutherford, "Race, Space, and the Polish Question," 72.

54. Minutes of departmental head meeting with Einsatzgruppe leaders under Heydrich on September 21, 1939, BArch R 58/825, 26–30.

55. Notes of envoy Schmidt at the Foreign Office, September 26, 1939, reprinted in *Akten zur deutschen auswärtigen Politik*, ser. D, vol. 8, doc. 138, 109–12.

56. Weizsäcker's memo on upcoming negotiations with Moscow on the same day, September 26, 1939, reprinted in *Akten zur deutschen auswärtigen Politik*, ser. D, vol. 8, doc. 137, 107.

57. Kroeger, *Auszug aus der alten Heimat*, 51.

58. Ibid., 50.

59. Himmler did in fact have to fight for this assignment: Hitler had first assigned it to VoMi, before Himmler managed to persuade him (Koehl, *RKFDV*, 49).

60. Rosenberg, *Politisches Tagebuch*, 80.

61. Minutes of departmental head meeting with Einsatzgruppe leaders under Heydrich on September 29, 1939, BArch R 58/825, 36–37. Partially reprinted in Pätzold, *Verfolgung, Vertreibung, Vernichtung*, 240.

62. Hitler to the Reichstag on October 6, 1939, quoted in *Verhandlungen des Reichstages*, 460: 51–63. On the speech's contemporary reception, see Wildt, "Neue Ordnung," 130.

63. Hitler to the Reichstag on October 6, 1939, quoted in *Verhandlungen des Reichstages*, 460: 56.

64. Wildt, "Neue Ordnung," 133–34.

65. Hitler to the Reichstag on October 6, 1939, quoted in *Verhandlungen des Reichstages*, 460: 51–63, here 56.

66. Ibid., 61.

67. Lammers to Pfundtner, September 7, 1939, Special Archive at the State Military Archives of Russia, Moscow, 720–5/2793, 1; Schenk, *Hitlers Mann*, 138; Epstein, *Model Nazi*, 124–26; Umbreit, "Auf dem Weg," 32–34; Rutherford, *Prelude*, 3; Rieß, *Anfänge der Vernichtung*, 244.

68. Umbreit, "Auf dem Weg," 11.

69. Ibid., 36.

70. Hitler to the Reichstag on October 6, 1939, quoted in *Verhandlungen des Reichstages*, 460: 62. See also memo for State Secretary Pfundtner, October 7, 1939, BArch R 1501/5401, 41.

71. Goebbels's diary entry for October 13, 1939, quoted in Alberti, *Verfolgung und Vernichtung*, 46.

72. Unsigned memo from Reich Interior Ministry on "responsibilities of the civil administration in the Polish territories," October 2, 1939, BArch R 1501/5401, 24–29.

73. Ibid.

74. Madajczyk, *Okkupationspolitik Nazideutschlands*, 548–52 and 564–73; Majer, *Fremdvölkische*, 395–404; on the Main Trustee Office for the East, see especially Rosenkötter, *Treuhandpolitik*, 81–88.

75. Umbreit, "Auf dem Weg," 39.

76. December 1, 1961, discussion between Dr. Hopf (of the German Federal Archives) and Ministerial Director Dr. Georg Hubrich, former head of the Reich Interior Ministry's Subdepartment I East, German Federal Archives, Bayreuth Branch, Ost-Dok. 13/157, 2–19, on questions about territories annexed during the war. It was apparently in spring 1935, at Stuckart's prompting, that Hubrich was brought into the Reich Interior Ministry, where he advanced in just a year to become group leader for the subject area of citizenship and race. Starting April 1, 1941, he became head of Subdepartment I East and acting head of Subdepartment I Sta R, Citizenship and Race, see Jasch, "Preußisches Kultusministerium."

77. Report from Wilhelm Keppler, a state secretary at the Foreign Office, quoted in Volkmann, "Zwischen Ideologie und Pragmatismus," 423. On the economic importance of this region, see Röhr, "Zur Rolle der Schwerindustrie," 10; Röhr, "Zur Wirtschaftspolitik," 223–24; Schwaneberg, "Economic Exploitation," 87–89; Kaczmarek, "Zwischen Altreich und Besatzungsgebiet," 348–49.

78. With its purpose achieved, the department was disbanded soon thereafter, see Haar, *Historiker im Nationalsozialismus*, 324.

79. Umbreit, "Auf dem Weg," 33; also Schenk, *Hitlers Mann*, 138.

80. Haar, *Historiker im Nationalsozialismus*, 328.

81. Vollert, "Proposal for the territorial border of West Prussia," undated (probably October 6, 1939), BArch R 1501/5401, 31–40.

82. On Schieder, see Aly, "Daß uns Blut zu Gold."

83. Aubin to Brackmann, September 18, 1939, BArch R 153/291, unpaged. See also Burleigh, *Germany Turns Eastwards*, 147.

84. Ebbinghaus and Roth, "Vorläufer des Generalplans Ost"; Haar, *Historiker im Nationalsozialismus*, 330–32; Burleigh, *Germany Turns Eastwards*, 147–48.

85. Pappritz to Aubin, October 4, 1939, quoted in Ebbinghaus and Roth, "Vorläufer des Generalplans Ost," 69.

86. This is also why Ingo Haar is mistaken in believing that Schieder's planning scenario, because it envisaged large-scale deportations of certain local population segments and their replacement by ethnic Germans from Eastern Europe, "did not stand in the tradition of the Prussia's Poland policy" (Haar, *Historiker im Nationalsozialismus*, 332). See also Ebbinghaus and Roth, "Vorläufer des Generalplans Ost," 76.

87. Schieder position paper, undated (probably October 7, 1939), BArch R 153/291, unpaged (emphasis in original). On the October 7 dating, see Ebbinghaus and Roth, "Vorläufer des Generalplans Ost," 70.

88. Note on message to Aubin drafted on October 7, 1939, quoted in Ebbinghaus and Roth, "Vorläufer des Generalplans Ost," 92.

89. Hitler's decree on the subdivision and administration of the eastern territories, October 8, 1939, reprinted in Pospieszalski, *Hitlerowskie "prawo" okupacyjne*, 84–88. In line with the earlier Prussian names, the two provinces were initially called West Prussia and Posen; only later were they renamed Danzig–West Prussia and the Wartheland, see *Reichsgesetzblatt Teil I* (1940), 251.

90. The city's name was Łódź before the German invasion and after liberation; Lodsch from September 1939 to March 1940; Litzmannstadt as of April 1940. On the annexation of Łódź, and for more precise details on the Wartheland's territorial extent and its administrative structure in general, see Marczewski, *Hitlerowska koncepcja*, 112–16. The

German ideological claim to Łódź was further justified by archaeological finds that allegedly indicated an early Germanic settlement; see Furber, "Near as Far," 557.

91. Decree on the strengthening of Germandom, signed by Hitler, Göring, Lammers, and Keitel, October 7, 1939, BArch R 43 II/1412, 575–77. Reprinted in Pospieszalski, *Hitlerowskie "prawo" okupacyjne*, 176–78; and Moll, *Führer-Erlasse*, 100–102. As Philip Morgan rightly notes, assignments like Himmler's were "a good example of standard fascist practice: creating 'shadow' fascist bodies" with powers that were inadequately separated from those of the state administration, and which began competing with the latter (Morgan, *Fascism in Europe*, 133–38).

92. Quoted in Jäckel, *Hitlers Herrschaft*, 34. Hitler had already become open to relinquishing South Tyrol by late 1922, as reflected in an article in the *Münchner Post* on his speech of November 11, in which he also abandoned its German populace (Jäckel and Kuhn, *Hitler*, 728). See also Gottfried Feder's officially approved commentary on the Nazi Party program, in which the party platform's first point, namely, the demand to unify all "Germans" into a "Greater Germany," also listed South Tyrol alongside the Sudetenland and Austria—but only until 1928. In the fifth edition, published in 1929, South Tyrol was no longer mentioned (Broszat, *National-Sozialismus*, 32–33). The clearest rejection of the claim to South Tyrol, with lengthy argumentation, is ultimately found in Hitler, *Hitlers Zweites Buch*, 189–215.

93. Aly, *Endlösung*, 64. On South Tyrol, see Stuhlpfarrer, *Umsiedlung Südtirol*, 1: 30–86.

94. August, "Entwicklung des Arbeitsmarkts," 306–8.

95. Tooze, *Wages of Destruction*, 291.

96. SS Senior Assault Unit Leader Rudolf Creutz to HSSPF Hildebrandt, March 1, 1940, archived in BArch BDCSSO file on Rudolf Creutz; thanks to Götz Aly for this document. See also undated presentation by Greifelt (probably January 1939), Bavarian State Archives, Nuremberg NO 5591, reprinted in Loeber, *Diktierte Option*, 4–7.

97. On the rivalry between SS Senior Group Leader Werner Lorenz and Himmler, see Stuhlpfarrer, *Umsiedlung Südtirol*, 1: 245–46.

98. Ibid., 1: 249–50.

99. Unsigned memo on meeting at office of HSSPF Southeast Erich von dem Bach-Zelewski, November 27, 1939, Nuremberg NO 5055, reprinted in Długoborski, *Polozenie ludności*, 139; see also Aly, *Endlösung*, 64; Umbreit, "Auf dem Weg," 125; Longerich, *Heinrich Himmler*, 434–37.

100. Himmler to Lorenz, Heydrich, Forster, Greiser, et al., October 11, 1939, Nuremberg NO 4613.

101. Decree on the strengthening of Germandom, signed by Hitler, Göring, Lammers, and Keitel, October 7, 1939, BArch R 43 II/1412, 575–77. Reprinted in Pospieszalski, *Hitlerowskie "prawo" okupacyjne*, 176–78; Moll, *Führer-Erlasse*, 100–102.

102. Himmler's first directive as RKFDV, undated (probably signed on October 17, 1939), Nuremberg NO 3078. On this dating, see Koehl, *RKFDV*, 56. See also Stuhlpfarrer, *Umsiedlung Südtirol*, 1: 251.

103. Chief of the Security Police and the SD to top-level Reich authorities, BArch R 43 II/1412, 55; Heydrich to top-level Reich authorities, October 13, 1939, BArch R 3001/20043, 1. See also Koehl, *RKFDV*, 54; Koehl, *Black Corps*, 187–88; Lumans, *Himmler's Auxiliaries*, 189–92; Leniger, *Nationalsozialistische Volkstumsarbeit*, 148–51. On the RKFDV, see Stiller, "Reichskommissar." On the EWZ, see Strippel, *NS-Volkstumspolitik*.

104. Himmler's first directive as RKFDV, undated (probably signed on October 17, 1939), Nuremberg NO 3078.

105. Umbreit, "Auf dem Weg," 6. Umbreit does not explore the remarkable parallels between this instituting of the CdZ (which did not significantly change thereafter) and the Reich Interior Ministry's plans for the future structuring of the occupation administration in Poland.

106. See Hess to Lammers, October 25, 1939, quoted in Stelbrink, *Preußischer Landrat*, 167.

107. Here, see particularly Frick's "second directive for implementing the decree of the Führer and Chancellor on the subdivision and administration of the eastern territories," November 2, 1939, reprinted in Pospieszalski, *Hitlerowskie "prawo" okupacyjne*, 89–92; also Frick's decree of December 27, 1939, reprinted in ibid., 92–95. Exceptions were made for the territories annexed to the provinces of Silesia and East Prussia. See also the legislation on the structuring of the administration in the Reichsgau of the Sudetenland, April 14, 1939, reprinted in Pospieszalski, *Hitlerowskie "prawo" okupacyjne*, 84–86.

108. Sommer to Stuckart, October 11, 1939, BArch R 1501/5401, 73.

109. Stelbrink, *Preußischer Landrat*, 103–11; also Pohl, "Reichsgaue Danzig-Westpreußen und Wartheland," 4–5. Pohl also explores the claim, repeatedly found in the relevant research, that a large proportion of the personnel were shunted to Poland for disciplinary actions or other transgressions, or else were particularly motivated by ideology, and he highlights this especially for the Wartheland, see ibid., 7. On this topic in the General Government, see Lehnstaedt, "'Ostnieten' oder 'Vernichtungsexperten.'"

110. Kaczmarek, "Zwischen Altreich und Besatzungsgebiet," 351; on their enhanced standing, see 351–55.

111. Jansen and Weckbecker, *Volksdeutscher Selbstschutz*, 61 and 67.

112. Witte et al., *Dienstkalender Heinrich Himmlers*, 49.

113. Frick's "second directive for implementing the decree of the Führer and Chancellor on the subdivision and administration of the eastern territories," November 2, 1939, reprinted in Pospieszalski, *Hitlerowskie "prawo" okupacyjne*, 89–92. See also the appointments of HSSPFs within the Reich itself on August 25, 1939, in Birn, *Höhere SS- und Polizeiführer*, 13.

114. Himmler's decree on the organization of the Gestapo in the eastern territories, November 7, 1939, reprinted in Pospieszalski, *Hitlerowskie "prawo" okupacyjne*, 101–3.

3 Consolidating Power

Reinforcing the German Occupation Regime through Population Policy

The Expulsion and Killing of Potential Opponents

The total defeat of Poland, alongside the agreement with the Soviet Union, gave the Nazis free rein on its side of the demarcation line, but also limited it to this.[1] Although this dependency on the Soviet Union was conceived from the outset as only a temporary arrangement, it nonetheless helped accelerate the projection of the "Lebensraum" dystopia onto Poland: if this central promise of Nazi ideology was not to be postponed even further, meaning to the time after the "final victory" in the west and the subsequent annihilation of the Soviet Union, then the *only* opportunity was in Poland.

The "Lebensraum" concept, although previously seen as a utopian daydream even by many Nazis, now became a driving force in conceiving occupation policy. Its political practicability seemed to face no obstacles, at least none that could not be overcome through the massive use of violence. Where a policy of ethnic cleansing had already begun during the war, the ethnocrats in Berlin and the occupied territories soon went a step further and prepared for a systematic selection process to be applied to the entire populace. The decision was who in the new "German east" was to be granted multitiered rights to residency as "Germans" or as members of the "intermediate class" ("Zwischenschicht"), which was a contemporary term for those who eluded ethnic classification; and denying those rights and even the right to life itself to the rest as "Fremdvölkische" (the "ethnonationally foreign"). These ideas were put into action with an unconditional readiness and radicalness that typified them as elements of a genuinely Nazi project. In essence, however, they can be traced back to intentions that had already been discussed at length in imperial Prussia and also in the debates over the "border strip," that is, the annexation plans entertained by the German government during the First World War.

Unsuccessful Prelude: The Nisko Campaign

In the first weeks after the German invasion, the main locations for the "ethnic cleansing of the soil" were Danzig–West Prussia and, to a somewhat lesser extent, the Wartheland. It was in the territories annexed to Silesia, however, that the ethnocrats undertook the first steps on the path toward a broader "Lebensraum" policy guided by the ideological premises of the Nazis.[2]

After his successes as the head of Vienna's Central Agency for Jewish Emigration (Zentralstelle für jüdische Auswanderung), Adolf Eichmann was tasked in July 1939 with bringing the same model to Prague. The outbreak of war had led to disruptions, however, forcing the relevant agencies to seek new strategies. Eichmann thought he had found his answer when he received an order from Reinhardt Heydrich on September 7, which mandated the arrest, dispossession, and expulsion of Polish Jews living within the Reich.[3] But then, after Eichmann collaborated with Dr. Franz Stahlecker, Prague's Commander of the Security Police and the Sicherheitsdienst (*Befehlshaber der Sicherheitspolizei und des SD*, or BdS), an alternative solution was put forward on September 10: instead of forced emigration, there would be state-organized deportation to a territory under German control.[4] This was the birth of the Nisko Plan. Since Stahlecker's idea also passed through Heydrich to reach Himmler, Claudia Steur may very well be correct in her interpretation of a remark made by Heydrich during a meeting on September 14, 1939.[5] At the meeting, he told his departmental heads that Himmler was submitting proposals to Hitler "that only the Führer could decide, because they would also be of major consequence in policy terms."[6] It is very probable that he was referring to this radicalization of policy, shifting from forced emigration to guided deportation.

If the Nisko campaign did in fact represent a major turning point, one must still ask: In what way? Miroslav Kárný's skeptical assessment from thirty years ago, that there are still "many unsettled questions in the history of Nisko," has not lost its validity.[7] These questions have remained unresolved because they were framed wrongly or, more precisely, based on false assumptions. Although scholars have explicitly emphasized that these deportations represented a radicalization of anti-Jewish policy, they also assume that this was simply the radicalization of an already existing policy—in other words, these were intensified efforts toward the same assumed goal, namely, to make the Reich "Jew-free" ("judenrein"). It is therefore no wonder that the deportation of Vienna's Jews, that is, Jews from the Reich, is assigned special significance here, although the Vienna group was certainly not the largest one. But what if the deportations to the vicinity of Nisko on the San River, or more precisely, to the village of Zarzecze across the San, were conducted not primarily to expel German Jews from the Reich, but instead to remove Polish Jews from the annexed territories; that is, that it was about Germanizing the annexed western Polish regions, and not Germany proper?

∗   ∗   ∗

The historiography of the Nisko campaign is divided even in the determination of its beginnings. It starts with the question of who first advanced this idea,

Eichmann or Stahlecker. But what is perhaps more important here is that both men responded to the assigned task with mass deportations to Poland, and at a time when this was not yet on the agenda even for the Reich Security Main Office.[8] The "official" beginning of the Nisko campaign is also not entirely clear. Scholars often cite Eichmann's memo of October 6, 1939, on an order from SS Senior Leader Heinrich Müller, chief of the Gestapo, in which Eichmann was asked to "make contact with the office of Gauleiter [Josef] Wagner in Kattowitz [Katowice]." The main goal of such discussions was to be the "deportation of seventy to eighty thousand Jews from the Kattowitz region . . . across the Vistula," while "at the same time" Jews might "also be deported from the vicinity of Mährisch Ostrau" (today Ostrava).[9] It should be noted: there was no mention of Vienna's Jews here. And although Seev Goshen rightly points out that only the memo survives, and not the original order itself, Michael Wildt's observation seems equally correct, that it is very likely an overestimation of Eichmann's capabilities when Goshen writes of Müller's *purported* order" (emphasis added), thereby casting doubt on the existence of such an order and conjecturing instead that Eichmann was attempting to attach Müller's blessing to the expulsion of Czech and Viennese Jews, thus providing it with the necessary authority.[10] It is much more likely that Eichmann simply saw an opportunity to take Müller's order and expand it to cover all territories he was tasked to rid of its Jewish populace. But no matter how exactly the operation started, this did not fundamentally change the course of events, which, in line with Müller's order, placed the focus clearly on the region around Kattowitz and—as it would turn out—on Polish Jews.[11]

This emphasis on Poland was mirrored by a shift in focus among the leadership of the Reich Security Main Office, who at this point were already concentrating their efforts on the Germanization of the annexed western Polish territories. After the expulsions and killing campaigns conducted by the Einsatzgruppen and "self-defense" units, it was now time to embark on the first systematic steps toward expelling the remaining undesired population segments. And it was probably no accident that this reorientation in the policy of violence took place on October 6, the same day that Hitler announced to the Reichstag an ethnic reorganization of eastern Europe.

As both Moser and Goshen correctly assert, it was not by the most direct route that Eichmann now traveled from Berlin to Kattowitz. He probably did not, however, stop off in Vienna on October 7—as both scholars have stated without citing sources, a claim subsequently repeated by Longerich, among others—in order to then travel onward via Mährisch Ostrau to Kattowitz; that would have been indeed a "marathon tour."[12] Instead, skipping Vienna, he made his way directly to Mährisch Ostrau, in order to inform his subordinates about Müller's order, before traveling on to Kattowitz on October 9. Here he met first with the administration head dispatched by Wagner, Otto Pfitzner, along with the head of

Border Commando III, Major General Otto von Knobelsdorff; then on the following day, he also finally met with the Gauleiter and Oberpräsident of Silesia, Josef Wagner, and spoke of starting with two trains each from the areas around Kattowitz and Mährisch Ostrau.[13] After that, Heydrich would write a progress report to Himmler that "would probably be passed on to the Führer," before a decision would finally be made about the "general removal" of all Jews. In any case, the first ones earmarked for expulsion here were Jews from the annexed territories, and not those from Austria or Germany itself.[14]

It can be assumed that when Eichmann spoke to his meeting partners about his intention to deport four thousand Jews to or across the demarcation line, he was "preaching to the choir"; after all, Wagner himself had already been planning to initiate the expulsion of the Jewish populace.[15] Somewhat unclear, however, was the figure of three hundred thousand Jews that Eichmann introduced here for the first time—and, specifically, Jews from Germany and Austria. In Kárný's view, this probably did not mean a program for deporting all Jews from Germany and Austria, since the number was too low for this. And ultimately, the meeting minutes state that Hitler had ordered a "reallocation" ("Umschichtung") of these persons but not their expulsion across the national border.[16]

With this train of events, it remains unclear how the deportations of Vienna's Jews came to pass at all, since mention of Vienna was absent—according to Eichmann's own records—from Müller's order, as was mention of what were now three hundred thousand Jews to be deported. Steur traces the increasing radicalization to Heydrich's visit with Hitler on October 7, when the topics under discussion included the "handling of Jews" ("Judenbehandlung").[17] And although it seems entirely possible that Heydrich thereby sought authorization to expand the deportations and passed the larger numbers on to Eichmann, who on that day was still in Berlin and not already on his way to Vienna, Steur's evidence nonetheless remains questionable because her conjecture is based on an extremely short entry in Halder's war diary. But the entry reveals little and seems to refer more to a conflict between the Wehrmacht and the SS over the killings conducted by a police unit in Mława.[18] In the entry, Halder simply wrote, "Complaint about Mława. Handling of Jews."[19]

Even if Halder's war diary is not enough to show that Hitler himself had approved large-scale deportations of Jews from the Reich itself, the likelihood that Eichmann received the number three hundred thousand from Müller or Heydrich before leaving Berlin is nonetheless much greater than the possibility that he simply invented it, thereby mentioning it to Wagner without any backing from above. Such a rapid escalation would not have been otherwise unusual for the overall Nisko campaign, nor for the subsequent deportation actions. In Mährisch Ostrau and Kattowitz, Eichmann did name Poland as the destination for the deportation trains, but what the exact locality would be, he did not know. It was only after the discussion with Wagner that Eichmann, along with Stahlecker, set out for Poland to settle this question as well. The initial ruminations focusing on the area around Kraków were made obsolete by the German-Soviet Frontier Treaty of September 28, which is why the area around Lublin now came into consideration. It was from there that Eichmann's wireless message of October 15, 1939, then reached the Gestapo in Mährisch Ostrau: "Railroad station for transports is Nisko on the San"—just in time to keep the entire operation from grinding to a halt.[20] It was only two days later that the Gestapo assembled the first transport, which left Mährisch Ostrau on October 18 as the first train in the Nisko campaign. On board were some nine hundred male Jews, who were considered by the Gestapo to be in good physical condition, and who were predominately Polish nationals—a crucial aspect, for it underlines the focus of the Nisko campaign.[21]

Just like its origins, the sudden termination of the Nisko campaign by an order from Berlin also raises some fundamental questions. The day after a train had left Mährisch Ostrau (which was to be followed by another from Vienna on October 20), a telex arrived in Kattowitz from Müller at the Reich Security Main Office. Sent only an hour after the transport had departed Mährisch Ostrau, Müller's message made clear that for every further transport, there needed to be, "in general, an authorization from this office."[22]

Since Eichmann, the addressee of this message, had already left the city, it was passed on to his deputy, SS Head Assault Leader Rolf Günther, who was at that moment supervising the dispatch of a deportation train carrying Jews who had fled from Kattowitz across the border after the German invasion and sought refuge in Mährisch Ostrau.[23] Günther decided against stopping the departure of the train and instead forwarded the telex to Eichmann. As a result, the latter immediately returned from Vienna to Mährisch Ostrau, where he learned from Günther that, in the meantime, the Reich Security Main Office had now ordered that "all transports of Jews are to be stopped."[24] After that, Eichmann immediately traveled on to Berlin in order to clarify the situation, for only half the originally planned transports had been sent. Nevertheless, it was no longer possible to undertake any more transports. Although one more train did leave Prague on November 1 with three hundred predominantly Polish Jews, it nonetheless had to be stopped at Sosnowitz (today Sosnowiec), especially since the bridge over the San had also collapsed in the meantime.[25] A third transport from Vienna also failed to come about.

Scholars have generally reckoned Eichmann to have been "successful," at least to the extent that the first deportation wave of October 18 and 20 was followed by a second one on October 26 and 27, during which—according to Moser—4,760 Jews were deported from Mährisch Ostrau, Kattowitz, and Vienna.[26] On the deportations from Vienna, the Austrian State Archive holds what would seem to be the most informative summary, one bearing the notation "Correct Nisko Lists," which shows a first transport on October 20 and a second one on October 26, with 669 persons assigned to the latter, recorded with car and seat numbers.[27]

The Austrian archive's list has not been mentioned in scholarship to date. But it is in fact also of questionable reliability, for it proves only that German ambitions to expel Vienna's Jews had already ripened quite far. It does not, however, answer the question of whether this second transport actually departed, or whether it too was halted at the last moment. Neither H. G. Adler nor Herbert Rosenkranz provide evidence about this, and neither do Moser or Goshen.[28] Goshen quotes a telegram sent from Berlin by Eichmann on October 24, in which the latter confirmed the cessation of deportations, but he nonetheless announced to his subordinates in Mährisch Ostrau that there would be one more, final, transport, "in order to maintain the prestige of the local [i.e., Mährisch Ostrau] Gestapo."[29] Meanwhile, Moser bases his claim on a telegram from the next day, in which Günther forewarned the camp superintendent in Nisko, Theodor Dannecker, of the arrival of a combined transport from Mährisch Ostrau and Kattowitz, which would depart from Kattowitz on October 27—but there is no mention of Vienna in the telegram.[30] More important: In a report on the history of the Austrian Jews under Nazism, compiled after the war by two members of the organized Jewish Community of Vienna (Israelitische Kultusgemeinde Wien, or IKG), Nisko is indeed mentioned—but with only the one transport that departed Vienna on October 20.[31] The same is true of the fifty-page report prepared by the former head of the IKG, Dr. Josef Löwenherz. He too describes Nisko as a traumatic wound and also lists one by one the deportations to Poland that started again in early 1941—but here too, there is no mention of a second transport to Nisko.[32] In the scholarly literature, however, apart from Tuviah Friedmann and Götz Aly, the second transport is taken for granted; for example, by Christopher R. Browning, Sybille Steinbacher, and Wolf Gruner.[33] No reliable evidence, in fact, exists for the second transport from Vienna apart from the aforementioned declarations of intent by the Nisko campaign's protagonists, which means they can be more convincingly seen as simply reflecting their eagerness to actually complete the project as envisaged. But at a time when the deportations had already come under heavy fire from Berlin, eagerness probably no longer sufficed to set more trains in motion.

Moreover, my doubts about the departure of this second transport from Vienna are further compounded by a message to Himmler on March 1, 1940, written by the state secretary at the Reich Transport Ministry, Dr. Wilhelm Kleinmann, listing all transports conducted since October 18, 1939, and still scheduled to happen by March 15, 1940.[34] Only three of them might have been part of the Nisko campaign: a transport carrying three thousand persons from Mährisch Ostrau on October 18 and two trains carrying a total of a thousand persons from Vienna on October 20. This would roughly match Moser's figure of 4,760 Jews deported to Poland, with the difference based on the lower number of Jews deported from Vienna, namely, a thousand persons instead of more than fifteen hundred.[35] Although Kleinmann's summary also raises some questions, in that it does not mention a train from Kattowitz, and the number of persons transported from Mährisch Ostrau appears somewhat high at first, both these discrepancies could be explained by the transport from Mährisch Ostrau having gone through Kattowitz, where it gained additional cars.[36] Furthermore, the entry for this transport differs from all others on the list in two regards: first, the train is not labeled a "Sonderzug" ("special train") but instead as a Wehrmacht train; second, it includes the notation "fifty freight cars."[37] Since the Wehrmacht also moved its troops in freight cars, each carrying around forty soldiers with all their gear, it is entirely conceivable that fifty freight cars were used in this case to deport three thousand persons.[38]

Kleinmann had compiled this summary after a meeting hosted by Göring, whose participants included the Gauleiters of the annexed eastern provinces, the head of the General Government Hans Frank, and Himmler. Discussions focused on the deportation of the Polish populace, and not least the question of available transport capacities. Here, it was Himmler who argued most strongly for a continuation of the deportations, and Kleinmann's summary was now intended to prove just how much the Reich Railroad had already done. This is why it can be safely assumed that Kleinmann really made an effort to list all transports known to Berlin—and, nonetheless, there is no mention here of a second set of deportations departing Vienna in late October 1939.

Unlike with the origins and early days of the Nisko campaign, the scholarly literature is in agreement about what forced its suspension: the resettlement of "Volksdeutsche" from Eastern Europe.[39] As early as October 15, 1939, the Reich had already signed an agreement with Estonia that provided for the emigration of its ethnically German populace. Similar agreements followed, with Latvia on October 30 and with the Soviet Union on November 16.[40]

As a consequence, the train with three thousand Jews from Mährisch Ostrau and Kattowitz was not the only deportation transport on October 18 that had been assembled by the Germans. That same day also saw the first "Volksdeutsche" from Estonia landing in Gdynia, which the occupiers had renamed Gotenhafen, and to make room for them, Forster's agencies had ordered the filling of a deportation train, which left the city—also on October 18—with 925 Poles bound for Kielce in central Poland, later to be followed by more.[41] The Reich Security Main Office, which had previously contravened Eichmann's original plan by shifting the Nisko campaign's focus to the deportation of Jews from Kattowitz along with Polish Jews in general, found itself forced to quickly change gears, for it had now become clear that tens of thousands of "Volksdeutsche" would be arriving in occupied western Poland in the coming weeks. With the strained transport situation, Himmler had to decide whether Eichmann's deportation of Jews or the accommodation of the "Volksdeutsche" should take priority. It is hardly surprising that Himmler decided to prioritize the deportation of the Polish populace in and around Gotenhafen, in order to free up the necessary housing and jobs for the "Volksdeutsche" who were now rolling in.

In the scholarly literature, there is now general agreement that the debarking of the Baltic Germans in Gotenhafen and Danzig was what stopped the deportations to Nisko. But the stoppage has often been mistakenly interpreted as a situation in which Nazi aspirations to expel Jews from the Reich had been subordinated, if only temporarily, to the needs of the ethnic Germans, when in fact the Nisko campaign should itself be seen as an early attempt to Germanize the annexed western Polish territories. Accepting this hypothesis also has implications for the position assigned to the Nisko campaign in the history of the annihilation of the Jews. David Cesarini, for example, suggests that Müller was already thinking ahead at this early date and had ordered the Nisko campaign in order to "broach an entirely new policy": the deportation of all Jews from the Reich, which included the annexed territories.[42] Michael Alberti likewise sees Nisko as "part of a much larger plan."[43] In this view, the Nisko campaign appears to be a first step toward a more comprehensive, but primarily anti-Jewish, policy. As far as could be found in the scholarly literature, it is only Ludmila Nesládková who contradicts this interpretation, viewing the stopping of the Nisko campaign as an effort to press ahead with what was the "most urgent concern" of the Reich Security Main Office at the time, making the *annexed Polish territories* "Jew-free."[44] I expressly concur with this analysis and would like to suggest situating the stopping of the Nisko campaign primarily within the context of the Germanization policy aimed at the western Polish territories. It is certainly true that Eichmann's and Stahlecker's initiative was originally aimed at deporting Jews from their area of responsibility and would have also signified a further step in the radicalization of the Reich's anti-Jewish policy. But it is equally true that these two men ultimately failed to push their plan through at the Reich Security Main Office. Here I would argue that Heydrich's and Himmler's attention had meanwhile become completely focused on the developments in Poland and on removing all people considered racially or politically undesirable from the annexed territories. Eichmann's plans for the deportation of Jews were a good fit here, but not in their original form, because the point was to expel Polish Jews, not German ones.[45]

The stopping of the Nisko campaign was the result of efforts by Heydrich and Himmler to fit this plan as well into the wider policy directed at Poland. Although their intentions cannot be used to also explain the inclusion of Viennese Jews, the Gestapo did nonetheless concentrate on selecting Jews with Polish citizenship in the deportations completed from Mährisch Ostrau and the one planned for Prague. The arrival of the "Volksdeutsche" in Poland certainly did force the Reich Security Main Office to reconsider the existing measures and ultimately to halt the Nisko campaign. But, as I have shown, and in contrast to the common view in the scholarly literature, it cannot be said that a project had thereby been stopped that had nothing to do with the Germanization of the annexed territories. If, as I have argued, the Nisko campaign is to be viewed more as a continuation of the Germanization policy begun by Udo von Woyrsch's Einsatzgruppe and the Wehrmacht's expulsion order, then the shifting of the deportation focus from Upper Silesia to Danzig–West Prussia, as necessitated by the arrival of the "Volksdeutsche," would have been an even easier choice for Heydrich and Müller to make, for in their eyes it would have simply been a shift in geographic focus for the Germanization policy from the south to the north of annexed Poland.

The Gotenhafen Model: Establishing a Circular Flow of Resettlement

The stopping of the Nisko campaign represented the failure of the first attempt by the Reich Security Main Office at also targeting an ideologically defined enemy—the Jewish populace—after having already subjected the Polish political elite to arrest and also murder. For the planners in Berlin, the debarkation of the Baltic Germans in northern Poland pushed Upper Silesia off the agenda for the moment, and the increasing dependency of the German economy (and its war machine) on the industrial zones there would further ensure that the local populace—and this also applied to the Jews for a while—was largely spared throughout the war from interventions like those in the two northern provinces.[46]

In the following months, the focus of the Nazi regime's Germanization policy would initially shift to Poland's northwest. The situation there was quite different from the one in Upper Silesia, and in many ways. Even during the interwar period, the Polish "Corridor" (i.e., the territory that separated East Prussia from the Reich) had already held a special place in German revanchist demands. After the conquest of Poland, the possibilities for a brutal course of action seemed greater here than in industrially important Upper Silesia, for example. Equally important was certainly the institutional framework, which remained considerably less solidified until late 1939 in the two newly established provinces of Danzig–West Prussia and the Wartheland, than in Upper Silesia or the Zichenau region. While these latter two territories were annexed to already existing provinces and immediately incorporated into their administrative structures, such structures—along with the relationship between the SS apparatus and the civil administration—were yet to be established in the two new "Reichsgaus" (meaning Gaus under the direct control of Berlin, allowing more overlaps between party and state).

But the occupiers went a step further in Poland's northwest and attempted for the first time to establish a systematic circular flow of resettlement, meaning that the local population segment considered "undesirable" would be deported and then replaced by "Volksdeutsche" immigrants from Eastern Europe. The development and implementation of these resettlement flows, which used Gotenhafen as their gateway, would prove characteristic of the future course of Nazi Germanization policy.

The decision to terminate the Nisko campaign, occurring just as another project in Nazi ethnopolicy was delivering its first successes at Gotenhafen, was at the same time a decision to combine two undertakings, originally conceived independently of one another, into a unified Germanization policy. As Wildt has noted, the decision to combine them tempers Aly's claim of a causal relationship between the immigration of the ethnic Germans and the deportation and ultimate annihilation of the Jews. Such a relationship did not exist, and neither was it intended at the very start, but had to be established first before it could unleash a radicalizing dynamic that has been correctly demonstrated by Aly.[47]

Even with the decision to evacuate the ethnic Germans, one can already see the inadequate state of preparation that typified Nazi projects, as shown, for example, in Hitler's promise to the leader of the German minority organization in Latvia, Erhard Kroeger, that all members of the German minority would be resettled, an action that was then carried out virtually overnight. But even here, Hitler's sudden decision can hardly have come as a surprise, in view of a policy proposal that had repeatedly surfaced over the decades, namely, to transfer Russia's "Volga Germans" to Germany's eastern provinces. In any case, the project progressed apace, so that by February 1940, two hundred thousand ethnic Germans from Eastern Europe had already been resettled in the annexed territories—a vanguard for the almost one million "Volksdeutsche" who were still to follow, celebrated by Nazi propaganda as "returners" ("Rückkehrer").[48]

*　*　*

The arrival and departure point for this forced population exchange was to be Gdynia, the most important Polish port city, formerly named Gdingen in German and now renamed Gotenhafen by the Nazis. On the same day that Himmler was appointed (Reichskommissar für die Festigung deutschen Volkstums, or RKFDV; Reich Commissioner for the Strengthening of Germandom), early rumors were already making the rounds that the city would soon be the first target for the settlement of ethnic Germans from the Baltics. Groscurth made this note in his diary: "Latvia: directive from the Führer: evacuate Germans regardless of situation. Organization of reception in Gotenhafen, which will be cleared of Poles for this."[49] These rumors were confirmed shortly thereafter by Heydrich on October 9, when he communicated to Ribbentrop that he considered a "substantial removal of the Polish populace from the city to be necessary."[50]

The reason for choosing Gdynia in particular cannot be conclusively ascertained. Certainly, it would seem natural to settle the inhabitants of Baltic port cities in yet another port city. But it seems likely that the choice was also influenced by Gdynia's symbolic significance in the German-Polish conflict. The place had long been an insignificant fishing village, until the Sejm (the parliament of the reestablished Polish state) resolved on September 23, 1922, that a deepwater port would be built there—within sight of Danzig—to host Poland's battle fleet and merchant marine and also to free the Upper Silesian mining areas from their dependence on German seaports, soon achieved with the construction of the Coal Trunk Line (Magistrala Węglowa).[51] By 1932, when Gdynia had caught up with the neighboring port of Danzig, it had long since become vital to Poland's foreign trade, and as the "pride of the Second Polish Republic," it came to symbolize Poland's success and will to survive.[52] Therefore, it might have been not only for pragmatic reasons that Gdynia had been selected: by choosing it in particular for launching the Germanization of the territories to be annexed, the occupiers were also making a symbolic statement. In any case, two days after Heydrich's message to Ribbentrop, Himmler also argued in favor of Gotenhafen, and ordered that members of the Polish elite were "to be expelled *first of all*."[53]

This dictate, that the first to be expelled should be those residents considered undesirable for political and ideological reasons, would have actually required a precise surveying of Gotenhafen's inhabitants, as had already been launched in other occupied locales.[54] But when Forster's agencies took over the organization of resettlement efforts in mid-October, there was no longer enough time for a survey. On October 14, a set of selection criteria was presented by Wilhelm Huth and Wilhelm Löbsack, the former being Forster's deputy (later a Regierungspräsident and the head of Department I at the Reichsstatthalter's offices), and the latter his ethnonationality officer (Volkstumsreferent).[55] These criteria demonstrated the pressure under which the authorities in Danzig–West Prussia were working, thereby contradicting Włodzimierz Jastrzębski's assessment of the deportations as a "carefully prepared evacuation measure."[56] Huth did not even bother to specify which groups were cleared for deportation and instead only stipulated those who could remain in the city: "Volksdeutsche" and—with some exceptions—Kashubians. In the process, he put down on paper what may well have been the first definition of the "Volksdeutsche" (singular: Volksdeutscher) in the annexed territories: "To be considered a Volksdeutscher is anyone who has belonged to one of the German organizations in Poland, or who as a nonorganized person has acknowledged German as his language, sent his children to a German school or raised them German, and can provide an impeccable ethnic German guarantor."[57]

The inhabitants of Gotenhafen and the adjacent locality of Adlershorst (today Orłowo) who had been labeled Kashubian by the Germans were to be spared if they had been born in the city. "The other Kashubians would be treated the same as the Poles, insofar as their dwellings are required for the Baltic Germans."[58] In this case, the German occupiers were not so interested in how much a dwelling's residents might be suitable for Germanization, but instead whether the dwelling itself was needed.

The emphasis on the housing question demonstrates how much the first deportation actions were shaped by the imperative to accommodate the incoming "Volksdeutsche"—a circumstance that would soon be repeated in the Wartheland. Tens of thousands were expected, and if they were to be accommodated here, then most of the roughly eighty thousand residents of Gotenhafen had to be expelled. A more nuanced survey, as had recently been begun in the rest of the province—dividing the local populace into "Volksdeutsche," autochthonous Poles, Poles that had migrated here in the interwar period, politically dangerous Poles, and finally Jews—was deemed unworkable here. Huth clearly felt it necessary to emphasize this in particular: "There exists no directive . . . according to which the populace born in West Prussia is to remain there." In view of the associated risk from the ethnonationalist perspective, Huth nonetheless sounded a note of caution: "But special attention must be given to the facts of whether there are German speakers among them and if these have raised their children German. If yes, then these cases are to be handled as borderline cases, in the sense that such are not to be treated as Poles."[59] According to Huth's instructions, the local municipal administration was solely responsible for the implementation of these measures—a provision that was intended to shut out the Immigration Central Office of the SS (Einwandererzentralstelle, or EWZ).[60]

That same day, Gotenhafen's police chief, SS Senior Assault Unit Leader Manfred Körnich, delegated the relevant responsibilities.[61] The Security Police were to select the "Volksdeutsche," register them, and provide them with identity documents—and to do so in accordance with the Gauleiter's guidelines. In his orders to the municipal police, however, Körnich inserted one more selection criterion. Although the housing needs of the immigrants had become virtually overnight the top priority dominating all others, it still needed to be balanced against economic necessities, and so he ordered that officers should identify not only the "Volksdeutsche," but also the Poles who worked in vital operations, in order to exempt them from deportations as well. Just a few days later, and after the first transport had already left the city, Körnich's instructions were further refined. Whereas the Gestapo-selected "Volksdeutsche"—along with some eighty long-established Kashubian fisher families and around five thousand skilled workers—were to be exempted from deportation, "all welfare benefit recipients" were to be rounded up, thereby adding social selection criteria to the ethnic and economic ones.[62]

The city lost around thirty-six thousand residents in total. Besides the 13,171 persons who were deported to Radom, Kielce, Lublin, and Siedlce in the General Government from October 18 to 26, another twenty-three thousand took matters into their own hands and simply fled—mostly to Posen and its vicinity.[63] The project could not have been judged a great success. First, not even half the city's residents had been expelled, and most of those had ended up not in the General Government, but in other parts of the annexed territories.[64] Second, even these first deportations had put the Reich Security Main Office into conflict with the German army's Chief Commander of the East (Oberbefehlshaber Ost), who gave his consent only "grudgingly," for he feared the loss of "irreplaceable workers."[65]

Therefore, although these transports were embedded within an ideologically charged grand project, namely, the Nazi regime's Germanization policy, the selection criteria were nonetheless tied to a logic guided by the functional needs of power. Whereas an ethnonationalist justification had protected the "Volksdeutsche" (and a few others) from deportation, it was economic reasons that exempted a much larger group: skilled Polish workers. This logic seems to have also defined the categories of those who were ultimately deported. The deportations included welfare recipients and, particularly, anyone seen as an obstacle to the settling of the ethnic Germans. The logic was also seen most explicitly in the case of the Kashubian populace, who were generally to be exempted on ethnic grounds—but the Kashubian exemption did not apply if the Kashubian in question had a good dwelling.

This new pragmatism becomes most obvious when compared with what happened in the deportations under the Nisko campaign. In early October 1939, when there was not yet a constantly growing number of incoming "Volksdeutsche" on the horizon, the Germans still believed they had all the freedom in the world to now tackle—in parallel to the mass executions of alleged political opponents—their ideologically central enemy, and so expel all Jews from Kattowitz Governmental Region (Regierungsbezirk Kattowitz). But this first deportation project—motivated solely by ideology—was immediately halted when it came into conflict with the looming needs of the ethnic Germans in need of settlement and was ultimately replaced by a second project that deported people from Gotenhafen and its vicinity. This second deportation project, however, was not about expelling Jews from Danzig–West Prussia: its exclusive goal was to make space for the incoming Baltic Germans, which was indeed a glaring difference from the Nisko campaign, one that signaled a shift in priorities that would define the deportation policy of the German occupiers in the annexed western Polish territories for the rest of the war.

In comparison with the number of anticipated "Volksdeutsche," the number of Poles deported with these transports seems very low. But nonetheless, Himmler had all further trains stopped. On October 26, he sent a message through the BdS of Kraków, Bruno Streckenbach, informing all involved agencies that the deportations from Danzig–West Prussia were to be suspended for the time being.[66] Besides complaints from the Wehrmacht, it was the rapid worsening of relations between the SS apparatus and the civil administration that was responsible for the stoppage.[67] Forster saw his authority as head of party and state in Danzig–West Prussia threatened by the SS apparatus and Himmler in his role as the RKFDV. On top of that were differences in agenda. From Forster's perspective, a somewhat more flexible attitude toward the bulk of the local populace was urgently needed if the goal was to quickly pacify the province—and also if he wanted to avoid further deepening the reliance on security agencies, that is, on Himmler. Unwilling to give Himmler free rein and let the SS apparatus implement the most extensive possible deportation policy in its efforts to transform Danzig–West Prussia into a mass settlement destination for the ethnic Germans from Eastern Europe, Forster "abruptly" blocked in late October any further settlement of Baltic Germans.[68] The order put into question all further SS resettlement plans, for the people could not be settled in the face of opposition from Forster as the head of the party and state institutions in the province.[69] Instead of constantly agitating the entire local populace, Forster decided early on that it would be better to pursue a policy course more in line with "traditional Prussian Polish policies."[70] Earlier than in other parts of occupied eastern Europe, in Danzig–West Prussia a conflict would emerge between the civil administration and the SS apparatus, one that could be boiled down to a dichotomy of "efficient exploitation versus racial ethnopolicy with systematic extermination," as it was described by Jansen and Weckbecker.[71]

There was another reason Himmler was able to so quickly adapt his priorities to the changed situation, one that tempered the importance originally assigned to Danzig–West Prussia in the first settlement plans. Just two days earlier, he had met with Arthur Greiser, Reichsstatthalter and Gauleiter of the Wartheland, to discuss the settling of Baltic Germans in his territory as well. During this conversation—which would turn out to be decisive for the later population policy of the Wartheland, as will be shown later—Greiser had shown himself more than ready to exploit the difficulties then emerging in Danzig–West Prussia and to redirect the Baltic Germans into his own province. When he explicitly reaffirmed this on October 26 to the head of the EWZ, Martin Sandberger, and the latter reported that Greiser had attached the "utmost importance to henceforth receiving continual transports from the Baltics to Posen [Poznań]," Himmler believed he was now able to change course and shift the focus of deportation and resettlement policy from Danzig–West Prussia to the Wartheland.[72]

The Reich Main Security Office Intervention

The halting of the Gotenhafen deportations by Himmler's directive of October 26, 1939, was the second time—after the Nisko Plan—that a large-scale expulsion project had been ended before it had really begun. While the causes discussed in the scholarly literature for this stop seem highly plausible, the question of causation is not the only one the directive raises. Other issues become clear if the order is interpreted not primarily as the last act of an undertaking that had failed in achieving its own ambitions, but instead as the expression of a new phase in Nazi population policy.

Despite the scanty surviving records, it is nonetheless apparent that wide-ranging organizational changes were happening within the SS complex. Besides the establishment of new institutions that would later play an important role in deportation policy, there was also a stronger centralization of deportation planning. Because the locally planned deportations could no longer keep up with the rapidly growing complexity of the regime's population policy objectives, and also because the SS apparatus in Danzig–West Prussia had come up against a Reichsstatthalter who had his own ideas about the Germanization of "his" province, a stronger involvement by SS headquarters seemed necessary. Headquarters involvement, especially Himmler himself, would not only allow Germanization policy to be coordinated across all occupied territories and better synchronized with the immigration of the ethnic Germans, but also give more weight to the population policy plans of the SS in the face of the Reichsstatthalter. This organizational metastasis of the SS apparatus in late 1939 has been only scantily investigated by researchers so far—an omission made even more serious by the fact that organizational decisions are always an expression of policy preferences as well.

Naturally, the first change that must be highlighted is the previously mentioned transformation of Greifelt's Coordination Office for Immigration and Return Migration, which became in the second half of October 1939 the Agency of RKFDV.[73] As a result, Greifelt was promoted to Himmler's "Reich Managing Director" ("Reichsgeschäftsführer") for his functions as the RKFDV.[74] In the scholarly literature, it is still largely unclear why Himmler selected Greifelt's office for this, thereby choosing what was still an extremely small team, comprising no more than twenty-nine staff members in December 1939.[75] According to Isabel Heinemann, "it made sense" to rely on Greifelt's office, because at least some of the South Tyroleans were to be resettled in the annexed Polish territories.[76] But in view of the fact that the SS already had its own dedicated Settlement Office (Siedlungsamt) as a subsection of the Race and Settlement Main Office (Rasse- und Siedlungshauptamt, or RuSHA), Heinemann's suggestion seems questionable. Himmler understood the "strengthening of Germandom" as not only the expelling of local "Poles," but, more important, the settling of "Germans," and so it would have been just as logical to assign these new powers to the head of the Race and Settlement Main Office, SS Group Leader Günther Pancke. And even more logical because the occupation of the Czech territory had allowed the Settlement Office to achieve considerable early "successes" in expropriation and resettlement policy.[77] The successes had earned the Settlement Office's head, SS Senior Leader Curt von Gottberg, the leadership of the Prague Land Office on May 17, 1939.[78] RuSHA managed to further expand its influence in settlement affairs during the invasion of Poland, in which its own surveying teams also participated, and their duties included providing services to the Einsatzgruppen and the establishment of a Land Office in Poland.[79] It initially seemed that Pancke's ambitions were even encouraged by Himmler: two days after his commissioning through Hitler's decree of October 7, it came time to prepare the implementation provisions for that decree, and here it was Pancke whom he chose for the task, not Greifelt.[80]

Therefore, when Greifelt was appointed Himmler's "Reich Managing Director" only a week later, it was a serious blow to Pancke. But Pancke did not give up, especially because the precise powers of Greifelt's new post had not yet been clearly defined. Hoping that Greifelt's ascent might yet be thwarted, he appealed to Himmler on November 20 and asked to be named the "personal representative of the Reich Commissioner . . . for all duties arising from the Führer's decree of October 7, 1939."[81] It was indeed no small request, and if Pancke had been successful, it would have subordinated Greifelt's newly established RKFDV headquarters to him and would also have led—especially in view of the other main responsibility of RuSHA, namely racial selection—to incalculable consequences for the entire future of Germanization policy. This foray by Pancke has been neglected in the literature to date, a surprising omission even in Heinemann's study, for she repeatedly quotes from this letter but nonetheless leaves this particular passage unmentioned. Instead, she too reinforces the dominant view that there was evidently no alternative to the ascent of Greifelt's agency.[82]

Pancke's ambitions were ultimately destined for a defeat that not only ended all hopes of his appointment as Himmler's personal representative but actually saw a considerable shrinking of his powers. But why did "Pancke and his office need to be pushed aside"—to take up a question posed by Rolf-Dieter Müller, who unfortunately left it unanswered.[83] In fact, enough points of contention had already accumulated between Himmler and Pancke in November 1939. One concerned the activities of the Race and Settlement Advisory Units (each known as a Rasse- und Siedlungsberatung, or RuS-Beratung) in Poland, with which Himmler was dissatisfied. Pancke's enthusiasm over a report from RuS-Beratung A, which he extolled as "extraordinarily interesting" when he forwarded it to Himmler on November 20, was in any case not shared by the latter. Here, the RuS-Beratung had made far-reaching proposals on population and land-use planning in eastern Upper Silesia, including the rerouting of the South Tyroleans to the Beskids. Himmler reacted coolly to this overreach into settlement planning: "The studies that have been done are certainly very interesting, but in my view, currently premature."[84] In contrast to Heinemann's conclusion, I find it difficult to see how one could surmise that in regard to this report, Himmler "expressly endorsed its observations."[85]

The coup de grâce in Pancke's failure may have come from the conduct of Curt von Gottberg, head of the Settlement Office. A perpetual jurisdictional struggle already existed with the Reich Minister of Food and Agriculture, Walther Darré, such as in questions of settlement planning, and the conflict escalated when Gottberg assumed the leadership of the Prague Land Office and began, among other things, to make arrangements for the settlement of South Tyroleans in Moravia.[86] Although Darré's earlier complaints to Pancke may have fallen on deaf ears, they were now given extra weight as Gottberg's conduct came under increasing fire in Prague itself.[87] When Gottberg was forced to undergo an internal audit, which would eventually expose a systematic misappropriation of state funds, the SD Command Precinct (SD-Leitabschnitt) in Prague screened his personnel and ultimately passed "a scathing verdict" on twenty-nine of his German employees.[88] Gottberg was dropped, on the one hand by Himmler, after Darré had written to "Heini" (a familiar form of "Heinrich") with a long list of Gottberg's misdeeds, threatening that there would be consequences if he allowed "Gottberg's case to pull in circles that neither you nor I would want" (here using the "Du" form, an informal "you" that again expresses intimate familiarity, in this case reflecting an old friendship that had fallen victim to more recent power struggles between Darré and Himmler).[89] On the other hand, Pancke also followed suit, as Gottberg had embarrassed him just as he was trying to expand the powers of RuSHA. This also certainly explains Pancke's harsh measures: he called on Gottberg to immediately register for sick leave, otherwise threatening him with "admittance to a concentration camp"—a threat that later earned Pancke the "sharpest disapproval" from Himmler.[90]

In any case, Himmler could no longer be persuaded to change his mind, and instead conferred these new responsibilities on a new and comparatively untarnished institution, because—as he let Pancke know—if RuSHA were tasked with this, then the entire assignment "would be threatened by the unavoidable confrontation with every ministry."[91] Thus, there was no more talk of entrusting Pancke with it. Upon the November 14, 1939, appointment of SS Group Leader Wilhelm von Holzschuher, the former Regierungspräsident of Lower Bavaria and the Upper Palatinate, to head the newly established Central Land Office (Zentralbodenamt) of the RKFDV, this area too was effectively removed from the jurisdiction of the Race and Settlement Main Office.[92] Pancke was made aware of this by November 29 at the latest, when Himmler summoned Pancke and

Holzschuher to come see him, in order to give them "detailed information on the structuring of the Reich Agency of the 'RKFDV.'" In Himmler's descriptions of the duties assigned to the new Central Land Office, RuSHA no longer came up at all.[93] A little later, Himmler put an end to any last remaining ambitions held by Pancke. According to Himmler, the oral briefing "also answered the question . . . of your own post."[94] This "plays no significant role for the moment in my work as Reich Commissioner." As a kind of consolation, Himmler nonetheless assured Pancke that the "settlement of people" would be transferred to him, and furthermore that Holzschuher would take over not only the Central Land Office, but also the RuSHA Settlement Office, purportedly to facilitate the flow of information, although Pancke was to be "officially not . . . involved."[95] The question of who would be in charge of the "settlement of people" was not detailed further in the message, and was then to be restricted exclusively to the racial selection of the settlers, and so Holzschuher's double role could hardly have been satisfactory to Pancke. When Holzschuher was appointed head of the RuSHA Settlement Office on December 14, it effectively amounted to a hijacking by the new agency of the RKFDV: after all, instead of incorporating the new Central Land Office into RuSHA, the Settlement Office had actually been taken over by one of Greifelt's subordinates. Even if Holzschuher's holding of both offices had actually been meant to simply promote better coordination between the two spheres while safeguarding the influence of RuSHA, this situation finally came to an end by June 1, 1940, when Himmler released Holzschuher from both positions at his own request; after that, they were never again occupied by the same appointee.[96] This is also why I think Heinemann is mistaken in assigning particular importance to RuSHA in the field of settlement policy. With his clear rejection of Pancke's ambitions, Himmler had begun a virtual dismantling of RuSHA, so that even the "Race and Settlement" in its name would soon become a misnomer, with its activities limited to the racial selection of individuals and no longer having anything to do with their settlement. Thus, describing RuSHA as a "key institution," let alone the "coordination headquarters of the SS race and settlement policy," seems to me to fundamentally misunderstand its rapid decline in influence.[97] On the contrary, RuSHA had already been shut out as a key player in Nazi population policy during the first months of the war.

* * *

Parallel to the ascent of Greifelt's agency and the freezing out of RuSHA, the Reich Security Main Office also underwent some important changes through which Heydrich intended to exert more control, in both conceptualization and institutional terms, over the migration already initiated (whether forced or not) of an ever-increasing number of people. This applied first to the EWZ, which on October 19, 1939, through an agreement between Departmental Heads III and IV, namely Otto Ohlendorf and Heinrich Müller, was subordinated to Ohlendorf.[98] For this area, Ohlendorf established the new Special Unit III ES (Sonderreferat III ES) on October 31, 1939, to be headed by Dr. Hans Ehlich, who was already head of the Unit for Race and Volk Health (Referat Rasse und Volksgesundheit).[99] As a unit for immigration and settlement (*Einwanderung und Siedlung*, thus ES), it was initially meant to handle all questions arising from the "Homeward into the Reich" ("Heim ins Reich") campaigns and to "establish connections among the Reich's central bodies" in this area.[100] But its scope soon expanded to cover "basic problems of eastern settlement" in general, so that it developed into the center of "Lebensraum" planning at the Reich Security Main Office.[101]

But for the context here under discussion, more important is the greater centralization of migration's other aspect as well, namely the expulsion of certain parts of the local populace, which was likewise the responsibility of the Reich Security Main Office and its agencies on the ground. After the negative experiences of deportation projects conducted so far, Heydrich wanted to establish stronger coordination in order to better synchronize the bidirectional population movements across all of occupied Poland while reconciling the movements with the interests of the relevant administration heads and other agencies. The aforementioned order of October 26, 1939, commanding an immediate suspension of deportations, was a first step in this direction. The order had been signed by Streckenbach, the BdS of Kraków, who was now "tasked with the centralized planning of settlement and evacuation efforts in the eastern area."[102] Thus, before the deportations from Gotenhafen could resume, "centralized planning" was to be conducted in order to bring together Germanization efforts all across the annexed western Polish territories, thereby coordinating the deportations while synchronizing them with the immigration of the "Volksdeutsche" now arriving from other parts of Eastern Europe.

The megalomaniacal dimensions of the leadership's thinking at the time are revealed by Himmler's Directive 1/II, signed in his capacity as RKFDV on October 30, 1939, thereby introducing the first phase of this centrally planned deportation policy. While deportations from the Reich itself were no longer mentioned in it, this was the first time that all annexed provinces were included, delegated responsibilities laid out, a timetable specified, and a hierarchy of targeted deportees established. According to the directive, around a million people were to be deported between November 1939 and February 1940, meaning more than eight thousand individuals per day. First, "all Jews" and "all Congress Poles" were to be deported from Danzig–West Prussia, along with an unspecified number of "the especially hostile Polish populace."[103] The preparation of the necessary "resettlement plan" was assigned to the relevant Higher SS and Police Leaders (Höherer SS- und Polizeiführer, or HSSPF), who gathered in Kraków for a first meeting on November 8, 1939, in order to be updated by Streckenbach on the latest planning status. At the meeting, he sketched out a three-phase deportation plan. In accordance with Himmler's directive, during a first phase "from mid-November" 1939 to February 1940, a million people including "all Jews and Congress Poles" were to be apprehended, dispossessed, and deported, in order to make space for around one hundred fifty thousand ethnic Germans from the General Government, Volhynia, and the Baltics. Around four hundred thousand people were to be expelled from Danzig–West Prussia, with some of the "returning transport trains" taking aboard the thirty thousand "Volksdeutsche" from the region around Warsaw. After that, in a second phase lasting until the end of 1940, the remaining populace was "to be evaluated on whether they should be graded as Poles or as Volksdeutsche, and where applicable, as Poles who were still desired." Then, from the beginning of 1941, the final phase would involve deporting the thereby identified "undesirable Poles."[104] With this, a plan was sketched out for the first time in Kraków that no longer subjected only a specific region to a Germanization policy, as previously seen in the cases of Kattowitz and then Gotenhafen, but instead considered the Germanization of all annexed regions together and dovetailing the deportation of undesired people with the settling of ethnic Germans.

By this meeting in Kraków at the latest, it must have become clear to the German ethnocrats that the objectives they were now setting would far surpass all previous killing and deportation campaigns. They would overwhelm German capacities in two ways at once, having set in motion a deportation project that would miss the specified deadlines from the very start and also fail to capture more than a small fraction of the people initially intended for expulsion.

After November 15, 1939, the original target date for resuming deportations, went by without a successful launch of the removals into the General Government—not even in just one province, and not even with people who were often already under arrest—the first train finally left Gladau (today Głodowo) in Danzig–West Prussia on November 22. When 9,250 people were deported by the end of the month, the targets for 1939 seemed to have been achieved.[105] The remaining 390,000—according to HSSPF Richard Hildebrandt on November 26, 1939—were to follow at the beginning of the next year.[106]

In contrast, the situation in Upper Silesia was considerably more complicated, just on account of the region's wartime economic importance alone.[107] Furthermore, uncertainty about the province's precise territorial extent continued into the year 1940. Josef Wagner and his deputy, Vice Oberpräsident Fritz-Dietlof von der Schulenburg, were from the very beginning against the annexation of the eastern counties into Silesia and called for their reintegration into the General Government.[108] The reasons Wagner cited were primarily "of an *ethnopolitical* nature," for the local "nationally Polish populace, numbering almost four hundred thousand individuals," would weigh heavy on the "ethnonational struggle [Volkstumskampf] in the contested eastern Upper Silesia" region.[109] With the implementation of a police border (*Polizeigrenze*) on

November 20, 1939, the distinction between the province's two parts was then given legal expression as well.[110]

On the question of who was first in line for deportation, Wagner was in agreement with Forster and Greiser: the goal was the "expulsion and eradication of the Polish people who had acted rebelliously against Germany."[111] The Regierungspräsidents were of the same view. In Kattowitz, the post was held by Walter Springorum, a member of the supervisory board at Hoesch AG (a huge steel and mining company) and former head of the Reich Interior Ministry's minorities unit specializing in the Upper Silesian question, and thus someone who combined economic expertise with ethnopolicy experience.[112] In fact, Springorum soon proved himself highly proficient at combining the Germanization of his governmental region with the security underpinnings and economic needs of Upper Silesia's heavy industry. He left no doubt about how these demands were to be balanced in uncertain cases. During a meeting on November 21, 1939, he placed "paramount importance" on the immediate deportation of those "Poles from the industrial populace" who had proved in the past to be "anti-German."[113] Only after that did he address the "cleansing of the rural districts," primarily meaning a forced rearrangement of the rural ownership structure, which was dominated by an abundance of small and very small farms. But Springorum did not intend to expel the individuals who became superfluous as a consequence but instead wanted to retain them as (industrial) workers. Since the settlement of ethnic Germans in Silesia was evidently not very far along at that point, he feared having to make up for the deportations of political activists with large numbers of "replacements from Galicia and Congress Poland"—and in this case, he would prefer to utilize "replacement workers from the farming districts."[114] Besides the political opponents, who in any case were to be expelled, the deportations still had to follow an economic rationale: here, the "superfluous" populace was considered redundant only in the context of the reduction in agriculture's need for labor in the wake of modernization, but that populace was then to be used in covering the anticipated labor shortages in the industrial sector, in a kind of officially enforced and guided "rural flight." What Springorum thus had in mind was a forcibly imposed modernization program that tried to increase industrial and agricultural production by eliminating what had already been singled out by German scholars even before the war as a central problem in Poland's backwardness, namely its "rural overpopulation."[115]

Practical issues were delegated to the resettlement working group that was established in November 1939.[116] The authorization for arrests and deportations was then issued on December 7.[117] The selection of the populace was conducted by a commission of the province's own Silesian Rural Development Company (Schlesische Landgesellschaft) under a man surnamed Klix, which acted in each rural county with a local committee to sort the inhabitants into three groups.[118]

In Group A were those who "fought against Germany with weapon in hand" and those who "actively operated against Germany and against Germans"—these were to be deported first.[119] Group B was reserved for those who "strongly sympathize with Polishdom, are markedly anti-German in attitude, but do not belong to the leading classes," and Group C consisted of those who "unquestionably belonged to the Polish minority"—the last word choice is worth noting here.[120] The deportations were initially to be limited to areas west of the police border, because Wagner still hoped he might yet unload the counties east of this back onto the General Government. In contrast to the situation in the other two eastern provinces, the annexation of these counties had not been justified by the need to accommodate the incoming ethnic Germans. Instead, part of the confiscated territory was to be used for the "strengthening of the locally long-established German peasantry."[121] With the remaining part, Springorum was now even prepared to exchange the "persons to be evacuated . . . with inhabitants of Poland's General Government, particularly agricultural workers from regions in which the ethnonational struggle was unknown."[122] Even though it evidently did not come to pass, this proposal nonetheless shows how much the German occupiers wanted to limit the economic damage resulting from the deportation policy. If the latter made it necessary to replace the deported politically active ones with other Poles from the General Government and thus push the Germanization of the province further into the future, then the occupiers were initially prepared to do so.

As in Danzig–West Prussia, such pragmatic policy ideas met with resistance in Silesia as well, especially from the SS complex. But the HSSPF of Breslau, Erich von dem Bach-Zelewski, found that his ability to act was considerably restricted by the strong position of the province's Oberpräsident. Bach-Zelewski was forced to accept that the "industrial area to a large extent . . . must be entirely spared for now from the evacuation measures for economic reasons," but the largely agricultural southern part of Upper Silesia was more suitable. This was particularly true of the rural county of Saybusch (today Żywiec), especially because the populace there allegedly was "almost entirely racially inferior and thus to be evacuated immediately."[123]

One could interpret the preceding quote as another piece of evidence pointing to the dominance of racial thinking. Such is the argumentation of Isabel Heinemann, for example, when she claims that such ideas formed "the foundation of sweeping deportation plans for eastern Upper Silesia" and thereby also sees further corroboration for the importance of RuSHA, whose expert reports supplied the argumentation for Bach-Zelewski.[124] A more illuminating approach, however, would be one that analyzes how the effectiveness of ideological tropes was derived from their functionality in consolidating German power in the region. In fact, the "racial qualities" of this region's populace had already been the subject of German research interest. After the conquest of Poland, the Reich Interior Ministry set up a commission under Ernst Vollert, which was tasked with developing proposals for the Reich's new borders. In studying the Beskids, and thus also Saybusch County, it was found that the Gorals also included people with "Nordic blood," which then conveniently helped justify the regime's claims to this region.[125]

Bach-Zelewski felt no affection for the Saybusch populace; they did not fit into his plans. He had learned that the SS ethnocrats in Berlin were preparing the resettlement of another group, the South Tyroleans, and had thereby brought Upper Silesia into the discussion. It was an opportunity he did not want to miss: taking control of what appeared to be an immediately available larger group of "Volksdeutsche" must have represented, for reasons of not only ideology but also security, a much better option for the accelerated Germanization of the area than the assimilation of the Gorals. As a result, Bach-Zelewski decided to recommend Saybusch County for "climatic and agricultural reasons, for the placing of South Tyroleans." The local populace became an inconvenience and so was cleared for deportation by Bach-Zelewski—and it was here where the fabrications of the RuS-Beratung served as an ideological justification for a much more complicated decision-making process.[126] Therefore, the causal connection has been interpreted backward by Heinemann. It was not, in fact, the report of the RuS-Beratung that caused Bach-Zelewski to call for the deportation of the Saybusch populace. The decision had already been made independently of this, and if Bach-Zelewski nonetheless made reference to it, he did so in order to also give ideological backing to his actions after the fact.

Bach-Zelewski's reasoning made little impression on the civil administration in Kraków. As Bach-Zelewski informed representatives of that government, the plan had been to start on November 15 with the deportation of four thousand people per day, which was "delayed week after week" by Kraków and finally reduced to a thousand people per day.[127] Just four days later, even that number met objections, as a delegation from Breslau learned in Kraków that the General Government currently found it beyond its abilities to accept even "a thousand people to accommodate."[128] The deportations did not take place and had to be postponed to the following year.

Ironically, it was from the Reich Security Main Office in Berlin that the definitive cancellation of all short-term deportation plans would overtake the SS ethnocrats in Silesia. In a telex dated November 28, 1939, Heydrich had once again intervened directly in deportation planning by informing the HSSPFs and the Inspectors of the Security Police and the SD (IdS) in the relevant provinces and in Kraków that the "evacuation . . . by general order" of Himmler was to be implemented by the Security Police. Future deportations would be guided by an "evacuation plan" that itself consisted of a long-range plan (*Fernplan*) and several short-range plans (each known as a *Nahplan*).[129] The long-range plan was currently being developed at the Reich Security Main Office (and thus no longer by Streckenbach), and its implementation was to be delegated to the IdS officeholders, who were the regional representatives of the Reich Security Main Office. With this decision, the HSSPFs were definitively ousted from direct stewardship of the deportation policy. After the census of December 1939, which had been ordered by Himmler and would finally deliver a more precise overview of the local populace, it would then be possible to schedule the long-range plan.[130] The first short-range plan, however, was to be launched before then—although only in the Wartheland. There, the task to be completed before the census was "to remove enough Poles and Jews so that the incoming Baltic Germans can be accommodated."[131] The goal was to replace eighty thousand local inhabitants with forty thousand ethnic Germans between December 1 and 17.[132]

It was probably just a few days later that Ehlich finished the long-range plan for the resettlement of the eastern provinces, thereby representing what Karl Heinz Roth calls the "first variant of the Reich Security Main Office's ethnopolicy plans for the East."[133] Pursuant to what had already been discussed in Kraków, the "settlement of the German east" could only be achieved through the "resettlement of members of foreign folkdom." Doing so would require a "plan that was thought out in all details" to avoid risking the "worst of upheavals in the economic life of the eastern provinces."[134] More than Streckenbach, Ehlich recognized what fundamental security-related and economic interests would be affected by deportations on such a scale—and not only in the General Government, but also in the Reich itself. For one thing, on military grounds the Wehrmacht voiced the "gravest of concerns" about a substantial increase in the population of the General Government, where the deficient food supply did not permit an increase, especially if the food riots feared by Hitler were to be avoided. For another, Ehlich was forced to recognize that the local populace were not simply undesirable "Fremdvölkische"—they were also a necessary workforce. One could not "ignore the reality" that the German economy, especially its agricultural sector, still depended on Polish workers. For example, in calculating the labor requirements for the following year alone, the Reich Food Estate (Reichsnährstand, a corporatist body covering food production and distribution) estimated that 1.7 million Polish forced laborers would be needed for Germany's agriculture. But in the annexed territories too, according to Ehlich, it would not be possible to do without Polish forced labor until sufficient numbers of ethnic Germans became available. As the ethnocrats of the Reich Security Main Office had to ask themselves, how could one, first, address the relevant economic and military needs; second, avoid the threat of a "political undermining and sabotage of the greatest magnitude" that came with the transport of a large number of forced laborers into the Reich's interior; and, third, hold on to the Nazi dystopian vision of a "settling of the German east"?

The answer to this complex of questions was not a new one: racial selection. Ehlich adopted the first phase sketched out by Streckenbach, which concentrated on expelling all Jews and political opponents into the General Government, but he then shifted the focus of all later considerations more toward "racial appraisals" ("rassische Musterungen"). Under Streckenbach, racial appraisals assessed only "racial suitability" and thereby determined the right of residence, but under Ehrlich they developed into a more nuanced arsenal of tools designed to harmonize ideological priorities with the German occupiers' other needs, particularly economic ones.

How Ehlich envisioned the practical handling of procedure can be read in the long-range plan. During the second phase, the remaining population was to be summoned into the employment offices. There, they were to be registered for the labor market while undergoing a "brief, imperceptible racial screening."[135] Even though such a brief, informal screening could not produce a nuanced assessment, it was nonetheless deemed enough for deciding whether the relevant individual was "suitable for dispatching into the Reich."[136] In a third and final phase, the local Landrat (rural councilor, the head of a rural county) also had to decide which of the remaining people were immediately available for deportation and which of them had to be replaced with corresponding workers from the Reich.

This three-phrase procedure that the Reich Main Security Office had brought into play was almost miraculous in reconciling the conflict between economic requirements and ideological dictates, transforming the forced recruitment of Polish workers that the economy demanded into an element of a truly Nazi Germanization policy. It assured the SS of approval from the hardliners: after all, by presenting a program that accorded with the racial premises of Nazi ideology, they upheld its relevance for political practice. And for the SS, a lasting implementation of the policy would have been a breakthrough with great political ramifications. Since the racial appraisals were naturally to have been conducted by the so-called "suitability assessors" ("Eignungsprüfer") from RuSHA, the SS would have then become a key player in the recruitment of labor. It is unsurprising that, from this perspective, Heydrich found it easy to argue that the coordination efforts now needed could be done only in Berlin, which meant that Streckenbach had to surrender his relevant powers to Ehrlich's planning team. But it is equally unsurprising that the more complicated demands of the overall deportation policy would also make the SS more reliant on the cooperation shown by the administration heads. In this regard, the conflicts with Forster's agencies must have seemed particularly uninviting, which resulted in one last shift of geographical focus, namely toward the Wartheland.

The First Short-Range Plan: Deporting the Polish Elite

Greiser's willingness to act with brutality was never in doubt. On September 28, 1939, when he told Hitler about his intention to liquidate "the Polish intelligentsia wherever he thinks it right," the Führer indicated he was "very satisfied" and faulted Forster's policy as "softer," which, especially "in regards to the intelligentsia . . . is not good."[137] Returning to Posen with this backing, Greiser instructed his Landrats "to compile, under the strictest secrecy, lists of Polish leaders and Polish intelligentsia—priests, teachers, major landowners, businesspeople, and industrialists—and to send these to me via official channels, labeled 'confidential Reich business,' to my personal address."[138]

At the same time the wave of killings was gradually abating toward the end of the year, the SS and police, working in close cooperation with the agencies of the newly installed civil administrations, began with the comprehensive registration of the local populace. The large-scale deportations in the Warthel-and, although beginning a little later than those in Danzig–West Prussia, were nonetheless directly related to the developments there, for Himmler's directive of October 11, 1939, named not only Gotenhafen, but also the city of Posen as a new home for the Baltic Germans.[139] And, in fact, Chief of Gestapo Heinrich Müller had already sent instructions just two days earlier to Erich Naumann, the head of Einsatzgruppe VI stationed there, telling him "to clear the Poles from a good neighborhood" and deport some of them to the General Government, in order to accommodate twenty thousand Baltic Germans.[140] But here, unlike in Danzig–West Prussia, the SS had found in Greiser a Gauleiter who not only tolerated the settlement of "Volksdeutsche" in his Gau, but actively promoted it—not least during a conversation with Himmler and Sandberger in late October, which ultimately prompted the latter to direct the bulk of settlers no longer to Danzig–West Prussia, but instead into the Wartheland.[141]

For the deportations from Posen, the first efforts were directed at establishing a reception camp for persons to be expelled, which was finally set up in the city's Glowno suburb (Polish: Główna) and could soon hold five thousand people.[142] Its first inmates were Posen residents who, as in Danzig–West Prussia, were considered either a political danger or a hindrance in the settling of Baltic Germans. The selection criteria also took into account the professions of the individuals. To make way for the 7,500 expected "Volksdeutsche," the expulsions were to include 450 families with members who had worked in professions of the intelligentsia and about whom "negative evaluations already exist," along with 300 families with members who had worked in the city's administration. Evidently because the Germans already felt so secure after completing the earlier waves of killings, however, the remaining 1,250 earmarked families had members who had worked only in industry, commerce, and the trades, namely economic

Figure 3.1. Glowno camp gate.
Source: Archive of Modern Conflict, album A10327.

Figure 3.2. Infirmary barracks and railroad siding at Glowno camp.
Source: Archive of Modern Conflict, album A10327.

Figure 3.3. Children at Glowno camp.
Source: Archive of Modern Conflict, album A10327.

Figure 3.4. Inside a barracks at Glowno camp.
Source: Archive of Modern Conflict, album A10327.

Figure 3.5. Machine-gun tower at Glowno camp.
Source: Archive of Modern Conflict, album A10327.

sectors that were to be filled by incoming "Volksdeutsche" as soon as possible.[143] On November 5, 1939, the first 217 individuals were brought to Glowno.[144]

At this point, it was still entirely unclear when the first transports were to leave the Wartheland, for a comprehensive plan for the Germanization of the annexed territories did not yet exist. As mentioned earlier, such a plan was first presented on November 8 to the HSSPFs gathered in Kraków. And, in fact, the agreements reached there did help speed developments in the Wartheland. SS Group Leader Wilhelm Koppe had attended as the representative from the Wartheland, having been appointed its HSSPF as of October 26, and in this position also becoming an appointee of Himmler in his role as RKFDV by November 1, 1939, at the latest.[145] After returning to Posen, Koppe began by establishing the institutional foundations for the population movements on November 11, 1939: first, a staff for accommodating housing and employment needs of Baltic and Volhynian Germans, and second, a staff for evacuating and transporting Poles and Jews to the General Government.[146] The institution Koppe founded was renamed the HSSPF's Office for Resettlement of Poles and Jews ("HSSPF, Amt für Umsiedlung von Polen und Juden") and was the precursor to the later Resettlement Central Office (Umwandererzentralstelle); it set the pace for deportation policy in the Wartheland and was led by SS Assault Unit Leader Albert Rapp, the head of the SD Command Precinct in Posen.[147]

On November 12—and time was pressing, the first transports having been scheduled in Kraków for November 15—Rapp had already completed a plan that Koppe then immediately forwarded to all relevant offices of the SS, police, and civil administration.[148] The inclusion of Landrats, Regierungspräsidents, and even the Reichsstatthalter in it was permissible because Koppe signed not only as the HSSPF, but also as the RKFDV appointee of Himmler, making use of this authority for the first time. As Reich Interior Minister Wilhelm Frick clarified in a subsequent explanation to the civil administrations in the annexed territories, the "technical directives of the Reichsführer of the SS [that is, Himmler] within the specified framework [that is, when it touched on matters pertaining to Himmler as RKFDV] are binding for you and your subordinate administrative branches."[149] Furthermore, each relevant HSSPF, as Himmler's RKFDV appointee, was allowed within this framework to also make use of the departments of the Reichsstatthalter's offices and subordinated bureaus, although in cases of conflict, the Reichsstatthalter was to decide. As a basic foundation for the subsequent deportations, Koppe's order specified the workflow, laid out the responsibilities, and, most important, also described guidelines for selecting persons to be deported.

According to the plan, the goal of the deportations was the "cleansing and securing" of the annexed territories.[150] To achieve cleansing and securing, three hundred thousand people were to be expelled by February 28, 1940. The number was to include one hundred thousand Jews (thus, besides thirty thousand in Lodsch, almost everybody in the vicinity outside Lodsch) and two hundred thousand non-Jewish Poles. The Jewish Poles were included without any further differentiation in the eyes of the German ethnocrats, since every Jew was to be deported regardless of individual case, but the situation was entirely different with the Christian Poles. In his selection guidelines for the latter group, Koppe tried to reconcile conflicting interests: the deportations were first to remove all Poles who were political activists, intellectuals, or criminals; second, selections were to be made in order to free up housing and employment opportunities for the incoming ethnic Germans; and third, they were not to adversely affect the Wartheland's economy. Thus, "manual laborers, low-level office workers, and civil servants" were to be spared as urgently required manpower unless they were "conscious Polish nationalists . . . or previously criminally convicted" but tradesmen were prioritized for deportation because this vocational group was particularly well represented among the "Volksdeutsche."[151]

Responsibility for the deportations was delegated to the Landrats, but in the selecting of targeted persons, they nonetheless had to cooperate with Rapp's new agency, which acted as a "central planning body and consultative organ."[152] Selection was to be based on a survey of each county's ethnic, political, social, and economic structure, which the Landrats had to submit within a week. To ensure that these surveys did not immediately lose their validity, Koppe prohibited Jews and Poles from changing residence.[153] Covering two pages, each survey was to state the relevant county's population, broken down into "Germans," Jews, and Poles (who were subdivided into long-established locals and Congress Poles), along with membership numbers for nationalist associations and parties, the number of criminals, and the county's occupational structure (subdivided into workers, farmers, and intellectuals).[154]

A few days later, Rapp issued implementing provisions for the selection of the non-Jewish Polish populace. For one, members of the intelligentsia were to be rounded up, which generally included all persons who "represent an obstacle to the implementation of Germandom in each individual county," which was also why the "sequential order of evacuation [was] to be determined according to the degree of dangerousness."[155] For another, all "anti-Reich and anti-German Poles," particularly the "Polish nationalist members of the anti-German, chauvinist, and class-struggle parties," were also to be rounded up. Finally, "criminal elements" were to be taken in, along with those "to be considered antisocial elements, such as the work-shy, beggars, prostitutes, etc."[156] To a greater extent than previously assumed by researchers, however, the deportations were a joint effort between Rapp's agency, the locally responsible Landrats, and the civil administration in general.[157] For example, the Posen municipal administration vetted the detained civil servants.[158] Meanwhile, the head of the provincial high court reviewed the apprehended captives.[159] Furthermore, the state archive and the Reich Railroad negotiated potential deferments with Rapp for workers who could not be replaced in the short term.[160]

Beyond such effects on the state apparatus, Rapp was also obliged to pay particular attention to economic interests. At a large meeting with representatives from the Reichsstatthalter's offices on November 23, 1939, Rapp assured them that he would not deport agricultural workers—except in the case of political activists.[161] But expelling political activists did not mean that the Reichsstatthalter's offices did not strive to exploit the labor of these people until their deportation, for example using those in deportation camps for forced labor.[162]

By late November, the preparations had advanced at least to a certain point, so that not only had the Landrats compiled an overview of the number of persons to be deported, but some of them had already been taken to the transit camps specially erected for the purpose. It was becoming clear that the deportation allotment assigned to the Wartheland during the meeting in Kraków, namely two hundred thousand Poles and one hundred thousand Jews, would be nowhere near enough—after all, the targeted number of deportees specified by just twenty-nine out of forty-one counties had already reached four hundred thousand.[163] It was by this point at the latest that the ethnocrats in the Wartheland also learned about the changes decided in Berlin, specifically about the centralization of deportation planning as well as the subdividing of further deportation waves into a long-range plan and several short-range ones, and at this point too it received the directive for the implementation of the first short-range plan. On November 28, 1939, Heydrich ordered the deportation of "eighty thousand Jews and Poles . . . into the General Government," to make space for the settlement of forty thousand Baltic Germans.[164]

Heydrich's order effectively forced a setting of priorities, meaning a decision on whom to deport first among the more than four hundred thousand people considered "undesirable." Unfortunately, the setting of priorities can no longer be reconstructed with certainty—which is surprising in light of the unusually extensive source materials on this first deportation wave. With the deportations beginning as scheduled on December 1 and ending a day late on December 17, 1939, Rapp's staff documented the number of transport trains (eighty), their times and places of departure, the total number of deported persons (87,883), and often their individual names too.[165] What is less clear is the criteria according to which these people were chosen, thus whether the Landrats had followed Himmler's instructions of October 30, 1939, thereby arresting primarily Jews and Congress Poles. It is also surprising that there is no summary of how many of these deportees were Jews, especially because the Nazis were generally very insistent on differentiating between "Jews" and "non-Jews," and they documented this distinction in later deportation waves.[166]

In recent research, highly divergent positions have been taken on the question of how the criteria were applied. For example, Alberti conjectures that the majority of the almost ninety thousand people deported during the first short-range plan must have been Jews, but Christopher Browning takes the opposite view and assumes that fewer than ten thousand were Jewish.[167]

Even where no deportation lists have survived, one can nonetheless attempt to extrapolate the identity of those deported by reconstructing the selection criteria. The original sources contain various remarks from which the objectives of these deportations can be inferred. For example, in his progress report on the first short-range plan, Rapp wrote that the deported people were primarily those "who represent an immediate danger to Germandom."[168] Meanwhile, a summary report from 1942 was equally vague when it described the goal of the first short-range plan as the "evacuation of the politically leading intelligentsia and to some extent Jews."[169] SS Chief Squad Leader Siegfried Seidl was more concrete in a report he presented in Eichmann's office in Berlin some five weeks after the conclusion of the first short-range plan, when he informed the latter that "so far, only politically contaminated persons and people with good dwellings were evacuated, so that space was made for the Baltic Germans."[170] He did not mention Jews. Furthermore, how very much this first short-range plan was aimed at those who either belonged to the social elite or possessed good dwellings (two conditions that naturally coincided in many cases), thereby following a logic more influenced by security-related and pragmatic concerns, is also demonstrated by the handling of the Congress Poles. They were similarly spared, despite always being named first alongside the Jews as part of the top-priority group for deportation. But as Seidl communicated to Eichmann, Congress Poles were generally "just simple laborers," thus having no "good dwellings . . . for the Baltic Germans," and furthermore were "to some extent indispensably engaged."[171] The same may have applied to many Jewish Poles.

In fact, only a single case has been documented in which Jewish Poles were deported under the first short-range plan—which tends to point more toward the lower priority given to deporting the Jewish populace. It was only in late November 1939 that the decision was made to also include Lodsch in the deportations; as a result, SS Assault Unit Leader Heinz Richter, an employee of Rapp, was dispatched there. Upon arriving in Lodsch, he discovered that the proscription lists were absent, because—according to city commissioner Franz Schiffer—everything was still "going pell-mell" and the chief of police was also not helping him.[172] As a quick solution, Schiffer suggested deporting the "Jewish proletariat" instead—because, after all, no selection process was required in that case. Richter also received little help from the local SD field office, which had allegedly compiled a list of the city's Polish intelligentsia and submitted it to the Gestapo—but no one had been able to find it afterward.[173] A new summary hastily assembled by the Gestapo would similarly prove to be of little help. Although three thousand persons were listed, it soon turned out that a third of them were no longer to be found at the listed addresses, and another portion were "even Volksdeutsche in leading positions," so that the police were finally able to take away just 2,600 political activists to the transit camp, along with their families. This result meant that the originally envisaged deportation of fifteen thousand "above all . . . politically suspect and intellectual Poles" had become impossible in any event. Richter thus concurred with the suggestion of Johannes Schäfer, the chief of police for Litzmannstadt: "In order to fill up the figure of fifteen thousand persons, it was therefore necessary to fall back upon the Jews."[174]

After evidently having made no attempt at all to earmark some of the Jewish populace for the first transports, the occupiers now turned hastily to the Jewish Council of Elders (Ältestenrat) "for the voluntary presentation of Jews willing to emigrate."[175] When only a thousand people registered, the police then surrounded entire blocks of houses, conducting what eyewitness reports described as a veritable "battue" ("Treibjagd") to flush out the Jewish populace there.[176] It is not clear, however, how many Lodsch Jews were caught up in these deportations. In Richter's report, which is primarily to be seen as an apology for the failures of the Gestapo and SD, the municipal administration alone is blamed for having neglected to register people before their deportation. This is why it is not possible to even cite a precise total: while the municipal administration reckoned 8,400, the SS and police estimated a figure between 9,600 and 9,900 deportees. But because no more than nine thousand Jews had actually been arrested, it seems questionable whether all of them were sent to the General Government. After all, those arrested for political reasons were certainly deported first, especially because the raids to arrest Jews did not begin until the night of December 14–15. But at that point, five of the ten transports had already left Lodsch, and none was supposed to be able to carry more than a thousand people.[177]

Therefore, if Jews were not listed as a separate group in the final deportation reports for the first short-range plan, it was because hardly any Jews were deported at that time—except for the makeshift solution for the shortfall in Lodsch. As for why even these Jews are not mentioned (except in Richter's internal report), Browning has already offered a possible explanation: their deportation "was evidence not of a success in deporting Jews but rather of a failure to identify and seize Polish political activists and intelligentsia," and so it was preferable not to list them separately in the statistics.[178]

If the deportations in Lodsch already demonstrate how important it was for the ethnocrats in the Wartheland to deport the politically active first, the impression is further reinforced by looking at the handling of deportations in the city of Posen. There, the registration work was not done by the authorities of the civil administration, as in the rest of the Wartheland, but instead by the ethnonationality officer of the SD Command Precinct in Posen, SS Junior Assault Leader Dr. Herbert Strickner.[179] For this, he set up a complex system of index cards that would soon become a kind of "training and testing center for all registration efforts."[180] First, all "members of the leading chauvinist Polish parties and associations" were registered in the central card catalog of the SD Command Precinct.[181] Those so registered soon amounted to more than a hundred thousand persons.[182] From this group, the occupiers then selected persons who "occupied positions that needed to be immediately filled by Germans (especially Baltic and Volhynian ones)."[183] These names were then compared against those in the "Volksdeutsche catalog," the "retainment catalog," and the "Ukrainians and Russians catalog" in order to exempt anyone who was categorized among the "Stammesdeutsche and Volksdeutsche" ("Stammesdeutsche" were "Germans by descent") or who was an indispensable worker, or was otherwise a non-Pole. Finally, an "evacuated persons catalog" was created, sorted according to street address, and with dwellings graded as very good, middling, or poor.[184] As Rapp claimed in his progress report, the selections were oriented toward "planning for the settlement of Baltic Germans": as a result, the victims of these deportations were not primarily Poles who had arrived after 1920, nor the remaining Jewish populace, but instead the Polish elite—graded according to their occupations and the quality of their dwellings.[185]

This fixation on Poland's social elite spared Congress Poles and—at least temporarily—Jews from deportation. But it did not necessarily spare people who were otherwise considered "Volksdeutsche." It is true that immediately after the deportations had begun, the Reichsstatthalter's offices had asked the SD to exempt those among whom "some external marker (German name, fluent German language, German ethnonationality vouched for by other Volksdeutsche) speaks in favor of this."[186] In Posen itself, the desire to exempt "Volksdeutsche" is why it had become routine to check names against the compiled "Volksdeutsche" catalog. Despite the civil administration's request, however, priorities were sometimes set differently. Strickner had been ordered to exempt "Volksdeutsche" and "persons of German blood"—but only if they were "politically uncontaminated persons."[187] And, in fact, when doubtful cases were adjudicated in Posen and the rural counties, the deportation of a political opponent took precedence over sparing "persons of German blood" or the "Deutschstämmige" (the "German-descended"); the latter expression was soon established as the relevant term because "German-blooded" (*deutschblütig*), a designation introduced with the Nuremberg Laws, was used in German jurisprudence only to distinguish Germans from Jews, and now a new term was needed "to differentiate . . . persons of German descent from those of Polish descent."[188] Thus, a progress report on the deportations in the rural county of Schrimm (today Śrem:), stated that "in the selection of persons to evacuate, less consideration has been taken of the German descent [*Deutschstämmigkeit*] of these persons than of their attitude toward Germandom."[189]

Outraged by this procedure, many German nationals turned to the Reich Security Main Office to protest against the deportation of their relatives, who after all—they claimed—had fought on the German side during World War I, had been decorated, and of course were "Germans." After several of these cases were reviewed, the relevant office in Posen received an admonishment and was urged to take more care in its assessments.[190] Rapp's self-defense reflects the logical knot in which the German ethnocrats had entangled themselves: in the absence of a "Reich directive," his agency had had to decide for itself the definition of the terms "Stammesdeutsche" and "Volksdeutsche." In this case, for "the Stammesdeutsche, blood-based belonging" was decisive, and for "the Volksdeutsche, the professing of Germandom during the past twenty years." The "professing of Germandom" ("Bekenntnis zum Deutschtum") was "understood extremely broadly," covering not only, for example, a family that "had publicly supported Germandom, belonged to German organizations, or sent its children to German schools"; in fact, it "sufficed" that they "had remained consciously German." It was more difficult to determine the "German-descended nature of those who were not simultaneously to be considered Volksdeutsche in the aforementioned sense [had professed their Germandom]," especially since, as Rapp reported, "the German-descended Poles in particular were supporters—sometimes leading ones—of the Greater Polish, anti-German effort."[191] And with these people, from Rapp's perspective, the security threat took precedence over any ideologically defined belonging. In any case, the German authorities in the Wartheland were working on the assumption that several thousand "Deutschstämmige" had already been deported into the General Government.[192]

Of course, there were good reasons for this concentration on the political elite of Polish society. The German occupation's authorities were, above all, precisely that: occupiers. It was thus necessary, in their own interests, to first lay the foundations for their own authority in these territories by eliminating any potential resistance before any further plans could be realized. Thus, from the German perspective, the prioritized deportation of all persons classified as security risks was only logical and was to some extent an extension of the killing campaigns seen in the early months, although through other means. This consideration is repeatedly mentioned in the orders, reports, and memoranda surrounding the first short-range plan, not only from the SS complex, but also the civil administration. The oft-repeated key concern was the need for the "securing and cleansing" of the province, always alongside the need to create "living and working spaces" or "accommodation and employment opportunities" for the "Volksdeutsche" destined for settlement.[193] Despite how very much the directives of Himmler and Heydrich may still have insisted on the implementation of ideological selection criteria, the ethnocrats in the Wartheland chose otherwise: it was not Jews and Congress Poles who were deported, but instead the potential opponents of the German occupation—particularly if they had good housing or employment positions. Even the "Deutschstämmige" were not exempt from such treatment. Security-related and economic considerations very clearly took priority over ideological ones.

The Integration of Loyal "German Ethnonationals"

In a greater part of the historical research literature, one could certainly get the impression that Nazi population policy was primarily one of exclusion (for example, in Jerzy Marczewski), as reflected in the killing sprees and deportations described in chapter 2.[194] The following will focus on demonstrating the opposite, showing how the Germanization policy of the occupiers was at least as much about inclusion too—and not only of people like the "Volksdeutsche" who were organized in German associations, but also of what would soon become an ever-expanding section of the local populace. Thus, if the occupiers felt that the Germanization of the Polish territories required the combining of what might be called "negative" population policy measures with "positive" ones, it is also unsurprising that the criteria deciding which persons were considered "German" or "Germanizable" were not so dissimilar to those that adjudicated the deportation of the Poles, namely in primarily following a logic guided by the functional needs of power.

Initiatives in the Individual Provinces

Silesia

In Silesia, it took a while for the registration of the "Volksdeutsche" to come up to speed. One reason was that Silesia, unlike the other two eastern provinces, was not initially under consideration as a new home for the ethnic Germans arriving from the Baltics. Another reason was that the final course of its eastern border was still not entirely clarified. Oberpräsident Josef Wagner was still fighting against the economically motivated expansion of his province into areas like the Dąbrowa Basin industrial region, because he feared that the Germanization of Silesia would be additionally hampered by its almost exclusively Polish populace.[195] The disagreement not only shaped the early stages of deportation planning but also meant that the registration of the local populace was very slow to begin.[196]

Danzig–West Prussia

The situation was entirely different in Danzig–West Prussia, which in the early days had already been a central focus of the killings perpetrated by the Volksdeutscher Selbstschutz and soon became a new deportation focus, with the debarking of the Baltic Germans and the ending of the Nisko campaign. This did not escape the attention of the local populace, such as those in the rural county of Bromberg, who—from fear of the SS and police—soon turned to Landrat Walther Nethe and asked him to issue "Volksdeutsche" identity documents. Nethe found himself ill-equipped to do so, and so on October 6, 1939, he delegated the task to his subordinated mayors and Amtskommissars (rural district commissioners), who were better informed on the local situations.[197]

A week later, the Landrat of the neighboring rural county of Dirschau went a step further and instructed his mayors and Amtskommissars to begin the selection process. Here, like everywhere else in Danzig–West Prussia at this time, the populace was sorted into four groups: "Volksdeutsche," Jews, "local" Poles already resident before 1918, and immigrant Poles from "Congress Poland and Galicia." The "Volksdeutsche" were those "who had *publicly professed being Germans and stood up for their Germandom*"; in contrast, locals who had "actively participated in the fight against Germandom" were assigned to the immigrant Pole category.[198] The security-oriented logic of this approach is clear. First, the original motivation for this order was not the speediest possible registration of all "Volksdeutsche" but the identification of the hostile populace, which was initially considered more important. The registration of the "Volksdeutsche" was considered necessary primarily as a way to prevent them from being "affected by measures that should only apply to Poles and Jews."[199] Second, the ultimately established criteria for the selection not only of "Poles" to be deported, but also of "Volksdeutsche" to be privileged, were primarily directed at one aspect: their conduct, especially politically. The mass-murder campaigns of the early months and the subsequent deportation waves had particularly targeted those who had been organized into Polish parties or associations and were thus considered especially dangerous. The stipulated "professing of Germandom" followed the same motivation: a "German" was a person whom the German occupation administration could rely on, which included above all the members of German minority organizations. These selection criteria were adopted for the first census in Danzig–West Prussia, which took place from December 3 to 6, 1939, and divided the resident populace into four groups: "Volksdeutsche," "local" Poles, "immigrant" Poles, and Jews.

THE ESTABLISHMENT OF THE DVL IN THE WARTHELAND

The dominance of this security-oriented paradigm was most clearly demonstrated by the founding in the Wartheland of the German People's List (Deutsche Volksliste, or DVL). Here, too, the selection process applied to the local populace by the civil administration had begun with the registration and elimination of political opponents, both real and presumed ones.[200] Preparations soon turned, however, to the registration of the "Volksdeutsche" as well. At the heart of these efforts was the jurist Dr. Karl Albert Coulon, the Reichsstatthalter's policy and ethnonationality officer (Volkstumsreferent), and in this function also head of the Gau Borderland Office (Gaugrenzlandamt).[201] Born in March 1906, Coulon had already joined the Nazi Party in 1926 during his university studies and subsequently also worked for the Nazi Party's Foreign Organization in Hamburg; thus, he already boasted previous experience in the field of ethnopolicy.[202] Arriving in the city of Posen on October 16, 1939, he began preliminary work on the DVL just three days later (according to his own report).[203] His work contacts would help him in this effort. Above all, he found a like-minded colleague in Herbert Strickner, the ethnonationality officer of the local SD Command Precinct, who shared Coulon's ideological beliefs and—ignoring institutional boundaries—became a close associate, even assuming important functions within the DVL offices.[204] Of course, this cooperation with the SD Command Precinct was hardly surprising, for it had been preparing for the upcoming deportations and had recently begun compiling an ethnonationality-based card catalog in order to avoid ensnaring politically uncontaminated "Volksdeutsche."

The existing situation that Coulon and Strickner found in Posen was, in the view of both ethnocrats, unsatisfactory. According to Strickner's extensive report on the activities of the DVL, by the time that the German troops marched in, the largest political organization of the German minority in Wielkopolska, the German Union (Deutsche Vereinigung), had already begun a multitiered registration of the "Volksdeutsche."[205] The German Union issued three different certificates. Certificate A was for individuals who had been members of German organizations before September 1, 1939; meanwhile, those who were considered "Deutschstämmige," but "for economic reasons did not profess Germandom," had to content themselves with Certificate B. Individuals who fell outside both categories but were nonetheless considered "loyal Poles," could apply only for Certificate C. The German occupiers, however, were critical of this system, not only because the German Union had ostensibly been "extraordinarily generous" in handing out Certificate B in particular, but also because a number of other organizations had been issuing similar ethnonational assessments, so that by late October, their number had reached forty thousand.[206] To the German occupiers, this situation was unacceptable. The "determination of ethnonational membership" ("Feststellung der Volkszugehörigkeit"), an expression suggesting objectivity, had to be wrested from the local "Volksdeutsche" and transferred to state control, as the first step in the Germanization of the newly established province.

The DVL was established by a decree from Greiser on October 28, 1939—meaning at a time when the other provinces were still experimenting with these questions at the county level, and mandatory guidelines had not yet been issued by the other Gauleiters or the Reich Interior Ministry. The earliness of this date could be a sign of the importance that Greiser and his subordinates attached to the task. In any case, it was certainly sped up by Himmler's aforementioned approval for the rerouting of a large part of the Baltic Germans to the Wartheland: what was probably the preferred hardline course of action, namely, the most comprehensive possible deportations of the local populace, now seemed feasible, because the "ongoing transports of Baltic Germans to Posen" would bring replacements.[207] It was thus a matter of urgency to register any locals who, as "Volksdeutsche," were to be safeguarded against deportation. It did not seem necessary to make compromises in the case at hand, as it had been in the other two provinces, in which there was an "intermediate class" allegedly living there. The DVL was to determine the ethnonational membership of each applicant as quickly as possible according to a uniformly regulated procedure, with results to be binding for all state agencies. According to the decree's central provision, "Whoever is registered in the DVL is German."[208]

The DVL was initially conceived as a two-level agency, with a central office at Coulon's unit in Department I of the Reichsstatthalter's offices and local branch offices under the Landrats and mayors. The adjudication committees consisted of representatives from the state administration, the SD, and the local "Volksdeutsche," and were chaired by the relevant Landrat or mayor.[209] The main work was to be done by the branch offices, which were to ask "Volksdeutsche" to come apply for induction into the DVL, hand out the necessary questionnaires, process them upon return, and announce their decisions "orally."[210]

The installation of the DVL offices initially had to be pushed through against resistance from the civil administration, particularly in the governmental regions of Posen and Hohensalza (today Inowrocław). Their selection work ultimately began in Posen, the region's political center and thus the epicenter of earlier confrontations between "Volksdeutsche" groups and Polish nationalist ones.[211] As a result, its branch office was exceptionally placed under Strickner and not the local mayor, and the "procedure tested before establishment in all other branches."[212] On November 3, 1939, Coulon informed the populace of this procedure with an announcement in the daily press. According to the announcement, questionnaires in duplicate would be distributed to applicants from November 8 to 18, 1939, which were to be returned with a photograph within three days, so that a decision could be received a week later. Eligible to apply were those who had belonged to a German minority organization before September 1, 1939, or who were "German-blooded, but due to the regime of terror, had been unable to act for the German cause or to openly present themselves as Germans."[213] All other offices were henceforth prohibited from issuing ethnonational membership certificates.

Although no detailed set of selection guidelines has been found to exist at that time, the announcement and the distributed questionnaires nonetheless point to the essential core of later selection practices, which did not fundamentally change for the rest of the war (see figures 3.6 and 3.7). The goal of the DVL

P 04685 **Zentralstelle**

Deutsche Volksliste

beim Reichsstatthalter im Warthegau

Zweigstelle _Po – H_

Fragebogen Nr. _7048_

_N° 1._
_15. 7. 41._

Name _W_ — Vorname _Heinrich_

Beruf — Wohnung _Posen, Martinstr. 25_

Geboren _02_ in _Pretzin a/Elbe_ Kreis _Torgau_

Seit wann in Posen? _21. Oktober 1939_

Derzeitiger Beruf _Apotheker_ Wo beschäftigt? _selbständig_

Wo vor dem 1. 9. 1939 beschäftigt? _in Jarotschin_

Von wo zugewandert? _Jarotschin_

Muttersprache _Deutsch_ — Bekenntnis: ~~gottgläubig~~ evangelisch ~~katholisch~~

ledig, ~~verheiratet, geschieden~~ (Unzutreffendes streichen)

Mit wem verheiratet: Name _/_ Geburtsdatum _/_

Geburtsort _/_

Kinder: Name _/_

Geburtsdatum

Geburtsort

Name, Vorname und Herkunft der Eltern und Großeltern.

Vater _Franz W_ geb. _1. IX. 1868_ in _Bennersdorf/Riesengeb._

Mutter _Helene S_ geb. _9. VIII 1874_ in _Beelitz/Mark_
(Geburtsname)

Großvater (vätl.) _Heinrich W_ aus _Greifenberg/Schlesien_

Großmutter (vätl.) _Johanna R_ aus _Wesel/Rhein_
(Geburtsname)

Großvater (mütl.) _Wilhelm S_ aus _Regenwalde (Pommern)_

Großmutter (mütl.) _Wilhelmine S_ aus _Wirsitz (Schlesien)_
(Geburtsname)

Welche Schulen besuchten Sie? deutsche _Progimnasium Jarotschin und Religion 2 Teil Geist in Breslau_

Welche Schulen besuchten Ihre Kinder vor dem 1. 9. 1939? deutsche _/_

polnische _/_

Welchen deutschen und polnischen Vereinen, Parteien, Vereinigungen, Kultureinrichtungen, Berufsverbänden, Genossenschaften, Stud. Vereinen usw. gehörten Sie vor dem 1. 9. 1939 an?

Jungdeutsche Partei für Polen, Bielitz von _1. V. 1934_ bis _zur Auflösung 9.V.39_

Verband für Handel z Gewerbe, Posen von _1927_ bis _heute._

deutscher Wohlfahrts Dienst, Posen von _1934_ bis _"_

deutscher Schulverein, Bromberg, Kreditverein, Posen etc. von bis

C. 13181279

Figure 3.6. The first questionnaire from the DVL branch in the city of Posen, filled out by an early Nazi activist prominent among the ethnic Germans of the Wartheland. He was enrolled in Group A, received ID no. 1, and was later transferred to Section 1, as shown by the stamp in the upper right corner.
Source: Polish State Archives in Poznań, under DVL Posen Stadt, 12126.

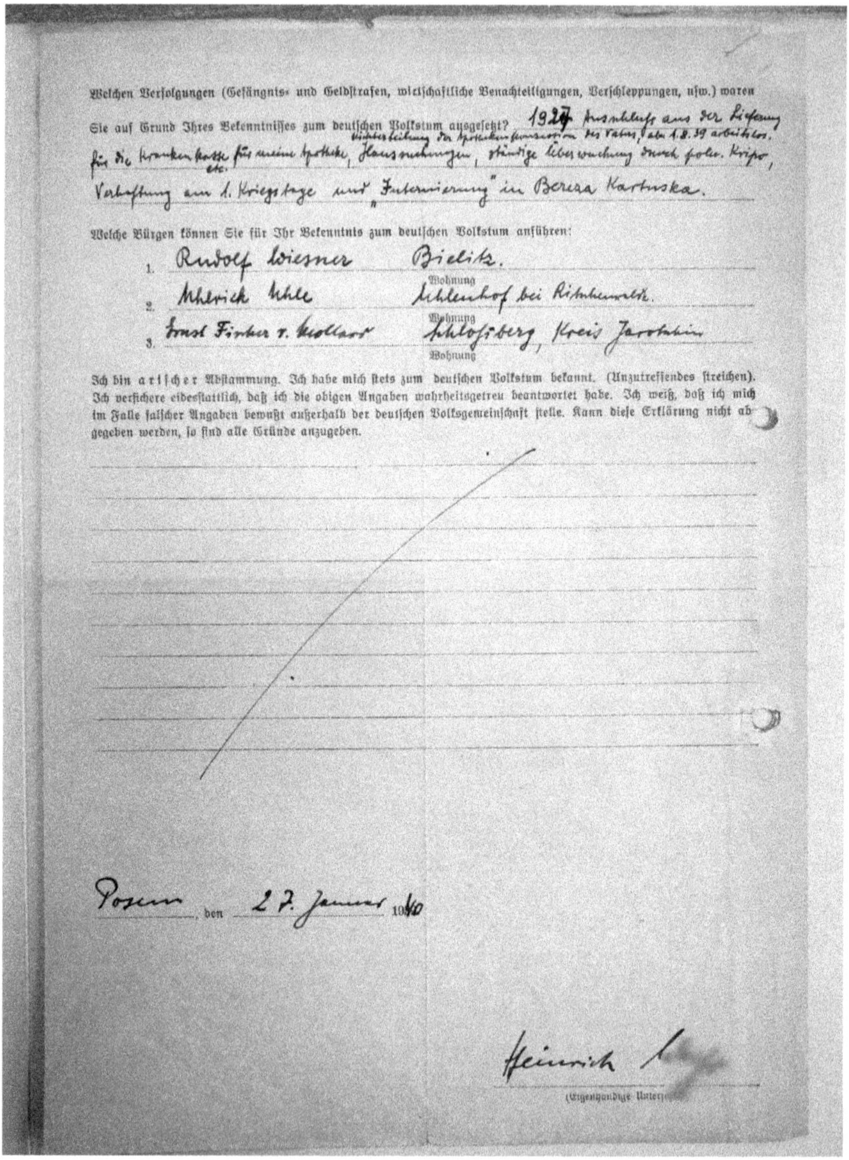

Welchen Verfolgungen (Gefängnis- und Geldstrafen, wirtschaftliche Benachteiligungen, Verschleppungen, usw.) waren Sie auf Grund Ihres Bekenntnisses zum deutschen Volkstum ausgesetzt? *1927 Ausschluß aus der Lieferung, Nichtbeteiligung der Apothekenkonzession des Vaters, ab 1.8.39 arbeitslos, für die Krankenkasse für meine Apotheke, Haussuchungen, ständige Überwachung durch polit. Kripo, Verhaftung am 1. Kriegstage und „Internierung" in Bereza Kartuska.*

Welche Bürgen können Sie für Ihr Bekenntnis zum deutschen Volkstum anführen:

1. *Rudolf Wiesner   Bielitz.*
   Wohnung
2. *Ulderich Uhle   Schlenhof bei Ritterswalde.*
   Wohnung
3. *Ernst Finke v. Mollard   Schloßberg, Kreis Jarotschin*
   Wohnung

Ich bin arischer Abstammung. Ich habe mich stets zum deutschen Volkstum bekannt. (Unzutreffendes streichen). Ich versichere eidesstattlich, daß ich die obigen Angaben wahrheitsgetreu beantwortet habe. Ich weiß, daß ich mich im Falle falscher Angaben bewußt außerhalb der deutschen Volksgemeinschaft stelle. Kann diese Erklärung nicht abgegeben werden, so sind alle Gründe anzugeben.

Posen, den 27. Januar 1940

Heinrich [Unterschrift]

(Eigenhändige Unterschrift)

Figure 3.7. Reverse side of figure 3.6.

was to register what soon became known as the *Bekenntnisdeutsche* ("professed Germans," primarily members of German organizations) and the "Stammesdeutsche" (who may not have been organized in German associations but could nonetheless prove their "German" descent). The DVL questionnaire investigated above all one's "conduct in the ethnonational struggle." For example, applicants had to state their mother tongue and religious denomination, when they had moved to Posen and from where, which schools their children had attended, and what German and/or Polish associations they had belonged to. They were asked, "What persecutions where you subjected to because of your professing Germandom?" and were also prompted to supply names of guarantors. And, finally, they had to state whether they were "of Aryan descent" and had "always professed Germandom."[214]

This focus became even clearer in another questionnaire that was designed only for those who had been awarded Certificate C from the German Union, meaning they were not classified as "Germans" at all, but as "loyal Poles." As Poles, they were not eligible for DVL enrollment, but because they had apparently proved themselves to be "loyal," they were nonetheless to be recorded. In both German and Polish, applicants were once again asked about membership in "political, economic, cultural, denominational, religious, military, paramilitary, or athletic associations, as well as student groups, parties, associations, cultural institutions, professional bodies, cooperatives, fraternities, etc." Instead of a declaration of belonging to "Germandom," there was instead an assurance that "I have never persecuted Germans nor actively or passively acted against Germandom."[215]

There are two ways in which this definition of "Volksdeutsche" applied by the Wartheland's civil administration would seem particularly noteworthy. First, it tied the purported "German ethnonational membership" above all to membership in organizations of the German minority. In view of the Nazi sympathies shared by most of these groups, the occupiers thereby also assumed general cooperation with the Nazi regime's "Lebensraum" project. Second, with this definition, the ethnocrats in the Wartheland had certainly decided against going it alone, in that their selection criteria very much drew on the longer tradition of Germany's naturalization practices, which was likely to attract broad support from large parts of the Nazi movement. The aspect of political loyalty had, for example, informed the "option" given to residents of Alsace-Lorraine and Northern Schleswig (when individuals were forced to opt for either German or non-German citizenship), which explains the importance of military service for the question of naturalization, as well as the discrimination seen against applicants who were accused of left-wing sympathies.[216] Moreover, the definition also corresponded with the new Reich citizenship law, which defined the Reich citizen (*Reichsbürger*) exclusively as a "national who is of German or kindred blood and who, through his conduct, demonstrates that he is willing and fit to faithfully serve the German Volk."[217] But even the Nazi Party's Racial Policy Office (Rassenpolitisches Amt der NSDAP) considered the DVL definition to be exemplary, and highlighted the selection process underpinned by political conduct as particularly positive. In the end, this definitional framework seemed capable of achieving widespread agreement in the annexed territories too, as it resembled the one applied during the deportations in Gotenhafen and also during the selections performed by the German Union's office in Posen. Although the generally broad consensus between the occupation administrations of Danzig–West Prussia and the Wartheland would soon acquire cracks and ultimately lead to two entirely different Germanization policies, it seems to have endured within the Wartheland itself between the German occupiers and the political elite of the local "Volksdeutsche."

As announced, the DVL branch office in Poznań began handing out questionnaires on November 8, 1939. They were supposed to be given only to persons who made a "German" impression on the DVL staff, so while 6,648 questionnaires were issued, some 3,000 applicants were turned away.[218] But before the assessment committee could evaluate the returned questionnaires, the ethnocrats were stopped in their tracks: the Reich Interior Ministry had meanwhile stepped in with a decree of its own and ordered the Wartheland "branch offices of the DVL . . . to immediately suspend their work."[219]

The Reich Interior Ministry's Introduction of German National Status in the Annexed Territories

At the Reich Interior Ministry, Greiser's efforts to establish the DVL caused a certain amount of uneasiness. Certainly, the law on the reintegration of Danzig into the Reich (coming into effect on September 1, 1939) and Hitler's annexation decree (coming into effect on October 26) had declared in general that the "Volksdeutsche . . . will become Reich citizens [Reichsbürger]" and the "residents of German or of kindred blood . . . will become German nationals [deutsche Staatsangehörige]."[220] In terms of implementation, however, reference was made to provisions that were still to come. The establishment of the DVL threatened to preempt those provisions and provoked resistance from the Reich Interior Ministry on two causes: the applied selection criteria were criticized as too exclusivist, and Greiser's rushing ahead was denounced as a usurpation of jurisdiction. Because German law tied national status to "ethnonational membership," induction into the DVL effectively predetermined the legal nationality of the affected persons—but this determination lay under the jurisdiction of the Reich Interior Ministry.

Although there was general agreement at the Reich Interior Ministry that this policy area should not be left to the Reichsstatthalters, its own ideas on the matter took some time to crystallize. Certainly, with the annexation of Austria, the Sudetenland, and the Memel Territory, a "strengthened trend from individual-based decisions to collective ones" had already become established, in which mass naturalization replaced traditional case-by-case assessments.[221] But in those situations, "völkisch [i.e. ethnonational] aspects remained . . . out of consideration." Now, with the annexation of western Poland, a change of course seemed necessary.[222]

The reasons for a change of course were elucidated in an overview from the Reich Interior Ministry to the other top-level Reich authorities, showing that even according to its own estimates, the German minority made up only 2.7 million of the 10.2 million inhabitants under consideration.[223] It is therefore unsurprising that several position papers addressing the question of mass naturalization in a territory where ethnic Germans were in a clear minority were circulated during precisely this period; political decision makers seized on them because they offered ideas on how German control of these territories could be consolidated without abandoning key elements of Nazi ideology. The focus of the debates was on how to decide the "ethnonational membership" of the local populace. The problem with the term "ethnonational membership"—namely that it referenced something imaginary and thus could not be managed through sharply delineated categories—was "solved" in a typical fashion: the term became a discursive weapon, its definition a question of power, guided exclusively by its political functionality. Even if it had to be accepted that only a small part of the populace were "Germans," then one could at least prevent the majority from being "Poles." The argumentative trick relied on the construction of a "mixed population" ("Mischbevölkerung") or a "wavering folkdom" (to borrow from the title of Robert Beck's trailblazing 1938 book), which might frequently display "Polish" linguistic, political, and cultural traits but was nonetheless allegedly undergoing a "shift in mindset" ("Gesinnungswandel") and gravitation toward "Germandom."[224]

Even before the invasion of Poland, the Reich Interior Ministry in particular had striven to further develop this line of argumentation. One of the projects promoted in the subsequent period with especial verve by the ministry's own publication office was the creation of an ethnographic atlas, which was intended to legitimize German claims to western Poland. Here, in his expert assessment of the maps for Upper Silesia, the Breslau-based professor of German ethnology, Walther Kuhn, argued for the extension of the term "Szlonzakians" ("Schlonsaken") from the Polish-populated county of Teschen to the German-populated region of Upper Silesia, in order to avoid using the "foolish name 'Water Polack' ['Wasserpolak']." Doing so would also allow one to emphasize the "community of identity and destiny shared by the two groups, and thus also the responsibility of the Upper Silesians for the Szlonzakians of Teschen." Furthermore, this was even more justified because the Szlonzakians were in terms of "descent and vernacular Polish, but in terms of culture and *mindset*, German," and—here borrowing from Beck—"in the east, in the mixed zone, national mindset is the only decisive factor." And if mindset was the decisive criterion, then on the map, the Szlonzakians had to be "represented as what they are: as Germans."[225]

In this debate, the Reich Interior Ministry was also assisted by other agencies, such as the Ethnic German Liaison Office (Volksdeutsche Mittelstelle, or VoMi). In his memorandum of August 25, 1939, on the "handling of the Masurian, Szlonzakian, Upper Silesian, and Kashubian questions," the head of the VoMi press office, Waldemar Rimann, also participated in the atomization of the Polish populace through the construction of various "ethnonational groups" ("Volksgruppen").[226] From the VoMi perspective, these groups could hardly be "labeled as Polish," nor "their customs and . . . home language as Slavic."[227] Unlike Kuhn, however, Rimann argued that the term "Szlonzakian" should be used exclusively for a certain population group in the Teschen region, meaning that four "ethnonational groups" lived there: Germans, Czechs, Szlonzakians, and Poles.

Rimann apparently felt that no further explanations were necessary for the differentiation of Germans and Czechs, but for differentiating between the other two groups, it was important to avert any misunderstandings. Thus, Poles were the "industrial workers who had immigrated from Galicia and Congress Poland," while the "local peasantry" were to be labeled not as Poles, but as Szlonzakians. Of course, he did not forget to point out that these fine distinctions had a short shelf life, which would expire with the occupation of this territory at the latest. At that point, "German terminology could recognize only German, Czech, and Polish," and the local Germans would be subdivided into the "urban populace, which are the quintessential Germans, and the German-Silesian rural people . . . the Szlonzakians." As a result, they were not to be listed separately, since the differing home language, meaning the fact that these people spoke Polish, was of little importance and was supposedly in the midst of "dying out anyway." Instead, what was important was the "professing . . . of Germandom," which allegedly existed beyond doubt among the Szlonzakians, thus making them Germans. The same applied to the populace in Upper Silesia heretofore known as the "Water Polacks," who in the future were to be simply called "Upper Silesians" ("Oberschlesier"). And, of course, in this view, the "Kashubians are not Poles" either. Despite the "temptation to use the term Slavic" here, the practice had to be "stopped, no matter what." Thus, in mapmaking, these groups were always "to be included, without any special indicators, as part of the German zone in terms of Volk and language."[228] Vollert was "fundamentally in agreement" with this and sought "an evaluation in light of the subsequently altered circumstances," meaning the occupation of these territories since then, in forwarding the memorandum to the Dahlem Publication Office for its opinion.[229] The reply came back positive, as might be expected. Beyond that, the Publication Office also recommended to the Reich Interior Ministry that it should emphasize "the will to German culture [deutsche Kulturwille] of the population groups in a suitable fashion."[230] Thus, in contexts like ethnocultural maps, "all those who have politically or culturally professed Germandom—regardless of what home language they speak—can be treated as Germans," and there could be "no more Masurians on any map."[231]

* * *

These questions acquired practical relevance as the end of the military occupation administration approached. The political decision makers in Berlin and in the provinces were in agreement that the Germanization of the annexed territories could not be achieved without large-scale deportations. There was great divergence, nevertheless, on the question of whom to deport. It was in this context that widespread attention was given to a position paper on "the issue of handling the populace of the formerly Polish territories according to racial policy aspects," which Dr. Erhard Wetzel and Dr. Gerhard Hecht from the Nazi Party's Racial Policy Office presented on November 25, 1939. Having recently returned from a research trip to Poland, where they had learned in Litzmannstadt about the workings of the DVL and probably also of the deportation authorities, they likewise supported the "atomization of the . . . entire populace into manageable segments" as a necessary measure.[232] Certainly, they began by declaring that Germans and Poles, "as a result of racial aspects, are deeply different in nature," meaning that Poles were to be deported.[233] But who exactly was a Pole? Wetzel and Hecht were able to reassuringly report that the German occupiers were not confronted with a united block of thirty-five million people, because half of them ostensibly belonged to non-Polish minorities, such as Ukrainians, Jews, Masurians, Kashubians, "Water Poles," Szlonzakians, and so on. And even with the nonetheless eighteen million people who remained, these race experts believed they could see great differences between the country's east and its west, where it was alleged that "millennia . . . before the infiltration of Slavic tribes" there had already been "Germanic peoples [Germanen]" living there. It was to them that the Poles owed not only "their becoming a Volk and state," but also a "not inconsiderable element of Germanic blood," which was followed by a "constant flow of German blood" with troop incursions from the Holy Roman Empire during the Middle Ages.[234] The desired conclusion: in the annexed territories, fewer than 6.5 million persons were to be expelled, because almost half the residents were either members of an ostensibly non-Polish minority or were, for other reasons, quite capable of being "Germanized." As for the deportations themselves, Wetzel and Hecht recommended planning for a longer time frame, for security-related, economic, and logistical reasons—a recommendation that also conformed with the thinking of the deportation bodies, which were intending precisely that. And, concerning the priorities set by them, there was also agreement from the Racial Policy Office:

the starting point was to be the "Polish chauvinists, members of Polish political and cultural policy parties," and the "Polish intelligentsia" in general.[235] In addition were finally the Jewish populace, "no matter whether observant Jews or christened ones, as well as the so-called antisocials, people with criminal records, inmates of penal institutions, and persons deemed incurably mentally ill."[236]

In light of the ongoing deportation planning, this discussion was not limited to the realm of ideological production. For example, the tight labor market prompted the Reich Labor Ministry on November 11 to push the Reich Interior Ministry for a speedy decision on how the "Kashubians are to be racially classified and as a result . . . are to be handled."[237] Attached to the message were two position statements written by the head physicians from the employment office of Danzig–West Prussia, who both argued for an economically amenable solution. Although Dr. Scharphuis was more cautious in warning against treating "a Kashubian . . . without further ado . . . as a Volksdeutscher," he nonetheless also assumed as a matter of course that the Kashubians were more German, since they had, "as a relict stock of Slavic origin, nothing in common with the Poles."[238] Dr. Petzsch was even more unequivocal. Complaining that there were "uncertainties about the assessment of the native rural populace (Kashubians)" at the state and party agencies in the counties of Neustadt, Karthaus, and Berent (today Wejherowo, Kartuzy, and Kościerzyna), he wrote that while the Kashubians were a "Slavic Volk fragment," they nonetheless had "many German words with Polish endings," counted "only with German numbers," and spoke at least an "imperfect German."[239] Most important, however, it was from among them that the Reich recruited the migrant workers urgently needed for agriculture, and they had "certainly delivered meritorious services." The "Kashubian upper class" and the "intellectuals" naturally had to be deported, but one would "need to carefully assess whether . . . native tribes might be considered for Germanization."[240]

∗　∗　∗

When Wilhelm Stuckart presented a draft version of "new regulations on the national status of Danzig residents and Polish nationals" on November 13, 1939, all such categorization questions initially remained unanswered. Instead, Stuckart referred to "difficulties" that momentarily made a "comprehensive legal arrangement . . . not possible." Certainly, it was undisputed that "persons of racially alien blood, especially Jews and Jewish hybrids ['Mischlinge']," were ineligible for German national status, and, of course, "no member of the Polish Volk could acquire Reich citizen rights, and thereby political rights." But it had to be "carefully examined . . . whether it lies in German interests to exclude all members of the Polish Volk from acquiring German national status." Here, for example, one conceivable solution was to summarily make into German nationals all those whose forefathers had been nationals of a German state. If the Reich Interior Ministry could not bring itself to implement such a solution in this case, it was primarily because no one could foresee who would ultimately fall victim to future deportations, and there should "not be a possibility that members of the Polish Volk, who are later evacuated, are first made into German nationals." What was thus arranged was a *provisional arrangement*" to register at least the "members of the German Volk." Stuckart attached a draft decree, which was to be discussed in Berlin on November 17.[241]

Frick signed the decree shortly thereafter on November 25, 1939, effectively unchanged. In regard to residents of the annexed territories, it restrictively stated that "subject to a final legal ruling . . . German nationals . . . are members of the German Volk" who had been nationals of Danzig on September 1, 1939, or else nationals of Poland on October 26, 1939.[242] The relevant determination was done according to the husband's status, in the patrilineal German tradition. If he was recognized as a "Volksdeutscher," then the status was extended to his wife and underage children; conversely, a female "Volksdeutscher" could not become a German national if she was married to a husband who was one of the "Fremdvölkische."

From the viewpoint of the Reich Interior Ministry, a more nuanced definition of "German ethnonational membership" was not necessary, as this seemed sufficiently covered by a decree issued after the occupation of the Czech rump state, dated March 29, 1939: "Of German ethnonational membership is whoever *professes* himself to be a member of the German Volk, as long as such professing is confirmed by certain facts, such as *language, schooling, culture*, etc. A more exact clarification of this term, 'of German ethnonational membership,' is not possible under the circumstances. But in general, there will nonetheless be no difficulties in determining accordingly whether someone is 'of German ethnonational membership' or not."[243]

In this definition, there are two important points worth noting. First, one cannot overlook the great importance given to the individual's own professing of ethnonational membership. As a consequence, another passage advises the citizenship offices that "German ethnonational membership . . . does not however require full or predominantly German descent. Since the professing of being a member of the German Volk is assigned major significance, it is also possible to view as a member of the German Volk someone who is partially or even *completely of foreign descent*. . . . Conversely, it is possible in individual cases that someone who is partially or fully of German descent, due to his professing, must be seen as a member of a foreign Volk."[244]

But, second, the Reich Interior Ministry was certainly not willing to leave the decision solely up to the applicant. Instead, the discretionary freedom of the citizenship offices, which was traditionally wide already, was further broadened. In doubtful cases, "above all is to be assessed whether the person claiming German national status on the grounds of his alleged German ethnonational membership represents, *in terms of his overall conduct, is a desirable addition to the population.* If this is the case, then in deciding the question . . . one should proceed *generously*; if this is not the case, then the requirements are to be strictly assessed."[245] To collect the necessary data for this, the relevant authorities (generally, this would be the local Regierungspräsident) were to hand out a questionnaire to the applicants (see figures 3.8 and 3.9).

I think it would be misleading, however, to describe this way of defining ethnonational membership as a "civic" one, as Tara Zahra does, because its relative openness worked less in favor of the applicants themselves but instead offered greater room to maneuver for the politicized bureaucracy.[246] As Gosewinkel argues, this was entirely deliberate, since labels like "German" and "Pole" were not to be consistently defined. Precisely because the Nazis were likely very aware that these terms "were not to be defined in an essentialist racial way, but only in a more political one," they had an interest in "keeping them open, so that they could be adjusted according to shifting political interests."[247] Indeed, the occupiers had no other choice, for a concise and practicable essentialist definition was intrinsically unachievable. In the end, the question of "who is a German" cannot be answered in essentialist terms, but only in formal ones, meaning the answer does not depend on personal—perhaps racially based—characteristics, but solely on the political act of acquiring German national status. Thus, even if every nationalist or racist movement needed to deny the decisionist, and thus political, quality of the act of acquiring German citizenship and to ground it instead in nature, its operationalization still had to be constructed in social terms—and was then generally tied to the conduct of the individual under consideration. Which is precisely what made the term "German" so flexible and subordinated to a political rationale.

With these restrictions on the registration of the "Volksdeutsche," the Reich Interior Ministry was in effect sanctioning the policy already applied in the annexed territories, which aimed at killing and increasingly deporting the political elite while registering the "Volksdeutsche" populace.[248] Two important caveats should be noted here. First, flexibility in applying the terms in no way represented an abandonment of the basic desire to turn the great majority of the local populace into German nationals, as already signaled. Prussia's former citizens, at least in large part, were clearly considered assimilable. Reluctance to give them German national status immediately was a concession to the momentary situation, to avoid making the fight against political opponents even harder. But, second, the Reich Interior Ministry was aware that the success or failure of the Nazi regime's Germanization policy would depend on the handling of the majority populace—and here, with the agreed decree, Frick intended to at least partially foreshadow the desired assimilation policy. This is also why reference was made to the preceding decree of March 1939, which gave decisive weight to

190/48

Deutsche Volksliste

ragebogen

rbs der deutschen Staatsangehörigkeit

gegliederten Ostgebieten

gstens 2 Wochen zu beantworten

Prokuratura Sądu Okręgowego w Lesznie
podprokurator V rejonu z siedzibą
w Wolsztynie

Frauen Geburtsname

(Vorname)

2. Familienstand: ~~ledig~~, verheiratet, ~~verwitwet~~, ~~geschieden~~ (Nichtzutreffendes streichen)
verheiratet mit Elisabeth geborene
geb. am 1904 in Schlieffenwalde

3. Geburtsjahr: 1906.
Geburtstag:
Geburtsort: Louisenthal
Politischer Bezirk: Elbing

4. Wohnort und Anschrift am 26.10.1939: Schlieffenwalde
Politischer Bezirk: Wollstein

5. Wohnort und Anschrift am 1.12.1939: Schlieffenwalde
Politischer Bezirk: Wollstein

6. Staatsangehörigkeit
a) Danziger Staatsangehöriger am 31.8.1939? ~~ja~~ nein
b) Polnischer Staatsangehöriger am 25.10.1939? ~~ja~~ ~~nein~~ nein
c) Staatenlos am 25.10.1939, aber früher polnischer Staatsangehöriger? ja
(Nichtzutreffendes streichen)

7. Beruf: [illegible]

8. Muttersprache: deutsch ~~polnisch~~ ~~tschechisch~~ ~~tschechisch~~
Sprachkenntnis: deutsch polnisch ~~tschechisch~~ ~~tschechisch~~
(Nichtzutreffendes streichen)

9. Haben Sie gedient?
a) bei einem deutschen Truppenteil?
b) bei einem österreichisch-ungarischen Truppenteil?
c) bei einem polnischen Truppenteil?
(Falls ja, bei welchem Truppenteil, von wann bis wann, welcher
Keine

Ausweis g. R. der Empfangsbescheinigung
1943
Amtskommissar

Gemäß Erlaß des R. Ministers des Innern v. 13.3.1941 in Gruppe 2 der Deutschen Volksliste, Zweigstelle Wollstein, aufgenommen. Sitzung der Prüfungskommission am 24.11.42 Reg. Prä.
Hat Ausweis Nr. 9254 der Zweigstelle Wollstein.

Gemäß Erlaß des Reichsministers des Innern v. 13.3.1941 in Gruppe 3 der Deutschen Volksliste, Zweigstelle Wollstein, aufgenommen. Sitzung der Prüfungskommission am 11.9.42
Hat Ausweis Nr. 10351 der Zweigstelle Wollstein.

A IIIa

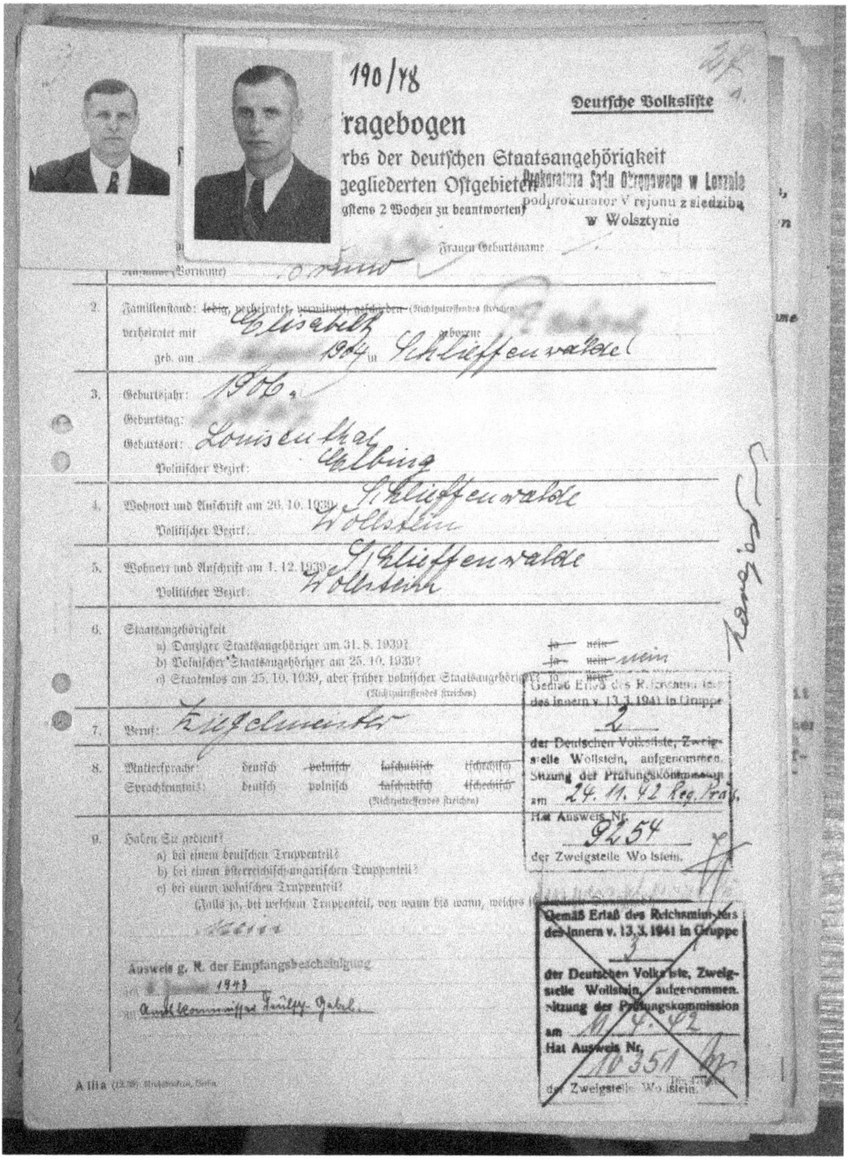

Figure 3.8. The new questionnaire that the Reich Interior Ministry, with its decree of November 25, 1939, had prescribed as mandatory for the acquisition of German national status, and which the DVL in the Wartheland then also had to adopt. This applicant was not initially accepted, because he was considered a Pole. When the DVL system in the Wartheland was expanded to five groups, he was entered into Section C and ultimately transferred into Group 3 when the Reich Interior Ministry introduced the DVL across the annexed eastern territories. The applicant's repeated protests finally resulted in his upgrading to Group 2. Although the "applicant was of Polish descent," according to the regional office, the upgrade was justified because, even before the invasion, he had already married an ethnic German and joined the German Union; furthermore, his employer—a German woman—had written a positive letter of recommendation for him.
Source: Polish State Archives in Poznań, under DVL Wollstein, 427.

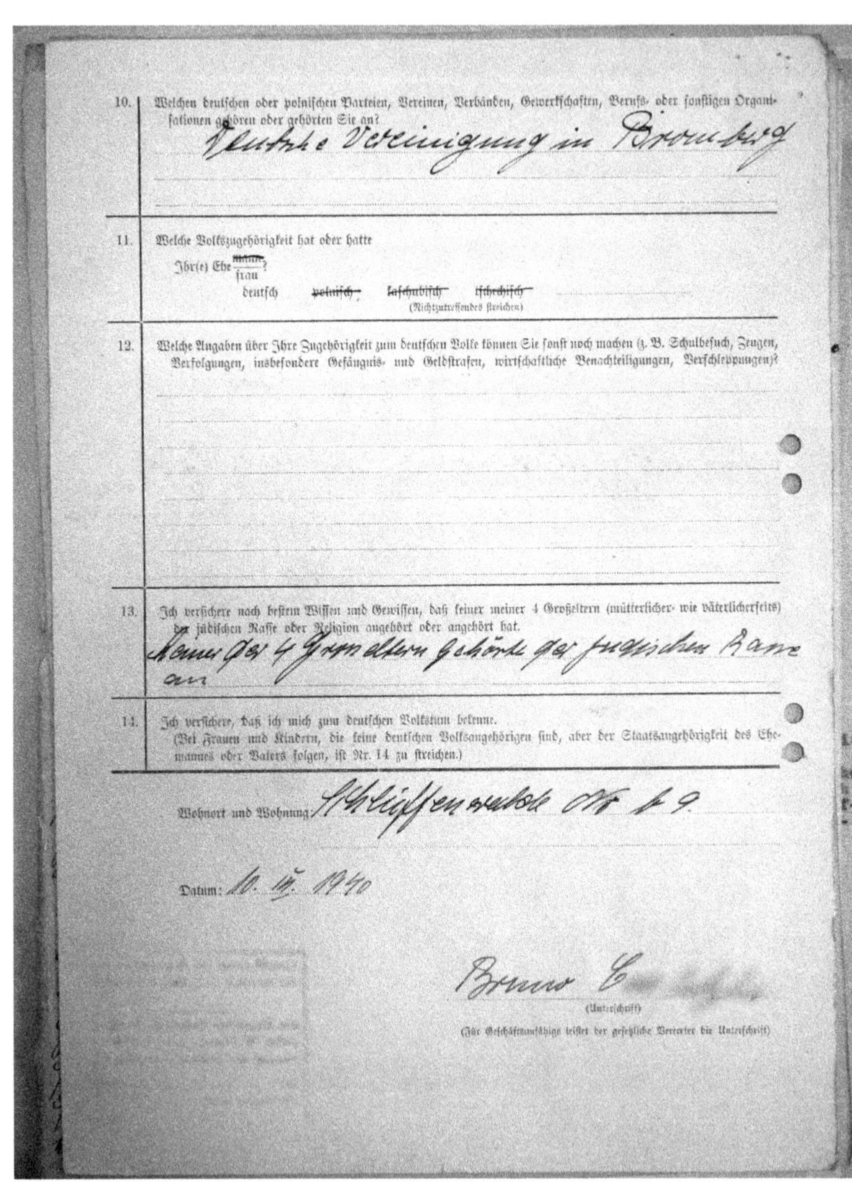

10. Welchen deutschen oder polnischen Parteien, Vereinen, Verbänden, Gewerkschaften, Berufs- oder sonstigen Organisationen gehören oder gehörten Sie an?

Deutsche Vereinigung in Bromberg

11. Welche Volkszugehörigkeit hat oder hatte Ihr(e) Ehe ~~mann~~/frau?

deutsch ~~polnisch~~ ~~kaschubisch~~ ~~tschechisch~~

(Nichtzutreffendes streichen)

12. Welche Angaben über Ihre Zugehörigkeit zum deutschen Volke können Sie sonst noch machen (z. B. Schulbesuch, Zeugen, Verfolgungen, insbesondere Gefängnis- und Geldstrafen, wirtschaftliche Benachteiligungen, Verschleppungen)?

13. Ich versichere nach bestem Wissen und Gewissen, daß keiner meiner 4 Großeltern (mütterlicher- wie väterlicherseits) der jüdischen Rasse oder Religion angehört oder angehört hat.

Keiner der 4 Grosseltern gehörte der jüdischen Rasse an

14. Ich versichere, daß ich mich zum deutschen Volkstum bekenne.
(Bei Frauen und Kindern, die keine deutschen Volksangehörigen sind, aber der Staatsangehörigkeit des Ehemannes oder Vaters folgen, ist Nr. 14 zu streichen.)

Wohnort und Wohnung: *Schließenwerbe Nr 19*

Datum: *10. 4. 1940*

Bruno C______

(Unterschrift)

(Für Geschäftsunfähige leistet der gesetzliche Vertreter die Unterschrift)

Figure 3.9. Reverse side of figure 3.8.

the (voluntary) professing of ethnonational membership and thus to the willingness to collaborate, at least passively.[249]

It was provisions like these that prompted Himmler to lodge a protest with the Reich Interior Ministry on January 13, 1940. After all, it could not be that the decision was made solely according to the "merely outward professing of Germandom (language, schooling, culture, etc.)," where in fact the "first criterion of German ethnonational membership must be the positive verification of racial membership."[250] Although the Reich Interior Ministry wanted to make membership in the German "Volksgemeinschaft" depend primarily on the readiness to collaborate as proven by the applicant's conduct, the SS argued for a racial assignment that was based on biometric characteristics and at least theoretically independent of conduct. Even if these irreconcilable viewpoints did not yet lead to open conflict during the winter of 1939–40, they nonetheless staked out the battlefield on which an increasingly acrimonious confrontation would take place in the coming years.

Notes

1. On the occupation policy seen in the Soviet-occupied part of Poland, see Häufele, "Deutsche und sowjetische Besatzungspolitik"; Häufele, "Zwangsumsiedlungen in Polen"; Musial, "Schlachtfeld"; Davies, *God's Playground*, 327–28, 331–35, and 343–65.

2. On this, more comprehensively, at Szefer, "Dywersyjno-sabotażowa działalność," 335; Jansen and Weckbecker, *Volksdeutscher Selbstschutz*, 26; Rossino, *Hitler Strikes Poland*, 77–82; Böhler, *Auftakt zum Vernichtungskrieg*, 54–146.

3. Rossino, *Hitler Strikes Poland*, 92.

4. Moser, "Nisko." See also Longerich, *Politik der Vernichtung*, 252; Rossino, *Hitler Strikes Poland*, 94.

5. Steur, *Theodor Dannecker*, 28–29.

6. (Signature illegible) memo on departmental head meeting of September 14, 1939, dated September 15, 1939, German Federal Archives [hereafter, BArch], R 58/825, 10–12.

7. Kárný, "Nisko," 69.

8. Although Goschen claims in his "Nisko" that the idea came from Eichmann, Moser, in his "Nisko," claims that it originated in a conversation between Eichmann and Stahlecker.

9. Eichmann's memo of October 6, 1939, quoted in Kárný, "Nisko," 74. See also Browning, "Nazi Resettlement Policy," 503.

10. Goshen, "Eichmann," 84; Wildt, *Generation des Unbedingten*, 469.

11. The cited figure of seventy to eighty thousand Jews would have encompassed three-quarters of the Jewish populace of the Kattowitz region, according to Steinbacher, *Musterstadt Auschwitz*, 113. See also the overview sent by Einsatzgruppe z.b.V. to Heydrich, November 8, 1939, Special Archive at the State Military Archives of Russia, Moscow [hereafter, SMR], 500–1/431, 178–79, which gives a figure of 57,010 Jews from towns of more than twenty thousand inhabitants.

12. On Eichmann's alleged route to Kattowitz, see Moser, "Nisko," and Goshen, "Eichmann," 89. The assertion was repeated in Longerich, *Politik der Vernichtung*, 256–57; Kárný, "Nisko," 75; and somewhat more reservedly in Wildt, *Generation des Unbedingten*, 471. Last quote is from Goshen, "Eichmann," 89. In addition, Longerich may have misinterpreted a memo reconstructed from two versions dated October 11 and 12, 1939, issued by Dr. Eugen Becker, special appointee for Jewish issues on the staff of Josef Bürckel, the Reich Commissioner for the Reunification of Austria with the German Reich. In the memo, Becker relayed a "strictly confidential message from the head of the Central Agency for Jewish Emigration," which stated that the "Führer has issued the order that, in starting the planned overall campaign, initially three hundred thousand Jews of limited means are to be relocated from the territory of the Greater German Reich to Poland." But the message makes no mention of a meeting between Becker and Eichmann (Botz, *Wohnungspolitik*, 186).

13. Ibid., 85; Longerich, *Politik der Vernichtung*, 256–57.

14. See the meeting minutes in Kárný, "Nisko," 77.

15. Safrian, *Eichmann*, 75.

16. See the meeting minutes in Kárný, "Nisko," 77. In contrast, see Gruner, "Von der Kollektivausweisung," 32.

17. Steur, *Theodor Dannecker*, 30; see also entry for October 7, 1939, at Halder, *Kriegstagebuch*, 1: 99.

18. Krausnick, "Hitler und die Morde," 66. On war crimes by this police unit, see Rossino, *Hitler Strikes Poland*, 103–5.

19. See entry for October 7, 1939, at Halder, *Kriegstagebuch*, 1: 99.

20. Safrian, *Eichmann*, 76.

21. Přibyl, "Schicksal," 297–342.

22. Telex from Reich Security Main Office to Security Police and SD in Mährisch Ostrau, October 19, 1939, quoted in Adler, *Der verwaltete Mensch*, 134. See also Goschen, "Eichmann," 92; Wildt, *Generation des Unbedingten*, 471.

23. Moser, "Nisko."

24. SS Head Assault Leader Rolf Günther's memo of October 21, 1939, quoted in Safrian, *Eichmann*, 79.

25. Besides Přibyl, "Schicksal," see also Nižňanský, "Aktion Nisko," 325–35. On the citizenship of the deportees, see also Nižňanský, "Aktion Nisko," as well as Přibyl, "Schicksal," 300.

26. Statistic from Moser, "Nisko." He is not the only one who assumes there was a second transport. See, for example, Goshen, "Eichmann," 89–91; Safrian, *Eichmann*, 78; Aly, *Endlösung*, 64; Longerich, *Politik der Vernichtung*, 258; Gottwaldt and Schulle, "Judendeportationen," 32.

27. Unsigned, undated transport lists for deportations leaving Vienna on October 20 and 26, Documentation Center of Austrian Resistance, Vienna, doc. 22142. See also unsigned, undated list in the Jewish Community of Vienna archival holdings [hereafter, IKG], Vienna holdings, A/Vie/IKG/III/Bev./Dep./1/4, which gives October 27 as the date of the second transport, with a few names featuring handwritten notes like "dep. again" and "in Vienna." Of course, since the Nisko campaign was not the last deportation action, but only the first one, such entries are not really conclusive.

28. Adler, *Verwalteter Mensch*, 135; Rosenkranz, *Verfolgung*, 217. Adler does briefly mention the second transport, but without citing a source.

29. Eichmann to Gestapo in Mährisch Ostrau, October 24, 1939, quoted in Goshen, "Eichmann," 92.

30. Moser, "Nisko."

31. The two compilers were Dr. Otto Suschny and Dr. Knut Weigel, who worked on the basis of materials submitted to the Jewish Historical Commission in Vienna under Tuviah Friedmann, which included Gestapo files, documents of the IKG, eyewitness accounts, and various other written sources. See Friedmann, *Tragödie.*

32. Undated report by Josef Löwenherz, Yad Vashem Archive, Jerusalem, O.2/595.

33. See Friedmann, *Tragödie,* 32; Aly, *Endlösung,* 64. Compare Browning, *Entfesselung,* 71, which cites Rosenkranz, *Verfolgung;* Steinbacher, *Musterstadt Auschwitz,* 114; and Gruner, "Von der Kollektivausweisung," 34. As evidence, Gruner points to a meeting of Vienna's municipal administration on the same day as the alleged second transport. But that transport is not mentioned in the minutes of this meeting either. Alderman Dr. Tavs mentions only that some three thousand Jews were then leaving the city every week "on the basis of voluntarily coming forward" (see undated minutes of first departmental meeting of the mayor with aldermen and departmental heads on October 26, 1939, signed "Schaufler," Austrian State Archives, Vienna, ZNsZ RK).

34. Kleinmann to Himmler, March 1, 1940, unpaged, BArch R 49/2791. Thanks to Peter Klein for this document.

35. The figure of 1,584 Jews is unanimously cited in, for example, Browning, *Entfesselung,* 70–71; Moser, "Nisko"; Goshen, "Eichmann," 89; Rosenkranz, *Verfolgung und Selbstbehauptung,* 217.

36. Moser, "Nisko."

37. Kleinmann to Himmler, March 1, 1940, unpaged. BArch R 49/2791. Thanks to Peter Klein for this document.

38. Thanks to Alfred Gottwaldt for these comparative figures.

39. Browning, "Nazi Resettlement Policy," 504.

40. For the Estonian and Latvian treaties, see the protocol on the resettlement of Estonia's German ethnonational group into the German Reich, October 15, 1939, reprinted in Loeber, *Diktierte Option,* 471–76; treaty on the resettlement of Latvian citizens of German ethnonationality into the German Reich, October 30, 1939, reprinted in ibid., 515–26. See also Browning, "Nazi Resettlement Policy," 504; Aly, *Endlösung,* 63–69; Łossowski, "Resettlement," 89–91.

41. Kleinmann to Himmler, March 1, 1940, unpaged, BArch R 49/2791. Thanks to Peter Klein for this document.

42. Cesarani, *Eichmann,* 77.

43. Alberti, *Verfolgung und Vernichtung,* 127. But see also Browning, *Entfesselung,* 65–74.

44. Nesládková, "Eine Episode," 352.

45. Browning, *Entfesselung,* 65.

46. On the situation of the local Jews, see Steinbacher, *Musterstadt Auschwitz,* 153–56.

47. See Wildt, *Generation des Unbedingten,* 462; Aly, *Endlösung.*

48. Unsigned, undated report of the RKFDV staff main office on the status of resettlements on June 1, 1944, BArch R 49/86, 46–55. Thanks to Götz Aly for providing a copy.

49. Groscurth, *Tagebücher,* 214. See also Schenk, *Hitlers Mann,* 177.

50. Heydrich to Ribbentrop, October 9, 1939, reprinted in Loeber, *Diktierte Option,* 127.

51. Kalisch, "Full Use," 57; Peiser, *Danzig und Gdingen*, 11–12; Cleef, "Danzig and Gdynia," 105.

52. For Gdynia's competition with Danzig, see Peiser, *Danzig und Gdingen*, 17. For its symbolic role, see Madajczyk, *Okkupationspolitik Nazideutschlands*, 243.

53. Himmler to Lorenz, Heydrich, Forster, Greiser, et al., October 11, 1939, Bavarian State Archives, Nuremberg [hereafter, Nuremberg], NO 4613 (emphasis in original).

54. See, for example, the survey of the populace in Dirschau the Landrat of Dirschau sent to the county's mayors and Amtskommissars, October 14, 1939, Institute of National Remembrance, Archive of the Main Commission for the Investigation of Crimes against the Polish Nation, Warsaw [hereafter, AGK], NTN/200, 111–13.

55. See first decree of the Regierungspräsident of Danzig, Fritz Hermann, November 7, 1933, BArch R 138-I/142, 47–49; also notes of Wilhelm Huth, October 14, 1939, Polish State Archives in Gdańsk [hereafter, APG], 279/1639, 9–11.

56. Jastrzębski, "Nazi Deportations," 5.

57. Notes of Wilhelm Huth, October 14, 1939, APG 279/1639, 9–11.

58. Ibid. As other examples will also demonstrate, this contradicts Jażdżewski's claim that Forster "did not consider the Kashubians a separate national group" (Jażdżewski, "Kaschuben," 82).

59. Notes of Wilhelm Huth, October 14, 1939, APG 279/1639, 9–11.

60. Ibid.

61. Memo from Körnich, October 14, 1939, APG 279/1639, 5.

62. Notes of meeting at city commissioner of Gotenhafen, October 20, 1939, APG 279/1639, 15–19.

63. Madajczyk, *Okkupationspolitik Nazideutschlands*, 407; also unpaged attachment to Kleinmann's message to Himmler, March 1, 1940, BArch R 49/2791.

64. These figures are supported by testimony on January 3, 1946, from the deputy mayor, Gerhard Cartellieri, who reckoned that some thirty-five thousand residents had been deported; see Federal Commissioner for the Records of the State Security Service of the former German Democratic Republic [hereafter, BStU] MfS-HA IX/11 1402, 2–4. Another estimate—probably inflated—of around fifty thousand persons departing or expelled from the city by October 26 is given in Jastrzębski and Sziling, *Okupacja hitlerowska*, 144–46.

65. See Umbreit, *Deutsche Militärverwaltungen*, 218; also status report of the armaments inspectorate under the chief commander of the east, October 28, 1939, Nuremberg EC-302-2.

66. Streckenbach to Hildebrandt, October 26, 1939, State Archives in Bydgoszcz, Poland [hereafter, APB], 9/2, 2.

67. For Wehrmacht complaints, see, for example, the status report of the armaments inspectorate under the chief commander of the east, October 28, 1939, Nuremberg EC-302-2.

68. Umbreit, *Deutsche Militärverwaltungen*, 218. See also Koehl, *RKFDV*, 62–63; Łuczak, "Ansiedlung," 196; Madajczyk, *Okkupationspolitik Nazideutschlands*, 480. As justification, Forster resorted to a claim that was not entirely unfounded, namely that the Baltic Germans tended to be older than the other settler groups. On the demographic composition of the settlers, see the report from 1st Lt. Dr. Rüdiger, head of a commission at the German Foreign Institute (Deutsches Ausland-Institut), April 21, 1940, BStU MfS-HA IX/11/143, 69, 4–18.

69. See Sandberger to Gestapo Command Office in Stettin, November 2, 1939, BArch R 69/854; Himmler's directive 4/II, November 3, 1939, AGK 68/5, 3. Thanks to Götz Aly for both

documents. As a stopgap measure, the settlers had to be given provisional accommodations at first, some of them even outside the province, in Mecklenburg and Pomerania.

70. Levine, "Local Authority," 349.

71. Jansen and Weckbecker, *Volksdeutscher Selbstschutz*, 179. The same sides faced off in two later conflicts, both of which Forster won again when he accomplished the disbanding of the Volksdeutscher Selbstschutz and halted the killings of the institutionalized in Danzig-West Prussia.

72. Sandberger to the EWZ, October 26, 1939, BArch R 69/490, 17–19.

73. Himmler's first directive as RKFDV, undated (probably signed on October 17, 1939), Nuremberg NO 3078.

74. Unpaged minutes by Ehlich, November 1, 1939, BArch R 69/493. See also Sandberger to EWZ, November 1, 1939, BArch R 69/426, unpaged. Thanks to Götz Aly for both documents.

75. Stuhlpfarrer, *Umsiedlung Südtirol*, 1: 251.

76. Heinemann, *Rasse, Siedlung, deutsches Blut*, 191. See also Leniger, *Nationalsozialistische Volkstumsarbeit*, 61–62.

77. Pancke to Heydrich, March 31, 1939, BArch NS 2/141, 61–63; Gottberg's memo of May 11, 1939, in Heinemann, *Rasse, Siedlung, deutsches Blut*, 129–30; see also Koehl, *RKFDV*, 43.

78. Gottberg's appointment by the Reich protector, Konstantin von Neurath, to act as provisional head of the Prague Land Office, occurred on May 17, 1939 (Heinemann, *Rasse, Siedlung, deutsches Blut*, 131–32).

79. Activity report of RuS-Beratung B, January 1, 1940, quoted in R.-D. Müller, *Hitlers Ostkrieg*, 86. See also Heinemann, *Rasse, Siedlung, deutsches Blut*, 201–8; Buchheim, *Die SS*, 224.

80. Pancke to Himmler, on the draft for implementing the Führer's decree on the strengthening of Germandom, October 23, 1939, BArch NS 2/60, 122. Unfortunately, the draft itself is not in the archives.

81. Pancke to Himmler, November 20, 1939, BArch NS 2/60, 51–59.

82. Heinemann, *Rasse, Siedlung, deutsches Blut*, 194–95 and 213.

83. R.-D. Müller, *Hitlers Ostkrieg*, 88.

84. Himmler to Pancke, November 28, 1939, BArch NS 2/60, 65.

85. Heinemann, *Rasse, Siedlung, deutsches Blut*, 205.

86. Longerich, *Heinrich Himmler*, 434–37.

87. Pancke's memo on a meeting at Darré's, May 17, 1939, reprinted in Müller, *Hitlers Ostkrieg*, 117–18. On criticism from the local chief of civil administration, the Reich Protector Konstantin von Neurath, see also Bryant, *Prague in Black*, 110.

88. Klein, "Curt von Gottberg," 97.

89. Darré to Himmler on Curt von Gottberg file, August 18, 1939, German Federal Archives, [hereafter, BArch—the BDC was amalgamated into the Bundesarchiv in Lichterfelde].

90. First quote is from the statement written by Pancke in the Curt von Gottberg file that Gottberg had to sign before the head of the Race Office, SS Senior Leader Otto Hofmann, November 13, 1939, BArch BDC. Second quote is from Himmler to Pancke, after a disciplinary hearing against Gottberg in which he was fully rehabilitated, undated, in the Curt von Gottberg file, BArch BDC.

91. Himmler to Pancke, December 12, 1939, BArch NS 2/60, 49–50.

92. Appointment of Holzschuher by Himmler, November 14, 1939, BArch NS 2/60, 83. See also Wilhelm von Holzschuher file, BArch BDC. Heinemann is thus mistaken when she assumes that the Land Offices remained under RuSHA until April 1940 (Heinemann, *Rasse, Siedlung, deutsches Blut*, 686). Similarly also Buchheim, *Die SS*, 223–24.

93. Holzschuher's note about briefing by Himmler, December 1, 1939, BArch NS 2/60, 60–63.

94. Himmler to Pancke, December 12, 1939, BArch NS 2/60, 49–50.

95. Ibid.

96. Himmler to Holzschuher, May 29, 1940, Wilhelm von Holzschuher file, Barch BDC.

97. Heinemann, *Rasse, Siedlung, deutsches Blut*, 42 and 10.

98. EWZ directive no. 12, signed "Sandberger," October 19, 1939, BArch R 69/228, 24.

99. Wildt, *Generation des Unbedingten*, 381–82; Roth, "Generalplan Ost—Gesamtplan Ost," 34. On the development of this unit until its merger into Departmental Group III B (Amtsgruppe III B), see Ehlich to Heydrich, February 12, 1940, SMR 500–4/72, 26–29.

100. EWZ directive no. 22, signed "p.p. Assault Unit Leader Roeder," November 1, 1939.

101. Ehlich to Heydrich, February 2, 1940, BA-DH, HA IX/11/ZR 890. Thanks to Götz Aly for this document.

102. Minutes of meeting with HSSPFs of occupied Poland and East Prussia in Kraków on November 8, 1939, reprinted in Łuczak, *Wysiedlenia ludności polskiej*, 3–5.

103. Himmler's Directive 1/II, October 30, 1939, reprinted in Łuczak, *Wysiedlenia ludności polskiej*, 1–2.

104. Minutes of meeting with HSSPFs of occupied Poland and East Prussia in Kraków on November 8, 1939, reprinted in Łuczak, *Wysiedlenia ludności polskiej*, 3–5.

105. The other deportation sites were Gotenhafen and Mewe (today Gdynia and Gniew).

106. Memo from Dr. Polthus, BArch R 75/3b, 9–10.

107. The most detailed on this topic is Sulik, "Bedeutung der Großindustrie," which also describes Upper Silesia's increasing importance after the German invasion of the Soviet Union, as well as its integration into an industrial network with the Donbass in the Soviet Union. See also Röhr, "Zur Rolle der Schwerindustrie."

108. The counties were Krenau, Olkusch, and Wadowitz (today Chrzanów, Olkusz, and Wadowice), as well as parts of the counties of Warthenau, Blachownia, and Saybusch (today Zawiercie, Blachownia, and Żywiec; Broszat, *Nationalsozialistische Polenpolitik*, 40; Steinbacher, *Musterstadt Auschwitz*, 112).

109. Wagner to Lammers, February 2, 1940, Nuremberg NG 3750 (emphasis in original). See also Broszat, *Nationalsozialistische Polenpolitik*, 40; Steinbacher, *Musterstadt Auschwitz*, 112–13. During the year, the involved parties did eventually agree in principal on a return to the old border, but the return did not ultimately happen, because Hitler and Göring wanted to settle the question as part of a wider European peace treaty (memo by Lammers, September 6, 1940, Nuremberg NG 3750). Göring made it clear, however, that any border demarcation had to be oriented above all to the economic needs of the region's heavy industry. See also Kaczmarek, "Deutsche wirtschaftliche Penetration," 259.

110. Steinbacher, *Musterstadt Auschwitz*, 110. The police border was later repeatedly adjusted and was upheld only as a formality after August 1, 1941, when its staffing was eliminated (Reichsführer of the SS, signed "p.p. von Kamptz," to the HSSPFs and Regierungspräsidents, July 27, 1941, State Archives in Katowice [hereafter, APK], 117/32, 3). It

was finally abolished on May 12, 1942 (Heydrich to the state governments outside Prussia and the Regierungspräsidents inside Prussia, May 12, 1942, APK 117/32, 50).

111. Wagner to Darré, December 9, 1939, quoted in Steinbacher, *Musterstadt Auschwitz*, 115.

112. Reich Interior Ministry personnel file for Walter Springorum, SMR 720–5/9624, 105.

113. Undated minutes of a meeting chaired by Springorum on November 21, 1939, reprinted in Długoborski, *Polozenie ludności*, 139–40.

114. Ibid.

115. On this, see, for example, Aly and Heim, *Vordenker der Vernichtung*; Esch, *Gesunde Verhältnisse*, 79–102 and 128–65.

116. Chaired by Schulenberg, its members included Reich Defense Departmental Head and Oberpräsident's Appointee for Resettlements Wolf von Wrangel; the head of the provincial employment office; the Silesian Rural Development Company; the HSSPF of Breslau and the head of his RKFDV office; the Regierungspräsidents of Kattowitz and Oppeln; several Landrats; the head of the provincial farmers' association; representatives of the regional agronomists; and the head of the provincial cultural office. See also Steinbacher, *Musterstadt Auschwitz*, 115.

117. Schulenburg to the Regierungspräsidents of Oppeln and Kattowitz, December 7, 1939, APK 117/826, 195–96, reprinted in Długoborski, *Polozenie ludności*, 143–44.

118. Each committee met under the chairmanship of the Landrat and included the Kreisleiter, the head of the county farmers' association, the county agronomists as representatives of the Silesian Rural Development Company, and one delegate each from the settlement authority and the Regierungspräsident. On this, see also (unsigned) Dept. I at the Oberpräsident's offices to the Regierungspräsidents of Kattowitz and Oppeln and the Silesian Rural Development Company, November 21, 1939, APK 117/826, 63–64. The involvement of the Silesian Rural Development Company is not so surprising, for it was the settlement company responsible here and had, furthermore, already begun in 1939 with the systematic purchasing and settling of land in the Hlučín region ([signature illegible], Reich Finance Ministry to the Reich Ministry for Food and Agriculture, June 24, 1939, BArch R 2/19014, unpaged). The Hlučín region had been assigned to Czechoslovakia after World War I and then occupied by Germany after the Munich Agreement. It was initially annexed to the Reichsgau of the Sudetenland and then in April 1939 to the Province of Silesia.

119. Schulenberg to Regierungspräsidents of Oppeln and Kattowitz, December 7, 1939, APK 117/826, 195–96, reprinted in Długoborski, *Polozenie ludności*, 143–44.

120. (Probably signed "Wrangel"), memo from Dept. I at Oberpräsident's offices, November 30, 1939, APK 117/826, 82–83. On the sorting of the local populace, see also the report of the Silesian Rural Development Company on activities in eastern Upper Silesia, prepared for the board meeting on February 1, 1940, dated January 12, 1940, BArch R 2/19014, unpaged.

121. Unsigned letter from Dept. I at Oberpräsident's offices to the Regierungspräsidents of Kattowitz and Oppeln and the Silesian Rural Development Company, November 21, 1939, APK 117/826, 63–64.

122. Signed "Bittner," Cultural Office of Kattowitz, to the Oberpräsident's offices in Breslau, December 8, 1939, reprinted in Długoborski, *Polozenie ludności*, 145–47.

123. See the unsigned minutes of a meeting at Bach-Zelewski's on November 26, 1939, dated November 27, 1939, Nuremberg NO 5055, reprinted in Długoborski, *Polozenie ludności*, 138–39.

124. Heinemann, *Rasse, Siedlung, deutsches Blut*, 205.

125. Burleigh, *Germany Turns Eastwards*, 159–60. In the beginning, even Himmler was not averse to such ideas. On Himmler's tour of the Beskids in the winter of 1939, the participant Hanns Johst, president of the Reich Literature Chamber, believed he had found evidence that the Gorals were of Germanic descent and rejoiced in the swastika carvings on the wooden houses as well as the allegedly endemic local hatred of Poles and Jews (Burleigh, *Third Reich*, 443–44).

126. Unsigned minutes of a meeting at Bach-Zelewski's on November 26, 1939, dated November 27, 1939, Nuremberg NO 5055, reprinted in Długoborski, *Polozenie ludności*, 138–39.

127. Ibid.

128. Minutes of Friedrich Borkenhagen, director of the Silesian Rural Development Company, of a meeting at the office of Helmuth Körner, head of the Department for Food and Agriculture in the General Government, on November 29, 1939, dated November 30, 1939, APK 117/826, 173–75.

129. Heydrich to the HSSPFs and the IdS officeholders of Breslau, Posen, Danzig, and Königsberg, and the HSSPF and BdS of Kraków, November 28, 1939, reprinted in Datner, Gumkowski, and Leszczyński, "Wysiedlanie ludności," 15–17. See also Madajczyk, *Okkupationspolitik Nazideutschlands*, 406–7.

130. From "p.p. SS Senior Group Leader Kurt Daluege, Reichsführer of the SS" to the administration heads, Regierungspräsidents, HSSPFs, and commanders of the order police (Befehlshaber der Ordnungspolizei, BdS) of Silesia, East Prussia, and the Wartheland, on the census in the formerly Polish territories now rejoining or newly joining the Reich, November 25, 1939, APK 117/826, 90–95.

131. Heydrich to the HSSPFs and the IdS officeholders of Breslau, Posen, Danzig, and Königsberg, and the HSSPF and BdS of Kraków, November 28, 1939, reprinted in Datner, Gumkowski, and Leszczyński, "Wysiedlanie ludności," 15–17.

132. Ibid.

133. Roth, "Generalplan Ost und der Mord," 55. On the dating, see Aly, *Endlösung*, 71, and Roth, "Generalplan Ost und der Mord," 57. Although Aly dates the long-range plan to the end of November, Roth believes it already existed at the time of Heydrich's telex. The latter interpretation cannot be drawn unambiguously from the telex, however, since Heydrich simply writes that it is being "planned from here," so that its completion could just as likely have happened a few days later. Whereas Aly attributes the long-range plan somewhat unspecifically to "Amt III" (Department III of the Reich Security Main Office; Aly, *Endlösung*, 70–71), Roth writes somewhat more precisely of a group under Ehlich. But it was more likely that Ehlich alone was responsible for this, just as he was likely alone shortly thereafter, in January 1940, in writing his proposal to establish resettlement centers; see Ehlich's memo to Heydrich on the establishment of resettlement central offices, February 2, 1940, BA-DH, ZR 890/A.2. Thanks to Götz Aly for this document.

134. Unsigned, undated long-range plan for resettlement in the eastern provinces, BArch R 69/1146, 1–13.

135. Ibid.

136. Ibid.

137. Entry for September 28, 1939, in Kotze, *Heeresadjutant*, 63.

138. Greiser to Landrats in the Wartheland, on guidelines for the administration structure in the counties and cities of the Province of Posen, confidential, September 29, 1939, AGK NTN/11, 1–2.

139. Himmler to Lorenz, Heydrich, Forster, Greiser, et al., October 11, 1939, Nuremberg NO 4613.

140. Müller to head of Einsatzgruppe VI, SS Senior Leader Erich Naumann, October 9, 1939, AGK 687/29, 1.

141. Sandberger to EWZ in Gotenhafen, October 26, 1939, BArch R 69/490, 17–19.

142. Inspector of the Security Police SS Regiment Leader Ernst Damzog to Greiser's deputy as Reichsstatthalter and Regierungspräsident of Danzig, August Jäger, October 26, 1939, BArch R 75/3b, 1.

143. Minutes of a meeting at city commissioner of Posen, November 1, 1939, AGK 687/29, 122–23.

144. (Signature illegible), memo from the SD in Posen, November 8, 1939, AGK 68/188, 3–10. See also Marczewski, "Nazi Nationality Policy," 35. On the conditions in Glowno, see Łuczak, *Pod niemieckim jarzmem*, 55.

145. On Koppe and the circumstances of his appointment and installation, see Klein, *Ghettoverwaltung Litzmannstadt*, 134–37.

146. Confidential order from Koppe, November 11, 1939, AGK 69/5, 8. On December 4, 1939, Koppe's position was strengthened by Greiser, who put him in charge of deportations on the state and party levels as well, order reprinted in Łuczak, *Wysiedlenia ludności polskiej*, 12–13.

147. On the personnel, see list (signed "SS Chief Squad Leader Blenk") of the persons engaged in the evacuation staff, January 12, 1940, AGK 68/83, 2–3. Thanks to Götz Aly for this document.

148. Rapp's plan, November 12, 1939, AGK 68/95, 4–7. See also Koppe's instructions to Reichsstatthalters, Regierungspräsidents, Mayors, Landrats, Sicherheitspolizei, Ordnungspolizei, etc., confidential, November 12, 1939, AGK 68/99, 1–5.

149. Frick to the civil administrations in the annexed territories, December 8, 1939, Polish State Archives in Poznań [hereafter, APP] 406/3, 15–17, reprinted in Pospieszalski, *Hitlerowskie "prawo" okupacyjne*, 179–80.

150. Order from Koppe, confidential, November 12, 1939, AGK 68/99, 1–5.

151. Ibid.

152. Rapp's report on experiences from campaigns conducted thus far and plans for future transports, December 18, 1939, SMR 500–1/88, 185–96, reprinted in Łuczak, *Położenie ludności polskiej*, 19–27.

153. Koppe's announcement in the *Ostdeutscher Beobachter*, November 15, 1939, AGK 68/4, 1. Since this was apparently not enough in Koppe's eyes, he later forbade the use of trains as well (Koppe to the Regierungspräsidents, January 16, 1940, AGK 68/4, 6).

154. As an example, see the overview for the county of Krotoschin (today Krotoszyn), undated (probably mid-November, 1939), AGK 68/237, 9–10.

155. Circular from Rapp, confidential, November 16, 1939, reprinted in Łuczak, *Położenie ludności polskiej*, 108–9.

156. Ibid.

157. On this, see Pohl, "Reichsgaue Danzig-Westpreußen und Wartheland," 402, which highlights the "virtually unparalleled symbiosis of the administration with the SS apparatus."

158. Rapp to municipal administration of Posen, November 16, 1939, AGK 68/144, 1–2.

159. Head of provincial high court to senior public prosecutors and correctional facilities, November 21, 1939, AGK 62/293, 4–6.

160. Rutherford, "Race, Space, and the 'Polish Question,'" 170–72.

161. Unsigned minutes of a meeting on November 23, 1939, dated November 25, 1939, AGK 68/107, 17–35.

162. Unsigned memo, Reichsstatthalter's offices, Department for Economy and Labor, to the Regierungspräsidents, November 18, 1939, AGK 62/334, 1–2; also Riediger to Landrats, November 27, 1939, reprinted in Łuczak, *Położenie ludności polskiej*, 9–10.

163. SS Senior Assault Unit Leader Hermann Krumey's memo of November 22, 1939, reprinted in Rutherford, "Race, Space, and the 'Polish Question,'" 139. Although Rutherford does not explicitly say so, the 409 transport trains he cites are probably a reference to the subsequently cited accounting by twenty-nine Landrats covering 402,000 persons. See, for example, Rapp's concluding report, December 18, 1939, SMR 500–1/88, 185–96, reprinted in Datner, Gumkowski, and Leszczyński, "Wysiedlanie ludności," 22–31; Łuczak, *Położenie ludności polskiej*, 19–27; and the overview attached to Rapp's report, divided by county, at SMR 500–1/88, 197–98.

164. Heydrich to the HSSPF and IdS of Posen, as well as the HSSPF and BdS of Kraków, November 28, 1939, reprinted in Datner, Gumkowski, and Leszczyński, "Wysiedlanie ludności," 18.

165. Number of trains is at Kleinmann to Himmler, March 1, 1940 (unpaged), BArch R 49/2791. Departure times and places at unsigned, undated (probably late December 1939 or early January 1940) summary of deportation transports under the first short-range plan, AGK 68/208, 20–23. Total deportee number is at Rapp, progress report on the resettlement of Poles and Jews from the Wartheland, January 26, 1940, AGK NTN/13, 39–50, reprinted in Datner, Gumkowski, and Leszczyński, "Wysiedlanie ludności," 46–57; according to Alberti, *Verfolgung und Vernichtung*, 137, the number was supplemented by some additional thirty thousand people who fell victim to locally organized expulsions. See also the unsigned handwritten list with the names, addresses, and occupations of the people deported from Posen on December 14, APP 834/10, 2.

166. On the lack of figures, see Marczewski, *Hitlerowska koncepcja*, 259.

167. Browning, "From Ethnic Cleansing," 9. That would be smaller than the number of deportees cited by Alberti for the city of Kalisch alone, namely sixteen thousand persons from December 2 to 15, 1939 (Alberti, "Exerzierplatz," 134–35). Alberti relies principally on Golczewski, "Polen," 428–29, who took his numbers primarily from Polish literature. In fact, Kleinmann's accounting of those deported from Kalisch during the first short-range plan shows "only" eight thousand persons in total, without any further details about whether they were Jews or Christians (Kleinmann to Himmler, March 1, 1940, BArch R 49/2791, unpaged). This figure is corroborated by an unsigned, undated county-by-county overview for the deportations up to and including the third short-range plan, giving a figure of 8,350 persons for Kalisch during the first short-range plan (AGK 62/76, 5). An argument similar to Alberti's had already been presented in Łuczak, *Pod niemieckim jarzmem*, 56. On the other hand, the latest study on the subject supports Browning's premise (Rutherford, "Race, Space, and the 'Polish Question,'" 156–57).

168. Unsigned (probably Rapp) progress report on resettlement of Poles and Jews from the Wartheland, January 26, 1940, AGK 68/208, 1–12.

169. Unsigned, undated concluding report on evacuations for the settling of Bessarabian Germans in the Wartheland (third short-range plan) from January 21, 1941, to January 20, 1942, AGK NTN/13, 99–106, reprinted in *Biuletyn Głównej Komisji* 21:106–10.

170. Seidl's memo about meeting with Eichmann, SS Chief Assault Leader Rolf Günther, and Dr. Erich Rajakowitsch in Berlin on January 22 and 23, 1940, dated January 25, 1940, AGK 68/107, 44, reprinted in Datner, Gumkowski, and Leszczyński, "Wysiedlanie ludności," 44–45. Seidl was a former staff member of the Central Agency for Jewish Emigration in Vienna and was transferred in mid-January 1940 to Rapp's agency.

171. Ibid.

172. Richter's undated report on his meetings in Łodsch on November 30, 1939, AGK 68/218, 13–14.

173. Ibid.

174. Richter's report on the deportations conducted in Lodsch from December 12 to 16, 1939, dated December 16, 1939, AGK 68/218, 27–35.

175. Ibid.

176. Alberti, *Verfolgung und Vernichtung*, 135.

177. Kleinmann to Himmler, March 1, 1940, BArch R 49/2791, unpaged.

178. Browning, "From 'Ethnic Cleansing,'" 9–10.

179. Rapp to Koppe, Damzog, etc., December 7, 1939, AGK 68/74, 1–2. After the first deportation wave was conducted, the city's card catalog office was permanently transferred to the SD (municipal administration to Rapp, December 19, 1939, AGK 68/100, 1).

180. Rapp progress report on the resettlement of Poles and Jews from the Wartheland, January 26, 194, NTN/13, 39–50,0, reprinted in Datner, Gumkowski, and Leszczyński, "Wysiedlanie ludności," 46–57.

181. Ibid.

182. Strickner's report on the formation and development of the DVL, undated (probably November 1942), reprinted in Pospieszalski, *Niemiecka lista*, 19–130, here 53.

183. Rapp progress report on the resettlement of Poles and Jews from the Wartheland, January 26, 1940, NTN/13, 39–50, reprinted in Datner, Gumkowski, and Leszczyński, "Wysiedlanie ludności," 46–57.

184. SS Chief Squad Leader Blenk to Rapp, January 20, 1940, AGK, 68/7, 10–13. Blenk was an employee of Rapp and head of the central card catalog. Thanks to Götz Aly for this document. Such lists can be found at APP 834/10, 122–313.

185. Rapp progress report on the resettlement of Poles and Jews from the Wartheland, January 26, 1940, NTN/13, 39–50, reprinted in Datner, Gumkowski, and Leszczyński, "Wysiedlanie ludności," 46–57.

186. Coulon to Rapp, December 4, 1939, AGK 68/159, 5.

187. Rapp to Koppe, Damzog, and city commissioner of Posen, December 7, 1939, AGK 68/74, 1–2.

188. Strickner's undated report (probably November 1942) on the formation and development of the DVL, reprinted in Pospieszalski, *Niemiecka lista*, 19–130, here 87. More comprehensively, see also Jürgen Arndt's memo on the definition of "Deutschstämmigkeit" in contrast to "deutsches Blut," "artverwandtes Blut," "deutschblütig," "stammesgleich," and "volksdeutsch," August 26, 1942, BArch R 186/35, unpaged.

189. (Signed "p.p. Mattern"), progress report from Landrat of Schrimm, March 22, 1940, reprinted in Łuczak, *Położenie ludności polskiej*, 121–22.

190. Unsigned (probably Eichmann), Department IV of Reich Security Main Office to IdS of Posen, December 29, 1939, AGK 68/159, 6–7.

191. Rapp progress report on the resettlement of Poles and Jews from the Wartheland, January 26, 1940, NTN/13, 39–50, reprinted in Datner, Gumkowski, and Leszczyński, "Wysiedlanie ludności," 46–57.

192. SS Assault Unit Leader Schmidt's consultation with chief of Warsaw police regiment Colonel Karl Brenner and SS Regiment Leader Josef Meisinger on January 8, 1940, dated January 10, 1940, AGK 68/253, 1–2; the latter two denied having filed complaints about the deportation of "Deutschstämmige."

193. Rapp's first draft for Koppe's order of December 12, 1939, dated December 10, 1939, AGK 68/95, 8–14; or, for example, Coulon's draft of a report to Reich Interior Ministry, February 9, 1940, AGK 62/297, 83–90.

194. Marczewski, "Nazi Nationality Policy," 33.

195. Wagner to the Reich Interior Ministry, February 2, 1940, with request to restore the old border, cited in Steinbacher, *Musterstadt Auschwitz*, 111–13. See also Burleigh, *Germany Turns Eastwards*, 143, Drozdowski, *Górny Śląsk*, 73 and Ehrlich, "Between Germany and Poland," 39.

196. In fact, during a meeting at Stuckart's on February 24, 1940, the attendees had already agreed to restore the old border. Göring, who had not been present, allegedly had no objections to the restoration, but only as long as the industrial zone was not torn apart (Stuckart to Himmler, Hess, and Göring, February 8, 1949, Nuremberg NG 3750; also, the unsigned letter, Oberpräsident's offices in Breslau to the Reich Interior Ministry, March 2, 1940, BArch R 43 II/647b, 38–40).

197. See his personnel files from the Reich Interior Ministry at SMR 720–5/6930 and SMR 720–5/6931. On the start of the registration effort, see Nethe to Amtskommissars and mayors, October 6, 1939, APB 9/2, 1.

198. Landrat of Dirschau to the county's mayors and Amtskommissars, October 14, 1939, AGK NTN/200, 111–13 (emphasis in original).

199. Ibid.

200. See, for example, AGK NTN/11, 1–2, Greiser to Landrats in the Wartheland, on guidelines for the administrative structure in the counties and cities of the Province of Posen, confidential, September 29, 1939.

201. Distribution of responsibilities at the Reichsstatthalter's offices in the Wartheland, December 15, 1939, APP 406/82, 1–53; undated (probably late 1939) distribution of responsibilities at the Gauleiter's offices in the Wartheland, APP 406/2, 50–52.

202. OPG (Oberstes Parteigericht) and PK (Parteikorrespondenz) files for Karl Albert Coulon, BArch BDC.

203. Coulon's report on the course and completion of the DVL process in the Reichsgau of the Wartheland, February 5, 1941, APP 406/1109, 320–32.

204. There is certainly no evidence that—as Richard J. Evans claims—"the SS leadership in the Wartheland persuaded Regional Leader [i.e., Gauleiter] Greiser to set up a German Ethnic List [i.e., DVL]" (Evans, *Third Reich*, 31). Instead, the reverse seems to be the case, with the initiative coming from Greiser. Similarly erroneous at Burleigh, *Third Reich*, 449–50.

205. Strickner's undated (probably November 1942) report on the formation and development of the DVL, reprinted in Pospieszalski, *Niemiecka lista*, 38. Strickner's statements are to be treated with caution, however, for they often ascribe more weight to his role and his agency than they deserve.

206. Ibid.

207. Sandberger to EWZ, October 26, 1939, BArch R 69/490, 17–19.

208. Greiser's decree of October 28, 1939, APP 406/1105, 1.

209. Coulon to DVL branch offices, November 15, 1939, APP 406/1113, 390–91. On April 4, 1940, Greiser instructed Coulon that if the offices of the Landrat and Kreisleiter were not held by the same person, then the latter was to be granted veto rights (Greiser to Coulon, April 4, 1940, APP 406/1108, 108–9).

210. Jäger's first implementing provisions for the DVL, October 28, 1939, APP 406/1105, 5–7.

211. Coulon's report on the course and completion of the DVL process in the Reichsgau of the Wartheland, February 5, 1941, APP 406/1109, 320–32. On the establishment of the DVL in the governmental regions, see messages from Coulon to Dr. Hans Burckhardt, the Regierungspräsident of Hohensalza, on November 15, 1939, APP 406/1113, 159, and also on November 27, 1939, APP 406/1113, 387. Presumably the same was also communicated to the Regierungspräsidents of Posen and Kalisch.

212. On the branch office's placement under Strickner, see unsigned memo from the ethnonationality unit (*Volkstumsreferat*) at the Reichsstatthalter's offices in Posen, July 25, 1940, APP 406/1109, 215–16. Quote is from Coulon to DVL regional office in Posen, July 1, 1940, APP 406/1113, 72.

213. Coulon's announcement on implementation of the order from the Reichsstatthalter of Posen on the establishment of a DVL, November 3, 1939, APP 406/1105, 4.

214. See also early draft from December 6, 1939, at APP 406/1109, 247–48; furthermore, Strickner's undated (probably November 1942) report on the formation and development of the DVL, reprinted in Pospieszalski, *Niemiecka lista*, 47–48. This focus on the schooling of the children was certainly not limited to the German occupiers in Poland. The occupation administration in the Czech territory proceeded similarly (Zahra, *Kidnapped Souls*, 187–89).

215. Strickner's directive for the city of Posen, November 29, 1939, AGK 68/159, 1–4.

216. See Gosewinkel, *Einbürgern und Ausschließen*, 191–93; Nathans, *Politics of Citizenship*, 142–43; Trevisiol, *Einbürgerungspraxis*, 135–37 and 163–65.

217. Reich Citizen Law of September 15, 1935, published in *Reichsgesetzblatt Teil I* (1935), 1146.

218. Strickner's undated (probably November 1942) report on the formation and development of the DVL, reprinted in Pospieszalski, *Niemiecka lista*, 56.

219. Riediger to Landrats and mayors, December 5, 1939, APP 406/1113, 384.

220. See law on reintegrating the Free City of Danzig into the German Reich, reprinted in Pospieszalski, *Hitlerowskie "prawo" okupacyjne*, 35–36. Quote is from Hitler's decree on the subdivision and administration of the eastern territories, October 8, 1939, reprinted in Pospieszalski, *Hitlerowskie "prawo" okupacyjne*, 84–88. The expression "of German or kindred blood" comes from the Reich Citizens Act. On the choice of words, see Essner, "*Nürnberger Gesetze*," 134–54.

221. Trevisiol, *Einbürgerungspraxis*, 203. See in detail at Ernst, "Das Staatsangehörigkeitsrecht," 72–87; Gosewinkel, *Einbürgern und Ausschließen*, 401–3.

222. Stuckart, "Die Staatsangehörigkeit," 233.

223. Calculations based on overview in Reich Interior Ministry to top-level Reich authorities, November 29, 1939, BArch R 1501/5401, 141–42. These calculations cover only the territories relevant to the present study, namely Danzig–West Prussia, the Wartheland, and the later Province of Upper Silesia.

224. On the "mixed population," see Stuckart, "Staatsangehörigkeit," 236. See also Beck, *Schwebendes Volkstum* [Wavering folkdom].

225. Kuhn to Pappritz, August 25, 1939, unpaged, BArch R 153/280 (emphasis in original).

226. On Rimann, see Lumans, *Himmler's Auxiliaries*, 139 and 143. See also Rimann's unsigned, unpaged VoMi memo on guidelines for the handling of the Masurian, Szlonzakian, Upper Silesian, and Kashubian questions, August 25, 1939, BArch R 153/280. Burleigh wrongly dates Riman's memo September 8, 1939, and claims that it was a revised version (Burleigh, *Germany Turns Eastwards*, 184). The relevant file, however, contains only this version, written before the invasion.

227. Rimann's unsigned, unpaged VoMi memo on guidelines for the handling of the Masurian, Szlonzakian, Upper Silesian, and Kashubian questions, August 25, 1939, BArch R 153/280.

228. Ibid.

229. Vollert to VoMi, September 5, 1939, BArch R 153/280. This file does not contain a revised version.

230. Unsigned letter, Dahlem Publication Office to Dr. Werner Essen, BArch R 153/280, unpaged. Essen was an adviser in Vollert's department at the Reich Interior Ministry and an established *Ostforschung* (eastern studies) expert (Haar, *Historiker im Nationalsozialismus*, 85, 89, 242, 245, and 302–3).

231. Unsigned letter, Dahlem Publication Office to Dr. Werner Essen, BArch R 153/280, unpaged.

232. Esch, *Gesunde Verhältnisse*, 330.

233. Erhard Wetzel and Gerhard Hecht, "Die Frage der Behandlung der Bevölkerung der ehemaligen polnischen Gebiete nach rassenpolitischen Gesichtspunkten" [The issue of handling the populace of the formerly Polish territories according to racial policy aspects], Nuremberg NO 3732, reprinted in Pospieszalski, *Hitlerowskie "prawo" okupacyjne*, 2–28, here 5. On Wetzel and Hecht, see Uhle, "Neues Volk," 112–16 and 119–21.

234. Wetzel and Hecht, "Frage der Behandlung der Bevölkerung," reprinted in Pospieszalski, *Hitlerowskie "prawo" okupacyjne*, 25.

235. First quote at Pospieszalski, *Hitlerowskie "prawo" okupacyjne*, 18; second quote at 17–18.

236. Ibid., 19. As would soon be seen, these proposals partially corresponded to the policies seen in the Wartheland. Contrary to the belief commonly revealed in the Nuremberg trials right up through the latest research, it was not the case that the DVL in the Wartheland represented the practical implementation of the memo from Wetzel and Hecht; in fact, the opposite was true: the memo found inspiration in the practices emerging in Posen and Lodsch.

237. (Signed "p.p. Dr. Martineck, Reich Labor Ministry"), to Reich Interior Ministry, November 11, 1939, BArch R 153/280, unpaged.

238. Report from Dr. Sharphuis, October 26, 1939, BArch R 153/280, unpaged. Here, Sharphuis drew on the ideas of Königsberg professor Erich Keyser, who would play an important role in legitimizing Forster's assimilation policy. On Keyser, see also Pinwinkler, "Volk, Bevölkerung, Rasse."

239. Report from Dr. Petzsch, October 15, 1939, BArch R 153/28, unpaged. See also Burleigh and Wippermann, *Racial State*, 130–31.

240. Report from Petzsch, October 15, 1939, BArch R 153/28, unpaged.

241. Stuckart to the Deputy Führer (attn. Dr. Sommer), Reichsführer of the SS (attn. Dr. Wetz), VoMi, and RKFDV, November 13, 1939, BArch R 1501/5378, 109–13 (emphasis in original).

242. Frick's decree on the acquisition of German national status in the territories incorporated into the German Reich, November 25, 1939, reprinted in Pospieszalski, *Hitlerowskie "prawo" okupacyjne*, 108–14.

243. (Signed "p.p. Pfundtner"), decree of the Reich Interior Minister, March 29, 1939, published in *Reichsministerialblatt der inneren Verwaltung* (1939), 783 (emphasis in original). This definition achieved a certain currency elsewhere as well. For example, it guided the EWZ in its selection of "Volksdeutsche" from Eastern Europe (document signed "Oberregierungsrat Duckart" [special appointee of the Reich Interior Ministry at the EWZ], guidelines for the naturalization of Volksdeutsche from Volhynia and Galicia, December 12, 1939, APL 205/6,1, 20–21). Furthermore, it outlasted the war and found its way—again in the selection of "Volksdeutsche" arriving from Eastern Europe—into West Germany's Law on the Affairs of Expellees and Refugees (Bundesvertriebenengesetz, or BVFG) of May 19, 1953 (Ernst, "Staatsangehörigkeitsrecht," 33–36).

244. (Signed "p.p. Pfundtner"), decree of the Reich Interior Minister, March 29, 1939, published in *Reichsministerialblatt der inneren Verwaltung* (1939), 783 (emphasis in original). Only excluded were the "completely foreign-blooded," meaning primarily Jews.

245. Ibid. Emphasis in original.

246. Zahra, *Kidnapped Souls*, 186. This is also why Mazower was mistaken in claiming that this regulatory framework "was actually *less* coercive" than Czechoslovakian nationality law, which had compelled the adoption of citizenship (Mazower, *Hitler's Empire*, 186 [emphasis in original]). See also Bryant's surprise at what he called an "open-ended definition," in *Prague in Black*, 73.

247. Gosewinkel, *Einbürgern und Ausschließen*, 411.

248. Stuckart to the Deputy Führer (attn. Dr. Sommer) and Reichsführer of the SS (attn. Dr. Wetz), VoMi, and RKFDV, November 13, 1939, BArch R 1501/5378, 109–13.

249. Only the "completely foreign-blooded" were excluded, meaning primarily Jews ([signed "p.p. Pfundtner"], decree of the Reich Interior Minister, March 29, 1939, published in *Reichsministerialblatt der inneren Verwaltung* [1939], 783).

250. Memo from Dr. Walter, RKFDV headquarters in Berlin, May 20, 1940, BArch R 49/61, 47–48.

4 "Lebensraum"

Population Policy in the Tug of War between Racial Hubris and the Rational Demands of Power

Racial Deportation Policy and Its Dilemmas for the Functional Needs of Power

With the invasion of Poland, the dystopian vision of a "German Lebensraum" had been put on the agenda as a war goal of the first rank. The Nisko campaign can be seen as an early example of the hubris of continuing to radicalize ideologically defined policy measures and then putting them into practice without any consideration. In following up on the October 1938 expulsions of Polish Jews from the German Reich, but also in adapting its goals to the new situation since the occupation of Poland, the Nisko campaign demonstrated the unfettered radicalized thinking of the Germans. Certainly, the halting of the deportation of Jews from Kattowitz as ultimately necessitated by the arrival of the Baltic Germans, and the shift to the deportation of primarily Christian Poles from Danzig–West Prussia, may appear to have been simply a pragmatic turn. But the central goal remained the same, namely the Germanization of the annexed territories. This was also true of the actions undertaken by the ethnocrats of the Wartheland, where the expulsion of Jewish Poles was temporarily suspended only in order to accommodate the Baltic Germans.

Attempts by the Berlin SS headquarters to reenergize the ideological thrust of the deportations came soon thereafter, first with Himmler's directive of October 30, 1939, and then a month later with Heydrich's long-range plan. Both these directives were aimed above all at the deportation of Jews, and both would ultimately fail. In the following months, deportation practices tended to drift further and further from the directives, for they missed precisely those groups whose deportation had been deemed particularly urgent in the directives, namely the Jews and the Congress Poles. Of course, to imagine that the forced compromises had turned the central authorities in Berlin and the ethnocrats on the ground into pragmatists would be to misjudge the weight of their ideological convictions. Instead, the measures conducted thus far were declared, as usual, to be temporary solutions—with the hope that each subsequent round of deportations would allow the realization of the ultimate racial goals. But the obstacles against finally building a Germanization policy solely guided by ideological premises would tend to increase over the following months, not decrease. The racists in the SS were soon forced to recognize that the need to accommodate ethnic Germans from Eastern Europe was not the only factor demanding a shift in priorities. Another was the reality that certain important power centers in the Reich saw the local populace not simply as an obstacle to the Germanization of the annexed territories but also as a useful workforce for the economy, or as soldiers for the Wehrmacht.

Intermediate Plan: Deporting Jews or Settling Ethnic Germans?

It was probably during the census period of December 17 to 23, 1939, and shortly after the conclusion of first short-range plan, that the Security Service (Sicherheitsdienst, or SD) Command Precinct in Posen presented a paper on "calculating deportation numbers" for the next wave of transports. The paper was still guided by the targets agreed in Kraków on November 8, 1939, which had allowed for the Wartheland to expel three hundred thousand persons by the end of February 1940. Although the SD wanted to target "a biological, a political, and a social component"—meaning Jewish Poles, political opponents, and the social elite—the occupiers had continued existing policy by initially concentrating on the latter two groups, and with disappointing results: although "the number of politically active Poles has been strongly reduced by flight, executions, and arrests," 50,780 members of political associations and parties remained to be deported, according to SD surveys, in twenty-nine out of forty-one counties alone.[1] On top of those were the members of the social elite, who numbered precisely 148,484 persons in thirty-four counties (here the SD was hinting at its own competence by citing "exact" figures).[2] This meant that the Wartheland's envisaged deportation of three hundred thousand persons would not be sufficient to deport "the entire intelligentsia and all political active Poles" and their families.[3]

Other concerns were expressed within the Reich Security Main Office in Berlin, with criticism directed at the inadequate number of deported Jews. Heydrich was determined to change this, and for the deportations of the second short-range plan (known as the "Zweiter Nahplan"), which would no longer be limited to the Wartheland but stretch across the entire annexed territories, he ordered the "comprehensive capture of all Jews in Germany's eastern Gaus regardless of age and gender and their deportation into the General Government of Poland." The goal was to expel six hundred thousand Jewish Poles between January 15 and the end of April 1940.[4]

With this, Heydrich was highlighting the desire by the Reich Security Main Office to dictate future deportation policy from Berlin. What stands out is that, on the one hand, he attempted to reideologize deportation policy by demanding the expulsion of primarily the Jewish populace, but on the other hand, he apparently found it necessary to considerably loosen the timetable set in Kraków. There the plan had still been to deport a million Jews and Poles by the end of February 1940, but the difficulties since then had now necessitated not only an extension of the deadline but also a major reduction in the total number of targeted deportees, cutting it by almost half. In order to secure control for the Reich Security Main Office and provide it with a more direct organizational conduit, Heydrich announced the appointment of Eichmann as a "special adviser" ("Sonderreferent") whose Unit IV R (Referat IV R) would now take over the "central handling of security-related matters during the implementation of the clearance of the eastern area."[5] Thus, while Ehlich was responsible for the "deportation and 'ethnoreversion' (Rückvolkung) strategy," Eichmann was now "responsible for the logistics."[6] It was through the units supervised by each that the strands of expulsion and selection policy in the German-occupied territories would run together for the rest of the war. In Poland, the agencies subordinated to them included not only the Immigrant Central Office (Einwandererzentralstelle, or EWZ), but also the regional deportation offices, which later became the Resettlement Central Offices (each known as an Umwandererzentralstelle, or UWZ).[7]

The first concrete preparations for the second short-range plan began with a meeting convened by Eichmann on January 4, 1940, whose invitees included administrative clerks from the various local IdS offices in the annexed territories and from the BdS office in Kraków. Convening the meeting was probably not another attempt by Eichmann, after the failed Nisko experiment, to impose his own will by putting the deportation of the Jews back on the agenda. Instead, he was now negotiating according to the express instructions of his superiors. Any modifications to be made were then the result of external pressures. The government in Kraków insisted on adherence to the "allotment stipulated by the General Government," obliging Eichmann to drastically reduce once again the number of Jewish Poles to be deported, this time down to three hundred fifty thousand, thereby reducing by almost half of Heydrich's recently demanded quota of six hundred thousand Jews.[8] Furthermore, the representatives from the Wartheland were also dissatisfied, as new caravans of ethnic Germans were arriving every day from Volhynia, Galicia, and the eastern Polish regions ceded to the Soviet Union, even though most reception camps in the Wartheland were still occupied by Baltic Germans whose settlement onward had been delayed.[9] In order to accommodate the new arrivals, it was not enough to deport only Jews: therefore, the Wartheland introduced the additional deportation of eighty thousand (in fact, as it would later turn out, primarily) Christian Poles, whose dwellings had been shown by experience to be the more useful ones.[10]

But it was not only the needs of the relevant occupation administrations that had to be coordinated: the Reich Security Main Office was soon confronted by the demands of the German economy as well. When it became clear that the rapidly increasing labor needs of the agricultural sector could be satisfied only briefly through the forced deployment of Polish prisoners of war, German covetousness quickly turned to the seemingly inexhaustible potential of the Polish civilian workforce. In the wake of Göring's directive on November 16, 1939 "to pursue to the maximum extent" the importation of Polish workers, the Reich Security Main Office was put on the spot because the control of foreigners within the Reich ultimately fell within its area of responsibility.[11] As early as November 1939, during the drafting of the long-range plan, Ehlich had been obliged to address demands from the Reich Food Estate (Reichsnährstand) for 1.7 million Polish farmworkers. And, in fact, this demand was later backed up by the Reich Food Ministry's State Secretary Herbert Backe on December 12, 1939, when he stipulated a need for 1.5 million Polish farmworkers.[12] Then, on January 5, 1940, Otto Ohlendorf, head of Department III and supervisor of Ehlich and Eichmann, had a meeting with Dr. Helmut Kästner, a senior civil servant from the Reich Labor Ministry. Ohlendorf was forced to make concessions, but he still tried to neutralize them in racial terms: although it was impossible to evade economic necessity and prevent the racially undesirable "recruitment" of foreigners, the Reich Security Main Office nonetheless insisted it would grant permission to enter the Reich only to workers who had first been racially appraised by the SS.

To clear up the practical details of these matters, Ohlendorf ordered a meeting in Posen on January 11, 1940. Chaired by Rapp, it was attended by Kästner from the Reich Labor Ministry, representatives of the deportation appointees at the IdS offices in Danzig–West Prussia and the Wartheland, and officials from the relevant provincial employment offices. At the meeting, the Wartheland was initially expected to deliver one hundred thousand workers for Germany's agricultural sector. Ernst Kendzia, head of the labor department at the Reichsstatthalter's offices, raised strong objections and pointed to the twenty thousand workers that the Wartheland had already supplied to the Reich in the past year. According to him, fulfilling the new demands would be "impossible" and the Wartheland could not afford to lose even more workers—on the contrary, the deportations needed to be suspended and workers retained.[13] Kendzia nonetheless had to subordinate himself to the needs of Germany's war economy, as did Ehlich as well, who admitted that even the originally envisaged racial appraisals would have to be waived for the time being. The necessary "suitability assessors" from RuSHA were not yet available, and of course, the recruitment of forced labor could not be postponed just because of ideological considerations. All that could be done was to try neutralizing the ostensible "threat" arising from the omission of racial appraisals. Thus, the plan was to limit recruitment to voluntary applicants only, who furthermore had to come from the annexed territories, since the General Government was expected to contain nothing but "enemies of the state" anyway.[14] In order to further minimize the imagined risk, Ehlich declared that the relevant persons would also need to be specially marked while inside the Reich. His threat then became reality with the introduction of the P badge for Polish forced laborers inside the Reich, beginning in March 1940—even before Jewish Germans were branded with the yellow star.[15] There was no doubt that these "voluntary" signups would be successful, since the alternative was removal to the General Government as penniless and homeless expellees, most likely to be exploited there by the local German authorities for forced labor.

The labor shortage had thus compelled yet another change of course in the overall Germanization policy, while also burdening the deportation authorities with an additional task. According to meeting notes prepared by Rapp's office, "on top of the existing evacuation campaign and the accommodation of Baltic and Volhynian Germans, there has now been added the deportation of Polish farmworkers demanded by the Reich."[16] The SD Command Precinct in Posen had already been forced to operate in a minefield of conflicting demands over the past weeks, as Himmler and Heydrich ordered above all the deportation of Jews and Congress Poles, while Greiser, his Landrats, and later also the SS Settlement Staffs (SS-Ansiedlungsstäbe) were targeting the social elite first of all, in order to eliminate the potential of political resistance against the German occupation and also accommodate the incoming ethnic Germans. Whereas Rapp had systematically opposed the ideologically based selection criteria and others like Eichmann criticized him for his opposition, he now found himself confronted by new demands, in which the deportations also had to be aligned with Germany's labor needs.

The demands from the Reich Security Main Office for an ideological handling of deportation policy, however, became increasingly overlaid with other interests during preparations for the upcoming deportations. Local worker shortages raised concerns as they threatened to become acute and more residents were recruited for Germany's war economy; the shortages could only be further exacerbated by the expanding deportations. The SD had begun taking workforce needs into account early on and had already created its own "retainment catalog" (*Rückstellungskartei*) for persons who were economically indispensable. The departments of the economy and of labor at the Reichsstatthalter's offices were not satisfied with retainment catalogs, and so the SD was ordered to coordinate their deselection process with the affected companies and employment offices, thereby taking "*into consideration, in any case, the declarations of indispensability.*"[17]

The crisis in the labor market also explains the impact that another criticism of the SD's selection practices was able to achieve, a criticism that ultimately affected Germanization policy as well. During a visit to Posen, Wilhelm Frick had apparently attacked what he felt to be excessive strictness in the SD's selection practices and asked Greiser, "in the evacuation measures, to give much more consideration than before to the so-called borderline cases."[18] Greiser seemingly agreed with Frick, since he passed this criticism on to Wilhelm Koppe and urged him, "more than before, to exercise the possibility of assimilation in regard to such persons." And Greiser also had a clear idea of what persons would be particularly suitable. In another corroboration of the Germanization policy's clear economic leanings, he let Koppe know that "the question of the tradesman is of particular importance here," meaning that this vocational group was particularly worth considering for assimilation.[19]

But, after the killing and deportation of the political opposition's elite, what had now become likely the most urgent problem—which the next deportations needed to help resolve—was the accommodation of the constantly growing number of incoming ethnic Germans, especially in the Wartheland. Even Ehlich and Eichmann began to accept the fact that the influx could not continue without consequences for the deportations. During a meeting on January 17, 1940, the size of the already existing problem became clear: in addition to the more than thirty thousand settlers from the Baltics who were still waiting in the camps for their final accommodation, another eighty thousand had since arrived from Volhynia. The "difficulties arising from the interaction between the settling of the Volksdeutsche and the evacuating of the Poles and Jews" had become so large that Ehlich and Eichmann felt they could be resolved only at a senior-level conference chaired by Heydrich. Until that happened, nothing could be done by the planners at the Reich Security Main Office except concur with the assessment of their colleagues at the SD Command Precinct in Posen "that for the Wartheland, whatever happens, space needs to be created, in the form of an evacuation."[20] Thus, for the Reich Security Main Office, the accommodation of German settlers had become more important than the expulsion of Jews and Congress Poles.

But to free up housing and jobs for the incoming ethnic Germans, it was necessary to overcome the increasing resistance of Hans Frank, head of the General Government, who did not want to accept any more deportees at all. Here, Eichmann knew how to leverage the strong position of the SS in the General Government. Just a day earlier, on January 16, he had turned directly to Bruno Streckenbach by telephone, who had "accepted the need for, in some measure, an *overriding* evacuation in the Wartheland" and approved the intake of forty thousand persons—apparently in disregard of Frank.[21] But it was clear to both that Streckenbach's intake would allow the housing of no more than twenty thousand German settlers, meaning that this measure was only an "emergency pressure release" in Ehlich's eyes.

Another problem confronting Ehlich and Eichmann was the promises that Ohlendorf made to the Reich Labor Ministry. The first in line for settlement were the Baltic Germans, for they had sat longer in the camps than the recently arrived settlers from eastern Poland. Because most of them had come from towns and therefore needed to be accommodated again in towns, it was already clear that most of the corresponding Poles to be expelled for this goal would—as help was needed above all in agriculture—"not be worth considering for manual labor in the Old Reich" (meaning the Reich's territory before the annexations). Ehlich and Eichmann were therefore forced to recognize not only that Himmler's and Heydrich's demands to deport Jews and Congress Poles conflicted with Ohlendorf's concessions to the Reich Labor Ministry (as it was anathema to Nazi ideologues not only in the SS to deport these two groups into the Reich), but also that both positions were irreconcilable with the necessities of accommodating the German settlers. The attempt by the Reich Security Main Office to micromanage the deportation planning was therefore in danger of falling apart. Before such a failure could be admitted, however, it was simply disguised instead, as usual. Ehlich preferred to speak of an "intermediate solution," which then grew into an "intermediate plan" ("Zwischenplan"), to be inserted before the second short-range plan.[22]

The aforementioned senior-level conference then took place in Berlin on January 30, 1940. Attended by very high-ranking figures, it would be the first time that an approved framework would be laid out for the year's deportations.[23] At the meeting, Heydrich departed significantly from the previous planning of the Reich Security Main Office and yielded for the first time to the realities on the ground: after an initial "mass movement" involving the expulsion of "40,000 Poles and Jews in the interests of the Baltic Germans" (which would become the intermediate plan), a second one would target "120,000 Poles in the interests of the Volhynian Germans" (which would become the second short-range plan).[24] The expulsion of the Jews, which had always been seen as a top priority by Himmler and Heydrich, was now to come last, in a third and final deportation wave. After that—and here, Heydrich was coming back to a scheme outlined in Kraków—"resettlement offices" ("Umwanderungsstellen") would be established to conduct racial appraisals of the remaining local populace in order to distinguish "Germans" from "Poles." Heydrich had thus accepted the setting of priorities forced through by the ethnocrats of the Wartheland, for whom the accommodation of the ethnic Germans was the first order of business.

In comparison with the concessions needed for the ethnic Germans, concessions required by Germany's labor market weighed even more heavily: according to Heydrich, eight hundred thousand to a million Polish workers would have to be recruited for Germany's agricultural sector rather soon, of which the Wartheland could only supply twenty thousand, and Danzig–West Prussia only eight

Figure 4.1. Poles at entrance of Mogilno Abbey transit camp, before their deportation into the General Government. This deportation occurred under the intermediate plan and was conducted with the help of Police Battalion 103, here assisted by local Volksdeutsche.
Source: Archive of Modern Conflict, album A10327.

thousand. As a result, the Reich Security Main Office was forced to approve an option that had always been precluded until now: the transport of Polish workers out of the General Government.

The selection practices developed by the SD Command Precinct in Posen during the first short-range plan, however, were not altered. Although Eichmann had demanded the prioritized deportation of Jews and Congress Poles just two days earlier, Strickner nonetheless instructed his subordinates to act as before in handling the "next evacuation," thus putting "members of the Polish intelligentsia who are *also* politically contaminated" on the deportation lists first, because doing so was the only way "to ensure the seizure of good dwellings."[25] There was no mention of targeting Congress Poles or Jews.[26]

The first deportation train under the intermediate plan, carrying a thousand persons, did not leave Posen's east station until February 10, 1940.[27] In the subsequent weeks up to March 15, 1940, there were 40,128 persons deported in forty transports to the General Government.[28] As with the first short-range plan, however, the figure was not broken down further in the surviving reports. As

Figure 4.2. Transfer from transit camp to train station in Mogilno.
Source: Archive of Modern Conflict, album A10327.

a result, one cannot determine with certainty the counties of the Wartheland from which the deportees came or how many of them were native Poles, Congress Poles, or Jews. But there is no reason to believe that the selection criteria had changed from before. Since the main goal was to accommodate urban dwellers from the Baltics, the main targets were Polish urban dwellers, particularly those who were political activists and/or occupants of good dwellings. In this situation, Jews were hardly affected. According to Alberti, of the more than twenty-four thousand people deported from Lodsch and Posen, no more than 2,018 were Jews.[29] And even these seem to have been more of an exception, at least in the case of Lodsch. For example, with the roundups of March 4, 1940, Jews were among those evicted from their homes—but only because their centrally located dwellings were required for the Baltic Germans. These evictions were then followed not by deportation to the General Government, but instead by relocation to nearby replacement homes, which were later incorporated into the ghetto. In contrast, the Christian residents of these homes were deported.[30] The Office for Resettlement was clearly serious about attuning the deportations to the needs of the Baltic Germans, as seen when Rapp confronted the Regierungspräsident's offices in Kalisch, which similarly to other civil administration agencies preferred the expulsion of welfare recipients over that of Jews: "The intermediate plan, which was established solely for the acquiring of dwellings and the final settling of the Baltic Germans, unfortunately will not tolerate any evacuations that do not simultaneously create employment opportunities and housing opportunities for Baltic Germans."[31]

The Second Short-Range Plan: Racial Paranoia and Worker Shortages

It was chiefly the planners at the Reich Security Main Office who were forced to come to terms with the situation, namely that the local populace earmarked for deportation were selected first according to security-related criteria and then to the extent that their removal helped in accommodating the incoming "Volksdeutsche"—but indeed not primarily according to racial or ideological criteria. The practice had become justifiable to the extent that the widespread exemption of Jewish Poles, although regrettable on ideological grounds, nonetheless expedited the settling of ethnic Germans, thereby very much helping to achieve the same ultimate goal: the Germanization of the annexed territories. In contrast, the agreement between the Reich Security Main Office and the Reich Labor Ministry marked a fundamental shift, for the ethnocrats found themselves confronted for the first time with the need to factor in a priority—namely, the alleviation of Germany's labor shortage—that was not only superficially inconsistent with the functional logic of Germanization policy to that point but also actually contradicted it. From a racial perspective, the threat was only too clear: it could be that persons earmarked for deportation are not transported, for example, into the General Government but, instead, because of their work abilities, carried into the Reich itself. The labor shortages in the Reich thus threatened not only to reshape the selection criteria in the annexed territories, but also to generate racial and ethnonational dangers within the Reich's home territory. If the Reich Security Main Office wanted to maintain its political effectiveness while adhering to its goal of centrally managing deportation policy from Berlin, it had to find a way to minimize precisely this risk. Its solution: the coordination of Germanization policy with labor deployment.

In the agreement wrested from him on January 5, Ohlendorf had still managed to make the recruitment of an initial one hundred thousand Polish forced laborers conditional on their racial appraisal, but he was soon forced to recognize that the SS did not actually have the necessary human resources to handle the task. In the event, no evidence exists of any mass recruitments of Polish forced laborers in the annexed territories during the first quarter of 1940, and it seems that the intermediate plan did not see anyone transported into the Reich for forced labor instead of into the General Government. Of course, this excludes the placement of "voluntary" workers by the local employment agencies, which had been given free rein in this regard by Heydrich on January 30, but only until the SS apparatus was able to secure the racial appraisal of larger numbers of people. Nonetheless, with forty-nine thousand workers, whether forced or not, sent from the Wartheland into the Reich by April 30, 1940, the actual number remained relatively low,[32] especially in light of the fact that some twenty thousand of that number had already been sent by the end of 1939.[33]

What makes the number even more remarkable is that the pressure from the Reich had not dwindled. Just a few days after the meeting at Heydrich's offices, the demand for Polish farmworkers was likewise reaffirmed during a meeting of the Council of Ministers on February 2, 1940.[34] It was heard again ten days later during a meeting at Göring's Karinhall residence, where Frank and the four Gauleiters of the annexed territories, along with Himmler, Max Winkler, and a number of state secretaries, had gathered on February 12, 1940, in order to discuss "eastern issues." What Göring considered foremost among them was made clear to the participants at the very start when he declared that "the highest objective of all measures to be taken in the east must be the strengthening of the Reich's war potential"—and not, for example, the fastest possible Germanization of the annexed territories. On the contrary: "the maximum possible agricultural production from the new eastern Gaus" could be extracted only when "sufficient workers remain in the provinces. These will largely be Poles." Of course, this did not mean that the deportation of workers was entirely forbidden, especially because the labor shortage in Germany's war economy was becoming increasingly dire. And so, according to the minutes, "all evacuation measures are to be oriented so that a viable workforce does not disappear. In addition, the entire eastern region must relinquish the envisaged number of workers to the Reich."[35]

With this deportation planning oriented toward economic criteria, Göring had certainly challenged Himmler's notions, as well as those of certain Gauleiters, but a clash of interests can hardly be detected in the brief written meeting minutes. For example, no comment is made when Himmler declared that in light of these economic considerations he is prepared to postpone the "absorption" of up to two hundred forty thousand "Volksdeutsche" from Lithuania, Bessarabia, and Bukovina, "in consideration of the difficulties of the resettlement and the necessities of war" and yet stood firm in wanting to accommodate two hundred thousand Baltic and Volhynian Germans, that is insisting on large-scale deportations necessary to achieve this.[36] Frank, for one, chalked up the latest planning developments as a success and optimistically noted two weeks later in his work diary that the plan to deport all 7.5 million Poles from the annexed territories into his responsibility was definitively off the table, and that he also been promised veto rights over any further deportations into the General Government.[37] Just to be sure, he also obtained a decree from Göring that told all relevant agencies "I forbid further . . . deportations lacking my authorization and lacking proof of agreement from the Governor-General [i.e., Frank]."[38] On top of that, he also put into play a proposal that had already been raised: instead of expelling persons from the annexed territories into the General Government, only to have them forwarded from there into the Reich as forced laborers, they could be transported directly into the Reich in the first place.

At this point, the problem remaining for the Reich Security Main Office was how to avert the alleged racial threat that resulted from opening the Reich borders to such a large number of Polish forced laborers. Ulrich Herbert seems to misjudge the political complexity of the situation when he suggests that the SS reacted to this solely with an intensified reign of terror.[39] Certainly, the growing dependence on ostensibly inferior persons was supposed to be made more acceptable through persecutory measures, leading to the "Polish decrees" of March 8, 1940, which subjected Polish forced laborers to a number of discriminatory restrictions and dictated that their persons be labeled inside the Reich with the letter P.[40] This "terror as a compromise serving the needs of power [Herrschaftskompromiß]," as Herbert calls it, may have helped contain the dangers associated with foreigners living inside the Reich, but from the SS perspective, it could not eliminate them.[41] Nazism's characteristic desire for "final solutions" would not let the ethnocrats at the Reich Security Main Office rest, which ultimately meant that the demand for racial appraisals was soon back on the agenda.

On February 2, 1940, Ehlich submitted a memorandum to Heydrich that would put racial appraisals at the heart of the second short-range plan for the first time. In it, he emphatically declared the "racial stocktaking of the entire Polish populace" to be the prerequisite for "the entire ethnopolicy in the German east." Although Heydrich had already stated during the conference on January 30 that the launch of this undertaking would be deferred until after the Jewish Poles were all deported, Ehlich pushed for a reconsideration just three days later. It had turned out that the RuSHA suitability assessors assigned to the EWZ would finish with the "funneling through" ("Schleusung") of the Volhynians and Galicians at the end of April. But that was also the time when the second short-range plan would likely begin, with the goal of deporting around one hundred twenty thousand persons. According to Ehlich, although the number of suitability assessors would not suffice for the "still to be conducted comprehensive survey," a "partial survey" was nonetheless possible, and even "essential." To achieve this, new bureaus would be established as "resettlement central offices" ("Umwanderungszentralstellen," or UWZs), which would integrate the racial appraisals into the deportation process. Doing so would ward off the ostensible danger that was tied in the Nazi imagination to the recruitment of so many workers from among the "Fremdvölkische" (the "ethnonationally foreign"). The UWZs would identify those individuals who "might be racially eligible for deployment with a farming family inside the Old Reich" and would "insert itself into the evacuation process as a filter, in order to divert the racially worthwhile segment of the Poles into the Old Reich."[42]

Ehlich's memorandum became a general guideline for reorganizing the resettlement apparatus on the Reich's periphery, which was accompanied by far-reaching changes at the Reich Security Main Office. Its Department III saw the establishment of a new Departmental Group III B (Amtsgruppe III B) under Ehlich, covering ethnonationality.[43] Meanwhile, Department IV saw the establishment of Departmental Group IV D (Occupied Territories), headed by Dr. Erwin Weinmann; under this was placed Eichmann's former Unit IV R (Referat IV R, covering *Räumung*, meaning evacuation), now known as Unit IV D 4 (Emigration and Evacuation).[44] Institutionally upgraded and better staffed, Ehlich and Eichmann were able to continue with their planning of Germanization policy and management of the relevant institutions in the annexed territories, which were now likewise reorganized with the founding of the UWZs, whose letterhead ultimately carried the appellation (as seen in the Wartheland), "The Chief of the Security Police and the SD, Resettlement Central Office." The heading referred to one of Heydrich's official titles, thereby demonstrating that he had now completely wrested this sphere of activities from the HSSPFs and placed it under the direct control of the Reich Security Main Office.[45]

Except for one important innovation, the tasks of the new agency UWZ had remained the same. First, it was still necessary to select individuals for deportation while remembering to uphold the "protection of German blood" as well as the "retainment of Poles engaged in operations essential to the war effort."[46] Second, the deportations themselves had to be prepared and supervised in cooperation with the local agencies. Third—and this was now new—the deportations no longer ran according to a two-step process, meaning first into the local camp on the county level and from there into the General Government. Instead, everyone was first deported to Lodsch, now renamed Litzmannstadt, where the UWZ built a multistage camp zone that put the relevant individuals through a complex selection process. The results determined whether they were deported to the General Government as before or they were transported to the Reich as (forced) laborers.

With the deportations expanded to include the other annexed territories of western Poland, the process was applied to the persons expelled from those places as well, so that all the "Pole trains" from the annexed territories to the General Government were soon channeled first through the camp complex in Lodsch.[47] The "Volksdeutsche" who traveled by train from Volhynia and Galicia had likewise arrived through the junction at Lodsch, and both Volksdeutsche Mittelstelle (Ethnic German Liaison Office, or VoMi) and the EWZ had also relocated their main work here.[48] All this meant that Lodsch—which would soon also host the largest Jewish ghetto on "German" soil—had ultimately become the epicenter of Nazi population policy in the annexed Polish territories.[49]

The structure of the UWZ was adapted to this expanded range of duties. Seven units (*Referate*) were established, assigned respectively to organizing, transport matters, and card catalog (Unit I); administration (Unit II); complaints/appeals (Unit V); and police deployment (Unit VII). There was also the inspectorate for the camp to be built in Litzmannstadt (Unit III), the camp's staff for medical "care," meaning the medical appraisal of the detainees (Unit VI), and an RuS office (Unit IV, with RuS standing for "Rasse und Siedlung," or "race and settlement"), which would later separate on November 1, 1940, to become the Litzmannstadt field office of RuSHA.[50] The leadership of the UWZ also saw a change in personnel, although not in structure. As before, it was subordinated to the head of the SD Command Precinct in Posen, which as of May 1940 had been a position occupied by SS Chief Assault Leader Rolf-Heinz Höppner.

The centralization of deportation planning at the Reich Security Main Office initially meant a huge loss of authority for the local HSSPFs. The fact that they nonetheless managed to assert themselves as influential players in Germanization policy was due to the simultaneous expansion of the regional RKFDV branch offices, which in Posen were placed under SS Senior Leader Hans Döring.[51] Parallel to the establishment of the UWZ, the cities of Posen and Litzmannstadt each saw the installation of an SS Settlement Staff (SS-Ansiedlungsstab), to which were then attached local SS Task Forces (SS-Arbeitsstäbe) in the counties earmarked for settlement by ethnic Germans. The assignment of each task force was, "to put it briefly, to make German" the county assigned to it.[52] These SS Task Forces would become the first to feel the pressures caused by each additional transport of incoming ethnic Germans. To secure work and housing for each of these new arrivals, they prepared village overviews, surveyed the individual farms on "farm maps" ("*Hofkarten*"), and planned consolidations when farms did not cover at least fifteen hectares (about thirty-seven acres), the last as a way to modernize the organization of local agriculture. The people living there were put onto a list of requested expulsions, which was then passed on—along with the overall pressure—to the UWZ, which then had to approve the lists and organize the deportations.

What was intended as a division of labor would later fail in practice, often because of jurisdictional struggles between these institutions or the narrow possibilities available to the German occupiers, which led to fierce confrontations again and again during the rest of the occupation period. Rapp got a foretaste of this when he dispatched SS Senior Assault Leader Rudolf Barth to Lodsch, where he was to set up a field office in preparation for the intermediate plan.[53] Hardly had he arrived on site when he collided with an emissary sent by Koppe, who likewise claimed authority over the organization of deportations in Lodsch.[54] Soon after the UWZ ultimately prevailed in this jurisdictional battle, Koppe pulled several senior SS officers from this institution that had slipped away from him; he transferred them into the settlement apparatus, thereby weakening the personnel of the UWZ.[55]

It is hardly surprising that Lodsch in particular would be the setting for these confrontations, considering the city's importance in Nazi population policy. But developments in settlement and deportation policy would further highlight the position of Lodsch in the wider topography of the regime's population policy. Whereas the first deportations had primarily targeted the western areas of the Wartheland along with its capital city of Posen, the deportations of the second short-range plan would mainly focus on the counties bordering the General Government.[56] This shift of focus to the province's eastern region led, for one thing, to the closing of the camp at Glowno.[57] For another, the Posen UWZ upgraded its Lodsch field office to a branch office in March 1940.[58] SS Senior Assault Unit Leader Hermann Krumey was named the new head in Lodsch, thereby becoming the second most important person in the organization after Höppner.[59] While Höppner worked from Posen on settling fundamental issues and communicating with agencies above his own, Krumey worked from Lodsch on the management and coordination of deportation activities.[60]

The decision to fundamentally modify deportation practice already with the second short-range plan, particularly the early introduction of racial appraisals, had led to a reorganization of the bureaus tasked with these matters, both at the Reich Security Main Office and on the Reich's periphery. This reorganization was also an expression of the growing complexity of deportation policy, which—in the view of the Reich Security Main Office—could be managed only through a more direct grip on the regional agencies. In contrast to the earlier deportations, eviction campaigns from then on were to involve all the eastern provinces for the first time. Furthermore, the selection of the affected persons was no longer to be oriented solely to the immediate needs of the incoming "Volksdeutsche," but were instead to be embedded within long-term Germanization plans that aimed to reshape the economy, society, and infrastructure, with plans prepared not only on Himmler's orders at the Staff Main Office of the RKFDV (Stabshauptamt des Reichskommissars für die Festigung deutschen Volkstums) headquarters in Berlin but also by other offices.[61]

Konrad Meyer, the new head of the RKFDV Planning Department and also head of the Institute for Agrarian Issues and Agrarian Policy at the University of Berlin, presented the first draft proposal, known as the "planning guidelines for the development of the eastern territories," probably in January 1940.[62] As was typical of all further reworkings of the General Plan for the East (Generalplan Ost), he argued that the problem of militarily securing and economically modernizing the new eastern provinces should be seen primarily in terms of population policy and that the problem could be solved by forcing changes in the ethnic and social composition of the populace.[63] While his colleagues at the Reich

Security Main Office were trying to push the deportation of Jewish Poles (and in vain, as has been shown), Meyer called for not only that but also the expulsion of another 3.4 million Poles, meaning Christian ones. Their places were to be taken by ethnic Germans: here, the "planning guidelines" offered suggestions on allocations of property and land to incoming settlers, as well as the size and number of their communities. These settlements were to be initially concentrated in the "settlement zone of the first order," which encompassed around 40 percent of the entire annexed territories, primarily in the counties of the Wartheland and Danzig–West Prussia that were closest to the General Government, along with counties forming two "ethnonational bridges" ("Volkstumsbrücken"), one crossing the former Polish Corridor and the other via Posen in order to connect the border strip to the Reich proper.[64]

It is difficult to say what practical consequences developed from these plans, if any. In the case of the extent of this first-order settlement zone, a certain skepticism would be justified, even more because any parallels between the plans formulated in Berlin and the policies practiced on the periphery are not necessarily enough to establish a causal relationship. For example, while Greiser did inform his Regierungspräsidents and Landrats on March 1, 1940, that the settling of ethnic Germans from Volhynia and Galicia was to take place in the province's east and justified his plan with the need to "create a firm, impenetrable wall of German people against Polishdom," it is entirely unclear how his instruction might be connected to Meyer's proposals.[65] It is unknown whether any correspondence on this topic took place around this date between the Reichsstatthalter's offices and the RKFDV headquarters or its bureau in Posen—and, in any case, the prioritization of the border area probably did not need professorial support from Berlin, for the priority was already obvious on military grounds alone. And, of course, the possibly intended strategy of "smothering" the Poles by encirclement was by no means invented by the ethnocrats at RKFDV headquarters. As previously mentioned, the last time such a scheme had developed appreciable influence was during World War I in discussions of the "border strip."

The shift of geographic focus for UWZ activities within the Wartheland can also be seen in the dense network of UWZ field offices that was rolled out over the eastern sections of Hohensalza Governmental Region and Litzmannstadt Governmental Region (as the latter would now be called).[66] Numbering twelve in total, these local bureaus were notified by Rapp on April 1, 1940, that the operations of the second short-range plan would begin on April 5, 1940.[67]

On the question of how these deportations were to be conducted, the ethnocrats drew on their previous experiences. Slight modifications were seen only in the question of who was to be deported. As before, the primary targets were people whose dwellings and jobs were needed for accommodating the ethnic Germans—which, in the case of Volhynians, usually meant Polish farmers.[68]

The SD did, however, make efforts to link this criterion with others, thereby establishing a more nuanced application of selection policy. To this end, the SD field offices were to set up so-called "resettlement catalogs" ("Umwanderungs-karteien"), in which were noted the specific individuals who were considered "politically undesirable," "economically superfluous," or "antisocial elements" in the eyes of the security forces and the Landrats.[69] Political opponents, seen as particularly dangerous by the Germans, were now to be deported no longer to the General Government, but to concentration camps in the Reich. As a result, in preparing for the second short-range plan, the Germans subjected the local populace to additional terror campaigns, picking up on the "Intelligenzaktion" ("intelligentsia campaign") by targeting those who, "in any way, stimulate the spirit of resistance and act against security interests."[70] The campaign began with the eastern border counties in and around the city of Litzmannstadt, as well as the Dąbrowa Basin industrial zone and other parts of Upper Silesia. Another wave of arrests occurred just a few weeks later, starting in the Wartheland's western part on May 15 and in its eastern part on May 17.

According to instructions from the Reich Security Main Office, the "Deutschstämmige" (the "German-descended") were to be spared. To accomplish this, the resettlement catalogs at the newly established UWZ field offices were supplemented with "Volksdeutsche" catalogs, whose source inputs also included the selection results of the German People's List (Deutsche Volksliste, or DVL) commissions. Unlike them, however, the SD went further by expanding the selection criteria of persons to be protected; for example, in considering "German names as an indicative factor"—after all, it was not only the "Volksdeutsche" who were to be spared, but also the "Deutschstämmige."[71] Furthermore, the deportations could not take in persons whose relatives were German nationals or were soldiers in the Wehrmacht.[72] The seriousness of this restriction for the UWZ was seen in an order sent shortly before, which imposed a general prohibition on deporting Protestants, as the assumption was made that Protestants would likely be German or of German descent.[73] The prohibition applied even to those counted among the political opposition, such as the followers of Juliusz Bursche, bishop of the Evangelical Church of the Augsburg Confession in Poland.[74]

It would be premature, however, to see this stronger emphasis on exempting the "Deutschstämmige" as a kind of racial turning point in deportation policy. After all, Jews were also initially spared deportation into the General Government after the consultations of January 30, 1940.[75] Some of the Polish populace also remained safe, as long as the Germans found it to be beneficial. On the one hand, exemptions were still being given to skilled specialists like railroad workers, tiled stove fitters, roofers, and chimney sweeps.[76] On the other, exemptions also applied to persons whose past conduct suggested a readiness for future collaboration. When the SD Command Precinct's new chief Höppner signaled that

Poles who had saved the lives of "Volksdeutsche" would no longer be spared, since the goal after all was an "ethnic and racial cleansing," he was soon pulled back onto the solid ground of security-oriented logic by—of all people—Ehlich:[77] "In the selection of Poles to be evacuated . . . politically unreliable elements are to be removed first of all . . . Poles who have verifiably saved Volksdeutsche from death or otherwise protected them, however, should be exempted from evacuation where possible, so long as a German-friendly attitude can be deduced from their conduct."[78]

Although concrete preparations for the second short-range plan had already begun in early April with the formal founding of the UWZ, it still took another month for the deportations to resume. The first train departed the Wartheland on May 6, 1940, carrying 987 persons to Petrikau (today Piotrków) in the General Government, as part of what was called the "Volhynian campaign" ("Wolhynien-aktion").[79] By the time the second short-range plan ended on January 20, 1941, another 178 transports would carry 133,506 people altogether, who came not only from the Wartheland but also from the provinces of Silesia, East Prussia, and Danzig–West Prussia. This was the first time that a short-range plan coordinated deportations not only from a single province but from all provinces within the annexed Polish territories.

Attempted Compromise: Racial Appraisal of (Forced) Laborers

The decisive innovation accompanying the second short-range plan was the introduction of racial appraisals, which now became an integral part of the deportation process. Since the still low number of suitability assessors prevented the dispatching of so-called "flying commissions" ("fliegende Kommissionen") to the various collection camps, it was decided to build a central camp complex in Litzmannstadt through which all deportees were to pass while undergoing a complex selection process, with the results deciding their fate. After arriving at one of Litzmannstadt's train stations, they went through the municipal delousing facility at Dessauer Strasse 6–11 and then brought to the "funneling-through camp" ("Durchschleusungslager") at Wiesenstrasse 4.[80] Here they underwent a "rough selection" ("Grobauslese") by RuSHA suitability assessors.[81] This preliminary screening was to select families that, "due to their appearance, seem suitable for transport into the Old Reich."[82] They were the only ones who were further subjected to a health inspection and political audit. While the screening determined their fitness for work, the health inspection and political audit examined their political loyalty and barred alleged political opponents from transport into the Reich.[83] Such barring happened regardless of whether they had been labeled "re-Germanizable" ("wiedereindeutschungsfähig") by the suitability assessors.[84] The final decision was ultimately made during the "fine selection"

("Feinauslese").[85] The fine selection was at first conducted at the UWZ camps and later, starting November 1, 1940, at the camp of the newly established RuSHA field office at Landknechtstrasse 73.[86] The creation of the RuSHA camp was based on a suggestion by Ehlich and had apparently become necessary in order to "eliminate disagreements between members of the other units of the UWZ and RuSHA."[87]

In Isabel Heinemann's analysis, these racial appraisals were more or less the same as the selection process developed for the enrollment of SS men, which was then transposed during the war onto the selections conducted by the EWZ.[88] In this, she is only partially correct. As evidence for her interpretation, she quotes from a message written by the head of the Race Office at RuSHA, Otto Hofmann, dated October 14, 1939, in which he informs the suitability assessors that for the upcoming racial appraisals at the EWZ, the "selection principles of the SS are authoritative."[89] But Hofmann certainly did not mean an exact copy of the selection process applied to SS applicants. Instead, in a later passage, Hofmann states that the racial selection of the ethnic Germans could be limited to surveying the shape of the body, head, and nose, along with hair texture, hair color, and eye color, because these characteristics were allegedly the "most important markers to be found in the racial constitution of the German Volk."[90]

In the racial appraisal of the Polish populace, however, the procedure was to be adjusted once again. Certainly, in the run-up to these appraisals, the designated head of the new RuSHA office in Lodsch, SS Senior Assault Unit Leader Erwin Künzel, had initially prevailed in his call to adopt the selection criteria already in use at the EWZ, which were less strict than those used in the SS selection process. But soon thereafter he received a message from Hofmann, who instructed him—"contrary to the agreement reached with you orally"—to tighten the selection criteria and to establish a "tangible difference between the appraisals for the Volksdeutsche and the current ones."[91] The suitability assessors were told to give up the previously applied "allowances" and "to create considerably stricter standards than had been necessary for one's own ethnonational group [this is, when compared to the appraisals of the incoming ethnic Germans by the EWZ]."[92] In the end, the purpose of this selection work was "to sift out the racially most valuable and politically uncontaminated part of the Polish Volk for a deliberate assimilation."[93] Thus, it was true that in October 1939 the SS had already begun to subject ethnic Germans to a selection process modeled—if only roughly—on the appraisals of SS applicants. In practice, however, a generous interpretation was used to ensure that, with the immigrants from Eastern Europe, as many as possible were recognized as "Germans." It was only with the introduction of the "fine selection" step at the RuSHA satellite camp in Litzmannstadt that these allowances were partially rescinded. Thus, from that point forward, two different standards were used in deciding the racial suitability of the persons in question: ethnic Germans from Eastern Europe could count on being treated leniently so that as many as possible would be recognized as "Germans," but the same allowances did not apply to the "Polish" populace of the annexed eastern territories.

Individuals presented to the suitability assessors were selected for one of three groups. While classification into the AR category (short for *Altreich*, or Old Reich) was reserved for those who, "in their overall impression, can be seen as racially valuable enough for a future merging into Germandom," in the case of "racially unfit and antisocial persons, as well as politically contaminated ones," the category of GG (General Government) was assigned.[94] Finally, the WR category (short for *Wanderarbeiter*, or migrant worker) was for those who had received a racially "positive" appraisal but came from a family that was labeled on the whole as "Polish."[95] Those in the WR category were "undesirable for assimilation . . . but usable as seasonal workers."[96] After selection, those classified AR and WR were transferred to the transit camp in Konstantynów near Litzmannstadt, while those classified GG went to the transit camp at Luisenstrasse 33. There they joined those who had already been classified as "not re-Germanizable" ("nichtwiedereindeutschungsfähig") during the "rough selection" process at the facility on Wiesenstrasse.[97]

Finally, before each transport into the General Government, the provincial employment office tried one last time to acquire additional workers, in parts also relying on local people who had worked in Germany before and were now tasked with persuading others to volunteer for work. But here at Luisenstrasse 33, the employment office wanted only "singletons" ("Einzelgänger"), which is what single adults were called in UWZ terminology. Before these persons could join the transports into the Reich, they had to be subjected to yet another racial appraisal, which from the perspective of the suitability assessors was a kind of "negative" selection, so that instead of choosing the "re-Germanizable," they had to exclude individuals who represented "glaring deviations from the European norm."[98] Those remaining, that is, the so-called volunteers, were then brought to the transit camp in Konstantynów like those selected by RuSHA for the AR and WR categories, where together they had to wait for transport into the Reich. In light of the role of the Konstantynów camp in the German economy, it is hardly surprising that although the camp's commandant and guards came from the UWZ, it was otherwise subordinated to the provincial employment office in Posen.[99]

The Re-Germanization Program

Just in time for the start of the deportations, Himmler in his role as RKFDV went a step further and signed directive 17/II on May 9, 1940, which took the racial appraisals already begun in the Wartheland and established them as a new field of activity reclaimed by the SS: the re-Germanization program.

This ideologically loaded concept cannot be understood without relating it to the economic logic that shaped not only the program's genesis and the setting of its goals but also the racial selection of workers at deportation camps. Without a doubt, Himmler was convinced—as seen in his directive—that many individuals in the annexed territories "on the basis of their racial suitability, come into question for a Germanization."[100] But this racial thinking achieved a real-world impact primarily because it could be tied to the rational demands of power, thereby becoming politically functional as well. Himmler could count on a practical realization of this racially motivated project because it also delivered an answer to real needs, especially economic ones, and thus drew the support of other powerful factions in the Reich.

The remaining provisions outlined by this and later directives on the re-Germanization program would ultimately establish a new, privileged form of forced labor.[101] Having arrived in the Reich, the "re-Germanizables" found themselves in a relatively advantageous situation, in that they could show an alien identity document issued in Litzmannstadt with the notation "national status yet to be settled, German?" which gave them—at least theoretically—a right to the same wages and food rations as the German workers at their new workplace.[102] Nevertheless, they were still forced laborers.[103] Their recognition as "Germans" largely depended on "proving themselves" in the workplace. If their work performance failed to satisfy the relevant company or HSSPF, it was taken as proof that they were not Germans after all, but Poles. They then faced the threat of being treated like the others transported from Litzmannstadt, who were subject to discriminatory special regulations as "P-Poles."

From the SS perspective, the re-Germanization program appeared to be a milestone development that could expand its sphere of influence while ideologically securing it. By tying the employment of foreign workers to a racial appraisal conducted by SS suitability assessors, not only did the SS manage to advance its position in the increasingly important policy area of workforce acquisition, but it could even hope to take the policy area over with a single master stroke. Even though the project was initially limited to the annexed Polish territories, SS ambitions encompassed all the occupied and yet-to-be-occupied territories of Eastern Europe, and had the potential to transform the SS into one of the Reich's top economic powers.

SS ambitions first, however, needed to be asserted above those of other political actors. Doing so was relatively easy in the case of the Nazi Party's Racial Policy Office. With the support of Hess, it asked to be "called in for the practical selection work in the east," but this was rejected by Pancke, head of RuSHA. In a message to Himmler on May 25, 1940, he argued for an "absolute separation of the fields of activity."[104] He wrote that while the Racial Policy Office, whose staff were "purely scientifically trained academics," could undertake the "educating" of the populace and assist with legislation, the SS needed to remain "solely responsible for the practical selecting and culling."[105] This division of labor was approved by Himmler, and Künzel was informed soon thereafter that any further "autonomous action" by the Racial Policy Office "cannot be tolerated."[106]

It was much harder to overcome the resistance from German economic players and the employment offices. Höppner had already found it difficult to assert the monopoly over worker placement that was claimed by the UWZ in the face of the Wartheland provincial employment office. When he then learned that individual employment offices had sought authorization to allocate Polish forced laborers to German enterprises directly, he immediately protested to their superior authority, namely the Department for Economy and Labor at the Reichsstatthalter's offices, and raised the "strongest of objections, as these families have not been racially inspected."[107] Just a short time later, a request from the Litzmannstadt employment office also had to be deflected, as it sought to disband the camp in Konstantynów and similarly deport the Polish workers directly into the Reich.[108] Although it is likely that Höppner was not always able to prevent the employment offices from bypassing the UWZ, it seems that he still managed to considerably restrict their activities in this sphere.[109]

* * *

In his maneuvering, Himmler could count on a number of important allies with a more ideological agenda. A decisive actor here proved to be the Nazi Party itself, in which a long-growing resentment about the country's "overforeignization" ("Überfremdung") was now becoming increasingly forceful. Thus, on July 20, 1940, during a meeting hosted by Hess on the employment of foreigners in mining, the Gauleiter of Halle-Merseburg, Joachim Eggeling, took the opportunity to criticize in particular the deployment of Polish workers in agriculture, pointing to the "unprecedented biological danger of current developments" and even warning of the "annihilation of our own Volk."[110]

The other attendees took up the thrust of Eggeling's attack and agreed to set a maximum on the number of foreigners deployed as (forced) laborers inside the Reich. Maybe unsurprisingly, they could not bring themselves to demand a reduction in the volume already reached. Setting a limit of three million persons simply stabilized the status quo.[111] The attack demonstrated, however, how intolerable it seemed, from the perspective of the ideologues, that the borders had been opened to millions of non-German persons. With its racial appraisals, the SS had offered a procedure that promised nothing less than the squaring of the circle. It posited the reconcilability of essentially contradictory political demands, emanating on the one hand from the racial premises of Nazi ideology and on the other hand from the functional needs of power, in this case the need for additional labor power.

Himmler's surprise move, however (his re-Germanization decree of May 9, 1940), represented only the practical policy spearhead of a new ideological offensive by the SS apparatus. Just a few days after the re-Germanization decree had upgraded the importance of the racial appraisals, originally limited to the UWZ, by declaring them to be a new goal of SS policy in occupied Poland, Himmler went a step further with his agenda-defining memorandum of May 15, 1940. With his "thoughts on the handling of the ethnonationally alien in the east," Himmler himself sketched out his goals as the RKFDV for the first time. In it, the racial appraisals moved to center stage, mutating from an instrument for recruiting needed labor into a kind of Archimedean fulcrum, one allowing the existing order to be dislodged in order to make room for the dystopian vision of the "German Lebensraum." In a crude application of "divide and conquer," Himmler intended to fragment the Polish populace into numerous "ethnonational splinter groups" ("Volkssplitter") in order to set them against one another. A rudimentary education system would teach them "to be obedient to the Germans, and also truthful, industrious, and well-behaved. I do not consider reading to be necessary."[112] Furthermore, the fragmenting of the populace was to lay the groundwork for "the racial sifting . . . which must form the basis of our ideas on fishing out the racially valuable from this mishmash, bringing them to Germany, and assimilating them there." In this way, Himmler thought the Kashubian identity could be obliterated within four to five years and hoped to see the "concept of the Jew . . . completely eliminated through the possibility of a great emigration of all Jews to Africa or elsewhere to a colony." On the other hand, the leftover unassimilable part of the Polish populace would be deported to the General Government, the new homeland "of a remaining inferior populace," to be joined by the "deported populace . . . from all parts of the German Reich, who are of the same racial and human type (segments of the Sorbs and Wends, for example)," where they would be at the Reich's disposal "as a leaderless worker Volk." This process might be "brutal and tragic" on the individual level, but it was, "if one staunchly rejects the Bolshevist methods for physically exterminating a Volk as being un-Germanic and untenable, still the mildest and the best"—at least according to what Himmler still believed at the time.[113] In a message written just a few days later to his HSSPFs in Poland, he further expanded on several aspects of his memorandum and, by pointing to the SS racial policy expertise that had now been proved in practice, he underlined the SS claim to leadership in this area, especially in comparison to the Nazi Party. Indeed, because the "natives . . . are not being Germanized by the party taking them into its charge and politically educating them," new ways had to be pursued: "The Germanization of the eastern provinces can only be done in accordance with racial understanding, by sifting the populace of these provinces. The racially valuable, to actually permit their blood to be taken into the body of our Volk without causing damage, some of them even being of benefit to us, must be transplanted to Germany as individual families."[114] The racial dystopian vision in which the treatment of local inhabitants was made dependent on the individual's "racial value," a constant fixation of all SS deportation planning, had achieved practical effect for the first time with the introduction of the re-Germanization program. This—at least in Himmler's vision—would be only the beginning.

The Madagascar Plan: Dystopian Flights of Fancy

Himmler's vision was destined to suffer the same fate as those presented by various SS bureaus during the preceding months: it failed because of practical problems on the ground. With no regard for the local populace and relying solely on the use of force, the occupiers soon had to admit that even their coercive methods were of limited success and that compromises were necessary.

It was among the planners in Berlin that this process took the longest. Thus, during a stopover in Litzmannstadt on May 16, 1940, Eichmann believed that the time had come for the local Gestapo to submit a detailed summary of the demographic and economic structure of the Jewish populace that had been forced into the ghetto. The ultimate purpose was preparation for the third "mass movement" (to use Heydrich's expression from January 30, 1940), meaning the expulsion of the Jews, which was "to happen immediately after the Volhynian campaign."[115] Although no timeframe had been set for this back in January, Eichmann now informed the UWZ on June 5, 1940, that the resettlement of the Volhynians was "to be completed by August 31, 1940."[116] September would then see the launch of the biggest deportations to that date; for example, the Litzmannstadt ghetto alone held 158,000 people.[117]

Eichmann's optimism was hardly shared by those handling practical implementation on the ground. One reason was the ongoing jurisdictional struggle between the SS apparatus and the Reich Ministry for Food and Agriculture.[118] A further delay resulted from the attempt to combine the settling of ethnic Germans with a modernizing of the allotment structure for agricultural land, which necessitated a more nuanced decision-making process and considerably slowed the placement of new settlers.[119] Even with an only slowly growing number of ethnic Germans, there were difficulties in settling them, because the SS Task Forces could not offer a sufficient number of suitable farms. The problem was initially caused by the fact that the available area had been artificially constrained; RKFDV headquarters had limited settling to the first-order settlement zone. It took only a month for the RKFDV branch offices and the SS Settlement Staffs to depart from the restriction and start settling ethnic Germans in rural counties outside the settlement zone.[120] By September 1940, half the settlement area lay outside this zone.[121] But there was another obstacle that could not be overcome with the stroke of a pen, namely the General Government's ongoing resistance to taking in more deportees. Even if it were defensible in political terms and achievable in policing terms, the administrations in the annexed territories, even in combination with the SS, could not manage to mobilize enough political pressure in Berlin to score a decisive breakthrough against Frank. There is a certain irony in the fact that the racial appraisals developed their greatest impact not in the "ethnonational struggle" ("Volkstumskampf") nor in Germany's labor market—for this, the number of people appraised was too small—but in deportation policy itself. The racial appraisals had given more options to the ethnocrats in the annexed territories, because—as Frank had hoped—the evictions no longer depended solely on the intake capacity of the General Government; instead, some of the dispossessed could be deported into the Reich, either as "re-Germanizable persons" or as "migrant workers." During the second short-range plan, however, ultimately only 11,912 persons were transported into the Reich after a "positive" racial appraisal.[122] This number hardly compared to the 292,158 locals who had been deported from the entire annexed western Polish territories by the end of 1940.[123]

The "way out" from this dilemma was offered by what was probably the most fantastical proposal seen so far in Nazi population policy: the Madagascar Plan.[124] Even if Madagascar had already been mentioned by Frank as a deportation destination for millions of Jews in a memorandum from January 1940, and Himmler had dreamed of deporting Jews "to Africa or elsewhere to a colony" in his "thoughts on the handling of the ethnonationally foreign in the east" from May 15, 1940, these remarks back then were more an expression of established antisemitic expulsion fantasies whose connection to Madagascar had already become virtually a tradition, and not so much portents of a new policy.[125] With France's looming defeat, however, the idea became concrete and propagated itself with "breathtaking speed."[126] Despite all the practical obstacles, not least of which were military ones, the project would have direct consequences for anti-Jewish policy, including the suspension of the envisaged deportation of Jews into the General Government.[127]

With the decision to pursue the Madagascar project, an entirely new situation had developed virtually overnight. By May 30, 1940, Frank was already reporting a fundamental change of attitude in Hitler, that he said for the first time that, after the Germanization of the annexed eastern provinces, the next step would be, "in the long run, the Germanization" of the General Government as well. An ideological justification for this abrupt change was quickly found: after months of occupation in which every brutality against the local populace was justified by citing its alleged racial inferiority, Frank now claimed to recognize "an absolutely German racial kernel" in it, one that would "bring this space . . . to Germandom."[128] In Frank's view, that is why radical changes were needed in deportation policy, since the General Government could no longer fulfill its existing function as a "deportation zone." Four days later, he wrote in a report to his departmental heads:

> Very important is also the Führer's decision, made in regards to my request, that no more Jew transports into the General Government take place. In terms of general policy, I would like to mention here that the plan is for the entire Jewish tribe . . . to be transported to an African or American colony as soon as possible after a peace agreement. Madagascar is under consideration . . . I have striven for the Jews of the General Government to be also included in this benefit. . . . This was accepted, so that in the foreseeable future, there will have been a colossal relief here as well.[129]

The sudden appearance of the Madagascar Plan would have its greatest impact on population policy in the Wartheland, where SS ethnocrats in particular saw it as a way out of the complete gridlock in deportation policy. Not only did it promise the final expulsion of the Jews, it also offered the possibility of increasing the number of Poles deported into the General Government instead of Jews and thus, finally, also speed up the settlement of the incoming ethnic Germans.[130] As a result, with Himmler's backing, Greiser sought to make an additional expansion to the second short-range plan, aiming to resettle in the Wartheland not only the Volhynians, but also around thirty thousand "Volksdeutsche" from Chełm in the General Government. Frank initially opposed this move and explicitly refused to take in any more than the one hundred twenty thousand Poles who had been dispossessed in order to settle the Volhynians. But the SS prevailed and was able to conduct deportations not only for the settling of Volhynians, but also for the settling of arrivals from Chełm.[131]

Another effect of the Madagascar Plan was that the settlement offices now discarded any last traces of concern for the settlement zone specified by Berlin. By the time the Chełm people arrived, half the settlement area lay outside the settlement zone, which—in view of the fact that the first-order settlement zone covered more than 40 percent of the Wartheland as well—ultimately meant that the limits of the zone had become de facto irrelevant in allocating the "Volksdeutsche." After the SS Settlement Staff found it necessary in the case of the Volhynians to ignore the stipulations of RKFDV headquarters, it seems that they also were then entirely disregarded with the settling of Chełm people.

Last, it was finally time to give more weight to the local "Volksdeutsche" as well. Their initial enthusiasm for the German invasion had given way—at least in part—to a certain disillusionment, for they felt they had not profited as much as they originally had hoped. Back when the higher state and party posts were being filled, the German minority organizations had already voiced criticism at being passed over. And now, the settling of ethnic Germans from other parts of Eastern Europe threatened to also dash their hopes of deriving material gain from the German invasion. Unwilling to trust the initiatives of the occupation administration alone, many "Volksdeutsche" turned directly to the SS Task Forces and UWZ field offices, and demanded the expropriation of their Polish neighbors. Recognizing the importance of "Volksdeutsche" support for German control, Krumey instructed his field offices for the first time on July 3, 1940, that they should accommodate such demands and take into account the Volksdeutsche who were "deserving."[132] The message here was that political loyalty paid dividends.

Of course, such accommodations did not signify any fundamental change in priorities, meaning that the deportations were to facilitate "first of all" the settling of new "Volksdeutsche."[133] It thus came as a surprise when an overwhelming crush of "bargain hunters" developed: as reported by the SD field office in Obornik (today Oborniki), "the hunt for eligible Polish farms is spreading more and more" among the local "Volksdeutsche."[134] For the UWZ, it was equally problematic that SS Task Forces, Landrats, county agronomists, and county farmers' associations had begun succumbing to this pressure and were now arbitrarily expelling people from their holdings, which were then reassigned to the rebellious "Volksdeutsche." These unauthorized expulsions circumvented the more nuanced selection process of the UWZ and undermined its control. But more important, they also threatened the deportation process itself and thus the placement of settlers, for people were being deported to the General Government without using their vacated homes for new settlers, and yet these deportees were counted by the General Government as part of the deportation quota allocated to the Wartheland.[135]

Attempted interventions by Höppner and the IdS of Posen, Ernst Damzog, directed at the relevant senior offices in Posen, were of little avail. When the head of the UWZ field office in Schroda, SS Senior Assault Leader Wilhelm Schmidtsiefen, forbade the SS Task Force commander, SS Senior Assault Unit Leader Herbert Hübner, from executing the intended expulsions aimed at "betterments" ("Besserstellungen") for the "Volksdeutsche," he was lambasted in return. If the SD did not want to help him, wrote Hübner, then he would go it alone. After all, similar actions had taken place in the neighboring counties, and in any case, he "could not understand how the SD has recently become so petty."[136]

Even after the Madagascar Plan was abandoned because of the course of the war, thus further aggravating the situation, the UWZ did not enjoy much more success than before. Pointing to the Wehrmacht's protests against additional transports to the General Government, Frank refused to receive any more. If these nonetheless continued, his administrators were instructed to "stop all transports and send them back into Reich territory."[137] Höppner believed that this development would lend greater weight to his own demands for a considerable curbing or even suspension of the deportations motivated by the aforementioned "betterments." Koppe, however, saw the situation entirely differently and chose instead to bring another kind of expulsion into play: if the dispossessed could no longer be deported into the General Government, then there was still the option of their "displacement" ("Verdrängung," in the jargon of the Nazis) within the Wartheland.[138]

Of course, Koppe's was not the solution that the UWZ had hoped for and amounted instead to the legitimization of a practice already used by several SS Task Forces. Höppner immediately highlighted the security threat posed by large numbers of homeless and destitute people and pushed for the displacements to be uniformly overseen by the UWZ. Pointing to the strained labor market, Höppner suggested that this was the only way to ensure that people were not simply thrown out of their homes but could be brought instead to wherever their labor was needed.

With these expulsions motivated by "betterments," it seems that the UWZ, despite its interventions, could only limit them at best and was unable to bring them under complete control. Damzog did manage to ask Greiser's deputy, Dr. August Jäger, to forbid the Landrats from deporting any more people except when necessary for settlers from Volhynia and Chełm, but the jurisdictional struggle with the SS Task Forces remained acute.[139] As Höppner informed Damzog, the "betterments" were still taking place "without any planning by a central authority." Koppe had purportedly decided that, although only in exceptional cases would what transports were still available carry persons dispossessed by "betterments," the identification of such cases fell within the discretionary power of each individual SS Task Force.[140]

These "betterments" represented yet another expansion of UWZ responsibilities, one that exceptionally did not spring from the activities of an occupation agency, but instead from the pressures exerted by local "Volksdeutsche." The local "Volksdeutsche" used actions comparable to those of the Volksdeutscher Selbstschutz—although with generally less deadly consequences—and were complicit in the demands by some settlers for the police to free up better housing, using such actions to actively inscribe themselves in the Nazi occupation and further radicalize its brutal population policy. How many people fell victim to these measures cannot be determined with certainty. The 5,114 cases cited by Seidl on November 9, 1940, are certainly too few, because his figure does not take into account the expropriations conducted autonomously by various agents.

Expanding the Deportations of the Second Short-Range Plan

The Germanization of the annexed western Polish territories had started with the deportation of Kattowitz Jews on October 18, 1939, and, with the abandonment of the Nisko campaign, the focus of the German deportation policy then shifted after just a few weeks, first to Danzig–West Prussia and finally to the Wartheland. It would take almost a year for the German ethnocrats to turn their attentions back to (Upper) Silesia, and soon afterward to Danzig–West Prussia as well.

The interruption was not intentional. Although one of the main reasons for transferring deportation planning from the HSSPFs to the Reich Security Main Office was the need to plan the deportation flows centrally and coordinate them with one another, the intention to coordinate in particular was a case of wishful thinking on Berlin's part. The reality looked quite different, from the very start. As I have shown, the abrupt shift of focus from Upper Silesia to Danzig–West Prussia was already an unplanned development, stemming from the circumstance that the Baltic Germans had traveled by sea and mostly landed at Danzig and Gotenhafen. As conflicts over the settling of these people escalated between the SS apparatus and the administration in Danzig–West Prussia, Himmler was forced to abruptly change strategy once again, so that most were rerouted to the Wartheland, where "appropriate" dwellings and jobs were to be made available to them under the first short-range plan. And when it turned out that the expulsion of nearly ninety thousand persons was still not enough, the Reich Security Main Office then interjected the intermediate plan, which, of course, also remained limited to this province.

Upper Silesia: Settlements Only on the Periphery

It was only at a relatively late date that Silesia drew the attention of the settlement planners. The first preliminary deliberations took place at a meeting of provincial planners from the eastern regions at the RKFDV headquarters in Berlin, where Meyer informed Silesian provincial planner Gerhard Ziegler about the intention to settle five hundred families from Volhynia in Kattowitz Governmental Region. Ziegler was in agreement with the settling of "Volksdeutsche" farming families, especially if it took place in the Beskid foothills, meaning Saybusch County, thereby allowing the establishment of a "cordon" to isolate the Polish-speaking populace from the Czech-speaking one.[141] His only dissatisfaction was the use of Volhynians, as South Tyroleans were preferred by the Silesian authorities. This possibility was soon discarded, for the population planners under Meyer gave the South Tyroleans an even more important task after France's defeat: their settlement in Burgundy, a part of the French heartland that was now to undergo Germanization, meaning that the "German Lebensraum" was to expand westward as well.[142]

In order to coordinate settlement efforts in Upper Silesia, Greifelt established an RKFDV branch office in Kattowitz, which—like those in other eastern provinces—was subordinated to the HSSPF, here Erich von dem Bach-Zelewski in Breslau. Apparently under pressure from Josef Wagner, it was his trusted associate and liaison to the Luftwaffe, Lieutenant Colonel Ernst Müller-Altenau, who was initially appointed to head the branch office, before preparations finally began in June for the settling of now five thousand Galicians on Himmler's orders.[143] Especially in comparison with the RKFDV branch office in Posen,

Müller-Altenau's office was originally given a rather subordinate role, delegating actions on the ground not to field offices of its own, but instead to agencies of the civil administration—above all the aforementioned Silesian Rural Development Company (Schlesische Landgesellschaft) and the settlement staff under the Landrat of Saybusch, Eugen Hering.[144] The arrangement changed only after the dismissal of Wagner, who had fallen victim to an internal power struggle within the party. Wagner was replaced by Fritz Bracht on April 27, 1940, and after the province's partition into Lower and Upper Silesia in January 1941, Bracht was formally appointed Oberpräsident and Gauleiter of Upper Silesia.[145]

With Wagner's downfall, a number of his supporters found their positions untenable, including Müller-Altenau, who was replaced by Dr. Fritz Arlt, previously head of population matters and welfare in the administration of the General Government.[146] Bracht also strengthened the position of the local RKFDV branch office. Settling was henceforth to be conducted solely by the forthcoming RKFDV field offices, while the civil administration, which had dominated until now, was no longer to participate "authoritatively," but to only assist "supportively."[147] The relevant tasks were delegated to the SS Settlement Staff under SS Senior Assault Unit Leader Hans Butschek.[148]

But why was Saybusch in particular chosen for these deportations? As a borderland, the Beskid foothills had always had a special place in the fantasies of German planners, and it was not only inside the Reich Interior Ministry that they had previously tried to convince themselves that the area's residents were not Poles at all. Even more recent were the musings of Ziegler, who had imagined that settling Germans in the Beskids would give rise to an "ethnopolitical cordon" that would demoralize the region's "Fremdvölkische" and facilitate the Germanization of the rest of the province. A progress report from the RKFDV branch office, however, offered somewhat more prosaic reasons for choosing Saybusch, showing that it was more of a makeshift solution, which in turn was typical for the overall settlement planning of the Nazis. While ethnopolitical considerations did play a certain role here, they went only to the extent that the area was assumed to have fewer "Volksdeutsche" than in the western part of the province, making it easier to avoid deporting "Volksdeutsche" and "Stammesdeutsche" by mistake. But the main factor speaking in favor of Saybusch was the region's relative economic insignificance. In contrast to all other counties in eastern Upper Silesia, deportations from here would not ensnare any industrial workers, which would affect the economic productivity of the Reich. As the RKFDV branch office admitted "an evacuation . . . of this very important workforce cannot be justified in view of this region's war-related production," the area remaining available for settlement was "almost exclusively the narrow eastern strip of the region."[149]

Concrete preparations for the deportations began when Bach-Zelewski informed the civil administration in early August 1940 about the allocation of eight hundred to one thousand "Galician-German hearths (families)."[150] During a meeting at Eichmann's offices a few days later, SS Chief Assault Leader Hans Dreier, who was the "Jew consultant" ("Judenreferent") of the Gestapo in Kattowitz, asked Krumey to dispatch a deportation specialist from Litzmannstadt, "for the purpose of local information and advice."[151] Dreier's participation in the meeting was probably explained by the fact that he had coordinated the deportations of Silesian Jews to Auschwitz that began in late February 1940 and thus was the local specialist in the field.[152] He did not play any further role in the subsequent deportations of the Christian Poles. The inclusion of Jews might still have been under consideration in the beginning, but the possibility was then definitively foreclosed by August 9 at the latest, with the guidelines prepared by Eichmann's Unit IV D 4.[153]

The—temporary—omission of Saybusch Jews certainly did not mean, however, that the Reich Security Main Office refrained from attempting another reideologization of the deportation regulations, meaning the inclusion of Jews and Congress Poles. Eichmann's guidelines provided for the expulsion of Congress Poles and allowed deviations from it only if they could not be rounded up in sufficient numbers. In this case, they were to be supplemented with members of manifestly anti-German organizations. As before, exempted persons included "Volksdeutsche" and "Stammesdeutsche," spouses in a German-Polish marriage, foreigners, members of other ethnic minorities, individuals unfit for transport, and Jews. Explicitly exempted also were persons who were important for the "operational performance of public facilities and industry."[154]

In contrast to events in the Wartheland—and also unlike what would soon occur in Danzig–West Prussia—the upcoming deportations from Saybusch were initially not to be organized by the UWZ that was now being established there too.[155] Instead, the "preparation and implementation of the evacuations" were at first "exclusively the task of the Gestapo Office in Kattowitz," where a dedicated staff was established under mid-level police officer Günter Wendland, beginning its duties in Saybusch on September 3, 1940.[156] As in the Wartheland, the local SS Task Force first surveyed the populace intended for deportation before passing along the corresponding "farm maps" to Wendland's staff, which then decided, according to the guidelines from the Reich Security Main Office, whether the relevant persons were to be cleared for deportation. A maximum of twenty thousand persons was stipulated to avoid violating the agreement with the General Government.[157]

It was thus after the preparations in eastern Upper Silesia were already in full swing, and the settling of several thousand Galicians was approaching, that the planners at RKFDV headquarters in Berlin turned their attention once again to this region. In Meyer's "planning guidelines" from January 1940 and the first-order settlement zone delineated therein, Silesia had still been left out, it being "a less ethnopolitically exposed area, and the question of the rural population [being] largely shaped by the expected expansion of the locally predominating industry."[158] After the county of Saybusch was designated a settlement focus for precisely this reason, the RKFDV headquarters also reactivated their attentions there.[159] In a move that typified the evolution of Nazi population policy, the decision makers in Berlin tried to at least retroactively adapt the existing "plans" to the rapidly changing practices on the ground and finally declared on September 11 that the entire territory south of the Vistula was now part of the first-order settlement zone.[160]

* * *

With the first transport that departed Saybusch on September 23, 1940, along with the seventeen more that followed up to December 14, 1940, the deportees may well have been—the records here are spotty—primarily persons whose farms seemed particularly suitable for the settling of "Volksdeutsche."[161] Expelled from their homes and robbed of almost all their possessions, these people were escorted by the occupiers first to transit camps in the towns of Saybusch, Rajcza, and Sucha (today Sucha Beskidzka). Before being sent onward to Litzmannstadt, they had to undergo racial appraisal by a RuSHA detachment dispatched for this purpose—which represented the first time that this procedure was applied outside the Wartheland. In Upper Silesia, the appraisal was the responsibility of the local bureau chief, SS Junior Assault Leader Kraus, who had been assigned two suitability assessors at once in the form of SS Section Leaders Thien and Schneider; they had to constantly shuttle between the camps, but nonetheless within eleven weeks they had managed to subject almost eighteen thousand individuals to a "rough selection"—in the truest sense.[162] The "findings" of this racial selection sent the individual subjects by rail cither in passenger cars to the RuSHA facility in Litzmannstadt or in mass transports—also via Litzmannstadt—to the General Government. The total number chosen for "fine selection" cannot be determined from the surviving records, but it certainly could not have been more than a few hundred; meanwhile, 17,413 individuals were deported to the General Government in eighteen transports between September 23 and December 14, 1940.[163]

Therefore, the total number of persons expelled during those weeks could not have exceeded eighteen thousand persons—falling short of the originally estimated twenty thousand. The disparity is remarkable in consideration of the zeal shown by the SS ethnocrats in fulfilling the deportation quotas and underlines the particularly difficult conditions—both those set in Berlin and those found in Silesia—under which the forced population exchange was conducted. The smaller number of deportees was also met with a significantly lower number of Galician settler families. Instead of the originally envisaged eight hundred to a thousand families, the number accommodated was only between 650 and 775, corresponding to between 2,876 and 3,709 persons.[164] One reason for the result was the stipulation that part of the province be reserved for settlement by "Reich Germans" ("Reichsdeutsche")—an area involving, according to instructions from Bach-Zelewski, three-quarters of the land under cultivation.[165] Furthermore, the farms in this region were primarily small ones, so that an average of seven or eight local families had to be expelled in order to settle two Galician ones.[166] As a result, lands available for settlement soon became scarce. It cannot be entirely discounted, however, that the lower number of deportees was also due to the disappointment setting in among the SS ethnocrats about the Galician "mountain farmers" allocated here. It had been determined "that the term mountain farmer in no way matched reality and that apparently in the Wartheland they had deliberately shifted the low-performing farmers out of their region"—an occurrence that over time would erode the trust between the settlement staffs in Silesia and the Wartheland, resulting in the centralizing of negotiations in Berlin.[167]

Danzig–West Prussia: Racist Discourse and Labor Shortages

Shortly before the conclusion of the expulsions from Silesia, a new deportation wave was also launched in Danzig–West Prussia, with a transport on December 5, 1940. The fact that the suspension of deportations had lasted a year is remarkable in itself, since the new logic in Nazi deportation policy—precipitated by the arrival of the Baltic Germans—had actually asserted itself here at first. The reason for this hiatus has already been addressed: Forster's criticism of the demographic structure of the Baltic Germans, along with—more decisively—his unwillingness to let the SS apparatus claim so much power over population policy in his domain. But when Himmler was forced to reroute the bulk of the Baltic Germans to the Wartheland, and Heydrich declared at the conference on January 30, 1940, that the Volhynians and Galicians would mostly be settled there as well, Forster apparently recognized the danger that his conflict with Himmler would leave him marginalized in the greater population movements.

As a result, Forster went on the offensive in March 1940 and demanded that forced resettlements also take place in Danzig–West Prussia. He did not appeal to the SS, however, but directly to Hitler and Göring, when he sought authorization for the deportation of forty-one thousand local inhabitants.[168]

This foray by Forster is highly significant. For one thing, he was opening another communication channel, one that allowed him to influence Nazi population policy while going over Himmler's head. Thus, on June 4, 1940, Göring instructed the SS apparatus to prepare the deportation of forty thousand persons, and Frank had no choice but to submit to this new situation on June 11, 1940.[169] For another thing, Forster's foray underlines once again the active role played by Göring in shaping Nazi population policy. In contrast to their portrayal in the literature, his interventions were not limited to curbing Himmler's high-flying deportation plans.

But for the time being, there were no more escalations between the civil administration of Danzig–West Prussia and the SS apparatus. Although Himmler had assured Göring and Frank during the meeting at Karinhall on February 12, 1940, that the resettlement of ethnic Germans from Lithuania, Bessarabia, and Bukovina would be postponed, the situation had changed completely with the occupation of these areas by the Soviet Union in June 1940. From Germany's viewpoint, the transfer of these people to Reich territory now needed to be tackled immediately. New settlement areas in Danzig–West Prussia were the perfect answer, even if they had now been virtually forced on the SS by Forster. And because Greifelt prematurely surmised that an agreement with the Soviet Union on the evacuation of Lithuanian "Volksdeutsche" would come "in the near future," he informed the HSSPFs in Danzig and in Königsberg on July 22 that each would absorb half these new settlers, and that in Danzig–West Prussia they were to be settled "in accordance with Settlement Zone I."[170] But because the zone here encompassed only six counties—envisaged as an "ethnonational bridge" between East Prussia and the Reich—Himmler unilaterally expanded it by three more counties on September 9, 1940.[171]

This largely pragmatically motivated decision now necessitated a first fine-tuning of the ideologically motivated selection criteria. Greifelt feared that the current deportation guidelines, which were aimed above all at the expulsion of Congress Poles, would be misinterpreted so that the bulk of the Kashubian populace would also be swept up. Because the expansion of Settlement Zone I had included counties containing many Kashubians, Greifelt found it necessary to make a clarification. On September 18, 1940, he ordered that Kashubians were to be deported only if they had "provably fought actively against Germandom" or else were living on farms too small for a livelihood as an independent farmer and were at the same time worth considering for assimilation.[172]

With this intervention, Greifelt was met with criticism from this own subordinate agencies, because he had thereby limited the options of the SS ethnocrats on the ground and confronted them even more emphatically with the contradictions of Nazi population policy. Then, in a message dated October 25, 1940, a radical about-face was demanded by SS Regiment Leader Theodor Henschel, head of the SS Task Force that had been established meanwhile in Danzig–West Prussia.[173] Because the population groups cleared for deportation, meaning the "Congress Polish property owners, as well as antisocial and criminal elements . . . live on farms that, already due to their condition, cannot be considered at all for occupation by returnees [Rückwanderer]," while the good farms "are almost entirely in the possession of the so-called 'West Prussian and Kashubian' populace," Greifelt's restriction was counterproductive.[174] If the latter could be deported only when an "emphatic anti-German attitude" could be proved, then there would necessarily be negative consequences on the settling of incoming "Volksdeutsche," as such for finding such proof was often "impossible." As Henschel clearly saw no way around it, he tried instead to undermine the ideological justification which had led to the Kashubians being exempted in the first place by questioning their categorization as an "intermediate class" ("Zwischenschicht"), thus questioning a basic assumption of existing Nazi ethnopolicy. In his view, these persons were "naturally Poles and represented, in the *unanimous* opinion of all experts acquainted with the local circumstances, the *most dangerous* class for an ultimate Germanization of this Gau. While the ethnonational membership of the Congress Poles is known, this so-called 'intermediate class' is, according to demand, Polish, German, and then again Polish."[175]

Henschel called for either a toughening of the selection criteria, with exemptions given to West Prussians and Kashubians only if they had relatives in the Reich or the Wehrmacht and with no more exemptions based on previous political good conduct, or else a complete abolishment of the current exemption rules—and this was in Henschel's view the more advantageous option. Here, all "indisputably Polish owners of agricultural landholdings" would be rounded up and transported first to a UWZ camp. There, they would be subjected to a more nuanced procedure like the one in Litzmannstadt, combining racial, political, and economic criteria, in order to divide them into four groups. Group I was to be reserved for those who seemed suitable for immediate assimilation inside the Reich. If a later assimilation could not be ruled out, and if the relevant persons were also "too valuable . . . for one to tear apart the families and send the able-bodied into labor brigades," they would land in Group II. On the other hand, if a later assimilation was ruled out, and a deportation into the General Government did not seem advisable, the families in question were to be selected for Group III, where they had to "stand ready for every work detail, include labor brigades." Only members of Group IV were to be deported into the General Government. Aware of the importance of economic factors in the shaping of Germanization policy, Henschel tried to shield his proposals against anticipated criticism from the regime's economic wing by explicitly indicating that with this procedure, no "stripping of the workforce" was to be feared.[176]

Soon thereafter, Henschel tried to push this concept at the RKFDV headquarters in Berlin as well, during a meeting at Ernst Fähndrich's offices on November 1, 1940, which saw the arrival of representatives from the German Resettlement Trust Company (Deutsche Umsiedlungs-Treuhand Gesellschaft, or DUT), along with Odilo Globocnik (the SS and Police Leader, or SSPF, of Lublin District), Ehlich, and Eichmann, among others.[177] The focus of discussion was the critical situation in the Wartheland, where the SS Settlement Staff in Posen had just reported that it could not settle any more people, and recently even had to turn away four hundred families originally allotted to the region. Hensch found an opportunity to exploit this situation, which happened to touch on his main interest: therefore, after describing the anticipated difficulties in accommodating the settlers acquired by Forster, he then offered to take in these four hundred families as well, but only if the local deportation guidelines could be toughened. And although the attendees failed to agree on the Kashubians, Henschel nonetheless seems to have achieved at least a partial success in how the rest of the "intermediate class" was to be handled. They were now to be shunted into a camp, where they would undergo a selection process conducted by the SD and RuSHA, ultimately to be deported into either the Reich or the General Government, thereby freeing up twenty thousand farms.[178] The exact organization of the procedure was what Fähndrich spelled out three days later in a submission to Himmler, which was prepared in consultation with the Reich Security Main Office and RuSHA.[179]

Here, one might be tempted to view Fähndrich's submission, as Isabel Heinemann does, for example, as evidence that "the question of racial selection played a key role."[180] It seems to me, however, that this interpretation fails to grasp the essence of Fähndrich's proposal, which did not actually support Henschel's demands, much less a selection process to be conducted primarily on a racial basis. Even Henschel himself had certainly not called for exclusively racial appraisals but instead for a multistage selection process that first applied a "racial, health, and political assessment" before weeding out individuals "as unsuitable for Germanization." His proposal also meant that—in Fähndrich's opinion—families chosen for assimilation should be compensated not according to their racial value but according to "their previously having politically proved themselves."[181] Such corrections were ultimately of minor importance, however, as Fähndrich was generally dissatisfied with Henschel's entire proposal. In his view, "such a rather contrived-seeming plan, *at present* can be reconciled only very poorly with the harsh realities." Already with reference to the functional interests of power alone, Fähndrich believed—here adopting the critique of the SD, as revealed in the marginalia to Henschel's proposal—that with "the intermediate class, one cannot proceed just like with the *Poles*." To him, such a "coercive solution" was counterproductive, because it would not only trigger a "flood of complaints" from relatives inside the Reich but also cause further unrest within the province itself, thereby threatening its Germanization in general. Fähndrich's own proposal was considerably more moderate. According to it, settlers should first be placed only on farms belonging to "indisputable Poles."[182] It was only afterward that racial appraisals should be considered, in order to identify the prosperous "racially bad" members of the "intermediate class" and the impoverished "racially good" ones; the former could be deported into the General Government, and the latter into the Reich. Only after that were the prosperous "racially good" members of the intermediate class also to be targeted. Since these last were generally to be compensated for their material losses, but a farmer would probably accept nothing less than reestablishment on another farm, the assimilation of this group would necessarily depend on the availability of farms inside the Reich itself—and thus should be postponed into the distant future.

But for Himmler, even this version, which was somewhat softened in racial terms, still went too far; instead, he shifted the focus back more strongly on the security-related function of the expulsions. In a message to HSSPF Richard Hildebrandt on November 28, 1940, he "agreed" that besides all Poles, the deportations were to take in only those members of the "intermediate class" who had "operated in an anti-German manner" or had "unquestionably . . . professed to Polishdom"—and in that order of priority.[183] He left open the question of whether this group was to undergo a racial appraisal as well.

The Reich Security Main Office, however, was against even Himmler's solution. At a meeting with Fähndrich and Henschel on January 7, 1941, which was also attended by other officials from the Reich Security Main Office and RKFDV headquarters, but to which—tellingly—nobody from RuSHA was even invited, Ehlich noted that expanding the deportations to include members of the intermediate class would also sweep up individuals who, "with the introduction of the DVL, would fall under Groups 3 and 4." There was no guarantee at the time that these persons would not be handled like Poles: "Under the existing procedure, after being authorized for removal, these families would go through the camp of the UWZ and there be subjected to aggressive selection by agents from RuSHA. As a result, and according to experience so far, the deportation of some 70 percent of the families in Groups 3 and 4 must be reckoned with." For Ehlich, this percentage was much too high, especially since this "result . . . contradicts the explicit order of the Reichsführer of the SS [i.e., Himmler], whereby Deutschstämmige families may not be moved into the General Government."

The Reich Security Main Office therefore pushed for a fundamental change. To be decided was whether "these Deutschstämmige families should be subjected to a racial examination" and thus whether they had to go through the UWZ camp before their transport into the Reich. The Reich Security Main Office prevailed here: in the future, there would be "no racial inspection" of these families. They were to be immediately separated from the other deportees and transferred to camps that the HSSPF would establish especially for this group.[184] There was also a solution to the problem of how these persons would be defined: "in the absence of another authority," the task would be delegated to the SD Special Unit (*SD-Sonderreferat*) at the SD Command Precinct in Danzig. Thus, another blow was dealt to RuSHA: with this "intermediate class," not only was a large part of the populace earmarked for deportation now slipping through the fingers of the suitability assessors, but the racial appraisals were also downgraded as a selection procedure for determining membership in the German "Volksgemeinschaft."

Heinemann notes in a preliminary observation that, on the part of the SS, "ever more ingenious methods for procuring space were drawn up," and this is valid at least to the extent that the scarcity of settlement land was the reason why this discussion had come up in the first place and it had also structured its course. But her resulting conclusion that these methods "amounted to a racial selection of ever more subgroups of the Polish and mixed-nationality local populace" is, however, wrong—this was out of the question, as Ehlich's intervention made clear.[185]

Typifying the self-contradictory nature of Nazi Germanization policy, Henschel had proposed the racial appraisal of the local populace just as it had become clear to him that he would be unable to accommodate the settlers assigned to him. The expansion of deportations that this would require, however, also needed to be underpinned ideologically, in that it ultimately affected members of the intermediate class, persons who in the ethnonational vision of the Nazis might be potential members of the German "Volksgemeinschaft" that was to be constructed. Henschel thought he could resolve this dilemma by calling for the racial appraisal of these individuals. With the high number of people excluded by the RuSHA procedure, the evacuation of urgently needed farms would thus be assured. But Henschel's racial underpinning of what was essentially a pragmatically motivated proposal was met by criticism—on ideological grounds—at the Reich Security Main Office, for it was clearly unacceptable for the intermediate class in Danzig–West Prussia to be subjected to the same selection procedure as the "Polish" natives of the Wartheland. In this "labyrinth of racial logic," the Reich Security Main Office was able to derail these racial appraisals by applying a racial rationale in opposition.[186]

As much as this metaphor applies to the present case, this can only be the starting and not the endpoint of the analysis. Instead, it is necessary to ask how this situation related to the power relationships between the involved actors and to the wartime needs of the Reich as defined by these actors. Although the existing documentation is scanty here too, one cannot fail to see that Ehlich's intervention strengthened the position of the Reich Security Main Office within the SS complex. The power to define who belonged to the intermediate class was snatched away from the RuSHA suitability inspectors and conferred on the SD. Furthermore, the German war economy was being supplied with ostensibly "German" (forced) laborers. What is clear is that the Reich Security Main Office had prevented the expansion of racial appraisals.

* * *

In Danzig–West Prussia, the first—and last—deportations under the second short-range plan were conducted in December 1940. The job of organizing and implementing them was assigned to the UWZ in Danzig, which had been founded on November 11, 1940, as an agency of the Chief of the Security Police and the SD (i.e., Heydrich).[187] Unlike the Wartheland case—but as was later done also in Silesia—formal leadership was given to the local chief of the Gestapo Command Office, which in Danzig was SS Senior Assault Unit Leader Hans-Helmut Wolff.[188] But the man who became de facto leader of the UWZ was SS Chief Assault Leader Franz Abromeit, who at the start of that year had already become administrative clerk for deportations on the staff of the Danzig IdS, SS Regiment Leader Helmuth Willich. In Danzig, the procedure was largely a copy of the one in the Wartheland and in eastern Upper Silesia. The SS Settlement Staff and local SS Task Forces prepared a list of farms that were suitable for accommodating settlers, surveyed the families currently living there, and forwarded the results to the special unit at the SD Command Precinct in Danzig, which then decided on the rightfulness of the deportation. After that, the deportation lists were forwarded to the UWZ in Danzig, which likely began on November 21 with the arrests of the subject persons, who were first concentrated in local reception camps before being transferred to the newly erected UWZ camp in Thorn (today Toruń).[189] There, they were subjected to a "rough selection" by a suitability assessor from the RuSHA field office in Litzmannstadt—and with this addendum, the procedure had become the definitive standard in the annexed western Polish territories.[190] While in these camps, they were also finally presented to representatives of the provincial employment office, the provincial farmers' association, and the chamber of industry and commerce, who then requisitioned indispensable workers on the spot. Labeled with a discriminatory letter P, the requisitioned were to be deployed as forced laborers within the local province.[191] The path of the other detainees led them through Litzmannstadt, where those with positive appraisals were transferred to the RuSHA re-Germanization camp, while the great majority, after a final listing by the local UWZ bureau, were deported into the General Government.

A total of 9,946 persons were deported in ten transports to the General Government between December 5 and 17, 1940—in addition to individuals removed as "re-Germanizable" or otherwise as forced laborers.[192] As with the other deportations so far, most of them had been selected because their dwellings or farms had seemed particularly suitable for the settling of incoming "Volksdeutsche." But in view of the complaints submitted by the SS Settlement Staff, the possibility cannot be excluded that the SD Special Unit exempted not only those who had relatives in the Reich or the Wehrmacht but also—here anticipating the regulations of January 7, 1941—persons who they thought might be able to make a valid claim for enrollment in Groups 3 or 4 of the DVL. On the other hand, it is certain that the deportations included the relatives of twenty individuals who were executed on Himmler's orders.[193] On top of that, the transports presumably included anyone "whose staying represents a danger and a burden for development work."[194] On the other hand, there is one aspect that remains unexplained: the 9,946 deportees included 3,259 Jews, representing a considerably higher proportion than in all previous deportations. But it may be that this reorientation was also a first practical response to the failure of the Madagascar Plan.[195]

With the second short-range plan, deportation planning, as conducted at the Reich Security Main Office from December 1939, went beyond the Wartheland to include the other provinces for the first time. From the viewpoint of the ethnocrats in Berlin and the various provincial capitals, the results were disappointing in two regards: although they had managed to expel 290,058 "Poles" from the annexed western Polish territories up to December 1940, replacing them with 176,442 "Volksdeutsche," their original hope was to have already expelled a million people by February, and to have conducted racial appraisals on the rest of the populace by the end of the year.[196] But these figures paled even more when set against the ethnographic structure of affected provinces at the time: although the number of "Germans" had been successfully increased to 831,062, the number of Poles still exceeded 8 million, thus representing 90 percent of the population. And in terms of the second short-range plan's goal of expanding the deportations geographically as well, the results were no better. Certainly, deportations in Upper Silesia had commenced, encompassing 17,413 persons, and the total in Danzig–West Prussia increased by almost 10,000 to reach 38,059 persons.[197] These numbers made up only one-eighth of the total deported persons to date, however, with the rest coming from the Wartheland.[198] And the stated hope that numbers would subsequently improve would also remain unfulfilled. As it would soon turn out, the deportations out of these two provinces were effectively suspended.

Third Short-Range Plan: Overtaken by the War's Progress

Just as he had done in January 1940, Heydrich convened a meeting in January 1941 to negotiate in Berlin the deportation and resettlement numbers for the coming year; he invited representatives from the Wehrmacht High Command and the relevant SS Main Offices, as well as the civil administrations in the annexed eastern territories and the General Government.[199] What is particularly notable here is how little the decision makers let themselves be disheartened by the difficulties of the past deportations, and so they ultimately agreed that the third short-range plan would encompass the deportation of 831,000 persons from the annexed eastern provinces into the General Government, where an additional 340,000 persons would be removed from their homes and displaced internally.[200] This outright exorbitant figure was also the result of the various interests expressed by various parties, which all demanded satisfaction. As a result, it was the first time that the deportations of Poles to accommodate ethnic Germans were no longer the overriding factor that decided everything: amounting to 438,000 persons, they failed to make up even half the overall total. They were to make room for 150,000 ethnic Germans, primarily from Bessarabia and Bukovina. Almost the same number, specifically 437,000, were to be removed for the Wehrmacht, which wanted to create large military training areas, while another 55,000 people were to make way for the expansion of the Auschwitz industrial area, and an additional 50,000 for providing "betterments" to local "Volksdeutsche." And finally, more than a year after the failure of the Nisko campaign, it was also necessary to fulfill the wishes of Baldur von Schirach, Reichsstatthalter and Gauleiter of Vienna: motivated by his city's housing shortage, among other factors, he wanted to expel 60,000 Jews from it. The representatives of the General Government, previously not shy about criticizing such deportation plans, were more subdued this time around.[201] In the wake of the Madagascar Plan's failure, Frank had received orders from Hitler himself, just a few weeks earlier: he was to immediately take in some of the Reich's Jewish populace and also to open the General Government to additional Poles from the annexed territories.[202]

From the perspective of the civil administrations in the eastern provinces, the agreed deportation numbers were a great success, in that they promised to advance the Germanization of the provinces at a rapid pace. Nonetheless, it was clear to the local experts that fulfilling the deportation numbers would not be enough to meet the envisaged settlement targets. And so, during the detailed planning phase that followed the conference in Berlin, the sobering reality became immediately apparent in every province: farms of adequate size, tradesmen's workshops, and urban housing were all in short supply. The seriousness of the situation is shown by the measures that the SS undertook: just two weeks after the meeting at Heydrich's, it seemed that the deportations aimed at "betterments" for local "Volksdeutsche," and probably also those for the creation of military training areas, were temporarily suspended.[203] With this, the number to be deported was reduced by half, and efforts could now be focused again on the evacuations for the accommodating of incoming settlers. In fact, at the first railroad timetable conference in mid-January 1941, it was only for this contingent that trains were made available.[204] On top of that, it was necessary to increase the lands available for settlement. As noted by a representative of RKFDV headquarters after a discussion with the head of the Posen branch office, Döring, it seemed that of the sixty-eight thousand farms originally earmarked for settlement, sixty thousand were already occupied, and no more than another two thousand were currently available.[205] In any case, the fifty-seven thousand settlers allotted to the Wartheland for 1941 could not be accommodated under these conditions.[206] After, as previously shown, the settlements had already been unilaterally expanded the previous summer to counties that did not belong to the first-order settlement zone, the settlement planners now definitively abandoned the guidelines of the RKFDV headquarters and opened the entire province to settlement.[207] Upper

Silesia followed shortly thereafter, when Himmler declared all of Upper Silesia part of the first-order settlement zone on January 16, 1941.[208]

In Berlin, the start of the deportations under the third short-range plan was set for February 1, except for Silesia, which would begin on March 1, 1941.[209] UWZ bureaus had now been established in Danzig and Kattowitz as well.[210] They were placed under the supervision of the regional IdS, but tied to the Gestapo and not the local SD Command Precinct as in the Wartheland, and they were responsible only for organizing the deportations, not for clearing individuals to be deported. Such selections remained in the hands of the regional SD, which established in each province a Special Unit III BS to handle this.[211]

The special units were supposed to ensure compliance with the selection criteria. As usual, various conflicting interests came into play. For one, the Reich Security Main Office again emphasized adherence to racial criteria, ordering that deportations were to take "only Congress Poles at first." Departures from this order were permitted only if their numbers were insufficient to fill the allotted contingent—and even then, only members of "manifestly anti-German organizations" were to be taken.[212] The civil administration agencies and the local RKFDV bureaus had other concerns, however, and furthermore had the right to nominate individuals for deportation. Thus, in Danzig–West Prussia, generally cleared for deportation were all those "who have professed to Polishdom," meaning people who had been politically conspicuous.[213] Meanwhile, in Silesia, the persons particularly targeted were those who were "not essential to the production process."[214] Furthermore, and in line with previous policy, it is clear that the settlement staffs were pushing above all for the deportation of persons whose homes were needed for the settling of ethnic Germans, while the mayors were also making every effort to get rid of "troublemakers" and welfare recipients. The UWZ and the special units first swung into action when it was time to go over the lists submitted to them from each county. They could cross off names only of persons who were exempted from deportations—although the officers on the ground sometimes overrode the decision from the regional capital anyway, on their own authority removing the subject persons from their homes. But it was agreed in all three provinces that before deportation, all detainees still had to undergo a selection process, so that RuSHA and the employment office could identify those who were suitable for forced labor in the Reich.[215]

This workflow would not survive for very longer, however, for preparations for attacking the Soviet Union had already begun. On February 21, 1941, Günther was already informing the UWZ bureaus that in the coming weeks, "for obvious military reasons," the Reich Railroad could probably provide just two trains per week—although seventeen would have been needed.[216] Then, on March 11, Greifelt informed the RKFDV appointees about the imminent halting of deportations.[217] With the forced termination of deportations on March 15, 1941, the third short-range plan had ended in failure before it could even really begin. By that point, "only" 19,000 persons had been deported from the Wartheland into the General Government, instead of the envisaged 230,000.[218] Meanwhile, in Danzig–West Prussia, it was probably no more than 11,000, instead of the planned 167,000 locals.[219] As for Silesia, where likewise 230,000 locals were supposed to be deported, there is no evidence that even a single deportation train had departed by mid-March. The Wehrmacht had to postpone their plans to create new military training areas, just as the local "Volksdeutsche" did their theft of neighboring properties. Instead of deporting a million persons by the end of the year, the occupiers had managed just 30,000.[220] Meanwhile, in the reception camps of VoMi, another 256,257 persons were forced to continue waiting.[221]

* * *

Views on this "fiasco" in the scholarly literature have been somewhat one-sided.[222] The deportation stop is either blamed mostly on the protests of the Wehrmacht, which claimed for itself all transport capacities and also expressed concerns about the security-related impact of the deportations on the staging areas in the General Government or on the inability of deportation planners at the Reich Security Main Office and RKFDV headquarters to balance the diverging interests between the Berlin central authorities and the regional civil administrations.[223] What has been either ignored or underrated here is another crucial factor: the rapidly growing need for workers both in the annexed territories and in the Reich itself. Above all, I believe it was this worker shortage that doomed the short-range plan to failure, before the strain on the rail network also ended it for practical reasons.

The conceptual transformation of Polish residents from dangerous or at least undesirable "Fremdvölkische" into indispensable workers had already been presaged during the first deportations. But with the upcoming attack on the Soviet Union, which meant a further prolongation of the war, the economic aspect acquired a new urgency. To mobilize all economic resources, Göring gave the following order at a meeting on January 29, that "foreign workers are to be brought in as much as possible. The Reich Marshall [i.e. Göring] has again determined that the concerns of population policy and racial policy must be set aside for now. Furthermore, the Reich Labor Minister has again and emphatically instructed the responsible German agencies in the occupied territories to move in this direction."[224] Shortly thereafter, the civil administrations in Poland were also explicitly instructed to supply the war economy with additional forced laborers without delay.[225]

At a hastily convened meeting, the head of the employment office in Litzmannstadt, Dr. Storch, informed attendees that Göring had ordered the delivery of two hundred fifty thousand Polish farmworkers in the near term.[226] Although the civil administrations of all Polish territories were meant to muster this number, and not just the Wartheland alone, its magnitude made it immediately clear that the existing deportation procedure was destined for the scrapheap.

This pertained above all to the racial appraisals introduced by the SS with the second short-range plan, which tied the selection of workers to a noneconomic yardstick and thereby artificially reduced the supply. The SS had been allowed to pursue this project as long as the negative consequences for the labor market remained manageable. These consequences will be examined later in detail, but suffice it to say here that the SS was forced to immediately suspend the racial appraisals when it became clear that they threatened the mustering of all economic capacities for the attack on the Soviet Union.

As the SS complex was soon forced to recognize, the implications of the worsening labor shortage went much deeper than this. At issue was not simply the procedural design of the deportations, but the deportations themselves. The head of the planning department of the settlement staffs in Posen and Litzmannstadt, Alexander Dolezalek, was already faced with this reality in February 1941. At a meeting with Greiser and his personal adjutant Harry Siegmund, he insisted that in accommodating the settlers, it was better to subdivide large estates than to consolidate small farms, which is what Greiser preferred. While Dolezalek reasoned that large estates would retard the Germanization of the province, because they could be tilled only with sufficient (Polish) farmworkers, whereas the consolidation of small farms depended on the deportation of considerably more people, which could not be assured in light of the fitful transport situation, Greiser pointed out that Hitler and Göring had tasked him with the "production of grain, grain, and yet again grain"—and that in this regard, large farms were simply more productive.[227] What Aly does not specifically underline here, although it actually represented an even more significant break, was Greiser's announcement that he no longer wanted to deport even some of the Poles to be dispossessed for the accommodation of ethnic Germans. In their role as a valuable workforce, the Wartheland could not do without them.

Of course, the civil administration had always been careful to avoid losing skilled workers. But the task had been manageable until now, for the deportations into the General Government and the delivery of workers into the Reich had been moderate. The third short-range plan promised—or from this perspective, threatened—to change all this by greatly multiplying the number of targeted people. The damage that this development could cause to the productive capacities of the annexed provinces was recognized in the respective capitals, and in Posen it had prompted Greiser to keep in the province at least some of the persons to be dispossessed by the resettlement project. How seriously Greiser judged this situation was ultimately shown in early March, when he himself issued a general prohibition on the deportation of Jews and instead ordered their internment in the ghetto of Litzmannstadt, which was developed into a production site.[228] Even as it was becoming clear at the Reich Security Main Office that the timetable of the third short-range plan was becoming untenable because of the Wehrmacht's deployment in the General Government, the provinces were already undergoing a change in thinking that would similarly put into question the current deportation planning, although for entirely different reasons.

As a result, the third short-range plan joined an ever-growing line of exuberant population policy projects that had abruptly collapsed. Its end differed, however, in one significant way from those of the preceding campaigns, which had failed primarily from the still incomplete surveying of the local populace and the transport arteries still partially suffering from the war's effects. Certainly, it was the overburdened infrastructure of the Reich Railroad that brought a practical end to the deportations this time as well. But in the scholarly literature, this circumstance has concealed a reevaluation on the part of the civil administration that was forced by the attack on the Soviet Union and which put into question the central premises of deportation planning at the Reich Security Main Office and RKFDV headquarters. What the civil administrators in Upper Silesia had already recognized from the very beginning was now becoming increasingly apparent to those in Posen and Danzig as well: however much the long-term goal of Germanizing these provinces could be achieved only by removing the populace declared "Polish," this same group was nonetheless proving indispensable in the short term for economic survival of a country at war. Confronted with a choice between pursuing a racial dystopia and satisfying the rational demands of power, the Gauleiters again opted for the latter. Beyond the planned increase in deportations to the General Government, the civil administrations were also faced with the threat of having to surrender more and more workers to the Reich, and so found themselves forced into a radical turnaround. At least the able-bodied among the local residents had been transformed virtually overnight from undesirable "Fremdvölkische" into valuable workers. Dolezalek noted this all too clearly in his discussion with Greiser and Siegmund: if it had actually been possible for all the deported Poles to be immediately replaced with equally qualified Germans from Eastern Europe or the Reich, the Wartheland would not be in the current dilemma. But, as Siegmund said: "You yourself know, what has become of all these big plans by the Reichsführer [i.e., Himmler]?"[229]

"Race" or "Volk"? Competing Visions for a "German Volksgemeinschaft"

By early 1941, the increasing dependence on the local populace had forced a radical turnaround in Nazi deportation policy. The full extent of this dependence is seen in the way the selection of individuals was carried out who seemed, in the eyes of the German occupiers, suitable for admission into the German "Volksgemeinschaft."

The intervention of the Reich Interior Ministry, as in Frick's decree on the acquisition of German national status from November 25, 1939, was initially met by heavy criticism in all three provinces. Here, each respective Gauleiter had a very specific vision of the best way to select the "Volksdeutsche" in his own province, and in cases of conflict, each was prepared to defend his vision against resistance from Berlin.

Provincial Divergences

THE WARTHELAND: "ABSOLUTELY NO ETHNONATIONALLY QUESTIONABLE ELEMENTS"

The strongest protest against Frick's decree came from the Wartheland. For the ethnocrats in Posen, the decree put into question their own selection policy as recently installed with the DVL, a policy through which the bulk of the local populace was not to be inducted into the state collectivity as "Germans," but instead expelled as "Poles." The criticism voiced by Karl Albert Coulon and his staff thus focused on the very vague definition of German ethnonational membership (who exactly belonged to the German Volk), and on what was meant by a "desirable addition to the population." This in turn made Coulon's demands even more stringent: "On the ethnonational battleground, there can remain absolutely no ethnonationally questionable elements who cannot guarantee they will be ready for the future burdens of their Volk consciousness."[230] Confronted with the task of implementing occupation policy and Germanization policy in a province where the occupiers and local "Volksdeutsche" altogether were only a small minority, Coulon thus cleaved to the notion that a German is primarily someone who, as proven by previous conduct, can be relied on in the implementation of occupation policy—a radical position that had seemed affordable in the beginning, as Himmler had after all promised to replace Poles with ethnic Germans.

It took a few weeks for the changes to the selection process, as necessitated by the Reich Interior Ministry's decree, to be completed so that the surveying could begin. Besides the need to choose suitable staff members, it was above all the preparation of an extra questionnaire that caused delay. In order to identify the "ethnonationally questionable elements," the ethnocrats of the DVL needed more information than what was collected though the questionnaire prescribed by Berlin. As Egon Leuschner, the section leader at the Nazi Party's Racial Policy Office and former appointee for population and race policy at the Gauleiter's offices in Silesia, wrote to Friedrich Uebelhoer (Regierungspräsident of Litzmannstadt), "this questionnaire in its one-sidedness was geared toward the acquisition of German national status, and not suited to facilitating the determination of German ethnonational membership in a responsible way."[231] Leuschner therefore developed a second one and pushed it through at the Reich Interior Ministry by way of Uebelhoer. Called the "supplementary questionnaire ("Ergänzungsfragebogen" see figures 4.3 and 4.4), it was attached to the ministry's own questionnaire—but only in the Wartheland.

Deutsche Volksliste

Zweigstelle _[Wollstein]_

Ergänzungsfragebogen

zur Ermittlung der deutschen Volkszugehörigkeit

Nr. _______

1. Bekenntnis: ~~gottgläubig~~, ~~evangelisch~~, katholisch.
   Bekenntnis des Ehegatten: ~~gottgläubig~~, evangelisch, ~~katholisch~~.

2. Wo beschäftigt: _______
   Tätigkeit vor dem 1. 9. 1939: _______

3. Name, Vorname und Herkunft der Eltern, Großeltern:
   Vater: _______ Ignatz _______ geboren _______ 1871 in Wabes
   Mutter: Bertha geb. _______ 2. 6. 1874 „ Bottchen
   Großvater (väterl.): Johann _______ „ Wabes
   Großmutter „ _______ Franz „ Neudörfchen
   Großvater (mütterl.): _______ „ Buda
   Großmutter „ _______

4. Zu Punkt 12 des vorstehenden Fragebogens:
   Welche Schulen besuchten Sie:
   a) deutsche _Volksschule_ von 1. 3. 1912 bis 31. 12. 1919
   b) polnische _______ „ _______ „ _______

5. Zu Punkt 9 des vorstehenden Fragebogens:
   Angabe der Nationalität oder Muttersprache im polnischen Militärpaß: _polnisch_

6. Zu Punkt 10 des Fragebogens:
   Welchen dort angeführter Vereinigungen usw. gehörten Sie vor dem 1. 9. 1939 an?
   von _1934_ bis _zur Auflösung_
   „ _______ „ _______

7. Zu Punkt 12 des vorstehenden Fragebogens:
   Welchen Verfolgungen (Gefängnis- und Geldstrafen, wirtschaftlichen Benachteilungen, Verschleppungen usw.) waren Sie auf Grund Ihres Bekenntnisses zum deutschen Volkstum ausgesetzt? _______

   Welche Bürgen können Sie für Ihr Bekenntnis zum deutschen Volkstum anführen?
   1. Name _______ Wohnung _______
   2. Name _______ Wohnung _______

Staatliche Druckerei in Posen

Figure 4.3. Supplementary questionnaire, used exclusively in the Wartheland as an attachment to the Reich Interior Ministry's own questionnaire, to facilitate the assessment of the applicant's ethnonational loyalty. Identified as German People's List, Branch Office [here: Wollstein], Supplementary Questionnaire, for the Assessment of German Volk Membership, it includes questions on the religion of the applicant and spouse, employment, names of parents and grandparents, schooling, passport nationality and mother tongue, prewar memberships, punishments suffered from "professing German folkdom," guarantors, children, and children's schooling. Point 10 declares "I have always, and before Sept. 1, 1939, professed to German folkdom. I know that in case of false statements, I have put myself outside the German Volksgemeinschaft. If this declaration cannot be affirmed, all reasons for it are to be specified." At the end is space for assessment notes.
Source: Polish State Archives in Poznań, under DVL Wollstein, 427.

8.	Kinderzahl:			
	1. Vorname	Geb.	Rel.-Bekenntnis	Muttersprache (Haussprache)
	2. „	„	„	„
	3. „	„	„	„
	4. „	„	„	„
	5. „	„	„	„
	6. „	„	„	„
	7. „	„	„	„
	8. „	„	„	„

9.	Welche Schulen besuchten Ihre Kinder vor dem 1. 9. 39?
	a) deutsche (genaue Bezeichnung der Schulgattung):
	b) polnische (genaue Bezeichnung der Schulgattung):

10.	Ich habe mich stets, auch vor dem 1. 9. 1939, zum deutschen Volkstum bekannt. Ich weiß, daß ich mich im Falle falscher Angaben außerhalb der deutschen Volksgemeinschaft stelle. Kann diese Erklärung nicht abgegeben werden, so sind alle Gründe dafür anzugeben.
11.	Ich versichere eidesstattlich, daß ich die obigen Fragen wahrheitsgetreu beantwortet habe. Ich weiß, daß ich mich im Falle bewußt falscher Angaben strafbar mache.

Schließenwalde, den 10. März 19 40

Bruno G

Eigenhändige Unterschrift.

Frei für Prüfungsvermerk:

Figure 4.4. Reverse side of figure 4.3.

Along with the questionnaires from the Reich Printing Office in Berlin, the DVL branch offices also received the twelve-page "green booklet"—as it was known internally—outlining the organization of the DVL and providing detailed procedural instructions. According to the booklet, the DVL now consisted of three organizational levels: a central office (*Zentralstelle*, attached to the Reichsstatthalter's offices), regional offices (*Bezirksstellen*, each at a Regierungspräsident's offices), and branch offices (*Zweigstellen*, each at a Landrat's offices). The personnel of each branch office included the Landrat (as chair) and the mayor of the county seat, along with one or two "Volksdeutsche," who needed approval from the central office and the local SD representative. Prospective enrollees had to request a questionnaire by visiting a branch office, where they were subjected to a first screening that turned away all those who they thought had definitely no chance at induction into the DVL. Upon the return of these questionnaires, which had to be completed for each family member, including children, they were assessed by the branch office's assessment committee, which assisted the Landrat as an "advisory body" and whose members had to be approved by Coulon.[232] Unlike before, however, the branch office could no longer pass a final binding judgment on each application, but were instead to notate it with a "preliminary decision" before forwarding to the newly established regional office.

Each regional office was attached to a Regierungspräsident. Besides its director, its personnel included two "Volksdeutsche" (who had to be proposed by the Regierungspräsident and approved by the central office) and the Regierungspräsident's departmental head for ethnonationality questions and citizenship matters (Dezernent für Volkstumsfragen und Staatsangehörigkeitsangelegenheiten). Besides coordinating the local branch offices, the primary responsibility of each regional office was to make a final decision on the applications from the branch offices, thereby awarding German national status if the applicant was selected for Group A ("Bekenntnisdeutsche," or "professed Germans") or Group B ("Stammesdeutsche," or "descent Germans"). If the application for admission was approved, an identity document was sent to the relevant Landrat for issuing to the applicant. Rejected applicants were to be notified in writing. Furthermore, each regional office also set up a card catalog to register all "Germans" and the rejected applicants, sorting them according to ethnopolitical criteria. Biethnic marriages were separately categorized (and then according to the mother tongue of the children), as were marriages involving a Jewish spouse.[233] For the authorities, this process laid the foundations for a more detailed differentiation in population policy.

But the greatest attention in the "green booklet" was devoted to the DVL selection criteria. To wit: the "basic prerequisite for German ethnonational membership is: *the professing to Germandom during the time of ethnonationally foreign rule.*"[234] This was generally tied to membership in a "Volksdeutsche" organization.

Approved persons were inducted into Group A and formed the basis of the Nazi Party in the Wartheland. As had been done during the initial and then aborted registration effort in Posen, the DVL was to take in not only these "Bekenntnis-deutsche," but also at least some of the "Stammesdeutsche," meaning persons "descended from German parents." Naturally, descent alone did not suffice. Instead, political conduct was to be surveyed for these persons as well, in order to differentiate between those who—despite being one of the "Deutschstäm-mige"—had "either professed to Polishdom . . . or had remained indifferent. With those who had professed to Polishdom, the decision is simple"—they were to be rejected. But if they had been classified as one of the "Deutschstämmige" and reckoned among the "indifferent," or else among those who "under the pressure of the Poles did not risk professing to Germandom," it was necessary to carefully consider whether the individual, according to the "overall impression of his personality and his conduct . . . can be recognized as a German" and sorted into Group B.[235]

Therefore, I think Włodzimierz Jastrzębski is mistaken when he claims that the German authorities in the Wartheland had "very broadly interpreted" membership in Group B.[236] The selection process for this group caused particular difficulties for the occupiers, already beginning with the determination of "German descent." Here, the problem lay precisely in formulating a definition of who was "German" and who was "Polish," regardless of a person's own self-identification—and, of course, the failure of the German occupiers to find a way of biologize being "German" as the sum of social practices necessarily affected all attempts at now deciding who was of "German" or of "Polish" descent. On the other hand, the German legal system had already gathered some practical experience with such contradictions, not least with the selection process applied to Jewish Germans, which was made dependent on the religious affiliation of the grandparents. In the Wartheland, it was decided to use a similar crutch, examining the names and surnames of the applicants and their ancestors as a way to infer ethnonational membership.

The difficulties encountered by the ethnocrats in determining the applicant's "German" descent were also seen in trying to decide whether a failure to participate in "Volksdeutsche" groups could be solely attributed to pressures from the Polish authorities. The assessment committees were provided with additional selection criteria, which in turn emphasized the central importance of the applicant's conduct. One such criterion was religion, in which Protestant was generally equated with German, and Catholic with Polish. Similarly important were documents from the Polish state in which the bearer had registered "German" under ethnicity or mother tongue. According to the DVL guidelines: "Anyone who has insisted on this inscription has thereby professed to Germandom."[237] But it was the applicant's name and language that were the decisive factors. The authorities were interested in what language was spoken at home and were instructed in doubtful cases to also summon the children, since it was their language skills above all that would decide what the "home language" was. Another datapoint was the language of instruction at the school selected by the parents for their children. Here, the authorities saw "the choosing of Polish schools very often as a professing to Polishdom," while children's attendance at a German-language school under a biethnic marriage was taken as evidence "that the German part of the marriage has prevailed." As for the names, every Polish spelling was negatively noted, with particular attention given to first names. "Whoever names their children Mieceslaw, Jadwiga, or Wojciech, is generally not a German. And if 'Karl,' born in 1920, is followed by 'Ceslaw,' born in 1934, one can infer a Polish outlook among the parents."[238]

This clear emphasis on the applicant's past and anticipated social practices, in regard to political conduct above all, may seem surprising: after all, Nazi Germany is seen first and foremost as a "racial state" in which biological selection criteria were to be imposed—at first domestically against the Jewish Germans, and then across occupied Europe against the rest of the oppressed populations. The ethnocrats in the Wartheland, however, clearly chose a different path and focused on "German mindset." The catalog of criteria in the "green booklet" did include a section on "racial markers (Rassemerkmale)," but they were to be applied only to "racially mixed-marriage cases as per the Nuremberg Laws"—that is, if the applicant was Jewish, which were to be set aside for the moment. But in the case of Christian Poles, the selection criterion of "race" was explicitly excluded:

> Certain racial markers are indeed a frequent indication that Germans were among the applicant's ancestors. But racial markers cannot be used as a reliable basis for assessing German ethnonational membership in the circumstances of the Reichsgau [i.e., the Wartheland]. On the contrary, it is often observed that the Nordic element is particularly evident among the Polishdom that was politically active, especially in the region around the city of Posen. Such politically active persons are the least likely to take a noncommittal stance in the ethnonational struggle. Especially with this Nordic-constituted Polishdom, one cannot cherish hopes of winning it over by accommodating it.[239]

After the hiatus caused by the Reich Interior Ministry's intervention from November 25, 1939, the DVL offices were instructed by the central office to begin operations by February 15, 1940, and to start handing out identity documents as early as April. In Posen Governmental District, everything went according to plan.[240] The first location to resume operations was the branch office for the city of Posen, which was directly subordinated to the central office. With most of the questionnaires having been handed out in November, the first sitting was convened here on February 1, 1940. Significantly, identity document number 1 was issued to Heinrich W., a pharmacist and leading representative of the ethnic German minority, who displayed all the desired attributes. Not only had he been a member of the Young German Party for Poland (Jungdeutsche Partei für Polen, or JdP) and other associations of the "Volksdeutsche," he could also boast about the official persecution he endured under the Polish authorities: "1927 disbarment of my pharmacy from health insurance deliveries, nonissuance of father's pharmacy license, unemployed as of August 1, 1939, house searches, constant surveillance by Polish police, apprehension on war's first day for 'internment' at Bereza Kartuska."[241] He was accepted for Group A, and as one of the "Volksdeutsche" members at the DVL central office, he would become an important collaborator of the German occupiers in selecting inductees from the local populace.

In contrast, startup problems were seen in Hohensalza Governmental District. During an inspection tour on February 26, 1940, Coulon discovered that most branch offices had yet to start their registration work and that Rudolf Schmidt-Berger, the local Regierungspräsident's departmental head for ethnopolitical questions, had not even begun setting up the DVL regional office.[242] Instead, he offered "quibbling criticisms" of the instructions from Posen.[243] The central office then appointed "former leading JdP member Hermann Brose" as head of the regional office, who would be assisted during the initial period by W. Geske and one of Coulon's staff members from Posen.[244]

Even these complications seemed minor in comparison to what happened in Kalisch Governmental Region (later renamed Litzmannstadt Governmental Region). Here, it was Egon Leuschner who took on the coordination of the DVL regional office, as well as the management of the most branch office in the city of Litzmannstadt encompassing by far the largest number of persons.[245] Unlike the procedure used elsewhere in the province, Leuschner's had implemented a more nuanced catalog of criteria also combining an *"ethnonational rating"* with a *"political* rating" (emphasis in original), but instead of using just two groups for enrollees, it put them into five, known as Groups A through E. The first two groups were reserved for those who—in their ethnonational rating—"have remained German in every regard," but still had to be sorted—in their political rating—into "active campaigners" and "staid citizens" ("biedere Bürger"). Persons who had already "fallen into the stream of ethnoconversion [Umvolkung]," but whose "ties to Germandom are only slightly decayed" and with whom only a "small push is needed, in order to remove the thin Polish veneer," belonged in Group C. Meanwhile, "reverse-poled Germans [verpolte Deutsche]," along with those "who already have the ethnoconversion process behind them and have in ethnonational terms become Poles . . . but without having fought against Germandom" were sorted into Group D; last, "actively and nationally reverse-poled persons" with a demonstrable track record of "anti-German activities with Polish national consciousness" were assigned as "renegades" to Group E.[246] These changes had to be pushed through by Kalisch Regierungspräsident Uebelhoer against the will of the DVL central office, where even Coulon could not escape the realization that they were probably unavoidable because of the different "political structuring of Germandom" in the region: whereas the Posen region had been "always an ethnonational battleground," where up to 20 percent of ethnic Germans were members of ethnic German organizations, "things were different in Congress Poland." There, the "Volksdeutsche" had "never had any hopes of coming to the Reich" and only 3 percent of them were in organized groups, which is why they were generally "much more subject to a long, unwarlike process of Polonization, a seeping away into ethnonationally foreign soil."[247] If a system as strict as the one in Posen had been imposed here, the German occupiers would have deprived themselves of individuals who were needed for the building of a "German Volksgemeinschaft" and the securing of Nazi rule.

Of course, the different selection criteria also resulted in different groups with different rights. For example, in the west of the Wartheland, all persons enrolled in the DVL were considered "Germans," but in Kalisch, this was true only of members in Groups A through C. Furthermore, the only de facto differentiation between the two groups in the west was in eligibility for appointment to the party and state apparatuses, whereas in Kalisch the more elaborate differentiation meant that "only A and B . . . are to be awarded Reich citizenship without hesitation," and members of Group C were granted, "for the time being, only German national status."[248] Some of these legal differences, however, become less significant upon closer inspection—and not only because the distinction between Reich citizenship and German national status had no real consequences in the annexed territories. The DVL regional offices in Posen and Hohensalza registered not only those inducted into the DVL, but also biethnic marriages in which the children spoke Polish and consequently made the whole family ineligible for Groups A and B. In, the regional office in Kalisch, the same people might simply have been enrolled in Group D. Even potential members of Group E were not ignored in the west—but they were initially registered not by the DVL branch offices there, but by the Gestapo and SD. Therefore, when the system was standardized in mid-1940 and the more nuanced method from Kalisch Governmental Region was imposed on the entire province, it was possible to do so without much adjustment. Nevertheless, identity documents attesting DVL membership were issued only to "Volksdeutsche," meaning persons in Groups A and B.

Upper Silesia: "The Term 'Volksdeutsch' Is . . . Not to Be Interpreted Narrowly"

In Silesia too, Frick's citizenship decree was met with criticism. In contrast to the case in the Wartheland, however, its regulations were seen here as too restrictive.

The Regierungspräsident of Kattowitz Governmental Region, Walter Springorum, asked Wilhelm Stuckart to intervene, and found in him a strong ally who supported his desire for a selection process that was as inclusivist as possible. Immediately after Frick's decree, Stuckart authorized the civil administration in Silesia to decide, according to "local circumstances," whether above all "the so-called Water Poles, Szlonzakians, Masurians . . . could be considered German ethnonationals."[249] Then on December 19, 1939, Springorum issued implementation provisions that instructed the relevant authorities to apply the most generous possible interpretation.[250] Stuckart defended this course of action in Berlin as well, when he explained to the Reich Propaganda Ministry on January 4, 1940, that with "the question of assessing and deciding German ethnonational membership . . . neither political loyalty . . . nor previous criminal convictions can play a role," and that it is "in Germany's interest to proceed as generously as possible, so that a large part of the nationally indifferent intermediate class, especially in eastern Upper Silesia and eastern Silesia, is also registered."[251]

Even though the final results of the census were still unavailable at that point, meaning that it was still not entirely clear how many residents of the annexed territories would declare themselves to be "Germans," the Reich Interior Ministry and the civil administration were already supporting the most "generous" possible treatment. Nonetheless, when the results of the census were finalized, they may have well been a surprise to everyone involved: although only 0.6 percent of residents east of the police border had labeled themselves "German," more than 95 percent of those west of it had done so.[252] In this context, Sybille Steinbacher is certainly correct in highlighting a message written by the chief of police in Kattowitz, Wilhelm Metz, for whom there was an obvious explanation: "Poles label themselves 'Volksdeutsche' for fear of evacuations . . . This is why statistics are now to be evaluated with caution."[253] After all, the German occupiers had repeatedly declared their intention of Germanizing the territories and had already begun with locally organized deportations as well as centrally organized ones by Eichmann, which, however—and this had been noticed—had taken place here exclusively in the formerly German and Austrian parts of Silesia.[254]

But Steinbacher's citation also needs to be expanded. It would be too easy to assume that the German administrators, in their quest to objectively determine the "nationality structure of eastern Upper Silesia," would be thwarted by the tactical behavior of the local populace.[255] Although the decree on the census had indeed stated "that for the question on ethnonational membership, the self-declaration of the subject person is basically decisive," the occupiers were naturally not prepared to leave the matter entirely up to the discretion of the respondent. The census takers were thus instructed to assess whether the claimed "ethnonational membership" was also "confirmed by certain facts, such as language, schooling, culture, etc." and did not "stand in contradiction to conduct so far."[256] If statistical reports are "ways of establishing the authority of certain visions of social order," so also are censuses: they were a part of the political process and influenced by its logic.[257] Therefore, if the census results caused surprise in their concrete form, there can be no doubt that the glaring contrast between the territories east and west of the police border was also a result of the occupiers' different expectations and political goals for the two zones. The civil administrators clearly shared a prevailing opinion that the former German and Austrian areas, along with their residents, belonged to the Reich; meanwhile, the "eastern strip" was felt to be "foreign" and a general threat to the successful Germanization of the whole province.

When the first partial results reached the Regierungspräsident's offices in Kattowitz, they reinforced Springorum's criticism of the time-consuming process precipitated by Frick's decree. In a message to Wagner, he outlined the fear that the "abundance of applications to be expected" west of the police border would certainly cause "very substantial difficulties."[258] The Landrat of Pless County alone expected some one hundred sixty thousand applicants but was unable to hand out more than a hundred questionnaires per day, quite apart from the considerably more time-consuming assessments that had to be done at his offices and then reviewed at the Regierungspräsident's offices. Springorum himself could see that his bureaucrats would be completely overwhelmed by the anticipated 1.5 million applications from across the entire governmental district, for it would take "many years of administrative work" to complete their processing.[259]

As a solution, Springorum proposed that registration be initially limited to persons who had been "Volksdeutsche" activists in the JdP or the German Volk Union (Deutscher Volksbund), along with those currently working for the state or Nazi Party—meaning persons who were immediately needed for the development of the occupation administration. But if the Reich Interior Ministry chose not to pursue his suggestion, then it needed to provide the necessary support for the most inclusive possible procedure, and soon. It was "of decisive importance, under what considerations one is to undertake the ethnonational incorporation of the extraordinarily numerous class of Upper Silesians who in the past twenty years, for the most diverse of reasons, have taken an indecisive and neutral stance toward Germandom, and thus will often be considered a wavering floating class."[260] For Springorum, the answer was obvious. Referring to the passage in the citizenship decree that recommended generosity in doubtful cases that represented "a desirable addition to the population," he explained that, in his opinion, "with by far the largest segment of native-born Upper Silesians, one would have to proceed according to the considerations specified here."[261] With this, Springorum was effectively addressing the treatment of the remaining populace as well, whose destiny, in the view of the Reich Interior Ministry, should be left for a later regulation. As a result, the Reich Interior

Ministry began by approving only Springorum's proposal to narrow down the selection process.[262]

It was ultimately because of the Wehrmacht's need for soldiers that Springorum's efforts to broaden the selection criteria would find success. For this, Springorum used the "guidelines for the registration procedure in the incorporated eastern territories" issued by the Reich Interior Ministry on March 7, 1940, which ordered that German nationals born in the years 1913 through 1920 were to be mustered by April 20, 1940.[263] While the authorities in the Wartheland and in Danzig–West Prussia reacted to this directive with restraint and summoned only the very small part of the local populace on whom German national status had already been conferred, those in Silesia decided to do the exact opposite. It is clear that Springorum immediately recognized the political leverage offered by this directive and played this card in his confrontation with the Reich Interior Ministry. On March 26, 1940, his deputy, Erich Kessler, instructed the subordinate bureaus in Kattowitz Governmental Region that, in implementing the Reich Interior Ministry's decree, they were to also summon the "Volksdeutsche who are resident and native here." After all, these persons had also acquired—according to this somewhat unconventional interpretation—German national status, even if the question had not yet been individually adjudicated. Thus,

> to be seen as Volksdeutsche are not only those who . . . have openly professed to Germandom through their activities and membership in German political groups and cultural associations, but also those who now profess to Germandom and did not act in hostility against Germandom during the Polish period. The term 'volksdeutsch' is therefore not to be interpreted narrowly, for the ethnopolitical goal vis-à-vis the Upper Silesian hybrid population is their complete Germanization. The Szlonzakians who designated themselves Silesians, German-Silesians, or Szlonzakians during the census of the Reichsführer of the SS are to be handled the same way."[264]

Since the general summons literally called for all "male German nationals and German ethnonationals [i.e., Staatsangehörige and Volkszugehörige]" to register and muster, the individual in question, "solely by appearing," would already be indicating that he "felt himself part of Germandom." In this case, one simply had to verify whether he could produce some proof of his German ethnonational membership—for example, the attestation of a German body, "so long as the word 'Volksdeutscher' is not missing therein." Apart from that, it was necessary to check whether he had indicated "German, Silesian, German-Silesian, or Szlonzakian" during the census. And even if this was not the case, it certainly did not have to result in disqualification, if he could now *"believably"* show that he had "mistakenly called himself a Pole"—a course of action that was otherwise not allowed.[265] Finally, he had to solemnly declare having never been criminally convicted nor a member of one of the more radical Polish nationalist associations.[266] The questionnaire for determining national status could then be filled out immediately and was to be notated on the spot by the mayor and the Ortsgruppenleiter (local group leader, the locality's leading Nazi official) with a suggested decision. This procedure shifted the preliminary decision down one administrative level, namely from the county's Landrat to the locality's mayor and also ensuring that the Nazi Party had an equal role to play in it.[267] The final decision was made in turn by the Regierungspräsident, and—here another new aspect—in the Kattowitz police district also by the chief of police.

Springorum received support from the bureau above him in Breslau. There, Vice Oberpräsident Fritz-Dietlof von der Schulenburg similarly ordered that in "deciding of the question of who is to be viewed as a Volksdeutsche resident," officials were to "proceed generously," and that the only persons to be excluded were those who "have *verifiably* professed to Polishdom and have *actively* operated accordingly."[268] An individual's "professed ethnonationality" ("Volkstumsbekenntnis") was to be based on his census response. Furthermore, Schulenburg instructed all other bureaus west of the police border to similarly implement the expedited naturalization of military recruits as practiced in Kattowitz. Springorum relayed these instructions to his subordinate bureaus on April 19, 1940. He wrote that the first priority was still the registration of organized "Volksdeutsche" along with those in the service of the state and party. However, this "restriction . . . cannot exclude the routine processing of particularly urgent individual cases at the same time. . . . Particularly pressing is the registering of male German nationals born in the years 1913 through 1921. I refer here to my administrative circular of March 26, 1940."[269]

Of course, it would not be just a few "individual cases." The chief of police for Kattowitz, whose authority covered a third of the governmental region's populace, declared that on the basis of this decree, "the average Silesian . . . is accordingly to be generally considered a German ethnonational."[270] In a message to the Regierungspräsident's offices, the Landrat of Pless, Bernhard von Derschau, also highlighted the great number of people who were to be recognized as "Germans" under this regulation, as well as the huge administrative burden resulting from this change to the existing procedure. Of the 160,000 applicants expected from his county, some 21,000 had been registered at that point, including 9,000 alone from the mustering of recruits born between 1913 and 1921. Another 37,000 to 39,000 applicants were to be processed in the near term, of whom almost half consisted of the 15,000 to 17,000 potential recruits from the next mustering phase, covering those born from 1900 to 1912.[271] With such a great number of applicants, the already repeatedly reworked selection procedure needed another review, and the Landrats needed more freedom to make decisions. From now on, they would decide "clear-cut cases" on their own and would no longer need to pass them along to the relevant Regierungspräsident or chief of police. Springorum did in fact allow Derschau to dispense with forwarding at least some of these applications and to adjudicate them locally instead, namely those of the military recruits.[272]

In Pless and other localities, however, the administrative capacities did not suffice for even this. Reinforcing the Wehrmacht was such a high priority that many men born in the relevant years were not even given a questionnaire and were instead inducted immediately—that is, before completion of the adjudication process, which was often skipped entirely. This tacit arrangement between the civil administration and the Wehrmacht was not exposed until the SS, in striving toward a more radical policy of exclusion, began investigating "misdeeds" in the Germanization policy implemented so far. On February 4, 1943, the RKFDV headquarters contacted the Oberpräsident's offices in the Province of Lower Silesia to ask how some forty thousand men could have been inducted into the Wehrmacht during the years 1940 and 1941 without any decision having first been made about their "ethnonational membership."[273]

Danzig–West Prussia: Becoming German through Upbringing

The situation was no different in Danzig–West Prussia, where—in the opinion of one party official—the Reich Interior Ministry had to accept the fact that it had been unable to "parry Forster's excessively powerful position."[274] Frick's citizenship decree was met with resistance in the province primarily because the Reich Interior Ministry had delegated the selection of the "Volksdeutsche" to the Regierungspräsidents, which Forster saw as an encroachment on his mandate from Hitler to oversee the Germanization of the annexed territories.[275] Like Greiser, Forster had delegated the selection process to party agencies, thereby marginalizing the Regierungspräsidents. But Forster seemed even less willing than Greiser to make any changes here. Civil administrators were told to hand out questionnaires only to persons who had already been recognized as "Volksdeutsche" by the offices of the local Kreisleiter (county leader, the head of a Nazi Party county-level branch) and had thereby received the green ethnonational identity document (*Volkstumsausweis*). Questionnaires were to be returned by the applicants within two weeks, notated by the Landrat or chief of police with the preliminary decision already reached by the party, and subsequently endorsed at the Regierungspräsident's offices.[276] The party's decisive role in the selection process becomes even clearer when one considers that Forster had successfully managed in almost every county to have a single trusted ally appointed simultaneously to the positions of both Kreisleiter and Landrat. In Preussisch Stargard, for example, Walter Hillmann first acted as Kreisleiter in deciding on awarding ethnonational identity documents in order to subsequently ensure as

Landrat that only these individuals also received a questionnaire, which he then notated with a preliminary decision and sent to the Regierungspräsident's offices, in order to obtain from it a citizenship certificate that he could issue to the applicant. The process was far removed from the stipulations of Frick's citizenship decree, according to which the Regierungspräsident was supposed to be the one who decided on awarding German national status.

Forster succeeded in implementing this process in the governmental regions of Marienwerder and Danzig. It was only the Regierungspräsident of Bromberg, Dr. Günther Palten, who proved unwilling to deliberately contravene Frick's decree or to let his own decision-making powers be limited by Forster. As a result, Bromberg differed from the other two governmental regions in calling on—here Palten used a formulation taken from the Reich Citizens Act (Reichsbürgergesetz) and repeated in Hitler's annexation decree—"all residents of German or related blood and of German ethnonational membership" to come make an application.[277] In Bromberg, the mayors and Amtskommissars (rural district commissioners) were explicitly forbidden from refusing to hand out a questionnaire—even if the applicant "has a Polish name or is of the Catholic religion."[278]

The questionnaires were evaluated everywhere in Danzig–West Prussia according to the same standards, however, guided by the criteria of the Reich Interior Ministry and focused above all on the applicant's conduct. The importance of having attended a German school was particularly highlighted, which exemplifies the inclusivist interpretation of these criteria, in that even the time before 1918 was taken into account and thereby enabled the inclusion of almost all former citizens of the German Empire. "An applicant's school attendance during the German period may weigh in his favor, if not conclusively. It represents a factor of upbringing that is not to be underestimated."[279] Thus, it was possible to become a member of the German "Volk" through one's upbringing.

Danzig–West Prussia's inclusivist selection policy is well demonstrated by the practices in the rural county of Neustadt (today Wejherowo), for which the surviving source materials are particularly extensive. Thus, of the 92,943 residents recorded in the census of December 1939, only 9,473 were accepted for Section I ("einwandfreie Volksdeutsche," or "impeccably ethnic Germans") and another 73,447 for Section II ("non-impeccable Volksdeutsche, obliging Poles, Kashubians"), who were allowed to stay for the time being.[280] In comparison, the number of persons earmarked for deportation was much smaller: 8,894 persons were placed in Section III ("Congress Poles, and others who are not impeccable"), and 482 in Section IV ("antisocials, Jews, criminals, and miscellaneous").[281] But, of course, the Jews had already been expelled from Neustadt in October 1939.[282] It is obvious that these numbers were also used by party agencies as yardsticks for the first round of selections. Thus, although the local Kreisleiter's offices received between 20,500 and 23,500 applications for an ethnonational identity document, only 5,500 were approved.[283] This roughly corresponded to the adult portion of the "Volksdeutsche."[284]

The province's inclusivist selection policy can also be seen in its school policy. During the census, only 10,120 individuals had indicated German as their mother tongue.[285] The number of persons recognized as "Volksdeutsche" was even a bit less. German-language schools, however, were now being established in great numbers, and they certainly did not limit enrollment to the 1,317 children of "Volksdeutsche"—instead, and in contrast to the Wartheland, they also took in 15,350 "children of the local populace," meaning those with parents selected for Section II.[286] Of course, as the mayor of Neustadt complained, "most of these children are not fluent in the German language," so that the schools, "as the first task, have to tackle the transmission of the German linguistic heritage."[287] The civil administration in Danzig–West Prussia was little concerned with how Himmler's "thoughts on the handling of the ethnonationally foreign in the east" had tried to effectively exclude the local populace from any schooling at all and to limit the knowledge of the German language to the understanding of orders issued by the occupiers. As noted in a report from the school board, on the contrary, "particular value is placed in all schools upon weaning pupils from speaking with a Polish timbre and accent, as they should be gradually brought to the point where they can speak the German language not only grammatically correctly, but also with a resonant richness. Of course, this also goes hand in hand with learning to write in German."[288] After just one year, the mayor was able to report an astounding success: "Today, all the children already have a perfect command of the German language."[289] Regardless of how willing to learn these children actually were, this linguistic Germanization policy, widely imposed and covering almost all children, was naturally a decisive factor in the ongoing development of selection policy. After all, by early 1941, the time had come for the "systematic Germanization of the intermediate class," a project in which German language proficiency would play a major role. While this was already widespread among the adult populace, because most of them had still been in school during the Prussian era, the civil administration now organized a crash course for their children and thus laid the groundwork for the desired outcome of the upcoming second selection phase.

The SS versus the Reich Interior Ministry

The major differences between the selection procedures of the individual provinces provoked a great deal of criticism, particularly at the Reich Interior Ministry and from Himmler in his role as the RKFDV. But what cut to the quick, particularly for SS planners, were the emerging efforts of the Gauleiters in Silesia and Danzig–West Prussia to ensure that a considerable fraction of the local populace, if it could not be recognized as "Volksdeutsche," was not to be excluded as "Poles" from future induction into the "German Volksgemeinschaft."

It had already become clear that the UWZs had long since changed course, and were no longer deporting only political opponents (both real and alleged) but also increasingly any person who stood in the way of settling ethnic Germans from Eastern Europe—which often enough led to the expulsions of ostensible "Stammesdeutsche" ("Germans by descent"), thereby provoking widespread criticism. This class of people was generally supposed to be exempted from deportation—on this point, Himmler and the civil administrations were in agreement for once. Thus, even as a matter of simply ensuring that the settlement of ethnic Germans happened as quickly and smoothly as possible, the SS had to be interested in seeing the local populace undergo a selection process that was rapid, universal, and exclusivist. Not even one of these attributes was fulfilled by the selection procedures used in Silesia and Danzig–West Prussia, where the selections were not keeping pace with the deportations, were not conducted consistently, and were overly generous in interpreting the already quite inclusivist selection criteria from Frick's citizenship decree. In Danzig–West Prussia, local procedure became a central problem for the SS apparatus, for the province played an important role in its settlement plans, second only to the Wartheland.

The SS Counterproposal: "The Decisive Criterion . . . Must Therefore Be Race"

As a solution, Richard Hildebrandt ultimately hit on the idea of establishing under the Ordnungspolizei a central complaints commission, which would be responsible for all complaints of the wrongful deportation of ostensible "Volksdeutsche."[290] This initiative seems to have met with great approval at RKFDV headquarters, as Greifelt sent a message to the RKFDV branch offices shortly thereafter on April 9, 1940, instructing them to follow this example and set up a bureau, similar to the headquarters' Main Department III (Compensation for Damage Claims), to hear "complaints against refusals to recognize Volksdeutsche" and about "allegedly wrongfully evacuated Volksdeutsche."[291] The political functionality of such a commission, operating under the control of the RKFDV apparatus, was clear: the complaints lodged by the affected individuals or their relatives in the Reich threatened to slow down the deportations—especially those that were to be decided by the civil administration—and the goal here was to prevent that. Furthermore, Greifelt was also probably trying to give more weight to his RKFDV branch offices on the ground. Although charged with the coordination of Himmler's tasks as the RKFDV since their creation over half a year earlier, their achievements so far had not been particularly impressive. Certainly, one could point to the work of the land offices, which had already stolen a great part of the usable farmland for the Reich. But in the field of ethnopolicy, the tone was set by other institutions, such as VoMi and the Reich Security Main Office. And although this changed somewhat with the establishment of the SS Settlement Staffs, their duties were still limited to the settling of ethnic Germans. The RKFDV branch offices were not involved at all in the selection of the local populace—but the complaints commissions promised to change that.

The Gauleiters were hardly pleased by this foray. Forster had already let Hildebrandt know that the clarification of ethnonational membership was not a matter for the police, but only for the state and party, and announced that he himself would establish "commissions for the reviewing of complaints about wrongfully conducted evacuations and about the nonissuance of recognition as Volksdeutsche."[292] The selection criteria used by these complaints commissions then confirmed all the fears of the SS complex. According to the criteria, the only persons to be automatically cleared for deportation were those who were undesirable for political or social reasons, as well as Jews and Congress Poles. But for the rest of the populace, there were strict rules. Above all, "members of the intermediate class" could be rounded up only if there also "exist *facts* from which their anti-German attitude can be demonstrated beyond doubt."[293] The problem for the SS complex was that the "intermediate class" had since become a rather expansive term in Danzig–West Prussia. The Reich Security Main Office was already appalled that this term in Danzig–West Prussia had come to effectively mean all persons born on the former territory of the German Empire before 1918.[294] But ethnonationality officer Wilhelm Löbsack had gone even a step further by now also including the Ukrainians living there, as long as they were willing to be "absorbed into Germandom."[295] The end effect was that the majority of the local populace had now excluded from the jurisdiction of the SS.

It is unclear whether Forster's complaint commissions were ever convened— or if they even needed to be. In any case, the head of the RKFDV branch office in Danzig, SS Regiment Leader Heukenkamp, did not stop complaining about what he saw as the "unbelievable mess in the Reichsgau of Danzig–West Prussia" and particularly about the weight given to political good behavior: after all, "it is not past political mindset or belonging to a party that define German ethnonational membership, but blood-based belonging." In any case, Heukenkamp was not able to implement Greifelt's directive in the face of resistance from the civil administration, and because the local situation allowed only the maintenance of the status quo, additional support was requested from Berlin for any further measures.[296]

Greifelt had no more luck in the Wartheland, where a highly nuanced selection mechanism already existed in the form of the DVL process, one that involved SD participation but again ignored the RKFDV branch office. For its head in Posen, SS Senior Leader Hans Döring, the goal was to change this situation. First he tried summoning Coulon to his offices in order to discuss the work of the DVL and the possibility of working together, but the latter refused, with the admonishment that the selection process was a matter for the civil administration. Döring had no more success with Coulon's superior, the head of Department I at the Reichsstatthalter's offices, Herbert Mehlhorn. Apparently Döring had become more explicit in formulating his demands, seeking "authoritative participation in all ethnonationality questions."[297] This request was rejected by Mehlhorn as well. When one of Döring's staff members, SS Senior Assault Unit Leader Wilhelm Laforce, then went to visit Coulon, it led to a "very animated confrontation" in which Laforce was also forced to accept that if the SS apparatus had any questions about or complaints against decisions made by DVL offices, they had to be presented through the corresponding SD officer.[298] Döring was unhappy with this result and began to gather material against Coulon, as the latter then learned from a trusted source.[299] "This minor incident," noted Coulon in a memo, "confirms the impression of an uncomradely and unobjective attitude from Döring's office."[300] Coulon's impression was further exacerbated when Döring began to collect DVL cases on his own and was alleged to have already compiled files on eighteen thousand individuals, a matter of withholding important material from the responsible authorities.[301] A complaint was brought up "in a huff" by Mehlhorn shortly thereafter at RKFDV headquarters.[302] Coulon asked Greiser to put his foot down, encouraging him to use his upcoming designation as Himmler's RKFDV appointee and simply forbid Döring from pursuing such activities.[303] But by that point, Döring had already conceded the futility of his undertaking and issued an order "to suspend for now the processing of ethnonationality questions."[304]

The efforts of the RKFDV branch office in Kattowitz also failed miserably. Shortly after Bach-Zelewski informed the Regierungspräsidents about Greifelt's directive, the Regierungspräsident of Oppeln, Dr. Johann Rüdiger, asserted that according to Frick's citizenship decree of November 25, 1939, deciding the ethnonational membership of local inhabitants was solely the prerogative of the Regierungspräsidents.[305] And his decision was binding for the SS as well, "in all those cases . . . in which German ethnonational membership is of significance for administrative activities."[306] As Springorum explained to Bach-Zelewski on May 21, 1940, he was not categorically denying the right of the SS to handle complaints, but they were nonetheless to be limited to the proceedings that were already pending there, and furthermore needed to be decided "in agreement with the administrative authorities responsible for the final determination of national status."[307] After that, it would seem that the local RKFDV branch office likewise suspended its activities in this sphere. This is at least the implication of a message from RKFDV headquarters in Berlin, which complained that inquiries on this with the RKF branch office in Kattowitz received only a cursory response, and anyway, in every case reaffirmed the decisions already reached by the civil administration.[308]

Instead of giving up, however, it seems that Greifelt then looked around for allies. He found them in the form of the Reich Security Main Office, which alone through its participation in the deportation process had already an interest in gaining more influence over the selection process. Both SS agencies agreed on two main points of criticism, which were briefly summarized by Dr. Johannes Walter from RKFDV headquarters in a stocktaking on May 20, 1940. First, there was still no success in establishing a uniform selection process. The decrees of the Reich Interior Ministry were "only partially . . . heeded" by the civil administrations in the annexed provinces or else were "quietly ignored as impracticable."[309] Second, the selection criteria prescribed by the Reich Interior Ministry had failed to stipulate that "the first criterion of German ethnonational membership must be the positive verification of racial membership," which is what Himmler had demanded.[310] Instead, the criteria were "intended solely for professing."[311] As a result, the Reich Security Main Office felt that the SS needed to push for the universal introduction of a procedure based on the DVL system in the Wartheland, which had "proved itself very well."[312]

During a joint session of representatives from RKFDV headquarters and the Reich Security Main Office on May 22, 1940, there was nonetheless a conflict, because when it came to the question of how a uniform selection process was to be implemented according to racial criteria and based on the Wartheland DVL system, each side claimed decision-making authority for its own agency. Here, the RKFDV headquarters demanded a particularly prominent position for its representative on the commissions so that it could "prevail in every case." But should the civil administrators be unwilling to give up this prerogative, then the RKFDV representative should at least be granted the role of a "public interests commissioner" in order to take up "randomly selected individual cases," or in general, to take up for "final decision-making the cases in which . . . the basic principles and guidelines of the Reichsführer of the SS in his role as the RKFDV have not been heeded."[313]

Such demands were hardly realistic, for they ignored the real-world division of powers in this policy field and would have meant not only the marginalization of the Reich Security Main Office, but also the neutralization of the civil administration. The Reich Security Main Office therefore responded with a counterproposal, drafted by Dr. Justus Beyer and forwarded by Ohlendorf to Himmler on May 24, 1940. It underlined once again the "great intolerability" of the existing selection procedure, which "neglects the racial aspect" and also is differently handled all across the region.[314] Although the local DVL system in the Wartheland elicited complete agreement, in Danzig–West Prussia, the Kreisleiter charged with the selection process had shown themselves to be "very uncertain about the demarcation of Polishdom" and were now even planning "to Germanize those of 'native Polishdom' in the hundreds of thousands," and in Upper Silesia, the administration was purportedly intent "on viewing the province's entire populace as Volksdeutsche . . . with the exception of those who . . . have actively worked for the Polish cause." What was needed was a procedure that, after having already completed the selection of the "Volksdeutsche," then registered the "passively or actively reverse-poled Deutschstämmige," before finally tackling the "question of the real intermediate class." Consequently, the Reich Security Main Office argued for the general introduction of a DVL in all of the incorporated territories. It was to consist of four sections whose selection criteria would generally follow those used in the Wartheland. "Deutschstämmige who have actively professed to Germandom" would be sorted into Section A, and those "who have not actively worked for Germandom but whose German mindset is not in doubt" would fall into Section B. Finally, Sections C and D were reserved for "passively" or "actively reverse-poled Deutschstämmige," meaning Poles who were not in organized Polish groups (Section C), and Poles who could be proved by the Germans to have been in such groups (Section D). Members of Sections A through C would receive "German national status," and those in A and B would additionally acquire "Reich citizen rights." After that, the legal status of the remaining populace would be decided in a last selection step. The "re-Germanization" and subsequent naturalization of the "renegades" in Section D could take place only after their transport into the Reich and was to depend on their political good behavior, but for the remaining "non-Deutschstämmige," it was necessary to make yet one more differentiation into two groups. There was a first group that could remain for now in the annexed territories, potentially receiving, "in view of their behavior, German national status"—failing that, they would be expelled into the General Government like the second group. Members of the first group would become "protected dependents [Schutzbefohlene] of the Greater German Reich" during this "transitional phase."[315] Thus, having already split citizenship status into Reich citizens and German nationals, the dynamic of ethnonationalist racial differentiation was now creating yet another legal status.

In order to ensure that the concrete selection practices were also put under the control of the SS apparatus, the idea was for the DVL offices to work "in tight cooperation" with the local RKFDV branch offices, Security Police, and SD. Furthermore, a Supreme Court of Review for Ethnonationality Questions (Oberster Prüfungshof für Volkstumsfragen) was to be established as a final appeals body, presided over by Himmler.[316]

Such a wide-reaching ambition was certainly not covered by the powers granted to Himmler by Hitler's decree of October 7, 1939. It had given Himmler authority in the handling of just two target groups, namely in the selection of ethnic Germans from Eastern Europe and in the removal of potential opponents against the German occupation. Thus, the proposal from the Reich Security Main Office was probably not aimed so much at the selection of individuals for

Sections A and B. For one thing, these "Volksdeutsche" fell under the jurisdiction of the civil administration agencies and party structures. For another, their registration was already more or less finished, namely within the framework of Frick's citizenship decree. It was quite different with Sections C and D, although in the case of the latter, the situation appeared clear-cut from the perspective of the SS apparatus: the members of Section D were political opponents who fell under the jurisdiction of the Reich Security Main Office anyway.

But for taking on Section C, more justification was needed. Justification was provided by calling attention to the "intermediate class." In the opinion of the Reich Security Main Office, the term was either being used wrongly or else referred to a very complicated situation in population policy. In both cases, the intervention of the SS was necessary. For instance, in Danzig–West Prussia, the term was "purely artificial," as in that the civil administration was using it to label everyone born in the region before 1918, without exception. And in places like Upper Silesia, where a "real 'intermediate class' exists, which in its racial substance is based on a mixture and in terms of mindset represents a wavering folkdom," the need was to first create clarity in defining the group. The premise was that the "linguistics-based concept of Slavicdom conceals the fact that Slavicdom, viewed in racial theory terms, does not represent a unity, but instead consists of very diverse groups. The decisive criterion for differentiation must therefore be race, and not cultural consciousness or language."[317] This definition not only conformed with the racial focus demanded by the SS apparatus, it also proved supremely functional in advancing SS power ambitions. On the one hand, control over an additional, not inconsiderable, proportion of the local populace could thereby be justified. On the other hand, it also offered justification for intervening in the existing selection activities of the DVL. As a result, the Reich Security Main Office called for the "racial selection" of the local populace, as it was already described in Kraków on November 8, 1939, to be delegated to the "resettlement centers" ("Umwanderungszentralen") and the RuSHA suitability assessors.

The Reich Security Main Office was not prepared to delegate this decision making entirely to RuSHA—instead, the appraisals should take place within the framework of the "resettlement centers," and thus under the aegis of the Reich Security Main Office. Aware that the highly exclusivist selection criteria of the RuSHA suitability assessors had already led to repeated confrontations with other authorities, including the SD, the Reich Security Main Office was careful to spell out certain fundamental considerations relating to the functional needs of power. For example, any Masurians, Kashubians, Upper Silesians, and Szlonzakians who "have demonstrably stayed on the German side" were generally to be spared the appraisals of the RuSHA suitability assessors. Instead, they were to be "given the opportunity to obtain recognition as Germans, even if their racial profile does not completely meet the requirements that are generally to be stipulated in the east."

The Reich Security Main Office also proved receptive to economic considerations, in stating that with regard to the "Water Poles," it was necessary to "take into account the population-policy concerns and economic concerns of the Oberpräsident of Silesia with respect to the danger of depopulating particular localities, by handling somewhat more generously the racial [appraisal] of the Upper Silesians."

Before forwarding the memorandum, Ohlendorf contacted RuSHA and VoMi, as well as the staff of the Deputy Führer. It was only after they had signaled their "complete agreement"—according to Ohlendorf—that it was then presented to Himmler, "with a request for your consideration and decision . . . on whether, on the basis of this proposal, the necessary further negotiations with the Reich Minister of the Interior can be undertaken."[318] In any case, the positions laid out in the memorandum became the basis not only for Himmler's main interventions, but also for the stances the SS institutions took in the negotiations of the following months. With the memorandum, the Reich Security Main Office had underscored once again its ambition to be the decisive force in ethnopolicy matters within the SS complex.

* * *

As has been shown, the SS apparatus was not alone in its criticism of selection practices on the ground. After the Reich Interior Ministry was forced to admit that the citizenship decree of November 1939 had not been successful in implementing a uniform process, its staff also began working intensively on a new set of guidelines during the following summer. Finally presented on July 3, 1940, the new draft proposal on the acquisition of German national status in the annexed territories would turn out to be a fruitless exercise, as it received no support from the Gauleiters and was ultimately torpedoed by Himmler; nonetheless, a brief outline of its basic principles is worth presenting here, because this example once again makes clear, especially when seen in contrast to the propositions of the Reich Security Main Office, just how far apart the Reich's relevant institutions had diverged on such an important issue.

Unlike the SS complex, the Reich Interior Ministry was not considering a fundamental change to the existing procedure: it still argued in favor of a two-step process in which the "Volksdeutsche" were to be identified first, before any decisions were to be made about the rest of the local populace. This first phase had eluded completion, particularly as the selection practices implemented thus far had shown that "in many cases, my circular of March 29, 1939 . . . was not taken as the foundation, and instead, one had proceeded according to very divergent viewpoints," and the selection criteria had been interpreted "sometimes too narrowly, sometimes too broadly."[319] But in the subsequent provisions, it became very clear that the Reich Interior Ministry was more critical of excessive narrowness, stating that with "recognizing members of the German Volk . . . one must proceed generously."[320] To ensure the looser interpretation in view of the divergent interpretations applied until then, more detailed instructions were now added. Their general thrust clearly remained the same: the main focus was still on applicant's conduct, and the main goal was the assimilation of individuals whose cultural proficiency made their inclusion seem most promising. In this context, it was political opponents who were excluded above all. Meanwhile, "German" descent did not seem to be particularly important: "For recognition as a German ethnonational, descent from German ancestors is not of decisive importance. The term 'German ethnonational member' ['deutscher Volkszugehöriger'] is not congruent with the term 'German-descended' ['deutschstämmig']. German-descended is anyone springing from German ancestors. Meanwhile, German ethnonational membership does not require either full or predominantly German descent."[321] As a result, persons "of German descent" were to be excluded here if they had "merged into a foreign folkdom," and conversely, if the other criteria were satisfied, "it is also possible to consider as a German ethnonational someone who is partially or fully of another descent, e.g., of Polish . . . descent."[322]

As the Reich Interior Ministry tried to make clear to its administrative officials by way of a few examples, ethnonational membership was above all a question of social praxis. Thus, members of German minority organizations were "routinely" considered to be "Volksdeutsche," and membership in a "Polish" party or political group was invariably taken as grounds for exclusion. Conversely, and in accord with the inclusivist orientation of existing policy, individuals who had joined "Polish" *cultural* groups were not to be automatically refused recognition as "Volksdeutsche." In general, "*active exertions for Germandom are not a prerequisite for recognition as a German ethnonational.* An indifferent or even a bad German still remains a German, and one must avoid pushing him against his will into the non-German camp, thereby supplying the latter with German blood . . . ethnonational membership and political loyalty are different things."[323]

The Reich Interior Ministry was thus adding further criteria that would enable individuals who had not been active participants in the German minority's cultural or political life to nonetheless be recognized as "Volksdeutsche." German language usage was assigned great significance as one of the "most important external markers of ethnonational membership." Individuals "who do not understand the German language cannot as a rule be recognized as members of the German Volk"—and it was certainly no accident that passive comprehension, instead of active usage, was considered sufficient. Corresponding attention was also focused on the applicant's name. If he had Polonized his name during the interwar period, this argued, "as a rule, for his Polish ethnonationality." And if names lacking German counterparts had been chosen by parents for their children, that fact could also be seen as indicating a "Polish orientation in the parents," and likewise the use of Polish schools in places where a German school was available.

The draft proposal cites "cultural connections" as an aspect that might justify recognition of certain local inhabitants as "Volksdeutsche." In this instance, the proposal's inclusivist orientation is especially obvious. In the Reich Interior Ministry's view, there were "in the formerly Prussian parts the greatest number of residents of Polish descent who, due to their growing up under German circumstances . . . had had strong points of contact with the German culture. Therefore, in doubtful cases, particularly with long-standing residents of the formerly Prussian territories, a sympathetic decision is indicated."[324] There were also distinct differences in its clarifications of the use of "race" as a selection criterion. The draft proposal does include a passage that could be initially seen as converging on the position of the SS apparatus: in considering whether a "German ethnonational" should be recognized, "besides the political and health-related requirements, particular importance is given to his racial assessment." But then in the implementing provisions, it states that "racial suitability is given particular importance to the extent that the foreign-blooded are not members of the German Volk. The fully foreign-blooded (Jews, Gypsies, members of non-European races) can never been viewed as German ethnonationals."[325] Race was thus used, as before, primarily as a way to exclude Jews, but explicitly not Poles. The Reich Interior Ministry was even prepared to make exceptions for "Mischlinge" ("hybrid persons"), as long as they had "made a particular sacrifice for the German cause." Therefore, as particularly loyal political allies, even "Jewish Mischlinge" could find a path to joining the "German Volksgemeinschaft," meaning that political loyalty actually took precedence here. But beyond the exclusion of Jews, race was explicitly not assigned particular significance as a selection criterion: "Beyond the case of having an element of foreign blood that . . . precludes recognition as a German ethnonational, the racial assessment alone is generally not a suitable guide for classification as a German ethnonational or a foreign one."[326]

To safeguard this inclusivist course of action, the SS was effectively shut out of the process. Although it was true that, unlike with the citizenship decree, the plan was now to let the SD send a representative to each of the "referee committees" that were to be established in an advisory capacity under the Regierungspräsidents and Landrats, the committees were to be convened only for "doubtful cases," and their decisions would not be binding anyway. Therefore, although the RKFDV headquarters still entertained dreams of taking over the entire selection process and the Reich Security Main Office strove to acquire at least a direct supervisory role, the Reich Interior Ministry was intent on maintaining the current exclusion of the SS apparatus.

The biggest differences, however, were over the question of what would happen to the rest of the populace. Although the Reich Interior Ministry insisted that the registration of the "Volksdeutsche" needed to be completed before any guidelines on the selection of the remaining populace could be issued, its draft proposal nonetheless offered an indication of its preferred course of action. It signaled its intention by referring to Hitler's annexation decree, which stated that those "of kindred blood" were generally at least eligible for German national status. The proposal stated that, in general, all "members of a foreign Volk who represent a desirable addition to the population are to become German nationals, and that these are thereby afforded an opportunity for full Germanization; once this has happened, they will henceforth as German ethnonationals have the possibility of acquiring Reich citizen rights as well."[327] In any case, the ministry felt that there was no alternative to this inclusivist strategy, because it would "not be possible to remove every member of a foreign Volk from the incorporated eastern territories."[328]

HIMMLER'S SUCCESS: THE DECREE ON ASSESSING AND WINNOWING THE POPULACE

By the time the Reich Interior Ministry's draft proposal was issued, it was clear that German ethnopolicy had already become a shambles. In any case, almost a year after the invasion of Poland, there was no trace of a uniform Germanization policy under Nazi rule. However much the concept of conquering "German Lebensraum" had defined Nazi ideology and at least its wartime propaganda, reaching even a vague consensus on what it actually meant had not been possible so far. For the main actors, the only point of agreement was that a selection process was necessary and that it was not acceptable to declare the entire local populace to be German nationals. But the questions of what criteria to apply, what procedure to use in applying them, and finally, who to assign to the task were points that provoked strongly divergent opinions.

Although the surviving sources offer no information on how these differences were resolved at the top, meaning between Frick and Himmler, one thing is clear: when movement came again in September 1940, it was the Reich Interior Ministry that had given way. Its defeat in the face of Himmler's demands was probably sealed on September 11, during a meeting that had been requested by Stuckart.[329] This would also explain how it was possible for Himmler, just a day later, to sign his "decree on assessing and winnowing the populace in the incorporated eastern territories," a foundational document that incorporated the main guidelines of the Reich Security Main Office's memorandum from May 1940. Instead of the two-phase inclusivist selection process applied to the local populace as preferred by the Reich Interior Ministry until then, there now came into effect a procedure aimed at processing the entire populace at once, one in which only a small proportion were to be taken into the German "Volksgemeinschaft" through a selection process to be oriented along racial lines.

Through his decree, Himmler intended to first separate part of the local populace as either "Volksdeutsche" or "Deutschstämmige" for enrollment into the four sections of the DVL, with each section given more rights than the one below; the DVL itself was now to be introduced in all the annexed provinces. Before the remaining populace was to be expelled, it was important to winnow out those "with whom a clear ethnonational classification is not possible," along with other "valuable Fremdvölkische."

Among those considered "ethnonationally difficult to categorize" were the Masurians, Kashubians, Szlonzakians, and Upper Silesians.[330] Probably to help prevent a Germanization policy like that seen in Danzig–West Prussia, where Forster had declared part of the local populace to be an "intermediate class" in order to justify their assimilation, Himmler also specified quotas for the first time. According to the quotas, 100,000 Kashubians could be enrolled in the DVL of Danzig–West Prussia, along with another "100,000 former Poles, who, as a result of mixed marriages and cultural influences, are leaning toward Germandom."[331] The decree does not explain why this latter group apparently existed only in Danzig–West Prussia, but it was probably inserted more as a signal of Himmler's readiness to compromise with Forster. The quotas for the "intermediate class" were also capped in Silesia, where the civil administration had similarly opted for what the SS saw as an excessively pragmatic Germanization policy.[332] It was alleged that this province contained no more than 120,000 Szlonzakians and 400,000 to 500,000 "Upper Silesians (Water Poles)"; the local DVL offices were given upper limits here as well.[333]

Meanwhile, the "valuable Fremdvölkische" were those individuals who had been earmarked for assimilation through the re-Germanization program introduced by Himmler in May 1940. The SS had already successfully monopolized this selection process: it was conducted by RuSHA suitability assessors and took place within the framework of the UWZ.

Thus, in accord with the recommendations of the Reich Security Main Office and based on the model of the Wartheland, the DVL was to register "Volksdeutsche" and "Stammesdeutsche" and sort them into four sections. "Volksdeutsche" were generally held to be only those who had "verifiably professed to Germandom before September 1, 1939," either by having "actively engaged in the ethnonational struggle" or at the very least by having "verifiably preserved their Germandom." They were to be correspondingly enrolled in Sections 1 or 2. Those who "had not verifiably professed to Germandom by September 1, 1939, but had made such a profession later on" were to be registered in Section 3. This primarily applied to individuals who were of German descent, that is, the "Stammesdeutsche," but were nonetheless considered "Fremdvölkische" by the German occupiers. They had "entered into ties with Polishdom but, because of their conduct, carry within themselves the prerequisite for becoming full members of the German Volksgemeinschaft."[334] However, Section 3 also included two other groups of "Fremdvölkische." One was "persons of non-German descent . . . in ethnonationally mixed marriages" in which "the German part . . . has prevailed." This verbatim adoption of the relevant stipulation from the Wartheland was significant in demonstrating Himmler's readiness to break with the patrilineal tradition of German citizenship laws. Thus, if a "German" woman was married to a "Polish" man, it was no longer the case that the entire family was lost to the German "Volksgemeinschaft"; instead, they had a right to claim German national status if the children were being raised "German." Section 3 also took in those groups that seemed to elude a "clear ethnonational classification," namely the Masurians, Kashubians, Szlonzakians, and Upper Silesians. If members of these groups "had verifiably professed to Germandom" before the German invasion, they were to be inducted into at least Section 3 of the DVL, even if "their home language is not German." Finally, Section 4 was to take in those individuals who had also "merged politically into Polishdom," meaning the "renegades." Enrollment in Sections 3 or 4 did not protect those persons from expulsions. In Himmler's view, the only way their "re-Germanization" might succeed was through immersion in a German environment, which meant being transported into the Reich itself. A major goal of the SS apparatus thereby seemed within reach, namely the deportation of the great majority of the local populace.

Himmler had not only stipulated a nuanced and exclusivist selection process, but had also assigned central importance to the criterion of "race" in the selections of the DVL. His decree contained no detailed guidelines on adjudicating applications, since his fundamental aim was first to introduce the DVL itself. Furthermore, part of the populace had already been selected under Frick's citizenship decree, with the resulting national status identity documents already issued. It would have been unrealistic for Himmler to try annulling this fait accompli, for he would have turned not only the Reich Interior Ministry against him, but also each of the Gauleiters. Therefore, it was much more realistic to try influencing the selection process for Sections 3 and 4, which had so far begun only in the Wartheland. It was only in this regard that Himmler's decree included a guideline for the adjudication of candidates: a "professing of Germandom" was to be required from members of Section 3 as well, but would be accepted only "if this professing is confirmed by facts, such as descent, race, schooling, and culture. In doubtful cases, the decisive factor is whether the person represents a racially valuable addition to the population."[335] In borrowing the previous written formulations of the Reich Interior Ministry, Himmler had completely changed their meaning by racially charging them. Even if it was no longer possible to exert any influence on the selection of individuals for Sections 1 and 2 as the selection into these groups was almost completed, the SS could at least hope to handle the rest of the populace with a selection process suited to their "racial suitability."

But even Himmler was forced to make compromises driven by the functional needs of power. For example, although Kashubians were considered "Fremdvölkische," they were not fundamentally precluded from assimilation into the "German Volksgemeinschaft," because they were allegedly "related by blood and represent a racially valuable addition to the population for the German Volk." As a result, the relevant process in their case was not considered an assimilation but rather a "re-Germanization, meaning a reclamation of lost German blood."[336]

As in the re-Germanization program, the racism of the SS proved to be politically adaptable to a certain extent. Its stance was politically functional in that it enabled the politically necessary integration of a particular section of the Polish populace without relying on the assimilation policy focusing on ethnonational criteria as advocated by the Reich Interior Ministry and other actors. A strict prohibition on any policy of assimilation was clearly dysfunctional, it was equally unacceptable to disengage from the ideological maxim that only the soil itself was Germanizable, which meant that Himmler's solution was more or less the only possibility: the selection of Poles through the re-Germanization program, and even their enrollment in the DVL, was no longer an act of assimilation, but instead a "recovery of lost German blood," one that could be seamlessly integrated into the racial narrative.

This racial charging of the selection criteria would have consequences for Section 4 as well. Having already succeeded in getting "Deutschstämmige" exempted from deportation even if they had been identified as political opponents, Himmler now issued a directive that these individuals were to be inducted into Section 4 of the DVL. This insistence on enrolling them as well was based on a truly racial imperative, the principle "that no German blood be made useful to a foreign folkdom."[337] This danger was taken very seriously by Himmler, as shown by the consequences facing these people if they refused to cooperate: "With those who refuse re-Germanization, security measures are to be undertaken. The children, who cannot be held responsible for the conduct of their parents, should not have to suffer under the culpability of their parents. For their upbringing, the German Reich will step in."[338] According to the provisions of this decree, the racial selection process would play an even more decisive role in the selections applied to the remaining populace. Harking back to the plan prepared in November 1939 by the HSSPFs in Kraków, which had been repeatedly discussed since then by various SS bodies, it had now come time to begin a "screening of the Polish populace" and the registering of "valuable Fremdvölkische" who "come into question for Germanization."[339] The UWZ, after having concluded the selection of deportees and transported them into the General Government, was to scrutinize the remaining residents who were not eligible for DVL enrollment in terms of "racial, health-related, and security-related considerations."[340]

Himmler was now connecting back to the re-Germanization project that had been set in motion with his directive of May 9, 1940. Typifying the ad hoc nature of the regime's Germanization policy, the project originally arose as a short-term solution for two pressing problems: the General Government's resistance to receiving more deportees and, more important, the worsening labor shortage in the Reich. With this last clause, consisting of just a few lines, Himmler had not only incorporated the existing re-Germanization program into a more comprehensive population policy but also given the UWZ a job that would dwarf even the registration efforts of the DVL. He left open the question of when, however, and according to what criteria this last and largest selection phase would be conducted by stating that he would issue "more detailed implementing provisions" at the appropriate time.[341]

The selection results would ultimately have major consequences for the legal status of the local inhabitants. Members of Sections 1 and 2, as German ethnonationals, acquired German national status and Reich citizen rights, thus putting them—at least formally—on an equal footing with the German occupiers. Those in Sections 3 and 4 fared much worse: as "valuable Fremdvölkische," they were generally earmarked for transport into the Reich, where they would be "re-Germanized." Until then, they would be denied Reich citizen rights. Although those in Section 3 were granted German national status, those in Section 4 received that status on a revocable basis only, meaning it could be withdrawn by the authorities at any time. Here, Himmler was drawing on a suggestion originally outlined by Wetzel and Hecht in their memorandum of November 25, 1939. But by far the largest group were those outside the four sections: as undesired "Fremdvölkische," these individuals became—as it was cynically called— "protected dependents [Schutzangehörige] of the German Reich with restricted inhabitant rights [Inländerrechten]," which effectively left them without rights.[342]

The belief in the absolute inequality of persons and the resulting impulse to differentiate between them had already led to the racial sorting of the German populace as introduced by the Nuremberg Laws, which turned Jews into persons with lesser rights. Himmler wanted to take this a step further in Poland. The entire populace of the annexed territories were to be subjected to a complex selection process in which the non-Jewish residents were also to be sorted according to ethnonational and racial criteria. In order to provide the selection process with a legal underpinning as well, the German national status framework was expanded once more, this time with the introduction of "revocable national status" ("Staatsangehörigkeit auf Widerruf"). And since most residents were to be expelled anyway, yet another legal status was created, the "protected dependent," a term whose colonial connotations were probably not accidental.[343]

With his decree, Himmler had given SS population policy a certain coherence for the first time, but—and this is generally overlooked in the scholarly literature—he had achieved coherence by largely adopting a system already practiced in the Wartheland. If he had actually succeeded in implementing it, then the selection of deportees and the selection of DVL enrollees would have both been processes bound by comparable, racially oriented criteria.

* * *

Of course, Himmler's decree also represented an effort to directly influence the balance of power on the ground. At least that was how it was seen by Greifelt, who decided to use the decree to mount another attempt to increase his agency's influence. What he seemed to find particularly irritating was his agency's exclusion from the DVL process, which had progressed the farthest in conducting selections on the local populace and also served as Himmler's reference model. Participating in this process, and perhaps even taking control of it, therefore promised wide-ranging ramifications that went far beyond the Wartheland.

On November 15, 1940, Greifelt went on the offensive by sending a surprisingly direct message to Greiser, announcing his desire to take direct control of the DVL process. After all, it was of "pivotal importance in ethnonational, political, and economic terms" and thus touched on his own sphere of responsibilities. Furthermore, this was to happen as quickly as possible: since Himmler's decree was going to change the division of responsibilities in this policy field anyway and was going to "directly" incorporate the RKFDV offices, this would also be the best way for him to follow up on the existing "complaints" about the operations of the "old DVL," whereby he named a few examples, "of which you will please take note."[344] For one thing, Greifelt criticized the excessively restrictive selection criteria, which purportedly "do not correspond to the principles that, in implementing the ethnonationality decree [Volkstumserlass] of the Reichsführer of the SS of September 12, 1941, are generally to be applied in the eastern territories"; beyond that was the harsh tone with which rejected applicants had been "fobbed off," so that even "German-descended people are so intimidated" that they do not dare at all to defend their own interests. Above all, however, he complained that the rejection letters had deceived applicants into believing there was no right of appeal. This was doubly wrong, because it was already possible to file an appeal with the Reichsstatthalter himself, and it would soon be possible to do so with the upcoming Supreme Court of Review for Ethnonationality Questions as well.

Greifelt's criticism culminated in a general attack on the DVL. He asked for "the issuing of such . . . questionnaires to be suspended right away. The new Volk List must come into play . . . with differently formulated questions for the applicants anyway." Furthermore, existing decisions would now be placed under the proviso of final confirmation from the relevant RKFDV branch office. In view of the failings seen thus far, "some of the DVL approvals issued until now must remain in dispute for the time being, namely until the creation of a possibility of subjecting each individual case to a detailed review. This possibility has not existed to date."[345] Meanwhile, for the intervening period until the "constituting of the new Reich legislative framework," Greifelt had a very clear idea of how the two agencies should work together. If the RKFDV headquarters should receive complaints about DVL rejections in the future, it would forward them to the RKFDV branch office in Posen for investigation. This would then deliver its findings to the DVL offices, and Greiser was to instruct them to use this as a fresh basis on which "to review once again their previous decision."[346]

Greiser responded in no uncertain terms. While he certainly agreed that the selection of the local populace "touches closely on the task of strengthening Germandom in the eastern territories," by no means did that mean that its implementation also had to be assigned to the RKFDV headquarters.[347] The question of whether this implementation

> is to be extended to the agency under your remit requires a general regulation. Since it has been implemented until now on a regional basis by my own state and party agencies in a proven manner, I see absolutely no reason to change or transfer the existing operation. This change is already made unnecessary by the fact that the entire leadership lies in the hands of the party, which after all is represented by myself within my Gau territory, and not by the Reich Commissioner [i.e., Himmler]. Furthermore, it lies within my jurisdiction, for the purposes of my appointment by the Reich Commissioner, to decide the extent to which I want to deploy the various offices of my Gau territory for completing the tasks of the Reich Commissioner . . . I plan to change nothing in the existing proven working methods, and instead will simply submit any appeals cases, as per the ethnonationality decree of September 12, 1940, to the Supreme Court of Review for judgment.[348]

Greiser was flatly rejecting Greifelt's detailed criticisms, along with his core demand for a review of all the complaints that had been brought to him. Furthermore, he had firmly decided that Greifelt's agencies would be kept out of the DVL selection process in the future as well:

> Regarding the . . . suggested collaboration between the agencies, I hereby state that I am unable to follow your line of thought. It is not the HSSPF who is the appointee [of Himmler as RKFDV]; instead, I myself am that. It remains solely and exclusively entrusted to my responsibility to decide who I will assign to the implementation within my Gau. I do not intend to tackle the ethnonationality process with the agencies of the police and the SS, but instead, solely and exclusively with the agencies of the party and state. Thus, there is no need for any of the collaboration between the different agencies as desired by you; instead, such collaboration will be initiated by me in the form that

> I . . . consider desirable. In order to avoid unnecessary paperwork concerning all such questions in the future, I consider it appropriate that you with your agency in Berlin remain a purely leadership-level authority . . . I cannot imagine another way of working together, nor do I want to.[349]

This last comment by Greiser was most certainly a reflection of reality. Himmler's decision to name the Gauleiters and administrative heads as his appointees in his jurisdiction as RKFDV can be best understood as a recognition of their power, for he could not hope to apply a coherent Germanization policy without their cooperation. This strategically expedient incorporation of powerful officeholders was meant to help the SS apparatus avoid undue friction with the agencies of party and state. Another fact supporting this reading is that Himmler excluded one Gauleiter only from this practice, namely Forster, with whom the conflicts had escalated too far in recent months. The others, however, had gladly accepted his offer, because it promised to increase their power merely in exchange for their cooperation in the future. Being named as Himmler's appointees also gave them direct access to the RKFDV branch offices. Greifelt could do nothing to counter this.

* * *

It was just a few days later that Himmler asked Frick on September 16, 1940, for the "speedy preparation of the necessary implementing orders" so that the DVL could also be established in reality across all the annexed eastern provinces.[350] The draft package, circulated by the Reich Interior Ministry in late October and containing the decree on the "acquisition of German national status by former Polish and Danzig nationals" along with the corresponding implementing provisions, was designed to replace the citizenship decree of November 25, 1939; beyond that, it also removed any doubt that Himmler was the one who had prevailed in this nearly year-long confrontation. The Reich Interior Ministry had acquiesced to all three of Himmler's core demands: a selection process (1) covering the entire populace that was (2) immediate and exclusivist, as already practiced in the Wartheland, and, in addition, now also (3) racially oriented.

In terms of the first core demand, the Reich Interior Ministry now embraced the idea of immediately subjecting the entire populace to a selection process, thereby declaring "great mass of the Polish populace" to be protected dependents, thus earmarking them for expulsion.[351] The remaining populace was no longer to be granted German national status without further ado but was instead to be endowed with graduated rights by being selected for the respective sections of the DVL, whose establishment was now ordered by the Reich Interior Ministry itself.

The Reich Interior Ministry, however, did not entirely bow to Himmler's demands. To be sure, it is undoubtedly true that the SS complex, in the pursuit of a maximally exclusivist selection policy justified by the alleged "racial" difference of the Polish populace, had successfully managed to universalize the racial discourse in a policy area where recourse to "race" had thus far been used in the isolation only of Jews and not of Poles. How hegemonic this racial discourse soon became is shown by the way that the Reich Interior Ministry, although forced to adopt it, nonetheless tried to hijack the racial terminology of the SS complex in order to achieve a contrary goal. Thus, already in the introduction to the implementing provisions, it was stipulated that "for enrollment in the DVL, the important thing is that no German blood may be lost and made useful for a foreign folkdom. . . . Even an indifferent German or a bad one still remains a German."[352] With this quote's first sentence, newly added since the July draft, the Reich Interior Ministry thus remained true to its established strategy of adopting the selection criteria put forward by proponents of exclusivism and then playing their own contradictions against each other. Whereas the highlighting of "race" was generally used by the SS complex to justify its demand for an exclusivist selection process, the Reich Interior Ministry was now attempting to achieve the exact opposite.

Also in terms of the four-group sorting system, extensive interpretations were now applied to the provisions already practiced in the Wartheland and taken up in Himmler's ethnonationality decree. Thus, according to the Reich Interior Ministry, Section 1 should generally admit members of all German minority organizations—even if they had "leaned toward Catholicism or Marxism." The "habitual use of the German language in public" also sufficed.[353] And regarding selections for Section 2, the Reich Interior Ministry pointed out that the self-employed, as well as civil servants and white-collar workers (*Beamte* and *Angestellte,* two classes that are distinct in German law), had professional reasons that naturally prevented them from exposing themselves politically and thus risking their jobs. As a result, even the use of Polish schooling could not be weighted negatively; in such cases, it was necessary instead to ascertain which language predominated in the home.

Whereas the desired professing of Germandom thus secured entry in Sections 1 or 2, enrollment into Sections 3 or 4 generally required "German" descent, as "the induction of foreign-descended persons into the German Volksgemeinschaft can happen only with the greatest of caution. In particular, if larger amounts of foreign blood were to be mixed into German blood, the resulting Volk, although speaking the German language, would no longer be, in terms of racial composition, the current German Volk."[354] As in Himmler's ethnonationality decree, the Reich Interior Ministry described three groups of persons to be selected for Section 3: first, "German-descended persons who over the years have entered into ties with Polishdom, but because of their conduct, there appears to exist the necessary requirement that they are once again becoming full members of the German Volksgemeinschaft"—a near verbatim adoption of the Wartheland regulations; second, "persons of non-German descent who live in an ethnonationally mixed marriage with a German ethnonational, wherein the German part has prevailed"—meaning "Polish" spouses; and third, "members of population groups that are ethnonationally not clearly to be classified, which lean toward Germandom in terms of blood and culture while speaking a Slavic home language." Here too, exceptions were made according to the applicant's political conduct. For example, individuals who had "professed to Germandom before September 1, 1939," were to be registered in Sections 1 or 2—even if their mother tongue was Polish. Correspondingly, members of this "intermediate class" were to be denied registration entirely if they were considered political opponents—therefore, they were not to be enrolled in Section 4, but instead excluded completely. Section 4 was exclusively reserved for political opponents who, as "German-descended persons . . . have politically merged into Polishdom."[355]

Whereas racial screening had been explicitly excluded in the past, both from the DVL process in the Wartheland as well as during the selections in the other two provinces, Himmler had now forced the Reich Interior Ministry to include it for the first time. According to the guidelines by the Reich Interior Ministry, however, racial screenings were to play only a minor role. First off, they were to be restricted to the applicants for group 3. And even amongst this group, applicants who could prove "German descent" were deemed automatically to be "racially suitable" and thus excluded from the need to undergo these screenings. Only if such proof was lacking, or if applicants could demonstrate "only a small percentage of German blood," induction into group 3 could only proceed "if there are no concerns regarding race. Here, racial suitability is of decisive importance." In contrast with the first draft of July 1940, the Reich Interior Ministry had thereby made a complete reversal and now declared in general: "The attempt to Germanize racially undesirable elements is already doomed to failure because their true Germanization is not even possible. This applies to the foreign-descended (Poles, etc.) as well as the foreign-blooded (Jews, Gypsies, members of non-European races). The foreign-blooded do not as a general rule have the required racial suitability. The fully foreign-blooded can never be recognized as German ethnonationals."[356] For the first time, and in clear contrast to the ministry's July draft, it was now possible to use "racial suitability" to exclude not only Jews but also Christian Poles.

Despite the more restrictive conditions, the Reich Interior Ministry still strove for an interpretation that was as inclusivist as possible, even with the selection process for Section 3. The first thing that stands out is an absence: despite Himmler's repeated demands to cap the number of "re-Germanizable" persons at one million, the Reich Interior Ministry had not done so. Because it was clear that, under the given selection guidelines, the great majority of DVL enrollees would fall into Section 3, the refusal to limit their number meant that the Reich Interior Ministry had left open a back door for an inclusivist selection practice. And this was precisely the option that the provincial chiefs in Danzig–West Prussia and Silesia would choose to use, much to the aggravation of the SS complex.

In contrast, it is less clear how the rules on national status were developed. In contrast to the Reich Interior Ministry's July draft, which still aimed to confer at least German national status on the great majority of the local populace, Himmler's ethnonationality decree was already much more restrictive in this regard. Like the exclusivist selection process specified there, the Reich Interior Ministry planned to award German national status to a smaller percentage than before, with the recipients to be subdivided into Reich citizens, German nationals, and revocable German nationals. Then, in the ministry's second draft, the regulations were tightened even further: German national status would no longer be summarily granted to members of Section 3, but only through case-by-case naturalization. Why the Reich Interior Ministry decided to do so, or under whose pressure, cannot be determined from the surviving source materials.[357]

Although the Reich Interior Ministry had shifted away from its previously held positions and by and large adopted Himmler's specifications, one area still existed in which it was not prepared to give up control: the practical implementation of the selection process. As in the model used in the Wartheland, the Reich Interior Ministry's draft proposal of October 1940 envisaged for the DVL a three-level hierarchy consisting of central offices, regional offices, and branch offices, with each linked to the corresponding level of civil administration. Furthermore, to maintain a unified rationale and act as a final appeals body, a Supreme Court of Review for Ethnonationality Questions was established—as demanded by Himmler's ethnonationality decree.

It was the DVL branch offices, operating on the county level, that would function as the main selection organ deciding on the induction of an applicant. The dominant position of party and state was secured through the choice of personnel, with each branch office staffed by the local Landrat (as the chair), the local Kreisleiter, a high-ranking representative from the Landrat's offices, another from the Kreisleiter's offices, and a representative of the local "Volksdeutsche." Here, in the DVL's most important committee structure, the SS apparatus was not represented at all. It was not much different at the other two levels, which functioned as appeals bodies. Although the SS sent one representative (from the IdS) to the seven-person committee at each regional office, and two representatives (from the HSSPF and the IdS) to the seven-person committee at each central office, the rest of the committee members from the party and state were subordinated to the chairman; in the case of the central office, this was the provincial chief, in his double role as the province's administration head and

Figure 4.5. Green identity document for DVL Section 3.
Source: Polish State Archives in Poznań, under DVL Wollstein, 427.

party leader.[358] The SS representatives were primarily marginalized by a particular regulation, taken from the July draft, in which applications and appeals were to be presented for discussion within the committee, but final decisions were to be made by its chairman alone. The SS representatives were not even granted a right of appeal, which would have allowed them to forward important cases to the next level up and finally to the SS-controlled Supreme Court of Review for Ethnonationality Questions.

In striving toward as inclusivist a selection process as possible, the Reich Interior Ministry did not rely solely on a de facto neutralization of the SS apparatus. It additionally ordered the continued acceptance of selections already performed under Frick's citizenship decree and also ordered that the thereby stipulated questionnaires were to be used in the future as well. Now, however, an identity document was to be issued to every person enrolled in the DVL: a blue one for members of Sections 1 and 2, a green one for Section 3, and a red one for Section 4.[359]

The final version of the draft was to be decided during a meeting at the Reich Interior Ministry on November 13, to which the appointed ethnonationality

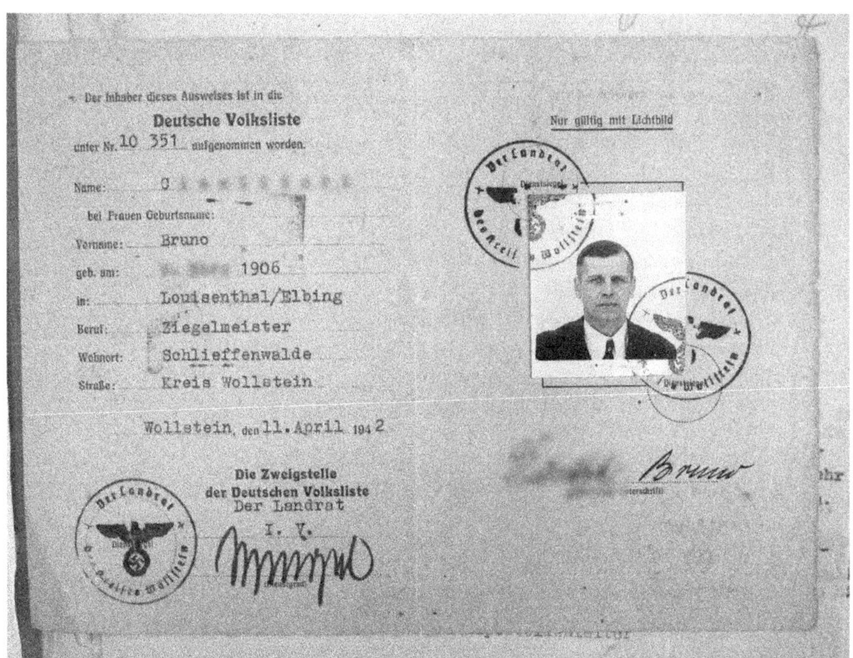

Figure 4.6. Inside of the figure 4.5 document.

officers (*Volkstumsreferenten*) from the annexed provinces were also invited. Coulon took this as an opportunity to push again for greater consideration of the applicant's conduct. Although the Reich Interior Ministry had completed an about-face, the ethnocrats from Posen's civil administration and SD nonetheless criticized the change as a half-hearted one, as the draft would still water down the criteria used in the Wartheland; but more important, it also attached too little importance to the ethnonational struggle.[360] Particularly revealing was their unanimous criticism of the newly introduced racial criteria in the selection process—a criticism that thus indirectly targeted Himmler, and not the Reich Interior Ministry. For example, Strickner, the ethnonationality officer from the Posen SD, rejected the idea that for those whose "German" descent could not be definitively verified, their enrollment was to depend on a racial selection yardstick, even if it had been determined that they had already been campaigning on behalf of German minorities before the German invasion. He felt that such persons should certainly be recognized as "Volksdeutsche."[361] Coulon summarized this criticism most clearly: while he did not doubt that the "conservation of German blood is necessary," putting this provision at the start of the implementing decree was nonetheless inappropriate, as it meant that behind this purely biological demand, the demands of the political present recede entirely. It leads to a politically untenable burden in the internal life of the newly incorporated eastern territories if the two tasks, namely the separating out of Germandom and of Polishdom, in other words the stocktaking of the past ethnopolitical struggle on the one hand and the winnowing of racially valuable blood on the other, are not sharply distinguished from one another. There develops within the ethnonational group [Volksgruppe] the impression that past dedication to the ethnonational struggle is only slightly valued, and that in end effect a racially well-rated Pole is judged better than a proven Volksdeutscher who may not appear as racially fortunate. But for development work in the east, politically or otherwise, the upkeep of political combat energy is just as important as the racial winnowing effort, which means that both should be taken into account. Therefore, the basis for adjudication must first be the individual's conduct in the ethnonational struggle.[362]

"Race" and political conduct followed different rationales as selection criteria, and thus could not be combined without creating contradictions, which was a problem that the Wartheland's civil administration decision makers had previously dealt with by simply excluding "race" as a selection criterion. Politically, this decision was made all the easier by the fact that even Posen's SD Command Precinct had sanctioned it. But with the particular weight given to racially oriented selection by Himmler's ethnonationality decree and more recently by the Reich Interior Ministry, Coulon was also forced to take a more tactical approach to the topic. To be sure, he was still not ready to let go of the demand that "first preference is to be given those who have proved themselves in the ethnonational struggle." But now, in contrast to his earlier assessment, he took these selection criteria tailored to the rational demands of power and tried to lend them a racial interpretation that better corresponded to Himmler's position. It was not particularly difficult to do so: he wrote that, in the end, "times of struggle are always times in which a selection process takes place. However, a selection process regarding suitability of character is always simultaneously a process of racial selection as well."[363]

For Coulon, the path to resolving the contradiction between political conduct and racial suitability was therefore clear. He then proposed the following interpretation: "During the time of struggle, the only people who would have professed to Germandom are those who have impeccable character, and thus are also racially impeccable. One's conduct during the time of struggle is therefore to be ascribed decisive significance."[364]

During the meeting at the Reich Interior Ministry on November 13, 1940, the criticism voiced by Coulon and others did not fall on deaf ears. As shown by a later draft from December 19, 1941, it was decided that members of the "intermediate class" who had imperiled themselves on the side of the German minorities were always to be classified in Section 1 or 2, and even if their descent was unclear, they were still to be exempted from undergoing racial selection.[365] Furthermore, Coulon also managed to universalize the supplementary questionnaire that had been formulated by the Wartheland authorities for their own province soon after receiving Frick's citizenship decree of November 25, 1939. It was now to become mandatory in all other eastern provinces as well. This ensured that the attention of the DVL offices stayed focused on the applicant's conduct, which was the primary line of inquiry on the supplementary questionnaire. Although the ongoing differences of opinion in Berlin would still delay the decree's release until March 1941, Coulon was nonetheless correct when he wrote "On the whole, it can be said that the now completed Reich-level regulations would not have happened and also would not have been conceivable without the groundwork and experiences of the Wartheland."[366]

The Power of the Gauleiters

Even if the Reich Interior Ministry and the SS complex mostly held contrary viewpoints in the confrontations just described, they nonetheless agreed on the acute need for a regulatory standard and that it was needed as soon as possible, because otherwise the competing procedures of the individual provinces would drift even further apart. One might expect that as the Reich Interior Ministry began to largely align itself with the positions of the SS complex, this would also affect the provinces by narrowing their ability to deviate from the directives coming out of Berlin. But this expectation would demonstrate a serious underestimation of the political power possessed by the Gauleiters. Although it can be shown that certain aspects and even phrasings from the circulating drafts also found their way into the selection policies of the provinces, the already established procedures of all three provinces nonetheless drifted even further apart. Berlin seemed far away, and as long as there was still no decree, the individual Gauleiters continued creating facts on the ground, ones that even a universal Reich-level regulation could no longer undo.

COMPLETION OF THE DVL IN THE WARTHELAND

In the Wartheland, the registration of the populace was already well advanced, and civil administrators had been discussing for months the possibility of a timeline for shutting down individual DVL offices. A universal Reich-level regulation would come too late for the Wartheland's selection process. Instead, it would affect only the subsequent treatment of each class after sorting. But the regulation's continual delay was in itself not inconsequential, for the legal ramifications of the selection process also needed to be settled. Greiser let the Reich Interior Ministry know that he was not prepared to wait any longer and had already drawn up a draft decree on the matter.

The main difference from the Reich Interior Ministry's draft proposals was that Greiser was defining not only each category's legal status, but also its general social status in a much more comprehensive manner. Thus, members of Groups A and B were to become German nationals, with further specifications on their relationship with the Nazi Party and their possibilities in economic life. Only members of Group A were immediately permitted entry into the party, its subgroups, and its associations and also to occupy all jobs in the civil service and the private economy. Meanwhile, members of Group B—like the majority of people in the Reich as well—could join the party only after a long qualifying period; furthermore, they could not become postsecondary instructors or "teachers in questions of worldview."[367] On the other hand, the "Stammesdeutsche" had to put up with much heavier discrimination. Members of Group C suffered particularly in economic terms. They were not allowed to become officials or leading staff members in public-service agencies, they were generally forbidden to work as teachers or managers, and their property could be confiscated, albeit with compensation. Members of Group D faced additional social sanctions. They had a right to the same wage levels, pension benefits, and food rations as all other members of the DVL, but they were not allowed to set up a self-employed operation or to join a party suborganization or the German Labor Front (Deutsche Arbeitsfront), and they were to be dispossessed with a "limited compensation payment as far as absolutely necessary for the establishment of a modest existence in the Old Reich." In fact, they were supposed to be transported there as quickly as possible. According to Greiser, "They must be removed from the struggle zone!"

Going beyond the draft proposals of the Reich Interior Ministry, Greiser now detailed for the first time the precise connection between "racial suitability" and the granting of German national status, thereby offering a view on how people were to be handled after their deportation from the Wartheland. Greiser did not deviate from the standpoint that "race" should play no role in sorting the populace under the DVL selection process, but when it then came time to decide on the national status of individuals in Groups C and D, which was to be done through case-by-case naturalization in accordance with the Reich Interior Ministry's latest draft, he wrote that these decisions should be tied to racial criteria as well. But even here, one can recognize an attempt to limit the consequences of the racial appraisal process by making the individual's evaluation dependent on previous conduct. Thus, members of Group C were to be considered for rejection only when it came to "eliminating the distinctly racially inferior, and not in selecting the best with members of a foreign Volk." In contrast, members of Group D were to undergo a "more stringent selection process, which however is less stringent than with Polish-descended persons."[368] Such differentiation rules were all the easier for Greiser because the subject individuals at the time of this second selection process would have already been deported to the Reich and would no longer be in the Wartheland. Therefore, when the expected protests emerged, it would be incumbent on bodies inside the Reich to deal with them.

To the Reich Interior Ministry, Greiser's decree represented just one more maverick action, the prevention of which was one of the main objectives of a universal Reich-level regulation. In any case, Stuckart did not let himself be pressured, and he informed Greiser that the ministry's decrees had already been sent "for the decision of the Führer," further threatening that if he continued to act independently, he would have to repeat the registrations done so far, as the regulations decided in Berlin differed "on a number of points from the guidelines that you have set up for recognition as a German ethnonational. Therefore, it will also be necessary in the Wartheland to review, based on the new guidelines, a not inconsiderable number of previous decisions."[369] Greiser ultimately shied away from defying Stuckart's explicit orders and issuing his own decree. He was also unwilling, however, to simply toss it aside. On the contrary, according to Coulon, its circulation was "absolutely necessary, no matter what."[370] Greiser therefore sent it as a memorandum to his top state and party officials—marked "confidential" and carried by personal messengers. This ensured that the Wartheland's key decision makers had a precise idea of the policy positions preferred by the Reichsstatthalter's office.

The policy developments of the Wartheland in late 1940 were also significant in another regard. The civil administration there had developed the most radical Germanization project, which had sought to link the exclusivist DVL selection process to promoting the settlement of ethnic Germans from Eastern Europe alongside large-scale deportations. So in terms of registering the "German" populace, Greiser's ideas were not only more radical than those of the other provincial chiefs, he was also quicker to synthesize them into a consistent policy and more vigorous in its pursuit, which also meant that he was the first one able to declare the process complete. But by then, the contradictions inscribed into Germanization policy from the very start had finally caught up with the civil administration.

With the completion of the DVL process, not only was the registration of the minority "Volksdeutsche" and "Stammesdeutsche" finally finished, but also that of the majority "Poles," meaning that the groundwork had now been laid for a comprehensive deportation policy. It was precisely this aspect that was confronted by new roadblocks. The concept of expelling locals from the province because of political, ethnonationalist, or other reasons had always been a weak point of Germanization policy, and not only in the Wartheland, as it could not convincingly answer two important questions: How were these persons to be deported, and to where? The Reich Railroad was already operating at maximum capacity in the region, and the General Government was raising increasing objections to the delivery of still more deportees. Even in Posen, it was soon recognized that continuing pursuit of the current course would ultimately be dysfunctional.

Coulon's memorandum of February 4, 1941, marked the completion of this turnaround while also pointing to its causes. In it, Coulon argued for a continuation of the Germanization policy while also favoring the deportation of individuals in Groups C and D. But, and this was a significant qualification, with the seriousness of the current situation, the deportation was to happen only if the resulting gaps in the labor market could be filled by arrivals from the Reich itself. The ethnocrats had been forced to recognize that the individuals earmarked for deportation were not simply undesirable "Fremdvölkische," but were also urgently needed workers whom they could not dispense with in the medium term. But if the "end goal," namely, "the removal of the entire Polish populace from the Wartheland," had to be taken off the agenda at least for now, then regulations for the interim period were required.[371] If the Poles could not be deported anytime soon, then it was all the more urgent to effect a "complete shift of ethnopolitical efforts to defending against the ethnonational adversary"[372] in order to maintain the ethnopolitical "advances" achieved to that date and consolidate the already accomplished beginnings of an ethnonationally hierarchized society. The forced realization that the dystopian vision of a "German Wartheland" would not soon become a reality, and that living alongside the hated Polish populace would be necessary for a while, inspired further oppressive impulses. An even stronger desire to expand the existing discriminatory measures emerged because of the necessity of maintaining a segregated society. In Coulon's view, two points needed to be clarified: "Germandom's relationship to Polishdom" and the upcoming "treatment of Polishdom."[373]

On the first point, the occupiers proved rather inventive in the Wartheland. Beyond the radical legal measures issued from Berlin, such as the directive introducing German criminal law in the incorporated eastern territories on June 6, 1940, Poles in the Wartheland were obliged to correctly greet every uniformed German and to accept the humiliations of an increasingly segregated public sphere, ranging from transit systems to eating establishments.[374] But the "German" populace was also subject to clearly defined rules of conduct. Greiser had tightened the relevant regulations with another directive on September 25, 1940—the same day that the DVL registrations were originally supposed to have ended, which would have allowed a "clear dividing line" to have been drawn at last. The police were instructed to take Germans into "protective custody" ("Schutzhaft") and possibly deport them to concentration camps if they failed to keep a certain required distance from Poles, or even worse, maintained a "friendly contact."[375] Sexual relations were also punished, with the German man put into "protective custody" and the Polish woman threatened with consignment to a brothel.[376] It was this aspect in particular that led to absurdly paranoid nightmares.[377] For example, when Coulon expressed his fear soon thereafter that Wehrmacht soldiers had fathered three thousand children with Polish women in the county of Konitz alone, it said little about reality and much about the author's ideological leanings.[378]

As to the second point, namely, the treatment of the local population segment that had been definitively declared "Polish," Coulon was confronted by the same dilemma as Greiser. Assuming that their separation from the German populace was secured, the Poles were now to be handled solely according to their necessity as a workforce. This meant that the regime of terror needed to continue, since "for the exploiting of the Polish workforce, the issue of supervising and coercing labor will always be decisive."[379]

Therefore, the sense of satisfaction over the speedy completion of the DVL process in the Wartheland soon gave way to sobering reality. The dystopian vision of a "German Volksgemeinschaft" was displaced by the expedient of an ethnonationally hierarchized society in which the privileging of a small "German" minority above a "Polish" majority had to be constantly supervised and regularly enforced. If, in pursuing the functional needs of power, a major goal of Germanization policy was to make occupation policy itself obsolete, for the remaining populace declared to be "Germans" would no longer see the Nazi presence as an occupation, then the Wartheland's civil administration would have to defer this dream for "perhaps a generation or more," as Coulon noted.[380]

The "Deutschstämmige Campaign" in Danzig–West Prussia

Forster proved to be even more willing to go it alone than Greiser was, despite the fact that he could not boast being very far along in the process. By the time the Reich Interior Ministry circulated its draft proposals in late October 1940, Danzig–West Prussia had done only the selection process precipitated by Frick's citizenship decree of November 25, 1939, meaning the registration of the "Volksdeutsche." Nonetheless, Forster had very clear ideas about the path forward. The ethnonationality department heads under the Regierungspräsidents got a first look at the future on May 17, 1940, from Forster's ethnonationality officer Löbsack. The registration of the "Volksdeutsche" ordered by the Reich Interior Ministry's citizenship decree of November 1939 would now be followed by the "systematic Germanization of the intermediate class," meaning the assimilation of the "Deutschstämmige" residing in Danzig–West Prussia to start on January 1, 1941.[381] Forster seems to have cared little that the universal Reich-level regulation of precisely this policy area was in fact the declared goal of the Reich Interior Ministry's decree package, which itself was on the verge of passing, or at least that was what Forster must have presumed. In this context, the announcement of an entirely new selection process should have been plainly out of the question.

Proving once again the great power of the provincial chiefs, however, Forster did not let himself to be deterred from giving the order for the "re-Germanization campaign" ("Wiedereindeutschungsaktion") on December 14, 1940.[382]

The chosen name of this campaign is in itself revealing in the insights it offers into the tactical strategy of the Reichssstatthalter's offices. During the constant quarrels with the SS complex over his allegedly too inclusivist selection policy, Forster must have seen how even the Reich Interior Ministry gradually shifted in line with Himmler's racial agenda. Therefore, if he was to maintain his existing policy, with a considerably greater percentage of local residents recognized as "Germans" than, for example, in the Wartheland, it would need stronger ideological backing than before. Here Forster displayed great tactical cunning in turning to the most renowned Nazi "race expert," Professor Hans F. K. Günther from Freiburg, who received an invitation stating that Gauleiter Forster would "place the greatest value on your expert opinion regarding the blood-based and settlement-based reconstruction of the Reichsgau of Danzig–West Prussia."[383] Günther did not fail to deliver what was expected of him. As Forster could later claim in his statements to the Reich Interior Ministry and Hitler, Günther had found after a ten-day "research tour" in September 1940 that, although the local populace represented an "inextricable racial mixture," the key question was nonetheless whether their "offspring could be a welcome addition to the German population." This he answered in the positive, declaring "that around four-fifths of the local Polish populace is not far removed from the Germandom of eastern central Germany."[384] Forster's inclusivist policy had thus received the sanction of racial theory.

In order to dispel from the outset any suspicions that he was aiming at the assimilation of "Poles," Forster introduced his re-Germanization decree with the claim that the planned actions would be strictly limited to the registration of individuals who "fit into our ethnonational and racial fabric, since only they can be fully absorbed without harming our ethnonational substance." But since it was only "spilled Germandom" that was "to be reexposed, and the lost recovered," in a process involving its "intellectual and spiritual absorption," then with the "Germanization campaign to be conducted in the next year, it will primarily be about a *re*-Germanization, a Germanizing *back*."[385]

These statements were more of a concession to the increasingly racialist discourse heard in Berlin and not an expression of a more restrictive selection policy. Forster did start accommodating the demand to put locals through a "racial evaluation," but it aimed only at the exclusion of "persons with an element of Mongoloid or Asiatic blood," meaning those with "racially alien blood" but not "kindred blood"; in other words, the "Fremdblütige" but not the "Fremdvölkische" (the "foreign-blooded" but not the "ethnonationally foreign" and thus not including Poles). According to Forster, two chief classes were to be considered for "Germanizing back," namely, the "lost splinter groups of Germandom from the nineteenth century and earlier periods" and the "formerly German families who in the last thirty to forty years have entered into ties with Polishdom or lapsed entirely into this." At least for the current phase, it was the latter group that should be targeted "first of all."

Of course, the criteria for recognizing formerly German families remained decidedly vague. For example, registration was to be limited to individuals whose parents or grandparents were born there, in other words the "local populace of West Prussia" (the province's name until 1919). Another aspect that did not really lead any further was the consideration of family names. Although the decree does state that German family names certainly offered an *"indication"* of German descent, the opposite conclusion was explicitly precluded.[386] After all, today's "carriers of Polish family names had, in many cases, German family names years ago." It is telling that the decree became more concrete at the point where "re-Germanizability" was tied to political loyalty. It was impressed on the responsible commissions that the "character-related and ethnonational conduct and mindset . . . are of particular importance as part of the overall evaluation," as reflected, for example, in the choice of schooling language or children's names. Once again, membership in Polish political organizations also played a role. But it was unlike earlier selection efforts in that the German occupiers in Danzig–West Prussia now felt they could afford a somewhat more generous treatment. Still excluded were individuals convicted of "crimes against the German Volk and the German Reich" after the German invasion. But previous membership in radical nationalist groups (such as Polski Związek Zachodni, the Polish Western Association) was no longer an insurmountable obstacle but simply a "tainting factor" that did not release the commissions from their "duty to evaluate the individual case with its particular circumstances and where appropriate to exceptionally undertake a re-Germanization."[387]

This new leniency toward individuals who just a few months earlier were still being persecuted as political adversaries is a reflection on just how secure the German occupiers had come to feel. It also points to a third selection criterion beyond "German" descent and political loyalty: the re-Germanization campaign also aimed to incorporate individuals without whom the province would collapse economically. How very much this issue had come to the fore after a year of German control was already shown by the happenings in the Wartheland. Forster's re-Germanization decree made it even clearer that this factor was starting to dominate Germanization policy.

The shortage of suitable workers in the Danzig–West Prussia had become such a serious problem that it ultimately reshaped the logic of the re-Germanization campaign, turning it into a virtual recruitment program for the local economy with Forster's order to "generally limit the re-Germanization campaign at first to farm and factory workers, tradesmen, and small-scale farmers." Proven economic productivity was enough to compensate for "deficits" in other areas, such as lack of evidence of "German" descent. After all, through the manifestation of "typically German skills and aptitudes that appear throughout the entire kindred, one can also indirectly deduce within the family the presence of a German blood influence (e.g., technical aptitude, a feeling for the upkeep and tidiness of equipment in the home and farmyard)."[388] Previously, Himmler had managed to force a specifically racial meaning onto the Reich Interior Ministry's indeterminate phrase "desirable addition to the population."[389] But in Danzig–West Prussia, it now acquired a much more pragmatic aspect—it was the "presence of vocational and performance-based proofs" that "in many cases will answer the question of whether this is a *desirable addition to the population.*"[390] This interpretation also helps explain the criteria that invariably denied recognition as "Deutschstämmige" to those considered socioeconomically undesirable or superfluous, "antisocial elements," "genetically diseased persons," or "habitual criminals."

Already with Forster's selection criteria, one can see how little moved he was by the compromise that had meanwhile been achieved between the Reich Interior Ministry and the SS complex. But then his implementing provisions on top of that must have seemed like an affront to the decision makers in Berlin. Regardless of the conflicts involving the Regierungspräsident of Bromberg, and in clear violation of all proposals discussed in Berlin, Forster put the implementation of the re-Germanization campaign again into the party's hands—and not those of the state administration, as demanded in the Reich Interior Ministry's latest draft. In order to record the details of all persons who came into question for a re-Germanization, a first "rough survey" was to be conducted by each Blockleiter (a party official responsible for the political supervision of a neighborhood). With a "form for preliminary registration" (figures 4.7 and 4.8), in which the personal data section included a blank for specifying a job, the family was first asked about its "German" descent: which family members had previously belonged to Germandom, when did Polonization begin and why, and which ancestors were "German" in terms of blood or professing; and Forster had already made clear in his decree that even a "minor element of German blood must suffice for preliminary registration."[391] In the next section, the Blockleiter was to answer a number of questions that all concerned the family's conduct, including political, leading up to the question of its "attitude toward the German Volk and state." He was then to summarize his impressions in the space for "general character evaluation," sign the form, and forward it for countersignatures from the Zellenleiter, Ortsgruppenleiter, and Kreisleiter (cell leader, local group leader, and county leader, which were the next three higher ranks in the Nazi Party hierarchy).

Admissions into the re-Germanization process were to be decided on the county level—although not by the Landrat, as envisaged in the Reich Interior

Kreisleitung der NSDAP   A   Steng vertraulich!   Nr.   Nr.

Formblatt der Vorerfassung

........................, den ....

Name .... Vorname ....

Wohnort .... Straße .... Hausnummer ....

geboren am .... in ....

Beruf .... verheiratet mit .... geb. .... Kinderzahl ....

I. Eigene Angaben der für die Wiedereindeutschung vorgesehenen Familie

1. Wer von der Familie gehörte früher dem Deutschtum an? ....

   Wann setzte die Polonisierung ein? ....
   und aus welchen Beweggründen? ....

2. Wer von den Vorfahren (väterlicher- oder mütterlicherseits) gehörte bluts- oder bekenntnismäßig dem Deutschtum an? ....

3. Womit begründet die Familie ihre deutsche Abstammung? (Dokumente?) ....

4. Leben Verwandte der Familie im Altreich? ....
   In welchem Verwandtschaftsverhältnis stehen sie zur Familie? ....
   Welcher Volkszugehörigkeit sind die Verwandten? ....
   Sind sie in der Partei und ihren Gliederungen? ....
   Zur Zeit in der Wehrmacht? ....

Ich versichere eidesstattlich, daß ich die obigen Fragen wahrheitsgetreu beantwortet habe. Ich weiß, daß ich mich im Falle bewußt falscher Angaben strafbar mache.

.... (Ort, Datum)   .... (Unterschrift des Familienvorstandes)

II. Stellungnahme des Blockleiters (auszufüllen auf Grund vorhandener Unterlagen, eigener Kenntnis bzw. Mitteilungen von vertrauenswürdigen Personen)

1. Welche von den unter I 1—4 gemachten eigenen Angaben der für die Wiedereindeutschung vorgesehenen Familie treffen zu? ....

   Welche Angaben sind falsch? ....

2. Wie war die Umgangssprache der Familie zu polnischer Zeit? ....

3. In welcher Sprache fanden die kirchlichen Feierlichkeiten statt? (Gilt vor allem für Mischehen) ....

   In welcher Sprache sind die Grabinschriften der in den letzten 30—40 Jahren verstorbenen Familienangehörigen? ....

Figure 4.7. Questionnaire for Deutschstämmige campaign in Danzig–West Prussia before introduction of DVL in annexed eastern territories.
Source: Institute of National Remembrance in Warsaw, NTN 196/201.

4. Wurde deutscher oder polnischer Gottesdienst besucht?

5. Verkehrte die Familie überwiegend mit Deutschen oder mit Polen?

6. Wie war die Einstellung gegenüber dem Deutschtum bis zum 1. 9. 1939?

In welchem Ansehen steht die Familie bei den Volksdeutschen?

7. Welchen polnischen Organisationen und Verbänden gehörte die Familie an? Träger polnischer Auszeichnungen und Orden?

An polnischen Aufstands- und Grenzkämpfen teilgenommen?

8. Sind starke poln.-katholische Bindungen vorhanden?

9. Wie war die Einstellung gegenüber dem polnischen Staat?

Wie war die Einstellung des polnischen Staates gegenüber dieser Familie (evtl. Bestrafungen wegen Beleidigungen des polnischen Staates usw.)?

10. Wie verhielt sich die Familie beim Einmarsch der deutschen Truppen?

11. Wie verhält sich die Familie seit dem 1. 9. 1939?

Wie ist im besonderen ihre Einstellung zum deutschen Volk und Staat?

Kann angenommen werden, daß die Familie Unruhe und Sabotageakte der Polen melden würde?

12. Allgemeine charakterische Bewertung.

13. Besondere Bemerkungen:

(Ort, Datum)   (Unterschrift des Blockleiters)

Stellungnahme des Zellenleiters:

(Ort, Datum)   (Unterschrift des Zellenleiters)

Stellungnahme des Ortsgruppenleiters:

(Ort, Datum)   (Unterschrift des Ortsgruppenleiters)

Prüfungsvermerk des Kreisleiters:

(Ort, Datum)   (Unterschrift des Kreisleiters)

Dem Geschäftsführer des Kreisbüros übergeben am:

Figure 4.8. Reverse side of figure 4.7.
Source: The holder's profession is given as master mason.

Ministry's draft proposal. Forster did order that each Landrat's offices establish a "County Bureau (Branch Office of the DVL)," meaning that he anticipated the DVL's imminent introduction. In formal terms, establishing the county bureaus represented a strengthening of the Landrat, although the leadership of the commission itself lay with the Kreisleiter. The practical effects of this distinction were generally immaterial, however, for the two positions were occupied by the same person in almost every county.[392]

The commissions were to begin with those who had already been named by the party apparatus during the "rough survey." They could even order an expert report into the "racial suitability of the family to be Germanized"—but from the Nazi Party's Racial Policy Office, and not from the RuSHA. However, these additional investigations were mostly to ensure that the persons in question were not a political threat and represented an asset to the imagined "Leistungsgemein-schaft" (meaning both "performance-based" and "high-performance" community). In the investigations, the criminal registry and files of the Security Police were examined, the health department was asked for a certificate of health, and finally the relevant occupational body was queried about the "vocational competence and performance of the family." Even the conduct of the children was not forgotten: the commissions were told to ask the school administration for an assessment report, which had "to go minutely into the child's character, performance, and demeanor."[393]

Until the required information had been gathered and a summons had been issued to the family, there was effectively no way for the subject persons to influence the selection process. In contrast with the Wartheland's registration process, where interested individuals could ask for a questionnaire and had to apply themselves for DVL enrollment, in Danzig–West Prussia, the initiative was entirely in the hands of the occupiers. In this regard as well, the Danzig–West Prussia process stood in clear contrast to the guidelines of the Reich Interior Ministry, which assumed a voluntary registration process. Rather, Forster's system did not consider the family's willingness to be inducted into the re-Germanization process until the last possible moment, namely during their appearance before the commission.

At their appearance, the family had to undergo an "objective assessment" as well as a "subjective" one. They had to present their supporting documentation and answer a number of questions, which were likewise specified in an appendix to Forster's decree and were related exclusively to the family's conduct. The final decision was to be made after considering all the assessment documents, meaning the Blockleiter's preliminary registration notes, the written results of the additional queries, and the commission's interrogation findings. Forster quite frankly admitted that it was "not possible to specify a precisely calculated formula as to whether a family can be Germanized or not." In doubtful cases, a "re-Germanization is to be undertaken if all factors are suggestive of a desirable addition to the population." And again: "If there is a lack of consensus, then the Kreisleiter makes the final decision." This verdict was final. No appeals process was outlined, and it was only with "doubtful questions of a fundamental nature" that an already passed ruling should be presented to Forster.

Finally, Forster also stipulated the end result of the re-Germanization campaign. The various Kreisleiters' offices were informed that Forster's ethnonationality officer Wilhelm Löbsack, with input from the "political science sphere in our Gau," in this case represented by Dr. Detlef Krannhals and Professor Dr. Erich Keyser, would be telling them in which locales this "lost Germandom can be found" and also set "quotas." The process was to be considered complete when the projected target of thirty thousand re-Germanizable families had been registered, thereby putting German control of the province on a broader footing.

It was only in defining the legal status of these people that Forster's plan converged again with that of the Reich Interior Ministry. Anticipating the soon-to-be-expected universal Reich-level regulation, Forster's decree stated that the families registered in the re-Germanization campaign would be assigned to Section 3 of the DVL. On the one hand, this meant that such persons could expect *"no equal status with the Volksdeutsche"* (emphasis in original) and were barred from holding positions of political or economic leadership. They were also denied the return of their confiscated assets, to ensure that they would not "hinder the settlement plans." On the other hand, it also meant that their legal status would be decided case by case, as stipulated in the Reich Interior Ministry's proposal, with no possibility of Reich citizen rights. Forster was much more explicit than the Reich Interior Ministry in highlighting the still precarious legal status of these individuals; despite their acceptance as re-Germanizable persons and their acquisition of German national status, they would certainly not be exempted from the coercive measures of the German occupiers. In a statement reminiscent of Germany's colonial administration, the alternatives for the affected individuals were laid out in all openness: "Those who prove themselves will have the great fortune of being allowed to call themselves Germans, and to take part in the rise of the German Volk and Reich. In contrast, if a person is not serious in his will to Germandom, he will be exterminated by the mighty German Reich, even if he believes himself safe in possessing a German national status certificate."[394]

Back in May 1940, Forster had already declared his willingness to follow up the registration of the "Volksdeutsche" with a second phase in 1941, during which the "Stammesdeutsche" would be registered. That he then actually implemented this pronouncement with his re-Germanization decree of December 14, 1940, might seem remarkable at first glance, in light of the fact that the Reich Interior Ministry and the SS complex were already far advanced in their efforts to develop a universal Reich-level regulatory framework for future Germanization policy and had already produced an October 1940 decree package in whose consultations Forster's relevant officials had also participated.

It may have been precisely this awareness of the negotiations in Berlin that inspired Forster to rush ahead once again. After all, it could not have been a positive development in his eyes, for the Reich Interior Ministry was not only enshrining the precedence of state agencies over those of the party (thereby also reaffirming the course it took in the confrontation with the Regierungspräsident of Bromberg), but also declaring itself in agreement with the more exclusivist selection policy demanded by Himmler, which above all put more emphasis on racial criteria. This position had little in common with Forster's own vision, namely, of a selection process conducted by party agencies and geared above all toward pragmatic criteria. With this confrontational course and planned induction of thirty thousand families, he hoped to seize the initiative by creating facts on the ground that even the anticipated universal Reich-level regulation could no longer undo.

"Polish Lists" in Upper Silesia

Considering the continual unilateral actions of the provincial chiefs Forster and Greiser, one might expect that the SS complex and particularly the Reich Interior Ministry were under increasing pressure to finalize the universal Reich-level regulatory framework as quickly as possible. But their work was delayed even further—not only because the party felt inadequately considered in its demands, but also because the Reich Interior Ministry wanted to embed the national status rules of the annexed territories within a general reorganization of the Reich's citizenship laws.

Unlike Forster and Greiser, Fritz Bracht initially refrained from taking unilateral action. But by January 1941, his patience had also run out. In a message to his province's state and party leaders, he highlighted the grievances resulting from the fact that a "clear and meticulous winnowing process and a clarification of population affairs . . . has so far not taken place." The situation was still leading "to many mistakes in the adjudication of countless cases of ethnonational membership," which exposed the affected individuals to fatal consequences in all spheres of life, from the "awarding of child benefits" to the enforcing of "confiscations."[395] Therefore, the situation would be remedied by a "special selection procedure," at least until the Reich Interior Ministry issued its final scheme.[396]

Brandt's responsiveness to the suffering of the local populace naturally had pragmatic reasons. An example was the confrontation over the employees of the Reich Railroad, launched by its division in Oppeln. As Friedrich Bachmann, the Regierungspräsident of Liegnitz temporarily charged with the Oberpräsident's affairs in Breslau, reported to the Reich Interior Ministry on January 29, 1941, the Reich Railroad in Oppeln had taken on 20,000 railroad workers, of whom only 69 had been granted German national status so far. Meanwhile, everyone else was forced to work for the wages of an unskilled laborer, regardless of actual position—and their morale was correspondingly "poor."[397] Just two days earlier, the Reich Railroad's Oppeln division had named 17 employees who urgently required a decision in their ethnonational membership proceedings.[398] Now another 605 names had been added. Of course, Bachmann understood that this specific case would not resolve the more fundamental problem, which is why he asked again for an "issuance of guidelines on the acquisition of ethnonational membership and citizenship in the incorporated eastern territories."[399]

If Bracht wanted to avoid endangering his province's economic performance and also wanted to stop testing at least its economically indispensable residents on their willingness to integrate into the German occupation regime, then he could no longer afford to wait for the repeatedly delayed decision of the Reich Interior Ministry. In accord with the already existing procedure, which assumed that a difference existed between the populations east and west of the police border, the civil administration in the west decided not to establish something like the DVL, but instead to implement a much less time-consuming process. Because the majority of residents in the west were considered "Germans" anyway, only the non-Germans would be registered there, on what was known as the "Polish List" ("Polenliste"); conversely, a "German List" ("Deutschenliste") would be established in the east. Worse off than all the others were only the Jews, who in the border strip fell under the responsibility of SS Senior Leader Albrecht Schmelt, Himmler's appointee for the labor deployment of "Fremdvölkische."[400]

The surviving records include the selection criteria only for the Polish List, in whose implementing provisions there was no doubt about the general goal, as outlined by Brach: "Until the introduction of the DVL, a winnowing of the populace in Silesia's incorporated territories is necessary in order to achieve for all residents, as long as they are not Poles or foreign-descended, a status equal to that of Reich citizens of the German Reich in economic and social terms."[401] This motivation, tailored to the rational demands of power, then dominated the selection criteria. There was as little talk of "racial suitability" as there was of "German descent"—and this latter dismissal was something new, even for avowed pragmatists in ethnopolicy. In fact, positive criteria were not specified at all. In this context, "Poles" were simply those considered nonlocal, politically unreliable, or socioeconomically undesirable, as well as those who had called themselves Poles during the census, had filled higher positions in Polish parties or economic or political associations, or else were "criminals and antisocial elements from the ethnonationally as yet unresolved class of the populace."[402]

Like Forster, Bracht delegated the process to party officials. The Ortsgruppenleiter were to issue a questionnaire to anyone they considered suitable, and "without regard to possession of a national status document or military identity card"; they were then to evaluate the result and, on that basis, draw up a "political conduct report with detailed substantiation." The resulting paperwork was then to be forwarded to a county-level assessment committee, chaired by the local Kreisleiter.[403] The approval process was complicated in Upper Silesia, where it required a "majority vote," but if agreement could not be reached in a particular case, it was automatically directed "to the RKFDV appointee for confirmation or amendment." An appeals committee was to be established there, chaired by Himmler's appointee (i.e., Bracht himself) or else the head of the RKFDV branch office, Fritz Arlt; the other members were to be a representative from the Gauleiter's offices, one from the Regierungspräsident, the Gestapo head of Kattowitz, and the registration department head from the RKFDV branch office. The decisions were to be reached "with a majority vote and conclusively."[404]

This majority voting is a remarkable deviation from the "Führerprinzip" ("leader principle," the idea that decision making lies solely in one person's hands). But what is even more remarkable is that the SS complex had in this case finally managed to break into a selection process thus far dominated by state and party agencies, intruding to an extent far beyond the participatory opportunities granted by the Reich Interior Ministry. Whereas Greifelt's plans had quickly foundered just a few months earlier in the face of Greiser's firm opposition, a similar plan was now prevailing under Bracht without much opposition. This was clearly the price that Bracht had to pay, for he was not yet firmly ensconced in his new post and still depended on Himmler's support. But any satisfaction the SS complex felt in this matter would not last long, because the corresponding registration work had probably not yet begun when Frick finally issued the universal Reich-level regulations that made the Polish List obsolete.[405]

Notes

1. Unsigned (probably SD of Posen) and undated (probably late December 1939) accounting of deportation numbers, Institute of National Remembrance, Archive of the Main Commission for the Investigation of Crimes against the Polish Nation, Warsaw [hereafter, AGK] 68/99, 17–22. On February 10, 1939, it was already seventy-five thousand persons, see Rapp to Eichmann of that date, AGK 68/7, 15–19.

2. Figure comes from a county-by-county summary by the SD on December 12, 1939, see Special Archive at the State Military Archives of Russia, Moscow [hereafter, SMR], 500–1/88, 199–200.

3. Unsigned (probably SD of Posen), on accounting of deportation figures, undated (probably late December, 1939), AGK 68/99, 17–22.

4. Notice from Heydrich, December 21, 1939, AGK 68/97, 1–7.

5. Heydrich to BdS in Kraków and IdS officeholders in Danzig, Posen, Breslau, and Königsberg, December 21, 1939, SMR 500–1/4, 67, reprinted in Datner, Gumkowski, and Leszczyński, "Wysiedlanie ludności," 32.

6. Roth, "Generalplan Ost—Gesamtplan Ost," 34.

7. An overview of the Reich Security Main Office's changing organizational structure at Wildt, *Generation des Unbedingten*, 358–62 and 381.

8. (Signed "SS Chief Assault Leader Franz Abromeit" of Danzig), minutes of meeting on January 4, 1940, January 8, 1949, reprinted in Łuczak, *Wysiedlenia ludności polskiej*, 29–31.

9. Between December 25, 1939, and February 9, 1940, the Wartheland received 119,771 arrivals, see German Federal Archives [hereafter, BArch], R 49/20, 11–28, report from the head of the VoMi deployment team in Łódź, SS Senior Assault Unit Leader Ludwig Doppler, undated. Thanks to Götz Aly for this document. At Lumans, *Himmler's Auxiliaries*, 164, the end date is incorrectly given as January 26, 1940.

10. (Signed "SS Chief Assault Leader Franz Abromeit" of Danzig), minutes of meeting on January 4, 1940, January 8, 1949, reprinted in Łuczak, *Wysiedlenia ludności polskiej*, 29–31.

11. Herbert, *Fremdarbeiter*, 79.

12. Ibid. See also Umbreit, "Auf dem Weg zur Kontinentalherrschaft," 258–64; Kroener, "Die persönlichen Ressourcen des Dritten Reiches," 774–78.

13. Unsigned (probably an employee of Rapp's), minutes of meeting on January 11, 1940, AGK 68/146, 3–9.

14. Ibid.

15. More comprehensively at Herbert, *Fremdarbeiter*, 74–82; also Spoerer, *Zwangsarbeit unter dem Hakenkreuz*, 93–94.

16. Unsigned (probably an employee of Rapp's), minutes of meeting on January 11, 1940, AGK 68/146, 3–9.

17. Koppe to Regierungspräsidents, Landrats, Gestapo, and SD, January 20, 1940, AGK 68/96, 8–10 (emphasis in original).

18. Greiser to Koppe, January 3, 1940, AGK 62/293, 21.

19. Ibid.

20. Ehlich's memo on intermediate solution for the second short-range plan, January 17, 1940, BA-DH, ZR 890/A.2. Thanks to Götz Aly for this document. See also Aly, *Endlösung*, 78–79.

21. Ehlich's memo on intermediate solution for the second short-range plan, January 17, 1940, BA-DH, ZR 890/A.2.

22. Ibid.

23. Unsigned minutes of Unit III ES (Referat III ES) meeting on January 30, 1940, Bavarian State Archives, Nuremberg, NO-5322, reprinted in Datner, Gumkowski, and Leszczyński, "Wysiedlanie ludności," 66–75. Besides Heydrich, the participants included the deputy head of the General Government, Reich Minister Seyss-Inquart; the HSSPFs of Danzig, Königsberg, Posen, and Kraków; Greifelt and his deputy, Rudolf Creutz; the SS and Police Leaders (SS und Polizeiführer, SSPF) and Commanders of the Security Police (Kommandeure der Sicherheitspolizei, KdS) officeholders from the General Government; the Gestapo chiefs from the annexed territories; and Werner Best, Ehlich, Eichmann, and other representatives of the Reich Security Main Office. On this conference, see also Rapp's memo for Koppe, Damzog, and Döring, February 1, 1940, AGK 68/109, 1–3. The gathering received surprisingly little attention from Aly, *Endlösung*, 82–83; Browning, *Entfesselung*, 98–100; Longerich, *Politik der Vernichtung*, 266–67.

24. Unsigned minutes of Unit III ES meeting on January 30, 1940, Bavarian State Archives, Nuremberg, NO-5322, reprinted in Datner, Gumkowski, and Leszczyński, "Wysiedlanie ludności," 66–75.

25. Strickner's work instructions to Dept. III, January 6, 1940, AGK 68/7, 1 (emphasis in original). Incidentally, the conference's plan was little affected by Koppe's subsequent order of January 14, 1940, which ordered above all the deportation of Jews, but also authorized the targeting of Christian Poles, as long as their expulsion was deemed necessary for accommodating ethnic Germans. The upper limit of 80,000 Christian Poles as previously negotiated at Eichmann's was not mentioned at the conference (Koppe to Reichsstatthalters, Regierungspräsidents, Landrats, etc., January 14, 1940, AGK 68/98, 1–4.

26. Head of central card catalog at the SD, SS Chief Squad Leader Blenk, to Rapp, January 20, 1940, AGK, 68/7, 10–13. Thanks to Götz Aly for this document. For preparatory work, see also Haussmann's summary of anti-German Polish organizations, January 3, 1940, BArch R 75/5, 11; Rapp to Eichmann on evacuation workflow at review and registration office, February 20, 1940, AGK 68/7, 15–19.

27. Kleinmann to Himmler, March 1, 1940, BArch R 49/2791, unpaged. Thanks to Peter Klein for this document. See also the undated overview with minor discrepancies, probably from just before the start of the deportations, at AGK 68/96, 22. The start was originally scheduled for January 7, 1940, and was postponed week by week until February 10 (Koppe to Greiser, January 4, 1940, AGK NTN/13, 36–37; Damzog to Rapp, January 12, 1940, AGK 68/114, 9–10; Koppe to Greiser and Landrats, February 1, 1940, AGK 68/98, 1–4).

28. Unpaged message, Kleinmann to Himmler, March 1, 1940, BArch R 49/2791. Kleinmann lists forty-one trains for this period, but one of them was from Stettin (province of Pomerania), departing on February 13, 1940, which represented the first time that Jewish Germans were deported to Poland, in this case to Lublin. Thanks to Peter Klein for this document.

29. Alberti, *Verfolgung und Vernichtung*, 141, which relies on figures from the UWZ.

30. Barth to Rapp, March 7, 1940, AGK 68/129, 1.

31. Rapp to Regierungspräsident's offices in Kalisch, March 6, 1940, AGK 68/96, 35–36. See also Gerhard Scheffler, mayor of Posen, to the HSSPF, March 5, 1940, AGK 68/153, 1.

32. Kroener, "Persönlichen Ressourcen des Dritten Reichs," 775.

33. Statement by Kendzia at a meeting on January 11, 1940, in unsigned minutes (probably taken by an employee of Rapp's) of the meeting, AGK 68/146, 3–9.

34. Herbert, *Fremdarbeiter*, 87.

35. Other attendees included State Secretary Paul Körner, Erich Neumann (Four-Year-Plan Office), Friedrich Landfried (Reich Economy Ministry), Herbert Backe (Reich Food Ministry), Friedrich Syrup (Reich Labor Ministry), Wilhelm Kleinmann (Reich Transport Ministry), Friedrich Alpers (Reich Forestry Office); conference at Göring's, February 12, 1940, Bavarian State Archives, Nuremberg, EC-305a.

36. Ibid.

37. See the sitting of the Reich Defense Committee (Reichsverteidigungsausschuss) on March 2, 1940, and assembly of county and city captains (*Kreis- und Stadthauptmänner*) for the district of Lublin, partially reprinted in Präg and Jacobmeyer, *Diensttagebuch des deutschen Generalgouverneurs*, 131 and 146–47; see also Browning, "From 'Ethnic Cleansing,'" 12–13.

38. Göring's directive on the interim ban on deportations to the General Government, March 24, 1940, reprinted in Pätzold, *Verfolgung—Vertreibung—Vernichtung*, 262.

39. Herbert, *Fremdarbeiter*, 81–85.

40. On the "Polish decrees," see Schminck-Gustavus, "Zwangsarbeitsrecht und Faschismus," 16–21.

41. Herbert, *Fremdarbeiter*, 81.

42. Ehlich's memo to Heydrich on the establishment of UWZs, February 2, 1940, BA-DH, ZR 890/A.2 (2). Thanks to Götz Aly for this document.

43. Ehlich to Ohlendorf and Heydrich, February 12, 1940, SMR 500–4/72, 26–29.

44. Wildt, *Generation des Unbedingten*, 352 and 381–82.

45. The process was a gradual one and was well illustrated by the agency's changing names, from "The HSSPF, Office for Resettlement of Poles and Jews," to "The IdS, Resettlement Office," to "The Chief of the Security Police and the SD, Resettlement Central Office" (also known as the UWZ). The official launch is dated April 24, 1940, when Best announced the establishment of a UWZ (Best to the Reichsstatthalter, HSSPF, and IdS of Posen, April 24, 1940, AGK 62/297, 101). For more background, see Klein, *Gettoverwaltung Litzmannstadt*, 138–41.

46. Unsigned concluding report on the evacuations for settling of Volhynian, Galician, and Chełm Germans (second short-range plan) in the Wartheland, with appendixes, undated (probably late January 1941), BArch R 75/6, 1–13, reprinted in *Biuletyn Głównej Komisji* 21: 89–105.

47. Ibid.

48. Best to top-level Reich authorities, February 3, 1940, SMR 1372–6/26, 13.

49. On the establishing of the ghetto in Łódź, see Alberti, *Verfolgung und Vernichtung*, 147–93.

50. Unsigned concluding report on the evacuations for settling of Volhynian, Galician, and Chełm Germans (second short-range plan) in the Wartheland, with appendixes, undated (probably late January, 1941), BArch R 75/6, 1–13, reprinted in *Biuletyn Głównej Komisji* 21: 89–105.

51. Holzschuher's memo on briefing with Himmler, December 1, 1939, BArch NS 2/60, 60–63; Himmler's directive 13/I, December 19, 1939, BArch R 138 I/33, 38, reprinted in Pospieszalski, *Hitlerowskie "prawo" okupacyjne*, 181; see also Greifelt's announcement, April 9, 1940, Polish State Archives in Katowice [hereafter, APK], 119/10701, 48–49, in which Greifelt ordered the establishment of a department to act as an appeals body reviewing decisions of the civil administration to clarify questions of "ethnonational membership," thereby putting the SS on a collision course with the DVL.

52. SSO (SS Offiziere) file on Georg Gloystein, Gloystein to RuSHA, April 20, 1940, German Federal Archives, Bunderarchiv Lichterfelde [hereafter, BArch BDC].

53. See also BArch BDC SSO file on Rudolf Barth and UWZ personnel file at AGK 358/6.

54. Unsigned telephone note on discussion with Barth, February 1, 1940, AGK 68/22, 7; Krumey to Rapp, February 1, 1940, AGK 68/22, 5; Barth to Rapp, February 2, 1940, AGK 68/12, 1–3; memo about division of responsibilities by head of RKFDV bureau in Posen, SS Senior Leader Döring, February 3, 1940, AGK 68/218, 53; Barth to Rapp, February 8, 1940, AGK 68/22, 9. See also interrogation of SS Chief Assault Leader Alois Schwarzhuber by the North Rhine–Westphalia state office of criminal investigation on March 28, 1969, BArch 162/20047. Thanks to Götz Aly for this last document.

55. Memo from Höppner, May 8, 1940, AGK 68/70, 1; Höppner to Krumey, May 14, 1940, AGK 68/68, 1; Ehlich to SD Command Precinct and UWZ in Posen, May 22, 1940, AGK 68/49, 1.

For more background on the conflict, see also Klein, *Gettoverwaltung Litzmannstadt*, 137–41.

56. Posen alone had deported twenty-nine thousand (Himmler to Lammers, concluding report on settling of Baltic Germans, July 26, 1940, BArch R 43 II/1412, 405–21).

57. The closure was planned for May 1, 1940 (Rapp to mayor of Posen, April 18, 1940 (AGK 68/186, 4). But it was actually on May 20, 1940, that the last inmates were transferred to the UWZ camp in Litzmannstadt (Rapp to Eichmann, Damzog, and Krumey, May 15, 1940, AGK 68/186, 11).

58. Rapp to UWZ field offices, April 1, 1940, AGK 68/130, 43–49.

59. UWZ personnel file at AGK 358/51.

60. Rapp to UWZ field offices, April 1, 1940, AGK 68/130, 43–49.

61. On the activities of other planning teams, see Roth, "Generalplan Ost—Gesamtplan Ost"; Schulz, "Nationalsozialistische Nachkriegskonzeptionen."

62. The plan, attached to an OKW message of March 8, 1940, is dated by Müller to February 1940. Reprinted in Müller, *Hitlers Ostkrieg*, 130–38.

63. Of course, Meyer was continuing an inglorious tradition here. Even before the war, German historians like Theodor Oberländer and Werner Conze were already outlining the negative consequences of a growing rural population. In his paper to be presented at a sociology conference planned for the fall of 1939 in Bucharest, Conze even intended to call for the "de-Jewing of the towns and market villages" (Haar, *Historiker im Nationalsozialismus*, 283–86 and 315–18). See also Aly and Heim, *Vordenker der Vernichtung*, 102; Aly, *Macht*, 153.

64. Planning guidelines for development of the eastern territories, reprinted in Müller, *Hitlers Ostkrieg*, 130–38 (in documentation for January–February 1940).

65. Greiser to Regierungspräsidents and Landrats, March 1, 1940, AGK NTN/36, 147–50; see also Aly, *Endlösung*, 87.

66. Apparently it was Friedrich Uebelhoer's wife who came up with the idea for the new name of Lodsch, which came into effect on April 1, 1940 (investigative report by Reich Interior Ministry Undersecretary Dr. Hans Eugen Stephan Fabricius on misappropriation charges against Uebelhoer, February 27, 1940, SMR 720-5/10244, 18–32.

67. Rapp to UWZ field offices, April 1, 1940, AGK 68/130, 43–49.

68. See also Eichmann to Rapp, March 14, 1940, AGK, 68/130, 35; Rapp to Landrat's offices in Dietfurt, April 5, 1940, AGK 68/130, 57.

69. Unsigned memo, regarding plans for the work of the UWZ, March 30, 1940, BArch R 75/3b, 72–74.

70. Gestapo in Posen to the Landrat's office in Jarotschin, May 4, 1940, German Federal Archives, Ludwigsburg branch, Ludwigsburg, Ger. [hereafter, BArchL], B 162/365h, 541–44. On the broader politicide, see Röhr, *Faschistische Okkupationspolitik*, 80–81; Madajczyk, *Okkupationspolitik Nazideutschlands*, 187–88; Musial, "Schlachtfeld zweier totalitärer Systeme," 13–18. Focusing more on Danzig–West Prussia, see Schenk, *Hitlers Mann*, 162–74; Jansen and Weckbecker, *Der Volksdeutsche Selbstschutz*, 136.

71. Rapp's guidance notes on technical preparations for work to be done under Volhynian campaign at UWZ field offices, March 20, 1940, AGK 68/145, 7–10.

72. It was first- and second-degree relatives for the former, and only first-degree ones for the latter (unsigned memo, on plans for the work of the UWZ, March 30, 1940, BArch R 75/3b, 72–74).

73. Seidl, on Volhynian campaign in Konin, March 18, 1940, reprinted in Rutherford, "Race, Space, and the Polish Question," 241. The prohibition was rescinded by Koppe on June 22, 1940 (memo from Krumey, June 24, 1940, State Archives in Posen [hereafter, APP], 834/2, 2), reprinted in *Biuletyn Głównej Komisji* 21: 84. On the negative criteria, see also Jastrzębski, *Hitlerowskie wysiedlenia*, 114.

74. Rapp to UWZ field office at Gostynin, April 5, 1940, AGK 68/252, 1. Bursche not only was decisively opposed to the power-seeking of German organizations in Poland during the interwar period, but also was a declared opponent of the Nazis; he was arrested as such immediately after the invasion and transported to the Gestapo jail on Berlin's Albrechtstrasse before finally dying in 1942 in the city's Moabit prison (Krebs, *Nationale Identität*). On the conflicts between Bursche and the German nationalist pastors within the Evangelical Church of the Augsburg Confession in Poland, see Kossert, "Protestantismus in Lodz," 88–93.

75. At any rate, this was the belief of Hans Frank, who assumed that the deportation of Jews would not resume before August 1940, according to his duty diary entry of April 5, 1940 (Browning, "Nazi Resettlement Policy," 508).

76. Railway workers cited at (signature illegible), UWZ branch office at Litzmannstadt to UWZ field office at Ostrowo, August 14, 1940, AGK 358/259, 42–45. Other workers cited at (signature illegible), letter Labor Dept. at Reichsstatthalter's offices to Damzog, January 16, 1941, AGK 68/146, 22. See also unsigned, on plans for the work of the UWZ, March 30, 1940, BArch R 75/3b, 72–74.

77. Höppner to Ehlich and Eichmann, June 1, 1940, AGK 68/158, 2–3.

78. Ehlich to SD Command Precinct in Posen, June 10, 1940, AGK 68/158, 4.

79. Unsigned concluding report on the evacuations for settling of Volhynian, Galician, and Chełm Germans (second short-range plan) in the Wartheland, with appendixes, undated (probably late January 1941), BArch R 75/6, 1–13, reprinted in *Biuletyn Głównej Komisji* 21: 89–105.

80. Krumey's instructions to UWZ camp in Litzmannstadt, April 17, 1940, AGK 69/144, 1–3.

81. Künzel to Hofmann, October 23, 1940, AGK 369/13, 85–86.

82. Krumey's instructions to UWZ camp in Litzmannstadt, April 17, 1940, AGK 69/144, 1–3.

83. Memo from Krumey on work of the UWZ from October 1, 1940, until September 8, 1941, AGK 69/26, 1–2. Thanks to Götz Aly for this document.

84. Barth to UWZ camp inspectorate and RuSHA bureau in Litzmannstadt, July 25, 1940, AGK 358/244, 2; (signed "p.p. SS Squad Leader Gerhart Drabsch, RuSHA head") to UWZ, October 1, 1940, AGK 358/247, 29; Krumey to Flottwellstrasse Camp, October 17, 1940, AGK 358/247, 34.

85. Directive from Himmler on selection of Polish ethnic groups to be Germanized, October 30, 1940, AGK 69/1, 31.

86. AGK 69/203, personnel file of health unit head, SS Chief Squad Leader Dr. Fähndrich; AGK 68/194, 2, Barth to Höppner, July 31, 1940; BArch 162/20047, interrogation of former RuSHA suitability assessor Johannes Preuss by the North Rhine–Westphalia state office of criminal investigation on May 23, 1969; AGK 69/1, 31, directive from Himmler regarding selection of Polish tribes to be Germanized, October 30, 1940; Greifelt to HSSPFs in the annexed eastern territories, December 5, 1940, State Archives in Łódź [hereafter, APL], 205/7, 12–13. For a brief overview of the selection process, see Marczewski, *Hitlerowska koncepcja*, 253–54; this also seems to be the most detailed description available.

87. Barth to Höppner, July 31, 1940, AGK 68/194, 2. The conflict apparently began with complaints from the RuSHA suitability assessors, who felt they were not taken seriously by the health unit physicians. But soon thereafter, RuSHA was also insisting on more independence from the SD. The conflict came up again a few months later at the EWZ, triggered by the head of the RuSHA bureau at the EWZ, Richard Kaaserer, who was refusing to acknowledge subordination to the Reich Security Main Office in his office's letterhead. But he was nonetheless forced to accept the subordination after Sandberger's agreement with Hofmann (Sandberger to Kaaserer, November 12 and November 26, 1940), AGK 369/1, 60 and AGK 369/1, 44–47; SS Chief Assault Leader Erwin Klinger to Kaaserer, December 2, 1940, AGK 369/1, 43 verso; Kaaserer to Hofmann, December 4, 1940, AGK 369/1, 42–43.

88. Heinemann, *Rasse, Siedlung, deutsches Blut*, 593–94.

89. Directive from Hofmann on instructions for suitability assessment of returnees, confidential, October 14, 1939, SMR 1372–6/26, 16–19; Heinemann, *Rasse, Siedlung, deutsches Blut*, 234–35.

90. Directive from Hofmann on instructions for suitability assessment of returnees, confidential, October 14, 1939, SMR 1372–6/26, 16–19.

91. Hofmann to Künzel, March 16, 1940, AGK 167/1, 15.

92. Unsigned RuSHA draft proposal on guidelines for selection of Polish ethnonationals in the new eastern Gaus, undated, AGK 167/1, 16–18 (probably prepared by Klinger in March 1940).

93. Ibid.

94. Krumey's instructions to UWZ camp in Litzmannstadt, AGK 69/144, 1–3; Rapp to UWZ field offices, Koppe, Damzog, Döring, Ehlich, and Eichmann, April 1, 1940, AGK 68/130, 43–49, reprinted in *Biuletyn Głównej Komisji* 21, doc. 4; unsigned RuSHA draft proposal on guidelines for selection of Polish ethnonationals in the new eastern Gaus, undated, AGK 167/1, 16–18.

95. Krumey's instructions to UWZ camp in Litzmannstadt, AGK 69/144, 1–3.

96. Unsigned RuSHA draft proposal on guidelines for selection of Polish ethnonationals in the new eastern Gaus, undated, AGK 167/1, 16–18.

97. Künzel to Hofmann, October 23, 1940, AGK 369/13, 85–86.

98. Barth's memo, on selection of workers under evacuation campaign, April 1, 1940, AGK 68/109, 16–17, reprinted in *Biuletyn Głównej Komisji* 21, doc. 5.

99. Ibid.

100. Himmler's directive 17/II, May 9, 1940, AGK 62/351, 2–3.

101. Greifelt to HSSPFs, on deployment of re-Germanizable Poles, July 3, 1940, AGK 68/259, 11–13. Also unsigned first-draft proposal from Main Dept. I at RKFDV headquarters on guidelines and notes, August 7, 1940, BArch R 49/2602, unpaged. Thanks to Götz Aly for this second document.

102. Rapp to UWZ field offices, April 1, 1940, AGK 68/130, 43–49. Starting in August 1941, these identity documents were issued to the subject individuals at their new workplaces (signed "Fähndrich, RKFDV headquarters"), to Reich Security Main Office, August 7, 1940, Bavarian State Archives, Nuremberg, NO-3095). Thanks to Götz Aly for this document. The change probably happened because of individuals refusing to accept this "privileged" status: they called themselves Poles and proved unwilling to sign the alien identity document. Apparently it was believed that such resistance would be easier to overcome when already inside the Reich, thereby speeding up the individual's work placement.

103. And were probably seen as such by the general public. For example, the bakery owner Rosa Hummel was allocated the re-Germanization candidate Wanda Jaskowska but then declined to call her a "German." For Hummel, she remained a "Pole," (deposition of Rosa Hummel, November 5, 1947, BArch 99 US 12/51490, doc. 91).

104. Pancke to Himmler, May 25, 1940, AGK 167/1, 32–33.

105. Ibid.

106. Unsigned memo on a meeting with Seitz at RuSHA on June 21, 1940, undated, AGK 167/1, 26–27.

107. Höppner to Kendzia, May 9, 1940, AGK 68/146, 18.

108. Memo from Höppner, May 21, 1940, AGK 68/190, 12.

109. Höppner to Müller, March 27, 1941, AGK 68/146, 42–43.

110. Manuscript of Joachim Eggeling's speech at meeting at Hess's on July 20, 1940, strictly confidential, August 3, 1940, AGK 62/346, 177–85.

111. Herbert, *Fremdarbeiter*, 122–24.

112. Himmler's memo "Einige Gedanken über die Behandlung der Fremdvölkischen im Osten" [A few thoughts on the handling of the ethnonationally foreign in the east], May 15, 1940, reprinted in Opitz, *Europastrategien des deutschen Kapitals*, 653–55. Himmler had initially shown his memo only to Hitler, who found it—according to Himmler—"very good and correct." This offered a great deal of political leverage. Himmler later presented it to Frank in order to pressure him (Longerich, *Politik der Vernichtung*, 274); Aly, *Endlösung*, 140–41.

113. Himmler's memo "Einige Gedanken über die Behandlung der Fremdvölkischen im Osten," May 15, 1940, reprinted in Opitz, *Europastrategien des deutschen Kapitals*, 653–55.

114. Himmler to the HSSPFs in the annexed territories, May 20, 1940, reprinted in *Biuletyn Głównej Komisji* 21: 74.

115. The Litzmannstadt chief of police, SS Brigade Leader Johannes Schäfer, to Höppner, May 16, 1940, AGK 68/26, 11.

116. Eichmann to Seidl, June 5, 1940, quoted in Aly, *Endlösung*, 101.

117. As the SD in Litzmannstadt reported, 158,000 persons were living in the ghetto, much less than the previously assumed two hundred thousand to three hundred thousand persons (reports from the precinct area, June 24, 1940, AGK 68/129, 3). Thanks to Götz Aly for this document.

118. Himmler to Greifelt, May 10, 1940, BArch R 75/3b, 70–71.

119. (Signed "p.p. SS Senior Assault Unit Leader Wagner"), memo from EWZ, July 30, 1940, APL 205/6 I, 196–97; (signed "Richard Rupp"), memo from farm allocation department at RKFDV bureau in Posen, September 20, 1940, BArch R 49 Anh. I/37, 5–16. Thanks to Götz Aly for the second document.

120. These were the rural counties of Krotoschin, Jarotschin, and Wongrowitz (Höppner to Ehlich and Eichmann, July 12, 1940, AGK 68/130, 89).

121. Memo from Krumey, September 13, 1940, AGK 68/130, 102. See also (signed "Richard Rupp"), memo from farm allocation department at RKFDV bureau in Posen, September 20, 1940, BArch R 49 Anh. I/37, 5–16. Thanks to Götz Aly for this document.

122. Specifically, 2,399 "re-Germanizable persons" and 9,513 "migrant workers" were transported into the Reich (undated overview, annex to concluding report on second short-range plan, AGK 68/228, 4–5, reprinted in *Biuletyn Głównej Komisji* 21: 96–97).

123. Unpaged and unsigned overview from Main Dept. I at Agency of the RKFDV in Berlin, on status of settlement and evacuation in the incorporated eastern territories, as of December 31, 1940, and planning for 1941, dated February 11, 1941, BArch R 49/303.

124. On Madagascar's function in antisemitic thought, see Brechtken, *Madagaskar für die Juden*; on the genesis of various European Madagascar plans, see Jansen, *Madagaskar-Plan*.

125. The January 1940 memo was titled "Rechtsgestaltung deutscher Polenpolitik nach volkspolitischen Gesichtspunkten" [Legal shaping of German Poland policy according to ethnopolitical aspects], anonymously drafted for the nationality law committee at the Academy for German Law; Hilberg and Browning speculate that Frank was the author (Schwaneberg, "Economic Exploitation," 69). Himmler's memo from May 15, 1940, was titled "Einige Gedanken über die Behandlung der Fremdvölkischen im Osten," reprinted in Opitz, *Europastrategien des deutschen Kapitals*, 653–55. Examples of the Madagascar tradition are at Longerich, *Politik der Vernichtung*, 273, and Browning, *Entfesselung*, 131.

126. Browning, *Entfesselung*, 133.

127. Ibid., 134.

128. Entry of May 30, 1940, in Präg and Jacobmeyer, *Diensttagebuch des deutschen Generalgouverneurs*, 210.

129. Entry of July 12, 1940, in ibid., 252.

130. Aly, *Endlösung*, 101–2.

131. Unsigned concluding report on the evacuations for settling of Volhynian, Galician, and Chełm Germans (second short-range plan) in the Wartheland, with appendixes, undated (probably late January 1941), BArch R 75/6, 1–13, reprinted in *Biuletyn Głównej Komisji* 21: 89–105. See particularly appendix 3, accounting of transport trains sent during Chełm campaign of second short-range plan with evacuated Poles from Litzmannstadt to the General Government.

132. Krumey to UWZ field offices, July 3, 1940, AGK 68/98, 11.

133. (Signature illegible), memo from UWZ, undated (probably late September or early October 1940), AGK 68/134, 9. Höppner received confirmation from Eichmann on October 17, 1940 (AGK 68/134, 15).

134. Unsigned report from SD main field office in Obornik, September 8, 1940. AGK 68/134, 6.

135. (Signature illegible), memo from UWZ, undated (probably late September or early October 1940), AGK 68/134, 9.

136. Schmidtsiefen to UWZ in Posen, October 30, 1940, AGK 68/134, 17.

137. Frank to Greiser, confidential, November 2, 1940, reprinted in Datner, Gumkowski, and Leszczyński, "Wysiedlanie ludności," 113. See also Browning, *Entfesselung*, 154–55; Höppner to Ehlich and Eichmann, November 5, 1940, reprinted in Datner, Gumkowski, and Leszczyński, "Wysiedlanie ludności," 113–14.

138. Höppner's memo on meeting of November 4, 1940, dated November 6, 1940, AGK NTN/36, 156–57.

139. Damzog to Jäger, November 6, 1940, AGK 62/299, 42–43.

140. Höppner's memo to Damzog, November 7, 1940, AGK 69/182, 1–2. Thanks to Götz Aly for this document.

141. Ziegler's memo on the meeting at Agency of the RKFDV in Berlin on March 5, 1940, dated March 9, 1940, reprinted in Długoborski, *Polozenie ludności*, 148–49.

142. Aly, *Endlösung*, 147–48.

143. Interrogation of Helmut Stutzke, first head of the Staff Main Office of the RKFDV, on March 12, 1963, BArchL, B 162/2438, 61–72. See also unsigned report on the development and activities of the settlement department for the period July 10, 1940, to May 31, 1941, dated June 7, 1941, BArch R 49 III/26, 120–131. Thanks to Götz Aly for this document.

144. Signed "Bach-Zelewski," appointee of the RKFDV, to Oberpräsident in Breslau, Regierungspräsident of Kattowitz, and Landrat of Saybusch, confidential, August 5, 1940, reprinted in Długoborski, *Polozenie ludności*, 161–63. On the settlements in general, see Szefer, *Przesiedleńcy niemieccy*; Szefer, "Deutschen Umsiedler." On Hering, see Kaczmarek, *Pod rządami gauleiteròw*, 75.

145. Lilla, *Stellvertretenden Gauleiter*, 19–20 and 25.

146. On Arlt, see Steinbacher, *Musterstadt Auschwitz*, 126–29, and BArch BDC SSO file on Fritz Arlt.

147. Friedrich Bachmann, Regierungspräsient of Liegnitz, minutes of meeting on September 5, 1940, undated, APK 119/39, 165–71.

148. Unsigned report on the development and activities of the settlement department for the period July 10, 1940, to May 31, 1941, dated June 7, 1941, R 49 III/26, 120–131. Thanks to Götz Aly for this document.

149. Unpaged and unsigned activity report of the RKFDV appointee in Upper Silesia, September 1939 to January 1943, dated March 30, 1943, BArch 186/42; excerpt of same also at Bavarian State Archives, Nuremberg, NO-5640. See also postwar debriefing of Landrat Eugen Hering by the German Federal Archives, Bayreuth branch, Bayreuth, Ger., Ost-Dok. 8/765, 14–23.

150. Signed "Bach-Zelewski," appointee of the RKFDV, to Oberpräsident in Breslau, Regierungspräsident of Kattowitz, and Landrat of Saybusch, confidential, August 5, 1940, reprinted in Długoborski, *Polozenie ludności*, 161–63. See also memo from police major Richard von Coelln, August 1, 1940, APK 119/4086, 4.

151. Memo from Eichmann, August 7, 1940, reprinted in Datner, Gumkowski, and Leszczyński, "Wysiedlanie ludności," 103–6.

152. Steinbacher, *Musterstadt Auschwitz*, 167.

153. Unsigned guidelines from Unit IV D 4 at the Reich Security Main Office on implementing the evacuation campaign in Saybusch County, Kattowitz Governmental Region, in the course of settling Galician-German mountain farmers (Volhynian campaign), undated (probably August 9, 1940), AGK, 69/1, 27–30. On this dating, see unsigned guidelines from Kattowitz Gestapo on implementing the evacuation campaign in Saybusch County, September 14, 1940, APK 119/4086, 11–17, reprinted in Długoborski, *Polozenie ludności*, 166–71.

154. Unsigned guidelines from Unit IV D 4 at the Reich Security Main Office on implementing the evacuation campaign in Saybusch County, Kattowitz Governmental Region, in the course of settling Galician-German mountain farmers (Volhynian campaign), undated (probably August 9, 1940), AGK, 69/1, 27–30.

155. For reference to the establishment of the UWZ, see the unsigned activity report of the RKFDV appointee in Upper Silesia, September 1939 to January 1943, dated March 30, 1943, BArch 186/42, unpaged; excerpt of same also at Bavarian State Archives, Nuremberg, NO-5640. In contrast, Jastrzębski ("Nazi Deportations," 4) claims that Himmler dispensed with establishing a UWZ in Upper Silesia, since only a small part of the populace was to be deported from there. This claim is probably incorrect: after all, the entire "Polish" populace

was supposed to be deported from there as well. The fact that it failed to happen was ultimately for other reasons that I will explore later.

156. Unsigned guidelines from Kattowitz Gestapo on implementing the evacuation campaign in Saybusch, September 14, 1940, APK 119/4086, 11–17; reprinted in Długoborski, *Polozenie ludności*, 166–71.

157. Ibid. See also, memo from adviser Nissen about a meeting on upcoming evacuation campaign in Saybusch, September 11, 1940 APK 119/4086, 7–10, reprinted in Długoborski, *Polozenie ludności*, 163–65.

158. Planning guidelines for development of the eastern territories, reprinted in Müller, *Hitlers Ostkrieg*, 130–38 (in documentation for January–February 1940).

159. (Signed "p.p. Heydrich"), Reich Interior Ministry to state governments outside Prussia and Reichsstatthalters in Posen and Danzig, August 13, 1940, BArch R 43 II/646, 83.

160. Unsigned memo for Agency of the RKFDV in Berlin, Main Dept. II, on meeting between Himmler, Bracht, Bach-Zelewski, and Greifelt, September 11, 1940, BArch R 49/2639. Thanks to Götz Aly for this document.

161. Contrary to Aly, who dates the first transport to October 1940—see *Endlösung*, 153—the earlier start is documented in an unsigned concluding report on the evacuations for settling of Volhynian, Galician, and Chełm Germans (second short-range plan) in the Wartheland, with appendixes, undated (probably late January 1941), BArch R 75/6, 1–13, reprinted in *Biuletyn Głównej Komisji* 21: 89–105.

162. Künzel to Hofmann, October 4, 1940, AGK 369/13, 74.

163. Unsigned concluding report on the evacuations for settling of Volhynian, Galician, and Chełm Germans (second short-range plan) in the Wartheland, with appendixes, undated (probably late January 1941), BArch R 75/6, 1–13, reprinted in *Biuletyn Głównej Komisji* 21: 89–105. A somewhat different figure of 16,400 persons is cited by RKFDV headquarters (unsigned overview from Main Dept. I at Agency of the RKFDV in Berlin, on settlement and evacuation in the incorporated eastern territories, status as of December 31, 1940, and planning for 1941, dated February 11, 1941, BArch R 49/303, unpaged.

164. The 650 comes from an unsigned memo dated November 21, 1940, reprinted in Długoborski, *Polozenie ludności*, 172–73, and the 775 comes from the unsigned 1940 annual report of Silesian Rural Development Company, BArch R 2/19015, unpaged. The figure of 2,876 persons is found in an unsigned overview from Main Dept. I at Agency of the RKFDV in Berlin on settlement and evacuation in the incorporated eastern territories, status as of December 31, 1940, and planning for 1941, dated February 11, 1941, BArch R 49/303, unpaged; then a slightly different figure of 2,950 persons is given by an undated document with Himmler's initials, probably also from the RKFDV headquarters, on the settling concluded up to December 1, 1940, BArch NS 19/3979, 11; finally, the considerably higher figure of 3,709 persons is found in the 1940 annual report of Silesian Rural Development Company, BArch R 2/19015, unpaged.

165. (Signed "Bach-Zelewski"), appointee of the RKFDV to Oberpräsident in Breslau, Regierungspräsident of Kattowitz, and Landrat of Saybusch, confidential, August 5, 1940, reprinted in Długoborski, *Polozenie ludności*, 161–63. See also unsigned first draft proposal from Main Dept. I at RKFDV headquarters on guidelines and notes, August 7, 1940, BArch R 49/2602, unpaged. Thanks to Götz Aly for this document.

166. Unsigned memo, November 12, 1940, reprinted in Długoborski, *Polozenie ludności*, 172–73.

167. According to Arlt, 95 percent of the farms in Saybusch were less than one hectare in size (2.5 acres; Arlt to Bracht, June 6, 1941, reprinted in Długoborski, *Polozenie ludności*, 187–92. See also an unsigned report on the development and activities of the settlement department for the period July 10, 1940, to May 31, 1941, dated June 7, 1941, R 49 III/26, 120–131. Thanks to Götz Aly for this document.

168. Madajczyk, *Okkupationspolitik Nazideutschlands*, 480. In further stating on the same page, however, that the relevant deportations began in April/May 1940, I believe Madajczyk is mistaken. Although two transports carrying a total of 1,519 Congress Poles did leave Thorn (today Toruń) for the General Government on May 12 and 14, 1940, they were probably not part of the second short-range plan. They are not included in any of the plan's surviving statistical records and, furthermore, no settlements were taking place in Danzig–West Prussia at this time. See, for example, reports by police officer Otto Lojak, Thorn police force, on May 12, 1940. (AGK NTN/192, 32), and May 19, 1940. (AGK NTN/192, 33). More important, they did not conform to the now-approved procedure, in that they skipped the racial appraisal process and the stopover in Litzmannstadt. It is more likely that they carried members of the Polish elite, who had been rounded up during the renewed widespread purges of that period, as already described. Madajczyk is probably also mistaken in claiming that another deportation wave happened between September and November 1940—which actually began a month later, see unsigned letter, Reich Security Main Office to railroad department at Reich Transport Ministry, September 13, 1940, Western Institute, Poznań, 1/71, unpaged.

169. Reich Security Main Office to railroad department, September 13, 1940.

170. Greifelt to the HSSPFs of Königsberg and Danzig, September 18, 1940, Political Archives of the Foreign Office, Berlin [hereafter, PAAA], R 100630. Thanks to Götz Aly for this document.

171. On the "ethnonational bridges" ("Volkstumsbrücken"), see planning guidelines for development of the eastern territories, reprinted in Müller, *Hitlers Ostkrieg*, 130–38 (in documentation for January–February 1940) and 157. The six original counties were Berent, Zempelburg, Bromberg, Schwetz, Kulm, and Graudenz; see (signed "Himmler"), RKFDV general directive 3/I, June 13, 1940, BArch R 186/35, unpaged. The three additional counties were Wirsitz, Neustadt, and Dirschau, see (signed "Himmler"), RKFDV general directive, September 9, 1940, BArch R 186/31, unpaged.

172. Greifelt to the HSSPFs of Königsberg and Danzig, September 18, 1940, PAAA R 100630. Thanks to Götz Aly for this document.

173. Short biography of Henschel at Heinemann, *Rasse, Siedlung, deutsches Blut*, 618.

174. Unsigned memo from head of Danzig–West Prussia Settlement Staff to RKFDV headquarters, October 25, 1940, State Archives in Bydgoszcz [hereafter, APB], 97/14, 1–5.

175. Ibid. (emphasis in original).

176. Ibid.

177. Globocnik's presence is explained by the fact that the settlers from Chełm and the Weichsel region came from the district of Lublin. See (signed "Dr. Kaumarms [DUT]"), minutes of meeting on November 1, 1940, BAP 1702/217. Thanks to Götz Aly for this document.

178. Ibid.

179. Fähndrich to Himmler, November 4, 1940, AGK 167/1, 52–53.

180. Heinemann, *Rasse, Siedlung, deutsches Blut*, 250.

181. Fähndrich to Himmler, November 4, 1940, AGK 167/1, 52–53.

182. Ibid.

183. Signed "Ehlich and Müller," minutes of the meeting of January 7, 1941, on procedure for resettling the so-called intermediate class in Danzig–West Prussia, January 8, 1941, BArch PL 170/67, 19–21.

184. Ibid.

185. Heinemann, *Rasse, Siedlung, deutsches Blut*, 250.

186. Essner, "Im Irrgarten der Rassenlogik" [In the labyrinth of racial logic].

187. Abromeit to Höppner, November 11, 1940, AGK 68/120, 2, reprinted in Datner, Gumkowski, and Leszczyński, "Wysiedlanie ludności," 116.

188. Heydrich to the Reichsstatthalter, HSSPF, IdS, and Gestapo in Danzig, January 23, 1941, SMR 500-3/22, 88.

189. At least this was the date specified by the provincial employment office, the head of the provincial farmers' association, and the chamber of industry and commerce, to allow them a chance to retain some of the detainees as forced laborers. See Wolff's minutes of a meeting on November 9, 1940, on resettlement in Danzig–West Prussia of Vistula Germans, as well as Volksdeutsche from Lithuania and Bessarabia, dated November 9, 1940, AGK 68/109, 10-15. Thanks to Götz Aly for this document.

190. Abromeit to Höppner, November 11, 1940, AGK 68/120, 2, reprinted in Datner, Gumkowski, and Leszczyński, "Wysiedlanie ludności," 116.

191. Wolff's minutes of a meeting on November 9, 1940.

192. Unsigned concluding report on the evacuations for settling of Volhynian, Galician, and Chełm Germans (second short-range plan) in the Wartheland, with appendixes, undated (probably late January 1941), BArch R 75/6, 1–13, reprinted in *Biuletyn Głównej Komisji* 21: 89–105.

193. Unsigned summary from UWZ Danzig, December 7, 1940, APB 97/14, 17.

194. Roeder to Reichsstatthalters, Regierungspräsidents, Landrats, December 9, 1940, BArch R 75/3b, 90–92.

195. In contrast, Jastrzębski, *Hitlerowskie wysiedlenia*, 81–82, cites 10,504 persons for this time period, of whom only 381 were Jews.

196. East Prussia is not included in these figures, but it also carries little weight here. At this time, there were still no settlers placed there, and around fifteen thousand locals had been expelled to the General Government (unsigned overview from Main Dept. I at Agency of the RKFDV in Berlin on accounting of the populace in the incorporated territories, February 13, 1941, BArch R 49/303, unpaged).

197. Unsigned concluding report of on the evacuations for settling of Volhynian, Galician, and Chełm Germans (second short-range plan) in the Wartheland, with appendixes, undated (probably late January 1941), BArch R 75/6, 1–13, reprinted in *Biuletyn Głównej Komisji* 21: 89–105.

198. Calculated according to unsigned overview from Main Dept. I at Agency of the RKFDV in Berlin, on settlement and evacuation in the incorporated eastern territories, status as of December 31, 1940, and planning for 1941, dated February 11, 1941, BArch R 49/303, unpaged.

199. Memo from Alexander Dolezalek on conference on January 8, 1941, dated January 10, 1941, BArch R 49 Anh. I/34, 7–8. See also preparatory meetings at Reich Security Main Office on December 17, 1940 (Eichmann to the Gestapo and SD offices in the annexed eastern

territories, December 12, 1940, BArch R 75/9a, 97), and at RKFDV headquarters on January 7, 1941 (memo from Butschek of South Silesia Settlement Staff, January 10, 1941, BArch R 49 Anh. III/26, unpaged; thanks to Götz Aly for this file). The numbers cited at this meeting are only slightly different from those ultimately agreed a day later. Largely in agreement also is unsigned accounting from RKFDV, February 11, 1941, BArch R 49/303, unpaged. On the conference, see also Madajczyk, *Okkupationspolitik Nazideutschlands*, 415–16.

200. Memo from Alexander Dolezalek concerning conference on January 8, 1941, dated January 10, 1941, BArch R 49 Anh. I/34, 7–8.

201. Ibid.

202. Meeting between Hitler, Frank, Schirach, Koch, and Bormann on October 2, 1940, reprinted in Seeber, *Zwangsarbeiter*, 264–67; meeting between Hitler and Frank on November 4, 1940, and meeting under Frank in Kraków on November 6, 1940, both reprinted in Präg and Jacobmeyer, *Diensttagebuch des deutschen Generalgouverneurs*, 302.

203. Höppner to Döring, January 20, 1941, AGK 69/182, 5–7. Thanks to Götz Aly for this document.

204. Höppner to Krumey, BArchL B 162/365b, 69.

205. Memo from Schröder on discussion with Döring, April 10, 1941, BArch R 49/2639, unpaged. Thanks to Götz Aly for this document.

206. This figure was specified at a meeting on January 8, 1941, see BArch R 49 I/34, 7–8, memo from Dolezalek, January 10, 1941.

207. Unsigned concluding report on evacuations for settling of Bessarabian Germans (third short-range plan) in the Wartheland from January 21, 1941, to January 20, 1942, undated, AGK NTN/13, 99–106, reprinted in *Biuletyn Głównej Komisji* 21: 106–10.

208. (Signed "Himmler as RKFDV"), directive 10/II, January 16, 1941, BArch R 186/31, unpaged.

209. Memo from Dolezalek, January 10, 1941, BArch R 49 I/34, 7–8.

210. For Danzig–West Prussia, it was in late January 1941 (Heydrich to Reichsstatthalter's offices and HSSPF in Danzig, January 23, 1941, SMR 500–3/22, 88). For Upper Silesia, it was mid-February 1942 ([signed "p.p. Dr. Rudolf Bilfinger"], Reich Security main office to the Oberpräsident and HSSPF in Breslau, February 14, 1941, BA DH 890 A2, 622A, 1–51). Thanks to Götz Aly for this document.

211. For Danzig, see head of Danzig SD Command Precinct to IV B 4 at Reich Security Main Office, February 28, 1941, APB 97/14, 51. For Silesia, see message from UWZ Kattowitz, undated (probably February 1941), APK 119/4088, 1–3.

212. See, for example, Eichmann's guidelines, undated (probably just before February 1, 1941), AGK 69/1, 38–41.

213. Unsigned summary from UWZ Danzig, February 3, 1941, BArch PL 170/46, 1–6.

214. General directive 4/41 from Bracht as appointee of the RKFDV, February 4, 1941, APK 119/4088, 13–17, reprinted in Długoborski, *Polozenie ludności*, 181–85.

215. Unsigned summary from UWZ Danzig, February 3, 1941, BArch PL 170/46, 1–6; unsigned summary from UWZ Kattowitz on development of the office, undated (probably February 1941), APK 119/4088, 1–3.

216. (Signed "Günther"), Unit IV D 4 at Reich Security Main Office to UWZ offices in the annexed eastern provinces, February 21, 1941, AGK 68/122, 35–36. A week later, Eichmann announced that, at least for the first week of March, two trains per day would probably be available after all, see Eichmann to UWZ offices in the annexed eastern provinces,

February 27, 1941, AGK, 68/122, 41; thanks to Götz Aly for this document. This assertion would turn out to be overhasty.

217. Greifelt to appointees of the RKFDV in the annexed eastern provinces, March 11, 1941, R 69/388, 247–49. See also Abromeit to the HSSPF, IdS, and SD Command Precinct in Danzig, March 11, 1941, APB 97/14, 47.

218. Summary from the UWZ of persons deported and displaced under third short-range plan, undated (probably late January 1942), AGK 62/76, 4. See also accounting from RKFDV headquarters, February 11, 1941, BArch R 49/303, unpaged.

219. Jastrzębski, *Potulice*, 9–12.

220. A figure of twenty-five thousand is given by Aly, *Endlösung*, 229. Although the precise numbers cannot be precisely determined, it nonetheless seems to be 11,123 persons from Danzig–West Prussia (Jastrzębski, *Potulice*, 22) and 19,226 from the Wartheland (unsigned concluding report on evacuations for settling of Bessarabian Germans [third short-range plan] in the Wartheland from January 21, 1941, to January 20, 1942, undated, AGK NTN/13, 99–106, reprinted in *Biuletyn Głównej Komisji* 21: 106–10). In any case, the results were clearly different from the self-imposed targets.

221. Aly, *Endlösung*, 229.

222. Ibid.

223. See, for example, Browning, *Entfesselung*, 158; Aly, *Endlösung*, 228–36.

224. (Signed "p.p. Jacobi"), Reich Interior Ministry to the Reich Security Main Office, Landesarchiv Berlin, B Rep. 057–01/448, A 26 (2). See also Adam, *Judenpolitik*, 290; Herbert, "Arbeit und Vernichtung," 393.

225. Höppner to Unit III B at Reich Security Main Office, March 13, 1941, BArch R 75/3b, 94–95, reprinted in Datner, Gumkowski, and Leszczyński, "Wysiedlanie ludności," 136–37.

226. Krumey to UWZ Posen and Ehlich, February 25, 1941, AGK 68/146, 23.

227. Aly, *Endlösung*, 231. See also memo from Dolezalek, February 12, 1941, BArch R 49 I/34, 43–47. Thanks to Götz Aly for this document.

228. Memo from Höppner for Koppe, Ehlich, and Krumey, on meeting with Kendzia et al. on March 4, 1941, dated March 7, 1941, AGK 68/146, 26–27.

229. Memo from Alexander Dolezalek, February 12, 1941, BArch R 49 I/34, 43–47. Thanks to Götz Aly for this document.

230. Coulon's report on the course and conclusion of the DVL process in the Wartheland, February 5, 1941, APP 406/1109, 320–32.

231. Leuschner's letter to Uebelhoer, undated (initialed on April 6, 1940), APP 406/1108, 54–61.

232. Guidelines for registering German ethnonationals in the DVL, headquarters copy, official use only, undated (probably late January 1940), APP 406/1106.

233. The card catalog was to establish the following six categories: "I. both parents German; II. husband German, wife Polish, (a) children German in schooling and home language, (b) children Polish in schooling and home language; III. husband Polish, wife German, (a) children German in schooling and home language, (b) children Polish in schooling and home language; IV. German from the General Government; V. husband German, wife foreign-blooded; VI. husband foreign-blooded, wife German." (ibid.).

234. Ibid. (emphasis in original).

235. Ibid.

236. Jastrzębski, *Hitlerowskie wysiedlenia*, 113.

237. Guidelines for registering German ethnonationals in the DVL, headquarters copy, official use only, undated (probably late January 1940), APP 406/1106.

238. Ibid. On the problems associated with using the family's surname as a guideline, see also Dzieciński, *Łódź*, 19.

239. Guidelines for registering German ethnonationals in the DVL, headquarters copy, official use only, undated (probably late January 1940), APP 406/1106.

240. Unsigned operational status report from DVL regional office in Posen to Coulon's unit, April 25, 1940, APP 406/1109, 226–28.

241. Heinrich W., response to questionnaire, APP VD Posen City/12126.

242. Memo from Coulon, February 26, 1940, APP 406/1113, 162–63.

243. W. Geske to Coulon, November 7, 1940, APP 406/1113, 189–91.

244. Coulon's report the on course and conclusion of DVL process in the Wartheland, February 5, 1941, APP 406/1109, 320–32.

245. Coulon to Uebelhoer, December 5, 1939, APP 406/1113, 224.

246. Unsigned memo on Litzmannstadt's Volk List system, undated (probably written by Leuschner in mid-1940), APL 897/53, 1–4.

247. Coulon's report the on course and conclusion of DVL process in the Wartheland, February 5, 1941, APP 406/1109, 320–32.

248. Unsigned memo on Litzmannstadt's Volk List system, undated (probably written by Leuschner in mid-1940), APL 897/53, 1–4.

249. Stuckart to Wagner, November 26, 1939, APK 119/10700, 10.

250. Springorum to chief of police in Kattowitz and Landrats, December 19, 1939, APK 119/10701, 1–4.

251. Stuckart to Reich Propaganda Ministry, January 4, 1940, APK 119/10695, 31. Political loyalty did in fact become a selection criterion, however, either in the positive sense as in the Wartheland as a precondition for registration, or in the negative sense, as in Danzig–West Prussia and Upper Silesia, where, at least in the beginning, individuals who had been recognized as Germans were expected to not have participated in organizations that were politically Polish.

252. Sroková, "K narodnostini politice," 283; Dziurok, "Zwischen den Ethnien," 224. For an overview organized by former partition zone, see Kaczmarek, "Niemiecka polityka," 118.

253. Metz to Springorum, March 7, 1940, reprinted in Steinbacher, *Musterstadt Auschwitz*, 117–18.

254. Ibid.

255. Ibid., 117.

256. Notes on the questionnaire, in attachment to Daluege's message, November 25, 1939, APK 117/826, 90–95.

257. Quoted in Walkenhorst, *Nation—Volk—Rasse*, 99.

258. Springorum to Wagner, January 21, 1940, APK 119/10702, 17–19.

259. Ibid.

260. Ibid.

261. Ibid.

262. (Signed "p.p. Ministerial Director Hermann Hering"), Reich Interior Ministry to Regierungspräsident's offices in Kattowitz, February 19, 1940, APK 119/10701, 13.

263. Vice Regierungspräsident Kessler to Landrats and chief of police in Kattowitz, March 26, 1940, APK 119/10695, 55–60.

264. Ibid.

265. Ibid. (emphasis in original).

266. Specifically named here were insurrectionary groups, paramilitary groups, and the Polish Western Association (Polski Związek Zachodni; Vice Regierungspräsident Kessler to Landrats and chief of police in Kattowitz, March 26, 1940, APK 119/10695, 55–60).

267. On the party's role, see memo from Schröder, March 3, 1940, APK 119/10701, 23. In doubtful cases, the relevant Kreisleiter was also to be consulted (Vice Regierungspräsident Kessler to county police authorities, April 1, 1940, APK 119/10695, 62–63; memo from Schröder, July 3, 1940, APK 119/10701, 87).

268. Schulenburg to Regierungspräsidents, April 5, 1940, APK 119/10700, 11–12 (emphasis in original).

269. Springorum to Landrats and chief of police in Kattowitz, April 19, 1940, APK 119/10702, 25–28.

270. (Signature illegible), chief of police in Kattowitz to Regierungspräsident's offices, May 30, 1940, APK 119/10701, 52–54.

271. Derschau to Regierungspräsident's offices, June 28, 1940, APK 119/10701, 79; see also Derschau to Regierungspräsident's offices, July 8, 1940, APK 119/10686, 126.

272. Derschau to Regierungspräsident's offices, July 8, 1940, APK 119/10686, 126.

273. Deputy head of the Staff Main Office, Rudolf Creutz, to the DVL central office in Kattowitz, April 2, 1943, SMR 1232/20, 67.

274. Memo from Storr, February 9, 1940, BArch NS 25/202; see also Levine, "Local Authority," 337.

275. Heukenkamp to RKFDV headquarters, June 25, 1940, BArch R 49/61, 83–87.

276. Dr. Meyer, ethnonationality officer at the Regierungspräsident's offices in Danzig, to Landrats and chiefs of police, April 27, 1940, APB 12/114, 3–5.

277. Summons by Günther Palten, January 8, 1940, APB 9/2, 3, which was announced by Landrat Nethe of Bromberg Rural County on January 19, 1940. Palten's defiant attitude ultimately caused Forster to push for his dismissal by the Reich Interior Ministry. He was replaced by Dr. Johannes Kurt Schimmel in June 1940 (unsigned Reich Interior Ministry memo, August 13, 1940, SMR 720-5/8949, 133–34). Sometime later, a similar fate befell the vice Regierungspräsident, Dr. Hubertus Schönberg, who had likewise criticized Forster's ethnopolicy. He was ultimately transferred to Troppau (today Opava); (unsigned Reich Interior Ministry letter to Schönberg, September 17, 1941, SMR 720-5/8949, 170).

278. Unsigned instruction, Walter Nethe to mayors and Amtskommissars, April 25, 1940, with reference to the circulars from the Regierungspräsident's offices on April 12 and 16, 1940, AGK NTN/198, 30–33.

279. Ibid. Nethe's personnel files from the Reich Interior Ministry are found at SMR 720-5/6930 and SMR 720-5/6931.

280. Unsigned summary of results from census of December 3–6, 1939, undated, AGK NTN/191, 7–56.

281. Ibid.

282. Accounting from mayor of Neustadt, September 16, 1940, APG 37/2, 143–53.

283. Heinz Lorenz, Kreisleiter/Landrat of Neustadt, annual report, September 18, 1949, APG 37/2, 259–319.

284. Of the 9,473 persons recognized as "German" by the authorities, only 7,017 were over the age of fourteen, and identity documents were issued only to legal adults, see unsigned

summary of overall results from census of December 3–6, 1939, in the county of Neustadt, organized by locality, as of January 1, 1940, undated, APG 37/469, 49–57.

285. Unsigned summary of results from census of December 3–6, 1939, undated, AGK NTN/191, 7–56.

286. Heinz Lorenz to Forster on Gauleiter visit on January 20, 1941, undated, APG 37/2, 327–49.

287. Accounting from mayor of Neustadt, September 16, 1940, APG 37/2, 143–53.

288. (Signature illegible), school board's annual report on school system developmental achievements in Neustadt County from September 11, 1939, to September 11, 1940, undated, APG 37/2, 229–39.

289. Accounting from mayor of Neustadt, September 16, 1940, APG 37/2, 143–53. A similar policy was also attempted by the German occupiers in the Czech territory, where the numbers reflected a considerably lower "success rate"; it is uncertain, however, whether the lower figure occurred because the occupiers met with more resistance there or because they were simply more honest, see Zahra, *Kidnapped Souls*, 193.

290. Hildebrandt to BdS of Danzig, confidential, February 27, 1940, AGK NTN/199, 3; see also Forster to Hildebrandt, March 21, 1940, BArch R 70 Polen/93, 52–53.

291. Message from Greifelt, April 9, 1940, APK 119/10701, 48–49 (without addressee, but found in files of Regeriungspräsident's offices in Kattowitz, and very likely sent to all RKFDV branch offices in the annexed territories).

292. Forster to Hildebrandt, March 21, 1940, BArch R 70 Polen/93, 52–53; (signed "p.p. Löbsack"), guidelines from the Reichsstatthalter's offices to the commissions for the reviewing of complaints about wrongfully conducted evacuations and about the nonissuance of recognition as Volksdeutsche, May 31, 1940, AGK NTN/199, 36–40. See also Forster to Palten, March 26, 1940, AGK NTN/199, 5.

293. (Signed "p.p. Löbsack"), guidelines from the Reichsstatthalter's offices to the commissions for the reviewing of complaints about wrongfully conducted evacuations and about the nonissuance of recognition as Volksdeutsche, May 31, 1940, AGK NTN/199, 36–40 (emphasis in original).

294. Ohlendorf to Himmler on clarification of ethnonational membership in the new eastern territories, May 24, 1940, BArch R 49/61, 70–77.

295. Report from representative of the Regierungspräsident of Bromberg, May 18, 1940, AGK NTN/199, 27–29.

296. Heukenkamp to RKFDV headquarters, June 25, 1940, BArch R 49/61, 83–87.

297. Memo from Coulon, July 25, 1940, APP 406/1109, 221–24.

298. Ibid.

299. Memo from Coulon, August 16, 1940, APP 406/1109, 214. The employee assigned to this task was Dr. Heinrich Bosse, head of the press/photo archive at the HSSPF.

300. Ibid.

301. Coulon to Dept. I, August 15, 1940, APP 406/1109, 212–13.

302. (Signature illegible), memo from Main Dept. I at RKFDV, August 31, 1940, BArch R 49/62, 42–43.

303. Coulon to Dept. I, August 15, 1940, APP 406/1109, 212–13.

304. (Signed "Laforce"), HSSPF of Posen to RKFDV headquarters, August 16, 1940, BArch R 49/62, 38.

305. Rüdiger to Oberpräsident's offices, May 5, 1940, APK 119/10701, 37–38.

306. Memo from Schröder to Prof. Dr. Arnold Köttgen, departmental head for police affairs, May 9, 1940, APK 119/10701, 40–41.

307. Springorum to Bach-Zelewski, May 21, 1940, APK 119/10701, 45–47.

308. (Signed "Amsberg"), summary from RKFDV headquarters, March 21, 1941, BArch R49/62, 118–19.

309. Memo from Dr. Walter, May 20, 1940, BArch R 49/61, 47–48.

310. Ibid.

311. Ohlendorf to Himmler, May 24, 1940, BArch R 49/61, 70–77.

312. Memo from Dr. Walter, May 20, 1940, BArch R 49/61, 47–48.

313. Unsigned memo from Main Dept. III at RKFDV headquarters, May 22, 1940, BArch R 49/61, 68–69.

314. Ohlendorf to Himmler, May 24, 1940, BArch R 49/61, 70–77. Beyer worked at Dept. III of the Reich Security Main Office and was also the latter's chief liaison to the Party Chancellery (Parteikanzlei); Wildt, *Generation des Unbedingten*, 75; Madajczyk, "Generalplan Ost," 91).

315. Ohlendorf to Himmler, May 24, 1940, BArch R 49/61, 70–77.

316. Ibid.

317. Ibid.

318. Ibid.

319. Draft proposal of Reich Interior Ministry on acquisition of German national status in the incorporated eastern territories, July 3, 1940, BArch R 49/61, 8–41.

320. Ibid.

321. Ibid.

322. Ibid.

323. Ibid. (emphasis in original).

324. Ibid.

325. Ibid.

326. Ibid.

327. Ibid.

328. Ibid.

329. Unsigned memo from RKFDV headquarters (probably for Himmler), September 11, 1940, BArch R 49/61, 2–7; Himmler to Frick, September 16, 1940, in which Himmler refers to discussion with Stuckart, APP 406/1109, 2–3.

330. Decree from Himmler as RKFDV, September 12, 1940, BArch NS 19/3979, 29–33, reprinted in Pospieszalski, *Hitlerowskie "prawo" okupacyjne*, 114–18.

331. Ibid.

332. Ibid.

333. There was also mention of 5,000 Masurians, but they were relevant only to Germanization policy in East Prussia (ibid.).

334. Ibid.

335. Ibid.

336. Ibid.

337. Ibid.

338. Ibid.

339. Ibid.

340. Ibid.

341. Ibid.

342. Ibid.

343. Protected dependent status (*Schutzangehörigkeit*) was formally introduced on April 25, 1943 (*Reichsgesetzblatt Teil I* [1943], 271–72). On protected dependent status, see Gosewinkel, *Einbürgern und Ausschließen*, 413–20, although Gosewinkel tends to strongly overemphasize the importance of the initially racial selection criteria.

344. Greifelt to Greiser, November 15, 1940, APP 406/1112, 28–34.

345. Ibid.

346. Ibid.

347. Greiser to Greifelt, November 24, 1940, APP 406/1112, 35–39.

348. Ibid.

349. Ibid.

350. Himmler to Frick, September 16, 1940, APP 406/1109, 2–3.

351. Reich Interior Ministry draft proposal on acquisition of German national status by former Polish and Danzig nationals, to Deputy Führer, Reichsführer of the SS, the Foreign Office, and administration heads in the annexed territories and General Government, etc., October 31, 1940, APP 406/1109, 20–35.

352. Ibid.

353. Ibid.

354. Ibid.

355. Ibid.

356. Ibid.

357. The new regulations also simplified matters for residents of Danzig. Unlike the rest of the populace, they were to be granted German national status wholesale. Instead of DVL branch offices, only a regional office was to be established there, in order to conduct a negative selection process identifying anyone who did not fulfill the criteria for Sections 1 or 2 and thus did not qualify for this summary bestowal of German national status.

358. This applied in principle to the regional offices as well. Either directly, as in the case of the Wartheland, where the Regierungspräsident was also Gau Inspector and thus head of the regional party agencies, or indirectly, because all committee members from the state administration and the party's regional subdivision were ultimately subordinated to the provincial head.

359. This color coding is reminiscent of an earlier attempt, initiated by the German Eastern Marches Society, to control foreign farmworkers by establishing a new FarmWorker Central Office (Feldarbeiter-Centralstelle) and to limit their stay in Germany, thereby balancing economic needs against fears of Polonization. The central office issued the necessary work permit cards, assigning a different color to each nationality. Polish seasonal workers received red cards (Conrad, *Globalisierung*, 162).

360. Memo from Coulon, November 7, 1940, APP 406/1109, 44. See also opinion from Hess, November 10, 1940, APP 406/1109, 67–73.

361. Opinion from Strickner, undated, APP 406/1109, 74–81.

362. Opinion from Coulon, November 12, 1940, APP 406/1109, 45–58.

363. Summarized comments from Coulon, November 13, 1940, APP 406/1109, 143–45.

364. Ibid.

365. Frick to Deputy Führer, version of December 19, 1940, BArch R 1501/5402, 305–35.

366. Memo from Coulon, November 18, 1940, APP 406/1109, 141–42.

367. Confidential message from Greiser to Gauleiter's office heads, party organization heads, Regierungspräsidents, etc., on impact of DVL process for state, party, and economy, February 15, 1941, APP 406/1130, 402–6.

368. Ibid.

369. Stuckart to Greiser, February 8, 1941, AGK 62/49, 83.

370. Coulon's report on the status of the ethnonationality unit's work as of February 1, 1941, and its continuation in the coming months, dated February 4, 1941, APP 406/1109, 305–11.

371. Ibid.

372. Coulon's report on the course and conclusion of DVL process in the Wartheland, February 5, 1941, APP 406/1109, 320–32.

373. Coulon's report on the status of the ethnonationality unit's work as of February 1, 1941, and its continuation in the coming months, dated February 4, 1941, APP 406/1109, 305–11.

374. For the June 1940 directive, see *Reichsgesetzblatt Teil I* (1940), 844–46.

375. Greiser's order of September 25, 1940, reprinted in Łuczak, *Położenie ludności polskiej*, 180–82.

376. In fact, Greiser gave this reason when he ordered the Gestapo to deliver six German men to a concentration camp and to consign two Polish women to a "public house" (i.e., a brothel; circular from Deputy Gauleiter Kurt Schmalz, April 19, 1941, APP 834/2, 23. In January 1942, Damzog argued for even tougher sanctions against Polish women accused of sexual intercourse with Germans. It was claimed that they pursued such sexual contact because they understood the severity of the punishment for Germans and could destroy their lives with sexual contact. By effectively declaring such women to be instruments in the ethnonational struggle, it was then possible to also demand longer prison sentences for them (Damzog to Reich Security Main Office, January 17, 1942, AGK 167/15, 5–9).

377. And not only in Poland; see Mühlhäuser, *Eroberungen*.

378. Coulon's report on the status of the ethnonationality unit's work as of February 1, 1941, and its continuation in the coming months, dated February 4, 1941, APP 406/1109, 305–11. See also Greiser's order of September 25, 1940, reprinted in Łuczak, *Położenie ludności polskiej*, 180–82.

379. Coulon's report on the status of the ethnonationality unit's work as of February 1, 1941, and its continuation in the coming months, dated February 4, 1941, APP 406/1109, 305–11.

380. Ibid.

381. Report from representative of the Regierungspräsident of Bromberg, May 18, 1940, AGK NTN/199, 27–29.

382. Forster's decree on the re-Germanization campaign, December 14, 1940, BArch R 49/76, 2–29. On this, see also Madajczyk, *Okkupationspolitik Nazideutschlands*, 483–84.

383. Staff office of the Reich farmers' association head to Günther, September 9, 1940, quoted in Weisenburger, "Rassepapst," 193.

384. Forster to Pfundtner, undated, quoted in Spittler, *Das höhere Schulwesen*, 185. See also entry for May 12, 1942, in Picker, *Hitlers Tischgespräche*, 286.

385. Forster's decree on the re-Germanization campaign, December 14, 1940, BArch R 49/76, 2–29 (emphasis in original).

386. Ibid. (emphasis in original).

387. Ibid.

388. Ibid.

389. See Himmler's ethnonationality decree (September 12, 1940, BArch NS 19/3979, 29–33, reprinted in Pospieszalski, *Hitlerowskie "prawo" okupacyjne*, 114–18) for the relevant provision, which was then included in the Reich Interior Ministry's draft proposal of October 31, 1940.

390. Forster's decree on the re-Germanization campaign, December 14, 1940, BArch R 49/76, 2–29 (emphasis in original).

391. Ibid.

392. Each commission also included the local Landrat, his designated clerk for ethnonationality questions, an agent of the RKFDV, a representative of the occupational body relevant to the candidate, and a physician from the Gau health department (ibid.).

393. Forster's decree on the re-Germanization campaign, December 14, 1940, BArch R 49/76, 2–29.

394. Ibid.

395. Bracht to the HSSPF and Oberpräsident in Breslau, Regierungspräsidents, Gauleiters' offices, etc., undated, APK 119/10702, 74–76. It must date from 1941, for it was attached to general directive 1/41 from the RKFDV appointee in Silesia. Furthermore, Bracht signed as Deputy Gauleiter, meaning it must have been sent in January 1941, before the province was formally divided at the end of January 1941 and he officially became Gauleiter and Oberpräsident of Upper Silesia.

396. Bracht to the HSSPF and Oberpräsident in Breslau, Regierungspräsidents, Gauleiter's offices, etc., undated (probably January 1941), APK 119/10702, 74–76.

397. Bachmann to Reich Interior Ministry, January 29, 1941, APK 119/10687, 14.

398. Oppeln division of Reich Railroad to Regierungspräsident's offices in Kattowitz, January 27, 1941, APK 119/10687, 12.

399. Bachmann to Reich Interior Ministry, January 29, 1941, APK 119/10687, 14.

400. On Schmelt's organization, which was unparalleled in occupied Poland, see Steinbacher, *Musterstadt Auschwitz*, 138–53.

401. Bracht's general directive 1/41, undated (probably late January 1941), APK 117/116, 104–6. Remarkably, Bracht signed this order in his role as RKFDV appointee. He might have done so because his official title was still only Deputy Gauleiter at that point, leaving him no alternative but to use the appointment received from Himmler just a few months earlier.

402. Ibid.

403. Ibid. The assessment committee also included the relevant Landrat, a representative of the local RKFDV field office, one from the local SD, and two local "Volksdeutsche." Except for the RKFDV field office representative, Bracht's specifications here corresponded to the Reich Interior Ministry's draft proposal.

404. Ibid.

405. Springorum to Landrats, Oberbürgermeisters, and chiefs of police, April 10, 1941, APK 117/116, 102.

5 Labor Deployment

Population Policy as a Tool of Exploitation and Assimilation

Forced Laborers for the Reich

Germany's invasion of the Soviet Union marked a decisive break in the history of World War II. The Reich's rapid mobilization of even its last human and material reserves would come to affect all policy spheres, which became increasingly subordinated to the needs of the war front. I will show how this also applied to the Nazi regime's population policy in Poland. As with the de facto collapse of the third short-term plan because of war preparations, the clogging of rail arteries by the Wehrmacht from March 1941 on also meant the practical end of deportations into the General Government. To the relevant administrators, the halt to deportation initially looked like just another bottleneck, and certainly not like the closing down of the deportation policy, which, after all, was a central pillar of Germanization policy, alongside the settling of ethnic Germans and the assimilation of certain parts of the local populace. But by the turn of 1941–42, it had become clear that their perception was false. The functional needs of power in the war against the Soviet Union quickly led to a radical reorientation of population policies in the annexed territories as well, transforming the deportations from a tool of Germanization policy into a tool of labor-market policy. The German occupiers did not stop expelling Poles from their homelands, but instead of traveling eastward into the General Government, they now traveled westward for labor deployment in the Reich. This arrangement would remain the same until Germany's final capitulation. In the annexed provinces, the regime's Germanization policy, and more generally its population policy, remained a variable dependent on the immediate demands placed on the Reich by the war.

The Failure of the Racial Appraisals

The preparations for the attack on the Soviet Union also forced the UWZs to suspend a pilot project that had not only extended the influence of the SS apparatus into yet another policy field, but also seemed to demonstrate the practicability of a policy motivated by racially dystopian visions: the racial selection of workers to be transported into the Reich. As I have shown, the UWZ had tried to monopolize the procurement of forced laborers for transport into the Reich at the start of the second short-range plan, arguing that the only viable candidates were either "re-Germanizable persons" to be settled there permanently or "migrant workers" to be deployed there temporarily as "racially harmless," single, unmarried persons. But the SS suitability assessors had generally approved no more than 10 percent of deportees for forced labor inside the Reich, thereby artificially restricting access to urgently needed workers.

According to Göring's instructions of January 29, 1941, "the concerns of population policy and racial policy" were henceforth to be "pushed into the background" when it came to labor-market policy.[1] On top of that, the occupation administrations in the annexed territories received a directive soon thereafter for another 250,000 farmworkers to be sent into the Reich in short order.[2] As a result, the racial selection procedure also collapsed. Krumey admitted to Ehlich on February 25, 1941, that the existing practice had failed. As an alternative, he suggested giving up the racial appraisals and henceforth diverting entire families actually earmarked for the General Government into the Reich instead. Otherwise, transports of persons already assigned to Sections C and D of the DVL, meaning "Polonized Germans" and "renegades," could begin.[3] Although this was exactly what Himmler had demanded in his ethnonationality decree of September 1940, it had always been impossible to implement. In the past, whenever plans in this direction had threatened to become more concrete, the Gauleiters had always pointed to the great unrest that such an action would necessarily provoke among the local populace; furthermore, the Gauleiters made their consent to such removals conditional on an explicit requirement, namely that removals could happen only in the context of a population exchange, in other words, with Germans taking their place.[4]

For the UWZ in Posen, the breaking point came shortly thereafter with a demand from the Reich Labor Ministry calling for the speedy recruitment of four thousand workers. Höppner informed Kendzia, head of the labor department at the Reichsstatthalter's offices, that "Polish families, as 'P' Poles, could go for labor deployments only through Litzmannstadt" and learned from the latter that the Reich Labor Ministry ostensibly knew nothing about this requirement.[5] After that, Höppner told Bruno Müller, an employee of Ehlich, that this requirement probably could not be maintained any longer.[6] A few employment offices had already begun sending forced laborers directly into the Reich, because the UWZ itself seemed unable to supply the four thousand forced laborers requested. The Reich Security Main Office then made an unambiguous pronouncement at the end of March, instructing Höppner to permit the employment offices to conduct direct transports into the Reich as well.[7] The UWZ insisted on receiving at least a list of the people transported directly so that they could be registered and later deported into the General Government after their labor deployment was finished. Höppner also took it on himself to get the rest of the Wartheland's SS apparatus to commit to this new course of action.[8] A commitment seemed particularly necessary with the Race and Settlement Main Office (*Rasse- und Siedlungshauptamt,* or RuSHA) field office in Litzmannstadt. Having been a proponent of racial appraisals in the past, Höppner now advocated compliance with the new regulations. Although the capitulation might be "regretted by everyone on racial and ethnonational grounds," it had to be "simply put up with during the Reich's current predicament regarding the shortage of workers."[9]

As a result, other methods were exploited in fulfilling the Reich's demand for forced laborers. In issuing an urgent order for a "combing campaign" ("Auskämm-Aktion"), Kendzia demanded that county farmers' associations start by listing the supposedly superfluous Polish workers on all farms over twenty-five hectares (just under sixty-two acres). They were to be rounded up in April 1941. After that, all the smaller farms were also to be scoured. For the first time, it was not only the unmarried who were to be transported into the Reich for forced labor, but also "usable families"—with "usability" no longer referring to "racial suitability," but solely to work fitness.[10]

The change of plans marked the defeat of a project that the SS apparatus had hoped would show the way. The disappointment lay not only in the failure to extend its own influence into a key area like labor recruitment. It lay also in the failure to prove the workability of a "Lebensraum" plan that operated according to racial criteria. It was realized early on that the systematic transport of foreigners for forced labor, as made necessary by the war economy, would bring the relevant political actors into a head-on collision with Nazi ideology. And repeated protests did emerge in the subsequent months, particularly from within the party itself. As a result, racial appraisals must have seemed like a magic bullet to the SS apparatus, for they promised to close the ever-widening gap between ideological agenda and political practice while also expanding the SS sphere of action. The introduction of racial appraisals promised to the German economy at least a restricted continuation of labor recruitment and furthermore took into consideration the loudly professed ideological misgivings of Nazi hardliners. After all, such appraisals were supposed to ensure that Poles sent into the Reich were only those who were, to some extent, "racially equivalent," and thus assimilable and did not represent a racial threat to the German "Volksgemeinschaft." Furthermore, transporting assimilable Poles would also facilitate a "weakening of Polishdom" (as Ehlich wrote in the long-range plan), in that it was "primarily . . . racially good Poles" who would be removed from the local populace.[11]

In this context, the forced abandonment of racial appraisals represented a major defeat, thereby threatening to undermine the vision propagated by a racially oriented "Lebensraum" policy. As I have shown, the period immediately after the conquest of Poland saw the SS already failing in its demand to have the entire Polish populace subjected to racial appraisals as soon as possible. Instead, it was necessary to settle for a minimal program of racial selections applied to those destined for deportation into the Reich. And, after less than a year, the war's increasing radicalization by the Nazi leadership was robbing the SS complex of even this partial success.

The defeat would prove indicative of the subsequent course of SS Germanization policy in the annexed eastern territories, one that repeated itself in adjacent policy spheres, such as in the attempt to impose racial appraisals on the members of the DVL. Here, too, the proponents of a more pragmatic course would prevail. As the SS ethnocrats were forced to recognize, the realization of racially based dystopian visions in political practice would always meet with stiff political resistance whenever it proved dysfunctional for the maintenance of power, that is to say, a threat to the functioning of policy areas necessary for the regime's survival.

Third Short-Range Plan, Part Two: Attempts at Compromise

The halt to forced deportation did not mean an end to expulsions in general, for it was only eastbound deportations that were initially prohibited. In fact, with the "combing campaign" of April 1941, the transport of Polish forced laborers continued in even greater numbers—only with people taken westward into the Reich. The causal link between Germanization policy and population policy was broken, and the latter was now forced to serve the economic logic of a country at war.

In order to decide on the question of how the further settling of ethnic Germans from Eastern Europe was to be secured under these conditions, Greifelt issued urgent invitations to attend a conference in Berlin on March 19, 1941. As before, the primary goal was to move ethnic Germans out of resettlement camps and into homes of their own—but now, it was even more important to consider the needs of the war economy. In essence, Greifelt committed the attendees to two main strategies. First, it was necessary to reduce the number of ethnic Germans who were still living in camps within the Reich but were actually destined for the annexed eastern provinces. Transporting them eastward was currently impossible anyway, for the Reich Transport Ministry had cut off the SS from the trains needed for this task as well. Therefore, work assignments in the Reich would no longer be limited to persons who had received from the EWZ an "A Notice" ("A-Bescheid," short for *Altreich* or "Old Reich"), which meant they were considered unsuitable for settlement in the eastern territories. Such work assignments would now be given to recipients of an "O Notice" ("O-Bescheid," short for *Osten* or "East decision") as well, meaning to persons actually earmarked for settlement in the annexed territories—and so economic policy trumped Germanization policy.[12] Second, Greifelt tried to loosen or entirely abolish the remaining provisions that restrained the settlement of ethnic Germans in the eastern provinces. With the first-order settlement zone already scrapped in every province, there was now a weakening of the regulation that reserved 60 percent of available settlement lands for allotment to soldiers after the final victory. Furthermore, each incoming settler would now receive considerably less land so that the remaining unassigned lands could accommodate a greater number of newcomers. But the overriding question was a different one: What would happen with the expelled Polish populace? For this too, Greifelt had answers at hand. These people would either be "displaced" (here using the new term "verdrängt") into the homes of other Poles within the province, be interned in "Polish camps," or be transported as forced laborers into the Reich.[13]

Greifelt's setting of priorities met with support in the provinces. A few days before the meeting in Berlin, similar conclusions had been reached in Upper Silesia. Arlt was certainly in favor of removing "Jews and non-able-bodied living ballast [Ballastexistenzen]," but he nonetheless wanted to ensure that the broader expulsions would not deprive the occupiers of an indispensable workforce. It was for this reason that he proposed the establishment of "reservations for Fremdvölkische . . . near planned industrial sites" wherever it was still impossible to forego the use of Polish workers.[14] This particularly applied to the area around Auschwitz, which the occupiers were expanding into a major industrial center.[15]

The other two provinces followed suit with similar ideas. On March 27, 1941, the HSSPF (Höherer SS- und Polizeiführer, Higher SS and police leader) in Posen had likewise ordered that the settlement of ethnic Germans was to continue under all circumstances. Able-bodied Poles were to be immediately deported into the Reich, with all others consigned to UWZ camps.[16] In contrast, the change of plans required a much greater organizational effort on the part of deportation authorities in Danzig–West Prussia. Dispossessed farmers were assigned to work as laborers on "German" farms or as a *Deputant* (a kind of indentured farmhand) on estates in the province's formerly East Prussian territories, but dispossessed urban families were threatened with separation by force. Because the UWZ in Danzig–West Prussia did not maintain an extensive camp system like the one in the Wartheland, such families were to be torn apart, with women and children lodged in the dwellings of other Polish families and able-bodied men interned in the labor camp at Thorn. The greater part of each man's wages was to be paid not directly to him but instead to his family so that the latter would not burden the German welfare system.[17] The expulsions—or in the jargon of the occupiers, "displacements"—for accommodating ethnic Germans from Bukovina and Bessarabia began in all provinces in late May 1941.

But just before that, a confrontation had taken place between Greiser and the relevant SS agencies, one that was symptomatic of Nazi population policy in Poland at the time. After the "combing campaign" of April 1941, Greiser had evidently decided that under no circumstances were any more Polish workers to be lost, and so he issued a prohibition of the further removal of able-bodied Poles from the Wartheland on May 10, 1941.[18] With Greiser's order, a paradigm reversal had been completed by the civil administration of the Wartheland, the province that had been the focus of Nazi population policy up to then; faced with the dilemma of choosing between accelerated Germanization and the safeguarding of local economic strength, Greiser had chosen the latter.

For the SS apparatus, the reorientation complicated an already difficult situation. If it had still been hoped that, with the suspension of deportations into the General Government, some of those expelled from their properties could now be transported to the Reich for forced labor, Greiser's move had forced a reevaluation. It was no longer enough for the SS Task Forces to simply submit lists to the UWZ specifying the families whose accommodations were needed for the settling of ethnic Germans. With Greiser's prohibition, the UWZ would now accept such lists only if the SS Task Forces had also specified for each family an alternative home nearby so that the local economy could keep its workforce. It was only then that the UWZ was able to assess whether the relevant families could be evicted at all before organizing the approved evictions.

The applied criteria had not fundamentally changed from those used in the deportations of February and March that year, and deportations still targeted those whose dwellings or farms could be used for ethnic Germans, as long as the current residents did not have relatives in the Reich or the Wehrmacht and were not "Deutschstämmige" or economically irreplaceable.[19] But here too, it seems that the criteria underwent a certain loosening: under the constantly growing pressure to accommodate the ethnic Germans still sitting in camps, the SS Task Forces were demanding the renewed assessment of families that had already been exempted from deportation. New deportations from among them would ultimately "free up" more farms for the settling of ethnic Germans from Bessarabia, according to Heinz Hochland, head of the UWZ field office in Kolmar (today Chodzież).[20]

Besides approving the submitted expulsion lists, the UWZ was still responsible for organizing the overall process, including requests for police deployments and the necessary transportation and the facilitation of selection activities by RuSHA and the employment office. But the SS suitability assessors were now limited to performing the "rough selection" of "re-Germanizable persons." The selection of able-bodied individuals (including those destined for transport into the Reich) was now under the exclusive responsibility of employment office representatives.

* * *

As I have already discussed, the prohibition on deportations also had consequences for the UWZ selection criteria. With the shortage of accommodations worsening with each additional wave of incoming settlers, the expulsions were suddenly extending to residents who had been exempted during earlier assessments, including "Deutschstämmige." A possible solution was suggested by Krumey as early as March 1941, when he broached the idea of establishing a gigantic "Polish reservation" ("Polenreservat") intended as an alternative deportation destination within the Wartheland instead of the General Government.[21] This suggestion was brought up again in May, when the Reichsstatthalter's offices asked the SS Settlement Staffs to find a contained area for the "creation of so-called Polish reservations."[22] But then, on May 12, 1941, this discussion was temporarily suspended in favor of forcibly lodging Christian Poles with other Polish families.[23] It is nonetheless of particular interest for two reasons. For one, because the halt to deportations was never lifted, the discussion was taken up again in the following year and did in fact lead to the establishment of "Polish reservations." For another, it also included talk of creating an enormous "Jewish reservation," intended to hold three hundred thousand Jewish Poles. It was in this context that Höppner wrote to Eichmann his infamous letter of July 16, 1941, telling him about an idea then under consideration at the Reichsstatthalter's offices, about whether the "most humane solution" before the onset of winter might be to "deal with the Jews unfit for labor through some fast-acting means."[24]

With the prohibition on deportations, the SS Task Forces often fell back on a different solution, simply ejecting undesired persons from their homes in unauthorized actions.[25] This action led to constant conflicts between the relevant German agencies, particularly involving repeated accusations that "Deutschstämmige" had also been subject to such treatment.

Such conflicts were certainly not limited to the Wartheland. In Danzig–West Prussia, one of the first confrontations emerged when the Landrat of Briesen County complained to his superior, the Regierungspräsident of Marienwerder, that the SS had taken away people he considered Germans and had wanted to register in the DVL. The Regierungspräsident then demanded that the Landrats be allowed more participation, including veto rights, in the preparation of deportation lists.[26] Meanwhile, in Upper Silesia, similar conflicts led to an open war of words, with the Landrats of Saybusch and Bielitz, and thus of counties at the heart of settlement efforts, attacking the responsible parties at the RKFDV branch office with accusations of "complete failure." It seems that the situation had escalated to the point that Bracht's deputy, Vice Oberpräsident Dr. Hans Karl Faust, found it necessary to intervene, paying a personal visit to work out a division of responsibilities that both sides could accept.[27]

But in the Wartheland, such conflicts became a regular accompaniment to the expulsions. Tasked with ensuring that the selection criteria were observed in the expulsion of local residents, the UWZ often found itself confronted by an alliance of local officials and SS Task Forces, who had very different motives in wanting to evict particular families.[28] Fears of a veto because, for example, the UWZ might consider the relevant family "Deutschstämmige," often led to abrupt unilateral expulsions. In fact, it was not very difficult to evade the control of the responsible UWZ field offices—after all, they were staffed by just three men on average and were generally responsible for three or four counties each.[29]

Such conflicts were multiplying, which is why they were put on the agenda of a conference in Schrimm on August 14, 1941, chaired by Koppe and attended by the SS Settlement Staff of Posen, its SS Task Forces, and the UWZ. The conference is particularly significant because the assembled SS deportation experts were also told about the future goals of German population policy. The head of the UWZ field office at Kolmar, Heinz Hochland, recorded the latest version of Berlin's fantastical planning in his own handwriting. Under the heading "future tasks" there was mention of deporting Poles from the Wartheland; but beyond that, there was also the "evacuation of Poles from the Gen. Gov., followed by settling of Germans," and the "solution of the Jewish question in Europe—UWZ, SS Group Leader Heydrich."[30] With this, the attendees were quite up to date, for it had only been July 31, 1941, when Heydrich had been empowered by Göring "to undertake, by emigration or evacuation, a solution of the Jewish question," thereby making "all necessary preparations . . . for a complete solution of the Jewish question in the German sphere of influence in Europe."[31] It can thus not be ruled out that, as Browning claims, Göring's message was seen in Berlin as a "'charter' to draw up a 'feasibility study' for the mass murder of European Jewry."[32] It is more likely, however, that even in Berlin the terms "emigration" and "evacuation" had not yet transformed into code words for mass murder. In any case, Hochland understood this passage as announcing yet another deportation wave, one that his office would also have to deal with.

In light of this megalomaniacal agenda, it is little wonder that Höppner and Krumey were not very successful in the pursuit of their actual interests, namely ensuring that the SS Task Forces adhered to the applicable guidelines. In this context, Koppe was clearly plagued by other worries. From his perspective, the all-important question was probably not the avoidance of wrongful expulsions, but rather how the deportations could be resumed at all, to prevent the population policy program from becoming entirely fictional. It was here that the SS Settlement Staffs served him as leverage. He therefore had little patience for any provisions that would limit their activities, and even less so as the situation from his perspective dramatically worsened in September and October 1941: on top of the need to accommodate some thirty thousand ethnic Germans from Bessarabia and Bukovina who still waited in the camps, Hitler had decided he could no longer wait until the end of the war to begin deporting Jews from the Reich, so that twenty thousand were now to be taken to the ghetto in Litzmannstadt. Even if I do not share Götz Aly's assertion that the deportation of Jewish Germans and

Austrians directly affected settlement policy, in that they did not actually use up any valuable living space while inside a ghetto, Aly is certainly correct in stating that this "self-created pressure" had a direct effect in radicalizing anti-Jewish policy in the region and also led to the establishment of the first German extermination camp, at Kulmhof.[33] It was against this backdrop that Koppe believed the SS Settlement Staffs should be granted maximum freedom of action: at a conference on settling the ethnic Germans, he called on the assembled members of the SS Task Forces to act "like the pike in the carp pond, a constantly roiling element," and to "keep under pressure all the agencies involved with the settlement efforts."[34]

Thus, the RKFDV branch offices, locally entrusted with the settlement of ethnic Germans, certainly knew what they were doing when, in the Wartheland, they flouted the racial selection criteria of the UWZ with Koppe's tacit backing, and when, in Danzig–West Prussia, they evicted people who had actually been earmarked by local party agencies for enrollment in the DVL. But this could only be a pyrrhic victory, as was apparently clear to the head office in Berlin, which had since been transformed into the Staff Main Office of the RKFDV (Stabshauptamt des Reichskommissars für die Festigung deutschen Volkstums).[35] Such actions, which steadily produced more and more potential for conflict, promised at most a short-term remedy, without fundamentally resolving the central problem posed by the worsening shortage of usable accommodations. On September 2, 1941, Greifelt described the catastrophic situation to Heydrich: the ongoing "herding together" of the Polish populace was encountering difficulties and thereby preventing the further settling of ethnic Germans, who were now increasingly assigned to go work in industry, even if they were actually farmers. The situation was depriving the Germanization project of its human resources, which is why Greifelt asked for an "investigation of the possibilities of resuming the evacuations of Poles in the incorporated territories."[36]

A highly revealing answer came a few weeks later from Eichmann. He informed the Staff Main Office of the RKFDV that a resumption of the deportations of Poles and Jews was not to be expected for now because there were still no "possibilities for reception" available. But in this regard, he also touched on his "efforts to find another territory as an interim alternative for the reception of evacuated contingents, with thoughts turning to the occupied Soviet Russian territories." But even here, one needed to "wait for a better transport situation."[37] Eichmann's answer points once again to the impasse into which Nazi population policy had now maneuvered itself. Unwilling to abandon their megalomaniacal plans in principle, the occupiers had bet everything on a single outcome, namely, the speedy conquest of the Soviet Union—and this also applied to their Germanization policy. But his answer also underlines how, after the Madagascar Plan, the Reich Security Main Office had ultimately returned to a deportation policy that was "integrated" in making no differentiation between removing Jews and removing Poles—a link that is often lost, particularly in studies of the Shoah.[38]

The Reich Security Main Office was so sure of the Red Army's imminent collapse in August 1941 that Eichmann tasked Höppner with submitting proposals for reorganizing the UWZs so that they would be ready to start with large-scale mass deportations, a project that had already been postponed repeatedly. Or, as Höppner put it, "After the end of the war, in the various territorial regions newly coming into Germany's possession, there will need to take place a large-scale evacuation of population segments that are undesired for the Greater German Reich. This is not only about the final solution of the Jewish question, which beyond the Greater German Reich will also cover all states under German influence, but above all about the evacuation from German settlement space of those members of primarily eastern and southeastern peoples who are racially incapable of Germanizing back."[39]

Höppner envisaged a massive expansion of the expulsion apparatus, one in which the UWZ would form its own Departmental Group (*Amtsgruppe*) directly under Department IV at the Reich Security Main Office and would need to establish field offices not only in the "sending territories" but also in the "receiving territories." The latter seem to have particularly stimulated Höppner's fantasies, in which he imagined them as *great spaces in the current Soviet Russia . . . entirely subordinated to the administration of the Chief of the Security Policy and the SD, or at least to that of the Reichführer of the SS.*"[40] The only thing left to clarify would be one last fundamental policy question: "Otherwise, the main thing is to have complete clarity from the very start about what is now to ultimately happen with these evacuated Volk segments not desired for the Greater German settlement spaces, whether the goal is to secure them some kind of life on a permanent basis, or whether they should be entirely eradicated."[41] Höppner's ideas here exemplify the extraordinary delusions of grandeur among German ethnocrats, for whom past failures had only strengthened their convictions that violence was the only way to achieve the goals they set for themselves and whose readiness for violence increased as the boundaries of the "German Lebensraum" project were steadily expanded with each German advance. Höppner had already distinguished himself in the past with his particularly monstrous proposals, such as the one concerning the mass murder of Wartheland Jews who were unfit for labor. And now he was opening for discussion the murder of all other "Volk segments not desired." As Marczewski correctly points out, Höppner's proposal by implication included the Polish populace for extermination as well.[42]

The Red Army ended such euphoric expectancy during the next two months.[43] In late 1941, the ethnocrats were also forced to acknowledge the disappointing results of their expulsion policy. Measured against the targets set during Heydrich's conference of January 8, 1941, by the end of 1941 the third short-range plan had proved to be an even bigger failure than all previous efforts. Instead of settling some 150,000 ethnic Germans as expected, the occupiers had managed to move only around 90,000 from the camps into new homes.[44] But to appreciate the full extent of the failure, it is necessary to also consider the deportation figures: whereas the intention from January to deport 831,000 people from the annexed eastern territories was still active, by the end of the year, the various UWZ branches were able to report the expulsion of "only" 177,758.[45] But of these people, 119,816 were not deported over the border but instead "displaced" within the province, while another 17,223 were transported not into the east but instead into the Reich as forced laborers. The approximately 50,000 people who were deported in the General Government must have disappointed the "German Lebensraum" planners in two ways at once, for this number was dramatically lower than the self-appointed deportation target and the General Government itself was now supposed to be Germanized as well.

The Extended Third Short-Range Plan: Final Collapse of the Circular Flow of Resettlement

As Adam Tooze convincingly argues, Germany's invasion of the Soviet Union was a go-for-broke gamble from the very start in that the Wehrmacht leaders had bet everything on a quick and complete obliteration of the Red Army. But if the Soviet Union should fail to collapse under this first assault, then the Reich would have to sustain a war that would logistically disadvantage the Wehrmacht with its increasing distance from its own supply bases and simultaneously overwhelm Germany's war economy.[46] At first, the Wehrmacht's plans seemed to be succeeding, just as in Poland and France. But the assurance of victory was soon shattered after the first few weeks as the Red Army inflicted the first painful defeats on the German troops.

The failure of its Blitzkrieg strategy forced the Reich into a fundamental reorientation. For the ethnocrats, although certainly accustomed to setbacks and postponements, this development signified a catastrophe of entirely new proportions: it was clear that the German economy would now exert even more pressure on ethnopolicy, pushing for its coordination with the worsening labor shortage. Furthermore, Nazi population policy was faced with a general gridlock for the first time: there was simply no destination territory for deportation available to the UWZs.

As a result, the end of 1941 saw the population planners in Berlin confronted with a structural dilemma that could no longer be resolved with the strategies employed thus far. Then, in January 1942, Heydrich hosted yet another conference, but in contrast to those of the previous two years, this meeting was not about coordinating settlement and deportation policy: for the moment, it appeared that practical policy measures would be incapable of bridging the gap between the real-world problems in the annexed territories and the megalomaniacal visions of Generalplan Ost. This was not true of every area of Nazi Germanization policy, however. Although the lack of victory over the Soviet Union had buried all hopes of acquiring a new destination for deportations, and thus of continuing the regime's deportation policy in the near future, the occupiers were only partially willing to accept the consequences. This applied not so much to the undesired Polish "Fremdvölkische." Already because of their numbers alone, it was clear that with these people—as well as the Russians and other peoples, as conceded by the authors of the RKFDV master plans—a solution was needed for the moment that would not further threaten German control of the relevant territories, either in security or in economic production. Such care was not considered necessary in the case of the Jews, however, which is why Ulrich Herbert's analysis, as also taken up recently by Tooze, seems highly plausible. In Herbert's view, it was this forced compromise, that is in regard to the treatment of the non-Jewish population, that opened up the possibilities for radicalizing antisemitic policy in the first place, up to and including systematic mass murder. The seemingly inexhaustible reservoir of Eastern Europeans for forced labor allowed for a devaluation of the Jewish workforce—according to this logic, the Jews, in fact, became "superfluous." The imperatives dictated by the rational demands of power, which had imposed certain limits on the German leadership in their treatment of at least certain segments of Eastern Europe's non-Jewish populace, did not apply to the Jews.[47]

Going beyond Herbert, I would argue that the abandonment of large-scale deportations was not only a precondition enabling the possibility of mass murder, meaning it was not only the framework within which antisemitic ideology could acquire practical shape, but was also a factor directly affecting the radicalization process itself. Although this interpretation cannot be directly derived from the statements of the perpetrators themselves, it can be deduced from the logic of their behavior. One can assume that with the failures in Germanization policy through January 1942, the responsible officials felt additional pressure to report some "progress," at least in certain subdomains. It thus would not be surprising that this pressure would particularly radicalize actions against the Jews even more—and not only because the regime's antisemitic policy at that point had already crossed the line into systematic mass murder, but also because a further radicalization in this policy area would provoke fewer conflicts between Nazi Germany's various power centers, and progress toward a "final solution to the Jewish question" could certainly be reported as a major victory. Of course, this situation does not fully explain the radicalization of antisemitic policy, but it certainly did contribute to the dynamic of failure that helped drive the decision-making process toward mass murder.

Therefore, the conference chaired by Heydrich on January 20, 1942, is also to be situated within the broader context of creating "German Lebensraum"—although the goal now was both broader and narrower than at the two previous conferences. At what became infamously known as the Wannsee Conference, it was once again the dystopian vision of the "German Lebensraum" that provided the central motif. It was no longer about trying to coordinate the general deportation of all Jews and "Fremdvölkische" from the Reich and the annexed and occupied eastern territories, but solely about the "evacuation of the Jews toward the east"—where "evacuation" was indeed most likely a code word for planned mass murder.[48] Thus, although the Wannsee Conference represented a decisive break, and one that had been, as Höppner wrote in his memorandum on the future of the UWZ, previously unforeseeable, namely the definitive separation of anti-Jewish policy from anti-Polish policy, it is nonetheless to be situated within the broader context of the violent population policy measures that are the focus of this book's analysis. The break was most obvious in the Wartheland and was particularly well illustrated by two contrasting ways that the ethnocrats responded to the suspension of deportations: although the Christian owners of homes needed for ethnic Germans were "displaced" within the province, the Litzmannstadt ghetto's imminent overcrowding problem in late 1941 was "solved" by the establishment of the first extermination camp, at nearby Kulmhof. Since the ideologically ordained deportation of the Polish populace was precluded by economic and security-related necessities, the occupiers struck out against the Jews even more radically.[49]

*   *   *

From 1942 on, the ongoing prohibition on deportations and, more important, the dependence on Polish labor would make all further attempts at better coordinating settlement and expulsion policies in the annexed territories even more difficult. A provincial patchwork predominated.

At the highest political levels, the power balance shifted between the various central institutions. Where the centralization of deportation policy had once allowed the Reich Security Main Office to successfully occupy a key area of population policy and thereby become the dominant player within the SS apparatus, the suspension of deportations now meant a relative loss of influence. The switch to "displacements" meant there was no longer a need for a universal procedure across provincial boundaries, because the general rule was for affected persons to be forcibly lodged with other Poles within the same county. A related consequence was that the Staff Main Office of the RKFDV became increasingly important in the following years. After all, the need to accommodate ethnic Germans was still unfulfilled and, in addition to those who waited in camps all over the Reich, refugees soon came fleeing the war as the front line began retreating in 1943.

The shift in power was also clearly reflected in the emergence of another player: the labor deployment administration, in the form of the General Plenipotentiary for Labor Deployment (Generalbevollmächtigter für den Arbeitseinsatz). The Reich Labor Ministry had asserted its presence from the very beginning, but its demands for Polish forced laborers had long lacked the power to decisively influence policymaking. With Germany's invasion of the Soviet Union, however, the demands of the labor deployment authorities acquired more weight and could no longer be sidestepped by the SS complex and various territorial heads. Nazi population policy in the annexed eastern provinces would not come to an end until Germany's surrender, but after 1941, it would no longer be solely a Germanization policy in every aspect. Nowhere was the shift clearer than in deportation policy. The removal of the local populace was no longer aimed at creating "German Lebensraum in the east," but was now yielding instead the exact opposite effect: a growing population of undesired "Fremdvölkische" in the heartland of the Reich itself.

These shifts on the level of the central authorities also had consequences for the apparatus implementing population policy on the ground, especially as the waning of the settlement work was further hastened by the Wehrmacht's constantly growing demands for personnel. Staffing reductions, consolidations, and finally closures of individual bureaus affected first the most numerous units of the RKFDV branch offices, meaning above all the SS Settlement Staffs and their subordinated SS Task Forces. But even the Reich Security Main Office's UWZs, which had much less personnel, were destined to suffer a similar fate, especially because their role as a selection body had been further reduced by the introduction of the DVL in all eastern provinces.

This turning point in population policy had already been presaged in 1941. Even before the ethnocrats in the annexed eastern provinces could present any plans for the coming year, Göring informed them of a change in priorities. On the same day as Hitler's decree of January 10, 1942, which launched a paradigm shift in Germany's armaments industry with its reorientation from a Blitzkrieg to a war of attrition, Göring ordered a centralization of labor deployment under the Four Year Plan's Labor Deployment Affairs Group (Geschäftsgruppe Arbeitseinsatz)—an intermediate step before the appointment of Fritz Sauckel, Gauleiter of Thuringia, to become General Plenipotentiary for Labor Deployment in March 1942.[50] Göring's decree declared that "the critical production of armaments . . . as well as agriculture must be supplied with the urgently needed workforce."[51] The Staff Main Office of the RKFDV quite reasonably interpreted this to also mean "stopping all measures that are likely to disrupt war-oriented manufacturing or agricultural work."[52]

From Berlin's viewpoint, the annexed eastern provinces were not all equally suitable for the recruitment of forced laborers. At least during the war's latter half,

Upper Silesia was largely spared from such demands because of the importance of its local heavy industry; meanwhile, the labor transports in Danzig–West Prussia were transacted within its own provincial boundaries. There, forced laborers were generally sent to go work in the counties of Marienwerder Governmental Region that had already been part of Germany's territory even before the invasion. In contrast, Greiser was confronted by a demand from the Labor Deployment Affairs Group around the end of January 1942 calling for the surrender of twenty thousand farmworkers within the shortest of time frames—a number that was doubled to forty thousand in early March.[53]

If the ethnocrats at the UWZ still nursed any hopes that the coming year might yet allow them to follow up on the deportations of the past, they were shattered for good by the Labor Deployment Affairs Group. What emerged instead was the "extended third short-range plan" ("erweiterter dritter Nahplan"), and despite the continuity suggested by its name, it had little in common with the previous deportations. The deportations under this short-range plan were limited to the Wartheland and were for the first time not intended to further the Germanization of the province but primarily to deliver the forced laborers demanded by the German war economy. The first preparatory meeting for these expulsions therefore took place not at an office of the SS Settlement Staff or the relevant UWZ, but in the labor department at the Reichsstatthalter's offices, on February 7, 1942. Because the last "combing campaign" had already rounded up all the Polish farmworkers who were not considered indispensable, Kendzia believed that additional workers could be freed up only if the smaller farms were consolidated—in other words, if cultivation could be made more efficient. Furthermore—and this highlighted the severity of the situation—such consolidated operations were no longer automatically assigned to ethnic Germans, at least not if there were any doubts about their ability to successfully run them. With any doubt, they were to be handed over to the "best earlier Polish owners."[54] In that case, the SS complex was forced to accept the fact that the transport of "Fremdvölkische" to go work in the Reich had now been separated from settlement policy. Furthermore, it was no longer possible for the SS Settlement Staffs to simply commandeer the vacated farms for their own purposes. In line with these revised objectives, new selection criteria and procedures were drawn up in the following weeks. The individual SS Task Forces were instructed to contact their local representatives of "Ostland" (short for Ostdeutsche Landbewirtschaftungsgesellschaft, or East German Land Management Company) in order to draw up plans for land consolidation with them, before listing the people who were freed up as a result. To ensure that only potential "agricultural workers" would be expelled, the lists for the UWZ had to be compiled in collaboration with the relevant employment offices.[55]

The forced recruitment of Polish workers was launched on March 2 and continued until June 23, 1942. Variously known as the "field hand campaign" or

"Z farm campaign" ("Feldarbeiteraktion" or "Z-Hof-Aktion," with the later standing for "Zusammenlegung", "consolidation"), this project was itself plagued by many difficulties. Once again, the occupiers found that news of the expulsion campaigns had spread very quickly, with many residents fleeing before the German raiding parties could arrive, and even with the ones rounded up, many had to be released again.[56] In addition to those few selected as "re-Germanizable persons," those released were, for example, families in which either half the children were under ten years old and thus incapable of work, or where any child was under one year old. According to the instructions of the Reich Labor Ministry, such families could not be deported. According to Krumey's orders, however, if families had a child under one, along with at least one child over twelve, then the exception did not apply—after all, the older child could take care of the baby. And even if families did have multiple children under ten years of age, they should still be brought to Litzmannstadt, "because this is where enough unaccompanied youths are available who, if added to these families, would make them capable of work."[57]

Particular ire was directed at pregnant women, who could not be recruited by the employment offices. In Krumey's view, such women were not only using pregnancy to shirk their labor obligations, but also to help "strengthen their own Volk, and thereby obstruct the desired goal of bringing about a reduction in the Slavs through biological means."[58] This imagined threat scenario accused Polish women of using a higher birth rate to counter the biopolitical tools of oppression introduced by the occupiers, such as increasing the permissible marriage age. Equally suspicious were those women who had been deported to the Reich to perform forced labor and were now being sent back in increasing numbers because they were expecting a baby. In another report, Krumey urged his superiors "to remind the agencies within the Old Reich that the German state must be ready to use every means possible to prevent the unbridled propagation of racially useless Polishdom."[59] It is hardly surprising that those at the UWZ no longer balked at anything—after all, it was just last year that Höppner had discussed the use of mass murder to murder a portion of the Wartheland's Jews, and furthermore, the Kulmhof extermination camp, not far from Litzmannstadt, had already begun operations. Ending on a word that—certainly not by accident—recalled Höppner's infamous letter, Krumey suggested that the best course would be "in every case, regardless of whether in the Old Reich or the Wartheland, to call upon every pregnant Polish person up to eight-and-a-half months for the fullest labor deployment. The thereby potentially resulting pregnancy discontinuation and impairment are not only desired, but also anticipated, and bring with them, beyond the educational effect, also an easing of the coming tasks. Exercising the sternest of influence on a circumstance is, according to the iron laws of nature, always the most humane."[60] If a birth could not be prevented, then it ought to be considered "whether or not these children, under certain conditions, should be removed from the mothers after a certain period. Children of good blood could be accommodated in care homes, while the others would have to be subjected to a special treatment [Sonderbehandlung]. In my opinion, this would quickly dampen the eagerness for children among these Polish women."[61]

Equally excluded from transport to the Reich were individuals who were sick, weak, or unfit for travel. Their numbers were relatively high, probably also because many of the young men were already living in prisoner-of-war camps or had been rounded up during earlier "combing campaigns." But in order to improve the productivity of local agriculture, it was nonetheless decided that persons evicted from their land could no longer remain in their home locality, even if they proved unable to work anywhere at all. Ever since the deportation moratorium of March 1941, however, it was already the case that most dispossessed locals were now forcibly lodged with other Poles, which meant that the SS Task Forces soon ran out of substitute accommodation addresses as demanded by the UWZ. Instead, the previously discarded idea of a "Polish reservation" was brought up once again, and this time it was actually implemented.

After the selection of forced laborers for the Reich, the remaining persons were catalogued by the local employment office and, as determined by labor needs, assigned to their new home localities.[62] It was only in the counties of Kalisch, Ostrowo, Welungen, and Kempen that persons incapable of work were transported to a new "Polish reservation," erected at the intersection of these four counties, which were a major focus of the expulsion efforts. This strategy would allow for supervision with less personnel and enable "an ethnonational . . . separation" despite the ongoing deportation moratorium.[63] Furthermore, if the deportations resumed, the reservation would allow a quicker reaction and these people would be transported right away. But this expedient seemed advantageous in economic terms as well. For one thing, it created a reservoir of readily available workers. For another, it seemed to offer a way for the occupiers to improve their own food supply. With food rations—already meager—issued only with the performance of forced labor, the rest of the populace was left to scrape out a living from the small plots allotted to them for subsistence agriculture—and this in a region that had been selected because of its poor soil. For these people, the "Polish reservation" turned into starvation zones.[64]

The extent to which the labor-deployment authorities had become a dominant player in population policy is reflected in the figures submitted in the annual report of the Wartheland's UWZ. With the transport of 38,168 forced laborers into the Reich, the ethnocrats in the Wartheland had almost fulfilled the quota demanded of them by Berlin. In order to do so, the UWZ had to first round up 171,947 individuals (although the annual report on the extended third short-range plan does contain surprisingly glaring inconsistencies here). During a first selection round, around half of them (82,403 persons) were immediately excluded on the spot because of illness, incapacity to work, young children, or current occupation—and apparently not all of them were actually evicted from their properties. After that came a second selection round, in which the employment office was forced to reject another 33,723 for similar reasons.[65] In the end, 99,074 were driven from their farms in the Wartheland during 1942, meaning that almost half the evicted were transported into the Reich for forced labor.

These figures help illustrate the paradigm shift that Nazi deportation policy underwent. In a first phase up to and including the first short-range plan in late 1939, the persons deported (or murdered) were still primarily those who, for political reasons, could not be considered for the "German Volksgemeinschaft" that was to be established here, including members of anti-German nationalist parties or groups. With the increasing numbers of ethnic Germans arriving from Eastern Europe, the occupiers had no choice but to change the selection criteria so that from the intermediate plan to the third short-range plan, they primarily targeted persons whose homes were needed. For the responsible officials, the deideologization of the selection criteria was made easier to accept by the fact that the roundups were still advancing the Germanization of the province. It was precisely this aspect that changed with the extended third short-range plan. This represented the first time since the moratorium of March 1941 that large numbers of locals could be deported, but the removals were no longer part of "German Lebensraum" plans, for the selection of these people was guided solely by their capacity to work for the Reich. Nazi population policy had been shifted onto a radically different track, which would remain the same for the rest of the war. Faced with the choice of either pursuing the Germanization of the eastern provinces as before or limiting the potential political fallout by adjusting policy to better fit the altered war situation, the Nazis opted for the latter.

Dismantling the UWZs

The possibilities had meanwhile become quite narrow, which was particularly evident to the ethnocrats in the Wartheland. To be sure, the expulsion of local residents for the accommodation of ethnic Germans continued to play a certain role in 1942, when the number of "Volksdeutsche" assigned to confiscated homes and farms still amounted to 21,576 persons.[66] But this was only a third of the previous year's number and represented barely 10 percent of all ethnic Germans settled in the Wartheland to that date.[67] Furthermore, these settlement opportunities were largely a by-product of the forced labor recruitments, with the newcomers placed mostly on farms whose owners had either been transported as forced laborers or rounded up during the process. With little actual work to do, Krumey and a greater part of his staff were then transferred to the General Government in order to organize the expulsion of the non-German populace from the town and county of Zamość—a first systematic attempt to similarly change the General Government into "German Lebensraum."[68]

The situation was similar in the other two provinces, except that they did not send appreciable numbers of forced laborers into the Reich. The ethnocrats in Upper Silesia were able to declare that the number of expellees and of settled newcomers had almost doubled, but these figures amounted to "only" 33,061 and 81,330 persons, respectively.[69] But the situation in Danzig–West Prussia was even worse. Although the settling of another 20,194 ethnic Germans meant that the overall number had reached 51,358 persons and thus almost doubled there too, the expulsion figures were quite different: 61,166 persons in total had been either deported out of province or "displaced" inside it by the end of 1942, only 4,705 of these cases took place in 1942 itself, which was less than in any previous year.[70] In all three provinces, such trends would not allow a full Germanization in the foreseeable future.

But particularly vexing for the SS complex was that an alternative path existed for the civil administrations. This will be examined later in greater detail, but for now, a short mention of the situation in Upper Silesia will suffice. In that province, Bracht certainly had no reason to complain about the progress of Germanization in his province. Whereas the SS had managed, with great effort, to settle 33,061 ethnic Germans, the civil administration had already registered 1,005,719 "Germans" over the same period, representing nearly half the populace—and the DVL was not even finished yet.[71] As in the other annexed provinces, the main players in Upper Silesian Germanization policy were not, in fact, the agencies of the SS.

* * *

The expulsions were effectively suspended in Danzig–West Prussia and Upper Silesia by the end of 1942. Instead of settlement activities, the "focus" of operations for RKFDV bureaus was now "shifted toward distinctly supervisory work," according to a report from Upper Silesia.[72] It was only in the Wartheland that the UWZ found itself confronted by new demands: those of labor deployment administration. On February 18, 1943, Ministerial Director Dr. Max Timm, tasked with workforce procurement under Sauckel, wrote to the Wartheland's provincial employment office about the farms in northern France supervised by "Reichsland" (the new name of the "Ostland" company), where the existing forced laborers, some seven thousand non-white French prisoners of war, had to be removed for "military reasons" and were now to be replaced by families from the Wartheland.[73] Kendzia forwarded this demand on February 23, 1943.[74] In order to avoid losing any more valuable workers, however, the required families were to be chosen from those previously rejected as "unsuitable" during earlier selections. Even if Reichsland administrators tried to insist that the selected persons, "in any case, had to be able-bodied, because they had to operate farms independently there," they would have to ultimately accept that the previous "yardstick . . . can no longer be maintained." Furthermore, "a family . . . with several small children or older persons" was now defenseless against deportation to France, just like "invalids with trachoma and other physical infirmities . . . are to be no impediment."[75] Still exempted from deportation were families with only one person capable of work (whether underage or adult) and, of course, any skilled workers that the Wartheland wanted to keep.[76] It ultimately took until the end of April for 16,772 persons to be rounded up and deported to France, via the camp at Litzmannstadt.[77]

The French recruitment campaign was hardly over when Lower Saxony's employment offices similarly reported an increase in need that was also to be covered with workers from the Wartheland. As a result, the local UWZ transported hundreds of people to Lower Saxony from May 25 to June 4, ultimately totaling 1,974 individuals by the end of the year.[78] This was followed by other demands for urgent deliveries, and the French recruitment campaign also picked up again. By the end of October 1944, 23,512 Polish forced laborers had been transported to France.[79]

Recruiting forced labor had thus become the main focus of work for the UWZ in the Wartheland. In a status report from August 1942, the "release of Polish workers for the Old Reich" was already listed as one of the "main tasks" of the UWZ.[80] A year later, Krumey also supplied concrete numbers. In December 1943, he spoke of transporting a quarter of all farm workers from the Wartheland, since they were ostensibly not needed there—an opinion certainly not shared by the civil administration.[81] The decisive factor here, though, was probably something else: because resumption of the deportation policy in the foreseeable future was an increasingly remote likelihood, the very existence of the UWZ needed new justification. The UWZ had originally been established during the peak of German power to manage the deportation of the local populace and thus facilitate the Germanization of the province—a goal pushed further and further away by the worsening war situation. Krumey reacted to this development early on. With the transition to "total war," recruiting the necessary workforce had become the "overwhelming preoccupation of the German war economy"—and it was precisely by answering this need that Krumey intended to legitimize the continued existence of his agency.[82] The rapid deterioration of the Reich's military position put a quick end to these plans as well. After most of the UWZ field offices had already been disbanded, its murderous mass expulsions inside the General Government likewise halted in the face of massive resistance, and the bulk of its personnel were dispersed to various trouble spots within the Reich's shrinking area of control, the UWZ effectively ceased its work in mid-1944.[83] Almost all its senior managers were pulled out in late March 1944, with a team under Krumey initially assigned to Einsatzgruppe F, where they were to implement the mass deportation of Hungarian Jews to Auschwitz, the largest single genocidal undertaking in the history of the Shoah.[84] According to a message from Krumey to his successor Hermann Püschel on August 14, 1944, the duties left to the remaining officials in Litzmannstadt included "the handling of queries, providing of information, etc.," along with "supervisory duties on the Ostwall" (the "eastern wall" defensive line).[85] Fortunately, time was running out for this as well. Łódź was liberated by the Red Army on January 19, 1945.

Assimilation

Nazi Germanization policy had initially focused on the deportation of individuals who allegedly threatened the dystopian vision of a German East, but as the war developed, the emphasis then shifted toward the assimilation of individuals without whom all hopes of expanding the "German Volksgemeinschaft" onto the future "German Lebensraum" would remain only a fantasy. But because the main players could agree on neither the path nor the goal, this policy area became another one rocked by bitter confrontations, which made any common approach impossible. A decisive shift in power, however, had seemed close at hand in the late summer of 1940, when Himmler managed to usurp the Reich Interior Ministry's authority over selection guidelines: in mid-September, Stuckart was forced to abandon his previous resistance to the promulgation of Himmler's decree on assessing and winnowing the populace in the incorporated eastern territories, which ordered the expansion of the DVL to all eastern provinces. In late October, the Reich Interior Ministry also consented in formal terms and sent a first draft of the order introducing the DVL, along with the associated implementation provisions.

It would be an exaggeration to call this a breakthrough for Himmler, however, and not only because it still took until March 1941 for the DVL to be introduced across the eastern provinces. The marginalization of the Reich Interior Ministry would prove to be a pyrrhic victory in the following period, especially because the SS complex would fail to end the increasing disparities in how the selection of the local populace was handled in the various provinces, or even to curtail the extent of local assimilation policy. Himmler's later attempts fared no differently—they too failed against the power of the Gauleiters. His initiatives in this area are of particular interest for the present investigation because they help illustrate the conflicts over the criteria for recognizing German national status and ethnonational membership, a struggle that would continue for the rest of the war; furthermore, Himmler's initiatives focused on one particular selection criterion that must be considered a Nazi innovation like no other, and yet was also highly contested among the Nazis themselves, namely "race." His repeated attempts at establishing race as the decisive selection criterion were overruled every time by the civil administrations, which rejected such race-based assessments as simply dysfunctional.

It was Germany's attack on the Soviet Union that would ultimately mark a decisive turning point not only in deportation policy but also in policy decisions about the remaining resident populace—more precisely, it was quickly realized in the late fall of 1941 that the Reich would need to equip itself for a longer war, one in which at least passive acceptance of the occupation by the bulk of the Polish populace would be indispensable to the Germans. In examining the related confrontations, it also becomes particularly clear that Nazi population policy can no longer be misinterpreted as primarily a policy of exclusion, but must instead be seen as one that increasingly aimed at the inclusion of more and more of the population. These people were subjected to an assimilation pressure that was unparalleled in German history, one that would soon dwarf its Prussian antecedents.

The Introduction of the DVL in All Annexed Territories of Western Poland

In looking back at Nazi Germanization policy in the annexed territories during the early war years, the relative weakness of the Reich Interior Ministry becomes particularly clear. Headed by a minister who lacked his own power base and who stood outside the Nazi leadership's inner circle, the ministry saw its influence crushed between two battling fronts, namely the party Gauleiters and the SS complex. But the claim that the Reich Interior Ministry "completely adopted Himmler's categories" is simplistic, in that it disregards the key role of initiatives on the periphery—in this case, the trendsetting influence of the Wartheland's DVL.[86] Himmler's decree was new in just one respect: "race" was a selection criterion now to be applied not only to Jews but also to Poles, with the former seen as "fremdblütig" ("foreign-blooded"), and the latter considered "fremdvölkisch" but "artverwandt" ("ethnonationally foreign" but "kindred"). As I will show, it was precisely this innovation—and thus, in a sense, the SS complex's own contribution to Nazi Germanization policy—that would ultimately fail to take hold.

It would be another four months before the decree on the DVL and German national status, along with the corresponding implementation provisions, were ultimately signed, in March 1941. Although the reasons for this delay cannot be conclusively determined from the surviving sources, it seems that the remaining differences had not been entirely ironed out at the meeting scheduled by the Reich Interior Ministry for November 13, 1940.[87] A core concern brought up by the introduction of the DVL across the annexed territories of western Poland was the need to work out a fundamental restructuring of German national status regulations, including the legal status of individuals who were to be denied membership in the state collectivity while nonetheless living within the German area of control. The introduction of the DVL and the creation of "revocable national status" ("Staatsangehörigkeit auf Widerruf") thus represented one more step—after the promulgation of the Nuremberg Laws—in undermining the institution of citizenship. On top of that was the establishment of "protected dependent status" ("Schutzangehörigkeit"), a legal innovation meant for individuals whose membership in another state collectivity was to be denied, but who were also to be refused entry into the German one.

Of course, from a Nazi perspective, this was a problematic development. As argued with indignation during an interministerial meeting at the Reich Interior Ministry on January 15, 1941, it was unacceptable that "those who may not be ethnoconvertible [umvolkbar], but are nonetheless Fremdvölkische of kindred blood, are only made into protected dependents . . . while the racially alien Jews are left in possession of German national status."[88] The suggestion from the Reich Interior Ministry, that the Jews be made into protected dependents too, was rejected by Hitler with the same argument: the Jews had to be made worse off than the Poles. As a logical consequence, the only remaining option was to declare them stateless—an idea that demonstrated in a most exemplary way the intertwined and mutually radicalizing relationship between anti-Jewish and anti-Polish policies. By the end of 1941, this declaration was also implemented in fact, at least for Jewish Germans who had been deported to extermination camps outside the Reich's borders.[89] But at the beginning of that year, consensus on the matter had yet to be achieved. Even though nobody objected to the repeated radicalization of anti-Jewish policy, there was still no agreement on whether Jewish "Mischlinge" ("hybrid persons") were also to be denied German national status. It was apparently such questions that ultimately helped make it seem advisable for the general overhaul of national status regulations to be disconnected from the introduction of the DVL across the annexed territories of western Poland, so that the latter project would not be delayed any longer. The draft decrees on the DVL were finally approved by Hitler, probably in February 1941.[90]

The decree on the DVL and German national status in the incorporated eastern territories was signed by Frick, Hess, and Himmler on March 4, 1941. On the one hand, it defined who could be enrolled in the DVL, namely former citizens of Poland or Danzig who resided in the annexed territories on October 26, 1939 (or September 1, in the case of Danzig).[91] On the other, it outlined the structure of the DVL, using the model from the Wartheland, with a central office (Zentralstelle) under the Reichssstatthalter or Oberpräsident, regional offices (Bezirksstelle) under the Regierungspräsidents, and branch offices (Zweigstelle) under the Landrats or mayors. As a central appeals body for all the annexed territories, the Supreme Court of Review for Ethnonationality Questions was established under Himmler as RKFDV. Furthermore, the resulting legal status was defined for each section: members of Sections 1 and 2 received German national status and Reich citizen rights, and members of Sections 3 and 4 had to seek naturalization through a separate procedure and thus undergo an additional selection process, and even then could become only revocable German nationals.[92] The rest of the populace was demoted to the status of protected dependents, but only as long as they still resided within the Reich. Deportation outside its borders would rob them of even this status.[93]

The implementing provisions were signed by Frick just a short while later, on March 13, 1941.[94] They too had only marginally changed from the draft proposal sent by the Reich Interior Ministry on October 31, 1940, which aimed at subjecting the entire populace to an exclusivist and nuanced selection process in which "race" also played a certain role in the selection criteria. This draft sealed the defeat of the Reich Interior Ministry in its conflict with the SS complex. Stuckart's claim, in an article published in the journal of the Academy for German Law in August 1941, that it was "clear from the outset that the Fremdvölkische will not become German nationals," certainly did not match the real-world developments in these acrimonious confrontations.[95] As previously shown, however, it cannot be said that the SS complex achieved unconditional success here, for key passages of the implementation provisions were quite vague and allowed considerable room for interpretation.

Enrollment in the DVL essentially depended on three criteria, which did not all need to be fulfilled simultaneously: conduct, descent, and to some extent in regard to enrollment in Section 3, race. The most important, as had also been practiced in the Wartheland, was the demonstration of acceptable political and social conduct in the time before the German invasion. The universal Reich-level regulation introduced in March adopted these criteria, as well as the privileging of "Bekenntnisdeutsche" over "Deutschstämmige" ("professed Germans" over the "German-descended"). Section 1 was for the enrollment of those who, for example, had belonged to German minority organizations, although simply presenting oneself as German in public was also sufficient. If a family did not qualify for Section 1, but was able to prove, for example, that it had joined a Polish association merely because of outside pressure but still spoke German at home, then it was assigned to Section 2.[96] In any case, enrollment in these two sections was not tied to proof of German ancestry let alone race—conduct was more important than descent.

"German descent" became a criterion only when it came to enrollment in Sections 3 and 4. Applicants who were accused of hostile political activities but who nonetheless had proof of their "German descent," were sorted into Section 4. In this logic, it was precisely this "German descent" that made such persons seem particularly dangerous, so that they had to be kept under surveillance. And even if not all these people could be reintegrated into the German "Volksgemein-schaft," such efforts applied at least to their children.

Finally, Section 3 took in applicants of "German descent" who had not pre-sented themselves as "Germans" during the interwar period, along with indi-viduals who were married to members of Sections 1 and 2 but would otherwise not be accepted into the DVL. Beyond these two was the largest group, those of the "intermediate class." It was only here that race also acquired a certain sig-nificance as a selection criterion. It applied to applicants labeled by the German occupiers as Kashubians, Water Poles, or Szlonzakians: as long as they had not already earned a right to enrollment in Sections 1 or 2 through their conduct during the interwar period or were not entirely excluded by activism as political opponents, then entry into Section 3 was open to them. The terminology chosen by the Interior Ministry is revealing: In contrast to what the SS would have pre-ferred, the selection was not to select those who were seen to be "racially suitable," but instead exclude those who seemed to be "racially unsuitable," that is, suggest-ing that the majority would qualify for inclusion into the DVL.

If the struggles over Section 3 ultimately became the main battleground for the players involved with Nazi Germanization policy, it was because of the sub-ject matter itself. After all, concepts like "German descent" and "racial suitabil-ity" were not only inherently impossible to nail down, but also because the Reich Interior Ministry showed little interest in restricting the associated freedom of interpretation by issuing more precise definitions. More detailed provisions on when a person's "German descent" could no longer be considered "reliably prov-able" failed to materialize, which was even more surprising when at least one proven model already existed, as in the legal test differentiating a first-degree Mischling from a second-degree one. According to what criteria, and by whom, a "racial appraisal" was to be conducted if necessary—on this too, the provisions were silent. In its decree, the Reich Interior Ministry had also failed to incorpo-rate Himmler's cap on assimilating those "of non-German descent," which had been set at one million persons in his ethnonationality decree.

The civil administrations in Danzig–West Prussia and Upper Silesia natu-rally used this freedom of interpretation to continue their existing policies, which were relatively inclusive in comparison with the Wartheland's policy and the ideas of the SS complex.[97] Most important, the provisions on the enrollment of "intermediate class" applicants into Section 3 allowed their number to grow to two million, ultimately representing two-thirds of all persons registered in the DVL. With this, Forster and Bracht implemented in their provinces a population policy that was only partially reconcilable with the Nazi ideal of a race-based "Germanization of the soil," thereby harking back much more to the German-ization policy of Prussia, meaning the forced assimilation of at least the former nationals of the German Empire.

THE WARTHELAND: "RENEWED ASSESSMENTS ONLY TO THE EXTENT ABSOLUTELY NECESSARY"[98]

The introduction of the DVL across the annexed territories of western Poland had the least impact on Germanization policy in the Wartheland, whose civil administration had managed to swing the preceding confrontations "in favor of the line established by the Wartheland's procedure," as Coulon noted with satisfaction.[99] And when the Reich Interior Ministry finally issued the implementation provisions for the new procedure, Herbert Mehlhorn received the assurance that the current registration process, begun under the old process and now almost complete, could be brought to an end before the results were reviewed and adapted to the new procedure.[100] Later, Greiser also ordered the reorganization of the province's DVL offices, in order to bring them in line with the specifications from Berlin.[101] But the selection process remained effectively unchanged. Here, the branch offices were simply to review the already enrolled persons according to the new guidelines and to do so before the relatively quick deadline of June 10, 1941. This seemed easiest with those enrolled in Group A of the "old" DVL, who were now to be transferred directly into Section 1 of the "new" DVL. As for transferring the other groups, Greiser pointed to the "somewhat more broadly drawn" provisions of the Reich Interior Ministry. On the other hand, he also impressed on his officials that one could "generally . . . assume" that Group B corresponded to Section 2, Group C to Section 3, and Groups D and E to Section 4. The relevant decisions were to be made on the basis of the existing files.

But if the Berlin guidelines were more broadly drawn than the ones originally issued from Posen, how should one handle those individuals denied a questionnaire because their chances of enrollment were considered too low by the local branch office? Here too, Greiser showed himself in no hurry to adopt Frick's provisions: he instructed his officials that, for the time being, "public notices of any kind on the new Reich-level regulation of the people's list procedure [i.e., DVL] are to be strictly withheld"; it was only after the completion of the reclassification process that the populace was to be informed of the new situation and invited one last time to come submit an application. This invitation, however, was only for unenrolled persons "of German descent" who sprang "at least 50 percent from German ancestors." The populace was to be informed "that applications from persons who are not of German descent are completely futile."[102] At first glance, this explicit emphasis on "German descent" appeared to signal a deviation from the existing position, which did not require it, at least not with the "Bekenntnis-deutsche." The resulting confusion was then resolved by the Reichsstatthalter's offices, which reaffirmed that, "for admission into Sections 1 and 2 of the DVL, having 50 percent German descent is of lesser importance, while the professing [of Germandom] is of crucial importance."[103] After all, "it is not acceptable that people who affirmed being Volksdeutsche during the Polish period are now barred admission to the DVL because of insufficient German descent."[104]

* * *

The branch offices began transferring names in May 1941. The time pressure was particularly intense in the larger cities, where thousands of decisions still had to be reviewed.[105] Uebelhoer therefore let his branch offices work according to a "reporting officer system" ("Berichterstattersystem"), in which a reporting officer prescreened application forms before "summarily presenting hundreds of identically constituted cases, because after close examination, they are convinced that each of these cases is constituted without any doubts."[106] At the DVL branch office for the municipality of Litzmannstadt, the second-largest in the entire province, these provisions were interpreted in such a way that decision making was effectively delegated to the administrative clerks.[107] They made their decisions "without producing written documentation," which made later review impossible. It was clear that hardly anyone was bothered by the fact that, "in most cases, the applicants possessed . . . no certificates of descent," which after all was still a decisive criterion for sorting individuals into Sections 3 and 4.[108] It was also here that the responsible departmental head for ethnonationality questions quickly realized it "could not possibly be true" that more than eighty thousand cases had been decided in just two sittings, making this branch office one of the first to report completion.[109] When this situation was finally exposed during a review of the branch office in mid-1944, the mayor defended himself by stating that a "by-the-rules induction of more than a hundred thousand persons through commission decisions . . . would have taken a very long time." Since the Regierungspräsident's offices and the mayor at the time, Werner Ventzki, had allegedly "expressly endorsed" this course of action—something that both immediately denied—and since many of the relevant subjects were now serving in the Wehrmacht anyway, it seemed hardly advisable to review all those applications once again.[110] Because apparently no review came to pass, the end result was that almost 20 percent of all persons inducted into the Wartheland's DVL had acquired German national status (on a revocable basis) through a process that no longer had anything in common with the province's otherwise restrictive guidelines.

However, the developments at the branch office for the municipality of Litzmannstadt seem to have been exceptional in their magnitude. Most of the other branch offices exceeded Greiser's deadline, which ultimately had to be extended again and again. But this did not lead to major changes. It was only in the Litzmannstadt Governmental Region that the DVL saw significant growth, inducting 31,878 persons from September 1941 to January 1942.[111] However, this was not the result of brand new applications, but instead the first adjudication of

12,644 applications already submitted but still unprocessed, as well as the review of some twenty thousand previously rejected but now approved. Most of them were probably sorted into Section 3. In combination with the "reporting officer system" used in the Litzmannstadt Governmental Region, the Reich Interior Ministry's implementation provisions had led here to the induction of some twenty thousand previously rejected individuals, which represented 10 percent of the governmental region's entire DVL membership. In the governmental regions of Posen and Hohensalza, the assessment committees seemed to adhere more closely to Greiser's guidance, resulting in only minimal changes. By the time a public call was issued to the Wartheland's newspapers around the turn of January/February 1942, in which the populace was informed about the new DVL and invited to submit membership applications, the changeover to the new procedure had already been completed without any significant changes to the selection practice.[112] Apart from in the Litzmannstadt Governmental Region, the Reich Interior Ministry's "ethnopolitically leniently . . . formulated" implementation provisions (as Strickner described them) had ultimately had no significant influence on the Wartheland's DVL—in this case too, it was the local actors who prevailed.[113]

Upper Silesia: Appeal to "All Those Upper Silesians Who Profess to Germandom"

In Upper Silesia, it was in the spring of 1941 that the first rumors about the looming introduction of the DVL made the rounds. At the time, the Reich was at the apogee of its strength, the situation seemed hopeless for the subjugated peoples of Europe, and the mass murders of the war's early period were still painfully fresh in people's memories; as a result, many feared the outbreak of another wave of violence, including the possible murder of persons excluded from the DVL.[114] Things would turn out differently, however—at least for those living west of the police border, in areas that had belonged to the German Empire until 1921.

Unlike the case of the Wartheland, the newly established Oberpräsident's office in Kattowitz was quick to inform its subordinated authorities about the introduction of the DVL, which replaced the "Polish List" and "German List."[115] Bracht then issued an appeal to the public on April 10, 1941: "I thus turn to the populace of Upper Silesia with an invitation to apply for admission to the DVL. I call upon not only those Volk comrades who belonged to German organizations during the time of Polish rule, but also all those Upper Silesians who profess to Germandom or are of German descent. . . . Through the DVL, the innate German character of German Upper Silesia will be clearly expressed outwards as well."[116]

With his public appeal, Bracht had made it clear that even Berlin could not divert him from his existing policy line. Naturally, he would ensure the "complete eradication of alien elements," as he let the Reich Interior Ministry know. But this should "cause relatively few difficulties" because the "influx from Congress Poland and Galicia has not been excessive"—which meant he generally intended to induct all other individuals west of the police border into at least Section 3 of the DVL. After that, the task would be "through peaceful development in the coming years, to strengthen their consciousness of belonging to Germandom, and if it has been buried, to reawaken it."[117]

The details were outlined by Bracht's implementation decree of May 25, 1941, which had probably been drafted by Fritz Arlt, head of the RKFDV branch office in Kattowitz. The "general principle" to uphold was that "wherever German blood exists, it must be retained for Germandom. If people are worthy, and their incorporation into the German ethnonational body [Volkskörper] represents an asset for Germany, they should undergo incorporation into the German ethnonational body."[118] If the applicant's social and political conduct was already an important criterion under Frick's implementation decree, and was the decisive one for induction into Sections 1 and 2, it would become even more significant in Upper Silesia. This fact was seen, for example, in the directive denying enrollment in Section 1 to anyone who had first described themselves as "Germans" during the census of December 1939 but then registered as "Poles" during the military conscription surveys of 1940 and 1941 in order to escape the draft. In contrast, informants working for Germany's military intelligence were "generally to be inducted into Section 1 as German activists," even if they were Poles—or as Bracht euphemistically put it, "despite their thereby required public Polish disguise."[119]

Particularly contentious were the selection criteria for Section 3; after all, Bracht knew about the fears, especially within the SS complex, that these could be interpreted in a way that would allow the majority of the local populace to be inducted under the pretext that they were all members of the "intermediate class." It was also for this reason that criticism had been directed at Frick's implementation provisions, for they had failed to set an upper limit like the one in Himmler's ethnonationality decree. As a corrective, Greifelt had already issued instructions in March 1941 to the RKFDV branch office in Kattowitz that such a development was to be prevented by all means: "Under all circumstances, it must be avoided that the formulation on page 10, at paragraph 6c [defining the 'intermediate class'], is erroneously used by the subordinated offices of the DVL to recognize too many Water Poles and Szlonzakians as Germans. I therefore order that this formulation be strictly interpreted according to the original sense of the fundamental decree issued by the Reichsführer of the SS on September 12, 1940."[120]

This made little impression on Bracht. In adopting Frick's implementation provisions, he too divided Section 3 into "Deutschstämmige who have entered into ties with Polishdom," "mixed marriages between Fremdvölkische and Deutschstämmige," and the "mixed populace residing in Upper Silesia . . . who have a Slavic home language." This last group was primarily defined by geography, and in Bracht's view, simply included the entire populace of formerly German or Austrian territories. In them, the only applicants who remained generally excluded were those not belonging to the autochthonous populace, meaning, for example, immigrants arriving after 1890 from the Russian or Austrian Partitions, along with anyone whose past political or social conduct left doubts about their ability to be integrated as loyal members of the "German Volksgemeinschaft." Reference was made to those who had arrived from the German Empire, especially Westphalia and western Upper Silesia, after the 1921 plebiscite, since this amounted to a declaration of loyalty to the newly established Polish state. And of course, members of the "intermediate class" could not be considered a "desirable addition to the population" if they had belonged to the Polish irredentist movement as German citizens before 1918, been functionaries in Polish parties or bearers of higher Polish distinctions during the interwar period, or joined the resistance movement after the German invasion. An exception was to be made only for Polish-speaking individuals west of the police border who could prove "German descent." They were enrolled in Section 4 as dangerous "renegades," and therefore kept under watch.

Although the SS complex had prevailed over the Reich Interior Ministry, its hopes of finally anchoring racial criteria in the selection of the local populace were dashed in Upper Silesia as well. Biometric criteria played only a minor role, if any. Bracht's implementation decree does include the instruction that, at least for members of the "intermediate class," such a person was to be enrolled in Section 3 only if the applicant was "worthy," wherein "racial grounds are decisive." But in terms of detailing this aspect, Bracht was satisfied with simply noting that it was "advisable" for Kreisleiters to involve the local head of the party's Racial Policy Office. Even then, it was not only "skull measurements and color chart comparisons that will be decisive; general life conduct and general life achievements must also be considered."[121] In Upper Silesia too, "Volksgemeinschaft" meant above all a "Tat- und Leitstungsgemeinschaft" (a "community of deed and achievement").

Like the Wartheland, Upper Silesia had also received assurance from the Reich Interior Ministry that it could introduce the DVL in stages, thus avoiding an abrupt shift from the existing enrollment process to the new procedure.[122] Therefore, when the branch offices in Upper Silesia took up their work in May 1941, they first continued with the registration of persons who could be eligible for Sections 1 or 2 (many of whom had already received a German national status document) or were working for the state or party—along with individuals who were threatened with dispossession and/or deportation. It was only afterward that the selection process would begin for the remainder.

But, as can be inferred from Bracht's implementation provisions, the Oberpräsident's offices had no doubts that a large part of the local populace similarly belonged in the DVL—if they lived west of the police border. According to an October 1941 message from Vice Oberpräsident Faust to the Reich Interior Ministry, the DVL intended to concentrate its registration efforts on a relatively small region of the province. To be excluded was naturally the extreme west of the province, which had previously remained inside the German Empire, meaning that its residents were already German citizens. But the eastern border counties were also largely excluded. As an example, Faust mentioned the county of Warthenau, formerly inside the Russian Partition, where the local branch office had already finished its work after processing just six hundred applications. The almost 120,000 remaining residents had been deemed not worth considering, in the view of the local civil administration. The DVL would therefore concentrate "for the most part on ten to twelve counties" of the Kattowitz Governmental Region, meaning areas that Germany and Austria had been forced to cede to Poland after World War I, in which some 1.8 million persons lived. So it was certainly no coincidence when Faust further stated that the DVL would enroll some 1.8 million persons, although two-thirds of them, in his view, would only be suitable for enrollment in Section 3.[123] Faust had thus informed the Reich Interior Ministry of the de facto continuation of existing local policy, meaning the general exclusion of persons residing east of the police border, even if they appeared to be "racially suitable" (as I will describe later in more detail), along with the general assimilation of those residing west of it, if they were not currently considered political adversaries.

As the civil administration soon discovered, this planned policy of assimilation would still be hampered by the Berlin guidelines, but not so much because of its stipulated selection criteria. As already shown, these had been interpreted by each province in a way that would allow the continuation of the local selection practice already established before the introduction of the DVL across all three provinces. A much bigger obstacle was presented by the procedure's material and labor costs, for the two questionnaires requiring delivery in triplicate, the case-by-case decisions involving in-person applicant interviews and on-site dwelling inspections, and the multistage appeals process. To make this problem clear to the Reich Interior Ministry, Faust described one example: of the 387,000 persons in Kattowitz Rural County, the local DVL branch office estimated that 300,000 were worth considering for enrollment. Only 15,352 applications had been processed by that time, however, because the Landrat lacked the resources to handle more.[124] For the province as a whole, the year-end balance sheet did not look much better, with only 190,000 applications processed of which 89 percent had been decided favorably.[125] But if the processing of the remaining 1.6 million was not to wait another five years, then the procedure would need to be expedited.

Danzig–West Prussia: "Kaminski" Means "Stein"

The DVL threatened to have far-reaching consequences for the selection process in Danzig–West Prussia. The threat had already become clear to Forster's representatives during the aforementioned meeting at the Reich Interior Ministry, which saw all provinces arguing for a grandfathering of their registrations completed thus far, along with a step-by-step introduction of the DVL. A conflict emerged when the Regierungspräsident of Danzig, Fritz Hermann, declared that Forster was not prepared to replace the existing procedure with the guidelines stipulated from Berlin and wanted to combine the two instead. As before, candidates would first be chosen through a "rough selection" conducted by the party before being handed over to the commissions of the DVL for final adjudication. Hermann promised that the principle of voluntary application would be preserved, in that applications from outside the preliminary registration process conducted by the party would also be processed—although the introduction of the DVL would not be publicized at first. Hermann Hering of the Reich Interior Ministry objected that the populace could hardly apply for enrollment in the DVL if they did not even know it existed; Hermann tried to rebut this by claiming "that this knowledge . . . would certainly spread quickly by word of mouth." Unable to hold Forster to the new procedure, the Reich Interior Ministry finally yielded here too "after lengthier debate," with assurances that the preliminary registration process would be conducted according to the guidelines "as they are stipulated in the minutes."[126]

Forster therefore began by continuing as before. Before the decrees on the DVL could arrive at his subordinated local authorities, they first received instructions on continuing the "Deutschstämmige campaign" ("Deutschstämmigenaktion") that had begun the previous year, meaning the registration of locals for "re-Germanization," with a quota specified for each county. The criteria and procedure of the 1941 "Deutschstämmige campaign" had undergone only minor changes from the previous year, as can be seen in a message from the Kreisleiter of Preussisch Stargard County (Danzig Governmental Region) to his Blockleiters, which instructed them to submit lists of persons already living there before World War I who also had relatives inside the Reich or were "of German descent" themselves, whereby it was enough to descend "from Germans in any parental proportion." Bilingual marriages were also to be considered, as well as families that had "behaved in a German-friendly and otherwise decent manner in the last twenty years," made a "German and/or racially favorable impression," or represented in general "a valuable addition for Germandom."[127] Thus, the registrations were to take in all those who, "in terms of self-professing, descent, and conduct, can be assimilated into the German Volk," wherein consideration was given to their "external appearance (cleanliness), language, vocational competence, name, previous membership in organizations, and birthplace (possibly of the parents and grandparents)."[128] These lists were sent to the Kreisleiters for review, who then returned them to the Blockleiters with questionnaires for preliminary registration. After that, the completed questionnaires were to be notated with short evaluations from the responsible Zellenleiter, Blockleiter, and Ortsgruppenleiter before delivery to a commission; after completion of the registration campaign, the commission then consulted with the relevant *Ortsgruppe* (local group, the Nazi Party organizational level below the county) to decide which persons should be proposed to the DVL branch office for enrollment. In contrast to those of the "Deutschstämmige campaign," each of these commissions now consisted solely of Forster's disciples: the local Kreisleiter, a representative from the Gauleiter's offices, and other "specially appointed men."[129] Since the final decision was to be made by the offices of the DVL, Forster no longer found it necessary to include even token representation from other interest groups like the SS complex.

It was only after this preliminary registration process had been completed in most counties that Forster then announced the introduction of the DVL in Danzig–West Prussia on May 21, 1941, while also issuing precise instructions on how Frick's implementation provisions were to be interpreted. The Reich Interior Ministry's new course was given due respect with the assertion that the "DVL does not aim to assimilate foreign folkdom." But, in fact, Forster's goal was to continue his assimilation policy, as illustrated in his definition of "German descent": beyond the usual criteria, such as membership in a Protestant congregation, he urged his officials to exercise a remarkable amount of understanding for applicants with Polish names. They were certainly not to be considered sufficient grounds for exclusion, since it was possible that the family name had been Polonized because of economic or political pressures: a "Kowalski" could be masking a "Schmidt," and a "Kaminski" could be disguising a "Stein." Furthermore, a Polish given name allegedly may have also resulted from a state authority's refusal to record the original German version in the official birth register.[130]

It is significant that Forster did not even specify when a candidate was to be rejected for insufficient "German descent." Whereas in the Wartheland individuals were considered "to be of German descent" only if they could produce at least two "German" grandparents, the DVL central office in Danzig–West Prussia permitted the enrollment of those who were "less than half of German descent"— without specifying whether even one German grandparent was necessary.[131] Forster showed a similar amount of understanding in the assessment of "conduct and mindset." After every political Polish organization had already been stamped out, with their leaders imprisoned or murdered, it was now believed that their former members need not necessarily be excluded if they had joined those organizations only "under duress." Not even a lack of German language skills was considered an impediment. Although the ability to speak German was a minimum requirement for members of Sections 1 and 2, that stipulation did not apply to members of Section 3, because, after all, the "mastery of the German language is not a significant marker of German descent."[132] The local-level authorities took this to heart, as seen when the Kreisleiter's offices in Neustadt organized language courses for those in Sections 3 and 4 who "are still not capable of speaking and writing in the German language."[133]

Nor did Forster fail in his communications with state and party officials to emphasize once again the importance of a speedy and inclusivist procedure. For example, on July 24, 1941, he instructed the Regierungspräsident of Bromberg, Dr. Johannes Kurt Schimmel, to immediately launch the work of the DVL branch offices in those counties where the preliminary registrations had already been completed. To Forster, the approval of the branch offices was a mere formality, since these candidates had already been scrutinized by the party. This is why differences of opinion were to be eliminated as quickly as possible: "If work is delayed by repeated objections from individual members on the commissions of the DVL branch offices, I expect you to remind the commissions of the importance of speedy decision making."[134] Schimmel immediately passed this instruction along, impressing on the Landrats that "your highest priority must be the effectuating of quick decisions."[135]

But Forster could also rely on party comrades on the ground like Waldemar Warras, the Kreisleiter in Thorn. According to the meeting minutes written by Mayor Dr. Zeitler, Warras began here with a historical sketch meant to justify a selection policy that was as inclusivist as possible: "The populace living here was systematically led into Polishdom by unwise German governments, so that they externally appear to be Polish; but the core is German, and it will simply depend on National Socialist educational work to make these people, who sometimes do not even know themselves where they belong, into valuable German people."[136] For Warras, it was the party that was in charge here, and not the DVL branch office. The persons chosen during the preliminary registration process and presented to the DVL branch office were no longer to be judged by the latter, as the party's decision was "final, and certainly cannot be overruled by short-sighted people, because it is not for the short term that we are sorting out the population structure here, but for the coming centuries. It does not matter whether small errors are made, the general line defined by the Gauleiter is correct."[137]

When Eduard Heinz, a school principal appointed as a "Volksdeutscher" to the DVL branch office, made the critical remark that this procedure would also likely abrogate Frick's implementation provisions, Warras gave the preemptory response "that one cannot engage in spiteful parliamentary bickering," before immediately declaring "that he would put before the party tribunal any DVL employee who did not submit to his orders on the DVL procedure." SS Junior Assault Leader Harbrecht fared no better when he let Warras know that he still wanted to abide by the Reich Interior Ministry's implementation provisions and would veto the induction of any "Polish-descended family group": "The Kreisleiter declared in response that when it came to resolving the ethnonational question in Danzig–West Prussia, responsibility rested solely with the Gauleiter, which is why the Gauleiter's command must be carried out. With this, he closed the meeting."[138] Forster was quite serious about this, as SS Section Leader Wellnitz of the SD would come to discover. Just two days after having fallen into an argument with Himmler about the DVL in Hitler's presence, Forster visited Neumark (today Nowe Miasto Lubawskie) on October 21, 1941, where he also took part in a sitting of the local DVL, which is something he had often done before.[139] To his great annoyance, he was immediately confronted with Wellnitz raising an objection against the first candidate proposed by the preliminary registration commission to the DVL branch office. According to the report of SS Assault Unit Leader Werner Böhm, who was head of the SD Precinct in Thorn and Wellnitz's superior, Forster reacted abusively, calling Wellnitz's objection "nonsense" and demanding that he withdraw it. When the latter refused and pointed to Frick's implementation provisions, Forster retorted, "You are too stupid to interpret the decree," and threw him out.[140] Of course, this episode further fueled ongoing animosities between Forster and the SS complex. As HSSPF Richard Hildebrandt knew only too well, this was not just an isolated incident. In a message to Himmler two days later, he fulminated that Forster had "absolutely no right" to launch attacks like this. They were "objectively so unjustified, as well as outrageous and insulting, that the SS cannot let the matter rest. After all, at some point it must be possible to put an end to the megalomaniacal and irresponsible goings-on of even a Gauleiter."[141] It was hardly surprising that the conflict between the SS complex and the civil administration would flare up again on precisely this question, because a major reason that Himmler had forced the introduction of the DVL was to shut out assimilationist selection practices, thereby advancing deportations and ultimately creating space for the ethnic Germans from Eastern Europe. But it was not only the civil administration's interpretation of the selection criteria that obstructed these goals. Equally irksome for the SS complex was Forster's order of May 15, 1941, which specified that the names of all persons earmarked for deportation were to be submitted to the relevant Kreisleiter, who would then decide whether the local DVL branch office should enroll them after all. Furthermore, even if they were already in a transit camp, such persons were expressly granted the right to apply for admission to the DVL.[142]

This possibility presented Hildebrandt with a problem: What would happen if a person had already been rounded and transported to a UWZ camp or the General Government but was then admitted into the DVL by a branch office? He predicted that it would be a particularly "great danger" if the subject was then sorted into Sections 1 or 2, as the RKFDV would then "be called on to provide

Figure 5.1. During a visit to Danzig–West Prussia, Goebbels (far corner of table) takes part in a sitting of the DVL branch office in Thorn. Gauleiter Forster sits next to him (on his right). *Source:* National Digital Archives of Poland, 2–3854.

recourse."[143] But classification into Sections 3 or 4 would also be problematic, in that such persons would be "German" and no longer subject to the same degree of SS control, meaning they would have to be taken from the transit camps for Poles and transferred to the "Germanization camp" erected for this purpose in Gosslershausen (today Jabłonowo Pomorskie).

Because the jurisdiction of the DVL in this matter could not be shaken, the SS complex chose to create a parallel structure that subjugated deportees to its own simulated DVL decision-making process as provided by the Reich Interior Ministry, in order to provide legal backing to their own actions in defiance of Forster. Field offices of the SD Special Unit were established at the UWZ camps in order to verify the ethnonationality of all persons transported there, as per Frick's implementation provisions of March 13, 1941.[144] If these individuals were "Deutschstämmige," they were to be immediately transferred to Gosslershausen, along with anyone certified to be ethnonationally non-Polish, as well holders of German national status documents or DVL Section 3 or 4 identity documents.[145] As for the individuals left behind in the UWZ camps, if they still wanted to submit enrollment applications, then the completed questionnaires were to be forwarded to the relevant DVL branch office, but with the notation that the SD

Special Unit considered the applicant ineligible for DVL admission. If the branch office did not agree with this recommendation, then the case went to the relevant IdS, allowing him to register an objection with the branch office.[146]

Of course, neither side was satisfied with this arrangement. The SD repeatedly complained that persons rejected by the SD Special Unit had nonetheless been enrolled by the local DVL branch office. According to Włodzimierz Jastrzębski, the SD field offices had been obliged to forward the application forms of 1,331 individuals up to the end of 1943, from which the DVL admitted 137 families. But it would be wrong to conclude (as Jastrzębski does) that, because the number of admissions was ostensibly small, most of them had been forced by the SD to submit an admission application even though they were "clearly" Poles.[147] For one thing, the DVL's enrollment of 137 families was not a small number at all, since every family member over the age of twelve had to fill out an application. Considering the average family size back then, it is certainly conceivable that around half the individual applications were approved. Furthermore, Jastrzębski has misunderstood the basic outlines of the conflict between the civil administration and the SS complex. While it is true that DVL questionnaires had to be filled out by all persons transported by the SS to UWZ camps—who in any case were already classified as not "Deutschstämmige"—the questionnaires were not distributed to facilitate induction into the DVL, but rather to reinforce the hopelessness of such an application and thus justify the decision by the SD to transport these persons. It is here that Jastrzębski's analysis misconstrues the Germanization policy of the SS, which in fact was pushing for a selection policy that was as exclusivist as possible, and thus, after its own agencies had deported these individuals to the UWZ camps, it had absolutely no interest in then pushing them to submit DVL application forms from there.

The offices of the DVL were just as dissatisfied. Certainly, the DVL central office had made clear that the SD was responsible for collecting completed questionnaires from persons in the UWZ camps, and the DVL branch offices had to make their decisions on the basis of the questionnaires sent to them by the SD—meaning that a summons was not envisaged.[148] But this did not prevent several DVL offices from contacting the relevant camps and asking them to transfer particular inmates to them. The UWZ rejected such requests.[149] The DVL regional office in Bromberg suspected that the SS was trying to use these questionnaires to prejudice decision making at the DVL offices, whose approach had been criticized as too inclusivist. After the UWZ camp in Thorn rejected further requests for the transfer of inmates, the DVL regional office finally turned to the central office on June 19, 1943, and demanded a change to the existing regulations because they were "hampering and/or preventing" decisions.[150] A similarly insistent call was heard from the Landrat of Bromberg, Walther Nethe, whose county included the largest UWZ camp, at Potulitz (today Potulice).[151] Citing a directive from February 9, 1943, in which the DVL central office instructed the branch offices to induct applicants into the DVL only after a face-to-face assessment, Nethe's deputy likewise pushed for the central office to issue a definitive decision.[152] There is no record of whether such a decision was issued in the remaining time. But a decision turned out to be unnecessary for the Bromberg Governmental Region, because the camp administration at Potulitz—with the approval of the IdS—ultimately acquiesced. On December 2, 1943, the first inmates were transferred to the DVL regional office, with more to follow.[153]

* * *

At the end of 1941, the DVL branch offices reported completion—not of the full population registration effort, but only of the "Deutschstämmige campaign" Forster had ordered in December 1940.[154] One reason for the very slow progress was that it relied not on the "voluntary" registration of the populace but instead on handpicked selection by the party, which had to register in each county a specific number of persons who also had to be employed in the most urgently needed occupations. But this obstacle was soon compounded by another problem. Even though the Danzig Regierungspräsident Fritz Hermann probably meant it as only a pretext when he claimed that the reason it was unnecessary to publicly announce the DVL before the completion of the "Deutschstämmige campaign" was because news of it would surely spread by word of mouth, this is precisely what began to happen.

For example, the Nazi Party organization in Thorn had been instructed to conduct a "rough selection" of the city's inhabitants, registering eight thousand of them for subsequent presentation to the local DVL branch office. But because it was very difficult to hide such an operation from the rest of the populace, the branch office soon found itself confronted by twelve thousand additional applications submitted directly by the general public, and not by the party's preliminary registration commission. Contrary to the Reich Interior Ministry's guidelines, the branch office was not allowed to process these applications on an equal footing and was forced instead to prioritize the ones sanctioned by the preliminary registration commission—although of these eight thousand individuals, only a thousand had actually requested a questionnaire on their own and subsequently submitted it to the branch office. For the local mayor, this was an untenable situation that required relief, so that the affected persons could be "helped to get their primary rights."[155]

This episode illustrates the general worry on the part of local authorities about the slowness of the selection process. During the census of December 6, 1939, the German occupiers had registered 3,417 "Volksdeutsche" in the city of Thorn—which was more or less the same number who received national status documents a little while later under Frick's citizenship decree, and was almost as many as the 3,983 who were subsequently enrolled in Sections 1 or 2 of the DVL after its introduction. But if the municipal administration in Thorn now wanted to also take a large part of the 57,166 persons listed as "resident" during the census and induct them into the DVL, then the registration of only eight thousand persons in a year meant that this process would drag on for a very long time.[156]

But even limiting the process to persons registered by the party left an enormous workload for the civil administrators. For example, the Landrat of Preussisch Stargard reported that he was managing to process the applications only because a teacher and several school students had agreed to help with the initial sorting. But the willingness of the students had noticeably dwindled since then.[157] Meanwhile, in the county of Neustadt, also in the Danzig Governmental Region, the Landrat was able to cope with the task only because he had drafted "youths as workers on the spot" and furthermore had convinced the Reich Labor Service to help out with the "women's war auxiliary." Nonetheless, according to the Landrat, it would have taken another year with three shifts working around the clock to process the rising flood of applications.[158]

Another good illustration is provided by the situation in the Bromberg Governmental Region, the only part of Danzig–West Prussia with more detailed surviving data for this time period. According to it, the local DVL branch offices had registered only 41,867 individuals by the end of December 1941, with a little more than 30,000 of them assigned to Sections 1 and 2.[159] But if the civil administration was serious about registering all the local "Volksdeutsche," along with every autochthonous resident who did not represent a political threat, then it was only a first step at best. The remaining gap becomes clear by considering the census results of December 1939, when almost 80,000 residents were classified as "Volksdeutsche" and more than 380,000 as "Einheimische" ("locals"), meaning that the remainder was ten times as great as the number inducted into the DVL to that date.[160] If Forster was serious about applying the selection process to the entire local populace as quickly as possible, then he too had a stake in changing the existing procedure.

Accelerating and Simplifying the Selection Process

The turning of 1941–42 marked an important watershed not only for deportation policy but also for the DVL. It had been over a half a year since the DVL branch offices had begun their work, and there were no longer any doubts that the selection process ordered by Frick's implementation provisions would require a great deal of time and labor. By then, such as effort was exactly what the German occupiers could less afford than ever before, as the failure of the Blitzkrieg strategy against the Soviet Union and the Reich's consequent reorientation toward a longer war became the defining factor in Germanization policy as well.

The situation was obvious with the need to once again expand recruitment for the Wehrmacht, which took personnel away from the German occupation apparatus in the eastern provinces and thus slowed the DVL selection process even more. On top of that, the Wehrmacht soon showed interest in the members of Section 3, by far the largest group in the DVL, which had so far escaped the draft only because the existing provisions stated that they were not German nationals, and would need to undergo case-by-case naturalization to receive that status. To change the law, Stuckart, Himmler, and Martin Bormann signed the "second order on the DVL and German national status in the incorporated eastern territories" on January 31, 1942, which conferred the newly created revocable national status on those in Section 3—at this point, at least 220,000 individuals, and ten times that number by the end of the war.[161] Revocable national status would automatically become regular national status if the right of revocation was not exercised within the first ten years. But the right of revocation could also "be waived earlier if worth has been fully demonstrated."[162] Stuckart wrote in retrospect that it had simply proved both "politically and psychologically necessary" for this group "to be legally bound to the Reich in some way." They could thus be promised "the prospect of full national status rights" but without freeing them from the direct control of the German occupiers, since a "negative selection at a later date" remained a possibility.[163] The pledge of a better legal status must nonetheless be seen as a "concession" on the part of the German occupiers, as rightly noted by Wacław Długoborski. Beyond the recruitment of soldiers, the cooperation of the noncombatant populace had also become more necessary than ever before, whether as suppliers of agricultural products or as workers in arms production.[164]

In Danzig–West Prussia, this situation led to yet another modification of the selection process in early 1942, which deviated even further from Berlin's guidelines. In order to further expedite the registration process, Forster issued instructions to DVL branch office personnel on January 9, 1942, that they too should attend the local preliminary registration commission's sittings, because in this way, the need for summoning candidates could "be avoided to an even greater extent than before." With this modification, DVL assessment commission members had truly become spectators in their own process. Further, Forster outlined the main target groups for registration: members of the "healing professions" and "understaffed professions," persons working in public service, those with relatives inside the Reich or on the front, and, finally, those who were to be deported.[165]

Forster had imitators in Upper Silesia. The trailblazer here was the Landrat of Kattowitz Rural County, who, as has been mentioned, had jurisdiction over some 387,000 residents and thereby reckoned with around 300,000 applications—which was almost as many as in the entire governmental region of

Bromberg. To help manage this crush to even a small degree, Philipp Heimann had ordered the establishment of local registration commissions in the various townships and cities. They were to first examine the questionnaires and compile the applicants who would be sorted into Section 3, so that the local DVL branch office could make a summary decision.[166]

This procedure was taken up by the Oberpräsident's offices. A memorandum from its ethnonationality unit, prepared in collaboration with the party, the RKFDV branch office, and the SD, similarly called for a change to the existing procedure, justifying it above all with the need "to identify as quickly as possible an adequate number of German ethnonationals to the offices of the Wehrmacht, in accordance with the requirement needed from you locally."[167] Compliance was to be ensured through public announcements inviting the "German populace of Upper Silesia" to come apply for enrollment in the DVL by March 1942. Whoever failed to do so without a valid reason would be "treated as not belonging to Germandom." The completed questionnaires would no longer be forwarded immediately to the DVL branch office at the county seat, however, but would instead (as in Kattowitz Rural County) be sent first to the relevant registration commission established at the local level, consisting of the mayor, the Ortsgruppenleiter, and an SD representative, who would then notate a proposed decision on each application. For those sorted into Section 3 by the registration commission, there would then follow "a summary decision by the DVL branch office, which is to use random spot checks only, in order to satisfy itself that the registration commission's proposal was correct." The DVL branch office's assessment committee would still make decisions only in terms of sorting into Sections 1, 2, or 4, and also in cases where disagreement remained within the registration commission after its regular proceedings. The names of applicants entered into Sections 1 through 3 were then to be communicated to the "military recruitment offices . . . immediately after the decision."[168]

Not even two weeks had passed before this draft proposal was adopted more or less verbatim by Himmler on February 10, 1942, who issued it as his directive on the "implementation of preliminary registration," to be mandatory for all provinces. The surprise is not only how quickly Himmler approved the decree, but the fact that he did so at all. Although the decree could not have aligned with his own interests, he nonetheless had little alternative, for Forster and Bracht had already reinterpreted Frick's implementation provisions in a way that allowed the continuation of their own assimilation policies—in his decree, Himmler was simply legitimizing an existing state of affairs that he could no longer change. Furthermore, a year-long selection process was certainly not desirable from his perspective either. And finally, he believed he had already secured certain control mechanisms. One was the proviso granting veto rights to each member of the preliminary registration commission, and thus to the SD as well, and a veto

meant that the application had to be processed according to the existing procedure. On top of that, Himmler ordered that if "additional local regulations for
the individual Gaus are necessary, these are to be arranged by the responsible
RKFDV appointees. They are to be brought to my attention through my Staff
Main Office."[169]

THE WARTHELAND: HIMMLER'S PROVISIONS "IMMATERIAL"

This acceleration of the procedure initially had only minor effects on the selection process in the Wartheland. There, the branch offices were just finishing
the transferal of names, and Greiser had already issued an ultimatum to the
"Deutschstämmige": whoever failed to apply for enrollment in the DVL by
February 28, 1942, would be treated as a Pole.[170] Himmler's provisions seemed
"immaterial . . . because a need for this did not exist."[171]

Nonetheless, the Wartheland did see developments aiming at least partially
along the same lines, if considerably later. On April 8, 1943, Greiser's deputy
August Jäger issued instructions to the DVL regional offices that all males in Section 4 born in 1923 and later were now to be transferred to Section 3, unless the
entire family was ineligible on racial grounds or was undesirable "in their social
conduct." This move was also open to older males in Section 4 if they voluntarily
requested it. They were all upgraded to Section 3 "in order to be able to prove,
through service in the Wehrmacht," that they were prepared "to fit themselves
into the German Volksgemeinschaft."[172]

But neither the easing of the enrollment procedure nor the transferring of
potential soldiers from Section 4 to 3 brought significant results. As the record
shows, DVL membership increased only marginally from the start of April to
the end of 1942, with just 44,786 new admissions. In comparison, the number of
rejections during the same period increased by 58.4 percent, which is certainly
revealing.[173] The DVL assessment commissions had clearly been unwilling to
apply their selection criteria more pragmatically, as can also be seen in the relative
weights of the sections. At the start of 1943, there were a total of 475,743 DVL members: 401,372 of them had been enrolled into the sections for the politically loyal
"Bekenntnisdeutsche" or "Volksdeutsche," representing 84.37 percent; in comparison, the 74,371 "Deutschstämmige" or "Wiedereinzudeutschende" ("persons
to be re-Germanized"), whom the Reichsstatthalter's offices wanted to transport
into the Reich as soon as possible, were a much smaller group, at 15.63 percent.[174]

UPPER SILESIA: APPRECIATING THE "OVERALL PERSONALITY"

The effects of Himmler's directive remained rather limited in Upper Silesia as
well, in that he was only legitimizing an already established procedure here.
During preparations for further registration efforts, Bracht's ethnonationality

officer Hohlfeld highlighted long-familiar priorities for a meeting at the Oberpräsident's offices on February 18, 1942. It was once again impressed on the DVL offices that registration activities were to be conducted "as a top priority before all other duties," and the importance of these registrations for the Wehrmacht's personnel needs was underlined. But the latter aspect was to be hidden from the local populace, which is why the assessments were "in any event . . . only to happen within the family framework, with the simultaneous induction of all family members (great-grandmother, grandmother, mother, and 'combat-capable' offspring)," meaning application forms were also "to be issued to families *without* combat-capable persons."[175]

After the meeting, the Regierungspräsidents and Landrats received Bracht's renewed call to the public, which was published in the local newspapers on March 1 and specified an application deadline of March 31, 1942. A comparison of its choice of words with those in Greiser's call reflected basic differences in Germanization policy. Whereas Greiser primarily emphasized the requirements whose lack would doom an application to failure, Bracht struck a considerably more inclusivist tone, simply calling on "all those persons who believe themselves eligible to submit an application for induction into the DVL to do so immediately." But Bracht apparently feared that his call would meet with little interest, which is why he preemptively blamed "work-shy and politically unreliable elements" for continually trying

> to convince you that Volk comrades inducted into the DVL (Sections 1 to 3) . . . are treated differently from other Germans, meaning that they are to remain second- or third-class Germans. Contrary to these senseless rumors, I once again explicitly affirm that all persons inducted into Section 3 of the DVL, in terms of property law, tax law, and labor law, are put on an absolutely equal footing as all other German Volk comrades within the Greater German Reich. The full enjoyment of your property, your assets, and all other civil rights, is assured to you.[176]

In a draft of a speech (probably by Hohlfeld) to be given at the DVL central office of Upper Silesia, whose first sitting was only just now happening on February 20, 1942, a full year after Frick's implementation provisions, its staff was committed to this inclusivist policy under which applicants who had been active in "German" organizations during the interwar period were to be sorted into Section 1, while even members of Polish economic and cultural associations might very well be inducted into Section 2, for such participation had been "often unavoidable." But it was in regard to Section 3 that Hohlfeld particularly exhorted his audience to exercise generosity. Examples of persons belonging in Section 3 included the "mixed population speaking a Slavic home language" who consisted "not solely of German elements," as well as individuals who had belonged to Polish political groups or even, "in certain cases," insurrectionary groups, paramilitary groups, or the Polish Western Association, meaning organizations espousing a radically anti-German policy. Ultimately, a person was to be assessed according to "overall personality," with judgments "not to be based on lifeless writings"—which probably also meant the provisions from Berlin. If a person was "worthy of incorporation into the German Volksgemeinschaft, then the person is to be admitted, and if not, then rejected."[177]

Starting in February 1942, the number of persons admitted into the DVL did indeed race to new heights. Whereas the DVL offices had previously registered 238,921 persons in the first nine months from May 1941 to January 1942, the number would surpass the million mark by the end of 1942.[178] The highly inclusivist interpretation of the provisions, especially in selecting for Section 3, is similarly apparent, becoming particularly obvious in comparison with the Wartheland. There, the two lower sections represented only 15.63 percent of DVL enrollment at the end of 1942, but in Upper Silesia, they added up to 754,414 persons, representing 75.01 percent.[179]

The particular emphasis on Section 3, which also illustrates the assimilationist thrust of Upper Silesia's selection practices, has often motivated past scholars to compare its Germanization policy with the one in Danzig–West Prussia. As correct as the association fundamentally is, one should not lose sight of an important difference in doing so: although both provinces certainly did induct more than 60 percent of the local populace into the DVL, the disparities east and west of Upper Silesia's internal police border are extreme to an extent found in no other province. The disparities are clearly seen, for example, in the data from late 1943 on Kattowitz Governmental Region, which had received the largest part of the western Polish territories annexed to Upper Silesia. At this point in time, the DVL branch offices had already inducted 60 percent of the local populace, but less than 2 percent were from the eastern part of the province, which was formerly in the Russian Partition, and more than 98 percent were from the western part, formerly in the Prussian and Austrian Partitions.[180]

To seek the reasons for this in the populace itself, which also would thereby essentialize it, would certainly give too much credence to the German propaganda of the time. When the occupiers proceeded differently in the west, it was not because, as Ryszard Kaczmarek suggests, "the populace living there represented part of the Aryan race, and thus were not subject to extermination on racial grounds."[181] Apart from the fact that an examination of German selection practices certainly does not allow one to draw any valid conclusions about the "racial" makeup of the populace, but only about the ideological makeup of the occupiers, it seems to me that Kaczmarek's conjecture is all the more misguided because it steers attention in precisely the wrong direction: "race" effectively played no role in the DVL selection criteria (and not only in Upper Silesia). Instead—and for this, it is precisely the east-west disparity in Upper Silesia that provides a conclusive piece of evidence—the province's DVL branch offices were much more guided by a combination of security-related and economic criteria on the one hand, and traditionally Prussian Germanization aspirations on the other. As a result, the populace in formerly German (and Austrian) territory was effectively faced with a choice: either assimilate or be rounded up in the next wave of deportations. Whoever felt compelled by these conditions to apply for admission to the DVL could count on leniency. But in the former Russian Partition, the occupiers showed themselves to be less open to compromise. In these counties, the lack of German language skills was taken as evidence that the applicant was a "Pole." Even recognition as a "Water Pole" or "Szlonzakian" was unavailable, because German ethnologists believed that these ethnic groups lived only in the former Prussian and Austrian Partitions. This territorial differentiation reveals the DVL process in Upper Silesia as less a Nazi innovation and more a continuation of Prussian tradition.

DANZIG–WEST PRUSSIA: "IMMEDIATE ENROLLMENT WITHOUT BUREAUCRACY"

As has been shown, Himmler had tried to avert the danger of an excessively inclusivist interpretation of his registration-accelerating decree of February 10, 1942, by inserting the stipulation that any local deviations were to be decreed solely by his RKFDV appointee for that region and were also to be communicated to him through the Staff Main Office of the RKFDV. This regulation was aimed primarily against Forster, the only civil administration head in the annexed provinces that Himmler had refused to name as one of his RKFDV appointees. In Danzig–West Prussia, the old arrangement was still in effect, with the HSSPF exercising this function. But if Himmler believed his stipulation would hold Forster in check, he would soon learn otherwise. Instead, Forster played Himmler's accelerating decree against Frick's implementation provisions, thereby freeing himself entirely of the restrictive guidelines of both Reich-level authorities.

In mid-1941, Forster was still refusing the Reich Interior Ministry's desire for a general call to the populace to help expedite DVL registration efforts and had relied instead on the party's own preliminary registration commissions; but now, this precautionary measure was apparently no longer necessary. On February 22, 1942, a general appeal to the public was launched by Forster as well. In looking back at the selection process so far, he once again underlined the civil administration's willingness to induct a large part of the populace, while also trying to defuse any doubts caused by the operation's slow progress:

> We have sought out the people who due to their conduct or descent can be considered Germans. . . . Now, with the enormous amount of work that had to be done over the last two-and-a-half years particularly in this area, it may be that

such-and-such an individual or family was forgotten by us. But in order that nobody be deprived of the possibility of returning to the German Volksgemeinschaft and professing to be German, a public invitation is hereby issued to all those who feel themselves to be German, or are demonstrably of German descent, or have relatives in the Old Reich, and who want to be counted among the German Volksgemeinschaft, to come register for admission to the DVL by March 31, 1942. No person who wants to return to the German Volksgemeinschaft and so far has been overlooked should be disadvantaged.[182]

But Forster did not want to rely solely on this promise of an inclusivist selection policy, and so he added a threat: "But whoever refuses this must be clearly mindful that, in the future, he will not be treated as belonging to Germandom, but will be outwardly labeled as a Pole, and subject to the regulations for Poles. That this is also tied to equal status with the worst enemies of the German Volk is likewise self-evident."[183] With this, the local populace was invited to make a "voluntary" application for the first time. This marked a "turning point" in existing policy, as rightly noted in the Polish underground press.[184] In order to ensure rapid processing of the applications, Forster went a step further than envisaged in Himmler's registration-accelerating decree and made summary decision making obligatory not only for selection into Section 3, but also into Sections 1 and 2. Who exactly was to be inducted here should "in general be clear; therefore, an immediate enrollment without bureaucracy is to be undertaken," meaning without the case-by-case assessments as before.[185] The latter were now to be limited solely to political opponents "of German descent" in Section 4. Furthermore, decisions would no longer depend on the Reich Interior Ministry's two questionnaires for each applicant; they were now dropped entirely.[186] Instead, as was tersely communicated to the DVL branch offices, "a form has been devised," which now covered a single page and was not to be filled out by the applicants but instead by the preliminary registration commissions, who were to directly question the relevant family during the application submission itself (see figure 5.2).[187] Beyond basic personal data, only five questions were of interest: whether German ancestors were determinable; whether relatives existed in the Old Reich; how the family's conduct was during the Polish period and also after September 1939; whether work performance had been good; and whether the household made a clean impression.[188] Thus, as in Upper Silesia, proof of "German" ancestors was no longer necessarily required for DVL enrollment in Danzig–West Prussia either.

Forster further stipulated how this information was to be handled in the next step. If there was nothing against the applicant, and "of the questionnaire's five questions, three can be answered in a positive manner . . . then the preliminary registration commission is to recommend enrollment in Section 3," unless Section 1 or 2 was still a possibility. This preliminary decision was then binding

Fragebogen
zur Vorerfassung für die Deutsche Volksliste

Familienname Gruß   Vorname Sylvester

geboren am 3.11.1882 in Garay   Kreis Scharnikau

Beruf (erlernter) Kaufmann   z. Zt. ausgeübter Kaufmann

Ehefrau (Vorname) Agnes   geborene Gruer

geboren am 31.7.1912 in Wordel   Kreis Flatow

Kinder: Vorname Wladislaus   geb am 9.5.1923   in Lobsens
                 Irene   „   „ 11.4.1931   „   Bromberg
            „   „   „   „
            „   „   „   „
            „   „   „   „
            „   „   „   „

Sonstige im Haushalt lebende Angehörige und sonstige Personen unter 21 Jahren:

Familienname	Vorname	geboren am	geboren in

Wohnort und Anschrift am 1. 12. 1939 Bromberg Kreis

1. Sind deutsche Vorfahren feststellbar?

    a) Ehemann ja — nein

    b) Ehefrau ja — nein

2. Sind Verwandte im Altreich vorhanden?

    a) Ehemann ja — nein

    b) Ehefrau ja — nein

3. Wie ist das Verhalten der Familie gewesen

    a) während der polnischen Zeit?

    b) seit September 1939?

4. Wie ist die Arbeitsleistung des Ehemannes und der Ehefrau, wenn auch diese berufstätig ist?

    gut — schlecht

5. Macht der Haushalt einen sauberen Eindruck? ja — nein

Vorschlag der Vorerfassungskommission:

Entscheidung der Zweigstelle der Deutschen Volksliste beim Oberbürgermeister in Bromberg

Entscheidung des M.d.I.:   Abt. 3

Bromberg, den 22. Juni   1942
Posener Str. 4/4

                            Zweigstelle der Deutschen Volksliste

Figure 5.2. Questionnaire for accelerating the DVL process in Danzig–West Prussia.
Source: Institute of National Remembrance in Warsaw, NTN 196/201.

on the DVL branch office. In sorting for Section 3, the "DVL branch office is to handle this application in such a way that an individual review of the recommendations is unnecessary." If the preliminary registration commission voted for Sections 1 or 2, then an "individual assessment is necessary, but with these two sections, one can proceed generously." On the other hand, if there was politically incriminating material, or fewer than three questions could answered in a positive way, then instead of rejecting the applicant, the case was to be referred to the DVL branch office with a corresponding opinion. The desired inclusiveness of the selection process was further underlined by the urgency with which the decision-making process was to be pursued: from "February 23 to March 15, 1942, the Landrats, mayors, and Kreisleiters are working exclusively for the DVL only, with all other tasks postponed." And every "Saturday . . . it is to be reported to me in Danzig . . . how many persons have been inducted into the individual sections of the DVL."[189]

The SS apparatus was again pressured not to slow down the decision-making process. The Security Police and the SD were told to answer inquiries about new applicants quickly, but with only a "yes" or "no," and to simply advise *whether* anything was against the subject person, but not *what*. Forster, in misrepresenting the registration-accelerating decree, went on to state that documents corroborating the applicant's German descent or political conduct before the German invasion were, "according to the directive of the Reichsführer of the SS, no longer required." They were nonetheless to be requested, but exactly "when this happens is unimportant. In no event can the decision be made dependent on presenting the documents."[190]

With this procedure, Forster had also removed any pretense of a universal Reich-level selection process. Naturally, the Reich Interior Ministry protested such unilateral interventions. Finally, in a letter to the DVL regional and branch offices on July 2, 1942, Forster informed them of an alleged agreement that the old questionnaires would be necessary only in cases where an assessment committee member contests the decision passed by the relevant chairman, so that the case is then referred to the next higher level.[191] Furthermore, of the five questions, applicants now had to answer at least the first two with "yes," meaning they would need to demonstrate of having "German" ancestors as well as relatives inside the Reich.[192]

But what should happen with the people enrolled in the past four months? For the Landrat of Bromberg County, Walther Nethe, the answer was clear: a "rectification" would only cause "difficulties," which is why the existing decisions were to be maintained.[193] There is no evidence that even a single branch office handled this any differently. Furthermore, there had already been problems in dealing with appeals cases. Those sent to the DVL regional office in Bromberg had been immediately sent back to the branch offices. In a message to the Landrats and mayors on June 27, 1942, Vice Regierungspräsident Walther Kühn noted that they had, "in accordance with the guidelines issued to you, made decisions largely without documentary paperwork, solely based on personal impressions and the unverified statements of the applicants themselves... The questionnaires stipulated in the Reich Interior Minister's circular of March 13, 1941, have also not been filled out."[194] The appeals could not be processed under these circumstances. The branch offices were instructed to proceed as before with such cases, meaning to have the questionnaires filled out and also all the necessary documents handed in. Simply claiming, as one applicant had done, to have subscribed to a German newspaper before the invasion, and thus to having lived as a "German" even then, would no longer suffice—the corresponding "receipts" would now have to be produced as well.[195]

Of course, such modifications had no effect on Forster's determination to implement a selection policy that was as inclusivist as possible. On July 2, 1942—the same day he had announced his own latest modifications—the branch offices received another message from Forster, in which he criticized them once again because the complaints of another authority—"including from the Chief of the Security Police and the SD"—had often been enough to make them rescind DVL enrollments. In order to prevent this, future complaints could be submitted only in writing and could be considered only after "all existing applications are processed"—meaning not at all for now. If a DVL branch office or regional office wanted to approve a request to remove someone from the DVL, the final verdict was, "after presentation of the files to the central office, to be pronounced, where required, by the Gauleiter and Reichsstatthalter."[196] In writing to the DVL offices a little later, Forster ordered that, in general, all persons receiving a "Volksdeutsche" identity document (from the party) during the first year of the German occupation and subsequently sorted according to Frick's implementation provisions into Section 3 were now to be inducted into Section 2 if they had worked for a party suborganization after the German invasion, or if nothing prejudicial against them existed from before the invasion. "If an objection is nonetheless raised by any commission member, such objection is not to be heeded."[197]

As in Upper Silesia, the number of persons registered in the DVL rose rapidly after Himmler's accelerating decree—or more precisely, after the expansion of Forster's inclusivist policy had thereby been facilitated: while the DVL in Danzig–West Prussia had contained a little more than thirty-one thousand members in December 1941, the number subsequently skyrocketed to nearly eight hundred thousand just ten months later.[198] Less striking than in Upper Silesia but nonetheless noticeable was that in Danzig–West Prussia too selection practices were more inclusive in the west of the province than in the east. Thus, in the counties of Leipe and Rippin, both formerly part of the Russian Partition, only 17 percent of the local populace had been registered in the DVL by the end of March 1943, but in the rest of the province, this share was 58 percent.[199]

For the individual DVL branch offices, this rapid expansion meant a massive upswing in decision making. For example, the branch office of Bromberg Rural County had registered a total of 1,380 persons by December 3, 1941, but at the first sitting "according to the new procedure" on March 7, 1942, it decided on 362 applications, and managed even more at the next meeting on March 14, with 2,203 applications. At this pace, 19,804 applicants were assessed by the end of June, with each weekly sitting processing an average of 1,238 applicants and a maximum of 2,587.[200]

The Final Marginalization of Racial Appraisals

From the perspective of the SS complex, the DVL selection practices, at least as seen in Danzig–West Prussia and Upper Silesia, must have confirmed the very fears that Himmler had tried to avert with his ethnonationality decree of September 1940 and with his pressure on the Reich Interior Ministry to introduce the DVL according to the Wartheland model. Above all, Himmler had failed to impose an exclusivist selection process, which he needed for his appointed task of accommodating the ethnic Germans from Eastern Europe, and which he also believed in as a racial ideologue. The corresponding demand that if applicants lacked proven "German descent," then their DVL enrollment should be tied to their "racial suitability," had failed to take hold in any province.

It was ultimately RuSHA that made a final attempt to influence DVL selection practices in favor of SS priorities. Referring back to Frick's implementation provisions, it presented its "guidelines for conducting racial assessments for the DVL" as early as April 25, 1941, in which enrollment in Sections 3 and 4 was tied to a racial appraisal. The assessments were to be conducted by RuSHA itself, which was to dispatch "expert commissions" to each governmental region, where they were to assess the relevant persons after completing the initial adjudication and to approve for enrollment in Sections 3 and 4 only those persons who, "on the basis of the racial evaluation, are found to be suitable."[201] This foray was considerably less ambitious than the earlier attempt by the Staff Main Office of the RKFDV to take over the entire process, but it nonetheless would have secured for the SS complex a veto over enrollments in Sections 3 and 4, thereby giving them a tool for ending inclusivist selection practices that obtained in Danzig–West Prussia and Upper Silesia.

* * *

Even before this new foray in the fight over DVL selection criteria became known in Danzig–West Prussia and Upper Silesia, meaning the provinces against which these guidelines were primarily directed, it met with strong opposition from the Wartheland. Egon Leuschner, who as a member of the Racial Policy Office had been invited to the meeting at RuSHA, was confronted on his return with fierce criticism from the Reichssstatthalter's offices in Posen and had to be defended by Uebelhoer.[202] The latter also used his powers to enable the fulfillment of the agreement achieved by Leuschner in Berlin, according to which the racial selection process would begin in Litzmannstadt Governmental Region, as a kind of field test. At least there, the logistical challenges would be fewer, because a RuSHA field office had already been established in Litzmannstadt.

At first, it was entirely unclear what "racial valuation group" ("rassische Wertungsgruppe") an applicant had to manifest in order to be enrolled in the DVL.[203] The original impulse at the RuSHA field office was to apply the same yardstick as the one used during the selection of Poles for deportation and during the re-Germanization program, meaning that only persons in Valuation Group I or II would be approved. But during a "test appraisal" of twenty families on May 10, 1941, it had to be admitted that only four of them fulfilled the requirements. Well aware of the opposition to yet another racial selection, the head of the local field office, SS Assault Unit Leader Fritz Schwalm, clearly understood that rejecting three-quarters of those in Sections 3 and 4 would not be politically viable.[204] Faced with opposition from the DVL regional office, Schwalm was forced to concede that "an admission of only racial Valuation Groups I and II into the DVL would lead to small-scale results." There was, however, no shyness at RuSHA about finding a solution nor about offering an ideological justification: given that people in Sections 3 and 4— unlike the ones to be "re-Germanized"—were "for the most part Deutschstämmige," they could also be admitted when selected into Valuation Group III. This would also allow equal treatment with the "Volksdeutsche" from the Baltics and other regions who had undergone the EWZ selection process, among whom it was likewise those in Valuation Groups I through III who were ultimately approved, with an "O Notice," for settlement "im Osten" or "in the East."[205]

This plan of action was problematic already on ideological grounds. For one thing, the two selection processes were not comparable in the eyes of the Nazis. Although an "O Notice" from the EWZ recognized the relevant family as suitable for settlement in the annexed territories, members of DVL Sections 3 and 4 were considered unsuitable in precisely this regard, and thus—at least theoretically—were to be transported to the Reich for "re-Germanization." For another thing, Schwalm neglected to mention how it came to be that migrants in Valuation Group III were ultimately recognized by the EWZ as equally worthy of an "O Notice": Himmler had been inspecting the selection process during a visit to the EWZ site in Gotenhafen on January 14, 1940, when he noticed how many people were being winnowed out by the suitability assessors as unfit for eastern deployment. Because a great number of settlers were needed for the "Germanization of the soil," Himmler ordered that instead of restricting "O Notices" to members of Valuation Groups I and II as before, they were now to be extended to those in Valuation Group III as well.[206] Schwalm, in justifying his concession to pragmatic necessities in Litzmannstadt, was thus relying on what itself had been a concession to pragmatic necessities.

Introducing Racial Selections into the DVL Process

The SS complex stepped up its efforts in the following months, as the racial appraisals were to be conducted not only in Litzmannstadt, but across the entire annexed eastern territories. The RuSHA field office in Litzmannstadt planned further "test appraisals" in June 1941 with the participation of RuSHA staff from Danzig–West Prussia and Upper Silesia, and the RKFDV headquarters coordinated operations in Berlin, deciding on August 12, 1941, in an agreement with RuSHA and the Party Chancellery (Parteikanzlei), that a dedicated assessment commission would be dispatched to each of the eleven DVL regional offices. Each commission was to subject six hundred persons per day to the racial selection process, thereby removing those in Section 3 "who due to their appearance are unsuitable for incorporating into the German Volksgemeinschaft."[207]

This plan was immediately rejected by the ethnocrats in the Wartheland. As Coulon explained to Dr. Gottfried Neesse from the Party Chancellery on August 26, 1941, the "most urgent problem" at the moment was that there were still too few Germans and too many Poles. In his view, the "racial policy question," meaning the further selection of the German populace, could not be tackled before the "ethnopolicy question," meaning the separation of "Germans" from "Poles," was settled. For that reason, all energies in Posen would be focused on the Polish majority populace, further policing their living conditions and suppressing as much as possible any remaining contacts with the "Germans" until they could be removed from the province. But to do so, it was necessary to maintain the active cooperation of the "German" populace, which therefore could not be unsettled with belated expulsions from the DVL. Coulon felt that instead of subjecting members of Sections 3 and 4 to racial selection right away, it made more sense to wait for their intended transport into the Reich. Since these were all persons of proven "German" descent, which, as has been mentioned, was a prerequisite in the Wartheland for enrollment in Sections 3 and 4 and meant they could be more dangerous than the Poles, they certainly could not be treated as Poles again if they failed to meet the standards of the suitability assessors. Coulon had thus tried to prevent the racial selections with a racial argument and had thereby set up an argumentative stalemate that could no longer be decided on the basis of ideology, a logical impasse that was necessarily produced by racial ideology but could be resolved only in terms of practicality.

Coulon's critique went even further, however. He feared that even if all members of Sections 3 and 4 were to be transported into the Reich independently of the racial appraisal results, the chronological order of their removals would nonetheless be prejudiced by the appraisals. In this regard, Coulon supported a decidedly different position on prioritization: "The order of the resettlements should again be done according to practical aspects, not theoretical ones. First in line are those who particularly strain the internal affairs of the ethnonational battleground."[208] Therefore, the ones who needed to leave the province first were all the politically dangerous members of Section 4, as well as those members of Section 3 "whose resettlement, due to ethnopolitical reasons . . . cannot be delayed." On the other hand, those engaged in locally understaffed occupations were to be removed last, regardless of their racial evaluations, and even then only if correspondingly qualified replacements came to the Wartheland from the Reich. "Aspects other than those defined by the circumstances of the ethnopolitical battle will meet with no sympathy among the Wartheland's German populace."[209] During these preparations for one last confrontation with the Polish populace, it seemed that race as a category was simply not functional.

In a later note to his superiors, which would also be sent to the Reich Interior Ministry, Coulon summarized once again the main arguments against introducing a racial selection process in the Wartheland. In doing so, he highlighted above all the basic incompatibility between the DVL selection process and the racial selection process proposed by the SS complex: "An incorporation of racial assessment into the procedure of the DVL . . . contradicts . . . its basic idea. The DVL is a summary registration of the Deutschstämmige based on the concept of professing, for Sections 1 and 2, and of descent, for Sections 3 and 4. . . . One must . . . maintain the principle of separating ethnonationality questions from race questions."[210] According to Coulon, the DVL had been introduced in order to enlist the "Volksdeutsche" and "Deutschstämmige," and with their support, to act against the Poles even more severely. But for this, it was imperative that "in terms of ethnonationality, a clarity and a reassurance are established among the German populace in the Wartheland as soon as possible, for this is the only way to create a truly united German ethnonational front against Polishdom." The "speedy completion of this process is henceforth the most urgent goal of ethnopolitical work in the Wartheland," which is why "an incorporation of racial assessments into the process itself is no longer possible." If the SS complex insisted on racial appraisals, then they should be done only after the subjects were transported into the Reich. But if they needed to happen in the Wartheland after all, then every precaution was to be taken in order to limit the feared negative consequences for the anti-Polish policy of the Reichsstatthalter's offices: "The dangers arising from culling the racially undesirable Deutschstämmige would necessitate in any case that the culled are removed from the Wartheland and placed in camps in the Old Reich, where it would then be still possible, through sterilization, to stop them from multiplying."[211] In any case, the administration in Posen was not willing to suspend the selection process until an agreement had been achieved with the SS complex in this matter. Although RuSHA explicitly demanded that identity documents be issued only after the relevant applicants had also been evaluated by its suitability assessors, its demand was ignored.[212] Schwalm ultimately had to accept the fact that the issuing of identity documents had created "established facts," and that only an assessment after the fact was still practicable. But doing so remained absolutely necessary, because if the relevant persons escaped removal and even managed to acquire revocable national status in the near future, then those who would later be disqualified from naturalization for insufficient "racial suitability" had to be selected now. Otherwise, there was a danger of these individuals achieving positions that could considerably complicate any future revocation of national status. Schwalm furthermore suggested a way to curb the negative labor-market effects feared by the Reichsstatthalter's offices: borrowing an idea from Coulon, he wrote that these persons could be "biologically neutralized through sterility but themselves retained as workers, while also making it unnecessary to relinquish them to an alien ethnonation."[213] The Reichssstatthalter's offices ultimately endorsed the restrictions laid out by Coulon. In response to a query from the Reich Interior Ministry, Jäger wrote on September 11, 1941, that the administration in Posen still favored the removal of all persons in Sections 3 and 4, but if this was not possible, then it would agree to racial selections—but only "after completion of the DVL," and only if the individuals thereby selected were to be immediately removed from the Wartheland, in order to avoid an "agitating of the local populace."[214]

The softening of Greiser's tone may have influenced Himmler's decision to attempt another major intervention in DVL selection practices. On September 30, 1941, he issued his directive on the "racial appraisal of the members of Section 3 of the DVL" and wrote separately to Greiser to approve a compromise arrangement for the Wartheland only. Greiser was asked to authorize the immediate start of racial selections and was assured in return that the rejection of affected individuals would become effective only if the SS could also guarantee their removal from the province, thus avoiding any agitating of the populace. To forestall the necessity of making similar concessions to Forster and Bracht, Greiser was further asked to treat these assurances as confidential.[215] With this secret assurance in place, the directive stipulated that all persons "earmarked for enrollment or already enrolled in Section 3 of the DVL whose German descent can no longer be verified with certainty are to be racially assessed. . . . A negative outcome from the racial assessment will necessarily result in rejection of the enrollment application or else expulsion from the DVL. To conduct the assessment, I appoint RuSHA in Berlin."[216]

Protests from the Gauleiters

The Wartheland

As might be expected, Coulon's initial reaction was less than enthusiastic. In an opinion he wrote for Jäger, he particularly highlighted the negative consequences for anti-Polish policy resulting from Himmler's directive, stating that it bore "no relationship at all to any of the practical political needs of the relevant Gaus." Jäger was asked to persuade Greiser to use corresponding implementation provisions, as with the earlier decrees from the Reich Interior Ministry, in order "to curb this decree's strongly agitating effect on the life of the Gau."[217] Coulon was somewhat pacified only after he was shown Himmler's supplementary message, which at least partially took into account the Wartheland's political needs and in any case had already received Greiser's approval, thus making any further opposition pointless.[218]

Others, however, were not so easily quieted. For example, the Regierungspräsident of Posen Governmental Region, Dr. Victor Böttcher, made little effort to hide his criticism in his status report and also addressed precisely the difference between the two selection processes: "It is becoming more and more apparent that the racial selection process is not simply a supplement to the DVL process, but that two different viewpoints are standing here in opposition to one another. While one, in deciding on Germanizability, is largely guided by the applicant's upbringing, conduct, and character, the other decides solely according to external appearance. History will ultimately decide which process is more correct."[219] It was probably criticisms like Böttcher's that caused RuSHA to stop concentrating solely on biometric markers—as had happened with selecting locals for deportation. According to plans prepared by the RuSHA field office, the DVL branch offices in the Wartheland would receive index cards for recording all persons enrolled in Section 3, to be sent back to Litzmannstadt by January 15, 1942. Besides the person's basic data, there was also a field for "notable aspects and social relations," where the "findings" of the assessment commission were to be recorded, such as "industrious, drunkard, hoodlum, criminally convicted, suspected of spying, etc."[220] After the conclusion of registrations, each DVL branch office would inform the RuSHA field office so that the local on-site selection process could begin.[221] After the RuSHA selection process was approved officially as well by the Reichsstatthalter's offices on March 3, 1942, the first summonses to appear were already issued to the relevant individuals in Posen Governmental Region.[222] To avoid any further agitation, the true nature of the assessments was to be left unclear—but of course, word got out.

Despite the original intention, RuSHA managed to extend its reach beyond Section 3 in Posen, and was racially appraising members of Section 4 as well—ostensibly for reasons of operational efficiency—along with candidates whose applications were either awaiting a decision at the DVL branch office, or had already been rejected for insufficient "German descent." The four investigatory commissions, each with two suitability assessors, visited the various DVL branch offices from early March to mid-April 1942 and evaluated 67,235 persons in just eight weeks, ultimately selecting 6,227 families for Valuation Group IV and 1,186 families for IVf (i.e., "fremdblütig," "foreign-blooded").[223]

The racial selection process had hardly finished when conflicts broke out again between the Reichsstatthalter's offices and RuSHA, from disagreements over how the results were to be used. An earlier conflict had already emerged before the selections had even begun, triggered by a criticism sent by Schwalm's successor, SS Chief Assault Leader Walter Dongus, to the Reichsstatthalter's offices on January 27, 1942.[224] The DVL was asked to enroll into Sections 1 and 2 only those applicants who could substantiate their "German descent." Of course, such a request attacked the very foundations of the entire DVL process in the Wartheland, which rewarded conduct above all; it was not for nothing that these two sections had been reserved for the "Bekenntnisdeutsche" ("professed Germans"), meaning applicants whose political and social conduct had proved satisfactory to the civil administration. For Sections 1 and 2, "German descent" was just as irrelevant as German language proficiency. It is thus no wonder that the Reichsstatthalter's office flatly rejected his request by writing a clear "Nein!" on Dongus's message.[225]

The next demand from the RuSHA field office was met with a similarly peremptory reaction from Posen. Immediately after the first selections were concluded, the field office had sent lists to the DVL branch offices naming persons who represented a "desirable addition to the population."[226] When the field office then went a step further and expressed a demand to the DVL branch office in Lissa (today Leszno) that it should enroll persons from Valuation Groups 1 and 2 even when they had failed to meet the DVL requirement of demonstrating two "German" grandparents, the branch office protested to its superior authority, the DVL regional office in Posen.[227] Regierungspräsident Böttcher prohibited this enrollment and immediately complained to the DVL central office, asserting that RuSHA "still" believed that persons already rejected by the DVL were nonetheless to be admitted solely on the basis of racial selections. He demanded that these interferences activity needed to stop.[228]

But Dongus was undeterred, and returned again to his demand in his concluding report. In his view, at least with persons set aside by the DVL branch offices because of insufficient "German descent," such applications should now be decided on the basis of their RuSHA valuation. He wrote that these were initially to be divided into two groups. On the one hand, applicants who had been sorted into Valuation Groups I or II, and who had also stood out in their "attitude and performance," should be admitted to the DVL after all, because "performance is equally an expression of the German person." With these people, the racial selections had ostensibly proved that "there must exist a much greater element of German blood than can be determined on the basis of parents' and grandparents' Polish names." On the other hand, if applicants were assigned only average performance scores, they were to be taken into the re-Germanization program. But an "accelerated and simplified re-Germanization process" was envisaged for people in this group, for they—unlike everyone else selected by RuSHA—were able to demonstrate at least one "German" grandparent, and thus "German blood." In contrast, "families rated as unacceptable (RuSHA IV and RuSHA IVf)" were to be excluded from the DVL. They were to be transported by either the employment office (into the Reich) or the UWZ (into the General Government).[229]

The first part of Dongus's demand was what drew particular criticism from the Reichsstatthalter's offices. It was only with great reluctance that the stance that racial selections should not be mixed up with the DVL process had been abandoned, and the negative selection process had been approved. But it was entirely out of the question to now let RuSHA also decide who would be enrolled in the DVL, because doing so would negate its essential purpose for the civil administration, which was to catalogue those whose support could be counted on, as well as those who required particular monitoring because of their political opposition to National Socialism as persons of "German descent." The Reichsstatthalter's offices did not stand alone in this conflict with RuSHA and could count on support from within the SS complex itself. For example, Höppner was already undercutting Dongus on May 13, 1942, when he informed the DVL offices that in the view of the SD Command Precinct in Posen, as well as the Reich Security Main Office, "racial suitability" alone was not sufficient grounds for enrollment in the DVL.[230] Höppner did not need to change his views when, in addition to his duties heading the SD Command Precinct, he became Coulon's successor in June 1942—first as ethnonationality officer at the Reichsstatthalter's offices, and finally as head of the Gau Office for Ethnonationality Questions (Gauamt für Volkstumsfragen).

It was under this new title that Höppner dealt RuSHA its next defeat. Although DVL assessment commissions either enrolled entire families or rejected them as a whole, RuSHA suitability assessors passed racial judgments on each individual, thereby threatening family members with being torn apart. Höppner forced through a pragmatic solution in such cases, stipulating that an individual could stay on the DVL despite a negative judgment if at least one family member was enrolled in Section 1 or 2.

I would like to illustrate this point with a hypothetical case reflecting a frequently seen situation. If a family included one parent who had been a member of a German association, this person was normally enrolled in Section 1—and without needing to substantiate "German" descent. But if the spouse had not also joined such an association, then that spouse needed to demonstrate at least two "German" grandparents in order to allow enrollment of the family. If that was not possible, then the decision depended on whether the children had been raised "German." If yes, then the spouse was considered "fremdvölkisch" ("ethnonationally foreign"), but nonetheless enrolled in Section 3, with the children in Section 1. The introduction of racial selections meant that the spouse, as a member of Section 3, had to report to the SS suitability assessors, possibly to be sorted into Valuation Group IV and thus expelled from the DVL. But because forcibly separating and deporting one family member was just as unthinkable as expelling the entire family, the ethnocrats were faced with a dilemma: in considering whether a person was to be incorporated into the "German Volksgemeinschaft," the candidate's political good conduct and "race" could justify two contradictory decisions, for these aspects did not necessarily coincide in the way suggested by Nazi ideology. In this situation, the ethnocrats remained true to the basic principle of the DVL, deciding against "race" and in favor of political good conduct.

An interesting aspect of this confrontation that deserves highlighting again is the formation here of two opposing fronts that do not correspond to the dominant constellation traditionally seen in scholarly research, pitting civil administration against SS apparatus. As already demonstrated during the selection of "re-Germanizable persons" in the UWZ camps, the SS apparatus again showed itself to be very much a heterogeneous power structure, with each of its Main Offices guided by its own internal logic and ready to pursue its own decisions against those of another Main Office, in alliance with other power centers if necessary. An example would be the discussion of Dongus's concluding report on June 19, 1942. As it turned out, Dongus and his far-reaching demands were not only opposed by Höppner (here representing the Reichsstatthalter's offices and the SD) and Heinz Hummitzsch from the Reich Security Main Office but they also failed to win the support of the RKFDV branch office in Posen and the Staff Main Office of the RKFDV. Höppner managed to impose his own position here, so that DVL members with a negative RuSHA valuation would not be expelled if they still had a close family member in Sections 1 or 2, or—in a new twist—if they could provide documentation that not only two, but all four grandparents were "of German descent."[231] In this, Höppner was supported by the Reich Security Main Office as well as the RKFDV branch office, and Dongus could offer nothing to counter Höppner.[232]

* * *

One issue that was sure to draw particular attention was the effect of these racial appraisals on the Wehrmacht's troop-replacement needs. The second decree on the DVL had been issued specifically so that members of Section 3 could also be drafted into the Wehrmacht, and the racial appraisals were now threatening to counteract this. As the commander of Military District XXI (which was responsible for the Wartheland) worriedly informed Greiser on July 17, 1942, he had been notified that 748 conscriptable members of Section 3 had been classified as "racially unsuitable" by the suitability assessors. Fifty-three of them were already "in the field," and one could assume that "a number of these people have proved themselves before the enemy." Although he had already contacted the RuSHA field office in order to discuss keeping these soldiers, he nonetheless wrote to Greiser to ask that this matter "be handled with particular generosity, if there are no criminal aspects or serious racial worries."[233]

Here too, Greiser took a stance against RuSHA when he wrote "It is self-evident that one must refrain from anything that could adversely affect the willingness of a soldier drafted into the Wehrmacht, let alone a soldier deployed to the front."[234] At the Reichsstatthalter's offices, it was agreed that of these fifty-three individuals, only those sorted into Valuation Group IVf (with f meaning "fremdblütig" or "foreign-blooded") would be removed from Section 3 and thus from the Wehrmacht. The rest "must be stomached."[235] Of these fifty-three people, none was actually expelled. As it soon turned out, thirty either had relatives in Section 1 or 2 or were themselves pure "Deutschstämmige," and, of the other twenty-three, only one was selected into Valuation Group IVf. But as Herbert Mehlhorn later stipulated in January 1943, such a person was to be exempted from expulsion if he was already serving on the front—which very likely applied here, as it had been more than half a year since this individual had been drafted.[236]

It is much more difficult to answer the converse question of whether anyone at all was harmed by the racial selection process, beyond the humiliation of such treatment by the occupiers.[237] This can probably be ruled out in the case of soldiers, and not only for the fifty-three initially specified by RuSHA, but also for the additional eighty-one who similarly received a negative RuSHA valuation during the second round of selections.[238] As Höppner wrote immediately after Stalingrad, in view of the "Wehrmacht's current troop replacement situation," negative consequences for soldiers could not be justified.[239]

But it seems that the rest of the affected persons also fared no worse, for the Reichsstatthalter's offices insisted on the upholding of Himmler's agreement, thereby tying expulsion from the DVL to removal from the Wartheland. But of removal there is no evidence at all. It is no small irony that combat-capable men who had been sorted by the suitability assessors into Valuation Groups IV or IVf probably found themselves in an even better situation now. As the DVL regional office in Litzmannstadt reported to Posen, hundreds of persons were in that governmental region and, as members of the DVL, possessed German national status (on a revocable basis) and enjoyed the associated advantages, but nonetheless were not drafted into the Wehrmacht.[240] And yet the Reichsstatthalter's offices still refused to deport them.[241] And when the Gestapo in Hohensalza complained to Damzog that Section 4 members were not being expelled even after a "negative" racial selection outcome, Mehlhorn here too pointed to Himmler's written agreement.[242]

The civil administration had been against racial selections from the very start but found itself either incapable of preventing them or unwilling to risk an all-out confrontation with Himmler. Instead, it torpedoed any attempt to enforce their ensuing consequences. After permitting RuSHA to initially subject 67,235 individuals to a racial selection process in March–April 1942, and then a few thousand more in March 1943, the civil administration prohibited the expulsion of persons labeled "racially undesirable" by the suitability assessors. In the view of the Reichsstatthalter's offices, the worsening war situation would not allow any further agitation of the "German" populace.

Dieter Gosewinkel is thus mistaken in his belief that it was in the Wartheland above all where "particularly restrictive racial criteria for 'Germanization' were applied."[243] Although the Regierungspräsident of Litzmannstadt Governmental Region would soon instruct his DVL branch offices that applicants were now to be routinely subjected to a racial selection process before enrollment into Sections 3 and 4, and Mehlhorn would then take up this practice for the entire Wartheland in mid-1942, not a single indication can be found that these instructions were actually implemented, especially because the DVL registrations were already effectively finished by then. This signified the failure of Himmler's final attempt to control the DVL selection process in the Wartheland through the imposition of racial criteria, and thus to open the central instrument of Nazi Germanization policy to the defining influence of the SS apparatus. In the Wartheland—to pick up on Coulon's aforementioned words—"ethnopolicy" came before "racial policy."

Upper Silesia

With Greiser having agreed to Himmler's request, thereby allowing his decree on the "racial appraisal of the members of Section 3" to be implemented at all, Otto Hofmann, the head of RuSHA, wrote to Himmler on November 22, 1941, and pushed for racial selections to be likewise implemented in Danzig–West Prussia and Upper Silesia as well.[244] Two months later, the relevant SS officials gathered in Kattowitz at a meeting hosted by Arlt on February 5, 1942, at which they agreed to establish ten commissions by the end of the month, each with one suitability assessor, so that racial selections could start in March 1942. Who exactly would be subjected to these racial selections was not specified and was likely still not clear either.[245] Such details were probably to be worked out at a meeting to which Himmler had summoned Greifelt, Hofmann, Ehlich, and Arlt, in order to discuss in general the handling of DVL members and the speeding up of the process. The racial selection process was also discussed at the meeting with Himmler—although this was later interpreted in entirely different ways by the attendees. In any case, although he had not been present, the head of the Race Office at RuSHA, SS Regiment Leader Dr. Bruno Kurt Schultz, believed that a reference to this meeting would allow him to send a rather bold request to Bracht on February 23, 1942: assuming permission from the latter for a racial selection process involving members of Sections 3 and 4, he asked him to "instruct the branch offices to provide cooperation" in this matter.[246] Reacting with indignation, Bracht responded that Arlt had told him exactly the opposite about this meeting. According to this account, Himmler had explicitly stated he wanted to refrain from such selections "for the moment." In addition, he told Schultz in no uncertain terms that the realization of his "intentions, in view of the current political situation, is absolutely undesirable" and that he "certainly cannot profess agreement" with this plan and must therefore reject it "categorically."[247] Bracht was willing to authorize racial selections only for the fifty thousand members of Section 4.[248] Beyond that, he proposed that RuSHA could also racially appraise the two hundred thousand persons who either were already earmarked for deportation or had been nominated by the Landrats for the re-Germanization program and who thus were all outside the remit of the DVL offices.

It is unclear why these additional groups were suddenly brought into play—after all, according to Himmler's directive of September 30, 1941, it was only the members of Section 3 who were to be racially selected. But it is also unclear how RuSHA expected to implement the selection process for the one million individuals in Section 3 with only ten suitability assessors available. Bracht certainly knew about RuSHA's lack of suitability assessors, and he advised RuSHA that, with the task of racially selecting the persons suggested by him, the assessors may have already "found enough to do during the war period."[249]

Bracht expressed himself even more clearly in a message that same day to Schultz's superior Hofmann. Besides complaining about the disrespectful manner of Schultz's request, Bracht proved to be particularly annoyed that, after "a number of discussions" with Himmler, a longer meeting with representatives from RuSHA in Kattowitz, discussions with Hofmann himself, and a "great number of written statements," he now had to deal with this topic "once again." Full of indignation, he let Hofmann know that, while he did not want to deny due recognition to "the energy, if not to say the fanaticism" of the RuSHA officials, he himself was "so comprehensively preoccupied . . . that I must regret I cannot let myself be engaged in further negotiations and correspondence concerning the aforementioned question complex."[250] Even a face-to-face discussion failed to move Bracht. Instead, Hofmann was told that applying racial selections to so many people would lead to "an intense agitation of the populace and with this an impairment of labor performance."[251]

On March 3, 1942, SS Senior Group Leader Heinrich Schmauser, the successor of Bach-Zelewski, entrusted SS Regiment Leader Walter Scholtz, the Breslau-stationed RuSHA head for SS Superior District Southeast (SS-Oberabschnitt Südost), with implementing the racial selections.[252] Pursuant to Bracht's orders, the RuSHA commissions were tasked with racially selecting members of Section 4, along with persons under consideration for a "re-Germanization."[253] From the surviving sources, it is not possible to determine exactly when the selections began. It was probably the middle of the year when the commissions first took up their work, initially with just a small number of persons to process. The main reason for the small number might have been that the Landrats were not particularly far along in cataloguing the local populace—neither in DVL enrollments nor in nominating those to be "re-Germanized," a task that had likewise been delegated to them. For this, RuSHA had issued brief guidelines in which the Landrats and Amtskommissars were advised that the goal here was "less an increase of the German Volk" and more "a qualitative decrease of the leadership class of foreign folkdom," a class that—allegedly—"exhibits a considerable amount of Nordic blood." The class was ostensibly easy to recognize and was in evidence particularly where a "family . . . through conduct, industriousness, cleanliness, and health, even under impoverished circumstances, sticks out from the rest of the Polish *and* the Volksdeutsche populace" or when they—literally—"stand out from the masses in general through the height of their stature."[254]

The racial appraisals had hardly begun when the old differences broke out once again. From his new posting in Prague, Schultz made a trip specifically to iron things out. But during a meeting on January 6, 1943, it soon turned out that the opposing viewpoints could no longer be reconciled, with Schultz and officials from the Kattowitz RuSHA office, SD Command Precinct, and RKFDV branch office on the one side, and representatives of Springorum, Hohlfeld, and several Landrats on the other. Schultz assured attendees that the racial selections looked not only at external appearance but also very much at "psychological stance," and he also emphasized the importance of "specific external markers" that allowed one to infer, "in many cases, internal attitude as well," such as the trait of "unbalancedness," which "would often be typical for wavering folkdom" in particular. In his view, this was why racial evaluations should also play "a decisive role in ethnonationality policy." He was backed up, however, only by his SS comrades—such as Weber from the RKFDV branch office—who voiced opinions that the racial selections were also necessary to counteract what was condemned as excessively "humane assessments," which were largely attributed to the Wehrmacht's need for replacement troops.

The civil administration was not interested, and unlike Coulon, did not even try to dress up its objections in ideological terms. Instead, the Landrats of Teschen and Saybusch, which were the rural counties most strongly affected by such coercive measures in population policy, pointed to the disastrous consequences that would further threaten their work as the local authorities of the German occupation apparatus. The racial selections threatened to jeopardize the entire ethnonationality policy, for the revocation of DVL branch office decisions meant that the "authority of the Landrat and the Kreisleiter would necessarily suffer greatly," and this in a situation already characterized by an "ethnopolitical crisis in confidence" among the populace. If the populace were to also start doubting the Gauleiter's recent promise that members of Section 3 would be made equal to those in the first two sections, the racial appraisals will have caused "damage that cannot be repaired," according to the Landrat of Saybusch, Eugen Hering. The Landrat of Teschen, Dr. Udo Krüger, and the Gauhauptstellenleiter Ditze (a senior official in the Upper Silesian Gauleiter's offices), agreed with Hering, likewise emphasizing that they considered the selection "not politically tenable."[255] Springorum put it in even more concrete terms: though he did not dispute the need for the DVL to work with RuSHA, he insisted unequivocally that "admission to the DVL is not to be refused just because, for example, the racial assessment says 'RuSHA IV.'"[256]

It was possible to find agreement only on those points that Bracht had already pushed through with Himmler the previous year, and which RuSHA had meanwhile accepted, particularly that the members of Section 3 were not to be racially selected. In all other points, agreement was effectively impossible—and unlike the case of the Wartheland, the civil administration in Upper Silesia no longer limited itself to blocking the consequences of the racial selections but soon aimed to stop them entirely. As a kind of preliminary foray, Springorum made clear to officials of the SS apparatus that the DVL offices would not be attaching decisive importance to racial selection results. They would be accepted by the civil administration as a decision-making aid at best, but the DVL offices were certainly not prepared to grant any veto rights to RuSHA. The DVL branch offices were to be advised that the recommended course of action "in doubtful cases is to make use of the RuSHA commission, and to use its evaluation as the basis for decision making. But it is to be pointed out to them that an exclusion from the DVL is permissible only if the evaluation says 'RuSHA IV,' and only if the relevant subject must be considered a clear member of the intermediate class, possessing a Water Polish vernacular."[257] The decision to treat the DVL selection process as separate from that of RuSHA was reaffirmed by Bracht in the following weeks. On January 25, 1943, Springorum announced Bracht's ruling that if a decision can also be made without the aid of a racial appraisal, then the latter is "without relevance, regardless of how it had turned out." This principle was "to be orally communicated" to the DVL branch offices. The relevant file also includes a short position statement by Bracht, again "for confidential information purposes," which deserves quoting at some length because of its decisiveness:

> My opinion was and is this: the induction of persons of German ethnonationality into the DVL can fundamentally not be made dependent on the result of a racial evaluation. . . . The RuSHA commission must therefore cease racial evaluations in connection to the DVL process. On the other hand, there are also cases in which a correct DVL decision can actually be derived from the positive result of a completed racial evaluation. Here I'm thinking of those cases where German descent cannot be unambiguously determined through genealogical documentation or subjective professing. . . . Here then, where the DVL offices possess no other convincing decision-making benchmarks, the RuSHA commission must become active, and it is from the results of its findings that the decision of the DVL must be derived. Of course, it is unacceptable for a whole family to be rejected just because one family member receives a finding of "RuSHA IV."[258]

When the racial selections finally resumed in March 1943, the DVL offices proceeded precisely according to Brandt's template. For example, during the selections conducted in the eastern rural counties of Warthenau and Blachstädt, very few members of Section 4 were actually sorted into Valuation Group RuSHA IV, and even with those who were, "a changing of the DVL decision was . . . not effectuated here. For the time being, nothing is to be initiated," according to Hohlfeld, referencing information from the local Landrat Curt Becker.[259] It seems that RuSHA was unwilling to accept this situation, and the responsible suitability assessor, SS Senior Assault Unit Leader Hansjürgen Siems, apparently put pressure on the Landrat to at least upgrade Section 4 members to Section 3 after a positive selection.[260] The matter was referred to the responsible authority, the Regierungspräsident's offices in Oppeln, which then responded that such upgrades were not to be done. Likewise informed about the issue, the Oberpräsident's offices supported the Regierungspräsident's decision unequivocally: "There is no connection between the racial evaluation and the DVL process. The DVL decision-making bodies may make use of the RuSHA commissions only if descent is not sufficiently clarified, or if other reasons make a racial evaluation seem advisable. By no means does a good racial evaluation result justify, for example, a better ranking of the applicant in the DVL, just like purely Polish ethnonationals, regardless of a good RuSHA grade, cannot be taken into the DVL, unless the special requirements for this have been satisfied."[261]

Similar conduct was seen in Kattowitz Governmental Region, where 95 percent of Upper Silesia's DVL members lived. It was probably no accident that the first protests against the racial appraisals came from Walrab von Wangenheim, the Landrat of Beuthen-Tarnowitz in the west of the governmental region, a county where RuSHA planned to racially appraise between ten and fifteen thousand individuals.[262] Wangenheim could count on the full support of his superiors when he reported on August 19, 1943, that although the suitability assessors had given him written objections against 321 enrollees in Section 4, he would "not process these for now, as they were not essential to the war effort." Despite the protests of the ethnonationality officer of the SD Command Precinct in Kattowitz, Perey, Wangenheim did not even forward the written objections to the DVL regional office. They remained without consequence for the relevant individuals.[263]

* * *

Springorum, however, was no longer satisfied with simply sidestepping the SS complex and its attempts to influence DVL decisions with its racial selections. With Wangenheim's letter attached, he wrote to Bracht that the "racial evaluation process, in the shape of these comprehensive mass screenings, should be shelved as not essential to the war effort, especially because no legal consequences of any kind have been drawn from these evaluations"—here referring to the civil administration's obstructionism. The only thing achieved by the racial selections was an agitation of the populace, and this "must be avoided now more than ever." In his view, the selections should "remain limited to isolated cases in which the DVL offices specially request them for the purposes of their decision making."[264]

The tour of the suitability assessors repeatedly triggered new complaints from the local authorities, which Springorum in turn immediately forwarded to Bracht, such as the message from the Landrat of Ilkenau, Dr. Heinrich Groll, dated June 2, 1943. Neglecting to first inform the Landrat, the local county bureau of the Kattowitz RKFDV branch office had summoned 228 individuals without reason and had them processed by the finally arriving commission "after hours of waiting . . . in a few minutes or fractions of a minute." The subjects had naturally interpreted this process as preparatory to an upcoming "evacuation measure, incarceration, transport to a concentration camp, etc." It also says something about the mood of the populace, or at least the Landrat's estimation thereof, that the real reason was seen as even more threatening: "The mood became even more agitated when word leaked out that this concerned Germanization measures. It has clearly been shown that, not only among the locally resident Polish populace but also among a large part of the summoned persons, a clear hostility toward rumors of Germanization efforts was to be seen."[265] It therefore comes as no surprise that Groll, making reference to an argument already brought into play by Springorum, also demanded an immediate cessation of the racial appraisals. Besides causing a general agitation that created an ideal "breeding ground for the resistance movement," the racial appraisals also meant that people were "provoked into a mood that impairs work enthusiasm to a great degree." Furthermore, the planned transport of "re-Germanizable" persons would have such dramatic repercussions that it was "simply not achievable at present." Since the racial selection results had no consequences anyway, he asked that they "be deferred until the end of the war."[266] As he had previously done with Wangenheim's complaint, Springorum forwarded Groll's message to Bracht, along with an accompanying note supporting the Landrat's argumentation and ending with the request "I therefore ask once again for at least an effective restriction to be placed on these racial appraisals."[267]

The complaints from Springorum and his Landrats finally landed at the RKFDV branch office, where Arlt, in a letter dated June 24, 1943, evinced a certain sympathy for the argument about the agitation of the populace.[268] But he was replaced at the end of the month by SS Senior Assault Unit Leader Friedrich Brehm, who—as a former member of RuSHA—was much more aggressive in defending the racial selections and willing to enter into a direct confrontation with Springorum.[269]

Although it is not clear when exactly the racial selections were suspended, it nonetheless seems certain that the suitability assessors had not visited all of Upper Silesia's counties. And, in any case, their decisions had consequences only for those still outside the DVL who were sorted into Valuation Groups I or II so that they could be swept up in the re-Germanization program. The racial selections had no effect at all on the decisions of the DVL branch offices, or on persons who already possessed a DVL identity document. The SS complex had thus failed in Upper Silesia as well.

Danzig–West Prussia

But it was again in Danzig–West Prussia that Himmler would experience his greatest defeat. As in Upper Silesia, race had played no role as a selection criterion here, so that it was only with the introduction of the DVL that Forster was forced to formulate a position in this regard. It turned out to be correspondingly equivocal: as he wrote on August 7, 1941, if a DVL branch office head had concerns about an applicant's "racial suitability," then the decision could be deferred and the Racial Policy Office called in. But Forster was clear on one point: responsibility for the racial selections would not fall on RuSHA but "*solely*" on the Racial Policy Office. In line with established practice so far, its "race experts" would not only focus on the applicant's "external appearance," but also assess whether the subject corresponded to the "mental image of a German person in terms of life outlook, living standards, and way of life."[270]

But even after this clarification, Forster was still dissatisfied with the work of the DVL branch offices, because he believed that many had still "repeatedly misunderstood" the question of the applicant's "racial suitability" as stipulated in Frick's implementation provisions. Thus, in a message to the Regierungspräsidents, Landrats, and mayors on October 30, 1941, Forster criticized DVL branch office personnel who rejected applicants for the sole reason that they "could not corroborate the presence of German blood with *certificates*" in the attempt to prevent a "large influx of foreign blood from endangering the German race." But in his view, this overlooked the fact that the "presence of German blood" also "can be assumed" if the applicants, along with their parents and their grandparents, are locals and "are impeccable in external appearance and cannot be racially distinguished from Germans." In any case, "Polish-sounding names are not to be ascribed decisive significance." Until a general regulation was issued by Himmler as RKFDV, it was solely Nazi Party officials who would be "called upon to judge racial suitability on the basis of external appearance" in cases where doubts existed about the applicant's "German descent." Forster was clearly aware that this directive was far removed from the fundament of Frick's implementation provisions. For that reason, its recipients were not to hand it over to anyone else: "This directive is to be orally communicated by the chairmen to the other members. They are to be strongly advised to adhere to it."[271]

Forster had another reason for such secrecy: there was no chance of an agreement with Himmler on this matter anytime soon. Shortly before another personal meeting in Danzig, Himmler referred directly to this directive when he wrote to Forster on November 20, 1941, and reminded him of their discussion of this topic at a lunch hosted by Hitler on October 19: "I am troubled, party comrade Forster, that despite the opinion you had at the end of our discussion in the Führer headquarters, in which you agreed with me that all must be racially inspected, you changed it again to such an extent within ten short days that you then wanted to permit racial examinations only in certain individual cases."[272] This claim that Forster had agreed to the racial selections is not a very plausible one, and not only because of his policy stance until then. After all, it was just two days later that the aforementioned clash happened at the DVL branch office session in Neumark (now Nowe Miasto Lubawskie) on October 21, 1941, when Forster threw out the SD official and thereby further escalated his feud with Hildebrandt. A little later, Forster dictated a letter to Himmler on November 13, 1941, in which he continued the discussion from Hitler's luncheon. The letter no longer survives, but from Himmler's answer of November 20 cited earlier, one does not get the impression that these two adversaries had converged even an inch.[273]

At the heart of the conflict stood once again Himmler's accusation that Forster was pursuing an excessively inclusivist Germanization policy. Forster had always defended his actions by claiming that the autochthonous populace mostly consisted of "Deutschstämmige" anyway. As I have described, in order to ideologically legitimize this racial theory, Prof. Günther was invited to come visit in 1940, and he ultimately delivered the desired information that four-fifths of the local populace was "Germanizable." A year later, Forster added fuel to the fire with a biased interpretation of central European settlement history, which again enraged Himmler and plummeted the two men into a historical wrangle. Himmler was particularly annoyed by the claim that the "German" settlement of the territory had survived the early medieval Migration Period and that this area "had been German except for a small region" right up until the defeat of the Teutonic Order. Himmler responded he had "never read anything about such a total German settlement in all my studies." Since it was clear to Himmler that Forster's policy stance was guided less by nationalist historians like Dr. Detlef Krannhals and Prof. Dr. Erich Keyser and more by pragmatic considerations, he showed understanding for the need, "during the war and the necessary war-related efforts, to have peaceableness and as little agitation as possible." "But I cannot agree," wrote Himmler, "when for the sake of a momentary wartime necessity you want to create permanent conditions." If Forster considered racial selections to be currently impracticable, then they simply had to be left undone—but under no circumstances could he then create facts on the ground through the DVL. In this situation, having "no decision on ethnonational membership would be better than a wrong one." After all, as Forster himself knew, "a single drop of wrong blood . . . can never be taken back out again." For that reason also, he rejected Forster's expedited procedure, which had fundamentally changed the DVL enrollment process, and declared categorically, "With your expedited procedure, which is absolutely in contravention of the Führer's intentions, I can agree only if it is a temporary measure necessary for the solving of momentary war-related issues, and if it is certain that all members of Groups III and IV are racially evaluated."[274] From the very start, Himmler had tried to exert a decisive influence in shaping the selection practices of the Gauleiters, and nowhere did he fail so thoroughly as in Danzig–West Prussia. Because Forster was vehemently resisting the introduction of racial selections as well, there was little that Himmler could do but threaten the nonrecognition of all enrollments in Sections 3 and 4—a threat that reflected his powerlessness in the dispute.

On November 20, 1941, Himmler traveled to Danzig. The next day, he took part in a sitting of the DVL branch office in Preussisch Stargard and also gathered information on the preliminary registrations conducted there by the party in order to finally meet with Forster and Hildebrandt on November 22.[275] Despite Himmler's note in his service diary of a "reconciliation between the two" (referring to Forster and Hildebrandt), reconciliation clearly did not occur.[276] Forster was not planning to make the DVL selection practice more restrictive; instead, he embarked on exactly the opposite course, as was mentioned earlier. Whereas the Gauleiters of Upper Silesia and the Wartheland tried to neutralize the unwelcome racial selections by restricting the circle of investigable persons and effectively preventing any negative consequences, Forster decided to simply forbid them by prohibiting RuSHA from operating within the DVL framework. Nonetheless, the suitability assessors in Danzig–West Prussia did not remain entirely inactive.

But it is not so much the handful of racial selections conducted for marriage petitions submitted by members of Sections 3 and 4 that are worth mentioning here.[277] Much more notable were the ones conducted on individuals who submitted applications for DVL enrollment after having been transported to internment camps by the UWZ. Placed beyond Forster's reach in the camps, they were the only group to undergo racial selections in significant numbers, although even those probably amounted to no more than a few thousand people. Of course, whether these racial selections had any influence on decision making at the DVL offices is another question altogether.

As has already been mentioned, the UWZ camp commandants had initially refused to transfer inmates to the responsible DVL offices for a personal evaluation, sending instead only the questionnaires that had been filled out under supervision, along with the concluding judgment of the field office established by the SD Special Unit in every UWZ camp. In February 1942, the field offices were told that from then on, they should "take the racial evaluation into account" when coming to a verdict.[278] But what is particularly interesting for the present investigation is that even within the decision-making process of the SS apparatus, the rulings of the suitability assessors were by no means decisive. Where RuSHA officials in the Wartheland had been unable to prevail against the civil administration with their demand that all persons selected into Valuation Groups I or II be generally admitted to the DVL, their colleagues in Danzig–West Prussia similarly failed—but this time against the resistance of the SD.

One example was the case of the Blaschkiewitz family, which submitted an application for DVL enrollment after having been brought to the "Germanization camp" at Gosslershausen. The local SD Special Unit had them fill out the questionnaires stipulated by Frick's implementation provisions before subjecting them to a racial selection process. The final judgment, also drawn up by the SD Special Unit, mentioned that the RuSHA suitability assessors had designated the family as still being very much a "desirable addition to the population." But for the SD, it was political criteria that were decisive, as they were, in terms of "appearance and life outlook . . . Polish people." And since "in no area is a leaning or effort toward Germandom ascertainable," and the "professing to Germandom is presented by both spouses in a completely indifferent way," the SD concluded that "an enrollment in the DVL must be denied." But the SD ruling was immaterial when it came to making the legally binding decision—this prerogative was the sole preserve of the relevant DVL branch office. Even though, in most cases, admission to the DVL did not mean immediate release from the camp, it was still of significance to the affected individuals, because a positive notification at least prevented a relocation to a "Polish camp" like Potulitz, where the living and working conditions were much worse. This was also the case with the Blaschkiewitz family, which was inducted into Section 3 by the relevant DVL branch office and probably released when the Gosslershausen camp was dismantled in June 1943.[279] Thus, for the DVL branch office's adjudication of the Blaschkiewitz family, the rulings of the SS complex played no role. When he wrote to the DVL regional and branch offices about how to proceed in this matter on February 9, 1943, Forster later added a separate directive that such adjudications were to be done with the rulings of the SS suitability inspectors in mind, but he also emphatically underlined that these SS rulings, "for the decision making of the DVL, are not to be seen as binding."[280]

When Isabel Heinemann states in her study of RuSHA that "almost two million people, members of DVL Groups 3 and 4, were earmarked for such a racial selection," she is indeed correct in outlining the declared intentions of Himmler and at least certain parts of the SS apparatus. But what is incorrect is her contention that "a greater part of them were also in fact subjected to it until the end of the war."[281] The fragmentary nature of the surviving records makes it impossible to gather precise data on the number of people in the annexed western Polish provinces who were subjected to a racial selection procedure by the suitability assessors under the DVL framework. It is nonetheless very unlikely that more than eighty thousand persons were affected by it in the Wartheland; in Upper Silesia it was certainly not even the fifty-one thousand members of Section 4; and in Danzig–West Prussia, the number must have been considerably smaller. This makes it highly improbable that any more than 150,000 persons were subjected to racial selection by the suitability assessors—meaning not even a tenth of the originally planned number.

Concluding the Registrations

In resisting the racial appraisals, the Gauleiters all pointed to one crucial aspect: they cost too much time and would further delay the conclusion of the DVL registrations by several months more. Which was exactly what the civil administrations were no longer prepared to do.

This time pressure was most apparent in the Wartheland. The ethnocrats in the Reichsstatthalter's offices had already announced in early 1940 that the DVL branch offices would close in the coming April. But in fact, they found it necessary to expand their local DVL system with additional sections in mid-1940, and finally to convert to the Berlin regulations in March 1941. The discontent within the Reichsstatthalter's offices was not only due to the amount of staff still tied up with the DVL process. Even more than that, Greiser wanted to begin the next phase of his ethnopolicy: after the selection of the "Germans," all energies were to be focused on dealing with the remaining Poles. The parameters of this policy aspect had already been under discussion for months in Posen. This intention to focus now on the remaining Polish population also helps explain the reasoning behind the appointment of SS Assault Unit Leader Rolf-Heinz Höppner, head of the SD Command Precinct and an expert in expulsions, as Coulon's successor.[282]

In his first memo as ethnonationality officer on May 27, 1942, Höppner declared that the DVL enrollments must finally come to an end. Whoever was not enrolled should now be treated as a Pole. Taking a swipe at the RuSHA suitability inspectors, he wrote that "a differentiation along the lines of whether he still has a drop of German blood will no longer be made."[283] Mehlhorn later instructed the DVL branch offices to conclude their operations by September 30, 1942. "This deadline is final." The DVL regional offices were then to inspect the branch offices over the following two weeks, submitting a report to the central office by October 15, 1942. After that, the regional offices and central office were to adjudicate the few remaining appeals cases, but otherwise, the DVL, as a German People's List, was complete.[284]

At least one DVL regional office, namely in Hohensalza, did in fact report completion.[285] Then on November 5, 1942, Jäger informed the regional offices that the DVL process was as good as finished; in appeals cases, the subject persons were to be given a deadline of one month, during which all necessary documents must be procured and the applications must be decided.[286] On November 19, 1942, the ethnonationality officer finally instructed the Gauleiter's offices to place announcements in the daily newspapers, informing the populace that from now on, no new applications for DVL enrollment would be accepted.[287] Things would turn out differently, however: although the DVL branch offices had considerably reduced their activities by the end of 1942, they still accepted applications until Nazi Germany's final defeat—but they amounted to only around twenty thousand additional enrollments. The originally planned closure of the branch offices had thus failed. It remained under discussion until the end of 1943, when the Reichsstatthalter's offices gave up their plan after protests from the Regierungspräsidents; the branch offices thus remained open.[288]

In Upper Silesia, the occupiers also wanted to conclude the DVL as quickly as possible—although for reasons contrary to those in the Wartheland. After the process had been radically simplified and accelerated by the beginning of 1942, the Oberpräsident's offices wanted to do something similar with the appeals cases still pending at the DVL regional offices: with the conclusion of the primary phase of the DVL process, the branch offices were to act as preliminary commissions evaluating each appeal and suggesting a verdict to the regional offices, thereby enabling summary decisions on those cases as well.

But here too, the conclusion of the primary phase of the DVL process would take longer than expected. The occupiers were facing increasing pressure from the populace, who were extremely unhappy with the entire process. In the opinion of the Landrat of Kattowitz, Philipp Heimann, it was less the "heavy repressive measures in the east" or the "whispered propaganda" of the Polish resistance movement that had precipitated a previously unknown "crisis of confidence" in recent months. He saw the main cause "above all in the effects of the ethnonationality policy practiced in Upper Silesia since September 1939. Nothing has ever stirred up feelings so much, or triggered such conflicts in every last family, like the DVL . . . which in the end, with all its differentiations coming from the Wartheland . . . was only suited for embittering and dividing Germandom in Upper Silesia."[289] In his view, the decisive issues had been mishandled. The German administration had not sufficiently favored the "German activists," had not sufficiently punished the "anti-German elements," and had not kept its promises to the "mass of seduced hangers-on." The Gauleiter's promise that the members of Section 3 would be made economically and socially equal to those of Sections 1 and 2 had still not been carried out and had now achieved the opposite effect, namely "to undermine the authority of the Nazi Party along with any confidence the Upper Silesians had in the actions of the party and state." Heimann concluded his general attack on the DVL, this "poisoned gift from the Wartheland," with a scathing verdict: "The past has taught us nothing and we've come full circle. The DVL is a tragedy for the Upper Silesian. But it is also a tragedy for the administration, that it was condemned to squandering its manpower and its reputation on an undertaking that can contribute nothing to the final victory, but is instead suited only to impeding, in unforeseen ways, the Gau of Upper Silesia in the fulfillment of its war-essential tasks."[290]

According to the postwar testimony of Bracht's ethnonationality officer Hohlfeld, this report had caused much furor at the time and had probably also influenced debates on what criteria were to be used by the DVL regional offices in adjudicating the appeals submitted against the decisions of the branch offices.[291] It turned out that the main proponent of further widening DVL admission practices was Bracht himself. During a meeting on November 17, 1942, again discussing the handling of appeals cases, Bracht declared with a new unequivocalness that not only "the Upper Silesian . . . who has acted neutrally, and whose ethnonational sensitivities had been shaken awake only since 1870 . . . is in general to be inducted as a German into the DVL, even if he had made certain concessions during the time of Polish rule." This was also to apply to the autochthonous population groups of the Prussian and Austrian Partitions who had "slid into the Polish camp." Even "active participation in the three Polish uprisings" (i.e., the Silesian uprisings of 1919 to 1921) would not result in exclusion if "close relatives (parents or siblings) are enrolled in the DVL, or if the wife is satisfactory and the full Germanization of the children is to be expected." In western Upper Silesia, this left very few people whose enrollment applications could actually be refused by the DVL offices. According to Bracht, only a small group came into question for this: "Persons who already professed to Polishdom during the Prussian or Austrian period, joined Polish organizations, and whose Polish stance throughout the subsequent years has also been documented."[292] Thus, while the civil administration began widening the selection criteria once again, the ideological backing for this was provided by the Gauleiter's offices. It is not surprising that it did not rely on the voluminous literature of racial anthropology.[293] Instead, preference was given to ethnonationalist authors like Robert Beck and his study of "wavering folkdom in a shift of mindset." Of course, Beck also lacked objective criteria for determining a person's ethnonationality, but instead had to admit that important criteria like German language skills were learnable. As the occupation authorities in Kattowitz asserted, "Even the Jew speaks German, but is nonetheless not a German." Of course, equally impermissible was the corollary of giving recognition to the subjective criterion of individual self-description, thereby conceding that "German is whatever wants to be German!" (as it was summed up in Kattowitz), which would de-essentialize national identity and relegate it to the sphere of personal responsibility as a chosen preference. The political capital tied to exercising hegemony over this ideological field could not be surrendered, meaning that ethnonationality had to be "determined"—in accordance with the applicable political goals—by the regime's own appointed bodies and could not be chosen by the individual. Beck therefore brought the concept of "subjective mindset" ("subjektive Gesinnung") into play, an absurd, self-contradictory construction that tried to offer a middle path, but without any suggestions for its concrete operationalization.

The debate was of no consequence for the Oberpräsident's offices, as the DVL selection practice was already decided and Beck was cited solely as an ideological prop. In this regard, his proposed conception was doubly attractive. First, it offered a way to deflect demands from the SS apparatus for the implementation of objective criteria, in this case racial ones. Naturally, Beck also worked from the assumption "that an ethnonational must carry the markers of his folkdom." But as the Gauleiter's offices wrote—and this was decisive—"Since these racial markers cannot be externally identified, they can only be inferred from mental comportment and character."[294] It was conduct, and not biometric markers, that decided a person's "race" and "ethnonationality." Second, Beck, with his scholarly treatment of long-established resentments against a "wavering" or "shaky folkdom," also offered the desired justification for the civil administration's particularly inclusivist approach.[295] As the Gauleiter's offices stated, echoing Beck, "participation in the political organizations of the foreign state are of course never a reliable marker, since even during their belonging to a foreign state, these people were part of a wavering folkdom."[296] One could not speak of a "wavering folkdom" and then enforce selection criteria that demanded impeccable conduct at every moment from each applicant. Therefore, the selection criteria also needed to admit individuals who had demonstrated a "swaying toward Polishdom," particularly because these "shortcomings" were "to be blamed on earlier state actions"—reflecting an astounding amount of sympathy on the part of the party, ultimately engendered by the political exigencies. These "earlier state actions" referred to the Germanization policy of the Prussian period, and not, for example, the Polonization policy of the interwar years: "In many cases, this swaying toward Polishdom took place because the Upper Silesian, due to his harsh German speech, was seen as inferior, and because he therefore felt himself to be 'inferior,' and sensed that he was not being included in the Volksgemeinschaft."[297]

This reading of Beck's study would seem paradigmatic of the way Nazi administrators used research from the humanities and social studies. Contrary to more recent claims about the influence of scholars on Nazi population policy, I could identify only a few cases where a requested expert opinion actually influenced an already chosen course of action. All too often, what presented itself as policy advice was simply scholarly justification in order to increase the political legitimacy of already settled decisions.[298] In the surviving records of Upper Silesia's ethnonationality unit, there is no evidence that Hohlfeld was even aware of contemporary research in this area—let alone actively engaging with it, or using it to shape his own policy. The same applies to the Gauleiter's offices, which presumably took an interest in Beck only when it came under ideological pressure and was forced to defend Bracht's course of action. The at times grotesque internal contradictions of Beck's argumentation went unnoticed or were at least not mentioned—after all, its policy practicability was not in question.

As the winter of 1942–43 was coming to an end, the DVL branch offices in Upper Silesia were able to conclude the processing of first-time applications and so devote themselves to the preliminary assessment of the fifty to sixty thousand appeals cases that had accumulated at the DVL regional offices.[299] At a conference of Landrats on June 24, 1943, Hohlfeld repeated the already established solution to the issue, namely that "the Upper Silesian, like the Szlonzakian, generally belongs in the DVL."[300] As the ethnonationality officer from the Regierungspräsident's offices in Kattowitz recalled after the war, "the judgments at the regional office gradually came to infer that an Upper Silesian whose ancestors came from the area that was Prussian until 1921 was to be inducted into the DVL."[301] And if a DVL regional office failed to do so in a few individual cases, then the applicant could still submit an appeal to the DVL central office, which would then ensure that the selection criteria were interpreted in an inclusivist way.

For example, when the Gabor family was first rejected by the local DVL branch office and then also by the regional office, they lodged an appeal, and their application was referred to the central office. From the documents available to the assessment commission, there was no denying that Mr. Gabor, at least, had "entered into strong Polish ties," had participated in the anti-German uprisings after World War I, and had later joined a radical nationalist insurgent group as well as a Polish military organization. The Polish state had awarded him the Cross of Independence, the Gold Cross of Merit, the Silesian Star, and the Cross of Merit for Bravery. But it spoke in his favor that he had fought on the German side during World War I, had been awarded the Iron Cross 2nd Class, and—according to his own testimony—had also shown support for Germans. In addition, he had subscribed to a German newspaper and had belonged "since 1936 . . . to the Professional Association for German Shepherd Dogs." It was probably decisive that both his parents were also "of Upper Silesian origin" and had relatives inside the Reich, and that other relatives in Upper Silesia had been enrolled in Sections 1 or 2. The lower-level judgments were vacated on August 14, 1944, and Mr. Gabor was now enrolled in Section 4 and the rest of his family in Section 3.[302]

*   *   *

According to the last available complete overview, the DVL in the annexed western Polish territories encompassed 2,819,072 individuals on April 1, 1944, meaning more than one-third of the local populace.[303] As has been shown, this overall figure is of only limited meaningfulness, because it cannot be said that a homogeneous Germanization policy existed in western Poland, for at least two reasons. First, the proportion of the populace inducted into the DVL varied greatly from province to province—ranging from 14 percent in the Wartheland to 66 and 69 percent in Upper Silesia and Danzig–West Prussia, respectively. This difference was a direct consequence of the sorting into Section 3, or more precisely, the ratio between the "Bekenntnisdeutsche" ("professed Germans") in Sections 1 and 2 on the one hand, and the "Stammesdeutsche" ("Germans by descent") in Section 3 on the other. In the Wartheland, with its exclusivist selection criteria, the number of people enrolled in the first two sections (namely 411,760) was six times as many as those in Section 3, and in the other two provinces, the proportion was reversed. There, it was Section 3 that encompassed three times as many people as the first two sections combined.[304]

A second disparity becomes apparent if one not only compares the selection practices of the various provinces but also considers the contrasts within each province on the county level. Only then does it become clear that even between the Germanization policies of Danzig–West Prussia and Upper Silesia, although at first glance similarly inclusivist, a significant difference existed. Unfortunately, the surviving source materials here are somewhat deficient. Less problematic is the fact that the latest available data covering all counties is for March 31, 1943—while the DVL was not yet completely concluded at that point, it would not grow significantly after then. More serious is the complication caused by the differing accounts of each province's total population figures, which vary by as much as 15 percent, thereby affecting all statistics based on them.[305] Certainly, the German occupiers in Danzig–West Prussia and Upper Silesia had recognized a similarly high proportion of the local populace as "German," and in both provinces, most of these enrollees had come from the former Prussian and Austrian Partitions, although the selection practices of the assessment commissions in the former Russian Partition turned out to be considerably more exclusivist. There were further striking differences between the two provinces. In Danzig–West Prussia, the number enrolled in the west was around three times that of those in the east—but even there, around one-fifth of the populace soon belonged to the DVL. The situation was quite different in Upper Silesia, where the civil administration had decided to limit the DVL to the former Prussian and Austrian Partitions—where almost the entire populace was inducted, meaning 1.2 of the 1.4 million residents. The only real effect of the DVL in Upper Silesia was in the greater restrictions placed on members of Section 3 than on members of Sections 1 and 2.[306] And even then, a major goal of Bracht's intervention in Berlin, as previously described, was the dismantling of these restrictions, particularly in their economic consequences, and thereby achieving equal treatment for members of Section 3. This stood in clear contrast to DVL selection practices in the former Russian Partition, where only 2 percent of the populace was admitted, equating to a little more than eighteen thousand people. It is from this perspective that Germanization policy in Upper Silesia was particularly paradoxical. In no part of the annexed western Polish territories were applicants confronted by lower hurdles to DVL registration than in Upper Silesia—provided that they lived west of the police border. At the same time, nowhere were the hurdles higher than in Upper Silesia—at least if the application was submitted east of the police border.[307]

* * *

By the end of 1943, the selection activities of the DVL were by and large concluded, with no more significant changes happening in the subsequent years. But the DVL did not suspend its work as planned. The German ethnocrats pursued their duties almost until they could hear the thundering cannons of the approaching war front. It required the advance of the Red Army to the Vistula river for the Oberpräsident's offices in Kattowitz to finally inform the Reich Interior Ministry on July 28, 1944, that "in view of the Führer's decree on total war deployment and in consideration of the strained situation," the administration had "suspended with immediate effect the sittings of . . . the DVL." Only "a few Wehrmacht cases" would still be processed.[308] A similar impetus soon emerged from within the Reich Interior Ministry as well, with instructions to the DVL offices in the annexed western Polish territories to suspend their activities on September 15, 1944. Here too, an exception applied to applicants who had already been drafted into the Wehrmacht or were otherwise of military conscription age.[309] According to this directive, the hiatus was initially supposed to be only half a year. A short time later, there was a little more realism in Berlin as well, with some starting to talk about destroying the files.[310]

In Upper Silesia, a representative of the ethnonationality unit had already traveled to Oppeln on October 23, 1944, where he gave his approval for the planned destruction of a large part of the local files. The DVL regional office had already suspended its sittings.[311] On November 5, 1944, Bracht signed in his role as Reich Defense Commissioner for Upper Silesia when he instructed the DVL offices to destroy the files of those enrolled in Sections 1 or 2, as well as those whose revocable national status had since been made irrevocable.[312] But the German bureaucrats would prove to be too hesitant. Although Hohlfeld would claim after the war that he had personally incinerated the files of the DVL central office in the boiler room of the Oberpräsident's offices, a great many of them still fell into the hands of the Red Army, enough so that the activities of the local DVL are actually documented in all significant aspects—and considerably better than those of the DVL central offices in Danzig and Posen.[313]

In the Wartheland, the initial decision apparently fell in favor of relocating the files instead of destroying them. For example, rather detailed information exists about such efforts by the DVL branch office for Litzmannstadt municipality, which however had chosen for its 114,000 membership files a rather unsuitable alternative site—one that would soon be needed by the local Landrat for the training of the Volkssturm (literally "people's storm," which was Nazi Germany's last-ditch national militia).[314] When the Reich Interior Ministry finally decided to notify the Gauleiters in January 1945 that all files were to be destroyed if they could not be kept safe, it was already too late in most cases.[315] As a result, the membership files of certain DVL branch offices, particularly those in Kempen, Schroda, Wollstein, and the rural and urban counties of Posen, have survived almost in their entirety. Besides the filled-out questionnaires, the files also contain correspondence between the applicants and the relevant DVL offices, including any appeals against an initially issued rejection notice, or against an unsatisfactory categorization.

After Germany's surrender, these files would shape the fate of the relevant individuals a second time, as they gave the Polish government some insight into the extent to which Polish citizens had collaborated with the enemy.[316]

Notes

1. (Signed "p.p. Jacobi"), Reich Interior Ministry to Reich Security Main Office, Berlin State Archive [hereafter, LAB], B Rep. 057–01/448, A 26 (2). A year later, during a discussion about deploying Soviet citizens en masse for forced labor, Heydrich similarly found himself arguing for a lost cause when he fought against all attempts "to postpone the racial and ethnonational question until after the war" (Herbert, "Arbeit und Vernichtung," 398).

2. Höppner to Reich Security Main Office III B, March 13, 1941, German Federal Archives, Berlin [hereafter, BArch], R 75/3b, 94–95, reprinted in Datner, Gumkowski, and Leszczyński, "Wysiedlanie ludności," 136–37.

3. Telex from Krumey to Ehlich and UWZ Posen, February 25, 1941, Institute of National Remembrance, Warsaw [hereafter, AGK], 68/146, 23.

4. But because this was not in the offing, the civil administrations asserted a new course of action during a meeting at the Reich Interior Ministry on May 16–17, 1941. Because of the objections, there was to be "a departure from the existing decision of the RKFDV in how the transplantation of this group into the Old Reich is to be conducted" (Bracht to DVL regional offices, May 26, 1941, Polish State Archives in Łódź [hereafter, APL], 176/387, 118–19).

5. Memo from Höppner, March 28, 1941, AGK 68/146, 47.

6. Höppner to Müller, March 27, 1941, AGK 68/146, 42–43.

7. Müller to Höppner, March 31, 1941, AGK 68/146, 50.

8. For example, with the SS Task Force at Grätz; Höppner to head of Settlement Staff at Posen, SS Assault Unit Leader Dr. Peter Carsten, April 4, 1941, AGK 68/259, 44–45).

9. Höppner to RuSHA field office, May 30, 1941, AGK 68/146, 59–60.

10. Kendzia to provincial farmers' association head and the East German Land Management Company (Ostdeutsche Landesbewirtschaftungsgesellschaft, Ostland), April 2, 1941, reprinted in Łuczak, *Położenie ludności polskiej*, 243–44.

11. Long-range plan for resettlement in the eastern provinces, undated (probably late November, 1939), BArch R 69/1146, 1–13.

12. Unsigned file note from SS Settlement Staff South in Upper Silesia, March 21, 1941, BArch R 49 II/26, 108. Thanks to Götz Aly for this document. The day after the conference, Himmler ordered labor conscription also for ethnic Germans waiting at camps inside the Reich, which was required until their transfer to the annexed eastern provinces (APL 205/2, 39–41, March 20, 1941).

13. Greifelt to the appointees of the RKFDV in the annexed eastern provinces, on the meeting of March 19, 1941, dated March 26, 1941, BArch R 75/2, 12–14.

14. Memo from Arlt to SS Settlement Staff South, March 14, 1941, BArch R 49/26, 78–81. Thanks to Götz Aly for this document.

15. Memo from camp commandant of Auschwitz, March 13, 1941, Federal Commissioner for the Records of the State Security Service of the Former German Democratic Republic, PA/770, 152–56; also Steinbacher, *Musterstadt Auschwitz*, esp. 178–94 and 205–52.

16. Krumey's directive to the UWZ offices, March 31, 1941, Polish State Archives in Poznań [hereafter, APP], 834/2, 10.

17. Franz Abromeit's minutes of meeting at HSSPF offices on March 21, 1941, dated March 22, 1941, BArch R 75/13, unpaged.

18. Siegmund to Koppe, confidential, May 10, 1941, APP 834/2, 36.

19. Eichmann's guidelines, undated (probably just before February 1, 1941), AGK 69/1, 38–41.

20. On Hochland, see Heinz Hochland UWZ personnel file at AGK 358/31. Quote is from Hochland to UWZ Litzmannstadt, October 20, 1941, APP 834/2, 184.

21. Memo from Krumey, March 21, 1941, AGK 68/146, 40–41.

22. Unsigned letter, Reichsstatthalter's offices to the SS Settlement Staffs, with request to find suitable location for a "Polish reservation," May 2, 1941, APP 834/2, 25.

23. Memo from Krumey, May 12, 1941, APP 834/2, 39–40.

24. Höppner to Eichmann, July 16, 1941, AGK NTN/36, 29–31.

25. An example of this is Krumey's confidential status report for the period May 6 to June 30, 1942, dated June 30, 1942, at BArch R 75/4, unpaged.

26. Jastrzębski, *Potulice*, 21–22.

27. Unsigned memo from ethnonationality unit on the inspection tour of November 12, 1941, Polish State Archives in Katowice [hereafter, APK], 117/140, undated, 184–85.

28. Unsigned concluding report on evacuations for settling of Bessarabian Germans (third short-range plan) in the Wartheland from January 21, 1941, to January 20, 1942, AGK NTN/13, 99–106, undated, reprinted in *Biuletyn* 21: 106–10.

29. See UWZ personnel file for SS Chief Assault Leader Fritz Jobski, signed "p.p. SS Senior Squad Leader Rudolf Bilharz," UWZ Litzmannstadt to head of UWZ field office in Grätz, July 8, 1941, AGK 69/206.

30. Hochland's unsigned notice, APP 834/2, undated, 146.

31. Göring to Heydrich, July 31, 1941, quoted in Longerich, *Politik der Vernichtung*, 421. After the war, Eichmann confirmed that the message had been written at the Reich Security Main Office (Longerich, *Politik der Vernichtung*, 696).

32. Browning, *Entfesselung*, 456–57.

33. Aly, *Endlösung*, 353.

34. Krumey to UWZ field offices on workshop conference of SS Settlement Staffs on October 2, 1942, dated October 7, 1942, APP 834/2, 169–74.

35. On the establishing of the Staff Main Office of the RKFDV, see Himmler's directive, June 11, 1941, Bavarian State Archives, Nuremberg [hereafter, BSA], NO-4057.

36. Greifelt to Heydrich, September 2, 1941, BSA NO-5011.

37. Eichmann to RKFDV Staff Main Office, September 29, 1941, AGK 69/1, 110. Thanks to Götz Aly for this document.

38. See, for example, Browning, *Entfesselung*, 455–75. In this section on the decision-making process during the second half of 1942, Browning does mention Höppner's memorandum of September 2, 1941, but presents the deportation of Poles and other undesirable "Fremdvölkische" as more an idea emanating from Posen, while the focus in Berlin was allegedly on the deportation of the Jews. This—as I think, mistaken—assumption then allows Browning to conclude that the course of action was "clear-cut" from late October onward: "The Jews had to die in their entirety" (Browning, *Entfesselung*, 460). In Longerich's corresponding chapter, the population policy in Poland is not mentioned at all (Longerich, *Politik der Vernichtung*, 427–34). And Aly, who discusses Eichmann's response in detail, places it only indirectly in the context of the deportations, highlighting instead—in accord with the main thesis of his study—its connection to the settlement efforts, which, however, are not specifically mentioned in Eichmann's response (Aly, *Endlösung*, 347–57).

39. Höppner to Ehlich and Eichmann, September 2, 1941, German Federal Archives, Ludwigsburg branch [hereafter, BArchL], B 162/339, 63–79.

40. Ibid. (emphasis in original).

41. Ibid.

42. Marczewski, "Nazi Nationality Policy," 41. The connection to the Polish populace is often overlooked, especially by Holocaust researchers. For example, Browning cites the same passage but then comes to a one-sided conclusion: "It seems that in late August, early September, not only in Posen but also in Berlin, there were planning efforts for a new phase in Jewish policy, whereby the 'complete eradication' of the Jews was also openly discussed" (Browning, *Entfesselung*, 466).

43. In his instructions on the restructuring of the EWZs and UWZs, Heydrich then chose not to pursue Höppner's far-reaching proposals, settling for smaller changes instead (provisions from the Chief of the Security Police and the SD on the structure and administration of the EWZs and UWZs, October 31, 1941, APL 206–1/1, 246–55).

44. At Heydrich's conference, it was agreed that 149,450 ethnic Germans would be settled (BArch R 49 Anh. I/34, 7–8). In fact, in Danzig–West Prussia, only 22,698 of the planned 53,350 were settled; in the Wartheland, only 54,052 of the planned 57,100; and in Upper Silesia, only 12,255 of the planned 39,000 (tallies calculated from two unsigned reports by the RKFDV Staff Main Office, BArch R 49/14, 1–33, April 30, 1943, and BArch R 49/303, unpaged, February 11, 1941).

45. This figure comes from adding up the data submitted for each province, although figures for Upper Silesia exist only for late August 1941. According to these data, 25,676 people were evicted from their homes in Danzig–West Prussia (unsigned overview of resettlements from UWZ Danzig in 1941, undated, BArch PL 170/39, 29); 130,826 in the Wartheland (unsigned concluding report on evacuations for settling of Bessarabian Germans [third short-range plan] in the Wartheland from January 21, 1941, to January 20, 1942, undated, AGK NTN/13, 99–106, reprinted in *Biuletyn* 21: 106–10); 21,256 in Upper Silesia (unsigned accounting of the RKFDV headquarters from February 11, 1941, BArch R 49/303, unpaged; Butschek to Statistics Dept. at Reichsführer of the SS, August 28, 1941, BArch R 49/317, unpaged). The exactness of these figures is dubious, not only because the data published by the central bodies in Berlin often differ from those of the authorities on location, but also because an unknown number of persons were expelled or deported through unauthorized expulsions that circumvented the UWZ. It can therefore be assumed that the specified deportation figures reflect the lower limits.

46. Tooze, *Wages of Destruction*, 452–60.

47. Herbert, "Arbeit und Vernichtung"; Tooze, *Wages of Destruction*, 526–38.

48. Meeting minutes of January 20, 1942, reprinted in Roseman, *Wannsee-Konferenz*, 170–84, here 174.

49. For a more detailed argument why the Wannsee Conference should better be situated not in the context of anti-Jewish policy alone but in the wider context of Nazi Germanization policy, see Wolf, "Wannsee Conference."

50. Eichholtz, "Vorgeschichte"; Herbert, *Fremdarbeiter*, 173–78; Tooze, *Wages of Destruction*, 513–51.

51. Göring's decree of January 10, 1942, reprinted in Eichholtz, "Vorgeschichte," 379–80.

52. Stier to selected HSSPFs, March 19, 1942, BArch R 49/73, 116–18.

53. Krumey's concluding report on extended third short-range plan, December 31, 1942, BArch R 75/9, 1–25, partially reprinted in *Biuletyn* 21: 115–22.

54. Krumey's confidential status report for October 1942, dated November 5, 1942, BArch R 75/4, unpaged.

55. Memo from Krumey, April 19, 1942, BArch R 75/10, unpaged, reprinted in *Biuletyn* 21: 111.

56. In the rural county of Turek, for example, only 12,391 of the 22,437 targeted persons could actually be expelled because the rest had already fled by the time the Germans arrived (report from head of UWZ special unit for Turek, SS Senior Assault Leader Wilhelm Koch, May 4, 1942, BArch R 75/10, unpaged). See also Koch's UWZ personnel file at AGK 69/209 and, similarly, concluding report from head of UWZ field office in Kempen, SS Chief Assault Leader Gustav Hütte, May 14, 1942, BArch R 75/10, unpaged.

57. Memo from Krumey, April 19, 1942, BArch R 75/10, unpaged, reprinted in *Biuletyn* 21: 111. The children were probably taken to the newly established youth custody camp (*Jugendverwahrlager*) in Litzmannstadt.

58. Krumey's confidential status report for the period May 6 to June 30, 1942, dated June 30, 1942, BArch R 75/4, unpaged.

59. Krumey's confidential status report for September 1942, dated October 2, 1942, BArch R 75/4, reprinted in *Biuletyn* 21: 114.

60. Ibid.

61. Krumey's concluding report on extended third short-range plan, December 31, 1942, BArch R 75/9, 1–25, partially reprinted in *Biuletyn* 21: 115–22. This report, alongside Krumey's participation in the murder of the Hungarian Jews in 1944, contributed to his sentencing to life imprisonment in postwar West Germany (BArchL B 162/1033).

62. Unsigned excerpt from a report by UWZ field office in Kempen, June 30, 1942, AGK 69/139, 43.

63. Unsigned confidential UWZ report for July 1942, dated August 5, 1942, BArch R 75/4, unpaged, reprinted in *Biuletyn* 21: 113–14.

64. On the "Polish reservations," see also Łuczak, *Pod niemieckim jarzmem*, 57.

65. Krumey's confidential status report for period of May 6 to June 30, 1942, dated June 30, 1942, BArch R 75/4, unpaged; Krumey's concluding report on the extended third short-range plan, December 31, 1942, BArch R 75/9, 1–25, partially reprinted in *Biuletyn* 21: 115–22. Despite their dramatic extent, the inconsistencies of the concluding report cannot be explained by means of the existing source materials. On the one hand, Krumey claims that the UWZ "evacuated a total of 216,136 persons in the reporting year." The figure included 167,417 persons who "were displaced" into reservations within the individual counties and another 99,074—and Krumey emphasizes this point—who were rounded up "outside the pursuit of farmworker acquisition . . . and the formation of Polish reservations." Of these, some remained "to the extent they were needed as workers, in situ." But they were likewise "displaced" if the "buildings were earmarked for settlers." In appendix 1 of his report, the total number of "evacuated and/or displaced Poles" is surprisingly listed as just 99,074 persons. Despite these inconsistencies, the last is the number that I will use in the present investigation because the UWZ also takes this number as the basis for all further summaries and there is no plausible reason why Krumey and his staff members would consciously choose to understate their work achievements. An explanation for this considerable discrepancy might be that these people were counted twice, or perhaps some were rounded up, rejected, and then allowed back to their homes instead of being "displaced."

66. A total of 220,308 ethnic Germans had been settled by December 31, 1941, a number that then increased only to 241,884 by December 31, 1942. For both numbers, see unsigned report from Staff Main Office on resettlements of 1942, dated April 30, 1943, BArch R 49/14, 1–33.

67. Unsigned accounting of the RKFDV headquarters up to January 16, 1941, dated February 11, 1941, BArch R 49/303, unpaged; unsigned report from Staff Main Office on resettlements of 1942, dated April 30, 1943, BArch R 49/14, 1–33.

68. The expulsions in Zamość also represented the first step in implementing an idea presented with the General Plan for the East, namely, the securing of population policy goals in the conquered territories through the establishing of SS and police outposts within German settlement zones (Marczewski, *Hitlerowska koncepcja*, 263–78; Wasser,

"Germanisierung im Distrikt Lublin"; more comprehensively at Wasser, *Himmlers Raumplanung*, 133–229; Aly, *Endlösung*, 380–81. See also Krumey's confidential concluding report on the work of the UWZ in the Wartheland and General Government, December 31, 1943, AGK NTN/13, 158–74.

69. Unsigned activity report of the RKFDV appointee in Upper Silesia, September 1939 to January 1943, dated March 30, 1943, BArch 186/42, unpaged; excerpt also at BSA NO-5640.

70. Unsigned overview from the UWZ in Danzig–West Prussia on internal resettlements in 1942, dated December 31, 1942, BArch PL 170/39, 1.

71. Of this 709,991 in Section 3, see the unsigned overview of the status of the DVL in the governmental regions of Kattowitz and Oppeln on December 1, 1942, APK 117/140, 232.

72. Unsigned activity report of the RKFDV appointee in Upper Silesia, September 1939 to January 1943, dated March 30, 1943, BArch 186/42, unpaged; excerpt also at BSA NO-5640.

73. BArch R 75/10, unpaged, Timm to provincial employment office, February 18, 1943. On Timm, see Herbert, *Fremdarbeiter*, 195.

74. Memo from Krumey, erroneously dated February 23, 1943, but no earlier than February 25, 1943, BArch R 75/10, unpaged, reprinted in *Biuletyn* 21: 122–23.

75. Memo from Krumey, February 24, 1943, BArch R 75/10, unpaged.

76. Report from Krumey, April 4, 1943, BArch R 75/4, unpaged.

77. Krumey's confidential concluding report on the work of the UWZ in the Wartheland and General Government, December 31, 1943, AGK NTN/13, 158–74.

78. Ibid.

79. Report from SS Chief Assault Leader Hermann Püschel, Krumey's deputy, November 1, 1944, reprinted in Łuczak, *Położenie ludności polskiej*, 158–60, and *Biuletyn* 21: 129.

80. Unsigned confidential UWZ report for July 1942, dated August 5, 1942, BArch R 75/4, unpaged, reprinted in *Biuletyn* 21: 113–14.

81. Krumey's confidential concluding report on the work of the UWZ in the Wartheland and General Government, December 31, 1943, AGK NTN/13, 158–74.

82. Tooze, *Wages of Destruction*, 513.

83. The redeployments of the SS personnel included Italy, France, and Estonia, and, of course, the deportation of the Hungarian Jews as well. See Krumey to Schwarzhuber, January 9, 1944, AGK 69/196, 26; Krumey to Prause, February 7, 1944, AGK 69/196, 32.

84. On Krumey's role in Hungary, see Gerlach and Aly, *Das letzte Kapitel.*

85. Krumey to Püschel, August 14, 1944, AGK 358/51, 9.

86. Heinemann, *Rasse, Siedlung, deutsches Blut*, 264.

87. Frick to Deputy Führer, December 19, 1940, BArch R 1501/5402, 305–35.

88. Unsigned minutes of meeting at Reich Interior Ministry on January 15, 1941, undated, Bavarian State Archives, Nuremberg, NG-300.

89. Eleventh provision of the Reich Citizens Act of November 25, 1941, *Reichsgesetzblatt Teil I* (1941), 721–24.

90. Broszat, *Nationalsozialistische Polenpolitik*, 198.

91. For former citizens of Danzig, however, who would have been sorted into Section 1 or 2 under the new guidelines, an exception was made. They were not inducted into the DVL but instead received German national status immediately.

92. Decree on the DVL and German national status in the incorporated eastern territories, March 3, 1941, *Reichsgesetzblatt Teil I* (1941), 118–20.

93. This also applied to deportations into the General Government (ibid.).

94. Frick's implementation provisions, March 13, 1941, APP 406/1105, 9–28, reprinted in Pospieszalski, *Hitlerowskie "prawo" okupacyjne*, 122–39.

95. Stuckart, "Staatsangehörigkeit," 236.

96. Frick's implementation provisions, March 13, 1941, APP 406/1105, 9–28, reprinted in Pospieszalski, *Hitlerowskie "prawo" okupacyjne*, 122–39.

97. Nor did it change anything that Greifelt had already written to his RKFDV branch offices in each province's capital on March 27, 1941, asking them to prevent "by all means" that this provision "is mistakenly used to recognize too many Water Poles and Szlonzakians as Germans," while also obliging them to observe the maximum numbers stipulated in Himmler's ethnonationality decree (Greifelt to RKFDV appointees, March 27, 1941, Special Archive at the State Military Archives of Russia, Moscow [hereafter, SMR], 1232/15, 38).

98. Greiser to Regierungspräsidents, Landrats, and mayors, April 6, 1941, APP 834/2, 13–22.

99. Memo from Coulon, November 4, 1940, APP 406/1109, 6–7.

100. Unsigned minutes of a meeting at the Reich Interior Ministry on January 15, 1941, undated, SMR 1232/15, 46–51.

101. One effect of this reorganization was that Coulon no longer headed the DVL central office (Greiser now had to exercise this function himself) and participated in consultations thereafter as a representative of the Gauleiter's offices (signed "p.p. SS Regiment Leader Karl Drendel," Wartheland Gauleiter's offices to the Reichsstatthalter's offices, April 11, 1941, AGK 62/35, 1).

102. Greiser to Regierungspräsidents, Landrats, and mayors, April 6, 1941, APP 834/2, 13–22.

103. Regierungspräsident's offices in Hohensalza, minutes by Dr. Senst of a meeting in Posen, September 6, 1941, APP 406/1120, 3–5.

104. Memo from Höppner to Dept. I of the Reichsstatthalter's offices in the Regierungspräsident's offices in Litzmannstadt, October 20, 1942, APP 406/1110, 164.

105. See, for example, Strickner's statements in his report on the formation and development of the DVL, undated (probably November 1942), reprinted in Pospieszalski, *Niemiecka lista*, 19–130, here 71.

106. Uebelhoer to DVL branch offices, September 18, 1941, APL 897/52, 84.

107. Hearing of Otto Triebe, administrative clerk at DVL branch office, August 14, 1944, APP 406/1113, 329–31.

108. Unsigned report from the mayor of Litzmannstadt for the Regierungspräsident, May 30, 1944, APP 406/1113, 314–15.

109. Memo from Schultheiss, August 5, 1941, APL 176/387, 130. See also memo from Coulon, July 29, 1941, APP 406/1120, 203.

110. Vice Regierungspräsident of Litzmannstadt, Dr. Ernst Hermann Riediger, to Reichsstatthalter's offices, June 26, 1944, APP 406/1113, 311–13.

111. Leuschner to Reichsstatthalter's offices, October 4, 1941, APP 406/1120, 46.

112. Draft of public call in the daily papers, due on February 28, 1942, undated (probably late January or early February 1942), APP 406/1115, 7.

113. Strickner's report on the formation and development of the DVL, undated (probably November 1942), reprinted in Pospiesyzalski, *Niemiecka lista*, 19–130, here 71.

114. Adamski, *Pogląd na rozwój*, 11–12.

115. Springorum to Landrats, mayors, and chiefs of police, April 10, 1941, APK 117/116, 102; also May 24, 1941, APK 117/116, 115.

116. Bracht's public call, April 10, 1941, APK 119/10731, 63.

117. (Probably signed by Vice Oberpräsident Faust), Oberpräsident's offices in Kattowitz to Reich Interior Ministry, October 1941, APK 117/140, 68–74.

118. Bracht's materials for preparing accounting of the implementation of the DVL, May 25, 1941, APK 117/116, 159–67.

119. Ibid.

120. Greifelt to RKFDV branch office in Kattowitz, March 27, 1941, SMR 1232/15, 38.

121. Bracht's materials for preparing accounting of the implementation of the DVL, May 25, 1941, APK 117/116, 159–67.

122. Unsigned minutes of meeting at Reich Interior Ministry on January 15, 1941, undated, SMR 1232/15, 46–51.

123. (Probably signed by Vice Oberpräsident Faust), Oberpräsident's offices in Kattowitz to Reich Interior Ministry, October 1941, APK 117/140, 68–74. See also (signature illegible), Kreisleiter's offices for Warthenau-Blächstadt, to Gauleiter's offices, June 26, 1941, APK 142/209, 141–54.

124. (Probably signed by Vice Oberpräsident Faust), Oberpräsident's offices in Kattowitz to Reich Interior Ministry, October 1941, APK 117/140, 68–74.

125. Overview of status of the DVL from Oberpräsident's offices on December 1, 1941, dated January 8, 1942, BArch R 49/467, unpaged.

126. Unsigned minutes of meeting at Reich Interior Ministry on January 15, 1941, undated, SMR 1232/15, 46–51.

127. Guidance notes for preliminary registration process from Kreisleiter of Preussisch Stargard, Walther Hillman, classified as strictly confidential and to be kept under lock and key, May 1, 1941, APG 532/919, 2–7. On Hillmann, see also personnel file from Reich Interior Ministry at SMR 720-5/3557.

128. Unsigned minutes of meeting of Landrats and mayors in Bromberg Governmental Region on May 14, 1941, undated, AGK NTN/201, 41–43. Cleanliness became a constantly recurring theme in the catalog of criteria separating Germans from Poles. More generally on the significance of cleanliness in the self-image of Germans and their separation from others, see Reagin, *Sweeping the German Nation*, esp. 181–217. On the significance of cleanliness in their separation from Poles, see Orłowski, *Polnische Wirtschaft*, 319–46.

129. Guidance notes for preliminary registration process from Kreisleiter of Preussisch Stargard, Walther Hillman, classified as strictly confidential and to be kept under lock and key, May 1, 1941, APG 532/919, 2–7.

130. Forster's confidential implementation provisions, May 21, 1941, AGK NTN/198, 56–63.

131. Implementation provisions from DVL central office, May 21, 1941, AGK NTN/198, 64–72.

132. Forster's confidential implementation provisions, May 21, 1941, AGK NTN/198, 56–63.

133. Circular from Nazi Party county organization head at Kreisleiter's offices in Neustadt, July 8, 1941, APG 266/4, 19–21.

134. Forster to Schimmel, July 24, 1941, APB 9/5, 107.

135. Schimmel to DVL branch offices, July 29, 1941, APB 9/5, 109.

136. Minutes by Mayor Dr. Zeitler of meeting at Kreisleiter's offices on September 24, 1941, dated September 24, 1941, AGK NTN/201, 50.

137. Ibid.

138. Ibid.

139. Entry of October 19, 1941, in Witte et al., *Der Dienstkalender Heinrich Himmlers*, 186. See also ibid., 209.

140. Memo from Böhm, October 21, 1941, BArch R 49/36a, 54.

141. Hildebrandt to Himmler, October 23, 1941, BArch R 49/36a, 52–53. On the further course of this conflict, see also Schenk, *Hitlers Mann*, 205–12.

142. Duckart, deputy head of SS settlement staff in Gdańsk, minutes of meeting of county task force leaders' caucus (*Kreisarbeitsstabsführersitzung*) on May 15, 1941, undated, APG 265/4492, 51–55.

143. Minutes of meeting at Hildebrandt's on October 28, 1941, reprinted in Jastrzębski, *Potulice*, 68–69.

144. Willich to SS Senior Assault Unit Leader Max Pauly and Abromeit, December 30, 1941, APB 96/351, 5–7.

145. Head of SD Special Unit at SD Command Precinct, SS Senior Assault Leader Dr. Pech, to UWZ camp at Thorn, January 15, 1942, APB 96/351, 3; Pech to UWZ Danzig and field offices of SD Special Unit at UWZ camps, January 26, 1942, APB 96/351, 11.

146. Head of SD Special Unit at SD Command Precinct, SS Senior Assault Leader Dr. Pech, to field offices of SD Special Unit, February 23, 1942, APB 96/351, 25–30.

147. Jastrzębski, *Potulice*, 54–57.

148. As again expressly stated in Raguse, Vice Regierungspräsident in Bromberg, to DVL branch offices of the governmental region, September 28, 1942, APB 9/5, 365.

149. See, for example (signed "p.p. Kluge"), UWZ Danzig to Regierungspräsident's offices in Bromberg, January 22, 1943, BArch PL 170/65, 97, in response to the latter's request for the transfer of camp inmates.

150. Unsigned DVL regional office in Bromberg to central office, June 19, 1943, AGK NTN/213, 27.

151. See also personnel file from Reich Interior Ministry at SMR 720–5/6930.

152. (Signed "p.p. Kistner"), Landrat's offices in Bromberg to Regierungspräsident's offices in Bromberg, July 10, 1943, AGK NTN/213, 32.

153. SD Special Unit at Potulitz to DVL regional office in Bromberg, December 2, 1943, AGK NTN/213, 34; Potulitz camp supervisor to DVL regional office in Bromberg, December 28, 1943, AGK NTN/213, 40.

154. See, for example, (signature illegible), status report from Landrat of Kulm to Regierungspräsident's offices in Bromberg, December 6, 1941, AGK 904/2, 121–25; (signature illegible), status report from Landrat of Wirsitz to Regierungspräsident's offices in Bromberg, January 9, 1942, AGK 904/2, 226–31.

155. Mayor of Thorn to Regierungspräsident of Bromberg, November 8, 1941, AGK 904/2, 16–17.

156. The census resulted in the following figures for Thorn, which purportedly had a total population of 69,151: 3,417 were in Tier I ("impeccable Volksdeutsche"); 57,166 in Tier II ("non-impeccable Volksdeutsche, obliging Poles, Kashubians"); 8,569 in Tier III ("Congress Poles, and others who are not impeccable"). A clearer picture of the city's ethnic composition was conveyed by the surveying of spoken language, according to which 9,280 spoke German and 59,481 spoke Polish (unsigned summary of results from census of December 3–6, 1939, undated, AGK NTN/191, 20–21). The last summary of DVL enrollments from the branch office for the city of Thorn is dated April 7, 1943. At that point, Sections 1 and 2 together contained 3,983 persons, Section 3 had 42,152, and Section 4 had just 10 persons. Not enrolled in the DVL were 10,864 persons who either came from the Reich or had been naturalized by the EWZ as ethnic Germans from Eastern Europe, along with around 16,000 Poles (Thorn

chief of police, SS Regiment Leader Alfons Graf, to Gestapo of Bromberg, April 7, 1943, AGK 904/4, 90–102). In Forster's view, Thorn had now become a predominantly "German" city, even though 59,481 residents had cited Polish as their mother tongue just four years earlier.

157. Landrat of Preussisch Stargard, Walther Hillmann, to Regierungspräsident's offices in Danzig, September 9, 1941, SMR 720–4/189, 7–8.

158. Unsigned report on activities of DVL branch office for Neustadt County, April 30, 1943, APG 37/2, 455.

159. Unsigned letter, Reichsstatthalter's office in Danzig to Reich Interior Ministry, March 7, 1942, APP 406/1120, 19–20. In the message, the author refers to the still inadequate statistical survey of the province. For example, in Danzig Governmental Region, it was known how many families had been sorted into each group but not how many individuals these families represented. The statistic was even more imprecise for Marienwerder Governmental Region, where again only families had been registered, but this time not even the how the groups sorted was known, only how many families in total had been inducted into the DVL.

160. Unsigned summary of results from census of December 3–6, 1939, undated, AGK NTN/191, 20–21. The fact that the numbers of German and Polish native speakers together exceeded the total number of people registered by the DVL results from the fact that some cited both languages as their mother tongue.

161. Second directive on the DVL and German national status in the incorporated eastern territories, signed by Stuckart, Bormann, and Himmler, *Reichsgesetzblatt Teil I* (1942), 51–52; overview of status of the DVL from the Reichsstatthalter's offices in Danzig–West Prussia, March 7, 1942, APP 406/1120, 19–20; in the Wartheland as of January 1, 1942 (January 9, 1942, APP 406/1120, 64–65); from RKFDV headquarters as of February 1, 1942, March 5, 1942, BArch R 49/467, unpaged.

162. Second directive on the DVL and German national status in the incorporated eastern territories, signed by Stuckart, Bormann, and Himmler, *Reichsgesetzblatt Teil I* (1942), 51–52.

163. Stuckart to top-level Reich authorities, RKFDV Staff Main Office, VoMi, August 4, 1942, APP 406/1110, 67–73.

164. Długoborski, *Polozenie ludności*, xxvii.

165. Forster to DVL branch offices, February 12, 1942, APB 9/5, 243–44.

166. (Signed "p.p. Schultze"), DVL branch office for Kattowitz County to mayors of the rural county, February 20, 1942, APK 82/691, 1–6.

167. Unsigned ethnonationality unit at Oberpräsident's offices in Kattowitz to Regierungspräsidents of Kattowitz and Oppeln, January 29, 1942, BArch R 49/3508, unpaged.

168. Ibid.

169. Himmler, RKFDV, directive 66/I, February 10, 1942, APB 9/5, 237–38. This simplification did not go unnoticed by the Polish resistance, see Gąsiorowski, "Niemiecka lista narodowa," 77.

170. Unsigned draft of public call from ethnonationality unit for publication in Wartheland newspapers, undated, APP 406/1115, 7.

171. Jäger to DVL regional offices, September 13, 1943, APL 176/387, 57.

172. Jäger to DVL regional offices, April 8, 1943, APP 406/1117, 16–17.

173. Overview from Reichsstatthalter's offices as of April 1, 1942, APP 406/1120, 91, and January 1, 1943, BArch R 186/32, unpaged.

174. Overview from Reichsstatthalter's offices as of January 1, 1943, BArch R 186/32, unpaged.

175. Hohlfeld's memo on meeting of February 18, 1942, undated, APK 117/140, 158–59 (emphasis in original). See also Kaczmarek, "Niemiecka polityka," 133–35.

176. Bracht's public call included in Faust to Regierungspräsidents and Landrats, February 19, 1942, SMR 1232/15, 65–60.

177. Draft text by ethnonationality unit at Oberpräsident's offices for lecture at first sitting of DVL central office, February 19, 1942, APK 117/140, 216–23.

178. As will be shown, DVL enrollments accelerated as of February 1942 in Upper Silesia as well, and not only in Danzig–West Prussia as claimed in Borodziej and Lemberg, *Unsere Heimat*, 43.

179. Overview from RKFDV Staff Main Office as of February 1, 1942, BArch R 49/467, unpaged, and May 1, 1942, BArch R 49/467, unpaged; overview from the Oberpräsident's offices as of December 1, 1942, APK 117/140, 232, and April 1, 1944, APK 117/140, 228.

180. Unsigned overview of population breakdown in Kattowitz Governmental Region, October 10, 1943, APK 117/140, 229.

181. Kaczmarek, "Zwischen Altreich und Besatzungsgebiet," 349.

182. Forster's public call of February 22, 1942, APB 5/3, 1–2.

183. Ibid.

184. Gąsiorowski, "Niemiecka lista narodowa," 75. In the Polish underground, the pushing of DVL enrollments was seen as proof of German failure and Polish resistance; as an article in the *Ziemiach Zachodnich Rzeczypospolitej* put it, "where enticements and promises have not brought satisfactory results, that is where force is applied," see Gąsiorowski, "Niemiecka lista narodowa," 76.

185. Forster's guidelines, February 22, 1942, APB 9/5, 261–69.

186. It was not until early 1944 that Forster brought Frick's questionnaires back into play. At his behest, Wilhelm Huth ordered that the old questionnaires, "to complement the operations of the expedited procedure, be filled out retroactively by DVL Section 3 members and put into the files, with copies sent to the Dahlem Publication Office as stipulated," see (signed "p.p. Huth"), DVL central office to regional and branch offices, January 31, 1944, APB 9/380, 233. There is no evidence that this actually happened.

187. Forster's guidelines, February 22, 1942, APB 9/5, 261–69.

188. Questionnaire from DVL branch office in Thorn, AGK NTN/201, 7.

189. Forster's guidelines, February 22, 1942, APB 9/5, 261–69. For a summary of the new procedure, see also unsigned overview at undated (probably late 1942), AGK NTN/200, 97–99.

190. Forster's guidelines, February 22, 1942, APB 9/5, 261–69.

191. This applied to assessments at a DVL branch office. At a regional office, objections had to be raised by two committee members for the case to be referred to the central office.

192. Forster to DVL regional and branch offices, July 2, 1942, APB 9/5, 352.

193. Nethe to head of Gestapo, July 9, 1942, AGK 904/3, 27–32.

194. Kühn to DVL branch offices, June 27, 1942, APB 9/392, 1–2.

195. Ibid.

196. Forster to DVL regional and branch offices, July 2, 1942, APB 9/5, 353. The following February, Forster mandated that in all cases, meaning also outside the appeals process, he alone could approve an expulsion from the DVL (Forster to DVL regional and branch offices,

February 9, 1943, APB 9/380, 81–82). It was not until February 7, 1944, that Forster delegated the power to revoke DVL identity documents to the Regierungspräsidents, although they could only do so themselves (Forster to DVL regional and branch offices, APB 9/380, 241–42).

197. Forster to DVL regional and branch offices, October 10, 1942, AGK NTN/197, 145.

198. HSSPF of Danzig to RKFDV Staff Main Office, December 3, 1941, BArch R 49/467, unpaged; unsigned overview of status of the DVL in Danzig–West Prussia on November 1, 1943 APP 406/1120, 28–32.

199. The figures for the local populace are based on the results of the second census in December 1940 (unsigned and undated overview, AGK NTN/189, 22) minus the reckoned 11,242 persons deported from the province between December 1940 and March 31, 1943 (unsigned overview from Reich Security Main Office as of November 15, 1940, BSA NO-5150, reprinted in Łuczak, *Wysiedlenia ludności polskiej*, 74–75). The DVL enrollment figures come from an unsigned overview of the status of the DVL in the annexed western Polish territories on March 31, 1943, undated, BArch R 186/32, unpaged.

200. Landrat of Bromberg Walther Nethe to Reichsstatthalter's offices, August 29, 1942, APB 9/702, 1–34.

201. Guidelines for implementing racial assessments for the DVL, April 25, 1941, AGK 167/39, 32–33.

202. Unsigned minutes of a meeting in Posen on the intended plans of RuSHA, undated, APP 406/1112, 79–83.

203. Racial valuation groups had been first used in the selection process applied to women who wanted to marry SS men, in order to ensure "racially healthy offspring." The women were sorted into Groups I through IV (Heinemann, *Rasse, Siedlung, deutsches Blut*, 53). This classification system may have drawn on earlier work by Egon von Eickstedt, see Klautke, "German Race Psychology," 27.

204. A short biography of Schwalm can be found at Heinemann, *Rasse, Siedlung, deutsches Blut*, 635–36.

205. Memo from Schwalm on a meeting at DVL regional office in Litzmannstadt on May 21, 1941, AGK 167/39, 3–5.

206. Otto Dietrich, directive 6, signed "SS Senior Assault Unit Leader Otto Dietrich," RuSHA head at EWZ, January 22, 1940, German Federal Archives, Berlin-Zehlendorf branch, Berlin Document Center, SSO file; Hofmann to Künzel, January 25, 1940, AGK 167/26, 27. According to Heinemann, RuSHA attempted to at least partially counteract Himmler's ordered expansion of "O Notice" recipient groups by tightening the selection criteria for Group III, see Heinemann, *Rasse, Siedlung, deutsches Blut*, 236.

207. Unsigned memo from Party Chancellery on meeting of August 12, 1941, dated August 14, 1941, APP 406/1131, 33–34. See also draft by RKFDV headquarters, undated, APP 406/1131, 12; draft by RKFDV headquarters, undated, APP 406/1131, 13–15.

208. Coulon to Dr. Neesse, August 26, 1941, APP 406/1131, 27–32.

209. Ibid.

210. Memo from Coulon, September 10, 1941, APP 406/1131, 41–45.

211. Ibid.

212. Schwalm to DVL central office, July 8, 1941, APP 406/1131, 3–5. In Litzmannstadt, for example, Uebelhoer had explicitly forbidden his DVL branch offices from waiting for a positive verdict from the assessment commissions before issuing identity documents (Uebelhoer to DVL branch offices, July 21, 1941, APP 406/1113, 254–58).

213. Schwalm to Mehlhorn, September 10, 1941, APP 406/1131, 9–11.

214. Jäger to Reich Interior Ministry, September 11, 1941, APP 406/1131, 46–48.

215. Himmler to Greiser, confidential, September 30, 1941, APP 406/1114, 3–4.

216. Directive 50/I by Himmler as RKFDV, September 30, 1941, APP 406/1114, 5–6, reprinted in Pospieszalski, *Hitlerowskie "prawo" okupacyjne*, 144–45. This decree thus shows that Himmler did not want to "simply create more" Germans in Poland, as Bergen believes, but actually wanted to curtail an inclusivist selection policy. But she is correct about the Nazi-occupied areas of the Soviet Union (Cf. Bergen, "The Nazi Concept of Volksdeutsche," 574).

217. Coulon's memo for Jäger, November 11, 1941, APP 406/1131, 53–57.

218. Greiser to Jäger, confidential, November 11, 1941, APP 406/1131, 68.

219. Böttcher to Greiser, January 13, 1942, APP 406/1131, 341–46.

220. Minutes by SS Senior Squad Leader Dr. Erich Sieder (tasked at RuSHA field office with conducting these selections) of meeting with Dr. Rössel (from RKFDV branch office) and Coulon, on December 11, 1941, dated December 11, 1941, APP 406/1131, 73–75.

221. Unsigned memo from ethnonationality unit at the Reichsstatthalter's offices, undated (probably after Coulon's meeting with Sieder and Rössel), APP 406/1131, 94–99.

222. Mehlhorn to Regierungspräsidents, March 3, 1942, APP 406/1114, 7.

223. Detailed report from RuSHA field office to Reichsstatthalter's offices, July 9, 1942, APP 406/1131, 163–75. See also Dongus's concluding report, confidential, May 29, 1942, APP 406/1131, 138–54. Of course, the ratio between the low number of suitability assessors and high number of selected individuals says much about the nature of the assessments. Although neither the daily working hours nor required commute times are known, I would suggest the following rough calculation: assuming 67,235 persons to be selected by eight suitability assessors, who in these eight weeks worked every day for twelve hours without breaks and used only a quarter of this time for traveling between the branch offices, then they had 3.5 minutes on average to sort each person into a valuation group. Thus, although Heinemann is fundamentally correct that the criteria of the racial appraisals stemmed from those used in the selection of new SS members, and that the SS had thus transplanted its racial ideals to the conquered territories, not only were these criteria differently valued, there was also much less time allowed for the actual selections. On this point, see Heinemann, *Rasse, Siedlung, deutsches Blut*, 13.

224. A short biography can be found at Heinemann, *Rasse, Siedlung, deutsches Blut*, 613–14.

225. Dongus to Reichsstatthalter's offices, January 27, 1942, APP 406/1131, 81–83.

226. Dongus to DVL branch office in Kalisch, April 27, 1942, AGK 167/10, 10–21.

227. Unsigned letter, Landrat of Lissa to Regierungspräsident in Posen, May 8, 1942, APP 406/1131, 125.

228. Böttcher's answer to Landrat of Lissa, undated, APP 406/1131, 126; Böttcher to DVL central office, May 14, 1942, APP 406/1131, 123–24.

229. Dongus's concluding report, confidential, May 29, 1942, APP 406/1131, 138–54.

230. SD Command Precinct Posen (signed "Höppner"), to Reichsstatthalter's offices, DVL central office and branch offices, May 13, 1942, APP 406/1131, 160–61.

231. Höppner to Ehlich, June 19, 1942, APP 406/1130, 63.

232. Unsigned (probably Höppner) memo, June 22, 1942, APP 406/1131, 417–18.

233. Commander of Military District XXI (signature illegible) to Greiser, July 17, 1942, APP 406/1117, 89.

234. Greiser to Jäger, July 24, 1942, APP 406/1117, 94.

235. Memo from Höppner, July 31, 1942, APP 406/1117, 103–5.

236. Mehlhorn to Military District Command XXI, January 1943, APP 406/1117, 150–51. This is also why Czesław Łuczak is mistaken when he claims that Greiser personally attached importance to removing those who did not fulfill the "racial criteria" of RuSHA (Cf. Łuczak, *Pod niemieckim jarzmem*, 60).

237. Łuczak, *Pod niemieckim jarzmem*, 60.

238. Military District Command XXI (signature illegible) to Reichsstatthalter's offices, September 25, 1942, APP 406/1117, 134.

239. Höppner to RuSHA field office in Litzmannstadt, February 15, 1943, APP 406/1117, 157–58.

240. DVL regional office Litzmannstadt (p.p. signature illegible) to Reichsstatthalter's offices, January 18, 1943, APP 406/1117, 12–13.

241. Höppner to Regierungspräsident's offices in Litzmannstadt, January 26, 1943, APP 406/1117, 14–15.

242. Unsigned letter, Gestapo in Hohensalza to IdS in Posen, March 13, 1943, APP 406/1131, 407–8; Mehlhorn to IdS in Posen, April 9, 1943, APP 406/1131, 409–10.

243. Gosewinkel, *Einbürgern und Ausschließen*, 410.

244. Heinemann, *Rasse, Siedlung, deutsches Blut*, 266; Witte et al., *Dienstkalender Heinrich Himmlers*, 270.

245. Unpaged memo from Arlt on a meeting with representative of SD Command Precinct and RuSHA, February 5, 1942, BArch R 49/3160.

246. Schultz to Bracht, February 23, 1942, BArch NS 2/80, 67. A short biography of Bruno Schultz can be found at Heinemann, *Rasse, Siedlung, deutsches Blut*, 634–35.

247. Bracht to Schultz, March 1, 1942, BArch NS 2/80, 68–70.

248. Section 4 encompassed 5,137 persons on February 1, 1942, but then had 52,780 on April 1, 1944. Bracht thus had a relatively clear idea of who was still to be enrolled. For DVL status on February 1, 1942, see BArch R 49/467, unpaged, and on April 1, 1944, see APK 117/140, 228.

249. Bracht to Schultz, March 1, 1942, BArch NS 2/80, 68–70.

250. Bracht to Hofmann, March 1, 1942, BArch NS 2/80, 65–66.

251. Memo from Hofmann, March 26, 1942, BArch NS 2/80, 51–53.

252. A short biography can be found at Heinemann, *Rasse, Siedlung, deutsches Blut*, 634.

253. Arlt to Oberpräsident's offices in Kattowitz, March 30, 1942, SMR 1232/34, 4–5.

254. (Signed "SS Regiment Leader Scholtz"), guidelines for the Germanization of Polish families, June 9, 1942, APK 119/10222, 49–50 (emphasis in original).

255. Unsigned minutes of meeting in Regierungspräsident's offices in Kattowitz on January 6, 1943, dated February 1, 1943, APK 119/10222, 82–85.

256. Hohlfeld's minutes of meeting on January 6, 1943, dated January 8, 1943, APK 117/140, 113–15.

257. Ibid.

258. Memo from Bracht, undated (probably January 25, 1943), APK 117/140, 116.

259. Memo from Hohlfeld, March 16, 1943, SMR 1232/34, 25.

260. Curt Becker to Regierungspräsident's offices in Oppeln, April 13, 1943, SMR 1232/34, 28.

261. Hohlfeld to Regierungspräsident's offices, June 9, 1943, SMR 1232/34, 29.

262. Unsigned letter, Landrat of Beuthen-Tarnowitz to Regierungspräsident's offices in Kattowitz, May 25, 1943, SMR 1232/37, 30. His personnel file from Reich Interior Ministry is at SMR 720-5/10599.

263. Wangenheim to Springorum, August 19, 1943, SMR 1232/37, 34–35.

264. Springorum to Oberpräsident's offices, May 30, 1943, SMR 1232/37, 30.

265. Groll to Springorum, private, June 2, 1943, SMR 1232/37, 31–32.

266. Ibid.

267. Springorum to Bracht, June 5, 1943, SMR 1232/37, 32.

268. Arlt to Faust, June 24, 1943, SMR 1232/37, 27.

269. Brehm to Springorum, July 6, 1943, SMR 1232/37, 26. In early 1944, when it came time to name someone new to the Gau Office for Ethnonationality Questions and the SS suggested Brehm, Bracht refused, not least because of his role in the racial appraisals, see SD Command Precinct (signature illegible) to Ehlich, February 19, 1944, SMR 500–4/71, 3.

270. Kühn to DVL branch offices, August 20, 1941, AGK NTN/200, 123–27 (emphasis in original).

271. Forster to Regierungspräsidents, Landrats, and mayors, October 30, 1941, APB 9/5, 179–81.

272. Himmler to Forster, BArch R 43 II/1332a, 84–87.

273. Himmler forwarded a copy to Lammers on November 26, 1941 (BArch R 43 II/1332,5, 83) and to Bormann with carbon copies for Heydrich, Greifelt, and Hofmann (BArch R 49/36a, 56).

274. Himmler to Forster, BArch R 43 II/1332a, 84–87.

275. Witte et al., *Dienstkalender Heinrich Himmlers*, 269.

276. Ibid., 270.

277. Heinemann, for example, mentions these alone in order to support her claim that "despite Forster's aversion to racial selections on a large-scale . . . such appraisals did take place" (Heinemann, *Rasse, Siedlung, deutsches Blut*, 271).

278. SS Senior Assault Leader Dr. Pech, head of SD Special Unit at SD Command Precinct, to field offices of SD Special Unit, February 23, 1942, APB 96/351, 25–30.

279. Unsigned memo from SD Special Unit, January 28, 1942, APB 96/334, 4; also Jastrzębski, *Potulice*, 58.

280. Forster to DVL regional and branch offices, February 9, 1943, APB 9/380, 243. It took more than a year for Forster to rescind this directive, see Forster to DVL regional and branch offices, May 9, 1944, APB 9/380, 261–62.

281. Heinemann, *Rasse, Siedlung, deutsches Blut*, 260.

282. Coulon would become head of the new Reich Headquarters for Eastern Research (Reichszentrale für Ostforschung), founded in 1943 by Alfred Rosenberg, which was to coordinate, finance, and, of course, control research in this area (Burleigh, *Germany Turns Eastwards*, 260–61).

283. Memo from Höppner, May 27, 1942, APP 406/1112, 303–4.

284. Mehlhorn's minutes of a meeting on June 23, 1942, dated June 24, 1942, APP 406/1110, 49–58.

285. Pickel to Reichsstatthalter's offices, October 13, 1942, APP 406/1120, 216–21; unsigned ethnopolicy status report from Regierungspräsident in Hohensalza, October 15, 1942, AGK 62/120, 75–78.

286. Jäger to Regierungspräsidents, November 5, 1942, APP 406/1120, 225–26.

287. Unsigned memo, ethnonationality unit to party leadership offices in the Wartheland, November 19, 1942, APP 406/1120, 233–34.

288. See correspondence between ethnonationality unit and Regierungspräsident on the closure of DVL branch offices at APP 406/1120, 239–45.

289. Heimann's status report for September to December 1942, undated, SMR 1232/26, 61–66.

290. Ibid.

291. Hohlfeld's statement on the DVL, February 8, 1961, BABt Ost-Dok. 13/6, 2–13.

292. Memo from Hohlfeld on a meeting at Bracht's on November 17, 1942, dated November 19, 1942, APK 117/140, 119.

293. For example, the sorry effort by Stengel-von Rutkowski, *Was ist ein Volk?*, which had been published shortly before, and examined precisely this question; it included an introduction by Otto Hofmann, head of RuSHA.

294. Unsigned memo from Gauleiter's offices, January 29, 1943, APK 142/206, 39–50.

295. Of course, the use of this construct was not restricted to German nationalists. In Poland, too, the border populace was accused of insufficient patriotism and labeled an "intermediate class," (Greiner and Kaczmarek, "Vereinsaktivitäten," 227.

296. Unsigned memorandum from Gauleiter's offices, January 29, 1943, APK 142/206, 39–50.

297. Ibid.

298. A good example was, of course, Forster's invitation to Prof. Hans F. K. Günther, whose scholarly report likewise served to legitimize already existing policy.

299. Memo from Hohlfeld on February 2, 1943 (SMR 1232/26, 51–53) and April 1, 1943 (SMR 1232/26, 67).

300. Memo from Hohlfeld on Landrats' conference on June 24, 1943, dated June 22, 1943, APK 117/140, 205–12.

301. Report from Dr. Alfons Woryna, June 3, 1962, BABt Ost-Dok. 13/8, 1–6.

302. Unsigned minutes of 48th sitting of DVL central office on July 14, 1944, dated August 13, 1944, SMR 1232/22, 23–27.

303. Overview from RKFDV Staff Main Office as of April 1, 1944, dated September 27, 1944, BArch R 49/467, unpaged.

304. The recorded population figures in the annexed territories vary considerably between sources. The numbers specified here lean more toward the lower range of recorded enrollments in the DVL and are based on the unsigned overview from the RKFDV Staff Main Office as of April 1, 1944, undated, BArch R 49/928, unpaged. For each province, the number of locals is calculated by taking the total number of residents and subtracting the German citizens who moved there from the Reich during the war, the ethnic Germans who were settled there from Eastern Europe, and the deported Poles.

305. For Danzig–West Prussia, the second census of December 1940 reveals 1,609,875 residents in the annexed areas of the province, but without differentiating between locals and people who moved there during the war (unsigned and undated overview at AGK NTN/189, 22). This differentiation is made in the "Kleiner Umsiedlungsspiegel" ("small resettlement mirror"), a twice-yearly report issued by the RKFDV Staff Main Office, with the number of locals (meaning Germans and Poles) given as 1,549,000 persons in the issue of February 1943 (BArch R 49/87, 3–6), and 1,543,000 persons in January 1944 (BSA NO-3568). In the RKFDV Staff Main Office's overview of April 1, 1944, the last one it provided, the number has shrunk to 1,375,000 persons (unpaged, BArch R 49/928). The figures for Upper Silesia show a similar fluctuation, with 2,374,000 persons given in the "Kleiner Umsiedlungsspiegel" of February 1943 (BArch R 49/87, 3–6), and 2,362,000 persons in January 1944 (BSA NO-3568). Once again, the lowest figure is found in the aforementioned RKFDV Staff Main Office's overview of April 1, 1944, with just 2,091,000 persons (BArch R 49/928, unpaged).

306. Himmler's directive 12/C as RKFDV on treatment of members of Section 3, February 9, 1942, APP 406/1107, 163–70, reprinted in Pospieszalski, *Hitlerowskie "prawo" okupacyjne*, 150–56; more detailed descriptions of the specific consequences in various areas of life at Majer, Fremdvölkische, 386–458; Kaczmarek, "Niemiecka polityka," 124–25.

307. Unsigned overview of results of second census of December 1940, undated, AGK NTN/189, 22; unsigned overview from Reich Security Main Office as of November 15, 1940, BSA NO-5150, reprinted in Łuczak, *Wysiedlenia ludności polskiej*, 74–75; unsigned overview of status of the DVL in the annexed western Polish territories on March 31, 1943, undated, BArch R 186/32, unpaged.

308. Unsigned memo Oberpräsident's offices to Reich Interior Ministry, July 28, 1944, APK 117/115, 95. A corresponding directive was sent to the Regierungspräsidents on August 27 (APK 82/689, 19).

309. Globcke to DVL offices in the annexed western Polish territories, September 15, 1944, APP 406/1107, 228–30.

310. Brandt to Stuckart, October 26, 1944, SMR 720–9/15, 28.

311. Unsigned memo from ethnonationality unit at Oberpräsident's offices in Kattowitz, October 25, 1944, APK 117/115, 5.

312. Reich Security Main Office III B (signature illegible) to SD Command Precinct Kattowitz, including protest from Reich Security Main Office, January 8, 1945, SMR 720–9/15, 14–15.

313. The main collection of files is housed in the former Special Archive at the State Military Archives of Russia, under fonds 1232.

314. Unsigned message, DVL branch office for Litzmannstadt municipality to Regierungspräsident's offices, November 21, 1944, AGK 360/3, 128; another such message from November 22, 1944, is at AGK 360/3, 139.

315. Unsigned message, Reich Interior Ministry to Reich Defense Commissioners in the annexed western Polish territories, January 1945, SMR 720–9/15, 13.

316. More detailed discussion and further reading on this are at Stryjkowski, *Położenie osób wpisanych*, and Stryjkowski, "Nachkriegsfolgen."

Conclusion

IN HIS STUDY of Hitler's war aims, Norman Rich drily noted that if Nazi Germany's plans were actually supposed to be based on Hitler's ideological beliefs, then they "had become very distorted indeed," for Hitler had become "so frequently and finally so completely . . . diverted from his ideological course."[1] There is probably no other policy field to which this observation better applies than the Germanization of the Christian Poles in the annexed territories. The "Germanization of the soil" demanded in *Mein Kampf* certainly did not translate into, for example, the racial selection policy demanded by the SS complex; instead, it yielded to an assimilation program whose logic pointed to its Prussian predecessor, but whose extent went far beyond it. How could it happen that the Nazis, who violently pursued the slogan of "Germany for the Germans" as had no government before, could nonetheless drive the percentage of non-Germans living inside the Reich to previously unseen heights through the importation of foreign forced laborers, thereby contravening their own racial antipathies? How could it be that the Nazis condemned Prussia's Germanization policy for its assimilationist goals, only to then implement the largest assimilation project ever seen in modern German history, with the establishment of the DVL during World War II?

These developments become particularly paradoxical if the Nazis are taken at their word, and their ideological imperatives are misunderstood as declarations of intended actions—a misunderstanding that muddies not only popular understandings of Nazism but certain strands of scholarly research as well. There are two reasons behind this, I would argue, and, although closely interconnected in historiographic terms, they are nonetheless worth analyzing separately here. First, there is the seldom examined assumption that the relationship between individual belief and social practice necessarily follows the sequence of first ideology, then planning, then practice. In this scheme, the relationship between theory and practice cannot be interpreted as a dialectic, but instead as a one-way street: practice manifests itself solely as an expression of ideology, while also being separated from it.[2] Second is the likewise rarely examined conception of ideology as a personal defect, instead of asking about the broader material conditions shaping its development and interpret ideology as a kind of historically dependent interface between the individual and the world, as an "ideational tool for forging a community from above," according to the research group "Projekt Ideologietheorie" ("Project on a theory of ideology").[3]

In the scholarly research on Nazism, these reductionist views have manifested themselves particularly in the intentionalist approach, according to which Nazi crimes are the direct and calculable consequence of conscious planning by a small group of Germans—or a large one, as Daniel Goldhagen claimed in the 1990s—who were driven by a homicidal ideology.[4] This personalizing view of history necessarily leads to a tautology, a simplifying conjecture on the cause of the Shoah: the reason the Nazi leadership (or the Germans in general) decided to annihilate the Jews was because they were antisemitic.[5] This error in reasoning comes from assuming a simple cause-and-effect relationship between ideology and practice. But I would not go as far as Franz Neumann did during the war, when he denied that any real ideology had been produced by Nazism at all. In his view, allegiance was not based, for example, on a belief in ideological promises but was instead created primarily through the "use of terror."[6] This fails to explain, however, why a regime would expend its energy on the production of ideology if the threat of violence was supposedly enough. Nonetheless, this doubt about the effectiveness of Nazi ideology is still a good analytical starting point in that it shifts attention to the question of practice. The most recent research into fascism, by Robert O. Paxton, for example, draws the conclusion "that what the fascists *did* tells us at least as much as what they *said*."[7]

Of course, this change in focus should not lead to the exact opposite of the mistake made by the intentionalist camp—that is, instead of reducing all practice to ideology, to now make the functionalist claim that ideology is simply an accessory for the legitimization of practice.[8] On the contrary, what is needed is an understanding of ideology that no longer analyzes it solely as a set of theoretical doctrines, but also as a practice. The focus would then be on the "performativity of the fascist Volksgemeinschaft," and with it the "materiality [of the ideological], its existence as an ensemble of apparatuses, intellectuals, rituals, and practices."[9] Althusser once illustrated this idea with a quote from Blaise Pascale: "Kneel down, move your lips in prayer, and you will believe."[10] Of course, Althusser was not talking about a trite inversion of the idealistic stance; instead, he was pointing to "an intricate reflective mechanism of retroactive 'autopoetic' foundation that far exceeds the reductionist assertion of the dependence of inner belief on external behaviour."[11] On the one hand, this perspective allows one to see the relationship between ideology and individual practice as a dialectic, and not simply as a unilinear cause-and-effect relationship.[12] On the other, it brings up the functionality of the ideological in the reproduction of power. For the individual subject, ideology offers, in the words of Stuart Hall, "the mental frameworks—the languages, the concepts, categories, imagery of thought, and the systems of representation—which different classes and social groups deploy in order to make sense of, define, figure out and render intelligible the way society works."[13] For the broader system, ideological confrontations are—according to Hall, with reference to Gramsci—"part of the general social struggle for mastery and leadership—in short for hegemony."[14]

My investigation has focused on the functional needs of power as an aspect of ideology; it is only through this, I believe, that one can understand the astounding fluidity of the selection criteria, as well as the contortions that the Nazi ideology producers were ready to perform in order to justify each new change. As I have shown, Nazi Germanization policy cannot be understood if it is reduced to its violent processes of exclusion, thereby failing to recognize that it was also a policy of inclusion. Even though the Jewish populace in particular—which was not the focus of the present book—remained categorically excluded from all assimilation efforts and were later systematically murdered, and even though political opponents (both alleged and real) and a large part of the Polish elite were murdered or else deported to the General Government alongside Jews, welfare recipients, and owners of desirable dwellings or productive farms, the lengthening war made the German occupiers increasingly dependent on a large part of the local populace. Of course, this does not mean that the German invasion had not dramatically worsened living conditions for most of them. Apart from those who had been successful in their applications for induction into Sections 1 or 2 of the DVL, thus becoming incorporated into the ruling apparatus and actually taking on the role of "master race members" within their Polish environment (at least as suggested by many examples), the rest of the populace was subject to constant surveillance and probably never able to shake the feeling that, in cases of doubt, they might yet be deported or even murdered. This applied somewhat less to those enrolled in Section 3 of the DVL, although the German occupiers did draft these men into the Wehrmacht and also made clear to all others that with the granting of German national status for a ten-year revocable term, future misconduct could be punished at any time. In contrast, the situation was completely unbearable for those who had been cynically downgraded by the occupiers to the status of "protected dependents" ("Schutzangehörige"), and thus had to bear the full brunt of German despotism.

But the threat of looming defeat caused some German ethnocrats to register doubts about the treatment of even this group, which suffered the most discrimination. Thus, propositions aimed at overcoming the DVL were seen in Upper Silesia that argued for a process that would improve the situation of those not enrolled in Sections 1 or 2, thereby binding them to German control. Of course, these propositions were aimed in particular at members of Section 3, for whose betterment Forster and Bracht were already striving, even as the DVL branch offices were barely managing to register the bulk of the populace. But as seen in a message from the civil administration in Upper Silesia, particular attention was also focused on those outside the DVL. Dated December 14, 1944, drafted by Hohlfeld and likely signed by Springorum, this missive, as a kind of logical conclusion of the ethnonationality policy in Upper Silesia, demanded from the Reich Interior Ministry "a change to the stance adopted until now toward Polishdom." After the Polish inhabitants had initially been "seen more or less as a populace that was hostile to the German Volk" and had only been tolerated for their "indispensability in the labor process," the "valiant demeanor" of the "many members of the younger Polish cohort who had been initially conscripted by the Wehrmacht without closer inspection of their ethnonational membership" had suggested the need for a "a certain loosening" of regulations. But such measures represented at most a "temporary stopgap" and needed to be extended in order to "prevent any further threat to security, and in the interest of continued trouble-free work in the armaments industry." On top of the already established privileging of Polish armaments workers, the Oberpräsident's offices now called for the cancellation of impediments for the rest of the Polish populace as well, such as their higher legal marriage age and their considerably lower wages. Furthermore, the tens of thousands of men who had been drafted into the Wehrmacht without determination of their ethnonational membership should "be made equal to the German populace in economic matters," if they were not already eligible for induction into Section 3 of the DVL. The forcefulness with which the Oberpräsident's offices urged the speedy implementation of these demands reflected the seriousness of the situation. As Springorum impressed on the Reich Interior Ministry, he was holding fast to this demand even if it was construed by the occupiers as a sign of weakness; according to his closing appeal, which was particularly astonishing from a Nazi occupation head in Poland, he did so because it was "perhaps the last time an opportunity exists to convince the preponderant part of the Polish populace, which has thus far been thinking loyally while also remaining in constant deployment for the war economy and thus for the security of our borders, of the will of the German Reich to recognize them as part of the European cultural nation."[15]

Now, one might object that it was hardly surprising that such ideas would emerge, particularly in Upper Silesia. But as I have shown, this tendency toward an ever more inclusivist selection policy was by no means limited to Upper Silesia—even in the Wartheland, the DVL was expanded early on. More revealing in this regard, however, were the plans that emerged with the completion of the DVL, which were aimed not at circumventing it as in Upper Silesia but instead at augmenting the existing selection process, for it had proved unable to keep up with the assimilationist goals of the occupation administrations.

As I have shown, Himmler's demand for racial appraisals to be conducted on certain sections of DVL enrollees met with intense resistance in the Wartheland as well, where it also came to nothing. But it would be a mistake to assume that this was tied to a fundamental rejection of race-based conceptions. At least in the Wartheland, one kept an open mind. Although race, from the perspective of the civil administration, was not suitable for differentiating between "Volks-deutsche" and Poles, there were fewer qualms about applying it in a second step, subjecting the rest of the Polish populace to a racial selection process. This is also why Greiser accepted Himmler's plan to conduct trial appraisals in three counties, which was intended to gather information on the racial composition of the Polish populace. The UWZ conducted the trial appraisals in early 1942 and found 7 percent of the local populace to be "re-Germanizable."[16]

But this new openness toward racial appraisals did nothing to alter the civil administration's determination that the next round of selections should also be geared as much as possible to the rational demands of power. This is also why the trial appraisals immediately led to a confrontation between the civil administration and the SS complex. On March 27, 1942, before his departure from the Wartheland, Coulon submitted a discussion paper, "The Polish Question in the Reichsgau of the Wartheland: Segmenting the Polish Volk according to Performance," in which he proposed subdividing the Polish populace according to performance, character, political conduct, and racial appearance into an amazing thirty-seven groups, thereby enabling a path into the German "Volksgemein-schaft" for those in the top groups. In this context, Coulon certainly did attach great importance to the "racial appraisal." But—probably with the exclusivist selection practices of the Rasse- und Siedlungshauptamt (Race and Settlement Main Office, or RuSHA) in mind—he was also quick to add that a considerable part of the local populace was in any case assimilable. For justification, he cited not only the idea that "for hundreds of years, German blood has flown into Pol-ishdom," which had since become part of the standard repertoire underpinning "re-Germanization" efforts, but he also pointed to a study by Hans Joachim Beyer, who claimed to have discovered that one "of the Slavic-speaking tribes from which the Polish Volk had emerged, namely the Polans, was Nordic." With such "scien-tific" buttressing, Coulon was little inclined to leave the racial appraisal results to the SS suitability assessors, instead preempting them by declaring that prob-ably 10 to 12 percent of the Polish populace was re-Germanizable—considerably more than the 7 percent cited by the UWZ after the trial appraisals. Coulon had very specific ideas about the selection process as well. He saw a need for an approach "that meets with the urgent necessities of war." And the answer was ultimately "evaluation according to work performance."[17] In the paper, Coulon had sketched a selection process that seemed almost ideal in combining the fur-ther Germanization of the province with the acquisition of "German" workers, thereby bringing together two policy spheres whose actors had frequently repre-sented opposing interests.[18]

For the local Gau chairman of the German Labor Front (Deutsche Arbe-itsfront), Albert Derichsweiler, even this proposal did not go far enough. Cer-tainly, in "later, calmer times," a link between "racial worth and quality of work performance" would have to be championed, but for the moment that was not an affordable option, and it was necessary to choose work performance alone. Derichsweiler tried to placate the ideological hardliners with the hair-splitting argumentation that using work performance as a criterion represented "in no way an abandonment of our fundamental stance toward Polishdom" because this "yardstick" simply drew on "one of the most important National Socialist principles, namely that of performance [Leistung]." Furthermore, it was

> an established fact that, unfortunately, it is not always the case that the racially good-looking are also highly qualified in terms of performance, and it unfortunately sometimes happens that an unremarkable appearance, perhaps even an unpleasant one, is capable of high performance levels, which on the other hand is not to say in general that performance capacity is not the consequence of good racial predisposition. But for us in these decisive months of the war, the most important thing is performance, which is why I believe that the idea of differentiated treatment for Poles according to the principle of performance is for the moment to be preferred over an adjudication according to racial principles.[19]

Herbert Mehlhorn concurred with this position, going as far as to say that eight hundred thousand to a million of the Wartheland's Poles were, "because of their outstanding performance, Germanizable," much to Höppner's consternation. As the latter subsequently remarked with resignation, such figures were commensurate neither with Hitler's stipulation of a million "re-Germanizable" persons across the entire annexed territories, nor with the results of the trial appraisals—and even more so since he was not even sure whether Mehlhorn's estimate already included associated family members. But even Höppner did not take the results of the trial appraisal all that seriously, as he himself cited 15 percent, meaning 550,000 persons, as "re-Germanizable." But what seems even more remarkable is that Höppner, with all his criticism of what he considered the excessively inclusivist plans of the civil administration, nonetheless supported the call to include performance as a selection criterion in the re-Germanization program, thereby revealing once again the differences that also existed within the SS complex itself, here between the Sicherheitsdienst (Security Service, or SD) and RuSHA:

> Experience has shown by and large that the selection of the populace solely according to racial aspects is in no way sufficient. Not only is the winnowing of *antisocial, genetically diseased,* and *politically contaminated persons* disregarded by this completely one-sided procedure that only considers phenotype, it also does not point in any way to the performance of the relevant persons in the community, or to their work performance at all, and thus to the question of whether or not these persons are a positive addition to the German Volk in terms of performance.[20]

After that, documents do in fact show a bundle of measures aimed at selecting the best-performing Polish workers—although it cannot be unambiguously proved whether they already represented the first steps toward the envisaged mass re-Germanization of the Polish populace. Greiser initially suggested to Himmler that citizenship legislation be further differentiated for particularly productive workers, who would then receive the special legal status of "attested ward of the Reich" ("testierte Schutzbefohlene des Reiches").[21] Himmler had refused, and agreed only to the labeling of "high-performing workers" ("Leistungsarbeiter"), who finally became known in the Wartheland as "high-performing Poles" ("Leistungspolen"); these labels did not result in a new type of national status but did guarantee the selected individuals certain material advantages not available to other Polish workers. In later statements, Greiser protested against considering this step a concession to the difficult war situation, claiming instead that the "establishing of the Association of High-Performing Poles" had been done only "in order to disrupt the unity of the Poles" and, furthermore, that every accommodation would apply only during a "transitional period," "in which the inferior ethnonation must be exploited to the very last, in order for it to disappear entirely."[22] Of course, one can also interpret this policy's practical application as representing the first steps of the assimilation policy favored by Mehlhorn and the Wartheland's labor deployment administrators, one targeting a not inconsiderable part of the Polish populace on the basis of racial criteria and the economy's labor requirements.

* * *

If the conceiving of the DVL as a four-level selection tool capable of incorporating almost two million people into Section 3, despite the fact that most probably spoke no German and did not see themselves as Germans, was already due to the realization that a long-term occupation policy was inconceivable without some assimilation of the local populace, the just described considerations in the Wartheland and Upper Silesia pointed to the further realization—in both cases, a forced one—that it was necessary to go beyond the existing policy still. It was above all the shortage of dependable workers and soldiers, along with the fear of a worsening security situation in the occupied territories, that had driven a further intensification of assimilation policy (however layered it might be), which no longer appeared to be assured by the existing instrument of the DVL—and on this point, Posen and Kattowitz were in agreement for once, as the two aforementioned examples show.

The reasons behind this realization, however, as well as the proposed solutions, pointed once again to the very different population policies of these two provinces. In the Wartheland, the DVL was conceived from the outset as a selection tool exclusively for the integrating of locals who had been proved politically loyal. And even if, with the introduction of Section 3, the province's DVL soon saw the induction of ultimately some seventy thousand individuals who were allowed a somewhat broader interpretation of this criterion, if only they could demonstrate at least two "German" grandparents, the civil administration had nonetheless held fast to the DVL as a catalog primarily of "Bekenntnisdeutsche" ("professed Germans"). With the conclusion of the DVL process, however, even the Wartheland's civil administration had to acknowledge that the Poles, instead of being expelled so that they could be replaced by Germans from Eastern Europe and the Reich as originally planned, still made up more than three-quarters of the total population and were simply indispensable, already for economic reasons alone. Greiser had this realization early on and forbade the deportation of workers at a time when deportation had not yet become impracticable by the course of the war. From this perspective, it seems only logical that Coulon, Mehlhorn, and Derichsweiler would then want to expand the assimilation policy to also incorporate those who were indispensable, namely the workforce's key performers. But because doing so was not compatible with the selection criteria and, ultimately, the purpose of the DVL, its further expansion was not an option at that time. Instead, the ethnocrats showed themselves open to a selection model that also allowed for racial appraisals, but only as one component within a broader criterion package in which work performance was decisive and in which the number of persons to be positively assessed was stipulated from the outset. With such a model, the DVL would be supplemented by an expanded re-Germanization program, one that would further differentiate the populace—entirely in accord with Nazi logic—while adding a new class of one million or more "re-Germanizable" people below the DVL, which was itself a hierarchical arrangement.

In Upper Silesia, the situation at the end of 1944 was viewed even more skeptically. With a more inclusivist selection policy having already been implemented in the west of the province and with the Red Army now within sight, the idea of supplementing the DVL with an additional assimilation program would not be enough to satisfy the Oberpräsident's offices—instead, a fundamental break with existing ethnonationality policy was demanded. As has been shown, the province's civil administration believed that the populace of the annexed territory could be clearly separated. The inhabitants of the former Prussian and Austrian partitions were all to be inducted into the DVL, while those of the former Russian partition were almost all to be excluded. But the resulting hierarchization of the populace had led to increasingly severe problems that started threatening the stability of the German occupation regime. First, although in the west of the province more than 90 percent of the local populace had been accepted into the DVL, doing so had failed to win them over. Instead, the majority complained about having to settle for Section 3, and thus having to accept disadvantages that members of Sections 1 and 2 did not. The civil administration therefore pushed for equal treatment to be extended to members of Section 3—as a result, of the two kinds of differentiation, namely internally between the DVL sections and externally in relation to the Polish populace, the first would fall away. This would have led to a state of affairs that the Reich Interior Ministry had already favored in the early months of the war, before it was derailed by Himmler and Greiser. But the radical thing about Springorum's demand was its attack on the second differentiation, between the Germans and the Poles. The radically different treatment of the province's eastern and western populations seemed no longer sustainable. The Poles should instead be recognized as "part of the European cultural nation." One could hardly be clearer in articulating the trend toward a more inclusivist population policy.

The assimilationist tendency of Nazi Germanization policy in western Poland certainly did not require a common selection practice. The question of what criteria to apply in dividing the local populace into "Poles" and "Germans" had been answered completely differently in each region, even after the general introduction of the DVL. This makes it even more surprising—and ironic—that unanimity reigned on one particular point: the rejection of race as a selection criterion. Here, Himmler already had to reckon with opposition for the simple reason that the Gauleiters feared losing part of their control over the selection process through the introduction of racial appraisals. But the decisive factor was the real-world practice of the RuSHA suitability assessors themselves, who confirmed every fear and dramatically demonstrated to the civil administrations that racial selections were incompatible with the respectively chosen DVL process. Even the Regierungspräsident of Posen had complained that criteria based on racial anthropology emphasized "appearance" instead of "character," and led to a highly exclusivist selection practice that rejected more than 90 percent of applicants as unsuitable—in other words, such criteria were simply dysfunctional.[23] In the ideological contest over who was German and how to determine German "ethnonational membership" ("Volkstumszugehörigkeit," as it was called back then), it was ultimately the category of "Volk" (in the sense here of "ethnonation") that prevailed over "race" as the defining difference. The reason was clearly not that the concept of Volk was any more able to offer precise answers, but instead because it allowed for a more flexible ideological discourse—for example, by emphasizing individual conduct and the readiness to assimilate—in which the rational needs of power could be better articulated, needs that had to be answered in order to put German control on a sustainable footing.

* * *

The assimilationist character of Nazi Germanization policy in annexed western Poland, along with—which was no less important—its ideological underpinnings, is reason enough to cast aside two basic assumptions that have been popular in scholarly research into Nazism and to venture instead a new hypothesis. The first concerns the purported dualism that sets pragmatists against ideologues, a concept that was popularized with the recognition of the Nazi regime's polycratic character. But in Nazi Germanization policy, one can see a clearly *ideological* battleground that no actor was able to escape; it was not, for example, a confrontation pitting the dispassionate strategists of the administrative apparatus against the doctrinaire soldiers of the SS complex, but instead a face-off between Volk-oriented ideologues and race-oriented ones. But the ideological character of this confrontation certainly did not mean that ideologically motivated conduct would necessarily be irrational or dysfunctional for serving the needs of power. For the civil administrations entrusted with governing and exploiting the annexed territories, it was highly functional to grant German national status to loyal and economically productive members of the local populace above all. As has been shown, the concept of Volk allowed for an ideological argumentation for a selection policy that met precisely these needs. But the same also applied to the racial discourse put forward by the SS apparatus. It is doubtlessly true that Himmler was a fervent supporter and leading proponent of the racial worldview. But for him, the demand for the introduction of racial appraisals was also highly functional, as it would have increased the power of the SS apparatus in exercising control over the selection process, while, as is more important, considerably expanding his possibilities in the settling of ethnic Germans from Eastern Europe. Certainly, racial appraisals were ideologically charged to an extraordinary degree. But from Himmler's point of view, this made them no less functional in serving the needs of power.

The second assumption concerns the widespread understanding of Nazi Germany as a "racial state." In view of the claims presented by a large part of scholarship on Nazism, particularly more recent works on Nazi occupation policy, one might well assume that in the struggle over selection criteria applied to the local populace, the side that brought race into play would gain the upper hand. But the opposite was the case. From the very start, the Gauleiters remained steadfastly convinced that race was entirely impracticable as a selection criterion for separating Germans from Poles—and ultimately prevailed over the SS complex. But in repelling Himmler's intervention, they not only prevented the shaping of the DVL according to racial criteria, they also dealt him a decisive defeat in his attempt to make race the main differentiating factor in designing the "German Lebensraum." These processes cannot be grasped with the seductive idea of Nazi Germany as a "racial state," which already needs revision for this reason alone.

This naturally brings up the question of how much my analysis is actually specific to the development of annexed western Poland in particular. In other words, is it possible to identify in the other German-occupied territories any assimilationist population policy tendencies that are comparable in orientation and extent to those seen in western Poland? The answer is a resounding yes, I think, when looking at the Germanization policies in Alsace, Lorraine, Lower Styria, Upper Carniola, and the Czech territory, along with the beginnings in the General Government, Ukraine, northern France, and Belgium. I will confine myself to briefly discussing two examples, for detailed research is still lacking here. The first example would be the Nazi population policy in the Protectorate of Bohemia and Moravia. The overblown deportation fantasies of the early days soon gave way to the sobering realization that, above all, the performance of the Czech economy had to be kept up. The head of the occupation administration, Reich Protector Konstantin von Neurath, and ironically the local HSSPF, State Secretary Karl Hermann Frank, both used every opportunity to push for a radical policy change in Berlin; after all—as the latter said to Hitler—although nobody had any idea of where to put the Czechs or who would replace them, one could well imagine how catastrophic the economic consequences would have been. It is not surprising that this occasion was also exactly when a receptive audience began emerging for an argument advanced by Prof. Karl Valentin Müller, director of the University of Prague's Institute for Social Anthropology and Ethnonational Biology (Institut für Sozialanthropologie und Völkerbiologie), who favored a comprehensive assimilation of the local populace in his new magazine *Deutsche Volksforschung in Böhmen und Mähren* (German ethnonational research in Bohemia and Moravia). If one would follow Chad Carl Bryant's argument and ascribe the German assimilationist tendencies in Bohemia and Moravia to Müller's power of persuasion, one would of course unilaterally sever the dialectical relationship between ideological discourse and political interests. After all, Müller's contention that the local population had been biologically "upgraded" over the centuries by intermarriage with German colonists, meaning that "German blood" still made up the foundation of the Czech people, seemed so persuasive precisely because it aligned with and provided an ideological expression for the rational interests of power for the German occupiers.[24] The latter soon agreed that at least half of all Czechs were Germanizable.

In Ukraine as well, clearly assimilationist intentions could be seen in the importation of the DVL, which was introduced there by order of the local Reich Commissioner in late 1942. The administration was instructed to "analogously" model its selection process on the one in the annexed western Polish territories, along with its principle that "no drop of German blood may be lost"—thereby committing it to an inclusivist procedure. Categorically excluded were only "Jewish Mischlinge," among whom even those with "some German blood are *mostly* to be given over to special treatment" (emphasis added), as well as "Fremdvölkische who have no ties of blood or marriage to Germandom."[25] As in Poland, the SS apparatus opposed this setup, because it was almost entirely shut out from the process. A demand for racial appraisals was aimed at changing this but very likely failed in Ukraine too, especially because the local Reich Commissioner preferred to rely more on the Nazi Party's Racial Policy Office than on RuSHA in the matter.[26]

Once again the question: How could such a population policy take hold in Nazi Germany, one involving not only mass murder and expulsion in its pursuit of imperialist goals on the Continent, but also forced assimilation (likewise on a mass scale), thereby transforming its territory less into a "Greater Germanic Reich" and more into a multiethnic empire? I have explored the main reasons, or more precisely, the political necessities behind the phenomenon at length in this book: with the slogan of a "people without space" ("Volk ohne Raum") quickly proving hollow, all schemes relying on the replacement of local inhabitants with German migrants were swept aside. And by the time Germany attacked the Soviet Union, it had already become clear that comprehensive expulsions and a further radicalization of despotic policies would sabotage not only the overtaxed German economy but also many German occupation regimes. The selective co-optation of the workforce's top performers, along with all others who were ready to accept German rule, therefore had to be seen as highly rational for serving the needs of power.

Of course, the discussion so far does not yet answer the question. After all, historical actors can also simply err in estimating their own capacities—especially when the political system is structured in a way that hampers corrective feedback, and no discursive framework is provided in which such feedback could be articulated. But such was not the case here. An assimilationist policy was not only rational in serving the needs of power, it could also be discursively justified by drawing on the concept of Volk, which ultimately linked back to an understanding of German identity whose symbolic significance had certainly lost nothing in magnetic appeal. This realization is not in itself surprising, for the word "Volk" was on everyone's lips in Nazi Germany, not least in formulations like "Volksgemeinschaft" ("ethnonational community"), which supplied the Nazis with the central rallying cries that explained their mass appeal in the first place.

More important for the context under investigation here, however, is another aspect. It would be a mistake to assume that in the German imagination during the first half of the twentieth century, Eastern Europe connoted a uniform space, one that was characterized—as, for example, in the anti-Polish stereotype—by squalor, underdevelopment, and wasteland starting immediately beyond the German border. The German ideological topography of Eastern Europe was more complicated and multilayered, making some historical regions seem close at hand (e.g., the Baltics) and pushing others into the distance (e.g., Galicia). The decisive factor was not the length of the connecting roads, but the depth of the historical relationships. It is along these lines that one can also read Edward Ross

Dickinson's concept of the "trans-imperial identity" of the German self-image.[27] This concept refers not only to the fact that "Volk" and "state" did not coincide in the understanding of most Germans, and that the "Lesser German solution" (i.e., the incomplete unification of German-speaking states) had instead established state borders incorporating national minorities while excluding various groups of "Germans"—and, of course, it was the Nazi regime that demanded "a new ordering of the ethnographic circumstances" as had no German government before.[28] More important, Dickinson points out that this "trans-imperial identity" was not only a political demand in Germany but also a lived reality, and much more so than in any other European nation. Thus, for a teacher like Maximilian Boehm, changing jobs from a German-speaking school in Livonia for another one in Lorraine was hardly anomalous—and also turned out to be extraordinarily formative for his son Max Hildebert Boehm, later a prominent ethnonationalist theoretician.[29] But Dickinson's argument also encompasses the opposite trajectory, namely where one could leave the German Empire without necessarily going into the foreign. Is it really so inconceivable that the German occupiers on their campaign eastward, although confronted by many foreigners, did not always imagine themselves as having arrived in entirely foreign places? Taking ideology seriously in this context would mean, for example, remembering the theory of German ethnonational and cultural soil, as already developed by Albrecht Penck and Wilhelm Volz during the Weimar Republic. The German cultural soil (*Kulturboden*) in Eastern Europe stretched across the territories "of the old German empire" (another term for the Holy Roman Empire) from Bohemia to Hungary, and even included what was called "island Germandom" (*Inseldeutschtum*), such as in Transylvania and the Crimea; meanwhile, the borders of the German ethnonational soil (*Volksboden*) approximated the German linguistic border.[30] But it was "different in the east," where a "German/Germanic ethnonational soil" ("deutsch-germanischer Volksboden") had allegedly been established three thousand years earlier, and historical events now meant that "language border is *not* ethnonational border," but instead that the "eastern German ethnonational soil includes the peripheral mixed peoples of Germandom." In this view, the region's resident "Kashubians and Masurians, the Upper Silesians and Wends, are of German culture, appendages of the German Volk, Germans even if the old idiom is not yet extinct; their ethnonational will and ethnonational consciousness is German . . . it is not race that decides folkdom . . . but rather the will and the ethnonational consciousness."[31] The fact that this theory was highly functional politically, and also provided scholarly ammunition for challenging the Treaty of Versailles, naturally increased its ideological power and furthermore connected to tropes such as Germany's ostensible "civilizing mission" in the east.

This imagining of Eastern Europe clearly seems to have also influenced the ideological discourse about the Germanization of these territories. What could be more obvious than for the political and economic pressures that compelled a more integrationist population policy to also activate an ideological discourse emphasizing a selection policy that revolved around *ethnonational* membership, all the more so in territories that had not been relinquished till after World War I and were still considered German ethnonational soil? A similar logic also arose for the German cultural soil that lay further eastward. The various versions of the General Plan for the East prepared by the SS apparatus are good examples. They have quite rightly come to epitomize the Nazi dystopian vision, one in which the annihilation of the Jews had already been predetermined, and the enslavement and execution of millions of others had been factored in as a prerequisite for building the "German East." Although it is still largely unclear how much these plans actually motivated the conduct of policy on the ground, or whether they instead lent retrospective coherence to the acts committed by the Einsatzgruppen and other homicidal groups, one aspect still cannot be overlooked. The planners under Konrad Meyer at the RKFDV Staff's Main Office, as well as those under Hans Ehlich at the Reich Security Main Office, were faced with a problem that was only too familiar to most German ethnocrats in occupied Eastern Europe: Where to get the people who would transform this territory into a "German Lebensraum"? As Ehlich declared during a lecture to the Reich Student Leadership (Reichsstudentenführung), this territory confronted the Germans with around seventy million people "of kindred, but not same-tribe blood" ("artverwandten, aber nicht stammesgleichen Blutes"), such as Poles, Ukrainians, and so on. Because living alongside them was not conceivable, and neither was their "complete displacement or . . . total physical annihilation," and "we would never have the people to replace these seventy million," the only remaining option—after a portion had been deported and another portion murdered—was the assimilation of the remaining populace. Of course, this is not the way that Ehlich chose to formulate it, for the Ukrainians and Poles still represented a racial threat in the eyes of the SS apparatus. On the contrary, he recalled that attempts at "assimilation, or we could also say in this case, Germanization, as we have witnessed in the past," have necessarily ended in failure. But, according to Ehlich, racial theory showed a path forward by claiming that "these peoples of southeastern Europe have soaked up, more or less to a large extent, valuable German high-performance genetic material."[32] It was now a matter of identifying this "percentage of German blood existing in the various peoples" and getting it *back*. "Racially suitable" Poles, White Russians, Ukrainians, and from other people in Eastern Europe were thus intended to fill the widening gap torn open by the "German Lebensraum," a gap that acquired ever more fantastic dimensions through the advances of the Wehrmacht: according to the "calculations" of Ehlich's men, some 15 to 20 percent of the Polish populace was "re-Germanizable," along with 25 percent of the White Russians and

35 percent of the Ukrainians; the estimates for the Latvians and Estonians were even more optimistic.[33] The interesting thing about these numbers was that they precisely added up to the fourteen million extra "Germans" that, according to the calculations of the Reich Security Main Office, would need to be found in order to secure the settlement of these territories. But of course as Ehlich emphasized to his student audience, this was certainly "not an ethnoconversion or a Germanization, but rather an ethnoreversion or a Germanizing back."[34] In places where the determining of German ethnonational membership did not promise the desired results, such as in territories where, for example, the proof of having "actively supported Germandom," as demanded for Section 1 of the DVL in western Poland, was likely to be "entirely precluded," and the evidence of "German descent" was also unreliable—as the SD critically noted, for example, in commenting on the DVL in Ukraine—one could always fall back on a "search for German blood," as was seen in the General Government.[35]

In any case, the policymaking efforts to safeguard Germany's war acquisitions did not fail because Nazi ideology proved too inflexible. No matter how the purportedly indispensable assimilation of a local population segment was justified, the Germanization policy in Poland shows that Nazi population policy aimed not only at the exclusion of the allegedly racially foreign, but to a large extent also at the inclusion of the ethnonationally similar, establishing with the DVL an assimilation program that was unparalleled in German history.

Notes

1. Rich, *Hitler's War Aims*, 2: xii.

2. Similarly Herbert, "Arbeit und Vernichtung," 385, in a reductionist analysis of anti-Jewish extermination policy.

3. Weber, *Faschismus und Ideologie*, 24.

4. Goldhagen, *Hitler's willing executioners*. On this school of intentionalist thought, particularly in West Germany, see Mason, *Intention and Explanation*.

5. For example, this is pointed out in Mason, *Intention and Explanation*, 28.

6. Neumann, *Behemoth*, 66–67.

7. Paxton, *Anatomy of Fascism*, 10 (emphasis in original). Paxton justifies the shift in focus by pointing to the unprecedented character of Nazi ideology. A similar sentiment was already expressed in an earlier recommendation to "attentively investigate what the fascists actually *do*" (emphasis added), see Weber, *Faschismus und Ideologie*, 72.

8. Thus, for example, Hans Mommsen's model of a "cumulative radicalization" has been rightly criticized for reducing individual actors to the level of supporting players (Mommsen, "Nationalsozialismus"); just as Götz Aly and Susanne Heim also had to acknowledge accusations of having ignored the antisemitism of the planning-level intelligentsia whom they called the "architects of annihilation," or of having underestimated its significance as a

tactical discourse (Aly and Heim, *Vordenker der Vernichtung*; translated by G. H. Blunden as *Architects of Annihilation*).

9. First quote is from Weber, *Faschismus und Ideologie*, 103; second quote is from Rehmann, "Ideologietheorie," 718. Althusser summed it up in a brief sentence: "Ideology has a material existence" (Althusser, *Ideologie*, 137). A similar foundation also underlies Wildt's conception of the "Volksgemeinschaft" as a kind of self-empowerment when he highlights the bonding power of "race defiler parades" (Wildt, *Volksgemeinschaft*). During these parades, the participants become integrated into the community of perpetrators, one in which they experienced their actions as "self-empowerment" while in fact having only acted out their "self-alienation through an enthusiastic self-activation" (Wildt, *Volksgemeinschaft*). See also Weber, *Faschismus und Ideologie*, 107. The nature of this forging of community from above is also made clear by the realization that the Nazis were certainly not thinking of generally giving up the state's monopoly on the use of force.

10. Althusser, *Marxismus*, 154.

11. According to Slavoj Žižek, who was taking up an idea from Isolde Charim (Žižek, *Mapping Ideology*, 12).

12. As one of the most recent examples, see Bloxham and Kushner, *Holocaust*, 129–30, with reference to the appropriation of antisemitic ideology in the exercise of anti-Jewish violence.

13. Hall, "Problem of Ideology," 29.

14. Ibid., 43.

15. Unsigned (probably Springorum), *Oberpräsident*'s offices in Kattowitz to Reich Interior Ministry, December 14, 1944, Polish State Archives in Katowice, 117/140, 245–46.

16. Krumey's preliminary final report from UWZ on trial appraisals of Polish populace in Wollstein Rural County and administrative districts of Schorda-Land and Königsbach, March 5, 1942, German Federal Archives, Berlin [hereafter, BArch], R 75/7, 12–16, reprinted in *Biuletyn* 21: 158–61, and in Pospieszalski, *Niemiecka lista*, 206–36.

17. Memorandum from Coulon, March 27, 1942, Institute of National Remembrance, Warsaw [hereafter, AGK], 62/53, 8–22. More comprehensively on Beyer at Roth, "Heydrichs Professor."

18. In a later revision dated May 14, 1942, on "solving the Polish question through the selection of re-Germanizable and Germanizable Poles and the final determination of those who would never come into question for a community with the Germans," Coulon further refined his selection process. The Polish populace was now to be divided into seventy-two subgroups, which were to be aggregated into four major groups. Members of the first major group were worth considering for "re-Germanization," but those of the last major group were "best eradicated immediately" (Coulon memo, May 14, 1942, AGK 62/53, 27–42).

19. Derichsweiler to Greiser, April 3, 1942, AGK 62/53, 53–66.

20. Unsigned memo from an SS Chief Assault Leader (probably Höppner), April 9, 1942 (emphasis in original), AGK 62/53, 43–49.

21. Greifelt's memo on the discussion at Himmler's, May 28, 1942, BArch NS 19/2743, unpaged.

22. Greiser's speech at a workshop conference of Gau Office for Ethnonationality Questions on March 20–21, 1943, AGK NTN/37, 678–85.

23. Böttcher to Greiser, January 13, 1942, APP 406/1131, 341–46.

24. Bryant, *Prague in Black*, 116–19. On Müller, see Harten, Neirich, and Schwerendt, *Rassenhygiene*, 245–47.

25. Signed "Dargl," Reich Commissioner of Ukraine to General Commissioner of Kiev, December 9, 1942, Special Archive at the State Military Archives of Russia, Moscow [hereafter, SMR], 720-2/49, 122–24.

26. Strippel, *NS-Volkstumspolitik*, 262. The SS complex was more successful when Ukraine was abandoned and the local "Volksdeutsche" were evacuated westward. It is probable that the EWZ selection procedure, in which "racial suitability" very likely played a role, was applied at least to those lacking identification documents from the Ukraine DVL. For a short description that particularly highlights the role of the SS complex, see Heinemann, *Rasse, Siedlung, deutsches Blut*, 448–53 and 465.

27. Dickinson, "German Empire," 153.

28. Hitler to the Reichstag on October 6, 1939, quoted in *Verhandlungen des Reichstages*, 460: 51–63, here 56.

29. Prehn, "Max Hildebert Boehm," 34–41, and more generally Michael Mann on the overrepresentation of "Volksdeutsche" and frontier Germans in the wholesale crimes of the Nazi regime, at Mann, *Dark Side*, 224. Boehm's most influential contribution to this debate during the Nazi period was "Das eigenständige Volk."

30. Quoted in Haar, "Leipziger Stiftung," 380. Albrecht Penck was director of the Geographical Institute in Berlin and head of the Museum for Marine Science; Wilhelm Volz was a professor in Breslau and chairman of the Silesian Society for Geography. See also Hruza, "Wilhelm Wostry," on the anti-Czech dimension.

31. Volz, "Zur Einführung" (emphasis in original). See also Haar, "Leipziger Stiftung," 378.

32. Presentation by Ehlich during the Salzburg conference of the Reich Student Leadership's Reich Ethnopolicy Unit on September 10–11, 1942, reprinted in Rössler and Schleiermacher, *Generalplan Ost*, 49–50.

33. Position paper by Dr. Erhard Wetzel from April 27, 1942, reprinted in Madajczyk, *Vom Generalplan Ost*, 50–81. See also Roth, "Generalplan Ost—Gesamtplan Ost," 41.

34. Presentation by Hans Ehlich during Salzburg conference of the Reich Student Leadership's Reich Ethnopolicy Unit on September 10–11, 1942, reprinted in Rössler and Schleiermacher, *Generalplan Ost*, 51–52. Ehlich's proposals were criticized by Helmut Schubert, for example, departmental head at the Main Department for Resettlement and Ethnonationality (Hauptabteilung Umsiedlung und Volkstum) at the RKFDV Staff Main Office, who argued in favor of further expanding extermination efforts against the populace of Eastern Europe, and that it was generally better not to extend the settlement zone borders so far east, rather than accepting that these territories could not be settled entirely by Germans. But as Roth convincingly notes, a critique using ethnopolitical argumentation to limit imperialist German expansion instead of justifying it was not a popular stance—not even within the SS apparatus. Schubert was later transferred to the front. Wetzel expressed similar views (Roth, "Generalplan Ost—Gesamtplan Ost," 41 and 61–67).

35. Comment on Ukraine in memo from KdS of Kiev, SS Senior Assault Unit Leader Erich Ehrlinger, undated, SMR 720-2/49, 66–70. On the search for German blood, see more comprehensively Wasser, *Himmlers Raumplanung*; also Madajczyk, *Okkupationspolitik Nazideutschlands*, 421–29 and 518–22.

Glossary

<table>
<tr><td>Title or term</td><td>English equivalent</td></tr>
<tr><td>Abteilung 1, 2, 3, 4 or previously A, B, C, D, E (der DVL)</td><td>Section 1, 2, 3, 4, A, B, C, D (of the DVL)</td></tr>
<tr><td>Alter Kämpfer</td><td>"Old fighter" from the Nazi Party's early period</td></tr>
<tr><td>Altreich</td><td>"Old Reich," meaning the Reich's territory before wartime annexations</td></tr>
<tr><td>Amtsbezirk</td><td>Rural administrative district</td></tr>
<tr><td>Amtskommissar</td><td>Rural district commissioner</td></tr>
<tr><td>AR category (RuSHA classification)</td><td>Altreich (Old Reich: racially suitable for labor deployment in the Reich and future assimilation into the German Volksgemeinschaft)</td></tr>
<tr><td>Arbeitsamt</td><td>Employment office</td></tr>
<tr><td>artfremden Blutes</td><td>Of racially alien blood</td></tr>
<tr><td>artverwandten Blutes</td><td>Of kindred blood</td></tr>
<tr><td>Auskämm-Aktion</td><td>Combing campaign</td></tr>
<tr><td>Auslandsdeutscher</td><td>A German abroad</td></tr>
<tr><td>Auslandsorganisation der NSDAP</td><td>Nazi Party's Foreign Organization</td></tr>
<tr><td>Außenstelle des Rasse- und Siedlungshauptamtes</td><td>Race and settlement field office</td></tr>
<tr><td>Befehlshaber der Ordnungspolizei, or BdO</td><td>Commander of the Order Police</td></tr>
<tr><td>Befehlshaber der Sicherheitspolizei und des SD, or BdS</td><td>Commander of the Security Police and the SD</td></tr>
<tr><td>Bekenntnis</td><td>Self-professing</td></tr>
<tr><td>Bekenntnisdeutsch</td><td>Professed German, (primarily members of German organizations)</td></tr>
<tr><td>Beschwerdeausschuss, Beschwerdefälle, Beschwerdeinstanz, Beschwerderecht, Beschwerdeverfahren</td><td>Appeals committee, appeals cases, appeals body, right of appeal, appeals process</td></tr>
<tr><td>Beschwerdekommission, Beschwerdestelle</td><td>Complaints commission, complaints office</td></tr>
<tr><td>Bezirkslandwirte, Kreislandwirte</td><td>Regional agronomists, county agronomists</td></tr>
</table>

Blockleiter	Block leader, a party official responsible for the political mobilization and supervision of a neighborhood
Blutseinschlag	Blood elements
asiatischer Blutseinschlag	element of Asiatic blood
deutscher Blutseinschlag	element of Germanic blood
fremdblütiger Blutseinschlag	element of foreign blood
geringer Bluteinschlag	minor blood element
germanischer Blutseinschlag	element of German blood
Bodenamt	Land office
Bodenständig	Autochtonous
Chef der Sicherheitspolizei und des SD	Chief of the Security Police and the SD
Chef der Zivilverwaltung, or CdZ	Chief of Civil Administration in occupied territories
deutschblütig	German-blooded
Deutsche Arbeitsfront	German Labor Front
Deutsche Stiftung	German Foundation
Deutsche Umsiedlungs-Treuhand Gesellschaft, or DUT	German Resettlement Trust Company
Deutsche Vereinigung	German Union
Deutsche Volksliste (DVL)	German People's List
Deutscher Ostmarkenverein	German Eastern Marches Society
Deutschstämmig	German-descended
Deutschtum	Germandom
Dezernent für Volkstumsfragen und Staatsangehörigkeitsangelegenheiten	Departmental head for ethnonationality questions and citizenship matters
Dienststelle des Reichskommissars für die Festigung deutschen Volkstums (RKFDV)	Agency of the Reich Commissioner for the Strengthening of Germandom
Dienststelle Vierjahresplan	Four-Year-Plan Office
Eignungsprüfer	Suitability assessor of the RuSHA
eingegliederte Ostgebiete	Incorporated eastern territories (of Poland)
Einwandererzentralstelle, or EWZ	Central Immigrantion Office
erwünschter Bevölkerungszuwachs	Desirable addition to the population
Feldarbeiteraktion	Field hand campaign
Fernplan	Long-range plan
fliegende Kommission	Flying commission

fremdblütig	Foreign-blooded
fremdstämmig	Foreign-descended
fremdvölkisch	Ethnonationally foreign
Führerprinzip	Leader principle: the idea that decision making lies solely in one person's hands
Gau	Geographic administrative subdivision (of the Nazi party)
Gauamt für Volkstumsfragen	Regional Office for Ethnonationality Questions
Gaugrenzlandamt	Regional Borderland Office
Gauleiter	Provincial leader, the head of a Nazi Party subdivision
Gauleitung	Gauleiter's office
Generalbevollmächtigter für den Arbeitseinsatz	General Plenipotentiary for Labor Deployment
Generalplan Ost	General Plan for the East
GG category (RuSHA classification)	General Government (racially unsuitable, antisocial, or politically too dangerous for settlement in the Reich)
Haupttreuhandstelle Ost	Main Trust Office for the East
Heim ins Reich	Homeward into the Reich
herrschaftsdysfunktional	Dysfunctional for serving the needs of power
herrschaftsfunktional	Functional for serving the needs of power
herrschaftsrational	Rational in terms of serving the needs of power
Höherer SS- und Polizeiführer, or HSSPF	Higher SS and Police Leader
Inspekteur der Sicherheitspolizei und des SD, or IdS	Inspector of the Security Police and the SD
Israelitische Kultusgemeinde Wien, or IKG	Jewish Community of Vienna
judenrein	Jew-free
Jungdeutsche Partei für Polen, or JdP	Young German Party for Poland
Kreisleiter	County leader, the head of a Nazi Party county-level branch
Landesarbeitsamt	Provincial employment office
Landkreis, Stadtkreis	County (whether rural or urban)
Landrat	Leader of a rural council
Lebensraum	Living space

Leistungsgemeinschaft	Performance-based or high-performance community
Leistungspole	High-performing Pole
Mischling	Hybrid
Musterung	Appraisal
Nahplan (pl., Nahpläne)	Short-range plan
Oberbefehlshaber des Heeres	Commander in Chief of the Army
Oberkommando der Wehrmacht	Wehrmacht High Command
Oberkommando des Heeres	Army High Command
Oberpräsident	Senior president, the head of a province
Oberpräsidium	Oberpräsident's offices
Oberster Prüfungshof für Volkstumsfragen	Supreme Court of Review for Ethnonationality Questions
Ordnungspolizei	Order police, or uniformed law enforcement officers
Ortsgruppe	Local group, the Nazi Party organizational level below the county
Ortsgruppenleiter	Local group leader, the locality's top Nazi official
Parteikanzlei	Party Chancellery
Persönlicher Stab Reichsführer-SS	Personal staff of the Reichsführer of the SS
politische Flurbereinigung	Political cleansing of the soil
Polizeipräsident	Chief of police (in a municipality)
Preussische Ansiedlungskommission	Prussian Settlement Commission
Rasse- und Siedlungsberatung, or RuS-Beratung	Race and Settlement Advisory Unit
Rasse- und Siedlungshauptamt, or RuSHA of the SS	Race and Settlement Main Office of the SS
Rassenamt	Race Office (of the RuSHA)
Rassenpolitisches Amt der NSDAP	Nazi Party's Racial Policy Office
rassische Musterungen	Racial appraisals
Rassische Wertungsgruppe (I through IVf)	Racial valuation group (of the RuSHA)
Regierungsbezirk	Governmental region (midlevel administrative division)
Regierungspräsident	Governmental region president
Reichsarbeitsministerium	Reich Labor Ministry
Reichsbahn	Reich Railroad

Reichsbürger	Reich citizen
Reichsbürgergesetz	Reich Citizens Act
Reichsbürgerrecht	Reich citizen right
Reichsdeutsch	Reich German
Reichsernährungsministerium	Reich Food Ministry
Reichsinnenministerium	Reich Interior Ministry
Reichskanzlei	Imperial Chancellery or Reich Chancellery
Reichskommissar für die Festigung deutschen Volkstums	Reich Commissioner for the Strengthening of Germandom
Reichsnährstand	Reich Food Estate (corporatist body covering food production and distribution)
Reichssicherheitshauptamt	Reich Security Main Office of the SS
Reichsstatthalter	Reich governor
Reichsstatthalterei	Reichsstatthalter's offices
RKF-Zweigstelle	Reich Commissioner for the strengthening of Germandom branch office
Rückdeutschung	Re-Germanizing
Rückstellungskartei	Retainment catalog
Ruckvolkung	Ethnoreversion, reclaiming of alleged Germandom
Schlonsaken	Szlonzakians (local Silesian population)
Schutzangehörig	Protected dependent
schwebendes Volkstum	Wavering folkdom
Sicherheitsdienst, or SD	Security Service of the SS
Sicherheitspolizei, or SiPo	Security Police of the SS
Siedlungsamt	Settlement Office (of the RuSHA)
Sonderfahndungsbuch Polen	Special prosecution book for Poland
SS- und Polizeiführer, or SSPF	SS and Police Leader
SS-Ansiedlungsstab	SS Settlement Staff
SS-Arbeitsstab	SS Task Force
SS-Hauptämter	SS Main Offices (top-level departments of the SS)
SS-Oberabschnitt	SS Superior District
Staatsangehörig	National
Staatsangehörigkeit auf Widerruf, Staatsangehörig auf Widerruf	Revocable national status, revocable German national
Staatsfeind	Enemy of the state

Stabshauptamt des RKFDV — Staff Main Office of the Reich Commissioner for the Strengthening of Germandom

Stammesdeutsch — German by descent

Stapo-Leitstelle — Gestapo regional command office

Stapo-Stelle — Gestapo office

Tat- und Leitstungsgemeinschaft — Community of deed and achievement

Umvolkung — Ethnoconversion

Umwanderungskartei — Resettlement catalog

Umwanderungszentrale — Resettlement center, of the SS

UWZ-Dienststelle — Resettlement field office, of the SS

verpolte Deutsche — Reverse-poled Germans

Volk — Variously means people, nation, or ethnonation

völkisch — Ethnonationalist

völkische Flurbereinigung — Ethnic cleansing

Volksbund für das Deutschtum im Ausland — Volk Alliance for Germandom Abroad

Volksdeutsch — Ethnic German

Volksdeutsche Mittelstelle, or VoMi — Ethnic German Liaison Office of the SS

Volksdeutscher Selbstschutz — Ethnic German Self-Defense Force

Volksgemeinschaft — Ethnonational community

Volksgenosse — Ethnonational comrade

Volkskörper — Ethnonational body

Volkstum — Folkdom or ethnonation

Volkstumsausweis — Ethnonational identity document

Volkstumsbekenntnis — Professed ethnonationality

Volkstumsdezernent — Ethnonationality officer of a mid-level authority

Volkstumsfrage — Ethnonationality question

Volkstumskampf — Ethnonational struggle

Volkstumskartei — Ethnonationality catalog

Volkstumspolitik — Ethnonationality policy, ethnopolitics

Volkstumsreferent — Ethnonationality officer of a Reich or provincial authority

Volkstumszugehörigkeit — Ethnonational membership, ethnonationality

Wartheland or Wartegau	Greater Poland or Wielkopolska (approximately)
Wasserpolak	"Water Polack," derogatory term for local Silesian population speaking a Polish-Silesian dialect
Wehrkreis	Military district
Wehrmacht	German regular army
Westmarkenverband	Polish Western Association (*Polski Związek Zachodni*)
Wiedereindeutschungsaktion	Re-Germanization campaign
wiedereindeutschungsfähig	Re-Germanizable
Wolhynienaktion	Volhynian campaign, the resettlement of ethnic Germans from the Volhynia region
WR category (RuSHA classification)	Wanderarbeiter (racially unsuitable for assimilation into the German *Volksgemeinschaft*, but suitable for forced labor in the Reich)
Zellen-, Ortsgruppen- und Kreisleiter	Cell leader, local group leader, and county leader, which were the bottom three ranks in the Nazi Party hierarchy
Zentralbodenamt	Central Land Office
Zentralstelle für jüdische Auswanderung	Central Agency for Jewish Emigration
Zweig-, Bezirks- und Zentralstellen	Branch offices, regional offices, and central offices
Zwischenplan	Intermediate plan
Zwischenschicht	Intermediate class

Bibliography

Archives

Austria

Austrian State Archives/Archive of the Republic (Österreichisches Staatsarchiv/Archiv der Republik, or ÖSta/AdR), Vienna

ZNsZ RK sections Bürckel Bureau (Dienststelle Bürckel)

Documentation Center of Austrian Resistance (DÖW), Vienna

Jewish Community of Vienna (Israelitische Kultusgemeinde Wien, or IKG), archival holdings

A/Vie Vienna Holding

Germany

Bavarian State Archives, Nuremberg
EC, L, NG, and NO documents

Berlin State Archive (Landesarchiv Berlin, or LAB)

B Rep. 057–01 District attorney at Berlin Appellate Court (Kammergericht Berlin), investigation files regarding Reich Security Main Office

Federal Commissioner for the Records of the State Security Service of the Former German Democratic Republic (Bundesbeauftragten für die Unterlagen des Staatssicherheitsdienstes der ehemaligen Deutschen Demkratischen Republik, BStU), Berlin

MfS-HA IX/11 Main Department IX at Ministry of State Security: investigations body

PA Personnel files

German Federal Archives (Bundesarchiv, or BArch), Berlin

NS 2 Race and Settlement Main Office (Rasse- und Siedlungshauptamt, or RuSHA)

NS 19 Personal Staff of the Reichsführer SS

PL 170 Resettlement Central Office (Umwandererzentralstelle, or UWZ), at microfilms F 73045–F 73047

R 43   Reich Chancellery

R 49   Reich Commissioner for the Strengthening of Germandom
                        (Reichskommissar für die Festigung deutschen Volkstums,
                        or RKFDV)

R 58   Reich Security Main Office

R 59   Ethnic German Liaison Office (Volksdeutsche Mittelstelle, or
                        VoMi)

R 70 Poland   Police departments in Poland

R 75   Umwandererzentralstelle, or UWZ, in Posen

R 138–1   Reichsgau of Danzig-West Prussia

R 153   Dahlem Publication Office (Publikationsstelle Dahlem, or PuSte)

R 186   Collection on ethnonationality and resettlement

R 1501   Reich Interior Ministry

R 3001   Reich Justice Ministry

BDC   Holdings of the former Berlin Document Center

German Federal Archives, Bayreuth branch (BArchBt)

Ost.-Dok. 8   Reports from members of political leadership class from eastern
                        German expulsion zones regarding events of 1939–45
                        (intelligence reports)

Ost.-Dok. 13   Reports on activities of German administration in the annexed
                        and occupied territories of Poland; also the Baltic states and
                        the Soviet Union

German Federal Archives, Dahlwitz-Hoppegarten branch (BArchDH)
ZR holdings

German Federal Archives, Ludwigsburg branch (BArchL)

B 162   Central Office of State Judicial Administrations for the
                        Investigation of Nazi Crimes

Political Archives of the Foreign Office (Politisches Archiv des Auswärtigen Amtes, or
        PAAA), Berlin

Israel

Yad Vashem Archive, Jerusalem (YVA)
O.2

Poland

Institute of National Remembrance, Archive of the Main Commission for the Investigation
        of Crimes against the Polish Nation (Archiwum Głównej Komisji Badania Zbrodni
        przeciwko Narodowi Polskiemu, or AGK), Warsaw

62	Reichsstatthalter of the Wartheland
65	Landrat of Schrimm County
68	Umwandererzentralstelle, or UWZ, Posen
69	UWZ Posen, Litzmannstadt bureau
167	Head of Rasse- und Siedlungshauptamt, or RuSHA, field office in Litzmannstadt
169	SD Command Precinct in Kattowitz
358	UWZ Posen, Litzmannstadt bureau
360	Mayor of Litzmannstadt
377	Nazi Party Wartheland, Kreisleiter's offices in Litzmannstadt
381	Regierungspräsident of Litzmannstadt
687	Gestapo of Posen
737	Gauleiter's offices in the Wartheland
800	Nazi Party Wartheland
826	Gauleiter's offices of Upper Silesia
865	HSSPF Southeast
904	Regierungspräsident of Bromberg
NTN	Najwyższy Trybunał Narodowy (Supreme National Court): Arthur Greiser, Albert Forster

National Digital Archives (Narodowe Archiwum Cyfrowe)

State Archives in Bydgoszcz (Archiwum Państwowe w Bydgoszczy, or APB)

5	Regierungspräsident of Bromberg
9	Landrat of Bromberg
12	Landrat of Konitz
96	SD Special Unit at Potulitz
97	Umwandererzentralstelle, or UWZ, Potulitz
98	UWZ Potulitz
189	Mayor of Bromberg

State Archives in Gdańsk (Archiwum Państwowe w Gdańsku, or APG)

37	Landrat of Neustadt
265	HSSPF of Danzig-West Prussia
266	Gauleiter's offices of Danzig
279	Municipal administration of Gotenhafen

State Archives in Katowice (Archiwum Państwowe w Katowicach, or APK)

82	Mayor of Myslowitz
117	Oberpräsident of Upper Silesia
119	Regierungspräsident of Kattowitz
142	Gauleiter's offices of Upper Silesia

State Archives in Łódź (Archiwum Państwowe w Łodzi, or APL)

176	Regierungspräsident of Litzmannstadt
206/I	Umwandererzentralstelle, or UWZ, Posen, Litzmannstadt office
897	DVL in Litzmannstadt Governmental Region

State Archives in Poznań (Archiwum Państwowe w Poznaniu, or APP)

406	Reichsstatthalter of the Wartheland
834	Umwandererzentralstelle, or UWZ, Posen
VD Posen City	Membership files of DVL branch office for Posen municipality

Western Institute, Poznań (Archivum Instytut Zachodni, or AIZ), archival holdings

Doc. 71	Evacuation of Poles
Doc. 199	Gendarmerie of Jarotschin

Russia

Special Archive at the State Military Archives of Russia (SMR), Moscow

500	Reich Security Main Office
519	Nazi Party
720	Reich-and-Prussian Interior Ministry
1232	Oberpräsident of Kattowitz
1372	Waffen-SS, care and provisioning bodies, military personnel, SS foreign legions

United Kingdom

Archive of Modern Conflict (AMC)

A10327	"Sonderkommando Mogilno" album

Literature

Adam, Uwe Dietrich. *Judenpolitik im Dritten Reich*. Düsseldorf: Droste, 1972.

Adamski, Stanisław. *Pogląd na rozwój sprawy narodowościowej w województwie śląskim w czasie okupacji niemieckiej*. Katowice: Księgarnia Św. Jacka w Katowicach, Pol., 1946.

Adler, H. G. *Der verwaltete Mensch: Studien zur Deportation der Juden aus Deutschland*. Tübingen, Ger.: J. C. B. Mohr, 1974.

Akten zur deutschen auswärtigen Politik 1918–1945. Baden-Baden, Ger.: Impr. Nationale, 1956–61.

Alberti, Michael. "'Exerzierplatz des Nationalsozialismus': Der Reichsgau Wartheland 1939–1941." In Mallmann and Musial, *Genesis des Genozids,* 111–26.

———. *Die Verfolgung und Vernichtung der Juden im Reichsgau Wartheland 1939–1945.* Wiesbaden, Ger.: Harrassowitz, 2006.

Alldeutscher Verband, ed. *Zwanzig Jahre alldeutsche Arbeit und Kämpfe.* Leipzig: Dieterich, 1910.

Althusser, Louis. *Ideologie und ideologische Staatsapparate: Aufsätze zur marxistischen Theorie.* Hamburg: Verlag für das Studium der Arbeiterbewegung, 1977.

———. *Marxismus und Ideologie.* Berlin: VSA, 1973.

———. "'Daß uns Blut zu Gold werde': Theodor Schieder, Propagandist des Dritten Reichs." *Menora: Jahrbuch für deutsch-jüdische Geschichte* 9 (1998): 13–27.

———. *"Endlösung": Völkerverschiebung und der Mord an den europäischen Juden.* Frankfurt: Fischer, 1999.

———. *Macht—Geist—Wahn: Kontinuitäten deutschen Denkens.* Berlin: Argon, 1997.

———. *Marxismus und Ideologie.* Berlin: VSA, 1973.

———. *Vordenker der Vernichtung: Auschwitz und die deutschen Pläne für eine neue europäische Ordnung.* Frankfurt: Fischer, 1997.

Anderson, Benedict. *Die Erfindung der Nation: Zur Karriere eines folgenreichen Konzepts.* New York: Campus, 1996.

Arendt, Hannah. *Elemente und Ursprünge totaler Herrschaft: Antisemitismus, Imperialismus, totale Herrschaft.* Munich: Piper, 1991.

Asmus, Helmut. *Das Hambacher Fest.* Berlin: VEB Deutscher Verlag der Wissenschaften, 1985.

August, Jochen. "Die Entwicklung des Arbeitsmarkts in Deutschland in den 30er Jahren und der Masseneinsatz ausländischer Arbeitskräfte während des Zweiten Weltkrieges: Das Fallbeispiel der polnischen Arbeitskräfte und Kriegsgefangenen." *Archiv für Sozialgeschichte* 24 (1984): 305–53.

Barker, Martin. *The New Racism.* London: Junction Books, 1981.

Beck, Robert. *Schwebendes Volkstum im Gesinnungswandel.* Vol. 1 of *Schriftenreihe der Stadt der Auslandsdeutschen,* edited by Hans Joachim Beyer. Stuttgart: W. Kohlhammer, 1938.

Bergen, Doris L. "The Nazi Concept of 'Volksdeutsche' and the Exacerbation of Anti-Semitism in Eastern Europe 1939–45." *Journal of Contemporary History* 29, no. 4 (1994): 569–82.

Berger, Hans-Hermann. *Das Staatsangehörigkeitsrecht im Hinblick auf die Gebietsveränderungen im Osten des deutschen Reiches.* Aussig, Czech.: Strache, 1940.

Berghahn, Volker. *Das Kaiserreich 1871–1914: Industriegesellschaft, bürgerliche Kultur und autoritärer Staat.* Vol. 16 of *Handbuch der deutschen Geschichte.* Edited by Bruno Gebhardt. Stuttgart: Klett-Cotta, 2003.

———. "Ostimperium und Weltpolitik: Gedanken zur Langzeitwirkung der 'Hamburger Schule.'" Connections: A Journal for Historians and Area Specialists, April 13, 2006. http://www.hsozkult.de/hsk/forum/2006-04-001.

Birn, Ruth Bettina. *Die höheren SS- und Polizeiführer: Himmlers Vertreter im Reich und in den besetzten Gebieten.* Düsseldorf: Droste, 1986.

Biuletyn Głównej Komisji Badania Zbrodni Hitlerowskich w Polsce 21 (1970).

Blanke, Richard, "The German Minority in Inter-war Poland and German Foreign Policy— Some Reconsiderations." *Journal of Contemporary History* 25, no. 1 (1990): 87–102.

Bloxham, Donald, and Tony Kushner. *The Holocaust: Critical Historical Approaches.* Manchester: Manchester University Press, 2005.

Bock, Gisela. *Zwangssterilisation im Nationalsozialismus: Studien zur Rassenpolitik und Frauenpolitik.* Opladen, Ger.: Westdeutscher Verlag, 1986.

Boda-Kręzel, Zofia. *Sprawa Volkslisty na Górnym Śląsku: Koncepcje likwidacji problemu i ich realizacja.* Opole, Pol.: Instytut Slaski w Opolu, 1978.

Boehm, Max Hildebert. *Das eigenständige Volk: Grundlegung der Elemente einer europäischen Völkersoziologie.* 1932. Facsimile reprint, Darmstadt, Ger.: Wissenschaftliche Buchgesellschaft, 1965.

Böhler, Jochen. *Auftakt zum Vernichtungskrieg: Die Wehrmacht in Polen 1939.* Frankfurt: Fischer, 2006.

———. "'Tragische Verstrickung' oder Auftakt zum Vernichtungskrieg? Die Wehrmacht in Polen 1939." In Mallmann and Musial, *Genesis des Genozids,* 36–56.

Borodziej, Włodzimierz, and Hans Lemberg, eds. *"Unsere Heimat ist uns ein fremdes Land geworden . . .": Die Deutschen östlich von Oder und Neiße 1945–1950.* Vol. 1, *Zentrale Behörden.* Marburg, Ger.: Herder-Institut, 2004.

Botz, Gerhard. *Wohnungspolitik und Judendeportation in Wien 1938 bis 1945: Zur Funktion des Antisemitismus als Ersatz nationalsozialistischer Sozialpolitik.* Vienna: Geyer, 1975.

Boysen, Jens. "Der Geist des Grenzlands: Ideologische Positionen deutscher und polnischer Meinungsführer in Posen und Westpreußen vor und nach dem Ersten Weltkrieg." In *Die Geschichte Polens und Deutschlands im 19. und 20. Jahrhundert.* Edited by Markus Krzoska and Peter Tokarski, 104–23. Osnabrück, Ger.: Fibre, 1998.

Brechtken, Magnus. *"Madagaskar für die Juden": Antisemitische Idee und politische Praxis 1885–1945.* Munich: R. Oldenbourg, 1997.

Breuer, Stefan. *Die radikale Rechte in Deutschland 1871–1945.* Stuttgart: Reclam, 2010.

———. *Die Völkischen in Deutschland, Kaiserreich und Weimarer Republik.* Darmstadt, Ger.: Wissenschaftliche Buchgesellschaft, 2008.

Bridenthal, Renate, Alina Grossmann, and Marion Kaplan, eds. *When Biology Became Destiny: Women in Weimar and Nazi Germany.* New York: Monthly Review Press, 1984.

Broszat, Martin. *Der Nationalsozialismus: Weltanschauung, Programm und Wirklichkeit.* Stuttgart: Deutsche Verlags Anstalt, 1960.

———. *Nationalsozialistische Polenpolitik 1939–1945.* Frankfurt: Fischer, 1965.

———. *Zweihundert Jahre deutsche Polenpolitik.* Frankfurt: Suhrkamp, 1972.

Brown, MacAlister. "The Third Reich's Mobilization of the German Fifth Column in Eastern Europe." *Journal of Central European Affairs* 19, no. 2 (1959): 128–48.

Browning, Christopher. *Die Entfesselung der "Endlösung": Nationalsozialistische Judenpolitik 1939–1942.* Munich: Propyläen, 2003.

———. "From 'Ethnic Cleansing' to Genocide to the 'Final Solution': The Evolution of Nazi Jewish Policy, 1939–1941." In *Nazi Policy, Jewish Workers, German Killers,* 1–26. Cambridge: Cambridge University Press, 2000.

———. "Nazi Resettlement Policy and the Search for a Solution to the Jewish Question, 1939–1941." *German Studies Review* 9, no. 3 (1986): 497–519.

Brudzyńska-Němec, Gabriela. *Polenvereine in Baden: Hilfeleistung süddeutscher Liberaler für die polnischen Freiheitskämpfer 1831–1832.* Heidelberg: Universitätsverlag Winter, 2006.

———. *Prague in Black: Nazi Rule and Czech Nationalism.* Cambridge, MA: Harvard University Press, 2007.

Buchheim, Hans. *Die SS—das Herrschaftsinstrument*. Vol. 1 of *Anatomie des SS-Staates*. Olten: Walter, Switz.: 1965.

Bundesministerium für Vertriebene. *Dokumentation der Vertreibung der Deutschen aus Ost-Mitteleuropa*. Edited by Theodor Schieder. With the assistance of Werner Conze, Adolf Diestelkamp, Rudolf Laun, Peter Rassow, and Hans Rothfels. Bonn: Bundesministerium für Vertriebene, Flüchtlinge und Kriegsgeschädigte, 1954–61.

Bundeszentrale für politische Bildung. *Deutsche und Polen*. Vols. 142–43 of *Informationen zur politischen Bildung*. Bonn: Bundeszentrale für politische Bildung, 1991.

Burleigh, Michael. *Germany Turns Eastwards: A Study of Ostforschung in the Third Reich*. Cambridge: Cambridge University Press, 1988.

———. *The Third Reich: A New History*. London: Pan Books, 2001.

Burleigh, Michael, and Wolfgang Wippermann. *The Racial State: Germany 1933–1945*. Cambridge: Cambridge University Press, 1991.

Caplan, Jane, and Thomas Childers, eds. *Reevaluating the Third Reich*. New York: Holmes and Meier, 1993.

Cesarani, David. *Eichmann: His Life and Crimes*. London: Vintage, 2005.

Chrzanowski, Bogdan. "Wypędzenia z Pomorza." *Biuletyn Instytutu Pamięci Narodowej* 5 (2004): 34–48.

Cleef, Eugene van. "Danzig and Gdynia." *Geographical Review* 23, no. 1 (1933): 101–7.

Conrad, Sebastian. *Globalisierung und Nation im Deutschen Kaiserreich*. Munich: Beck, 2006.

Czapliński, Władysław. "The Protection of Minorities under International Law (Comments on the Alleged Existence of a German Minority in Poland)." *Polish Western Affairs* 25, no. 1 (1984): 121–36.

Czubiński, Antoni. "Poland's Place in Nazi Plans for a New Order in Europe in the Years 1934–1940." *Polish Western Affairs* 21, no. 1 (1980): 19–46.

———. "Die polnische Historiographie des Zweiten Weltkrieges: Hauptrichtungen der Diskussion in den Jahren 1945–2000." *Studia Historica Slavo-Germanica* 25, no. 1 (2004): 3–28.

Datner, Szymon, Janusz Gumkowski, and Kazimierz Leszczyński. *Genocide 1939–1945. War Crimes in Poland*. Warsaw: Wydawnictwo Zachodni, 1962.

———. "Wysiedlanie ludności z ziem polskich wcielonych do Rzeszy." *Biuletyn Głównej Komisji Badania Zbrodni Hitlerowskich w Polsce* 13 (1960): 5–180.

Davies, Norman. *God's Playground: A History of Poland*. 2 vols. New York: Columbia University Press, 1982.

Day, Graham, and Andrew Thompson. *Theorizing Nationalism*. Basingstoke, UK: Palgrave Macmillan, 2004.

Dickinson, Edward Ross. "The German Empire: An Empire?" *History Workshop Journal* 66, no. 1 (2008): 129–62.

Dingell, Jeanne. *Zur Tätigkeit der Haupttreuhandstelle Ost, Treuhandstelle Posen 1939 bis 1945*. Frankfurt: Peter Lang, 2003.

Długoborski, Wacław, ed. *Polozenie ludności w Rejencji Katowickiej w latach 1939–1945*. Vol. 11 of Instytut Zachodni, *Documenta Occupationis*.

Dobroszycki, Lucjan. "Polish Historiography on the Annihilation of the Jews of Poland in World War II: A Critical Evaluation." *East European Jewish Affairs* 23, no. 2 (1993): 39–49.

Domarus, Max. *Hitler: Reden und Proklamationen*. Vol. 2, bk. 1, *1939–1940*. Wiesbaden, Ger.: Löwit, 1965.

Döring, Stefan. *Die Umsiedlung der Wolhyniendeutschen in den Jahren 1939 bis 1940.* Frankfurt: Peter Lang, 2001.

Drozdowski, Marian Marek. "Górny Śląsk czasów Drugiej Rzeczypospolitej: Rzeczywistość, stereotypy, mity." In *Rola i miejsce Górnego Śląska w Drugiej Rzeczypospolitej.* Edited by Marii Wandy Wanatowicz, 65–83. Bytom: Museum Górnośląskie, Pol., 1995.

Dzieciński, Paweł. *Łódź w cieniu swastyki.* Łódź: Krajowa Agencja Wydawiczna, 1988.

Dziurok, Adam. "Zwischen den Ethnien: Die Oberschlesier in den Jahren 1939–1941." In Mallmann and Musial, *Genesis des Genozids,* 221–33.

Ebbinghaus, Angelika, and Karl Heinz Roth. "Vorläufer des 'Generalplans Ost': Eine Dokumentation über Theodor Schieders Polendenkschrift vom 7. Oktober 1939." *1999: Zeitschrift für Sozialgeschichte des 20. und 21. Jahrhunderts 7,* no. 1 (1992): 62–92.

Ehrlich, Adam. "Between Germany and Poland: Ethnic-cleansing and Politicization of Ethnicity in Upper Silesia under National Socialism and Communism 1939–1950." PhD diss., Indiana University, 2005.

Eichholtz, Dietrich."Die Vorgeschichte des 'Generalbevollmächtigten für den Arbeitseinsatz.'" *Jahrbuch für Geschichte* 9 (1973): 339–83.

Einhart [Heinrich Claß]. *Deutsche Geschichte.* Leipzig: Dieterich, 1909.

Eley, Geoff. *Reshaping the German Right: Radical Nationalism and Political Change after Bismarck.* New Haven, CT: Yale University Press, 1980.

Epstein, Catherine. *Model Nazi: Arthur Greiser and the Occupation of Western Poland.* Oxford: Oxford University Press, 2010.

Ernst, Alexander. "Das Staatsangehörigkeitsrecht im Deutschen Reich unter der Herrschaft der Nationalsozialisten und seine Auswirkungen auf das Recht der Bundesrepublik Deutschland." PhD diss., University of Münster, 1999.

Esch, Michael G. *"Gesunde Verhältnisse": Deutsche und polnische Bevölkerungspolitik in Ostmitteleuropa 1939–1950.* Marburg, Ger.: Herder-Institut, 1998.

Essner, Cornelia. "Im 'Irrgarten der Rassenlogik' oder nordische Rassenlehre und nationale Frage 1919–1935." *Historische Mitteilungen 7,* no. 1 (1994): 81–101.

———. *Die "Nürnberger Gesetze"; oder: Die Verwaltung des Rassenwahns 1933–1945.* Paderborn, Ger.: Schöningh, 2002.

Evans, Richard. *The Third Reich at War.* London: Penguin, 2008.

Fahlbusch, Michael. *Wissenschaft im Dienst der nationalsozialistischen Politik? Die "Volksdeutschen Forschungsgemeinschaften" von 1931–1945.* Baden-Baden, Ger.: Nomos, 1999.

Fiedor, Karol. "The Attitude of German Right-Wing Organizations to Poland in the Years 1918–1933." *Polish Western Affairs* 14, no. 2 (1973): 247–69.

Fink, Carole. "The Minorities Question at the Paris Peace Conferences: The Polish Minority Treaty, June 28, 1919." In *The Treaty of Versailles: A Reassessment after 75 Years.* Edited by Manfred F. Boemecke, Gerald D. Feldman, and Elisabeth Gläser, 249–74. Cambridge: Cambridge University Press, 1998.

Fischer, Fritz. *Griff nach der Weltmacht: Die Kriegszielpolitik des kaiserlichen Deutschland 1914–18.* Düsseldorf: Droste, 2000.

Forgus, Silvia P. "German Nationality Policies in Poland: Bismarck and Hitler." *East European Quarterly* 20, no. 1 (1986): 107–18.

Frensing, Hans Hermann. *Die Umsiedlung der Gottscheer Deutschen: Das Ende einer südostdeutschen Volksgruppe.* Munich: R. Oldenbourg, 1970.

Friedlander, Henry. *The Origins of the Nazi Genocide: From Euthanasia to the Final Solution.* Chapel Hill: University of North Carolina Press, 1994.

Friedmann, Tuvia, ed. *Die Tragödie des österreichischen Judentums: Bericht und Dokumentensammlung.* Haifa: Institute of Documentation in Israel for the Investigation of Nazi War Crimes, 1958.

Frymann, Daniel [Heinrich Claß]. *"Wenn ich der Kaiser wär"': Politische Wahrheiten und Notwendigkeiten.* Leipzig: Dieterich, 1914.

Furber, David. "Near as Far in the Colonies: The Nazi Occupation of Poland." *International History Review* 26, no. 3 (2004): 541–79.

Gąsiorowski, Andrzej. "Niemiecka lista narodowa na Pomorzu Gdańskim w świetle publikacji konspiracyjnych." *Zapiski historyczne* 49, no. 4 (1984): 69–93.

Geiss, Imanuel. *Der polnische Grenzstreifen 1914–1918: Ein Beitrag zur deutschen Kriegszielpolitik im Ersten Weltkrieg.* Lübeck, Ger.: Matthiesen, 1960.

Gerlach, Christian, and Götz Aly. *Das letzte Kapitel: Realpolitik, Ideologie und der Mord an den ungarischen Juden 1944/1945.* Stuttgart: Deutsche Verlags-Anstalt, 2002.

Goguel, Rudi. "Die Bedeutung der 'Reichsuniversität Posen' für die Germanisierungspolitik in Polen im Zweiten Weltkrieg." *Wissenschaftliche Zeitschrift der Humboldt-Universität zu Berlin* 17, no. 2 (1968): 189–95.

———. "Die Nord- und ostdeutsche Forschungsgemeinschaft im Dienste der faschistischen Aggressionspolitik gegen Polen 1933–1945." *Archivmitteilungen* 17, no. 3 (1967): 82–89.

———. "Über die Mitwirkung deutscher Wissenschaftler am Okkupationsregime in Polen im Zweiten Weltkrieg, untersucht an drei Institutionen der deutschen Ostforschung." PhD diss., Humboldt University of Berlin, 1964.

Golczewski, Frank. "Polen." In *Dimension des Völkermords: Die Zahl der jüdischen Opfer des Nationalsozialismus.* Edited by Wolfgang Benz, 411–97. Munich: R. Oldenbourg, 1991.

Goldendach, Walter von, and Rüdiger Minow. *"Deutschtum erwache!": Aus dem Innenleben des staatlichen Pangermanismus.* Berlin: Dietz, 1994.

Goldhagen, Daniel J. *Hitler's Willing Executioners: Ordinary Germans and the Holocaust.* New York: Knopf, 1996.

Gosewinkel, Dieter. *Einbürgern und Ausschließen: Die Nationalisierung der Staatsangehörigkeit vom Deutschen Bund bis zur Bundesrepublik Deutschland.* Göttingen, Ger.: Vandenhoeck & Ruprecht, 2001.

Goshen, Seev. "Eichmann und die Nisko-Aktion im Oktober 1939: Eine Fallstudie zur NS-Judenpolitik in der letzten Etappe vor der 'Endlösung.'" *Vierteljahrshefte für Zeitgeschichte* 29, no. 1 (1981): 74–96.

Gottwaldt, Alfred, and Diana Schulle. *Die "Judendeportationen" aus dem deutschen Reich 1941–1945: Eine kommentierte Chronologie.* Wiesbaden, Ger.: Marix-Verlag, 2005.

Greiner, Piotr, and Ryszard Kaczmarek. "Vereinsaktivitäten der Deutschen in Polnisch-Oberschlesien 1922–1939." *Zeitschrift für Ostmitteleuropa-Forschung* 45, no. 2 (1996): 221–35.

Groscurth, Helmuth. *Tagebücher eines Abwehroffiziers, 1938–1940: Mit weiteren Dokumenten zur Militäropposition gegen Hitler.* Edited by Helmut Krausnick und Harold C. Deutsch. Stuttgart: Deutsche Verlags-Anstalt, 1970.

Gruner, Wolf. "Von der Kollektivausweisung zur Deportation der Juden aus Deutschland 1938–1945: Neue Perspektiven und Dokumente." *Beiträge zur Geschichte des Nationalsozialismus* 20 (2004): 21–62.

Günther, Hans F. K. *Rassenkunde des deutschen Volkes*. Munich: J. F. Lehmanns, 1923.

Haar, Ingo. *Historiker im Nationalsozialismus: Deutsche Geschichtswissenschaft und der "Volkstumskampf" im Osten*. Göttingen, Ger.: Vandenhoeck & Ruprecht, 2002.

———. "Leipziger Stiftung für deutsche Volks- und Kulturbodenforschung." In Haar and Fahlbusch, *Handbuch der völkischen Wissenschaften*, 375–82.

Haar, Ingo, and Michael Fahlbusch, eds. *Handbuch der völkischen Wissenschaften*. Munich: K. G. Saur, 2008.

Hadler, Frank. "Drachen und Drachentöter: Das Problem der nationalgeschichtlichen Fixierung in den Historiographien Ostmitteleuropas nach dem Zweiten Weltkrieg." In *Die Nation schreiben: Geschichtswissenschaft im internationalen Vergleich*. Edited by Christoph Conrad and Sebastian Conrad, 137–64. Göttingen, Ger.: Vandenhoeck & Ruprecht, 2002.

Hagen, William. *Germans, Poles, and Jews: The Nationality Conflict in the Prussian East, 1772–1914*. Chicago: University Press of Chicago, 1980.

———. "National Solidarity and Organic Work in Prussian Poland, 1815–1914." *Journal of Modern History* 44, no. 1 (1972): 38–64.

Halder, Franz. *Kriegstagebuch*. Vol. 1, *Vom Polenfeldzug bis zum Ende der Westoffensive*. Edited by Hans-Adolf Jacobsen. Stuttgart: Kohlhammer, 1962.

Hall, Stuart. "The Problem of Ideology: Marxism without Guarantees." *Journal of Communication Inquiry* 10, no. 2 (1986): 28–44.

Hansen, Georg. "'Damit wurde das Warthegau zum Exerzierplatz des praktischen Nationalsozialismus': Eine Fallstudie zur Politik der Einverleibung." In *September 1939: Krieg, Besatzung, Widerstand in Polen*. Edited by Christoph Kleßmann, 55–72. Göttingen, Ger.: Vandenhoeck & Ruprecht, 1989.

Harten, Hans-Christian. *De-Kulturation und Germanisierung: Die nationalsozialistische Rassen- und Erziehungspolitik in Polen 1939–1945*. Frankfurt: Campus, 1996.

Harten, Hans-Christian, Uwe Neirich, and Matthias Schwerendt. *Rassenhygiene als Erziehungsideologie des Dritten Reichs: Bio-bibliographisches Handbuch*. Berlin: Akademie-Verlag, 2006.

Hartenstein, Michael. *Neue Dorflandschaften: Nationalsozialistische Siedlungsplanung in den "eingegliederten Ostgebieten" 1939 und 1944*. Berlin: Klöster, 1998.

Hasse, Ernst. *Das Deutsche Reich als Nationalstaat*. Munich: J. F. Lehmann, 1905.

Haubold-Stolle, Juliane. "Imaginative Nationalisierung des Grenzregion Oberschlesien 1918–1933/39." In *Deutschsein als Grenzerfahrung: Minderheitenpolitik in Europa zwischen 1914 und 1950*. Edited by Mathias Beer, Dietrich Beyrau, and Cornelia Rauh-Kühne, 215–24. Essen, Ger.: Klartext, 2009.

Häufele, Günther. "Deutsche und sowjetische Besatzungspolitik in Polen zwischen 1939 und 1941: Der ökonomische Aspekt." *Studia Historiae Oeconomicae* 22 (1997): 53–67.

———. "Zwangsumsiedlungen in Polen 1939–1941: Zum Vergleich sowjetischer und deutscher Besatzungspolitik." In *Lager, Zwangsarbeit, Vertreibung und Deportation: Dimensionen der Massenverbrechen in der Sowjetunion und in Deutschland 1933 bis 1945*. Edited by Dittmar Dahlmann and Gerhard Hirschfeld, 515–33. Essen, Ger.: Klartext, 1999.

Hauser, Przemyslaw. "Die deutsche Minderheit in Polen 1918–1933." In Jacobmeyer, *Die deutsch-polnischen Beziehungen*, 67–88.

Hehn, Jürgen von. *Die Umsiedlung der baltischen Deutschen: Das letzte Kapitel baltisch-deutscher Geschichte*. Marburg, Ger.: Herder-Institut, 1982.

Heiber, Helmut. "Dokumentation: Der Generalplan Ost." *Vierteljahrshefte für Zeitgeschichte* 6, no. 3 (1958): 281–325.

Heinemann, Isabel. *Rasse, Siedlung, deutsches Blut: Das Rasse- und Siedlungshauptamt der SS und die rassenpolitische Neuordnung Europas.* Göttingen, Ger.: Wallstein, 2003.

Herbert, Ulrich. "Arbeit und Vernichtung: Ökonomisches Interesse und Primat der 'Weltanschauung' im Nationalsozialismus." In *Europa und der "Reichseinsatz": Ausländische Zivilarbeiter, Kriegsgefangene und KZ-Häftlinge in Deutschland 1938-1945.* Editetd by Herbert. Essen, Ger.: Klartext, 1991, 384–426.

———. *Best: Biographische Studie über Radikalismus, Weltanschauung und Vernunft, 1903–1989.* Bonn: Dietz, 1996.

———. *Fremdarbeiter: Politik und Praxis des "Ausländer-Einsatzes" in der Kriegswirtschaft des Dritten Reiches.* Bonn: Dietz, 1999.

Herwig, Holger H. "Geopolitik: Haushofer, Hitler and Lebensraum." *Journal of Strategic Studies* 22, nos. 2–3 (1999): 218–41.

Hettling, Manfred. "Volk und Volksgeschichten in Europa." In *Volksgeschichten im Europa der Zwischenkriegszeit.* Edited by Manfred Hettling, 7–37. Göttingen, Ger.: Vandenhoeck & Ruprecht, 2003.

Hillgruber, Andreas. "Deutschland und Polen in der internationalen Politik 1933–1939." In Jacobmeyer, *Deutschland und Polen,* 47–61.

Hitler, Adolf. *Hitlers zweites Buch: Ein Dokument aus dem Jahr 1928.* Edited by Gerhard L. Weinberg. Stuttgart: Deutsche Verlags-Anstalt, 1961.

———. *Mein Kampf.* Munich: Eher, 1943.

Hobsbawm, Eric. *Nationen und Nationalismus. Mythos und Realität.* Munich: Deutscher Taschenbuch Verlag, 1996.

Hoensch, Jörg K. "Deutschland, Polen und die Großmächte 1919–1932." In Jacobmeyer, *Die deutsch-polnische Beziehungen,* 19–34.

———. *Geschichte Polens.* Stuttgart: Ulmer, 1998.

Hofmann, Wolfgang. "Das Ansiedlungsgesetz von 1904 und die preußische Polenpolitik." *Jahrbuch für die Geschichte Mittel- und Ostdeutschlands* 38 (1989): 251–85.

Horne, John, and Alan Kramer. *Deutsche Kriegsgreuel 1914: Die umstrittene Wahrheit.* Hamburg: Hamburger Edition, 2004.

Hruza, Karel. "Wilhelm Wostry." In Haar and Fahlbusch, *Handbuch der völkischen Wissenschaften,* 772–76.

Hutton, Christopher M. *Race and the Third Reich: Linguistics, Racial Anthropology and Genetics in the Dialectic of Volk.* Cambridge: Polity Press, 2005.

Instytut Zachodni. *Documenta Occupationis Instytutu Zachodniego.* Poznań, Pol.: Instytut Zachodni, 1983.

Izdebski, Zygmunt. *Niemiecka lista narodowa na Górnym Slasku.* Katowice, Pol.: Instytut Śląski, 1946.

Jachomowski, Dirk. *Die Umsiedlung der Bessarabien-, Bukowina- und Dobrudschadeutschen: Von der Volksgruppe in Rumänien zur "Siedlungsbrücke" an der Reichsgrenze.* Munich: R. Oldenbourg, 1984.

Jäckel, Eberhard. *Hitlers Herrschaft: Vollzug einer Weltanschauung.* Stuttgart: Deutsche Verlags-Anstalt, 1986.

———. *Hitlers Weltanschauung: Entwurf einer Herrschaft.* Stuttgart: Deutsche Verlags-Anstalt, 1986.

Jäckel, Eberhard, and Axel Kuhn, eds. *Hitler: Sämtliche Aufzeichnungen, 1905–1924*. Stuttgart: Deutsche Verlags-Anstalt, 1980.

Jacobsen, Hans-Adolf. *Nationalsozialistische Außenpolitik 1933–1938*. Frankfurt: Metzner, 1968.

Jansen, Christian, and Arno Weckbecker. "Eine Miliz im 'Weltanschauungskrieg': Der 'Volksdeutsche Selbstschutz' in Polen 1939/40." In *Der Zweite Weltkrieg: Analysen, Grundzüge, Forschungsbilanz*. Edited by Wolfgang Michalka, 482–500. Munich: Piper: R. Oldenbourg, 1990.

———. *Der "Volksdeutsche Selbstschutz" in Polen 1939/40*. Munich: R. Oldenbourg, 1992.

Jansen, Hans. *Der Madagaskar-Plan: Die beabsichtigte Deportation der europäischen Juden nach Madagaskar*. Munich: Herbig, 1997.

Jasch, Hans-Christian. "Das preußische Kultusministerium und die 'Ausschaltung' von 'nichtarischen' und politisch mißliebigen Professoren an der Berliner Universität in den Jahren 1933 bis 1934 aufgrund des Gesetzes zur Wiederherstellung des Berufsbeamtentums vom 7. April 1933." *Forum Historiae Juris*, August 28, 2005. http://www.forhistiur.de/zitat/0508jasch.htm.

Jastrzębski, Włodzimierz. *Hitlerowskie wysiedlenia z ziem polskich wcielonych do Rzeszy 1939–1945*. Poznań, Pol.: Instytut Zachodni, 1968.

———. "Nazi Deportations of Polish and Jewish Population from Territories Incorporated into the Third Reich." Paper presented at International Scientific Session on Nazi Genocide in Poland and in Europe 1939–1945. Warsaw: Główna Komisja Badania Zbrodni Hitlerowskich w Polsce, 1983.

———. *Potulice: Hitlerowski obóz przesiedleńczy i pracy*. Bydgoszcz, Pol.: Bydgoskie Towarzystwo naukowe, 1967.

Jastrzębski, Włodzimierz, and Jan Sziling. *Okupacja hitlerowska na Pomorzu Gdánskim w latach 1939–1945*. Gdańsk, Pol.: Wydawn. Morskie, 1979.

Jażdżewski, Leszek. "Die Kaschuben in der deutschen Armee in den Jahren 1942–1945." In *Annexion et nazification en Europe: Actes du colloque de Metz, November 7–8, 2003*. Edited by Sylvain Schirmann, 81–100. Metz: Metz University, 2003.

Kaczmarek, Ryszard. "Die deutsche wirtschaftliche Penetration in Polen (Oberschlesien)." In *Die "Neuordnung" Europas: NS-Wirtschaftspolitik in den besetzten Gebieten*. Edited by Richard J. Overy, Gerhard Otto, and Johannes Houwink ten Cate, 257–72. Berlin: Metropol, 1997.

———. "Niemiecka polityka narodowościowa na Górnym Śląsku 1939–1945." *Pamięć i Sprawiedliwość* 2, no. 6 (2004): 115–38.

———. *Pod rządami gauleiterów: Elity i instancje władzy w rejencji katowickiej w latach 1939–1945*. Katowice, Pol.: Wydawn. Uniw. Śląskiego, 1998.

———. "Zwischen Altreich und Besatzungsgebiet: Der Gau Oberschlesien 1939/41–1945." In *Die NS-Gaue: Regionale Mittelinstanzen im zentralistischen "Führerstaat"?* Edited by Jürgen John, Horst Möller, and Thomas Schaarschmidt, 348–63. Munich: R. Oldenbourg, 2007.

Kalisch, Johannes. "'Full Use': Der Kampf der Freien Stadt Danzig gegen Gdynia 1930–1932." *Wissenschaftliche Zeitschrift der Wilhelm-Pieck-Universität Rostock: Gesellschafts- und Sprachwissenschaftliche Reihe* 30, no. 2 (1981): 57–63.

Kárný, Miroslav. "Nisko in der Geschichte der 'Endlösung.'" *Judaica Bohemiae* 23, no. 2 (1987): 69–84.

Kershaw, Ian. *Hitler 1889–1936: Hubris*. London: Allen Lande, 1998.

———. *Hitler 1936–1945: Nemesis*. London: Allen Lane, 2000.

———. "Improvised Genocide? The Emergence of the Final Solution in the 'Warthegau.'" *Transactions of the Royal Historical Society* 2 (1992): 51–78.

Klautke, Egbert. "German 'Race Psychology' and Its Implementation in Central Europe: Egon von Eickstedt and Rudolf Hippius." In *"Blood and Homeland": Eugenics and Racial Nationalism in Central Europe and Southeast Europe, 1900–1940*. Edited by Marius Turda and Paul J. Weidling, 23–40. Budapest: Central European University Press, 2007.

Klein, Peter. "Curt von Gottberg: Siedlungsfunktionär und Massenmörder." In *Karrieren der Gewalt: Nationalsozialistische Täterbiographien*. Edited by Gerhard Paul and Klaus-Michael Mallmann, 95–103. Darmstadt: Wissenschaftliche Buchgesellschaft, Ger., 2004.

———. *Die "Gettoverwaltung Litzmannstadt" 1940 bis 1944: Eine Dienststelle im Spannungsfeld von Kommunalbürokratie und staatlicher Verfolgungspolitik*. Hamburg: Hamburger Edition, 2009.

Kleßmann, Christoph, and Wacław Długoborski. "Nationalsozialistische Bildungspolitik und polnische Hochschulen 1939–1945." *Geschichte und Gesellschaft* 23, no. 4 (1997): 535–59.

Koehl, Robert L. *The Black Corps: The Structure and Power Struggles of the Nazi SS*. Madison: University of Wisconsin Press, 1983.

———. "Colonialism inside Germany: 1886–1918." *Journal of Modern History* 25, no. 3 (1953): 255–72.

———. "The Deutsche Volksliste in Poland." *Journal of Central European Affairs* 15, no. 4 (1956): 354–66.

———. "The Politics of Resettlement." *Western Political Quarterly* 6, no. 2 (1953): 231–42.

———. *RKFDV: German Resettlement and Population Policy 1939–1945*. Cambridge, MA: Harvard University Press, 1957.

Kolb, Eberhard. "Polenbild und Polenfreundschaft der deutschen Frühliberalen: Zu Motivation und Funktion außenpolitischer Parteinahme im Vormärz." *Saeculum* 26 (1975): 111–27.

Komjathy, Anthony, and Rebecca Stockwell. *German Minorities and the Third Reich: Ethnic Germans of East Central Europe between the Wars*. New York: Holmes & Meier, 1980.

Kopp, Kristin. "Arguing the Case for a Colonial Poland." In Langbehn and Salama, *German Colonialism*, 146–63.

Koselleck, Reinhart, Fritz Gschnitzer, Karl Ferdinand Werner, and Bernd Schönemann. "Volk, Nation, Nationalismus, Masse." In *Geschichtliche Grundbegriffe: Historisches Lexikon zur politisch-sozialen Sprache in Deutschland*. Edited by Otto Brunner, Werner Conze, and Reinhart Koselleck, 7: 141–432. Stuttgart: Klett-Cotta, 1992.

Kossert, Andreas. "Protestantismus in Lodz 1918–1956: Die evangelische Bevölkerung der mittelpolnischen Industriemetropole im Spannungsverhältnis zwischen Deutschland und Polen." In *Deutsche und polnische Christen*. Edited by Martin Greschat, 86–116. Stuttgart: Kohlhammer, 1999.

Kotowski, Albert S. *Polens Politik gegenüber seiner deutschen Minderheit 1919–1939*. Wiesbaden, Ger.: Harrassowitz, 1998.

Kotze, Hildegard von, ed. *Heeresadjutant bei Hitler 1938–1943: Aufzeichnungen des Majors Engel*. Stuttgart: Deutsche Verlags-Anstalt, 1974.

Kramer, Alan. *Dynamic of Destruction: Culture and Mass Killing in the First World War.* Oxford: Oxford University Press, 2007.

Krausnick, Helmut. "Hitler und die Morde in Polen: Ein Beitrag zum Konflikt zwischen Heer und SS um die Verwaltung der besetzten Gebiete (Dokumentation)." *Vierteljahrshefte für Zeitgeschichte* 11, no. 2 (1963): 196–209.

———. *Hitlers Einsatzgruppen: Die Truppen des Weltanschauungskrieges 1938–1942.* Frankfurt: Fischer, 1985.

Krebs, Bernd. *Nationale Identität und kirchliche Selbstbehauptung: Julius Bursche und die Auseinandersetzung um Auftrag und Weg des Protestantismus in Polen 1917–1939.* Neukirchen-Vluyn, Ger.: Neukirchner Verlag des Erziehungsvereins, 1993.

Krekeler, Norbert. "Die deutsche Minderheit in Polen und die Revisionspolitik des Deutschen Reiches 1919–1933." In *Die Vertreibung der Deutschen aus dem Osten: Ursachen, Ereignisse, Folgen.* Edited by Wolfgang Benz, 15–28. Frankfurt: Fischer, 1985.

———. *Revisionsanspruch und geheime Ostpolitik der Weimarer Republik: Die Subventionierung der deutschen Minderheit in Polen 1919–1933.* Stuttgart: Deutsche Verlags-Anstalt, 1973.

Kroeger, Erhard. *Der Auszug aus der alten Heimat: Die Umsiedlung der Baltendeutschen.* Vol. 4 of *Veröffentlichungen des Instituts für deutsche Nachkriegsgeschichte.* Edited by Herbert Grabert. Tübingen, Ger.: Verlag der deutschen Hochschullehrer-Zeitung, 1967.

Kroener, Bernhard R. "Die persönlichen Ressourcen des Dritten Reiches im Spannungsfeld zwischen Wehrmacht, Bürokratie und Kriegswirtschaft 1939–1942." In *Das Deutsche Reich und der Zweite Weltkrieg,* 5, bk. 1: 691–1001. Stuttgart: Militärgeschichtliches Forschungsamt, 1988.

Kroll, Frank-Lothar. *Utopie als Ideologie: Geschichtsdenken und politisches Handeln im Dritten Reich.* Paderborn, Ger.: Schöningh, 1998.

Kulczycki, John J. *School Strikes in Prussian Poland, 1901–1907: The Struggle over Bilingual Education.* New York: Columbia University Press, 1981.

Laak, Dirk van. *Über alles in der Welt: Deutscher Imperialismus im 19. und 20. Jahrhundert.* Munich: C. H. Beck, 2005.

Lask, I. M., ed. *The Kalish Book.* Tel Aviv: Societies of Former Residents of Kalish and the Vicinity in Israel and U.S.A., 1968.

Lehnstaedt, Stephan. "'Ostnieten' oder 'Vernichtungsexperten': Die Auswahl deutscher Staatsdiener für den Einsatz im Generalgouvernement Polen 1939–1944." *Zeitschrift für Geschichtswissenschaft* 55, no. 9 (2007): 701–89.

Leitz, Christian. *Nazi Foreign Policy, 1933–1941: The Road to Global War.* London: Routledge, 2004.

Lemkin, Raphael. *Axis Rule in Occupied Europe: Laws of Occupation, Analysis of Government, Proposals for Redress.* Clark, NJ: Lawbook Exchange, 2008.

Lempart, Matthias. "Die deutsche Volksliste in Oberschlesien: Normative Regelungen und praktische Umsetzung." *Confinium* 2 (2007): 190–206.

Leniger, Markus. *Nationalsozialistische "Volkstumsarbeit" und Umsiedlungspolitik: Von der Minderheitenbetreuung zur Siedlerauslese.* Berlin: Frank & Timme, 2006.

Leuschner, Egon. *Nationalsozialistische Fremdvolkpolitik.* Berlin: Rassenpolitisches Amt der NSDAP, 1940.

Leuschner, Thorsten. "'Die Sprache ist eben ein Grundrecht der Nation, das sich nur bis zu einer gewissen Grenze gewaltsam verkümmern läßt': Deutsch-polnische Gegensätze in der Entstehungsgeschichte des preußischen Geschäftssprachengesetzes von 1876." *Germanistische Mitteilungen* 52 (2000): 149–65.

Levine, H. "Local Authority and the SS State: The Conflict over Population Policy in Danzig-West Prussia 1939–1945." *Journal of Central European Affairs* 11, no. 4 (1969): 331–55.

Lilla, Joachim, ed. *Die Stellvertretenden Gauleiter und die Vertretung der Gauleiter der NSDAP im "Dritten Reich."* Vol. 13 of *Materialien aus dem Bundesarchiv.* Bremerhaven, Ger.: Wirtschaftsverlag, 2003.

Lindemann, Gerhard. "Die preußisch-deutsche Reichsgründung 1870/71 und die polnische Minderheit." *Kirchliche Zeitgeschichte* 15, no. 1 (2002): 24–51.

Loeber, Dietrich A., ed. *Diktierte Option: Die Umsiedlung der Deutsch-Balten aus Estland und Lettland 1939–1941.* Neumünster, Ger.: Karl Wachholtz, 1974.

Longerich, Peter. *Heinrich Himmler: Biographie.* Berlin: Siedler, 2008.

———. *Politik der Vernichtung.* Munich: Piper, 1998.

Łossowski, Piotr. "The Resettlement of the Germans from the Baltic States." *Acta Poloniae Historicae* 92 (2005): 79–98.

Lück, Kurt, and Alfred Lattermann, eds. *Die Heimkehr der Galiziendeutschen.* Vol. 14 of *Unsere Heimat.* Posen, Pol.: Historische Gesellschaft für Posen and the Gaugrenzlandamt of the Nazi Party in the Reichsgau of the Wartheland, 1940.

Łuczak, Czesław. "Die Ansiedlung der deutschen Bevölkerung im besetzten Polen (1939–1945)." *Studia Historiae Oeconomicae* 13 (1978): 193–205.

———. *Pod niemieckim jarzmem (Kraj Warty 1939–1945).* Poznań, Pol.: PSO, 1996.

———. *Polityka ludnościowa i ekonomiczna hitlerowskich Niemiec w okupowanej Polsce.* Poznań, Pol.: Wydawn. Poznańskie, 1979.

———, ed. *Położenie ludności polskiej w tzw. Kraju Warty w okresie hitlerowskiej okupacji.* Vol. 13 of Instytut Zachodni, *Documenta Occupationis.* Poznań, Pol., 1990.

———, ed. *Wysiedlenia ludności polskiej na tzw. ziemiach wcielonych do Rzeszy 1939–1945.* Vol. 8 of Instytut Zachodni, *Documenta Occupationis.* Poznań, Pol., 1969.

Lukas, Richard C. *The Forgotten Holocaust: The Poles under German Occupation 1939–1944.* Lexington: The University Press of Kentucky, 1986.

Lukowski, Jerzy, and Hubert Zawadzki. *A Concise History of Poland.* Cambridge: Cambridge University Press, 2001.

Lumans, Valdis O. *Himmler's Auxiliaries: The Volksdeutsche Mittelstelle and the German National Minorities of Europe 1933–1945.* Chapel Hill: University of North Carolina Press, 1995.

Mackensen, Rainer, Jürgen Reulecke, and Josef Ehmer, eds. *Ursprünge, Arten und Folgen des Konstrukts "Bevölkerung" vor, im und nach dem "Dritten Reich": Zur Geschichte der deutschen Bevölkerungswissenschaft.* Wiesbaden, Ger.: Verlag für Sozialwissenschaften, 2009.

Madajczyk, Czesław. "Generalplan Ost." *Przegląd Zachodni* 3 (1961): 66–103.

———. *Die Okkupationspolitik Nazideutschlands in Polen 1939–1945.* Ost-Berlin: Akademie-Verlag, 1987.

———, ed. *Vom Generalplan Ost zum Generalsiedlungsplan.* Munich: K. G. Saur, 1994.

———. "Zur Besatzungspolitik der Achsenmächte: Ein persönliches Forschungsresümee." In *Das organisierte Chaos: "Ämterdarwinismus" und "Gesinnungsethik": Determinanten nationalsozialistischer Besatzungsherrschaft.* Edited by Johannes Houwink ten Cate and Gerhard Otto, 303–38. Berlin: Metropol, 1999.

Majer, Diemut. *"Fremdvölkische" im Dritten Reich: Ein Beitrag zur nationalsozialistischen Rechtsetzung und Rechtspraxis in Verwaltung und Justiz unter besonderer Berücksichtigung der eingegliederten Ostgebiete und des Generalgouvernements.* Boppard, Ger.: Boldt, 1993.

Majewski, Piotr. "Sage nie, du gehst den letzten Weg: Deutsche und Polen nach dem Novemberaufstand." In *Polenbegeisterung: Deutsche und Polen nach dem Novemberaufstand 1830.* Edited by Zamek Królewski w Warszawie, 29–40. Warsaw, 2005.

Mallmann, Klaus-Michael, Jochen Böhler, and Jürgen Matthäus, eds. *Einsatzgruppen in Polen: Darstellung und Dokumentation.* Darmstadt, Ger.: Wissenschaftliche Buchgesellschaft, 2008.

Mallmann, Klaus-Michael, and Bogdan Musial, eds. *Genesis des Genozids: Polen 1939–1941.* Darmstadt, Ger.: Wissenschaftliche Buchgesellschaft, 2004.

Mann, Michael. *Dark Side of Democracy.* Cambridge: Cambridge University Press, 2005.

Marczewski, Jerzy. *Hitlerowska koncepcja polityki kolonizacyjno-wysiedleńczej i jej realizacja w "Okręgu Warty."* Poznań, Pol.: Instytut Zachodni, 1979.

———. "Hitlerowska polityka narodowościowa na ternie Okręgu Warty 1939–1945." In *Przymus germanizacyjny na ziemiach polskich wcielonych do Rzeszy Niemieckiej w latach 1939–1945: Materiały z konferencji.* Edited by Włodzimierz Jastrzębski, 59–82. Bydgoszcz, Pol.: Wydawnictwo Uczelniane WSP w Bydgoszczy, 1993.

———. "The Nazi Nationality Policy in the Warthegau 1939–1945 (an Outline)." *Polish Western Affairs* 30, no. 1 (1989): 31–49.

Mason, Timothy W. "Intention and Explanation: A Current Controversy about the Interpretation of National Socialism." In Hirschfeld and Kettenacker, *Der Führerstaat,* 23–42.

Massin, Benoit. "Rasse und Vererbung als Beruf: Die Hauptforschungsrichtungen am Kaiser-Wilhelm-Institut für Anthropologie, menschliche Erblehre und Eugenik im Nationalsozialismus." In Schmuhl, *Rassenforschung,* 190–244.

Matuschek, Herbert. "Das Polnisch der Oberschlesier: Zu den Kontroversen um ein Idiom." Parts 1 and 2. *Oberschlesisches Jahrbuch* 13 (1997): 93–120; 14–15 (1998–99): 193–214.

Mazower, Mark. *Dark Continent: Europe's Twentieth Century.* New York: Vintage Books, 2000.

———. *Hitler's Empire: Nazi Rule in Occupied Europe.* London: Allen Lane, 2008.

Merkenschlager, Friedrich. *Götter, Helden und Günther: Eine Abwehr der Güntherschen Rassenkunde.* Nuremberg, Ger.: Spindler, 1926.

Ministerialblatt der inneren Verwaltung [Ministerial gazette of the interior administration]. Published by the Reich Interior Ministry. Berlin, 1936–45.

Moll, Martin, ed. *"Führer-Erlasse" 1939–1945.* Stuttgart: Steiner, 1997.

Mombauer, Annika. *The Origins of the First World War: Controversies and Consensus.* London: Longman, 2002.

Mommsen, Hans. "Der Nationalsozialismus: Kumulative Radikalisierung und Selbstzerstörung des Regimes." In *Meyers Enzyklopädisches Lexikon,* 785–90. Mannheim, Ger., 1976.

Morgan, Philip. *Fascism in Europe.* London: Routledge, 2003.

Moser, Jonny. "Nisko: The First Experiment in Deportation." *Simon Wiesenthal Center Annual* 2 (1985). http://motlc.wiesenthal.com/site/pp.asp?c=gvKVLcMVIuG&b=394999.

Moses, A. Dirk. "Hannah Arendt, Imperialisms, and the Holocaust." In Langbehn and Salama, *German Colonialism*, 72–92.

Mühlhäuser, Regina. *Eroberungen: Gewalttaten und intime Beziehungen deutscher Soldaten in der Sowjetunion 1941–1945*. Hamburg: Hamburger Edition, 2010.

Müller, Michael G. "Deutsche und polnische Nation im Vormärz." In *Polen und die polnische Frage in der Geschichte der Hohenzollernmonarchie 1701–1871: Referate einer deutsch-polnischen Historiker-Tagung vom 7. bis 10. November in Berlin-Nikolassee*. Edited by Klaus Zernack, 69–95. Berlin: Colloquium-Verlag, 1982.

Müller, Michael G., and Bernd Schönemann. *Die "Polen-Debatte" in der Frankfurter Paulskirche*. Frankfurt: Diesterweg, 1991.

Müller, Rolf-Dieter. *Hitlers Ostkrieg und die deutsche Siedlungspolitik: Die Zusammenarbeit von Wehrmacht, Wirtschaft und SS*. Frankfurt: Fischer, 1991.

———. "Das Schlachtfeld zweier totalitärer Systeme: Polen unter deutscher und sowjetischer Herrschaft 1939–1941." In Mallmann and Musial, *Genesis des Genozids*, 13–35.

Nathans, Eli. *The Politics of Citizenship in Germany*. Oxford: Oxford University Press, 2004.

Nesládková, Ludmila. "Eine Episode in der Geschichte des Dritten Reichs: Das Lager in Nisko und die Juden aus dem Ostrauer Gebiet." *Hefte von Auschwitz* 22 (2002): 343–62.

Neubach, Helmut. *Die Ausweisungen von Polen und Juden aus Preußen 1885–86: Ein Beitrag zu Bismarcks Polenpolitik und zur Geschichte des deutsch-polnischen Verhältnisses*. Wiesbaden, Ger.: Harrassowitz, 1967.

Neumann, Franz. *Behemoth: Struktur und Praxis des Nationalsozialismus 1933–1944*. Cologne, Ger.: Europäische Verlags-Anstalt, 1977.

Niendorf, Mathias. *Minderheiten an der Grenze: Deutsche und Polen in den Kreisen Flatow und Zempelburg 1900–1939*. Wiesbaden, Ger.: Harrassowitz, 1997.

Nižňanský, Eduard. "Die Aktion Nisko, das Lager Sosnowiec (Oberschlesien) und die Anfänge des 'Judenlagers' in Vyhne (Slowakei)." *Jahrbuch für Antisemitismusforschung* 11 (2002): 325–35.

Oldenburg, Jens. *Der deutsche Ostmarkenverein 1894–1934*. Berlin: Logos, 2002.

Opitz, Kurt, ed. *Europastrategien des deutschen Kapitals 1900–1945*. Bonn: Pahl-Rugenstein, 1995.

Orłowski, Hubert. *Polnische Wirtschaft: Zum deutschen Polendiskurs der Neuzeit*. Wiesbaden, Ger.: Harrassowitz, 1996.

Ostdeutscher Beobachter: Organ der NSDAP; Verkündigungsblatt des Reichsstatthalters und seiner Behörden. Published by the Nazi Party and the Reichsstatthalter of the Wartheland, 1939–1945.

Pätzold, Kurt, ed. *Verfolgung, Vertreibung, Vernichtung: Dokumente des faschistischen Antisemitismus 1933–1942*. Leipzig: Reclam, 1991.

Paxton, Robert O. *The Anatomy of Fascism*. London: Allen Lane, 2004.

Peiser, Kurt. *Danzig und Gdingen: Vortrag, gehalten im Februar 1933*. Danzig: Danziger Allgemeine Zeitung, 1933.

Peukert, Detlev J. K. "Die Genesis der 'Endlösung' aus dem Geist der Wissenschaft." In *Zerstörung des moralischen Selbstbewußtseins: Chance oder Gefährdung?* Edited by Forum für Philosophie in Bad Homburg, 24–48. Frankfurt,: Suhrkamp 1988.

———. *Die Weimarer Republik: Krisenjahre der klassischen Moderne*. Frankfurt: Suhrkamp, 1987.

Picker, Henry, ed. *Hitlers Tischgespräche im Führerhauptquartier*. Stuttgart: Seewald, 1976.

Pilichowski, Czesław. "Nazi Genocide in the Light of German Plans and their Implementation." *Polish Western Affairs* 24, no. 2 (1983): 181–214.

Pinwinkler, Alexander. "Volk, Bevölkerung, Rasse, and Raum: Erich Keyser's Ambiguous Concept of a German History of Population, ca. 1918–1955." In *German Scholars and Ethnic Cleansing 1920–1945*. Edited by Ingo Haar and Michael Fahlbusch, 86–99. New York: Berghahn, 2005.

Piotrowski, Tadeusz. *Poland's Holocaust.* Jefferson, NC: McFarland, 1997.

Pohl, Dieter. "Die Reichsgaue Danzig-Westpreußen und Wartheland: Koloniale Verwaltung oder Modell für die zukünftige Gauverfassung?" In *Die NS-Gaue: Regionale Mittelinstanzen im zentralistischen "Führerstaat"?* Edited by Jürgen John, Horst Möller, and Thomas Schaarschmidt, 395–495. Munich: R. Oldenbourg, 2007.

Polish Ministry of Foreign Affairs. *German Occupation of Poland: Extract of Note Addressed to the Allied and Neutral Powers; Polish White Book.* New York, 1942.

Polish Ministry of Information. *The Black Book of Poland.* New York, 1942.

———. *The German Invasion of Poland.* London, 1940.

———. *The German New Order in Poland.* London, 1943.

———. *The Quest for German Blood.* London, 1943.

Pospieszalski, Karol Marian. "Hitlerowska polemika z 'Generalplan Ost' Reichsführer SS." *Przegląd Zachodni* 2 (1958): 346–69.

———, ed. *Hitlerowskie "prawo" okupacyjne w Polsce: Wybór documentów i próba syntezy; Ziemie "wcielone."* Vol. 5 of Instytut Zachodni, *Documenta Occupationis.*

———. "Nazi Attacks on German Property: The SS Reichsführer's Plan of Summer 1939." *Polish Western Affairs* 24, no. 1 (1983): 98–137.

———, ed. *Niemiecka lista narodowa w "kraju warty."* Vol. 4 of Instytut Zachodni, *Documenta Occupationis.*

Präg, Werner, and Wolfgang Jacobmeyer, eds. *Das Diensttagebuch des deutschen Generalgouverneurs in Polen 1939–1945.* Stuttgart: Deutsche Verlags-Anstalt, 1975.

Prehn, Ulrich. "Max Hildebert Boehm und die geistige Mobilmachung der 'Volksgemeinschaft': Radikales Ordnungsdenken vom Ersten Weltkrieg bis in die frühe Bundesrepublik." PhD diss., University of Hamburg, 2010.

Přibyl, Lukáš. "Das Schicksal des dritten Transports aus dem Protektorat nach Nisko." *Theresienstädter Studien und Dokumente* 7 (2000): 297–342.

Prior, Robin, and Trevor Wilson. "Review Article: The First World War." *Journal of Contemporary History* 35, no. 2 (2000): 319–28.

Proctor, Robert N. *Racial Hygiene: Medicine under the Nazis.* Cambridge, MA: Harvard University Press, 1988.

Puchert, Berthold. *Der Wirtschaftskrieg des deutschen Imperialismus gegen Polen 1925–1934.* Ost-Berlin: Akademie-Verlag, 1963.

Puschner, Uwe. *Die völkische Bewegung im wilhelminischen Kaiserreich: Sprache, Rasse, Religion.* Darmstadt, Ger.: Wissenschaftliche Buchgesellschaft, 2001.

Rak, Romuald. "Die deutsche Volksliste (1941) und ihre sittliche Beurteilung." *Oberschlesisches Jahrbuch* 7 (1991): 223–30.

Raphael, Lutz. "Die nationalsozialistische Weltanschauung: Profil, Verbreitungsformen und Nachleben." In *Kriegsende 1945: Befreiung oder Niederlage für die Deutschen? Gedanken über die Hintergründe des Rechtsextremismus in der Bundesrepublik Deutschland.* Edited by Günter Gehl, 27–42. Weimar: Bertuch, 2006.

Reagin, Nancy R. *Sweeping the German Nation: Domesticity and National Identity in Germany, 1870–1945*. Cambridge: Cambridge University Press, 2007.

Rehmann, Jan. "Ideologietheorie." In vol. 6, bk. 1, of *Historisch-kritisches Wörterbuch des Marxismus*, 717–60. Hamburg: Argument, 2004.

Reichsgesetzblatt Teil I [Reich law gazette, part I]. Published by the Reich Interior Ministry, 1922–45. Berlin.

Rich, Norman. *Hitler's War Aims*. 2 vols. New York: Norton, 1973.

Rieß, Volker. *Die Anfänge der Vernichtung "lebensunwerten Lebens" in den Reichsgauen Danzig-Westpreußen und Wartheland 1939/40*. Frankfurt: Peter Lang, 1995.

Riga, Liliana, and James Kennedy. "Tolerant Majorities, Loyal Minorities and 'Ethnic Reversals': Constructing Minority Rights at Versailles 1919." *Nations and Nationalism* 15, no. 3 (2009): 461–82.

Röhr, Werner, ed. *Faschismus und Rassismus: Kontroversen um Ideologie und Opfer*. Berlin: Akademie-Verlag, 1991.

———. "Faschismus und Rassismus: Zur Stellung des Rassenantisemitismus in der nationalsozialistischen Ideologie und Politik." In Röhr, *Faschismus und Rassismus*, 23–65.

———. "Die faschistische Okkupationspolitik in Polen 1939 bis 1945 und die Stellung dieses Landes in den Plänen für eine 'Neuordnung' Europas." *1999: Zeitschrift für Sozialgeschichte des 20. und 21. Jahrhunderts* 7, no. 3 (1992): 43–63.

———, ed. *Die faschistische Okkupationspolitik in Polen 1939–1945*. Vol. 2 of Schumann and Nestler, *Nacht über Europa*. Ost-Berlin: Deutscher Verlag der Wissenschaften, 1989.

———. "'Reichsgau Wartheland' 1939–1945: Vom Exerzierplatz des praktischen Nationalsozialismus zum 'Mustergau'?" *Bulletin für Faschismus- und Weltkriegsforschung* 18 (2002): 28–54.

———. "Zur Rolle der Schwerindustrie im annektierten polnischen Oberschlesien für die Kriegswirtschaft Deutschlands von 1939 bis 1949." *Jahrbuch für Wirtschaftsgeschichte* 4 (1991): 9–58.

———. "Zur Wirtschaftspolitik der deutschen Okkupanten in Polen 1939–1945." In *Krieg und Wirtschaft: Studien zur deutschen Wirtschaftsgeschichte 1939–1945*. Edited by Dietrich Eichholtz, 221–51. Berlin: Metropol, 1999.

Romaniuk, Marek. *Podzwonne okupacji: Deutsche Volksliste w Bydgoszczy 1945–1950*. Bydgoszcz, Pol.: Artpress,1993.

Roseman, Mark. *Die Wannsee-Konferenz: Wie die NS-Bürokratie den Holocaust organisierte*. Berlin: Propyläen, 2002.

Rosenberg, Alfred. *Das politische Tagebuch Alfred Rosenbergs aus den Jahren 1934/1935 und 1939/1940*. Edited by Hans-Günther Seraphim. Göttingen, Ger.: Musterschmidt, 1956.

Rosenkötter, Bernhard. *Treuhandpolitik: Die "Haupttreuhandstelle Ost" und der Raub polnischer Vermögen 1939–1945*. Essen, Ger.: Klartext, 2003.

Rosenkranz, Herbert. *Verfolgung und Selbstbehauptung: Die Juden in Österreich 1938–1945*. Vienna: Herold, 1978.

Rosenthal, Harry K. *German and Pole: National Conflict and Modern Myth*. Gainesville: University Press of Florida, 1976.

Rossino, Alexander B. *Hitler Strikes Poland: Blitzkrieg, Ideology, and Atrocity*. Lawrence: University of Kansas Press, 2003.

Rössler, Mechtild, and Sabine Schleiermacher, eds. *Der "Generalplan Ost": Hauptlinien der nationalsozialistischen Planungs- und Vernichtungspolitik*. Berlin: Akademie-Verlag, 1993.

Roth, Karl Heinz. "'Generalplan Ost'—'Gesamtplan Ost': Forschungsstand, Quellenprobleme, neue Ergebnisse." In Rössler and Schleiermacher, *Der Generalplan Ost*, 25–95.

———. "'Generalplan Ost' und der Mord an den Juden: Der 'Fernplan' der Umsiedlung in den Ostprovinzen aus dem Reichssicherheitshauptamt vom November 1939." *1999: Zeitschrift für Sozialgeschichte des 20. und 21. Jahrhunderts* 12, no. 2 (1997): 50–70.

———. *Geschichtsrevisionismus: Die Wiedergeburt der Totalitarismustheorie*. Hamburg: KVV Konkret, 1999.

———. "Heydrichs Professor: Historiographie des 'Volkstums' und der Massenvernichtung; Der Fall Hans Joachim Beyer." In *Geschichtsschreibung als Legitimationswissenschaft, 1918–1945*. Edited by Peter Schöttler, 262–342. Frankfurt: Suhrkamp, 1997.

Rutherford, Philip T. *Prelude to the Final Solution: The Nazi Program for Deporting Ethnic Poles, 1939–1941*. Lawrence, KS: University Press of Kansas, 2007.

———. "Race, Space, and the 'Polish Question': Nazi Deportation Policy in Reichsgau Wartheland, 1939–1941." PhD diss., Pennsylvania State University, 2001.

Safrian, Hans. *Eichmann und seine Gehilfen*. Frankfurt: Fischer, 1997.

Sauer, Wolfgang. "Das Problem des deutschen Nationalstaates." In *Moderne deutsche Sozialgeschichte*. Edited by Hans-Ulrich Wehler, 407–36. Königstein im Taunus, Ger.: Athenäum, 1981.

Schenk, Dieter. *Hitlers Mann in Danzig: Gauleiter Forster und die NS-Verbrechen in Danzig-Westpreußen*. Bonn: Dietz, 2000.

Schmidt, Rainer. *Die Außenpolitik des Dritten Reiches 1933–1939*. Stuttgart: Klett-Cotta, 2002.

Schmidt-Rösler, Andrea. *Polen: Vom Mittelalter bis zur Gegenwart*. Regensburg, Ger.: Pustet, 1996.

Schminck-Gustavus, Christoph R. "Zwangsarbeitsrecht und Faschismus: Zur 'Polenpolitik' im 'Dritten Reich.'" *Kritische Justiz* 13 (1980): 1–27 and 184–206.

Schmuhl, Hans Werner. *Rassenhygiene, Nationalsozialismus, Euthanasie: Von der Verhütung zur Vernichtung "lebensunwerten Lebens" 1890–1945*. Göttingen, Ger.: Vandenhoeck & Ruprecht, 1987.

Schneider, Wolfgang. *"Vernichtungspolitik": Eine Debatte über den Zusammenhang von Sozialpolitik und Genozid im nationalsozialistischen Deutschland*. Hamburg: Junius, 1991.

Schramm, Gottfried. "Der Kurswechsel der deutschen Polenpolitik nach Hitlers Machtergreifung." In *"Unternehmen Barbarossa": Zum historischen Ort der deutsch-sowjetischen Beziehungen von 1933 bis Herbst 1941*. Edited by Roland G. Foerster, 23–34. Munich: R. Oldenbourg, 1993.

Schulz, Karsten. "Nationalsozialistische Nachkriegskonzeptionen für die eroberten Gebiete Osteuropas vom Januar 1940 bis Januar 1943." Master's thesis, Technical University of Berlin, 1996.

Schumann, Wolfgang, and Ludwig Nestler, eds. *Europa unterm Hakenkreuz: Die Okkupationspolitik des deutschen Faschismus*. 8 vols. Berlin: Deutscher Verlag der Wissenschaften, 1988–96.

———, eds. *Nacht über Europa*. Cologne, Ger.: Pahl-Rugenstein, 1989.

Schwaneberg, Sonja. "The Economic Exploitation of the Generalgouvernement in Poland by the Third Reich." PhD diss., Oxford University, 2006.

Seckendorf, Martin. "Kulturelle Deutschtumspflege im Übergang von Weimar zu Hitler am Beispiel des Deutschen Auslands-Instituts (DAI): Eine Fallstudie." In *Völkische Wissenschaft: Gestalten und Tendenzen der deutschen und österreichischen Volkskunde in der ersten Hälfte des 20. Jahrhunderts*. Edited by Wolfgang Jacobeit, Hannjost Lixfeld, and Olaf Bockhorn, 115–35. Vienna: Böhlau, 1994.

Seeber, Eva. *Zwangsarbeiter in der faschistischen Kriegswirtschaft: Die Deportation und Ausbeutung polnischer Bürger unter besonderer Berücksichtigung der Lage der Arbeiter aus dem sogenannten Generalgouvernement 1939–1945*. Ost-Berlin: Deutscher Verlag der Wissenschaften, 1964.

Sharp, Alan. "The Genie That Would Not Go Back into the Bottle: National Self-determination and the Legacy of the First World War and the Peace Settlement." In *Europe and Ethnicity: World War One and Contemporary Ethnic Conflicts*. Edited by Seamus Dunn and T. G. Fraser, 9–28. London: Routledge, 1996.

Smith, Woodruff D. *The Ideological Origins of Nazi Imperialism*. New York: Oxford University Press, 1986.

Spittler, Botho. *Das höhere Schulwesen in der "polnischen Ecke" Westpreußens im Spannungsfeld der Nationalitätenpolitik*. Dortmund, Ger.: Forschungsstelle Ostmitteleuropa, 1986.

Spoerer, Mark. *Zwangsarbeit unter dem Hakenkreuz: Ausländische Zivilarbeiter, Kriegsgefangene und Häftlinge im Deutschen Reich und im besetzten Europa 1939–1945*. Stuttgart: Deutsche Verlags-Anstalt, 2001.

Sroka, Irena. "Die Organisation von Zwangsarbeitereinsatz in den eingegliederten Gebieten in der ersten Phase des Krieges (am Beispiel Oberschlesiens)." *Studia Historiae Oeconomicae* 14 (1980): 267–81.

Sroková, Irena. "K narodnostini politice nemecke treti rise v katoviskem vladnim obvodu." *Slezský Sborník* 84, no. 4 (1986): 274–85.

Stefanski, Valentina M. "Nationalsozialistische Volkstums- und Arbeitseinsatzpolitik im Regierungsbezirk Kattowitz 1939–1945." *Geschichte und Gesellschaft* 31, no. 1 (2005): 38–67.

Steinbacher, Sybille. *"Musterstadt" Auschwitz: Germanisierungspolitik und Judenmord in Ostoberschlesien*. Munich: K. G. Saur, 2000.

Stelbrink, Wolfgang. *Der preußische Landrat im Nationalsozialismus: Studien zur nationalsozialistischen Personal- und Verwaltungspolitik auf Landkreisebene*. Vol. 255 of *Internationale Hochschulschriften*. Münster: Waxmann, 1998.

Stengel-von Rutkowski, Lothar. *Was ist ein Volk? Der biologische Volksbegriff: Eine kulturbiologische Untersuchung seiner Definition und seiner Bedeutung für . Wissenschaft, Weltanschauung und Politik*. Erfurt, Ger.: Stenger, 1943.

Steur, Claudia. *Theodor Dannecker: Ein Funktionär der "Endlösung."* Essen, Ger.: Klartext, 1997.

Stiller, Alexa. "Reichskommissar für die Festigung deutschen Volkstums." In Haar and Fahlbusch, *Handbuch der völkischen Wissenschaften*, 2008, 531–40.

Stone, Dan. "Beyond the 'Auschwitz syndrome': Holocaust Historiography after the Cold War." *Patterns of Prejudice* 44, no. 5 (2010): 454–68.

Stossun, Harry. *Die Umsiedlung der Deutschen aus Litauen während des Zweiten Weltkriegs: Untersuchungen zum Schicksal einer deutschen Volksgruppe im Osten.* Marburg, Ger.: Herder-Institut, 1993.

Strippel, Andreas. *NS-Volkstumspolitik und die Neuordnung Europas: Rassenpolitische Selektion der Einwandererzentralstelle des Chefs der Sicherheitspolizei und des SD, 1939–1945.* Paderborn, Ger.: Schöningh, 2011.

Stuckart, Wilhelm. "Die Staatsangehörigkeit in den eingegliederten Gebieten." *Zeitschrift der Akademie für Deutsches Recht* 8, no. 15 (1941): 233–37.

Stryjkowski, Krzysztof. "Nachkriegsfolgen der 'Deutschen Volksliste' in Großpolen und das Schicksal der verbliebenen Deutschen." In *Deutschsein als Grenzerfahrung: Minderheitenpolitik in Europa zwischen 1914 und 1950.* Edited by Mathias Beer, Dietrich Beyrau, and Cornelia Rauh-Kühne, 261–77. Essen, Ger.: Klartext, 2009.

———. *Położenie osób wpisanych w Wielkopolsce na niemiecką listę narodowościową w latach 1945–1950.* Poznań, Pol.: Instytut Historii UAM - Uniwersytetu im. Adama Mickiewicza, 2004.

Stuhlpfarrer, Karl. *Umsiedlung Südtirol: 1939–1940.* Vienna: Löcker, 1985.

Sulik, Alfred. "Die Bedeutung der Großindustrie Oberschlesiens in der Kriegswirtschaft des Dritten Reiches (1939–1945)." *Studia Historiae Oeconomicae* 20 (1993): 203–26.

———. "Volkstumspolitik und Arbeitseinsatz: Zwangsarbeiter in der Großindustrie Oberschlesiens." In Herbert, *Europa und der "Reichseinsatz,"* 106–26.

Szefer, Andrzej. "Die deutschen Umsiedler in der Provinz Oberschlesien in den Jahren 1939–1945." In *Tradition und Neubeginn: Internationale Forschung zur deutschen Geschichte im 20. Jahrhundert.* Edited by Joachim Hütter, Reinhard Meyers, and Dietrich Papenfuss, 345–54. Cologne, Ger.: Heymanns, 1975.

———. "Dywersyjno-sabotażowa działalność wrocławskiej Abwehry na ziemiach polskich w przededniu agresji hitlerowskiej w 1939 r." *Biuletyn Głownej Komisji Badania Zbrodni Hitlerowskich w Polsce* 32 (1987): 271–372.

———. *Przesiedleńcy niemieccy na Górnym Śląsku w latach 1939–1945.* Katowice, Pol.: Śląski Instytut Naukowy, 1975.

Taguieff, Pierre-André. "From Race to Culture: The New Right's View of European Identity." *Telos* 98–99 (1994): 99–125.

Ther, Philip. "Beyond the Nation: The Relational Basis of a Comparative History of Germany and Europe." *Central European History* 36, no. 1 (2003): 45–73.

Tims, Richard W. *Germanizing Prussian Poland: The H-K-T Society and the Struggle for the Eastern Marches in the German Empire 1894–1919.* New York: Columbia University Press, 1941.

Tooze, Adam. *The Wages of Destruction: The Making and Breaking of the Nazi Economy.* London: Penguin, 2007.

Trevisiol, Oliver. *Die Einbürgerungspraxis im Deutschen Reich 1871–1945.* Göttingen, Ger.: Vandenhoeck & Ruprecht, 2004.

Trzeciakowski, Lech. *The Kulturkampf in Prussian Poland.* New York: Columbia University Press, 1990.

———. "Die polnische Frage in Ideologie und Politik der deutschen Liberalen vor 1870." *Jahrbuch für die Geschichte Mittel- und Ostdeutschlands* 35 (1986): 53–71.

———. "Preußische Polenpolitik im Zeitalter der Aufstände (1830–1864)." In *Polen und die polnische Frage in der Geschichte der Hohenzollernmonarchie 1701–1871: Referate einer deutsch-polnischen Historiker-Tagung vom 7. bis 10. November in Berlin-Nikolassee.* Edited by Klaus Zernack, 96–110. Berlin: Colloquium-Verlag, 1982.

Uhle, Roger. "Neues Volk und reine Rasse: Walter Gross und das rassenpolitische Amt der NSDAP." PhD diss., Technical University of Aachen, 1999.

Umbreit, Hans. "Auf dem Weg zur Kontinentalherrschaft." In *Das Deutsche Reich und der Zweite Weltkrieg*, vol. 5, bk. 1: 3–345. Stuttgart: Militärgeschichtliches Forschungsamt, 1988.

———. *Deutsche Militärverwaltungen 1938/39: Die militärische Besetzung der Tschechoslowakei und Polens.* Stuttgart: Deutsche Verlags-Anstalt, 1977.

Verhandlungen des Reichstages [Proceedings of the Reichstag]. Stenographic reports, Berlin.

Volkmann, Hans-Erich. "Zwischen Ideologie und Pragmatismus: Zur nationalsozialistischen Wirtschaftspolitik im Reichsgau Wartheland." In *Ostmitteleuropa: Berichte und Forschung.* Edited by Ulrich Haustein, Georg W. Strobel, and Gerhard Wagner, 422–41. Stuttgart, 1981.

Volz, Wilhelm. "Zur Einführung." In *Der ostdeutsche Volksboden: Aufsätze zu der Frage des Ostens.* Edited by Wilhelm Volz, 5–6. Breslau: Hirt, 1926.

Wagner, Gerhard. "Die Weimarer Republik und die Republik Polen, 1919–1932: Probleme ihrer politischen Beziehungen." In Jacobmeyer, *Die deutsch-polnischen Beziehungen*, 35–48.

Walkenhorst, Peter. *Nation—Volk—Rasse: Radikaler Nationalismus im deutschen Kaiserreich 1890–1914.* Göttingen, Ger.: Vandenhoeck & Ruprecht, 2007.

Wasser, Bruno. "Die 'Germanisierung' im Distrikt Lublin als Generalprobe und erste Realisierungsphase des 'Generalplans Ost.'" In Rössler and Schleiermacher, *Der Generalplan Ost*, 271–93.

———. *Himmlers Raumplanung im Osten: Der Generalplan Ost in Polen 1940–1944.* Basel, Switz.: Birkhäuser, 1993.

Weber, Klaus, ed. *Faschismus und Ideologie: Projekt Ideologietheorie.* Hamburg: Argument, 2007.

Wehler, Hans-Ulrich. *Das deutsche Kaiserreich 1871–1918.* Göttingen, Ger.: Vandenhoeck & Ruprecht, 1994.

———. "Deutsch-polnische Beziehungen im 19. und 20. Jahrhundert." In Wehler, *Krisenherde*, 201–17.

———. "Von den 'Reichsfeinden' zur 'Reichskristallnacht': Polenpolitik im Deutschen Kaiserreich 1871–1918." In Wehler, *Krisenherde*, 181–202.

Weisenburger, Elvira. "Der 'Rassepapst': Hans Friedrich Karl Günther, Professor für Rassenkunde." In *Die Führer der Provinz: NS-Biographien aus Baden und Württemberg.* Edited by Michael Kißener and Joachim Scholtyseck, 161–99. Konstanz, Ger.: Universitätsverlag Konstanz, 1997.

Weitz, Eric D. "From the Vienna to the Paris System: International Politics and the Entangled Histories of Human Rights, Forced Deportations, and Civilizing Missions." *American Historical Review* 113, no. 5 (2008): 1313–43.

Wildt, Michael. "'Eine neue Ordnung der ethnographischen Verhältnisse': Hitlers Reichstagsrede vom 6. Oktober 1939." Zeithistorische Forschungen 3, no. 1 (2006): 129–37.

———. *Generation des Unbedingten: Das Führungskorps des Reichssicherheitshauptamtes.* Hamburg: Hamburger Edition, 2002.

———. "Radikalisierung und Selbstradikalisierung 1939: Die Geburt des Reichssicherheitshauptamtes aus dem Geiste des völkischen Massenmordes." In *Die Gestapo im Zweiten Weltkrieg: Heimatfront und besetztes Europa*. Edited by Gerhard Paul and Klaus-Michael Mallmann, 11–41. Darmstadt, Ger.: Wissenschaftliche Buchgesellschaft, 2000.

———. *Volksgemeinschaft als Selbstermächtigung: Gewalt gegen Juden in der deutschen Provinz 1919 bis 1939*. Hamburg: Hamburger Edition, 2007.

Wippermann, Wolfgang. *Der "deutsche Drang nach Osten": Ideologie und Wirklichkeit eines politischen Schlagwortes*. Darmstadt, Ger.: Wissenschaftliche Buchgesellschaft, 1981.

———. *Der Ordensstaat als Ideologie: Das Bild des deutschen Ordens in der deutschen Geschichtsschreibung und Publizistik*. Berlin: Colloquium-Verlag, 1979.

———. *Totalitarismustheorien: Die Entwicklung der Diskussion von den Anfängen bis heute*. Darmstadt, Ger.: Wissenschaftliche Buchgesellschaft, 1997.

Witte, Peter, Michael Wildt, Martina Voigt, Dieter Pohl, Peter Klein, Christian Gerlach, Christoph Dieckmann, and Andrej Angrick, eds. *Der Dienstkalender Heinrich Himmlers 1941/42*. Hamburg: Hamburger Edition, 1999.

Wolf, Gerhard. "The Wannsee Conference in 1942 and the National Socialist Living Space Dystopia." *Journal of Genocide Research* 17 (2015), 153–75.

Wollstein, Günter. "Die Politik des nationalsozialistischen Deutschlands gegenüber Polen 1933–1939/45." In *Hitler, Deutschland und die Mächte: Materialien zur Außenpolitik des Dritten Reiches*. Edited by Manfred Funke, 795–810. Düsseldorf: Droste, 1976.

Woolsey, Theodore S. "The Rights of Minorities under the Treaty with Poland." *American Journal of International Law* 14, no. 3 (1920): 392–96.

Wright, Jonathan. *Gustav Stresemann 1878–1929: Weimars größter Staatsmann*. Munich: Deutsche Verlags-Anstalt, 2006.

Wynot, Edward Jr. "The Polish Germans 1919–1939: National Minority in a Multinational State." *Polish Review* 17, no. 1 (1972): 23–76.

Zahra, Tara. *Kidnapped Souls: National Indifference and the Battle for Children in the Bohemian Lands, 1900–1948*. Ithaca, NY: Cornell University Press, 2008.

Zimmer, Oliver. *Nationalism in Europe 1890–1940*. Basingstoke, UK: Palgrave Macmillan, 2003.

Žižek, Slavoj. Introduction to *Mapping Ideology*. London: Verso, 1994.

Zorn, Gerda. *"Nach Ostland geht unser Ritt": Deutsche Eroberungspolitik zwischen Germanisierung und Völkermord*. Berlin: Dietz, 1980.

Index of Persons

Only historical figures are listed

Abromeit, Franz, 182, 242, 253, 255, 340, 347
Alpers, Friedrich, 243
Amsberg, Felix von, 259
Arlt, Fritz, 173, 241, 250, 252, 267, 291, 322, 323, 328, 340, 352, 353
Aubin, Hermann, 64, 74

Bachmann, Friedrich, 239, 240, 250, 262
Bach-Zelewski, Erich von dem, 75, 98, 99, 135, 136, 172, 173, 176, 206, 250, 251, 259, 324
Backe, Herbert, 147, 243
Barth, Rudolf, 157, 243, 244, 246, 247
Batocki, Adolf, 29
Beck, Robert, 121, 122, 141, 335, 336, 385
Becker, Curt, 326, 352
Bernhard, Ludwig, 30
Best, Werner, 52, 54, 71, 242, 244
Bethmann-Hollweg, Theobald von, 28, 29, 31
Beutel, Lothar, 53
Beyer, Hans Joachim, 360, 371
Beyer, Justus, 207, 259
Bilfinger, Rudolf, 254
Bilharz, Rudolf, 341
Bismarck, Otto von, 23, 24, 25, 26, 28, 32
Blenk (SD Command Precinct Posen), 137, 139, 243
Boehm, Max Hildebert, 368, 386
Böhm, Werner, 297, 347
Borkenhagen, Friedrich, 136
Bormann, Martin, 254, 302, 348, 353
Bosse, Heinrich, 258
Böttcher, Victor, 317, 318, 351, 371
Bracht, Fritz, 15, 173, 239, 240, 241, 251, 252, 262, 269, 281, 287, 290, 291, 292, 293, 303, 304, 305, 316, 323, 324, 325, 326, 327, 328, 334, 336, 338, 339, 340, 345, 346, 349, 352, 353, 354, 358
Brackmann, Albert, 64, 74

Brauchitsch, Walther von, 45, 58, 59
Brehm, Friedrich, 328, 353
Brenner, Karl, 140
Brose, Hermann, 195
Brüning, Heinrich, 39, 40
Burckhardt, Hans, 141
Butschek, Hans, 173, 254, 342

Canaris, Wilhelm, 57
Carsten, Peter, 340
Class, Heinrich, 24, 28
Conze, Werner, 18, 245, 387, 393
Coulon, Karl Albert, 115, 116, 139, 140, 141, 189, 192, 195, 196, 205, 206, 225, 226, 227, 229, 230, 231, 255, 256, 258, 260, 261, 288, 314, 315, 316, 317, 319, 322, 324, 333, 345, 350, 351, 353, 360, 363, 371
Creutz, Rudolf, 75, 242, 257

Dahlerus, Birger, 60, 61
Daluege, Kurt, 53, 57, 71, 136, 256
Damzog, Ernst, 137, 139, 170, 171, 242, 243, 245, 246, 247, 249, 261, 322
Dannecker, Theodor, 82, 129, 130
Dargl (Reich Commissioner's office in Ukraine), 372
Darré, Walther, 93, 133, 135
Derichsweiler, Albert, 360, 361, 363, 371
Derschau, Bernhard von, 200, 201, 257
Dietrich, Otto, 350
Ditze (Gauhauptstellenleiter in Upper Silesia), 325
Dolezalek, Alexander, 187, 188, 253, 254, 255
Dongus, Walter, 318, 319, 320, 351
Doppler, Ludwig, 000
Döring, Hans, 157, 184, 205, 206, 242, 244, 247, 254
Drabsch, Gerhard, 246

GERHARD WOLF is Senior Lecturer in history at the
University of Sussex.

CPSIA information can be obtained
at www.ICGtesting.com
Printed in the USA
BVHW030536290420
578800BV00001B/1